IN MANORS AND ALLEYS

**Recent Titles in
Contributions to the Study of Popular Culture**

Behold the Mighty Wurlitzer: The History of the Theatre Pipe Organ
John W. Landon

Mighty Casey: All-American
Eugene C. Murdock

The Baker Street Reader: Cornerstone Writings about Sherlock Holmes
Philip A. Shreffler, editor

Dark Cinema: American *Film Noir* in Cultural Perspective
Jon Tuska

Seven Pillars of Popular Culture
Marshall W. Fishwick

The American West in Film: Critical Approaches to the Western
Jon Tuska

Sport in America: New Historical Perspectives
Donald Spivey, editor

Screwball Comedy: A Genre of Madcap Romance
Wes D. Gehring

Buckskins, Bullets, and Business: A History of Buffalo Bill's Wild West
Sarah J. Blackstone

S.J. Perelman: A Critical Study
Steven H. Gale

The Rhetorics of Popular Culture: Advertising, Advocacy, and Entertainment
Robert L. Root, Jr.

IN MANORS AND ALLEYS

A Casebook on the American Detective Film

JON TUSKA

Contributions to the Study of Popular Culture,
Number 17

Greenwood Press
NEW YORK · WESTPORT, CONNECTICUT · LONDON

Library of Congress Cataloging-in-Publication Data

Tuska, Jon.
  In manors and alleys.

  (Contributions to the study of popular culture,
ISSN 0198-9871 ; no. 17)
  Bibliography: p.
  Includes index.
  1. Detective and mystery films—United States—
History and criticism. I. Title. II. Series.
PN1995.9.D4T795   1988   791.43′09′09355   87-17737
ISBN 0-313-25007-3 (lib. bdg. : alk. paper)

British Library Cataloguing in Publication Data is available.

Copyright © 1988 by Jon Tuska

All rights reserved. No portion of this book may be
reproduced, by any process or technique, without the
express written consent of the publisher.

Library of Congress Catalog Card Number: 87-17737
ISBN: 0-313-25007-3
ISSN: 0198-9871

First published in 1988

Greenwood Press, Inc.
88 Post Road West, Westport, Connecticut 06881

Printed in the United States of America

The paper used in this book complies with the
Permanent Paper Standard issued by the National
Information Standards Organization (Z39.48-1984).

10 9 8 7 6 5 4 3 2 1

Copyright Acknowledgments

The author and publisher gratefully acknowledge permission to reprint material from the following copyrighted sources.

Excerpts from STEP RIGHT UP! AN AUTOBIOGRAPHY OF WILLIAM CASTLE. Copyright 1976 by William Castle. Reprinted by permission of The Putnam Publishing Group.

Excerpts from the SELECTED LETTERS OF RAYMOND CHANDLER. Copyright 1981 by Columbia University Press. Reprinted by permission of Columbia University Press.

Excerpts from KILLER IN THE RAIN, copyright 1964 by the Helga Greene Literary Agency, and THE MIDNIGHT RAYMOND CHANDLER, copyright 1971 by Helga Greene, reprinted by permission of Houghton Mifflin Co., Boston, and Hamish Hamilton, Ltd., London.

Excerpts from DASHIELL HAMMETT. Copyright 1984 by Dennis Dooley. Reprinted by permission of Crossroads-Ungar-Continuum.

Excerpts from THE WORLD OF RAYMOND CHANDLER edited by Miriam Gross. Copyright 1977 by Weidenfeld and Nicolson. Reprinted by permission of Weidenfeld and Nicolson, London.

Excerpts from THE NOVELS OF DASHIELL HAMMETT, copyright 1965 by Alfred A. Knopf, Inc., from THE COMPLETE POEMS AND STORIES OF EDGAR ALLAN POE WITH SELECTIONS FROM HIS CRITICAL WRITINGS, copyright 1976 by Alfred A. Knopf, Inc., from DASHIELL HAMMETT: A LIFE by Diane Johnson, copyright 1983 by Diane Johnson, and from AGATHA CHRISTIE: A BIOGRAPHY by Janet Morgan, copyright 1985 by Alfred A. Knopf, Inc., reprinted by permission of Alfred A. Knopf/Random House, New York.

Excerpts from THE CASE OF ERLE STANLEY GARDNER by Alva Johnston, copyright 1947 by Morrow Publishing Company, and ERLE STANLEY GARDNER: THE CASE OF THE REAL PERRY MASON by Dorothy B. Hughes, copyright 1978 by Dorothy B. Hughes, reprinted by permission of William Morrow & Co., New York.

Excerpts from THE VAGRANT MOOD by W. Somerset Maugham. Copyright 1949, 1950, 1952 by W. Somerset Maugham. Reprinted by permission of Doubleday & Company, New York, and A. P. Watt, London.

Excerpts from CEASELESSLY INTO THE PAST by Kenneth Millar. Copyright 1981 by Kenneth Millar. Reprinted by permission of Capra Press, Santa Barbara.

"First Fig" by Edna St. Vincent Millay. From COLLECTED POEMS published by Harper & Row. Copyright 1922, 1950 by Edna St. Vincent Millay. Reprinted by permission of the Estate of Edna St. Vincent Millay.

Excerpts from THE SOUND OF DETECTION: ELLERY QUEEN'S ADVENTURES IN RADIO by Francis M. Nevins, Jr. Copyright 1983 by Francis M. Nevins, Jr. Reprinted by permission of the author. Excerpts from DASHIELL HAMMETT: A LIFE AT THE EDGE by William F. Nolan. Copyright 1983 by William F. Nolan. Reprinted by permission of Contemporary Books, Inc. Excerpts from CONAN DOYLE: A BIOGRAPHY by Pierre Nordon translated from the French by Frances Partridge. Copyright 1966 by John Murray, Ltd. Reprinted by permission of John Murray, Ltd., London.

Excerpts from WATTEAU'S SHEPHERDS: THE DETECTIVE NOVEL IN BRITAIN 1914–1940 by LeRoy Lad Panek. Copyright 1979 by Bowling Green University Popular Press. Reprinted by permission of Bowling Green University Popular Press.

Excerpts from IN AND OUT OF CHARACTER by Basil Rathbone. Copyright 1962 by Basil Rathbone. Reprinted by permission of Bertha Klausner International Literary Agency, Inc., New York.

Excerpts from THE FILMS OF SHERLOCK HOLMES by Chris Steinbrunner and Norman Michaels. Copyright 1978 by Chris Steinbrunner and Norman Michaels. Reprinted by permission of Citadel Press, Secaucus.

Excerpts from MORTAL CONSEQUENCES: A HISTORY FROM DETECTIVE STORY TO THE CRIME NOVEL by Julian Symons. Copyright 1972 by Julian Symons. Reprinted by perimission of Curtis Brown, Ltd., London.

Excerpts from PHILO VANCE MURDER CASES by S. S. Van Dine. Copyright 1936 by Willard Huntington Wright. Reprinted by permission of Elisabeth Marton, New York.

Excerpts from EDITOR TO AUTHOR: THE LETTERS OF MAXWELL E. PERKINS edited by John Hall Wheelock. Copyright 1950 by Charles Scribner's Sons. Reprinted by permission of Charles Scribner's Sons, New York.

An
ENCORE
for
Patricia Joy

Veritas nimis sæpe laborat;
exstinguitur nunquam.
                    Livy

Contents

	Illustrations	xi
	Introduction	xiii
	Prologue: Edgar Allan Poe and the Birth of the Detective Story	1
1.	The Adventures of Sherlock Holmes	9
2.	The Life and Times of S. S. Van Dine	49
3.	The Master Detectives	89
4.	Oriental Detectives	161
5.	The Song of the Thin Man	197
6.	Adventurers and Thieves	241
7.	The Detective Film in Transition	307
8.	Raymond Chandler in Hollywood	351
9.	Crime in the Streets	393
	Notes	409
	Bibliography	437
	Index	445

Illustrations

Illustrations follow page 240.
1. John Barrymore on location filming SHERLOCK HOLMES (1922)
2. Basil Rathbone and Nigel Bruce in THE HOUND OF THE BASKERVILLES (1939)
3. Nicholas Rowe and Alan Cox in YOUNG SHERLOCK HOLMES (1985)
4. Williard Huntington Wright during his halcyon days as S.S. Van Dine
5. Robert Wade, Eugene Pallette, Warren William and Robert Barrat in THE DRAGON MURDER CASE (1934)
6. Erle Stanley Gardner in his study at his desert ranch
7. Winifred Shaw, Warren William, Claire Dodd, and Eddie Acuff in THE CASE OF THE VELVET CLAWS (1936)
8. Publicity poster for the first Ralph Bellamy/Ellery Queen film
9. Margaret Rutherford as Miss Marple in MURDER SHE SAID (1962)
10. Albert Finney interrogating Anthony Perkins in MURDER ON THE ORIENT EXPRESS (1974)
11. Warner Oland in CHARLIE CHAN IN EGYPT (1935)
12. Warner Oland and H. Bruce Humberstone on the set of CHARLIE CHAN AT THE RACE TRACK
13. Norman Foster directing a scene from CHARLIE CHAN IN RENO (1939)
14. Boris Karloff and Grant Withers in MR. WONG IN CHINATOWN (1939)
15. John P. Marquand joins Norman Foster and Peter Lorre on the set of a Mr. Moto film
16. Keye Luke, Harold Huber, and Peter Lorre in MR. MOTO'S GAMBLE (1938)
17. William Powell with Dashiell Hammett and director W.S. "Woody" Van Dyke during the production of THE THIN MAN (1934)

18. W.S. Van Dyke directing William Powell, Myrna Loy, and Sam Levine in a scene from AFTER THE THIN MAN (1936)
19. Peter Lorre and George Raft in BACKGROUND TO DANGER (1943)
20. Director John Huston with Walter Huston and Humphrey Bogart on the set of THE MALTESE FALCON (1941)
21. Louis King directing John Howard, Reginald Denny, and E.E. Clive in a scene from BULLDOG DRUMMOND COMES BACK (1937)
22. Warren William, Eric Blore, Fred Kelsey, and Thurston Hall in a typical scene from a Lone Wolf film
23. Harriet Hilliard and Chester Morris in a scene from CONFESSIONS OF BOSTON BLACKIE (1941)
24. George Sanders and Wendy Barrie in a scene from THE GAY FALCON (1941)
25. Barbara Hale, Sheldon Leonard, and Tom Conway in THE FALCON IN HOLLYWOOD (1944)
26. Publicity for CRIME DOCTOR (1943)
27. Lloyd Nolan and Marjorie Weaver in MICHAEL SHAYNE, PRIVATE DETECTIVE (1940)
28. Lizabeth Scott, Marvin Miller, and Humphrey Bogart in DEAD RECKONING (1946)
29. Kirk Douglas and Burt Lancaster in I WALK ALONE (1947)
30. Billy Wilder directing Barbara Stanwyck and Fred MacMurray in DOUBLE INDEMNITY (1944)
31. Raymond Chandler on a Los Angeles street
32. Edward Dmytryk directing Claire Trevor in MURDER, MY SWEET (1944)
33. Robert Montgomery directing Lloyd Nolan in LADY IN THE LAKE (1946)
34. A script conference on THE BIG SLEEP (1946)
35. Robert Altman directing Nina van Pallandt and Elliott Gould in THE LONG GOODBYE (1969)
36. Clint Eastwood in DIRTY HARRY (1971)

Introduction

> A sticker on the rear bumper of the Cadillac read, "Honk if you love Jesus." The children's dark eyes looked out at me in solemn question. Was this the promised land?
>
> Ross Macdonald[1]

My original design had been simply to write a trilogy having to do with three major themes of the American cinema. In practice I found I had to modify this design somewhat. The Western film proved too unwieldy to deal with adequately in a single book. It had to be divided into two volumes. THE FILMING OF THE WEST (1976) is in the process of revision; it is concerned exclusively with the production history of the Western film. While accumulating data for it, I found that I had so much on the formation and history of Mascot Pictures that I published it as a separate history, THE VANISHING LEGION (1982). THE AMERICAN WEST IN FILM (1985) is focused on the ideological contents of Western films, on *what* was filmed, and is also concerned with varying critical approaches to the Western film. The second book in this trilogy was THE DETECTIVE IN HOLLYWOOD (1978); and the third, which became DARK CINEMA: AMERICAN FILM NOIR IN CULTURAL PERSPECTIVE (1984), was an outgrowth of the second.

The present volume is a revised version of the second and I intend this to be its definitive form so that all that ever need be added to any future edition would be an update concerning detective films and trends in detective films issued subsequently to its publication. The book has been rewritten and restructured to incorporate all the new facts and details which have come to light and the corrections of numerous errors which were kindly called to my attention by readers.

My focus has been historical and threefold: the popular detectives and the authors who created them; how those detectives changed, or were changed, when they were brought to the screen; and the lives and personalities of those who played in detective films, or adapted them for the screen, or directed them. Many of the interviews contained in this book, beyond their intrinsic interest, are also of historical significance since so many of those to whom I did speak over the years have now passed from the scene.

Through it all there can be seen to emanate a generating line in the treatment and perspective of the detective from what it was in SHERLOCK HOLMES BAFFLED (Biograph, 1900) to what it became in the evolution of the cinematic detective story.

About one thing I am sure. No player in detective films will ever be vexed at me if I say that in his personal life he little resembled his image on the screen. The same definitely cannot be said of actors who played movie cowboys. Many of them took offense at how I tried in THE FILMING OF THE WEST to penetrate behind the Hollywood illusion, even when I knowingly and discreetly did not penetrate very far. One movie cowboy's wife broke into tears because I had not included an illustration of her husband in his cowboy outfit. William Boyd once told me that he wanted to be remembered as Hopalong Cassidy. Gene Autry insisted I preserve the screen fiction and ignore entirely the real human being. Ken Maynard regaled me because I mentioned that he drank. A movie cowboy, it would appear, wanted to be thought of as he was on the screen, as if that projective fantasy had some ontological substance. The identification proved all-encompassing which is why a definitive version of THE FILMING OF THE WEST must await attrition. Fortunately, Humphrey Bogart did not think of himself as Sam Spade any more than Peter Lorre regarded himself as Mr. Moto or George Sanders confused himself with the Saint or the Falcon. Actors who have portrayed screen detectives tend not to lock us into a personal fantasy about life without which we might all be better off—the actors do not, but oftentime the plots of the stories do.

Authors such as Rex Stout who have immense literary significance within the genre have had to be overlooked because only two films were made of his detective stories. Others whose work did not make the transition to the screen have had to be excluded on this basis alone, and none other.

All detective fiction is written to formula. This is scarcely adequate for much of it also to be abominably written, but such remains frequently the case. Some rather eminent critics of the genre have sought to arrogate the detective story to a metaphysical sphere. For me, that is not where it belongs. Its affects, I believe, are more psychological and sociological.

There is some fiction which it behooves every person of culture to have read. This fiction belongs to the world and its concerns and sympathies extend beyond the spiritual milieu in which it was produced. Insofar as this is true, these works are vital to everyone's education; but the list, I fear, is not a long one. I rather imagine a single bookshelf would hold those volumes of fiction without which, to have come and gone and not to have read, would leave us impoverished and less as human beings. This shelf would contain Homer's ILIAD and ODYSSEY, Æschylus' ORESTEIA, the plays of Sophocles and Euripides, Virgil's AENEID, Horace's CARMINA, Shakespeare's plays, Cervantes' DON QUIXOTE, Goethe's FAUST, Austen's PRIDE AND PREJUDICE, Stendahl's LE ROUGE ET LE NOIR, Balzac's LE PÈRE GORIOT, Flaubert's MADAME BOVARY, Tolstoy's WAR AND PEACE, Dickens' DAVID COPPERFIELD, Dostoyevsky's THE BROTHERS KARAMAZOV, Melville's MOBY-DICK; and from this century, only because we are of this century and it is closest to us, Hesse's DEMIAN, Mann's DER ZAUBERBERG, Proust's À LA RECHERCHE DU TEMPS PERDU, and perhaps Hemingway's A FAREWELL TO ARMS and Somerset Maugham's OF HUMAN BONDAGE. I am not sure it would include any short stories, although they are the most difficult prose fiction to write well; and I am quite certain it would contain no generic fiction at all and, therefore, no detective stories.

I read a great many detective stories between the ages of twelve and sixteen. I preferred the puzzle stories which S. S. Van Dine can be said to have pioneered. They represent a challenge to the mind and, provided the author is fair with the reader, the possibility of legitimately solving a problem. Hence, my early interest in detective fiction led me into an interest, far more compelling, in logic, philosophy, languages, and ultimately world literature. Following adolescence, I read few detective stories, except when I traveled. It was not until I was at work on the first draft of this book that I read them again in any quantity and then I read them systematically, by chronology and by author, studying both the genre as a whole and an individual author's contribution to it. The same has been true while I have been at work on this revision. What preferences I may have among the detective stories I have read will be found in the text; but these preferences are purely idiosyncratic and are definitely to be binding on no one. I have also, in the course of my work, studied American Western fiction extensively. I know that I shall never attempt to study any other category of generic fiction; two have been, I sometimes think, more than sufficient for a single lifetime.

In seeking out so many people personally to interview in order to write this book, my objective remained merely to learn as much as I could about the past, much after the fashion of a detective story itself, so that I could adequately and to my satisfaction reconstruct what had happened in the development of the detective story and the detective film. Yet, this alone could not completely fulfill my purpose. In order to approach my subject critically, I have had upon occasion to analyze the plots of detective stories, first to understand the significance of these plots as plots, to evaluate them as plots, and perhaps to contrast fictional plots with motion picture treatments of them, because the media are *not* the same and what works on the printed page often cannot work on the screen. It is also impossible to write intelligently about a plot the sole reason for which is to identify a murderer without sometimes remarking on the techniques by which that murderer is exposed and the plausibility, cogency, fairness with which motives are adduced and the exposure accomplished. I might apologize for this practice, but why, since it is really unavoidable; and, to be sure, there are so many thousands of detective stories and hundreds of detective films not subjected to this kind of analysis that a reader or viewer will still have many a surprise in store.

It is my conviction that so much detective fiction and, by implication, quite a number of detective films fall into this category of a story intended for people who like surprises because the majority seeking this type of entertainment actually want to be surprised, rather than working along with, or even ahead of, the detective to arrive at the correct solution. I recall when I arranged a screening of THE DRAGON MURDER CASE (First National, 1934) for Lucky Humberstone who had directed the picture nearly forty years before, about midway through he leaned over to me in the projection room where we sat at the Burbank Studios.

"Do you know how this thing comes out?" he asked.

"Yes."

"Don't tell me. I know I directed it, but I've forgotten who did it."

The shock of revelation, however, need not be only in discovering who committed a crime. There is another kind of detective story, the kind that becomes increasingly prevalent toward the end of this book. Here, the detective film, altered by the bleak vision of *film noir*, is not so concerned with who did it, or even why, as with the social and psychological environment which produced the crime and with the ways of dealing with that. Sometimes, in the far-reaching corruption indigenous to the American way of life, even the detective himself becomes corrupted. When you cannot escape from corruption, or successfully immunize yourself against it, all you might hope to do is to depict it, or to confront it as a vigilante would.

For a number of detective story writers, their lives, often the very settings of their stories or the incarnation of their detectives, converge, intersecting in Hollywood. This is not merely because a series of motion pictures was inspired by their characters or stories. It goes beyond that insofar as the milieu in which the detective is placed is that of the uninhibited, conservative, frank, suspicious, predatory, almost fascist, frequently bewildered, always contradictory society of Southern California. Having lived there, I am not in the least sympathetic with the view, currently somewhat in vogue, that if you want to know the truth about Southern California you should read Raymond Chandler. Leigh Brackett, who worked on the screenplays for Chandler's THE BIG SLEEP (Warner's, 1946) and THE LONG GOODBYE (United Artists, 1973), made no bones about it as we sat in the living room of her desert home. "You know where Ray got most of his characters, don't you? He went to the movies in the 'Twenties and 'Thirties. So many of his characters aren't real at all. They're movie conceptions of people." Many detective story writers have come from the East, or the Middle West; but, whether they only visited Southern California or in fact settled there, it had a measurable effect on them. The late Ross

Macdonald, talking to me in a vacant dining room in a cafe in Santa Barbara filled with sunlight, told me earnestly:

"Everything good *and* bad begins in California. Then it moves East."

He believed that; and it was from that perspective that he wrote his detective stories.

It is very difficult to write a successful novel without sympathetic characters. Noel Coward once said of W. Somerset Maugham that in a long literary career he never managed to draw a sympathetic character. Maugham loved detective stories. I suspect what must have appealed to him is the fact that detective stories rarely, if ever, contain sympathetic characters other than the detective. Maugham solved this problem in his own work by creating a sympathetic persona through writing in the first person singular. Many detective stories employ this same device, whether they are narrated by a friend or associate of the detective or by the detective himself. Since this book is very much an investigation, I have tried to adapt this technique to achieve my own ends. What I have discovered will be found in what follows with, I hope, more than a few characters capable of engendering sympathy. But then, of course, the author of a detective story is under no obligation to have us like his characters. He can expose them or kill them off, all the while indulging us in an antisocial orgy that might, under other circumstances, be regarded as morally suspect. Yet he has to accomplish more than this to win lasting favor in a world in which "lasting" means the span of his lifetime. He must conjure ideal characters. When a detective story writer's favor with the public outlasts him, it is usually the ideal characters who account for it and seldom, if ever, the stories in which those ideal characters are to be found.

I have made no attempt to mention every detective film ever made in the United States. This would be as pointless as to attempt a critique of every detective story ever written. I am aware that there are books which purport to have achieved the latter; and, therefore, it has been with some amusement that I have read reviews which have demonstrated that the author or authors of these mammoth tomes have indeed *not* read every book they criticize and have even cribbed some of their assessments from other sources. The only warranty I would make is that I have seen all the films which I cite in passing; but, conversely, I have never mentioned the title of a film just to include it if I have had nothing more than that to say about it; and the same applies to the detective fiction I have cited.

Since detective story writers, by and large, expended great energy in creating their fictional detectives, in those cases when the time came to bring their creations to the screen, the respective authors were very anxious lest the screenplay destroy overnight what it had taken them years to construct. Some authors, such as Erle Stanley Gardner and Rex Stout, became so disgusted with the Hollywood treatment of their characters they refused to license further photoplays featuring them. In other cases, the movies devised detective characters based only loosely, if at all, on fictional prototypes. These scored better, if not always with the public, at least with producers who did not have to cope with irate authors. In still other cases, men such as Dashiell Hammett and Raymond Chandler became involved in working on the screenplay versions of their fictional works. Chandler, of the two, was very much an annoyance, but as he himself said his detective, Philip Marlowe, was really all he had to sell. Notwithstanding, it was this tendency on the parts of certain detective story authors to become scenarists for their detectives that assured that their world-view, their contributions to plot treatment and dialogue ended up having such a widespread currency among detective film productions with which they themselves might have nothing to do.

"The Eighteenth-century Enlightenment had transformed men's minds, and men now were in the process of transforming their world," Aaron Marc Stein wrote in his essay, "The Mystery Story in Cultural Perspective" (1976). "The detective-story hero, therefore, emerged as this Nineteenth-century man, the devotee of fact, the child of reason. Of just such stuff Sherlock Holmes was made."[2] As a popular version of the scientist, this kind of detective represented the forces of reason, truth, and justice in a more or less absolute sense. Yet, this image diminished under the influence of Hammett, Chandler, and others from what is termed the BLACK MASK school.[3] Repeated questioning slowly overshadowed all certitude with what Hamlet described as "the pale cast of thought." Truth and justice, if not reason, may have remained the domain of the detective, but increasingly society itself became his opponent and who actually committed a crime frequently was ambiguous.

William Ruehlmann's book, SAINT WITH A GUN (1974), is an indictment of American detective fiction of the hard-boiled variety. "The private detective who not only tracks down his quarry but executes him too is reenacting the American retributive morality," Ruehlmann wrote; "the eye's city is Salem Again where ritual deaths expiate our helplessness in more real regions."[4] From this perspective, far from supporting order in a chaotic world, the detective becomes his own law and administers justice according to his own bias. As impressive as this interpretation appears at first glance, what is being ignored is the rather sad fact that money and power, as opposed to some abstract principle or some eternal, incontrovertible ideal, determine justice, if not also truth; which is why I began this book by quoting Livy: "Truth is often much too hard pressed . . . ," although he did add (and I must tentatively agree): "it is never extinguished." The detective who creates his own justice is doing nothing differently in principle than the judge whose opinion was bought long before he ever assumed the bench or the police officer who is victim to a system which gives him a daily quota of arrests to make if he wishes to keep his job. Accepting what Ruehlmann had to say, I am still compelled to assert that the detective, no matter how outlandish his behavior, is himself the product of a corrupt social order and so how should we hope that he could escape from it totally untarnished?

"Didn't it strike you as curious," I asked John Huston in 1975 as we talked together in his suite at the Beverly Hills Hotel, "that you should have directed THE MALTESE FALCON in 1941 and that Sam Spade emerged such a hero, only now to have played the villain in CHINATOWN [Paramount, 1974], where money, power, and influence alone rule the day?"

Huston leered at me, then leaned forward, his features grimacing into a consummate smirk.

"It wasn't any different when I made THE MALTESE FALCON than it is now," he replied. "It's only that we were less able or willing to accept it then."

In 1981, in Puerto Vallarta, asking Huston the same question, this time to be filmed, he refused to respond. Later, in Los Angeles, I voiced my frustration in getting any straight answers out of Huston to Orson Welles.

"I can understand that," Welles said. "He isn't saying anything about anything or anybody that is likely to get him in trouble because he wants to receive the Life Achievement Award from the American Film Institute."

Obviously the strategy worked. Shortly thereafter, Huston did receive the award. It is one of the ironies of American society that those artists most likely to be fêted and honored are those who support the Establishment, at least verbally. How else should it be when Louis L'Amour is the most decorated author in the history of American letters?

There is no getting around it. Human nature is often willfully self-deceptive. In living our lives, most of us find this such a difficult state of affairs with which to contend that we try to close it out of our minds and prefer not to think about it. It is otherwise for the detective. He is by nature suspicious. He expects everyone to lie to him. In this sense, detective stories permit us to have a catharsis in which we can at once admit the almost universal deceit of human beings and yet hold on to the belief that not all men are so because the detective himself remains such a daring exception. The furor aroused in those cases where the detective is revealed to be the culprit, albeit almost comic, is also readily comprehensible. We prefer our illusions. Yet, emphatically, we cannot really arrive at the identity of the wrongdoer without ourselves becoming, for the duration of a detective story, pathologically vigilant about believing anyone. "Watch them," Robert Montgomery as Philip Marlowe says into the camera in LADY IN THE LAKE (M-G-M, 1946), "they're tricky." And so they are.

One of the principal charms, I believe, of Conan Doyle's stories is the remarkable friendship between Sherlock Holmes and Doctor Watson. Or witness that amazing professional relationship between Perry Mason and his loyal Della Street and his enduring friendship with Paul Drake of the Drake Detective Agency. I would submit that this special emotional affinity accounts for much of the appeal of certain kinds of detective stories. Yet it can be otherwise. Particularly since the Second World War, the detective in film has increasingly become a loner with the viewing audience as his only intimate companion. When romance enters the story in the form of a girl friend, she may, as often as not, be a suspect; in fact, with a surprising consistency she is frequently the murderer. Only isolation can follow upon such ubiquitous suspicion and a detective's life is necessarily a lonely one. Existential separation has emerged as a dominant cinematic theme in the detective film. But then, is there not a certain reassurance to be had in the knowledge that we are not completely alone in our loneliness, in our feelings of separation and alienation?

The detective traditionally has been a truth-seeker. Almost everyone else, to a greater or lesser degree, is a variety of truth-hater. Resentment of the truth-seeker is one of the oldest human dramas. It is this tension between the natural human impulse to conceal the truth and the bold flourish to expose it which provides the detective genre with its most fundamental *raison d'être*. The Age of Reason asserted that knowledge is power. But knowledge in the contemporary world has been found to be a source of suffering, despair, even sickness unto death, reminding us resoundingly of the pessimism of Ecclesiastes; and power—power is money. Because in a materialistic society money consorts with greed amid economic pressures and exigencies of all kinds, the lack of money has become irrefragably confused with the emptiness and dissatisfaction inevitable when more romantic illusions fail. The Enlightenment neglected the maxim that "in much wisdom is much grief; and he that increaseth knowledge increaseth sorrow." For the modern detective, knowledge imposes a permanent loneliness. The Enlightenment also placed the highest value of all on human life. Individual, premeditated murder is a deep-seated taboo that, despite its prosaic ubiquity, still prompts sufficient emotional turmoil to sustain our interest. Too many and too much, however, have brought about a transition from a brave and open willingness to arrive at the truth, to at first a clandestine, then even a brazen consent to reject it, or not to discover it at all. The detective has passed through all of these phases, from inspiring awe and security to being an offensive intrusion even to those who propose to employ him, to becoming a self-appointed avenger in a society that wishes only concealment and the *status quo*.

I may be an antiquarian, but I am totally incapable of nostalgia. When once I was sitting in a cafe near the Studios de Boulogne in Paris with Roman Polanski, I handed him an illustrated book of the screenplays from his first three feature films. There were many candid photos of him directing.

"Have you seen this?" I asked him.

"No," he said, taking the book at once and avidly paging through it, intrigued by the illustrations. "You know," he remarked after a time, "it is strange, I was so unhappy when I made these pictures, but when I look at these photographs, I feel nostalgic."

I could not genuinely relate to what he was saying. I may as well confess here that I was deeply unhappy when I wrote the first version of this book; and, when I began again to go over it, all those emotions came over me once more as a cresting wave. I would not want in the least to go back, or even to reflect nostalgically on that time. Rather, I am grateful to have lived past that point in my life so that, from a much more pleasant sense of well being, I could expunge what I felt to be inferior from this book so as to write it as I think it ought best to be written. Yet, if the detective story is to be believed, or the lives of many of those who chose to write detective stories, the individual past is not only filled with anguish, but it is anguish which cannot be overcome. It is nearly intrinsic to the technique of the detective story that this should be so, since it begins with a crime and attempts to reconstruct from the past how that crime necessarily and inevitably came to happen.

I have found that all I need do is change my physical surroundings, move to a different city, establish a new life amid new friends, and I think scarcely at all of where I once lived, nor do I in any sense miss it. Perhaps this is in part the case because when I was still a university student, working my way through school employed as an announcer for a classical music radio station, I interviewed Leopold Stokowski for the first time when he was almost eighty. I wanted very much to know just how one went about living to an advanced age and remaining active. "Forget the past," he told me. "You can do nothing about the past." Then, cupping his magnificent hands, he smiled. "The future," he said, "that is something you can mold."

One thing you might notice, as I have, were you to change your physical surroundings completely and then return to your former setting. The people who were once so close to you when you lived there are still wound up in the same emotional and psychological concerns they had when you left. It will all seem strange to you because you are no longer part of it. The same sense of strangeness is often embodied in modern dectective stories, especially in the novels of Ross Macdonald; and, as the past is unraveled through investigations and interrogations, patterns are revealed and you slowly become aware of the powerful emotional grasp of the past on individuals, be that past a reality or only a fantasy. I trust in this book I have been able to reconstruct the past of the detective film in the United States without either anguish or nostalgia, albeit not without a certain poignance.

IN MANORS AND ALLEYS

Prologue: Edgar Allan Poe and the Birth of the Detective Story

> If the phantasmagoria of Coleridge and De Quincey were inspired by drugs, then it might be said—in the equivocal sense—that Poe's manuscripts were found in bottles.
>
> Harry Levin[1]

In literary history, the detective story was born in April, 1841 when Edgar Allan Poe's "The Murders in the Rue Morgue" appeared in GRAHAM'S MAGAZINE. Poe's detective was C. Auguste Dupin. He is French. He lives in Paris. He prefers the night hours. He solves nearly all his "problems," as he calls them, through ratiocination which does not require him to leave the shuttered rooms which he shares with the anonymous narrator of his exploits. Poe's second Dupin story was "The Mystery of Marie Rogêt." It was first published in LADY'S COMPANION in November, 1842. It embodied Poe's attempt, using Dupin, to explicate the actual circumstances of a contemporary murder case based on newspaper accounts. The third Dupin story, "The Purloined Letter," was featured in THE GIFT in 1845.

Howard Haycraft in MURDER FOR PLEASURE (1941) claimed that "the first tale exemplified, loosely, the *physical* type of the detective story. In the second, Poe reverted to the opposite extreme of the purely *mental*. Finding this (presumably) equally unsatisfactory, the artist in him led, inescapably, in the third story to the *balanced* type. Thus, swiftly, and in the brief compass of only three slight narratives, he foretold the entire evolution of the detective romance as a literary form."[2] Yet, when it came to attributing a motive to Poe for creating the detective story as a literary *genre*, Haycraft came to a rather curious conclusion. "There is assuredly much to be said," he wrote, "for Joseph Wood Krutch's brilliant oversimplification: 'Poe invented the detective story that he might not go mad.' Men still read them for the same reason today."³

My own suspicion is that the detective story as an antidote for madness might be more relevant to a consideration of Poe's literary art than as an explanation of why people read such fiction. After all, Poe is best remembered for the fantasies about the grave which he wrote. In his story, "Berenice," for example, Egaeus is in love with his cousin, Berenice. Egaeus narrates the story. "In the strange anomaly of my existence," he confides, "feelings with me, *had never been* of the heart, and my passions *always were* of the mind. Through the gray of the early morning—among the trellised shadows of the forest at noonday—and in the silence of my library at night—she had flitted by my eyes, and I had seen her—not as the living and breathing Berenice, but as the Berenice of a dream; not as a being of the earth, earthy, but as the abstraction of such a being; not as a thing to admire, but to analyze; not as an object of love, but as the theme of the most abstruse although desultory speculation."⁴ A messenger tells Egaeus that Berenice, who has been so ill that her hair has completely changed its color, has died. While she has been suffering, Egaeus has been haunted by visions of Berenice's teeth. In an earlier version of the story there is an episode which Poe subsequently suppressed in which Egaeus, seeing Berenice in her coffin, is horrified when the bandages around her jaws break and her exposed teeth seem to grin hideously at him. It is unfortunate that Poe removed this episode since it reinforces Egaeus' obsession and perhaps assists a reader in better understanding why Egaeus later disinters the body and with instruments belonging to the family physician extracts all thirty-two of her teeth. The ending is irony. Egaeus learns that Berenice was not really dead, but rather in a cataleptic state. She comes to consciousness during this brutal act and screams wildly.

It is stories with plots of this kind which, in this century, have made Poe the object of psychoanalytic investigation. Stefan Zweig in DIE WELT VON GESTERN [THE WORLD OF YESTERDAY] (1944) called her "the wonderful Princess Maria Bonaparte" and Freud's "most faithful pupil" for her part in rescuing Freud from Hitler's Vienna⁵; and it was Maria Bonaparte who in EDGAR POE, ÉTUDE PSYCHOANALYTIQUE (1933) wrote the most ambitious psychoanalytic treatise on him. She had been preceded, however, by Joseph Wood Krutch whose EDGAR ALLAN POE: A STUDY IN GENIUS (1926) had appeared in the previous decade and which also sought to apply psychoanalytic interpretations to Poe's life and works. "It seemed to me then," Krutch wrote in his autobiography, MORE LIVES THAN ONE (1962), "(as it still does) that if the psychoanalytical approach to literature, just then beginning to be made here and there, would work anywhere it should be on so obviously abnormal a writer as Poe."⁶ Krutch wholly identified the man and his work to such an extent that in his study of Poe he could remark " . . . the forces which wrecked his life were those which wrote his works."⁷ Yet, as Claudia C. Morrison observed in FREUD AND THE CRITIC: THE EARLY USE OF

DEPTH PSYCHOLOGY IN LITERARY CRITICISM (1968), Krutch nowhere mentioned Freud or any specific psychoanalytic doctrine. "Essentially," she wrote, "the book was a portrait of a neurotic rather than an analysis of the neurosis in causal terms, Krutch's main interest being to trace the evidences of a neurotic imbalance in Poe's character and in his works. It might be added that one motive behind the study seems to have been to discredit Poe both as an artist and as a man. The term 'neurotic' in Krutch's hands was more than a scientific description; it had a distinctly pejorative connotation. In his portrait, Poe emerged as mean, hypocritical, envious, spiteful, inordinately quarrelsome, weak, and overwhelmingly egocentric. Krutch's judgments on Poe's creations were equally harsh: they were found to be narrow, morbid, lacking in reality, and full of specious rationalism—in short, a little more than morbid products of a morbidly neurotic individual. It is not merely that Krutch was not in sympathy with Poe; he even implied . . . that anyone who was sympathetic to this type of writing was so because of his own peculiar neurosis."[8] In his actual analysis of Poe, Krutch made no attempt to diagnose his unconscious necrophilia as being caused by his mother's early death and as at least a contributing factor to his mental condition. Maria Bonaparte had no such reservations. In her study, Poe's infantile sexual desires with attendant castration anxiety and unconscious necrophilia were quite obvious from the fiction he wrote, as was his psychic impotence.

Yet, ironically, the reservation I have to this sort of approach was voiced by Freud himself, in a comment he once made to Stefan Zweig: " 'There is as little one hundred percent truth as there is one hundred percent alcohol!' "[9] For Maria Bonaparte, the "solution" to the story "Berenice" rested in the concept of *vagina dentata*, in effect a castration fear displaced from below to above the waist. Such a view may be interesting, but there is no way it can be verified. Or take "The Murders in the Rue Morgue" itself. In it an old woman and one much younger are brutalized by an orangoutan who has escaped from his owner and who swung into the open window of their fourth-storey room one night only to lock the window behind him when he departed. Since Poe, at the time that he wrote this story, was living with his child-wife, Virginia, and her mother, one might suppose that some secret hostility toward them is to be found concealed behind the fate of the two women in the story. For Maria Bonaparte, it was otherwise. "At an unbelievably early age," she wrote, "the child already possesses larval instinctual mechanisms which allow it to store upon impressions of adult sex acts performed in its presence. That Poe, as a child, was present at such times, when sharing the room with his actress mother, the crime of the ape is almost certain testimony."[10] Both suppositions, it strikes me, might be correct, or neither; we cannot know.

What Joseph Wood Krutch was all too inclined to accept from psychoanalysis was the prevailing view that art is the product of neurosis. Yet this acceptance really undermined his position as a critic with regard to Poe: if all art is neurosis, why is Poe's particular neurosis any worse or better than anyone else's neurosis? Similarly, Howard Haycraft, in citing Krutch's view that Poe wrote detective stories to prevent himself from going mad and making an inductive leap by this means to supposing this to be the reason why others read them, appears to have made a further induction, albeit totally consistent: that one's neurosis determines what kind of neurotic writers one is going to read. In contrast, I believe a more balanced view is that some art, as some fantasy, is the result of unhealthy causes and attitudes, and that we must learn to distinguish the difference. Moreover, as George Orwell pointed out, when reviewing Salvador Dali's autobiography and Dali's obsession with necrophilia, "mere moral disapproval does not get one any further. But neither ought one to pretend, in the name of 'detachment,' that such pictures as 'Mannequin rotting in a taxi-cab' are morally neutral. They are diseased and disgusting, and any investigation ought to start out from that fact."[11]

The major difference between Poe's necrophiliac fantasies and his detective stories is presumed to reside in the circumstance that the detective stories make use of reason and logic and are, therefore, on a more elevated plane. "As the strong man exults in his physical ability," Poe wrote at the very beginning of "The Murders in the Rue Morgue," "delighting in such exercises as call his muscles into action, so glories the analyst in that moral activity which *disentangles*. He derives pleasure from even the most trivial occupations bringing his talent into play. He is fond of enigmas, of conundrums, hieroglyphics; exhibiting in his solutions of each a degree of *acumen* which appears to the ordinary apprehension preternatural. His results, brought about by the very soul and essence of method, have, in truth, the whole air of intuition."[12] Notwithstanding this eloquent plea, there is nothing rational or logical about this story or the methods Dupin uses to arrive at a solution. When Dupin infers the existence of a French sailor belonging to a Maltese vessel from his discovery of a small piece of ribbon at the scene of the crime, he calls this an induction, whereas he is merely reasoning from one particular to another.

In his book, MORTAL CONSEQUENCES: A HISTORY FROM THE DETECTIVE STORY TO THE CRIME NOVEL (1972), Julian Symons had occasion to quote Laura Riding's criticism of "The Murders in the Rue Morgue." "If only the lower sash moved," she wrote, "then the ape, grasping the shutter and kicking himself backwards (frontways is impossible) into the room, would have been obstructed by the upper half of the window from landing directly on the head of the bed, which was pressed close against the window. If only the lower half moved, then it was only the lower half that was open. If, however, the upper sash moved too, the ape, on climbing out and shutting the window behind him, as he is said to have done, could not have fastened this upper sash by the secret 'catch.' . . . The window would have remained open."[13]

The same is the case with "The Mystery of Marie Rogêt," based on the real murder of Mary Rogers. Poe claimed to have successfully solved the murder and to have identified the culprit. The truth, as Julian Symons rightly insisted, is that "it remained unsolved, with the balance of probability being that Mary

Rogers died accidentally following an abortion. A year before his death, Poe, who had said in the story that 'it was at once evident that murder had been committed,' admitted this in a letter. 'The "naval officer" who committed the murder (rather the accidental death arising from an attempt at abortion) confessed it . . . but, for the sake of relatives, I must not speak further.' The naval officer existed, although we have only Poe's word for his confession: but the point really is that the story was based upon the idea that Mary Rogers had been murdered, and if she died accidentally the logic of the argument is destroyed at its base."[14] These criticisms are important because, as Symons himself concluded, "the prime merit claimed by Poe for his puzzle stories was that they were model exercises in accurate reasoning. If the reasoning is faulty, the merit of the stories is much reduced."[15]

Faulty reasoning and preposterous plots have plagued the detective story ever since Poe originally fell into these traps. Another influence Poe exerted on subsequent authors was his rather shoddy erudition. When Egaeus begins to list the books he was reading at the time of his growing obsession, he includes "St. Austin's [sic] great work, 'The City of God' "[16] among the titles. Poe's reading was obviously wide and desultory and he was fond of quoting Latin authors, from Seneca to Tertullian. At the conclusion of "The Mystery of Marie Rogêt," Poe himself remarked that "nothing, for example, is more difficult than to convince the merely general reader that the fact of sixes having been thrown twice in succession by a player at dice, is sufficient cause for betting the largest odds that sixes will not be thrown in the third attempt. A suggestion to this effect is usually rejected by the intellect at once. It does not appear that the two throws which have been completed, and which lie now absolutely in the Past, can have influence upon the throw which exists only in the Future. The chance for throwing sixes seems to be precisely as it was at any ordinary time—that is to say, subject only to the influence of the various other throws which may be made by the dice. And this is a reflection which appears so exceedingly obvious that attempts to controvert it are received more frequently with a derisive smile than with any thing like respectful attention. The error here involved—a gross error redolent of mischief—I cannot pretend to expose within the limits assigned me at present; and with the philosophical it needs no exposure."[17]

This view of probability could only have come from Pierre Simon de Laplace who set it forth in his THÉORIE ANALYTIQUE DES PROBABILITIÉS (1812). I doubt that Poe actually read this work, but he may well have read Laplace's companion to this treatise, a very lucid and non-technical exposition of his theory titled ESSAI PHILOSOPHIQUE SUR LES PROBABILITIÉS (1814). Laplace wrote in the latter that " . . . we find that an event having occurred successively any number of times, the probability that it will happen again the next time is equal to this number increased by unity divided by the same number, increased by two units. Placing the most ancient epoch of history at five thousand years ago, or at 1826213 days, and the sun having risen constantly in the interval at each revolution of twenty-four hours, it is a bet of 1826214 to one that it will rise again tomorrow." [18]

Laplace's interpretation of the universe in this work as well as in his others was a strictly deterministic one. Such a view is a perfect embodiment of the confident Enlightenment that the past can be described and the future predicted from a single accurate observation in the present. Dupin's orientation to reason and deduction, and that of Sherlock Holmes and numerous others in the future, was derived from this firm belief in determinism. Correct deductions could lead only to a single determination which must also be correct if the deductions were correct. Poe's detective stories, and those which followed in his wake, assured and reinforced such belief. It is, to say the least, comforting. Modern logic with its principles of co-presence and polarity, as modern physics with its principle of indeterminacy and modern probability theory with its calculus of relative frequencies, has discarded the deterministic model of the universe as inadequate. Notwithstanding, I suspect it constitutes one of the major attractions of the story of pure ratiocination which Poe created.

Dupin, who was fond "of enigmas, of conundrums, hieroglyphics," liked them because he was confident that he could solve them. To T. S. Eliot, writing about Poe, this was indicative of a clever adolescent who is better at puzzles than at the complications of life. Fyodor Dostoyevsky, in his preface to a Russian translation of Poe's stories, found even the unworldly tales to be strangely materialistic in their point of view. "Even in his most unbounded imagining," Dostoyevsky wrote, "he betrays the true American." [19] The materialism in the detective stories is, if anything, far more pronounced: all mystery—to use Poe's typical adjectives—no matter how grotesque, how bizarre, how *outré* could be reduced to a basic, materialistic explanation. The whole medieval perspective which attributed virtually every phenomenon to an other-worldly cause was banished from this deterministic universe.

Finally, Poe provided detective fiction with the character of the sympathetic avenger. This image again is uniquely American. For example, in the short story, "La Grande Bretêche," written between 1839 and 1842, Honoré de Balzac told the unhappy events of M. le Comte de Merret and his unfortunate wife. When Merret discovers that his wife has a lover, and realizes that the lover is hiding in a small alcove, he attempts to expose her. She denies that anyone is hiding in the room. He then has the alcove sealed up with mortar and bricks and sits by her side for the next twenty days. When she would intercede, M. le Comte hastens to remind her that she had sworn on the cross that no one was there. Mme. de Merret wastes away and soon dies. As for M. le Comte, it is told how he came to a miserable end, going to Paris and flinging himself into every kind of dissipation until an early death brought him final release. For Poe such a termination to a story of revenge must have seemed a lot of sentimental nonsense.

Montresor says at the start of "The Cask of Amontillado" (1846): "I must not only punish, but punish with impunity. A wrong is unredressed when retribution overtakes its redresser. It is equally unredressed when the avenger fails to make himself felt as such to him who has done the wrong."[20] Just what wrong Fortunato did to Montresor which must be avenged is never stated, but Fortunato's weakness is that he is a connoisseur of wine. It is by this means that Montresor lures him to his wine cellar and manages to seal him up inside an alcove. As Montresor informs Fortunato, the motto of his family is *"Nemo me impune lacessit"* [No one provokes me with impunity].[21] It is a motto that has been shared by the many avengers in detective fiction, right down to Mike Hammer and the tough cop played by Chuck Norris in CODE OF SILENCE (Orion, 1985). The influence it has exerted has been almost as significant in the history of the detective story as has been Poe's conclusion in EUREKA: A PROSE POEM (1848): "There is no such thing as spirituality. God is material."[22]

Of the three Dupin stories, "The Purloined Letter" has yet to be filmed. The garish elements of Poe's other fiction certainly are to be found in the cinematic renderings of the other two stories. MURDERS IN THE RUE MORGUE (Universal, 1932) directed by Robert Florey was Leon Ames' first picture. His name on the credits is given as Leon Waycoff. He was cast as Pierre Dupin, a medical student. The film was primarily a vehicle for Bela Lugosi who is touring carnivals in France with a pet ape with which he regularly converses and which he uses to assist him in murdering Parisian streetwalkers in an effort to mingle human and animal blood. This story idea was subsequently purchased by Warner Bros. and used as the basis for PHANTOM OF THE RUE MORGUE (Warner's, 1954) directed by Roy Del Ruth. Steve Forrest played Paul Dupin, a French medical student. Karl Malden was cast as the deranged head of the Paris zoo who, having repressed apparently the memory of driving his wife insane, sets out on a campaign to avenge her death by enticing a giant ape to kill women in the gaslit streets. MURDERS IN THE RUE MORGUE (American-International, 1971) directed by Gordon Hessler was filmed in Spain. It does not feature Dupin as a character and, although there is an ape in a stage play, the murders are committed with acid by a man intent on vengeance.

THE MYSTERY OF MARIE ROGET (Universal, 1942) was strictly a low-budget affair directed by Phil Rosen. Lloyd Corrigan was cast as Inspector Gobelin and Patric Knowles played Dr. Paul Dupin, the chief medical officer of the Paris police. This team undertakes to solve the disappearance and murder of a famous stage actress. The dialogue was so absurd that even in 1942 it must have been viewed by audiences as more a comedy than a mystery.

Yet, while Poe may have created the detective story and fashioned the first amateur consulting detective, it was to be Sherlock Holmes who first came to the screen.

1
The Adventures of Sherlock Holmes

> As Cuvier could correctly describe a whole animal by the contemplation of a single bone, so the observer who has thoroughly understood one link in a series of incidents, should be able accurately to state all the other ones, both before and after.
>
> Sherlock Holmes[1]

I

Arthur Conan Doyle was born on 22 May 1859 in Edinburgh. He was surely named for King Arthur and for his great uncle and godfather, Michael Edward Conan. The latter worked as a literary, music, and dramatic critic. The Doyle family was profoundly Roman Catholic. Arthur's father, Charles Doyle, was the least successful of the five sons of Irish caricaturist, John Doyle. Charles was epileptic and emotionally disturbed; he became an alcoholic. Ten years before Arthur was born, Charles Doyle secured employment as an architect for the Scottish Office of Works and, to supplement his income, would also do free-lance illustrations, mostly of criminal trials and for children's books. Arthur's mother, née Mary Foley, known later simply as "The Ma'am," was a woman obsessed with family. She could trace her lineage back to the Plantagenets. Arthur could remember her stirring porridge with one hand while reading LA REVUE DES DEUX MONDES. She would discuss the Goncourts and Flaubert with Arthur while darning socks and hold him spellbound whole nights narrating adventures about her ancestors. It was her only means of escape from an unhappy husband and the difficulties of raising a family in relative poverty.

While growing up, Arthur's favorite author was Mayne Reid who had spent only a brief time in the United States and wrote almost all of his fifty-odd American frontier sagas while living in London. Reid's dramatic stress in his novels was on action and most of his characters serve a purely functional role: they propel the plot. He disliked Indians and regarded them invariably as the enemy. He also detested Roman Catholic priests and was not above drawing them as villains. His distrust of Mexicans was even more vitriolic than his attitude toward Indians; and, equally, he condemned the Mormons for their polygamy. His most memorable adventures—including Arthur's favorite, THE SCALP HUNTERS (1851)—were narrated in the first person, a technique in storytelling which Arthur would perfect in his maturity. Reid was a pantheist and evoked this image of God in his stories. Charles Higham is probably accurate in his THE ADVENTURES OF CONAN DOYLE (1976) when he attributes to Reid the beginnings of Arthur's rejection of the religion of his family. Certainly it was to Reid, as opposed to any more reliable source, that Arthur went when he was at work on the long section of A STUDY IN SCARLET (1887) set in Utah and concerned with the lives of the Mormons. Reid with his constant use of weak heroines in distress who have ineffectual, or unscrupulous, brothers and therefore must be rescued by strong and chivalrous heroes undoubtedly reinforced Arthur's already strong sense of chivalry and idealism learned from his mother and his reading of one of his mother's distant relatives, Sir Walter Scott.

Arthur was large of frame and athletic. He studied first at Jesuit institutions: Hodder, a preparatory school; and then at Stonyhurst which had a complementary school in Austria which permitted him to complete his final year at Feldkirch. Homosexuality was not even tacitly allowed at these Jesuit schools, as it was in many English preparatory schools, and sports accordingly were promoted as a preferable alternative. This posture toward sexual repression would accompany Conan Doyle all his life and would be true, as well, of his most successful literary creation, Sherlock Holmes. However unnatural it may appear to a later generation, I suspect that Doyle was impressed by the physical and mental control the Jesuits exercised over themselves; not only was this kind of control regarded by Doyle personally as among the highest virtues, but he must have admired to a degree the Society's discipline which required each member to master the classical languages, theology, philosophy, as well as one or more scientific or cultural areas of knowledge. Holmes himself embodies both an interest in ancient cultures and languages as well as a mastery of modern science to the extent that it can be put to use in his profession. Yet, by the time Arthur left Stonyhurst for Feldkirch, he also found himself repelled by the Jesuit teaching methods and quite prepared to reject Roman Catholicism and all belief in Heaven and Hell. It was while in Austria that Arthur discovered Edgar Allan Poe. His own mental landscape was more than a little haunted by ghosts. During these years, Arthur's father had become increasingly subject to fits and hallucinations. Arthur himself was in the throes of conflict between the dreamy side of his personality and the rational. There is no question that Poe's stories of ratiocination would exert a tremendous affect on him, since he subsequently consolidated and perfected Poe's techniques in fashioning his own stories; but at this time Poe's strange combination of fascination with the preternatural and fundamental materialism may have held more appeal.

After a short trip to Paris to visit with his godfather, Arthur returned to Edinburgh. It was a family decision in which he concurred that he study medicine. He entered the University of Edinburgh where he qualified for a bachelor of medicine degree in 1881 and graduated a doctor of medicine in 1885. In 1879, while still an undergraduate, Arthur wrote his first story, "The Mystery of the Sasassa Valley," and sold it to CHAMBERS' JOURNAL. He began writing other stories. In the meantime, his father's condition worsened to the point that he entered an insane asylum where he would die in 1893. This added an increased burden on the family—there were three older daughters and four younger children, of which Arthur's brother, Innes, was the youngest. It was Arthur's hope that his writing might supplement the family's income until he could begin practicing medicine.

The year 1880 was an important one. Whenever he could find time, Arthur sought to replace his father in the upbringing of Innes. That year Arthur also attended his first lecture on spiritualism titled "Does Death End All?" Arthur was unconvinced. His spiritual mentors were rather Renan, Carlyle, and Winwood Reade, men who believed that Nature was ordered, coherent, harmonious. In sharp contrast to this, and to the homilies of Roman Catholicism, was the procession of the sick and dying which he encountered. Christianity did not seem to hold any answer for the riddle of human suffering. Arthur made the decision to lapse in the practice of his religion, an act which caused The Ma'am severe consternation. Finally, to help further with the family's flagging resources, Arthur accepted a position as a ship's surgeon (in those days a medical degree was not required in this job) aboard a whaling vessel, the *Hope*.

In all, he was at sea seven months. He fell in love with the Arctic Ocean. Visions from this journey were to remain with him the rest of his life. In 1881, Arthur again accepted a position as surgeon aboard the *Mayumba*, bound for Africa's Gold Coast. The ship ran into gales in the Bay of Biscay and, from that point on, the trip became a series of nightmares, of malaria, blackwater fever, with Arthur himself succumbing to typhoid fever in Nigeria. He was narrowly missed by a shark when swimming and, on the return voyage, the ship was swept by fire; it was still smoking when it was tugged back into the Liverpool docks.

After a brief experience in partnership with a quack, Arthur opened his own practice in Southsea, Portsmouth in 1882. Since patients were few, he turned once more to writing, producing stories which, as Charles Higham noted, show "the influence of Poe in their manner of conveying the wildest excesses of fancy in an atmosphere of documentary realism."[2] Again and again in these stories, Conan Doyle evoked the theme of love and death. In "The Captain of the 'Pole-Star,' " a story obviously inspired in part by his Arctic voyage and published in TEMPLE BAR magazine in 1883, the first-person narrator is a ship's doctor who describes the events which occur when the whaling vessel which he is on is moored to an ice floe. The captain of the ship, a neurotic haunted by visions of his dead mistress calling him to join her in the spirit world, makes the crew nearly mutinous with his strange carryings on. Finally, seeing her drifting across the ice floe, he jumps ship and disappears into the night. When finally his body is found, the narrator observes that "sure it is that Captain Nicholas Craigie had met with no painful end, for there was a bright smile upon his blue, pinched features, and his hands were still outstretched, as though grasping at the strange visitor who had summoned him away into the dim world that lies beyond the grave."[3] Nor is this fixation upon necrophilia confined to fiction written during the 1880s; rather it is a generating line running through Conan Doyle's work from beginning to end which culminated with his conversion to spiritualism. In "The Ring of Thoth," a story published in THE CORNHILL in 1890, an Egyptologist has a nocturnal encounter in the Egyptian room of the Louvre with an ancient Egyptian high priest whom he discovers kissing a mummy perfectly preserved in all her beauty until exposed to the air at which point she disintegrates. The high priest's name is Sosra and he tells the Egyptologist his story, how he found the secret of extending his life indefinitely. Yet, before he could convince the woman he loved that she, too, should take the potion, she died of a plague. An antidote to the potion was hidden in the ring of Thoth. After centuries of searching for that ring, he has now found it and can die. " 'I have found my quest,' " he says. " 'The old curse is broken. I can rejoin her. What matter about her inanimate shell so long as her spirit is awaiting me at the other side of the veil!' "[4] The next day Sosra is found dead, embracing one of the mummies. "So close was his embrace that it was only with the utmost difficulty that they were separated."[5] In Charles Higham's words, "the extraordinary perversion of the theme surpasses Poe,"[6] and it does foreshadow the belief in spiritualism and the nightly séances during which Conan Doyle would converse at length with a number of his deceased relatives. As the American writer, Harvey Fergusson, once put it, "a man's destiny is a thing he discovers, a mystery that unfolds,"[7] and while the future course of Conan Doyle's life may seem to follow a pattern to a would-be biographer, to Conan Doyle in 1882 it was still very much a mystery. One of his patients invited him to attend séances in Southsea, but he found them a disappointment. In fact, he felt the entire affair a hoax and put the matter before a friend, Major-General A. W. Drayson, a mathematician and astronomer, who glibly informed the young doctor that he had been victimized by mischievous spirits from the "other" world. Conan Doyle rejected this explanation out of hand, but when THE CAPTAIN OF THE "POLE-STAR" AND OTHER STORIES (1890) appeared in book form he dedicated the book to Drayson and they did remain friends. Conan Doyle began attending séances at Drayson's home in Portsmouth. Doyle was impressed by the psychic phenomena accompanying these sessions, including showers of butterflies descending from the ceiling, followed by profusions of flowers and vegetables. One of the mediums was a Mrs. Maggs. Her control came from

Brooklyn, as did spirit letters and even a large pigeon which fluttered around the heads of those at the table and left unspiritual liquid siftings fall to stain the Major-General's carpet.

Arthur's younger brother, Innes, came to live with him. Patients were few and Arthur computed how to live on twopence a day. Sometimes there was not even that and he and Innes subsisted on only crusts of bread. The stories he wrote in the late hours, once Innes was alseep, might be accepted, but it was the custom of the day that such magazine fiction be published anonymously and Conan Doyle was appalled to realize that his income from writing amounted only to fifty pounds a year.

In the summer of 1885, Conan Doyle made the acquaintance of Louise Hawkins who had come with her mother and brother to take the sea air. The brother fell ill and Conan Doyle diagnosed his condition as cerebral meningitis. The boy became a resident patient; there was no cure then. The boy died and on 6 August of that summer Conan Doyle and Louise, whom he called "Touie," were married. Louise had a tiny private income and Conan Doyle's married status increased the number of female patients willing to come to him. Conan Doyle's wife was neither gifted nor well-read, but she had been reared to be the ideal Victorian housewife, sewing, mending, cooking, and cleaning. Conan Doyle might be wrestling with some problem of metaphysics; Louise could fix him a cup of tea. Conan Doyle might be exhausted after writing one of his horror stories or having returned from a séance; Louise would take off his shoes or massage his brow. As he became more prosperous and cheerful, Conan Doyle gained weight, began playing cricket and soccer with the local teams, and was able to send Innes off to boarding school.

As much as he wanted it to be otherwise, Conan Doyle could not bring himself to believe that the mind and spirit survived death. "When the candle burns out," he wrote in THE NEW REVELATION (1918), after his conversion to spiritualism describing the way he once felt, "the light disappears. When the electric cell is shattered, the current stops. When the body dissolves there is an end of matter."[8] He had written a novel, presumably an autobiographical work which he titled THE NARRATIVE OF JOHN SMITH, but it was lost in the mails; he wrote another novel, THE FIRM OF GIRDLESTONE, only for it to be rejected by every publisher he approached. The success of his short stories kept him going. It was then he decided to try his hand at a detective story. He read Poe again, and Émile Gaboriau. From the former he got the idea of a narrator and an extraordinarily brilliant detective, from the latter the notion of a detective adept at disguises. Originally, he was going to name his detective Sherringford Hope, but he finally settled on Sherlock Holmes. He discarded the name Ormon Sacker for his narrator, settling on Dr. John H. Watson. One of his favorite books was Robert Louis Stevenson's NEW ARABIAN NIGHTS (1882). Some of these stories had appeared in THE CORNHILL. In fact, occasionally Conan Doyle's anonymous stories were opined to have been written by Stevenson. In these stories, Conan Doyle found many elements he could use, including Stevenson's title for one of them, "The Adventure of the Hansom Cab," which supplied the matrix for the initial Sherlock Holmes short stories. Stevenson was a romantic, as was Conan Doyle, and his stories are filled with exotic and bizarre and even terrifying events which occur behind the bland, staid, comfortable Victorian exteriors. Lieutenant Brackenbury Rich in "The Adventure of the Hansom Cab" is a veteran, returned from the Indian hill wars, prostrated by a sabre wound and jungle fever, feeling himself a foreigner in London, much as would Conan Doyle's narrator who had been disabled in the Second Afghan War.

Conan Doyle titled his novel A STUDY IN SCARLET. Working on it, he devised a methodology for the composition of detective fiction which he would never abandon. He would think of a crime and its solution first; then he would begin telling the story, concealing as much of the truth as he could until the solution was arrived at by the detective in the last pages. A number of writers had turned to detective fiction, of course, since Poe, but Doyle did something none of the others had thought to do: he made his detective far more interesting than the problem being investigated. For his human model, Conan Doyle chose Dr. Joseph Bell, a skilled surgeon who gave extracurricular lectures on clinical surgery at the Edinburgh Infirmary when Arthur was a medical student. Bell had taken a liking to Conan Doyle and had engaged him as his outpatient clerk. Arthur played much the same role to Bell as Watson would to Holmes. Bell took great pleasure in "deducing" the biographies of patients he was seeing for the first time, amazing his clerk by his incredible accuracy. Naturally, I do not know if Bell referred to this process as deduction; obviously neither Poe nor Conan Doyle had studied formal logic, or there would never have been the confusion rampant in their fiction between what is properly deduction and what is induction.

Jacques Barzun maintained, I believe with justification, that "the short story [is] the true medium of detection. Pleasant as it is to begin a novel that promises a crowd of actors and incidents, of clues and disquisitions upon clues, the pleasure is soon marred by the apparently unavoidable drawback of a subplot and its false leads."[9] Conan Doyle was unable to solve this problem in A STUDY IN SCARLET; in fact it was S. S. Van Dine in his Philo Vance stories who hit upon the idea of *multiple* murders to sustain a reader's interest throughout a detective novel, a device that was shamelessly imitated by a legion of writers after him. What Conan Doyle did was to pad his book with an explanatory subplot, a very lengthy flashback of events which led up to the crime in London, events which showed the Mormons to be evil conspirators and which was directly from the pages of Mayne Reid. Conan Doyle even accepted as fact the notion of the Great American Desert, telling his reader that "from the Sierra Nevada to Nebraska, and from the Yellowstone River in the north to the Colorado upon the south, is a region of desolation and silence."[10]

Conan Doyle sent the completed manuscript first to THE CORNHILL, only to have it returned. He commenced work on an historical novel, MICAH

CLARKE, and sent it out again. It was only when he tried Ward, Lock, a firm which published a number of his favorite writers, including Sir Walter Scott and Bret Harte, that Conan Doyle was successful. The firm purchased the copyright for twenty-four pounds but said that the story would not be published for a year. It appeared in BEETON'S CHRISTMAS ANNUAL in December, 1887.

Charles Doyle was subject to *grand mal* epileptic seizures and no doubt sedative drugs, such as hyascin and morphine, were administered to him. Conan Doyle merely reversed the process: Holmes took cocaine to stimulate his cerebral faculties. When A STUDY IN SCARLET was issued in book form in 1888, the publisher contacted Charles Doyle in the asylum and hired him to do the illustrations. These drawings were done by a man under great mental duress, and for Holmes Charles Doyle used himself, as he looked when a younger man, a tall figure with a pale beard. These are, in fact, the only illustrations in the history of the stories which picture Holmes with a beard.

Conan Doyle's primary ambition was to write historical fiction. Here he was a victim again of Mayne Reid. Reid liked to have his characters speak in the vernacular, to such a degree that what they say is incomprehensible to a modern reader. In MICAH CLARKE (1889), set during the time of the Rebellion and when James, Duke of Monmouth, was a pretender to the crown, Conan Doyle used a deliberately antiquated period diction for dialogues which was pronounced historically incorrect for the Seventeenth century by an editor at Blackwoods who turned down the book. However, when Longmans, Green published the novel, it met with a critical reception that was favorable and which coincided with the birth of Conan Doyle's first child, Mary Louise, named after The Ma'am and Touie. Conan Doyle set to work at once on THE WHITE COMPANY (1892) which, when it appeared in serial form in THE CORNHILL in 1891, was declared by the editor to be the greatest historical novel since IVANHOE. It was set in the Fourteenth century.

Conan Doyle was invited to a supper at the Langham Hotel by Joseph Marshall Stoddart, editor of LIPPINCOTT'S MONTHLY MAGAZINE in Philadelphia. Oscar Wilde was also present, telling entertaining stories and even praising MICAH CLARKE. Stoddart commissioned a new Sherlock Holmes novel from Doyle and from Wilde the novella he would call PICTURE OF DORIAN GRAY. Conan Doyle's novel was titled THE SIGN OF THE FOUR. Holmes' character was further fleshed out. At the very beginning, he injects himself with a seven-percent solution of cocaine. We learn that as Garboriau's Lecoq he is a specialist in footprints and tobaccos and that as Dupin he can read his friend's past history from simple observations in the manner of Dr. Bell. Holmes' client is Mary Morstan, Conan Doyle's image of the perfect woman. Of course, Holmes' deductions are superficially impressive, although ultimately they occasionally lack substance or logical necessity. For example, Holmes informs Watson that " 'I knew you had not written a letter, since I sat opposite to you all morning. I see also in your open desk there that you have a sheet of stamps and a thick bundle of postcards. What could you go into a post office for, then, but to send a wire? Eliminate all other factors, and the one which remains must be the truth.' "[11] Yet, as commentators have pointed out, Watson might have gone for a money order or a postal order, or to inquire the cost of sending a package, or even to buy stamps of a different value than those on his sheet. Holmes did *not* eliminate all the other factors. Jonathan Small's assistant in this novel is an Andamanese Islander whom Conan Doyle totally misrepresented. Charles Higham found that Conan Doyle based his impression of these aborigines on a "harrowing and xenophobic account"[12] which he had read in THE INTERNATIONAL REVIEW. Holmes insists that the Andamanese Islanders " 'have always been a terror to shipwrecked crews, braining the survivors with their stone-headed clubs, or shooting them with their poisoned arrows. These massacres are invariably concluded by a cannibal feast.' "[13] T. S. Blakeney, commenting on this passage, remarked that the aborigines "are *not* cannibals—I was told in 1936, while on a visit to the Andaman Islands, by the Chief Commissioner, that when the aborigines had been questioned about this practice, they expressed horror at the idea. . . . Holmes' gazetteer gave a very untrue picture of the Andamanese; they were rather attractive little people, whose treatment at the hands of the Government of India was nothing less than tragic."[14]

At one point in the narrative, Holmes counsels Watson that " 'Women are never to be entirely trusted—not the best of them,' " which Watson dismisses as an "atrocious sentiment."[15] The reader's credulity is really strained when Conan Doyle has a Scotland Yard man allow Watson to take a chest, thought to contain a treasure but so far unopened, to Mary Morstan to open it while the official remains outside in a cab; and he accepts glibly Watson's assurance, upon returning with the chest having been opened, that it was found to be empty! In Jonathan Small's statement, the other three signatories who make up the "Four" are declared to be Sikhs, whereupon Conan Doyle gave all three of them Mohammedan names Sikhs would never have. It would be equivalent, wrote one commentator, Dr. Andrew Boyle, to Watson claiming an intimate "knowledge of Scotland and then [to] set down a tale about three simple Highland soldiers named Venizelos, Vasco de Gama, and Voroshilov."[16]

"I have never been nervous about details," Conan Doyle confessed years later in his autobiography, "and one must be masterful sometimes."[17] It is largely due to this happenstance—which accounts for such oddities as John Watson's wife referring to him on one occasion as James or the fact that Conan Doyle became confused as to just *how* Watson had been wounded in Afghanistan—that there emerged so much critical commentary on the stories over the years in a collective effort, similar to Biblical Higher Criticism, either to point out errors, omissions, implausibilities, contradictions, and impossibilities, or to reconcile these somehow into a more encompassing unity in which everything is explained logically. This would indicate to me, at least, that the principal attraction of the Sherlock Holmes stories was their ostensible appeal to logic which was inevitably at odds with Conan Doyle's inherent irrationality.

At this time, based on a casual conversation with a Harley Street physician, Conan Doyle decided to give up general practice and become an ophthalmologist. Leaving little Mary behind with The Ma'am, Conan Doyle and Louise went to Vienna for a period of six months so Arthur could study the human eye at the Krankenhaus. Finding himself unable really to grasp complex medical terminology in German, Conan Doyle spent most of his time ice skating with Louise at the Prater, drinking with English journalists, and writing a rather disappointing fictional piece. When he returned, he set up a small office in London as an eye specialist despite his having no supporting diplomas. Rather predictably, he was unable to attract a single patient. However, it did not greatly matter. He soon struck an agreement with H. Greenough Smith, editor of THE STRAND MAGAZINE, to write a series of stories for that publication featuring Holmes and Watson as continuing characters. These stories, too, are filled with improbabilities. The reader of "A Scandal in Bohemia" is to believe that the King of Bohemia, seeking to conceal his identity, would nonetheless arrive at Holmes' rooms dressed so sumptuously he could not help but stand out among the people in the street. In "The Red-Headed League" the reader is to accept as the most natural thing that a pawnbroker would show only the slightest of suspicions when being set to work copying the ENCYCLOPEDIA when he doubtless was aware that it was readily available. However, once again, it did not greatly matter. These stories entranced the reading public and established Conan Doyle as the most popular British writer of his time; they made Sherlock Holmes a household word. Why? I believe it was because readers did not care in the least about the plots of the stories; what concerned them, above all, was the personality of Sherlock Holmes and, of course, his friendship with Watson; and, yes, the personality of Watson himself. " 'From a drop of water . . . ,' " Sherlock Holmes had assured Watson in A STUDY IN SCARLET, " 'a logician could infer the possibility of an Atlantic or a Niagara without having seen or heard of one or the other. So all life is a great chain, the nature of which is known whenever we are shown a single link of it.' "[18] This was Holmes' religion; and it was a religion his readers and admirers were only too willing to believe.

"As the creation of a doctor who had been soaked in the rationalist thought of the period," Pierre Nordon wrote in CONAN DOYLE: A BIOGRAPHY (1964), "the Holmesian cycle offers us for the first time the spectacle of a hero triumphing again and again by means of logic and scientific method. And the hero's prowess is as marvellous as the power of science, which many people hoped would lead to a material and spiritual improvement of the human condition, and Conan Doyle first among them."[19] Conan Doyle did his best to imagine grotesque, even terrifying, situations which, when subjected to Holmes' analytic methods, could readily be reduced to the commonplace. Nothing is so reassuring as this. Contrast twelve-year-old Edgar's first experience of life in Stefan Zweig's novella, "*Brennendes Geheimnis*" [Burning Secret] (1911): "For the first time he now became aware that he had grown up in an atmosphere of evident comfort and that to the right and to the left of his life gaped abysses deep into darkness, which he had never seen before. For the first time he sensed something of it, that there were callings and occupations, that there were thronged around his life secrets, near to the grasp and still never noticed."[20] The dark abysses, set forth in the opening pages of a Holmes story, usually right after some demonstration by Holmes of the superiority of his method of observation, are dissipated by the end. Holmes and Watson may live in rooms surrounded by fogs and mists, but Holmes is a beacon in the night; he restores to all "the atmosphere of evident comfort" in which they have grown up.

While there are crimes of blood in the cycle of short stories Conan Doyle wrote about Holmes, there are no scenes of slaughter and certainly nothing even remotely resembling the "serial" murders which S. S. Van Dine was to make popular in detective stories. In some of the stories there is not so much as a corpse and in the twelve stories contained in THE ADVENTURES OF SHERLOCK HOLMES which ran in THE STRAND, nine contain no murder whatsoever. Later, of course, murders figure more prominently, but only for accentuation, never as the source of the drama itself. The criminals we encounter are usually professionals or from the privileged class. The threats to property and the social order are always made by immoral individuals, not by those classes who might have good reason to oppose the Establishment. Most of the women we meet are almost unbelievably innocent and almost always insipid. They exist to move along the plot, as they do in Mayne Reid's fiction, and Conan Doyle took so little interest in them that in four cases their Christian names are Violet. As Pierre Nordon observed, "this name is as common in the stories as dukes in Shakespeare's plays."[21] Holmes frequently breaks into houses, but this is acceptable because his objective is wholesome; and, when he feels a murderer justified, he is not above letting him go free. These proclivities were to have distant ramifications in the development of detective fiction and in the history of the detective film. Thanks to Watson, the reader is also given a stylized portrait of London, a city fascinating in its diversity, as a fashion center, its literary and artistic society, its business district, its hotels and theatres, galleries and concert halls, and London as a sea port. The imagery is so intensely imagined that it becomes cinematic before there was a cinema. "Sherlock Holmes was never at fault," Watson wrote in THE SIGN OF THE FOUR, "and he muttered the names as the cab rolled through squares and in and out by tortuous by-streets. 'Rochester Row,' said he. 'Now Vincent Square. Now we come out on the Vauxhall Bridge Road. We are making for the Surrey side, apparently. Yes, I thought so. Now we are on the bridge. You can catch glimpses of the river.' We did indeed get a fleeting view of a stretch of the Thames, with the lamps shining upon the broad, silent water; but our cab dashed on, and was soon involved in a labyrinth of streets upon the other side."[22]

W. Somerset Maugham, who was himself rather adept at writing short stories, noted in his essay, "The Decline and Fall of the Detective Story," how when he was preparing his anthology, TELLERS OF TALES (1939), he re-

read the collected stories of Conan Doyle. "I was surprised," he wrote, "to find how poor they were. The introduction is effective, the scene well set, but the anecdote is thin and you finish the tale with a sense of dissatisfaction. . . . You know no more of Sherlock Holmes after you have read fifty stories than you did after reading one, but the constant reiteration has broken down your resistance; and this lay figure, decked out with theatrical properties, has acquired the same sort of life in your imagination as is held by Vautrin or Mr. Micawber. No detective stories have had the popularity of Conan Doyle's, and because of the invention of Sherlock Holmes I think it may be admitted that none has so well deserved it."[23] The magic of these stories also, it seems to me, is a direct consequence of the way in which Conan Doyle structured them, as if they were all part of an elaborate saga only some parts of which have been made accessible to the reading public. The stories are filled with internal references to other stories, some of which have been told, some of which were not to be told. There is the counterpoint between Holmes and Watson: " 'Excellent!' I cried. 'Elementary,' said he." However, this is as close as Conan Doyle ever came to the apocryphal, "Elementary, my dear Watson."

In THROUGH THE MAGIC DOOR (1907) Conan Doyle himself diagnosed the chief attraction of Boswell's THE LIFE OF SAMUEL JOHNSON, LLD. (1781). "It is just these pen pictures of his of the big, uncouth man, with his grunts and his groans, his gargantuan appetite, his twenty cups of tea, and his tricks with the orange peel and the lamp-posts, which fascinate the reader and have given Johnson a far broader literary vogue than his writings could have done."[24] Surely this is what Conan Doyle had in mind himself as a literary model when he began his series of the Adventures in THE STRAND. In the very first story, "A Scandal in Bohemia," Holmes comments: " 'I am lost without my Boswell.' " As Pierre Nordon discerned, "if the dramatic element is abstracted from the Adventures, leaving only the human relationship between Holmes and Watson, the cycle seems to be a sort of anecdotal biography."[25]

When Doyle's first stories, "A Scandal in Bohemia" and 'The Red-Headed League," arrived on H. Greenough Smith's desk, he read them and then this usually staid man went at once to the publisher, George Newnes, shaking with such excitement that the manuscript pages trembled in his hand. "They're two stories by Dr. Conan Doyle!" he is said to have cried out. "This is the greatest short-story writer since Edgar Allan Poe."[26] Needless to say, Conan Doyle, who was even then plotting out in his mind his next historical novel, did not agree with their high estimation, although he was pleased with the prospect of handsome remuneration.

There was still one more factor in Holmes' sudden popularity. By mistake, Sidney Paget was summoned to do the illustrations; it was his brother, Walter, who should have been engaged, but Sidney accepted the assignment and used Walter, who was tall, elegant, dark-haired, and good-looking, for his model. Paget's image of Sherlock Holmes, in Charles Higham's words, "had hundreds of thousands of young women yearn for this fictional character as they might yearn for a stage actor, and a similar number of men wanted to emulate his flawless tailoring and various forms of headgear. Sherlock Holmes became a star before movies were born, and through no wish of his creator."[27] It was Paget, not Conan Doyle, who provided Holmes with the inimitable deerstalker.

Both in serial form in THE STRAND and in newspapers in the United States and then in book form, the Sherlock Holmes stories proved sensationally successful. Conan Doyle indulged his desire to travel and he took Louise, when pregnant, on a trip to Norway during which they experienced a stormy crossing. At home in England, he had taken her tricycling with him in wet weather; and they went to Switzerland where they encountered severe snowstorms and cold; it was here that Conan Doyle first observed the three-hundred-foot Reichenbach Falls. Back in London, the pains in Louise's side and her cough became worse and Conan Doyle had her consult another physician and then a third: the opinion was unanimous. Louise had tuberculosis, a death sentence in 1893. Conan Doyle blamed himself for not having suspected her condition earlier and he came, increasingly, to resent the deadlines for the Sherlock Holmes stories and the necessity of having constantly to think up new puzzles. He decided to kill off Holmes, which he did in "The Final Problem," Holmes supposedly plunged over the cliff at the Reichenbach Falls, locked in a deathgrip with his adversary, the Napoleon of Crime, Professor James Moriarty.

The reaction was instantaneous. More than twenty thousand cancelled their subscriptions to THE STRAND. Tens of thousands wrote letters of protest, terming it a foul act of murder. Women appeared in mourning and men wore black silk bands around their hats or on their coat sleeves.

The Conan Doyles were not in England at the time, but in Switzerland, at the Kurhaus Hotel in Davos, where better weather and care might ease Touie's condition. Two months prior to Holmes' death, Charles Doyle had swallowed his tongue during an epileptic seizure; this personal torment, combined with Louise's illness, and being surrounded by dying consumptives sparked Conan Doyle's interest again in spiritualism. When Touie had shown no interest in séances, and The Ma'am had condemned such things out of hand, Conan Doyle's enthusiasm had become dormant, but now he began increasingly to brood on the possibility of the survival of the human soul.

In the years immediately ahead, Conan Doyle, now retired completely from medicine, devoted himself to writing. He came to the United States on a lecture tour. With Louise, he visited Egypt, which was then a British Protectorate, and he became a special investigator for the Society for Psychical Research. He moved his family into the country and was often irritable and given to despair. Then, in March, 1897, he fell in love with Jean Leckie. She was the quintessential Victorian woman insofar as she believed men ought to be worshipped and she did worship Conan Doyle. She was extremely well read, had studied voice although she was not a professional vocalist; and she was a brilliant conversationalist. She rarely quarreled with Conan Doyle, although, at the time, she did not share his interest in spiritualism. However, Conan Doyle was adamant about one thing. There had been no intimacy between him and Touie since her condition had been diagnosed, but he would not be unfaithful to her as long as she lived. E. W. Hornung, who would create the Raffles character named after Conan Doyle's alchemist, Raffles Daw, had married Conan Doyle's sister, Connie, and both he and Connie urged Arthur to consummate his relationship with Jean. Conan Doyle would not hear of it and in this The Ma'am, who had once impressed on her son her own rapture with the fantasy of a pure and shining knight of honor, upheld him now in his decision. But Conan Doyle did become more and more haunted by nightmares and unable to sleep. Spiritualism for him as for many people at that time was a form of rebellion against the rationalism of the new age of science in which everything might be explained and even the straight line would be replaced with a curve that is a continuous function without a differential co-efficient. Philo Vance, one of Sherlock Holmes' successors, would aptly sum up the problem: " 'No human being, however, intellectual, can escape the results. The mathematician who repudiates nature's laws is nevertheless amenable to those laws. Indeed, his rapt absorption in hyperphysical problems merely increases the pressure of his denied emotions. And outraged nature, in order to maintain her balance, produces the most grotesque fulminations—reactions which, in their terrible humor and perverted gaiety, are the exact reverse of the grim seriousness of abstruse mathematical theories. The fact that Sir William Crookes and Sir Oliver Lodge—both great mathematical physicists—became confirmed spiritualists, constitutes a similar psychological phenomenon.' "[28]

Conan Doyle decided to revive Sherlock Holmes, this time as a stage play, to prove, among other things, that he did not really hate the sleuth. The plot of the play would take place before the incident at the Reichenbach Falls, but it would feature the diabolical Professor Moriarty. Originally, Conan Doyle had thought of Herbert Beerbohm Tree to play Moriarty; but after a meeting with Tree, where the actor proposed playing *both* Moriarty and Holmes, and Holmes with a beard so the audience could tell the two characters apart, he dismissed that idea. Charles Frohman, the leading theatrical producer in New York, met with Conan Doyle and they got on famously. It was agreed between them that William Gillette would be ideal for the part of Holmes. "It will be perfectly all right, Mr. Frohman," Conan Doyle said. "But I make one stipulation. You are a genius of the romantic production. There must be no love business in SHERLOCK HOLMES."[29]

Gillette was taken with the idea, but he extensively revised Conan Doyle's stage version, adroitly combining plot ingredients from several of the short stories. At the end, Gillette had Holmes falling in love with the heroine. Conan Doyle liked Gillette's revised version, although the romantic ending nettled him. He was anxious to meet with the actor and in May, 1898, the actor crossed the Atlantic. He met Conan Doyle at the train station dressed in a deerstalker, an ulster, and carrying a silver-topped cane. He was, indeed, the drawings of

Sidney Paget brought to life. Gillette took out a large magnifying glass and began to inspect Conan Doyle's face. "Unquestionably an author," was his conclusion. Conan Doyle broke out in thunderous laughter.[30] Once at Hindhead, in conversation with Conan Doyle, he told the former medical man something of his life. Ordinarily cold, reserved, even taciturn, he had a mocking sense of humor and a cruel logic. Women were no longer of any interest to him. Despite his fame and agreeable countenance, his heart had been broken by the death of his wife. He read widely and had an interest in spiritualism. The two hit it off so well that when Gillette returned to New York he cabled Conan Doyle with a question: "May I marry Holmes?" Conan Doyle cabled back: "Marry him or murder him or do what you like with him."[31] The play went on to become a phenomenal success. After its long New York run—216 performances—Gillette brought it to the United Kingdom. On this British tour and in the London revival of 1905 the role of Billy, the young page who represents the Baker Street Irregulars, was played by a juvenescent Charlie Chaplin.

In the meantime, Conan Doyle devoted himself to working on another stage play which enjoyed a modest success, wrote a sentimental novel filled with glimpses of his marriage to Louise, rode to hounds along with Jean Leckie, played cricket and soccer although past forty, and produced some of his most haunting horror stories. I would strain the credulity of the reader were I to ignore completely the terrible tension which must have persisted in Conan Doyle's life at this time, in love with two women and continent with both. Perhaps in part as an escape from this intolerable situation, he became caught up with the Boer War in 1900, enlisting for service as a physician and an unofficial attaché. When he was ready to embark for South Africa, Jean Leckie had his stateroom filled with flowers.

This was not "modern" warfare as he would later witness in France, but it was, notwithstanding, an overwhelming experience. The Langman Hospital, where he served, was overflowing with patients. For a long time, there was no water—it had been cut off by the Boers—and typhoid was epidemic. The physician-in-chief, Robert O'Callaghan, quit in frustration and returned to London. Conan Doyle was among those left in charge. In quarters intended to house three hundred, there were a thousand men. They were unable to sleep, water pimples erupted on their skins, their tongues became dessicated and turned black while their gums rotted, stools poured out of them, soaking through the beds and onto the parched grass of those housed outside the pavilion, delirium and death stalked through the compound. Thousands of flies, attracted by the offal, swarmed over the patients, crawling on their faces and invading all their orifices, nearly smothering them. Sixty victims a day were buried in shallow graves, wrapped in hospital blankets. One morning, out riding, the wind blew at him from the hospital, and Conan Doyle had to vomit. That evening he came down himself with a mild version of the fever.

After he recovered, he managed to go to the front during a brief leave of absence. In July, 1900, he was released from active service and went to Pretoria to make a report on the conduct of the Langman Hospital, which had been the subject of criticism in the South African, British, and American press. He saw Lord Roberts, commander of the British forces. Lord Roberts was concerned about charges of poor hygiene and incompetence among the staff at the field hospital. Conan Doyle apparently satisfied him. On 11 July, he set out on the return voyage to England. Once there, he began to work indefatigably on THE GREAT BOER WAR (1900), a history of the conflict which appeared that same year. He saw Jean Leckie as much as he could without, he believed, Louise's knowledge. Accordingly, most of Conan Doyle's biographers have gone along with the supposition that Louise remained in the dark about the relationship. Not only in this highly fanciful, in view of the fact that even Louise's mother knew about it and was scarcely sympathetic, but the affair was a constant source of family dissension. When Conan Doyle came to London for a cricket match, shortly after his return from South Africa, both Hornung, who was known familiarly as Willie, and Jean Leckie had been present. Conan Doyle later wrote to The Ma'am that "Willie's tone was that of an attorney dissecting a case, instead of a brother standing by a brother in need. Among other remarks he said that I attached too much importance to whether the relations were platonic or not—he could not see that 'that made much difference.' I said 'the difference between guilt and innocence.' But could you conceive such nonsense. Of course when I saw this carping tone I refused to speak further on so sacred a matter, and I left the house not angrily but in a serious frame of mind which is more formidable."[32]

It strikes me as improbable that Louise—who did not die until 4 July 1906 at the age of forty-nine—should not herself have been troubled. Certainly Conan Doyle was tortured by his mixed and divided sympathies. Little trace of Louise is to be found in Conan Doyle's fiction, although Mary Morstan (who also died at an early age of illness in the Sherlock Holmes stories) was probably based on her; and there is nothing about her in Conan Doyle's private papers. However, Mary Conan Doyle did write to Pierre Nordon on 31 January 1957 that some two months before the end her mother had called her to her room for a talk. "She told me that some wives sought to hold their husbands to their memory after they had gone—that she considered this very wrong, as the consideration should be the loved one's happiness. To this end she wanted me not to be shocked or surprised if my Father married again, but to know that it was with her understanding and blessing."[33]

In his personal life, Conan Doyle's attitude toward women was in contrast to his indifference toward them in the Sherlock Holmes stories. He was staunchly opposed to suffrage for women, yet he was in favor of liberalizing the divorce law. Prior to 1857, no legislation regarding divorce had been in existence; divorce could only be had as a result of a parliamentary decision, an expensive and complicated procedure to say the least. The 1857 law made civil divorce possible, but on unequal terms. The husband need only prove adultery; the wife had to prove not only adultery but also that she had been deserted for an uninterrupted period of two years or that she had been brutalized. Conan Doyle felt the grounds should be the same for both sexes. This position brought him into violent opposition with the Church and was another inducement for him to seek in spiritualism a moral perspective that might replace what he felt was the antiquated morality of Christianity.

During the early years of the new century, Conan Doyle became a man in search of causes, or responded affirmatively when causes came to him. He wrote a pamphlet in defense of the British position in the conflict with the Boers titled THE WAR IN SOUTH AFRICA, ITS CAUSE AND CONDUCT. It was this pamphlet, when combined with his earlier history of the war, which led to his nomination for knighthood shortly after King Edward VII assumed the throne. Conan Doyle became a tireless defender of the oppressed native population of the Belgian Congo being mercilessly exploited by King Leopold II. He became a consultant in the defense of a number of men falsely accused and even convicted of crimes on the flimsiest circumstantial evidence. He went so far as to issue pamphlets explaining in concise Holmesian fashion the facts in these cases, gave of his time and effort without expectation of remuneration, and definitely in the Oscar Slater case, although the matter dragged on for years, succeeded in securing the man a retrial at which he was exonerated. Conan Doyle used the world-wide fame Sherlock Holmes had brought him in the service of humanity. This is something that virtually no other prominent author of detective fiction, with the notable exception of Erle Stanley Gardner, ever did. In fact, shortly after S. S. Van Dine was revealed to be Willard Huntington Wright, he was made an honorary police chief of Bradley Beach, New Jersey, near where he owned a dog kennel, only to confess himself utterly baffled by the hold-up and murder of a bank messenger. Conan Doyle may have modeled Sherlock Holmes on Dr. Joseph Bell, but the character was nonetheless very much an expression of one side of his complex personality.

In 1902, the year Conan Doyle was knighted, Sherlock Holmes made his reappearance in THE STRAND, this time in the novel, THE HOUND OF THE BASKERVILLES. It was still a story which had taken place before the tragedy at the Falls, but it was a new Holmes adventure and it was greeted with great enthusiasm by the reading public. The next year, as he privately became convinced that not only might the spirit survive the death of the brain but that it could be contacted by certain persons who were still alive and gifted with mediumistic qualities, he was also presented with a check for $5,000 by S. S. McClure of McCLURE'S MAGAZINE in New York to write a new series of Sherlock Holmes stories. The only condition was that these stories must come after the episode at Reichenbach Falls, that, in short, Holmes must be shown to have survived. Some years earlier, while on his lecture tour in the United States, Conan Doyle had lent McClure a similar sum to keep his magazine afloat. The money, nostalgia perhaps about McClure's gratitude, combined with his general feelings that death is not final and his political conviction that the

United States and Great Britain should join in managing the rest of the world (and thus, with his stories, to bring the American and British people closer together) comprised a temptation that was irresistable. In the summer of 1903, in "The Adventure of the Empty House," to Watson's immense astonishment and joy, and by now to that of millions of readers around the world, Sherlock Holmes made his dramatic return. Mycroft Holmes had seen that his brother's Baker Street lodgings had been maintained throughout his three-year absence. Professor Moriarty had died at the Reichenbach Falls, but not Holmes. Instead, Holmes had traveled about the world, living for a time in Tibet. He had had to keep his identity a secret because, even now, one of the professor's most desperate minions, Colonel Sebastian Moran, was in pursuit of him. Through a ruse, in which Mrs. Hudson, Holmes' landlady, also plays a part, Holmes and Watson capture Colonel Moran in the abandoned Camden House, across the street from the Baker Street diggings.

"There is only one house on the whole of Baker Street that answers the description," Vincent Starrett quoted Holmes specialist, Dr. Gray Chandler Briggs, "and when I told Sir Arthur that the sign 'Camden House' was over the door, he was amazed. He told me, with such seriousness that I could not doubt him, that he did not believe he had ever been in Baker Street in his life; if he had, it had been many years before—so long that he had forgotten!" Dr. Briggs added: "There is something spooky about Doyle, anyway."[34]

Conan Doyle did not dislike Holmes, as some would insist later. "I do not wish to be ungrateful to Holmes, who has been a good friend to me in many ways," Conan Doyle wrote subsequently. "If I have sometimes inclined to be weary of him it is because his character admits of no light or shade. He is a calculating machine, and anything you add to that simply weakens the effect. Thus the variety of stories must depend upon the romance and compact handling of the plots. I would say a word for Watson also, who in the course of seven volumes never shows one gleam of humor or makes one single joke. To make a real character one must sacrifice everything to consistency and remember Goldsmith's criticism of Johnson that 'he would make little fishes talk like whales.' "[35]

Conan Doyle quoted a Cornish boatman who had written to him to say that when Holmes had fallen over that cliff he may not have been killed himself, but that he was never quite the same man afterwards. Holmes, for one thing, was no longer a drug addict. Holmes was also now both judge and jury in certain cases. Conan Doyle's efforts on behalf of victims of the British judicial system had made him anything but a supporter. In "The Adventure of Charles Augustus Milverton" Holmes allows the murderer to go free, as he does in "The Adventure of the Devil's Foot." In the latter, Holmes comments: " 'I think you must agree, Watson, that it is not a case in which we are called upon to interfere. Our investigation has been independent, and our action shall be also. You would not denounce the man?' " To which Watson replies: " 'Certainly not.' "[36] Also in the latter, although Doyle resorted to the somewhat illegitimate device of a poison unknown to science, Holmes remained the clear-sighted rationalist. " 'I fear,' said Holmes 'that if the matter is beyond humanity it is certainly beyond me. Yet we must exhaust all natural explanations before we fall back upon such a theory as this.' " The theory Mortimer Tregennis would have Holmes fall back on is that the method of the crime " 'is not of this world.' "[37] But it is Holmes' belief in material causes and human agencies, and not Tregennis' preternatural proclivities, which emerges triumphant at the end.

As the cycle of Holmes stories continued, the decline continued; and so poorly executed are some of the very late ones—Conan Doyle wrote the last Holmes story in 1927—that Sherlockians take almost the same position toward THE CASEBOOK OF SHERLOCK HOLMES (1927), Conan Doyle's last collection of tales, that the Council of Nicea took toward what it regarded as spurious and apocryphal books which must needs be excised from the Bible. Two of the tales in this collection are narrated in the first person by Holmes himself and the third by a narrator who is neither Holmes nor Watson. "By universal consent," Jacques Barzun and Wendell Hertig Taylor wrote of the CASEBOOK in A CATALOGUE OF CRIME (1971), "these twelve stories are deemed inferior to every previous collection. The reason is not in their conception, which is often splendid, but in their execution, which is slovenly. Doyle was tired of Sherlock Holmes, he had picked up a great deal of American slang, and the effort to recreate the Victorian or Edwardian scene was beyond his strength. Still, there are fragments of dialogue and of desription in these tales that equal or surpass anything done earlier, and some of Holmes' most frequently quoted *mots* come from these decried adventures."[38]

Howard Haycraft was somewhat more acerbic, pointing out that even "so faithful a disciple as Vincent Starrett pairs a sizable group of earlier and later tales, bearing plot resemblances that seem more than accidental: 'A Scandal in Bohemia' and 'The Norwood Builder'; 'The Blue Carbuncle' and 'The Six Napoleons'; 'The Greek Interpreter' and 'The Solitary Cyclist'; 'The Naval Treaty' and 'The Second Stain.' Any discerning reader can easily expand the list. Repetitions of stock-characters, implements of crime and of detection, and similar minutiae are even more numerous throughout the long saga. All these are integral weaknesses that cannot be explained away, as certain others may be, by the obvious fact that Holmes came first in his particular field and has suffered from his imitators."[39] Haycraft was similarly harsh in his over-all judgment that, "aside from his masterly creation of character, little real originality or inventiveness can be claimed for Doyle."[40]

I incline toward E. M. Wrong who, in the Introduction to his collection of detective fiction, CRIME AND DETECTION (1926), quoted Horace, "*vixere fortes ante Agamemnona multi*" [there lived many brave heroes before Agamemnon],[41] only to conclude that in much the same way we "tend to think of the pre-Holmes detectives as of the pre-Shakespearean drama; to call them precursors only. Holmes was a really great achievement. From him dates the expansion of the last thirty years, and the crystallizing of one type of detective story. The canon is not exclusive but it is fixed; a friend of the detective tells the tale, as he did in Poe; he sees or can see all that the detective does, but never understands what deductions to draw from the facts. Thus the chief relevant incidents are in reality concealed from the reader though there is an ostentatious parade of openness. The detective's friend acts in the dual capacity of very average reader and of Greek chorus; he comments freely on what he does not understand."[42] Where I do not agree with Wrong is in his belief that "what one loves in Holmes, in truth, is not his logic but his habits and his colleague."[43] In fact, I suspect that one of the principal reasons it became commonplace among Sherlockians to deny Conan Doyle's authorship of the stories, insisting instead that he was but Dr. Watson's literary agent, is because many of those who loved the stories precisely because of their commitment to science and to reason rejected Conan Doyle on the grounds of *his* commitment to spiritualism.

Less than a year after Louise's death in 1906, Conan Doyle married Jean Leckie. Innes was best man and Conan Doyle's two children, the eighteen-year-old Mary and fifteen-year-old Kingsley, were there and welcomed their new stepmother warmly. In Constantinople, on their honeymoon, Sir Arthur and Lady Doyle both received high awards from Sultan Abdul-Hamid who, it turned out, was enamored of the Sherlock Holmes stories. Later, on a trip to Canada, the Conan Doyles received an enthusiastic reception in New York and Joseph Hodges Choate, former U.S. ambassador in London, introduced Conan Doyle to well-wishers as "the best known living Britisher."[44] In Canada, as Pierre Nordon wrote, "he was the official guest of the government, and had a chance to see the scenery that he had dreamt about ever since reading the works of Parkman, the historian. He went to stay at the national reserve of Jasper Park, made a trip to the Great Lakes, and journeyed from one end of the country to the other in the special train placed at his disposal."[45]

Conan Doyle, by virtue of the fame brought to him by Sherlock Holmes, became the intimate of a number of political figures, from King Edward VII to Prime Minister Herbert Asquith and Winston Churchill. He had always been a man in search of a cause and for a time he thought it might rest in a political career; twice unsuccessfully he ran for a seat in Parliament. He bought a new country estate, Windlesham, and it was here that he settled with his family and where his children with Jean were born, Denis, Malcolm (better known as Adrian), and Jean Lena (called Billy). It was finally in spiritualism that Conan Doyle found what he believed to be the *cause célèbre* of *his* career; he would bring to the world the wonders of its emancipation and his reputation as a physician and man of science would, he hoped, lend credence to his endorsement. What it did, as a matter of fact, was cost him a peerage, turn against him many of his highly influential friends, including King George V, Lloyd George, as well as Asquith and Churchill.

Conan Doyle's biographers have never quite known how to deal with this issue. John Dickson Carr avoided almost all mention of it. Pierre Nordon sought to explain, if not justify, it on the basis that Conan Doyle perceived in the tenets of spiritualism an antidote to the prevailing materialism in the Western world. Charles Higham narrated somewhat objectively Conan Doyle's immersion in spiritualism, but not even he was willing to see in it a recurrence of mental illness which had run in the family. Conan Doyle had been converted to spiritualism long before the Great War began; the conflict did not influence his behavior, but it did perhaps prompt him to go public with his convictions.

It is difficult today to understand the naive reaction to modern science and modern life which spiritualism posed for its many believers. Spiritualism postulated that life after death was a life of the mind as in the world there had been a life of the body. Food, money, and sexuality no longer existed, but the arts of music, painting, poetry and fine prose were avidly pursued. The dead lived in communities and marriages between them were purely incorporeal. Here, at last, could be found the happiness which eluded human beings when physically alive. There is no question that his belief in spiritualism forestalled a complete mental breakdown, since the Great War would claim the lives of all the young men of the family: Jean's brother, Malcolm Leckie; Arthur's nephews, Oscar Hornung and Alec Forbes; his brother, Innes; and his eldest son, Kingsley.

Jean's resistance eventually broke down and she became a passionate convert as well. In 1919, Conan Doyle accepted what he regarded as the greatest challenge of his life, to bring news of this joyous gospel to the peoples of the world. He lectured widely and indefatigably. The money earned by his lectures went to the spiritualistic cause and, in addition, he invested 250,000 pounds of his own money. Probably the best analogy to the spiritualistic waves following the global conflict would be the emergence in the United States of religious cults and "born-again" fundamentalism after the defeat in Vietnam.

Conan Doyle's gullibility was such that he believed obviously faked photographs of ectoplasmic manifestations to be authentic. Nor did it stop at this. Photographs, declared to be of fairies, showing young women wearing recent Paris fashions, were exposed as a fraud by a man from the Eastman laboratories. Conan Doyle immediately rallied to the defense of these photographs and wrote a book, THE COMING OF THE FAIRIES (1922), not only defending the photographs but promulgating his own belief in the existence of fairies and assuring readers of their essential neighborliness.

Séances became a nightly ritual at Windlesham and all members of the Conan Doyle family regularly participated. Conan Doyle also attended séances elsewhere. Once, at Merthyr Tydfil, in Wales, Conan Doyle wrote of how "for two hours my wife and I sat listening to the whispering voices of the dead, voices which are so full of earnest life, and of desperate endeavors to pierce the dull barriers of our sense."[46] In the darkness, Kingsley and Innes seemed to shimmer and grow in amplitude before their eyes. When Oscar Hornung, Willie and Connie's dead son, appeared, Arthur clutched at Jean's sleeve and cried out through his tears, "My God, if only people knew—*if only they could know!*"[47]

In instance after instance, no sooner would Conan Doyle make a public statement on behalf of some medium or some mediumistic experience, than the medium would be exposed by investigators to be a fraud. In some cases, as, for example, after The Ma'am had died and she was brought back during a séance and Conan Doyle grasped at her to embrace her only to pull back in horror at her large, very corporeal biceps, he would say nothing, feeling that ridicule of charlatans and imposters would weaken the cause. When the Conan Doyles came to the United States in 1922 on a tour in behalf of spiritualism, THE NEW YORK TIMES ran an editorial the following day, describing the once believed author as a pathetic figure and concluding that "with each of the interviews he gives it becomes harder to be patient with him."[48] When Conan Doyle would lecture, accompanied by a slide show of ostensibly authentic "spirit" photographs, with eerie music played on a gramophone, women would faint upon seeing the strange glowing faces, or scream, or wander up and down the aisles sobbing, calling out for news of loved ones who had died, many of them husbands or sons lost in the Great War. Newspapers in New York reported that Conan Doyle's seven lectures in that city had led to a rash of suicides by people anxious to visit the next world. One woman, Maude Fancher, after listening to Conan Doyle on the radio, murdered her two-year-old son and then consumed a bottle of Lysol, convinced that she could be of even greater service to her husband on the other side. She left burial instructions which indicated that she was to be placed sitting up in her tomb, holding her baby in her arms. Confronted with these numerous occurrences, Conan Doyle's pat answer was that these people misunderstood the true nature of spiritualism.

During the Great War, Conan Doyle had toured the front. It had been his intention to write a definitive history of the conflict, along the lines of his narrative of the Boer War. The scenes of carnage, on a scale and beyond anything he had witnessed or imagined in Africa, were overwhelming to him. When he visited General Humbert in the Argonne, the General fixed Conan Doyle with a hard look.

"*A propos,*" he said, "*Sherlock Holmes, est-ce-qu'il est un soldat dans l'armée anglaise?*"

"*Mais, mon général,*" Conan Doyle responded in halting French after an awkward pause, "*il est trop vieux pour service.*"[49]

In the world which emerged after the Great War, Sherlock Holmes, in Conan Doyle's opinion, no longer held any answers, if he ever had. "Why was this tremendous experience forced upon mankind?" he asked aloud in THE VITAL MESSAGE (1919). "Surely it is a superficial thinker who imagines that the great Designer of all things has set the whole planet in a ferment and strained every nation to exhaustion, in order that this or that frontier be moved, or some fresh combination be formed in the kaleidoscope of nations. No, the causes of the convulsion, and its objects, are more profound than that. They are essentially religious, not political."[50] The Great War was sent to humanity in order to arouse it from its spiritual torpor and put it in a position to recognize at last the enduring truths of spiritualism. The imagination which could so vividly imagine Sherlock Holmes, recreate history, transfix with tales of science fiction, fantasy, and horror, now conjured before Conan Doyle's eyes the spirits of his dead loved ones; his natural inclination toward morbidity now indulged itself so that he spent almost as much time with the dead, conversing with them, as he did with the living. Not for him was Horace's invocation: *"dum loquimur, fugerit invida aetas: carpe diem, quam minimum credula postero"* [even while we are speaking, the jealous time of life may have fled: seize the day, trusting as little as possible in what follows].[51]

II

The first film to feature a recognizable detective and, therefore, the first detective film was SHERLOCK HOLMES BAFFLED (Biograph, 1900). It opens to a burglar robbing the silverware. A man, obviously Holmes, enters the room smoking a cigar. He espies the burglar. Through trick photography, the burglar vanishes. The cigar explodes and the burglar reappears. Holmes shoots at him and, once again, the burglar vanishes. When he next reappears, Holmes grabs his loot. That is how it all began. Arthur Marvin was the cameraman. The film was 49 feet in duration.

Maurice Costello played the detective in the next film to be made, THE ADVENTURES OF SHERLOCK HOLMES (Vitagraph, 1903). This one ran 725 feet. But perhaps the most important very early Holmes films were those made by Viggo Larsen. Larsen was born on 14 August 1880 and, entering the military at the age of fourteen, he was sent to the Belgian Congo. When he saw an advertisement for the Nordisk Film Kompagni of Denmark, he applied and so became one of the first actors and directors working for the firm. He made a series of short Sherlock Holmes films for Nordisk, starring as Holmes, and then, in 1910, he emigrated to Germany where he stayed until 1945. In Germany as well he appeared as Sherlock Holmes in several films. Also in the 'Teens, Georges Treville starred in a series of twelve British-made Sherlock Holmes films which were distributed in the United States. William Gillette even made a stab at the role, starring in SHERLOCK HOLMES (Essanay, 1916). This film was based, of course, on Gillette's stage play which had been touring for almost two decades. Gillette was over sixty when this film was made. The MOVING PICTURE WORLD in its review of the film commented that "a few more years and it would have become impossible for Mr. Gillette to take the part with the physical vigor that would recall his best efforts of the old days to his international admirers, and at the same time would leave in comparatively permanent form his Sherlock Holmes for the delight of future generations."[52] Unfortunately no prints of Gillette's SHERLOCK HOLMES are known to survive.

All of this notwithstanding, unquestionably the most notable portrayal of Sherlock Holmes during the silent era was that of Eille Norwood in a series begun by Stoll Picture Productions in Great Britain in 1921. Conan Doyle wanted to be very much involved in this aspect of his creation. "Films . . . were unknown when the stories first appeared," he wrote, "and when these rights were finally discussed and a small sum offered for them by a French company it seemed a treasure trove and I was very glad to accept. Afterwards I had to buy them back again at exactly ten times what I had received, so the deal was a disastrous one. But now they have been done by the Stoll Company with Eille Norwood as Holmes, and it was worth all the expense to get so fine a production. Norwood has since played the part on the stage and won the approbation of the London public. He has that rare quality which can only be described as glamour, which compels you to watch an actor eagerly even when he is doing nothing. He has the brooding eye which excites expectation and he has also a quite unrivalled power of disguise. My only criticism of the films is that they introduce telephones, motor cars, and other luxuries of which the Victorian Holmes never dreamed."[53] Film rights were not the only rights Conan Doyle had had to buy back; in order to bring out all the Holmes stories in a collection he had had to buy back rights to A STUDY IN SCARLET for five thousand pounds!

Norwood was close to sixty when he first apeared as Holmes, but this seemed to bother no one. "My idea of Holmes is that he is absolutely quiet," Norwood commented. "Nothing ruffles him but he is a man who intuitively seizes on points without revealing that he has done so, and nurses them up with complete inaction until the moment when he is called upon to exercise his wonderful detective powers. Then he is like a cat—the person he is after is the only person in all the world, and he is oblivious of everything else till his quarry is run to earth."[54] Norwood was a master of make-up and he had the requisite control of his face muscles which, when combined with wax and wigs, could significantly transform his appearance. Since the silent film was *only* a visual medium, this emphasis on disguises no doubt contributed to the popularity of these films with viewers. For Chris Steinbrunner and Norman Michaels in their book, THE FILMS OF SHERLOCK HOLMES (1978), which includes eleven illustrations of Norwood's Holmes in various disguises, the fact that Stoll chose to make these films as contemporary vehicles constitutes no problem since "the portrait these films present of a vanished London has great charm" and, in their view, "despite this mild and almost unobtrusive updating, the rendering of Sherlock is accurate, the mood very much on target, and the adaptations (despite the necessity of title cards rather than spoken words) both well done and absolutely straight."[55]

I have quoted them because many of the Norwood films survive at the British Film Institute where I had occasion to screen them and my response was not nearly so positive. For me, these short films slavishly reproduce the short stories on which they are based and no real effort was made to adapt these fictions to the screen. THE MAN WITH THE TWISTED LIP (Stoll, 1921), with William J. Elliott credited for the screenplay, opens with establishing shots of the beggar through the arch of Barclay's Bank off Regent Street at Piccadilly Circus and proceeds to recount the story in a straight-forward fashion. Norwood physically is an interesting Holmes; Hubert Willis played Dr. Watson. However, THE BERYL CORONET (Stoll, 1921), with these same principals, narrates most of the story through a reconstruction via flashbacks, as does THE DYING DETECTIVE (Stoll, 1921). Obviously the filmmakers, confronted with a first-person narrative, did not quite know how to treat it; and, if these films are any indication, this narrative technique simply could not be managed viably in a silent film. On the other hand, Norwood's impersonation of Holmes does remain impressive despite the passage of time.

THE SIGN OF THE FOUR (Stoll, 1923) was Norwood's first Holmes feature. Arthur Bell played Athelney Jones of Scotland Yard and Arthur Cullin was cast as Dr. Watson. Much of the story is told by flashbacks, this time with Isobel Elsom as Mary Morstan telling Holmes about her father's mysterious death and his previous life in a Colonial prison. By the last reel, Holmes and Jones are in a speed boat chasing Jonathan Small and his dwarfish assistant along the Thames. The picture concludes with a close-up of the announcement of Watson's marriage to Mary Morstan.

Outside of this series and many other films, both short and long, about Sherlock Holmes, very little was done by way of filming detective stories in the silent era. Detectives did appear occasionally in chapter plays—Charlie Chan's first appearance was in a serial, albeit he was scarcely the central character—and in feature films as well, but their roles were usually comic. When Buster Keaton came to spoof a detective in SHERLOCK, JR. (M-G-M, 1924), Holmes was really the only one on whom he could base his film. It may well be that filmed detective stories ideally require the sound medium, a question which I address at further length in the next chapter. As it stands, the one detective film made during the silent era which continued to excite praise subsequently in the years following its release was SHERLOCK HOLMES (Goldwyn, 1922) directed by Albert Parker and starring John Barrymore as Holmes, Roland Young as Watson, and Gustav von Seyffertitz as Professor Moriarty. It, too, was based on Gillette's stage play. Some of the exteriors were filmed in London and in Switzerland. "I came over to England after Barrymore had arrived," Albert Parker later recalled, "and I was told that Barrymore couldn't be seen or found anywhere. I finally tracked him down to a tiny little attic room at the Ritz Hotel, and I went in and there was Barrymore sitting up in bed blind drunk. The room was in a terrible state. There were even gin bottles in his shoes! Eventually I got him to work, and I can tell you I had a pretty rough time with him on location in England. We had rows; it was a very tricky time. We went to Switzerland on location; more rows. They loaned us a whole train for filming, and even shifted a whole load of snow on one of the mountain tops when we got to the top and found there wasn't any! It was all done with great difficulty, as Barrymore was drunk most of the time. We returned to the States when we had all the location shots, and then I really had it out with Barrymore, a *real* row. I told him he was killing himself, and so forth. I really let him have it. And Barrymore must have seen the strength of what I was saying, and you know, he never touched a drop while we were filming all the interior scenes. I did it because I was fond of Barrymore, and I think he gave a very good, restrained performance in those scenes."[56]

Barrymore was a man of somewhat diminutive stature and one casting problem with him, as would later be the case also with George Raft, Edward G. Robinson, and Alan Ladd, was to find actors whose height did not exceed his and who were yet capable of carrying off their roles. "When the modest, self-effacing Roland appeared on my horizon," Barrymore recalled in his typically exaggerated manner of speaking concerning the casting of Roland Young as Dr. Watson, "I took a great liking to him; so much so that I began to feel sorry for him during our scenes together. For once in my life, I decided to be somewhat decent towards a colleague. I suggested a little stage business now and then, so that such a charming, agreeable thespian might not be altogether lost in the shuffle. When I saw the completed film, I was flabbergasted, stunned, and almost became an atheist on the spot. That quiet, agreeable bastard had stolen, not one, but every damned scene! This consummate artist and myself have been close friends for years, but I wouldn't think of trusting him on any stage. He is such a splendid gentleman in real life, but what a cunning, larcenous demon when on the boards."[57]

There are, of course, a good many scenes in which Holmes is not accompanied by Watson; and here, the chief attraction is Barrymore's physical appearance, not his acting. Steinbrunner and Michaels found that much of the dialogue, carried over from the stage play, only served to slow down the film. I tend to agree with them and in their conclusion that "there are surprisingly few visual highspots. Even the Stepney gas chamber scene (in the theatre version the climax of the second act), with its darting cigar and sleight-of-hand misdirection, fails to stun. And, strangely, many of the crackling lines in the final confrontation between detective and criminal are dropped."[58]

Carol Dempster, D. W. Griffith's favorite ingenue from this period, was cast as Alice Faulkner and Barrymore so detested her he even refused to film scenes with her. Notwithstanding, on screen, as on the stage (albeit with Holmes' recitations of his faults cut to a minimum), the film retains the romantic ending.

MORIARTY: You do not think that this is the end?
HOLMES: I rather hoped so, Moriarty. I start on my honeymoon tomorrow.

Basil Rathbone had occasion to work with Barrymore on ROMEO AND JULIET (M-G-M, 1936) directed by George Cukor. In his autobiography, he recalled the scene where Barrymore, as Mercutio, tries to conjure up Romeo, ending with the line, "He heareth not, he stirreth not, he moveth not." "As he approached this line," Rathbone wrote, "Barrymore took a deep breath, flexing his eyebrows and bulging his eyes. Then he said, 'He heareth not, he stirreth not.' Long pause, then with much relish, 'He pisseth not!'

"George groaned, 'Jack, *please.*'

" 'Strange how me heritage encumbereth my speech,' was Jack's reply. 'Dear Mr. Shakespeare, I beg you hear me yet awhile. I am but an improvident actor [pronounced actor-r-r] and yet I would beg you to consider an undeniable fact, I have improved upon your text. "He moveth not" is not so pertinent to the occasion as "he pisseth not." '

"And so it went on until nearly lunch time. Thalberg was sent for and came onto the set. Very gently he pleaded with Jack to speak the line as it was written.

" 'Very well,' rejoined Jack, 'just once I will say it that thou mayest see how it stinketh.' And he did, and that's the only 'take' they got from him that day and of course the one that appears in the picture."[59]

Despite the persistent problems producers and directors had with Barrymore, he continued to make films almost to the end of his life; although he would not appear in a detective film after SHERLOCK HOLMES until the Bulldog Drummond series at Paramount in the late 'Thirties. By that time, his excessive drinking had so affected his brain that he could no longer remember a single line and giant cue cards had to be held up for him to read even the simplest dialogue.

THE RETURN OF SHERLOCK HOLMES (Paramount, 1929) was the first sound Holmes film. David O. Selznick, at the time head of production at Paramount, told Clive Brook, who was under contract to the studio, that he looked very much like Sherlock Holmes. Brook did not agree. When he was aboard the *Olympic*, on his way to the States, he received a telegram informing him that he was to play Holmes in his next film. Basil Dean was the director and H. Reeves Smith was cast as Dr. Watson. The photoplay was filmed at Paramount's Astoria studio.

"We had a lot of trouble during the shooting of the film," Brook later recalled. "The director's work had hitherto been confined to the theatre, and he had little experience of movies, and how they are made; and he was misguided enough to try to teach the studio personnel their job. He insisted on having four-sided sets constructed, to assist the actors in a feeling of reality, not understanding that cameramen and sound-recordists could not operate in such a set-up. Finally, he left before the picture was completed and I finished directing the film myself. . . . I very much enjoyed Holmes. I characterized him larger than life and this permitted much comedy."[60]

THE RETURN OF SHERLOCK HOLMES is intolerably dull. Watson has a flapper daughter who is getting married. Holmes is retired from practice. Here is a sample of the dialogue.

HOLMES: And the motive wasn't simply robbery, either, Watson.
WATSON: How do you know that?
HOLMES: I deduced it.

Holmes spends two middle reels reconstructing what the viewer has already seen in the first reel. Donald Crisp was cast as Colonel Sebastian Moran, "the second most dangerous man in England," and Harry T. Morey was hardly competent as Professor Moriarty. The film is perhaps only important for its final exchange.

WATSON: Amazing, Holmes.
HOLMES: Elementary, my dear Watson, elementary.

At the same time as Holmes made his debut in a talking film, so did Conan Doyle. He appeared in a newsreel insisting on the validity of spiritualistic phenomena. He had announced the retirement of Sherlock Holmes with the publication of "Shoscombe Old Place," but this time there was no popular reaction. His identification with the spiritualist cause had alienated most of his once large readership. He had become, in fact, a laughing-stock. He had enjoyed John Barrymore in his portrayal of his detective, but in 1930 he was too ill to see either Clive Brook or THE HOUND OF THE BASKERVILLES (German, 1929) made at UFA in Berlin with Carlyle Blackwell as Holmes. He died in a large basketchair, surrounded by his loving family, looking out across Jean's rose garden to the golf links. The date was 7 July 1930. On 28 July 1930 Jean announced to the press that she had communicated with her late husband by means of a spirit photograph and, until her own death in 1940, she maintained contact with him. She insisted that he had diagnosed her terminal disease as cancer in 1936 before other doctors could. After Jean died, the Conan Doyle children also received messages from her while they went about, in less than a generation, dissipating utterly Conan Doyle's sizable estate. It is of no consequence. Sherlock Holmes has retained his popularity among contemporary readers, while most of what Conan Doyle wrote other than the Holmes stories, no less than Conan Doyle and even spiritualism itself, have faded irretrievably into the past.

III

Father Ronald Knox, who wrote detective stories himself and who was one of the most articulate critics of the genre, in 1911 when he was Chaplain at the University of Oxford published a satire about the Sherlock Holmes stories. His objective was to denounce the extremes to which theologians, in their *soi-disant* Higher Criticism, had gone in their analysis of Holy Writ. To make his case, he used the Conan Doyle tales as a suitable subject for textual exegesis, trying to date the stories in terms of a logical chronology. Sydney Roberts, a professor of literature in Cambridge, had just published a book on Samuel Johnson and it had involved him with certain problems in writing biography. He took up the controversy and devised his own chronology for the stories which had been published so far, and even addressed cases mentioned but not so far recorded by Watson. This activity gave rise to a number of works by others who also wanted to engage in the literary game. H. W. Bell in SHERLOCK HOLMES AND DR. WATSON, THE CHRONOLOGY OF THEIR ADVENTURES (1932) produced the most ingenious chronology for the adventures both recorded and unrecorded; but his book only invited further controversy and, to date, no less than four complete biographies have been published devoted to the life of the fictional detective, the most impressive yet fantastical of which remains William S. Baring-Gould's SHERLOCK HOLMES OF BAKER STREET (1962). T. S. Blakeney in SHEROCK HOLMES: FACT OR FICTION? (1932) made what he felt were compelling arguments that Holmes indeed was a real person and all of the subsequent biographies have assumed this premise as the basis on which they have been written. A book has even been published devoted to Holmes' knowledge of music.

Vincent Starrett wrote the first of the biographies of Sherlock Holmes in THE PRIVATE LIFE OF SHERLOCK HOLMES (1933), which had its beginnings as a series of essays, some of which had been published while Conan Doyle was still alive. Starrett had sent these early essays to Conan Doyle and the latter wrote back to him that "it was really very kind of you to write so heartily about Holmes. My own feelings towards him are rather mixed, for I feel that he has obscured a good deal of my more serious work, but that no doubt will right itself in time—or if not, it does not greatly matter."[61]

On 6 January 1934 Christopher Morley organized the Baker Street Irregulars which met on this date for the first time at the old Hotel Duane on Madison Avenue in New York City. An order of toasts was worked out and, in time, a constitution with bylaws. The dinners became more or less an annual affair and in time a number of eminent detective story writers, as well as others from varying walks of life, became members. Perhaps the most illustrious member of the group was President Franklin D. Roosevelt. During the Second World War, he christened the Intelligence Department of his headquarters Baker Street and his correspondence concerning Holmes has been included in Philip A. Shreffler's THE BAKER STREET READER: CORNERSTONE WRITINGS ABOUT SHERLOCK HOLMES (1984). It is worth noting that among the Baker Street Irregulars, and all the other clubs and associations which have risen since, Conan Doyle's name is not to be mentioned; the stories are regarded as the biography of a real man written by another real man.

In the meantime, Holmes also continued to enjoy a lively career on the screen. What would prove to be a series of Holmes films was begun in England at the Twickenham Film Studio. THE SLEEPING CARDINAL (Twickenham, 1931) starred Arthur Wontner in the role of Holmes with Ian Fleming as a very polished Dr. Watson. The plot had Holmes foiling a scheme involving counterfeit bank notes at the bottom of which was Colonel Sebastian Moran played by Louis Goodrich. Wontner, although he was in his late fifties when he made this film and would be sixty-two in the last film in the series, looked the part almost as much as Norwood had. His delivery was reserved, his bearing thoughtful, and his characterization was dignified.

"The studio wasn't much more than a big tin shed, really," Wontner once remarked of Twickenham, "not like film studios today. We used to start filming early in the morning, and continued until pretty late at night, with very few breaks. Of course, we had to stop shooting quite often when a train went by, because of the noise. But we couldn't afford much time for retakes, and there were no elaborate rehearsals or anything like that."[62]

THE SLEEPING CARDINAL was released in the United States under the title SHERLOCK HOLMES' FATAL HOUR. It won the New York Cinema Award as the best mystery drama of the year and it just happened to be shown at the same time as William Gillette was touring the country in a farewell engagement in the stage play which had brought Holmes and Gillette's portrayal to fame early in the century. In March, 1975, when I went to see the play in its Broadway revival, following its successful run in London, the house was packed, had been for weeks previously, and was sold out weeks in advance. The play, critics said at the time, was so bad that it was good; at least the audience laughed a lot.

THE SPECKLED BAND (British & Dominion, 1931) starred Raymond Massey who was making his screen debut playing Holmes. Massey's Holmes had obviously read the Philo Vance mysteries and perhaps even a few by Ellery Queen: he is utterly modern, somewhat cynical in his attitudes, and totally cerebral, without even a hint of a curved pipe and a deerstalker. The anteroom to Holmes' study is filled with bustling secretaries, intercoms, and automated filing systems. The clacking office machinery creates a frightful din. There is nothing remarkable about Athole Stewart's Dr. Watson, but Lyn Harding, cast as Dr. Grimesby Rylott (the name changed a bit from Conan Doyle's rendering: Roylott), came to his role with genuine relish, having first appeared in the stage production of the story. Intimidating, glowering, exuding menace, he is an apt foil for Massey's urbane reserve. For all the modernity of Holmes' quarters and methods in this film, visually the film readily combined a view of Rylott in a horse-drawn vehicle and the heroine's suitor in a sports car. Because of his emotional reticence during most of the photoplay, Massey was able to make the parting image of Holmes quite touching, with its brief glimpse into a loneliness which borders on despair.

THE HOUND OF THE BASKERVILLES (Gaumont, 1931), released the same year as THE SLEEPING CARDINAL and THE SPECKLED BAND, hoped no less to cash in on the new market for detective thrillers and the resurgence of interest in Sherlock Holmes. Robert Rendel was cast as Holmes and Frederick Lloyd played Watson. Although parts of the picture portion of the film survive, the sound track is lost completely.

The two most significant entries in 1932 both featured Arthur Wontner again in the role of Holmes. THE MISSING REMBRANDT (Twickenham, 1932) was based on Conan Doyle's story "The Adventure of Charles Augustus Milverton" and was directed by Leslie S. Hiscott who had directed THE SLEEPING CARDINAL. An opium den, graphically photographed, and Holmes disguised as an old woman and as a clergyman added to the visual interest of the film. "Arthur Wontner's performance as Holmes was magnificent," Michael Pointer wrote in THE PUBLIC LIFE OF SHERLOCK HOLMES (1975). "Here at last, we felt, was Sherlock Holmes, come to life before our eyes; the type of Holmes described by Watson in many of the stories. Arthur Wontner adopted the 'half-humorous, half-cynical vein which was his habitual attitude to those about him,' and presented a cultured and gentlemanly Holmes, with 'a remarkable gentleness and courtesy in his dealings with women.' He made the character seem very natural by the 'quietly genial fashion' in which he adopted the mannerisms of the great detective. The words are Watson's, and they fit Wontner beautifully."[63] Ian Fleming again played Watson as a self-effacing, well-bred gentleman, albeit a trifle fatuous, as was appropriate to the character.

Even before filming had commenced on THE MISSING REMBRANDT, Wontner had signed to appear a third time as Holmes, but for a different studio. THE SIGN OF FOUR (Associated Radio Pictures, 1932) was produced by Rowland V. Lee and directed by Graham Cutts. Ian Hunter was given the role of Watson. RKO Radio in the United States purchased American distribution rights for the film. THE SIGN OF FOUR is, in my opinion, the finest of the films in which Wontner played Holmes. In part, I suspect, this is because of the presence of Lee who at the time had been directing the Dr. Fu Manchu films at Paramount. When Sholto is murdered, the effects are appropriately eerie, and the recreation of the scene is quite as memorable as it is in the novel. Holmes wears a modified fedora and his detection sequences are among the best to be found in any Holmes film. Wontner is equally effective in the brief scene where he is disguised as an old sea captain and the picture concludes with a thrilling fight. The pacing is more typically American than in any of the other Wontner entries, which is to say there is constant motion, physical or psychological, impelling the denouement.

The Fox Film Corporation was disinclined to let the British studios alone cash in on Holmes' renewed popularity. Clive Brook was again drafted for the role. "That was a terrible film," Clive Brook said later about SHERLOCK HOLMES (Fox, 1932). "It was made by Fox. I was under a long-term contract with Paramount and they loaned me to Fox. The studios used to do very well out of loaning us actors to other studios for large sums of money. We were under contract and were just paid the same salary anyway. So Fox asked Paramount for me for a Holmes film and I foolishly thought—Sherlock Holmes, fine! I'll do it—and I didn't have a script, which was unusual for me. I usually read a first copy of the script to see what I was doing. I got on to the set and began reading this thing and I discovered that it was ghastly from my point of view, bringing it up to date with gangsters from America, and Holmes engaged. . . . ''[64] The girl to whom Holmes is engaged is Alice Faulkner, an upper-class English ingenue played by Miriam Jordan. Here is a sample of their dialogue.

ALICE: Sherlock Holmes, Esquire!

HOLMES: What is it? Why, Alice, my dear! (They kiss very affectionately).

ALICE: Wasn't I an optimist to think I could charm you away from all these jobs and bottles with a new frock!

HOLMES: Why, it's charming. I noticed it was new the moment you came into the room.

ALICE: Humbug, you didn't see me come into the room. Besides, I've worn it seven times already.

Curiously, Bertram Milhauser, who would work on the Basil Rathbone series at Universal in the 'Forties, did the screenplay; William K. Howard directed. Ernest Torrence played Moriarty who, once he escapes from jail, imports Chicago mobsters to assist him in a reign of terror. Holmes goes to battle against him. When the conflict is over, Holmes and Alice declare their intention for him to retire from his practice and take up chicken farming.

Yet, as bad as SHERLOCK HOLMES is, A STUDY IN SCARLET (World-Wide, 1933) is worse. Edwin L. Marin directed. Reginald Owen was cast as a very weak Holmes who helps Alan Mowbray, as Inspector Lestrade, find a murderer preying upon members of a secret society because the society is heir to a rich estate. This is the tontine plot and it would occur repeatedly in subsequent films.

Following THE SIGN OF FOUR, Arthur Wontner was retained by still a third studio to portray Holmes in THE TRIUMPH OF SHERLOCK HOLMES (Gaumont-British, 1935) based on Conan Doyle's novel, THE VALLEY OF FEAR. Ian Fleming was back as Watson and Lyn Harding was cast in the role of Professor Moriarty. The film remains faithful to its literary source, even to the extensive flashback in the middle section. Chris Steinbrunner and Norman Michaels in THE FILMS OF SHERLOCK HOLMES rate this film more highly than I do, regarding it as Wontner's best film. "Only," they have noted, "in one particular does it grievously improvise: instead of allowing Professor Moriarty to remain in a shadowy background as the instigator of the evil—as he was in the book—he is brought for a few scenes into center stage. And this is almost forgiveable for that outrageously dramatic actor Lyn Harding—the menacing Dr. Rylott in Raymond Massey's THE SPECKLED BAND—was for this film (and the next) cast as the wicked Professor, purloining every bit of dialogue in which he shares.''[65] For me, it is precisely this overemphasis of Professor Moriarty which weakens these films. It is far too simplistic to reduce villainy again and again to this evil genius, removing the focus from the ingenuity and individual culpability of a crime to the mere melodrama of a super hero and a master villain locked in a clash of titans.

Leslie S. Hiscott directed THE TRIUMPH OF SHERLOCK HOLMES. He was replaced by Thomas Bentley for the fifth and final Arthur Wontner entry, SILVER BLAZE (Twickenham, 1937). Ian Fleming was once more cast as Watson and Lyn Harding was back as Professor Moriarty in a story which, as originally conceived by Conan Doyle, had nothing to do with him. When SILVER BLAZE opened in London, a Friday evening performance was ragged by the audience and the film had to be withdrawn from the program for a couple of days. When it was quietly restored, nothing further of an untoward nature occurred and the Friday-night audience had been duly castigated in the press. But, as Michael Pointer observed, "this incident has some significance. With hindsight it clearly would not have been wise to have made any more of the Wontner series of Sherlock Holmes films in the same form. The age of the gifted amateur detective had ended, like so many aspects of Victorian life, with the changes in society wrought by the Great War. The clever solvers of puzzles gave way to the heroes of crime and mystery adventures, the police inspectors and the agents who came in from, or stayed out in, the cold. The amateur detective could no longer function plausibly in the altered environment, and had become an anachronism. Sherlock Holmes set in the 1930s was out of place, for his type and style of detection is based on a totally different era. It was largely the portrayal by Authur Wontner that sustained the acceptance of this situation."[66]

It was a similar kind of ridicule and rather malicious amusement which came to plague Basil Rathbone after he assumed the role. "In the upper echelon of my very considerable following as Mr. Holmes," he reflected in his autobiography, "there has always been a somewhat patronizing, if polite, recognition of my modest achievement. In the lower echelon I have experienced nothing but embarrassment in the familiar street-corner greeting of recognition, which is inevitably followed by horrendous imitations of my speech, loud laughter, and ridiculing quotes of famous lines such as 'Quick, Watson, the needle' or 'Elementary, my dear Watson,' followed by more laughter at my obvious discomfiture. Quite frankly and realistically, over the years I have been forced to accept the fact that my impersonation of one of the most famous fictional characters in all literature has not received that respectful recognition to which I feel Sir Arthur Conan Doyle's masterpieces entitle him. Has it been my fault? I do not think so. . . . Professionally it has always been conceded that both pictures and broadcasts were of an exceptionally high quality. Could it be that our efforts somewhat resembled museum pieces? Here possibly may be a clue to the problem, i.e., the word 'museum.' . . . It would seem that our *timing* was bad. Nineteen thirty-nine was far too late for a serious presentation of THE ADVENTURES OF SHERLOCK HOLMES."[67]

It was early in 1939 that Darryl F. Zanuck, head of production at Twentieth Century-Fox, engaged in a dinner conversation with two of the studio's personnel, Gene Markey, a writer, and Gregory Ratoff, an actor/director. Markey made the suggestion that someone ought to film Conan Doyle's classic, THE ADVENTURES OF SHERLOCK HOLMES. While Zanuck proved receptive to the proposal, he wondered who ought to play Holmes. Markey suggested Basil Rathbone for the role and Nigel Bruce as Watson. Within days, both actors had been signed to appear in THE HOUND OF THE BASKERVILLES (20th-Fox, 1939).

Rathbone was born at Johannesburg, South Africa on 13 June 1892. He had worked for years on the stage, preferring Shakespearean roles, when he made his sound debut in THE LAST OF MRS. CHENEY (M-G-M, 1929). Except for playing Philo Vance in 1930, Rathbone had built a substantial reputation as a calculating, cold-hearted villain. Off screen, he was infinitely charming, totally devoted to his second wife, Ouida Bergere Rathbone, who had formerly been married to film director George Fitzmaurice. Ouida managed Rathbone's career and specialized in giving the most elaborate parties in Hollywood. For example, a joint guest of honor party was thrown for Artur Rubinstein and Leopold Stokowski by the Rathbones in typical grand style. The dining room was extended for the occasion out into the garden. On the mirrored surface of the largest table was a lucite grand piano and a couple of lucite violins. From the piano stemmed lilies of the valley, forget-me-nots. Scattered above were Dubonnet flowers. Place cards were one continuous scroll of silvery gray material inscribed with the name in Dubonnet lettering. Between the names ran the score of one of Chopin's *polonaises*, also in Dubonnet. A vast Dubonnet rug covered the entire floor. Silver lamé flashed from the walls. Just below the ceiling ran a three-foot frieze of cellophane, scored with black notes. Over the fireplace was a banner of red cellophane declaring "The world of Music knows no boundaries." Ouida Rathbone, according to Artur Rubinstein, was "the most extravagant hostess I had ever known." Although he neglected to mention Stokowski toward whom he had a personal antipathy, Rubinstein did recall in his autobiography, MY MANY YEARS (1980), how "at the entrance of their beautiful house in Bel Air, a butler would receive one with a large dish of caviar with the accompanying drinks. All the famous actors and producers of Hollywood were their guests. Two photographers were busy taking snapshots of different groups of us. . . . That was the evening we met Charlie Chaplin, Charles Laughton, Bette Davis, Leslie Howard, Rex Harrison, Ethel Barrymore, Nigel Bruce, Merle Oberon, Hitchcock, Errol Flynn, and Marlene Dietrich. I was also delighted to find Charles Boyer, my old friend from Paris, who had married a charming Scottish actress."[68]

It was his portrayal of Sherlock Holmes on screen and on the radio which enabled Rathbone to afford this life-style. I do not doubt for a moment that he accepted the role initially because he saw in it a means to top billing. He may have been billed second in THE HOUND OF THE BASKERVILLES, but after that he was always the star; and he had not starred in a film since THE BISHOP MURDER CASE (M-G-M, 1930). When I met him, very late in his life, he was somewhat bitter and disillusioned about his career; unquestionably he had had higher expectations. He told me a witty story which, in the retelling, has about it something of the pathetic. "I was asked recently," he said, "how much I earn. I answered five thousand dollars a week. That sum seemed to impress my interlocutor until he asked the inevitable question: and how many weeks did you work last year? One, I said." I believe he was sincere in his comment in his autobiography that "had I made but the one Holmes picture, my first, THE HOUND OF THE BASKERVILLES, I should probably not be as well known as I am today. But within myself, as an artist, I should have been well content."[69]

Since Nigel Bruce's parents were traveling at the time he was born, his birthplace is variously given as Ensenada, Mexico, or San Diego, or somewhere in between. The date was indisputably 4 February 1895. He started on the British stage appearing in plays such as BULLDOG DRUMMOND with Sir Gerald du Maurier. Bruce was known to his friends as Willy. He made his motion picture debut in COMING OUT PARTY (Fox, 1934) and in his very next film he played a detective. As far as Rathbone was concerned, "Nigel Bruce was the ideal Dr. Watson, not only of his time but possibly of and for all time. There was an endearing quality to his performance that to a very large extent, I believe, humanized the relationship between Dr. Watson and Mr. Holmes. It has always seemed to me to be more than possible that our 'adventures' might have met with a less kindly public acceptance had they been recorded by a less lovable companion to Holmes than was Nigel's Dr. Watson. . . . "[70] Steinbrunner and Michaels are somewhat more critical than this in THE FILMS OF SHERLOCK HOLMES. "Portly and blustering," they wrote, "and perhaps a shade too old-appearing to be a true Watson—actually he was only 44 in HOUND, three years younger than Rathbone, surprisingly— Nigel's approach to the role was essentially comedic. Made increasingly bumbling and silly by later films, Bruce has not found favor with Sherlockian film students."[71]

THE HOUND OF THE BASKERVILLES was superior to all the films that went before it and most that followed it; and it was prudently set in the Victorian period. Irving Cummings was originally set to direct it, but he was replaced at the last moment by Sidney Lanfield. Casting was very effective, with Richard Greene as the Baskerville heir and Lionel Atwill as Doctor Mortimer. Baskerville Hall was constructed in its entirety on a Fox sound stage and was actually a leftover from a Charlie Chan film. This staginess, oddly enough, only amplified the sense of terror and the vicious hound was more horrifying than it had been in previous versions and than it would be in the later Hammer production. Ernest Pascal wrote the screenplay and I tend to agree with Steinbrunner and Michaels that his script "followed closely the Conan Doyle book, making few changes other than purifying the relationship between the Stapletons (they are brother and sister in the screenplay, rather than secretly husband and wife) and adding spiritualism as an interest for Mrs. Mortimer so that a séance could be included in the film for atmosphere. Pascal's feelings were obviously that one shouldn't tamper too much with a masterpiece, and as a result the film comes across as slightly heavy."[72] Far more effective is THE ADVENTURES OF SHERLOCK HOLMES (20th-Fox, 1939) which came next. George Zucco is intensely menacing as Professor Moriarty and, in my opinion, more convincing than Lyn Harding and the others who had preceded him. Ida Lupino is persuasive as the imperiled heroine pursued by a club-footed gaucho as part of a decoy plot to keep Holmes off the scent of Moriarty's real scheme, theft of the crown jewels from the Tower of London.

These were both major productions, but after their release the studio had no intention of continuing. It was then that Jules Stein of MCA, Rathbone's agent, put together a package which included a weekly radio series to be broadcast on NBC and a series of films to be produced by Universal Pictures. Holmes, of course, had been on the radio since 1930 when William Gillette had starred in the role. The series with Rathbone and Bruce began on NBC in October, 1939 and, although it would switch along the way to the Mutual Broadcasting Network, it continued with Rathbone in the role of Holmes until May, 1946. After that time, Tom Conway assumed the role, with Nigel Bruce continuing as Dr. Watson. On 25 March 1942 it was announced in the trades that Universal had acquired from Denis P. S. Conan Doyle, representing the estate, rights to 21 stories to be filmed at the rate of three a year for a period of seven years; no novels were to be used as the basis for any screenplay. The contract consisted of a year-to-year option, so that Universal could drop out in any given year if it chose. Were the studio to film all 21 of the stories, the estate would receive $255,000. Stein's concept for the films was that Holmes should be updated to the 1940s. The idea appealed to Rathbone who had only appeared in period Holmes films. Yet, ironically, as Steinbrunner and Michaels have noted, while no previous "Holmes film had been deliberately put back in the Victorian era before Twentieth Century-Fox did it in 1939, . . . in a rapidly changing American where a Holmes film other than at Fox had not been produced for nearly a decade, the fact that before Rathbone *all* Sherlocks were contemporary had been forgotten."[73]

When it is all said and done, perhaps Michael Pointer, and even Conan Doyle before him, were correct and Holmes could not be made contemporary; certainly he could not plausibly be made contemporary with the 1940s. In the first release, SHERLOCK HOLMES AND THE VOICE OF TERROR (Universal, 1942), Rathbone's portrayal was as poised as ever, but he wore his hair swept forward and at one point when he would reach for his deerstalker, Nigel Bruce's Dr. Watson admonishes him, "Holmes, you promised!" The plot of the film finds Holmes battling to save England from a Nazi invasion. John Rawlins was the director. Roy William Neill replaced him on the next film, SHERLOCK HOLMES AND THE SECRET WEAPON (Universal, 1942), which cast Lionel Atwill as Professor Moriarty only too willing to sell the coveted scientific invention to the Nazis. Neill stayed on to direct all the subsequent entries. I think, generally, that Steinbrunner and Michaels are apt in their assessment of these Universal films and that even the least of them is "saved by the vigorous and electric playing of Basil Rathbone, who at times seemed to invest far more into the role than the script demanded, and often treaded so close to the raw edge of dramatic hysteria that we riveted our attention on him and away from the paucity of the script. Most of the films, too, are saved by the masterful direction of Roy William Neill ('dear Mousie,' Basil often called him, and relates that while the films had nominal producers and writers Mousie was the final word in all these departments as well, and in general control). Neill, an unsung genius of the camera, brilliantly plumbed every shadow and created the atmosphere that often was the series' primary asset. It's not easy to forget the dread, shrouded moors of THE SCARLET CLAW [Universal, 1944]— far more cloaked in mystery than the Fox Dartmoor of HOUND—or when Holmes (and, simultaneously, the camera) first realizes in SHERLOCK HOLMES FACES DEATH [Universal, 1943] that the Main Hall floor of Musgrave Manor is a gigantic chessboard."[74]

Hillary Brooke appeared in several of the entries, most substantially in SHERLOCK HOLMES FACES DEATH and THE WOMAN IN GREEN (Universal, 1945). "Basil and Willy knew each other off the set," she told me. "They were very good friends and it came across on the screen. Basil loved ice cream cones and he would frequently go to the Universal back lot to look at the animals they kept there when he had a free moment. Basil and Willy made up a lot of scenes as they went along, although our director, Roy Neill, knew the scripts and knew both what he wanted and how he could get it on the budget he had. Every afternoon while we were shooting we would stop for tea at four o'clock. It was all very English."

Rathbone enjoyed Bruce's humor and he became more the buffoon than ever in these films, although, doubtless, Neill exercised a restraining hand. Mary Gordon had played Mrs. Hudson in the Fox films and she was retained in that role throughout the Universal series, while Dennis Hoey was something of a regular playing the unimaginative Inspector Lestrade. The tontine plot seemed a particular favorite among the screenwriters. In SPIDER WOMAN (Universal, 1944) Gale Sondergaard was cast as the master villain, using a rare spider to induce men to suicide who have named her their insurance beneficiary. In THE HOUSE OF FEAR (Universal, 1945) Holmès is called in to prevent the continuing murders of members of a private club known as The Good Comrades. He exposes the plot at the end: none of the men are dead; it is an insurance swindle.

William S. Baring-Gould in SHERLOCK HOLMES OF BAKER STREET has recorded that Holmes was consulted in the matter of the Jack the Ripper slayings and, indeed, that the identity of the Ripper was none other than Inspector Athelney Jones of Scotland Yard! The closest this series came to the same idea was in THE WOMAN IN GREEN in which, according to the screenplay, the Yard is "confronted with a series of the most atrocious murders since Jack the Ripper." Young women are being killed and their thumbs are being hacked off. Professor Moriarty, this time played by Henry Daniell, with Hillary Brooke as his assistant is behind the plot. At one point Hillary is supposed to hypnotize Holmes with Moriarty looking on. Both she and Basil could not help breaking out in laughter as this improbable sequence was being filmed. PURSUIT TO ALGIERS (Universal, 1945) was the slowest of all the films, with virtually all the action taking place aboard a ship, Holmes acting as bodyguard to the heir to the throne of Rovenia played by Morton Lowry who had been cast as Stapleton in THE HOUND OF THE BASKERVILLES.

TERROR BY NIGHT (Universal, 1946) may be the finest of the Universal series with the action set entirely on a train with Alan Mowbray in the cast, ostensibly Watson's old military friend from India but in actual fact the notorious Colonel Sebastian Moran. DRESSED TO KILL (Universal, 1946) was last. Patricia Morison was cast as the enterprising female villain who very nearly succeeds in killing Holmes. "Basil told the most marvelous jokes on the set," she told me. "He was a very warm man, but, you know, he was also very high strung, jittery. He could never relax."

Darryl F. Zanuck, when he was released from the service, set about to wrench back control of Twentieth Century-Fox from Bill Goetz who had taken over in his absence. Goetz was Louis B. Mayer's son-in-law and Mayer assisted Goetz in founding International Pictures which merged with Universal in 1946. With Goetz in charge of production, it was announced that Universal would no longer be making "B" pictures, Westerns, or serials. The Holmes films were definitely a "B" series. On 4 June, Universal allowed its contract with the Conan Doyle estate to lapse. Roy William Neill, who had four years to go on his seven-year contract, settled with the studio and went to England on vacation where, shortly later, he died of a heart attack. Rathbone could see that no other studio was likely to renegotiate a deal with the estate; and he also realized, very much to his dismay, that playing the same role for almost seven years meant that he was hopelessly typecast. To salvage his career, he would have to try something else. He went East to resume work on the stage. The radio series by itself could do nothing for him except further identify him with a role he wanted to divorce himself from completely. Rathbone also had second thoughts about Holmes' personality, similar to those Conan Doyle had had. " . . . Toward the end of my life with him," Rathbone wrote, "I came to the conclusion (as one may in living too closely and too long in seclusion with any one rather unique and difficult personality) that there was nothing lovable about Holmes. He himself seemed capable of transcending the weakness of mere mortals such as myself . . . understanding us perhaps, accepting us and even pitying us, but only and purely objectively. It would be impossible for such a man to know loneliness or love or sorrow because he was completely sufficient unto himself. His perpetual assuming of infallibility; his interminable success (could he not fail just once and prove himself a human being like the rest of us!); his ego that seemed at times on the verge of a superman complex. . . . "[75]

Yet, the identification with Holmes was something Rathbone could never shake; it dogged him to the end of his days, although it did not bring him theatrical success when, in 1953, he appeared in SHERLOCK HOLMES, a stage melodrama written by Ouida, nor when he made an isolated appearance as Holmes on CBS earlier that same year. The sad irony in this is that Basil Rathbone was an extraordinary actor. "On one occasion," Michael Pointer wrote, "Basil Rathbone and Nigel Bruce appeared as guests on a comedy radio show and swapped their regular parts, with Rathbone as a bumbling Watson and Bruce as a sharp decisive Holmes. It is reported that Rathbone's imitation of Nigel Bruce stopped the show. But then Rathbone was such a talented actor that he could deal with that sort of situation with ease. . . . "[76] Rathbone sold his Bel Air home and, henceforth, made New York the center of his activities. At his death, he left an estate of less than $20,000.

Little, if any, distinction attaches to most subsequent Holmes films and it is worth noting that Holmes did not return to the screen until THE HOUND OF THE BASKERVILLES (United Artists, 1959), produced by Hammer Films fifteen years after the Rathbone series ended. Peter Cushing was cast as Holmes with André Morell as Watson. The only attribute of this film perhaps worth mentioning is that is was made in color. The hound is laughably tame and, as Steinbrunner and Michaels concluded, "while the opening Baker Street sequences were acceptable and affectionate, once the story proceeded into the moors it veered far from the Doyle source, adding . . . Satanism, altering the character of Stapleton and changing Beryl completely, making her a hot-blooded, scheming Spanish beauty who is Stapleton's unlikely daughter and the true perpetrator of the horror of the hound."[77]

The only notable fact about A STUDY IN TERROR (Columbia, 1965) in which John Neville played Holmes and Donald Houston was cast as Watson is not that the screenplay pitted Holmes against Jack the Ripper, but that Ellery Queen wrote a novelization of the movie, a fact about which I shall have more to say when I come to the section devoted to him. When I asked Billy Wilder what, in retrospect, he thought of his THE PRIVATE LIFE OF SHERLOCK HOLMES (United Artists, 1970), a film which implies that Holmes may have been homosexual, he looked at me sharply and snapped: "Can't we change the subject?"

THE SEVEN PERCENT SOLUTION (Universal, 1970), on the other hand, is excellent, although the plot is pure camp. The screenplay was by Nicholas Meyer, based on his novel by the same title. The plot proposes that Holmes, following his encounter with Professor Moriarty at the Reichenbach Falls, did not go to Tibet, as was related by Watson, but instead, at Watson's instigation, went to Vienna to Sigmund Freud to be cured of his cocaine addiction. The casting by the film's director, Herbert Ross, was little short of brilliant, with

Alan Arkin as Freud, Nicol Williamson as Holmes, and Robert Duvall as Watson. The premise, developed far more effectively in the film than it is in the novel, is that Professor Moriarty, Holmes' boyhood tutor, was also his mother's lover and, thus, Holmes' unconscious hatred of Moriarty is the consequence of sexual repression manifested consciously as the projection of Moriarty as a master criminal. Vanessa Redgrave was cast as a courtesan, Lola Deveraux, with whom Holmes spends what remains of his three-year sabbatical after his successful cure. Yet, as Steinbrunner and Michaels pointed out, "Watson's deep concern for his friend's well-being, the lengths to which he goes to cure him, his tears and his joy at Holmes' recovery—all tell us that the underlying twosome in this film is, after all, not Holmes-Freud nor Holmes-Deveraux but—as always—Holmes and Watson. It is a very human Holmes and Watson (as scripted, *both* men have occasion to shed tears on screen), and we sense even more strongly than in the Billy Wilder film which explored the same feelings, the deep affection and love passing between them."[78]

Yet, how far have we moved from the original conception of Sherlock Holmes as presented in Conan Doyle's stories? As interesting as the characters are in this film, and as effective as is the drama, ultimately THE SEVEN PERCENT SOLUTION is a pastiche which deals with characters other than those which Conan Doyle created. This film may well mark the demise of Sherlock Holmes' cinematic career. If there was already something absurd about him in the Arthur Wontner and Basil Rathbone films, to update him a century after the time he flourished would seem impossible and it may well be no less impossible to return to Conan Doyle's naive portrait of London as he imagined it to have been and as he projected it in the stories. What I am saying comes to this: our image of a human being has altered too much for us to accept, without tampering, the character of Sherlock Holmes as he would be if he existed today or as he would have been had he existed in the past. His existence is truly confined to and circumscribed by Conan Doyle's imagination, where he was born to begin with and where his existence was sustained. Vincent Starrett's words were never more apt than they are now:

> A yellow fog swirls past the window-pane
> As night descends upon this fabled street;
> A lonely hansom splashes through the rain,
> The ghostly gas lamps fail at twenty feet.
> Here, though the world explode, these two survive,
> And it is always eighteen ninety-five.[79]

What has come to replace the efforts to resurrect Holmes in new stories or impersonate him in new films is Holmesian criticism. "At the present time," Philip A. Shreffler wrote in his Introduction to THE BAKER STREET READER, "there are more publications—from mimeographed newsletters to little magazines, from chapbooks to major hardcover volumes—devoted to Sherlockian analysis than ever before. . . . Just as the 1970s seemed to be the decade of the Sherlockian pastiche (beginning with Nicholas Meyer's SEVEN PERCENT SOLUTION), the 1980s are proving to be the decade of Sherlockian criticism."[80] Such a phenomenon is not really new in intellectual and cultural history. Euhemerus in the Fourth Century B.C. sought to keep the memory of the gods alive by denying them their divinity and instead suggesting that their origin could be traced to idealized portraits of kings and heroes. He proposed, in his own way, a Higher Criticism as a viable substitute for blatant disbelief. The detective who reigns in contemporary films is not a man of reason, of intellection; he is a man of action; he is not an amateur; he is a professional; he does not need to deduce the identities of wrong-doers; he knows who they are and we are expected to share his professional satisfaction and appreciate his superior skill as he kills them. In the brutalized world of late Twentieth-century blood fantasies, Sherlock Holmes has no place. If proof were needed of this, one need look no further than YOUNG SHERLOCK HOLMES (Paramount, 1985) which was produced by Steven Spielberg and directed by Barry Levinson. Nicholas Rowe was eighteen when he played Holmes and Alan Cox was fourteen when he played Watson. A disclaimer appears on the film which explains that, while Sir Arthur Conan Doyle "did not write about the very youthful years of Sherlock Holmes," the film "is an affectionate speculation about what might have happened had the sleuth and his partner met during their college years." The stress is all on action. There is a series of brutal murders, induced by hallucinogenic drugs, masterminded by the head of a fanatic blood cult from Egypt who manages to kill Holmes' girl friend before the two engage in a spectacular sword fight on the frozen Thames.

2
The Life and Times of S. S. Van Dine

> However unethical—theoretically—it may be to take another's life, a man's own life is certainly his to do with as he chooses. Suicide is his inalienable right. And under the paternal tyranny of our modern democracy, I'm rather inclined to think it's about the only right he has left, what?
>
> Philo Vance[1]

I

There was a time, from about 1950 to 1980, when Philo Vance vanished from the scene of American popular culture. The mystery novels which featured him and the films based on them were known principally to antiquarians. This was both sad and unfair. THE BISHOP MURDER CASE (1929), THE "CANARY" MURDER CASE (1927), and THE GREENE MURDER CASE (1928), in just about that order, remain literary landmarks in the puzzle variety of detective stories; while THE KENNEL MURDER CASE (1933) and THE DRAGON MURDER CASE (1933) have two of the most interesting settings you are likely to encounter in detective fiction.

It was in 1970 that I first published "The Philo Vance Murder Case" in VIEWS & REVIEWS Magazine. The next year, together with other essays which had appeared in the same issue, it was published as a chapbook, PHILO VANCE: THE LIFE AND TIMES OF S. S. VAN DINE, by Bowling Green University Press.[2] In this form, it was used as a teaching aid in college literature courses. Subsequently, I expanded that essay to form a chapter in THE DETECTIVE IN HOLLYWOOD, kept somewhat at a minimum, however, since my editor had an antipathy for S. S. Van Dine's fiction. Yet this activity was in the vanguard of a rediscovery of Philo Vance which has resulted, by 1985, in seven of the twelve S. S. Van Dine novels being reprinted in paperback editions by Scribner's, following in the wake of the first six novels having been re-issued in handsome cloth-bound library editions by the Gregg Press, edited by Otto Penzler and with new introductions by Chris Steinbrunner. In their ENCYCLOPEDIA OF MYSTERY AND DETECTION (1976), Steinbrunner and Penzler used for an illustration of S. S. Van Dine the pen drawing which appeared on the covers of both VIEWS & REVIEWS and my chapbook.[3]

No other author of detective fiction, save Sir Arthur Conan Doyle, had so meteoric a rise in sudden popularity as S. S. Van Dine; and absolutely no other author of detective fiction eclipsed so swiftly and so completely. Van Dine was a most interesting man. But to tell of how he came to create Philo Vance requires that you concern yourself to a degree with the story of his life.

Willard Huntington Wright was born of a good family, the younger of two sons, at Charlottesville, Virginia, on 15 October 1887. Early on, this date became changed to 1888 and Willard never sought to correct the error.[4] He was educated at Pomona College in California and elsewhere, but he was a troublesome, if not always indifferent, student. He was accepted as a special student at Harvard during the first semester of 1906–1907; but his habit of attending lectures with a small glass of absinthe perched on his desk irritated his instructors. He told the administrators that he wanted really only to write and it was suggested to him that actually writing would perhaps be a more prudent course than seeking a university education. His older brother, Stanton MacDonald-Wright, became together with Morgan Russell the co-founder of Synchronism in Paris before the Great War and emerged as one of the most important post-Impressionist painters in the United States. According to Stanton, when they were children, he and Willard would lie awake in the morning and describe the monsters which their youthful imaginations conjured before their eyes; frequently their imaginings were identical. Archibald Wright was reputedly a weak and ineffectual father, their mother indulgent, and it was to his mother, Annie Van Vranken Wright, that Willard became especially close. To Stanton's consternation and resentment, she always protected Willard. A profound sibling rivalry developed between the two, so strong that it outlasted Willard by more than thirty years. When Stanton and I became friends in the 1970s, Willard was still very much alive to him. He would frequently urge me, if I wanted to understand Willard truly, to read Balzac's ILLUSIONS PERDUES (1837–1843). In his studio at his home in the Pacific Palisades, Stanton kept a complete edition of Balzac in French, always to be near at hand. Nor was this passion his alone. At the very beginning of THE "CANARY" MURDER CASE, Willard wrote that the case revealed "a hidden page of passional melodrama which, in its essence and organisms, was no less romantic and fascinating than that vivid, theatrical section of the COMÉDIE HUMAINE which deals with the fabulous love of Baron Nucingen for Esther van Gobseck, and with the unhappy Torpille's tragic death."[5] For Stanton I know, and for Willard I suspect, much that was encountered in life was compared with some incident to be found in Balzac.

Willard, as Stanton, had a sharp, cynical, even brutal manner upon occasion, offset unquestionably by a personal charm and sophistication. Willard claimed the absinthe he drank at Harvard was to assist the lectures down his throat. Later, when he was engaged in hack writing, he used his mother's maiden name as a pseudonym, writing as Frederick Van Vranken. He felt his mother quite conventional and justified the name because he was writing for the conventional masses.

Stanton wanted to be a painter. Willard wanted to be a poet. To his dismay, Willard had little facility with languages. He once confessed to his only daughter, Beverly, that he knew only restaurant French and that he envied Stanton's mastery of French and Italian. Yet, this weakness so nettled him that in the Philo Vance stories he invariably introduced foreign words and phrases to give the impression that he was far better versed in European languages than he was and even claimed that he was by profession a philologist as one of his philosophic idols, Friedrich Nietzsche, had been. The situation resulted in an often absurd exhibition. Vance might be all right if he stuck to Latin terminology from the law profession, such as when Willard had him remark, " 'Really, y'know, I must devote more time to the caressin' art of *suggestio falsi* and *suppressio veri* . . . ,' "[6] but when Vance wanted to say that every man after his death is revealed as having been better than he was by virtue of the passage of time, which would have required of him use of the dative of advantage, what Vance ended up saying was, " '*Omnia post obitum fingit majora vetustas.*' "[7] This is literal nonsense. It probably should read, *Omne post obitum fingitur maior vetustati.* Raymond Chandler was a Latin and Greek scholar. As a student he translated Cicero into English and back into Latin and placed third out of six hundred candidates examined by the civil service in England in English, French, and Greek. Yet it is a curiosity worth noting that in all of the carping and nitpicking he did in his books and his private correspondence about Philo Vance he *never* questioned his intellectual pretensions. Dashiell Hammett, however, in reviewing THE BENSON MURDER CASE (1926) observed that "this Philo Vance is in the Sherlock Holmes tradition and his conversational manner is that of a high-school girl who has been studying the foreign words and phrases in the back of her dictionary."[8]

What it came to, apparently, was that while Willard longed for recognition of his erudition, he lacked the trained discipline of the true scholar. For him, fame, wealth, and success included appreciation of his mental acumen. It was this last which was to prove the most elusive. Following his departure from Harvard, Willard secured a job on THE LOS ANGELES TIMES as a cub reporter and assistant literary critic. This was in 1907. By 1910, he was writing under his own byline and was considered a literary authority of considerable merit. His father had been a railroad contractor and Willard watched over the family's real estate holdings in California. He was compelled to leave work early one day in 1910 with the onset of a sudden migraine headache just minutes before the TIMES building was dynamited by the McNamara brothers.

Many were killed. It was the first time that Willard's fitful nervous disposition would bring him truly good fortune. It would again. But in the end it would kill him. He had less than thirty years before him.

While still a literary critic for the TIMES, Willard reviewed a book on Nietzsche by H. L. Mencken. Mencken thanked him and a correspondence sprang up. It was through Mencken's efforts that Willard was contracted to succeed Percival Pollard as editor of TOWN TOPICS. In October, 1912, Willard came East. Besides his editorship of TOWN TOPICS, Mencken also got him a position as a sub-editor of THE SMART SET. John Adams Thayer, who started in the magazine business with the Munsey publications, purchased THE SMART SET for a dear price with the hopes of creating a journal of letters that would appeal to a more sophisticated audience. It was not very long before Willard's cleverness overwhelmed Thayer to the extent that he agreed to give him editorship of THE SMART SET for an entire year with a guarantee of *carte blanche* as to its contents. H. L. Mencken was THE SMART SET's book reviewer, George Jean Nathan its drama critic.

Willard talked Thayer into financing a trip to Europe for himself and Nathan. The two were to join with Mencken in writing a series of essays to be titled EUROPE AFTER 8:15. Mencken, who had already been to Europe, was to contribute his share from American shores. Willard had Stanton, who was then living in Paris, show them around to all the better baudy houses. Within six months, Willard had totally altered the tone of THE SMART SET. But the series of articles published as a book in 1914 with the outbreak of hostilities in Europe proved a financial bust. When he was ostracized by long-time acquaintances and as hard-won advertisers began to cancel their contracts, Thayer got cold feet. Willard was released before his editorship was scheduled to terminate, receiving a cash settlement only after much haggling.

With Europe at war, Stanton returned to the United States and he and Willard again became close. Stanton possessed much the same vituperative wit and audacious mixture of obscenity and erudition which made Willard such an iconoclastic editor. I recall Stanton once in all sincerity telling me that he rejoiced every year when the death tolls for automobile accidents were computed: there were that many fewer people in the world! Willard put similar sentiments into Philo Vance's monologues. " 'If society were omniscient . . . ,' " Vance is quoted as saying, " 'it would have a right to sit in judgment. But society is ignorant and venomous, devoid of any trace of insight or understanding. It exalts knavery, and worships stupidity. It crucifies the intelligent, and puts the diseased in dungeons. And, withal, it arrogates to itself the right and ability to analyze the subtle sources of what it calls "crime," and to condemn to death all persons whose inborn and irresistible impulses it does not like. That's your sweet society . . . ,—a pack of wolves watering at the mouth for victims on whom to vent its organized lust to kill and flay.' "[9]

Willard and Stanton had both married for the first time within close proximity to each other while they were still in their teens. Willard was eighteen when he married Katherine Boynton. She accompanied him to California when he went to work for the TIMES. He left her and Beverly behind in Glendale when he went East to edit THE SMART SET. Stanton was no more enthusiastic about conjugal bliss than Willard was; in fact, he would be married three times in his life. At the time, Willard was a believer in Nietzsche's philosophy that when a man goes to a woman, he must go armed with a whip. His lifestyle in New York brought him into contact with a number of high society flappers who took an interest in him; nor was he above forcing them to stand in a corner for several hours if their talk irritated him. Yet, as Stanton soon learned, Willard's living expenses were mostly being paid by the women he knew rather than by what he was earning as a writer.

After numerous conversations with Stanton, Willard plunged into a series of articles for FORUM and other publications on the futuristic tendencies in painting. He even tried composing pieces for the piano, largely in imitation of Debussy. He became addicted to opium. Stanton also fell victim to the drug; he confessed to me that even in his eighties some nights his muscles would spasmodically contract while he was asleep. Willard began to write books feverishly. WHAT NIETZSCHE TAUGHT (1915) and MODERN PAINTING, ITS TENDENCY AND MEANING (1915) were published in the same year. The two brothers went for a time to England. Here, Willard tried to overcome his opium addiction by sealing himself in a hotel room. He failed. But he wrote his first novel, THE MAN OF PROMISE (1916), and followed it with THE CREATIVE WILL: STUDIES IN THE PHILOSOPHY AND THE SYNTAX OF AESTHETICS (1916). H. L. Mencken lauded the novel in FORUM. It did not sell. Nor did it later, when Scribner's re-issued it after Willard's fame as S. S. Van Dine.

Following their short, and abortive, trip abroad, the brothers returned to New York. Stanton had been hired by Willard to help research the books on modern painting and aesthetics, but money was tight and, increasingly, Willard met Stanton's requests for funds with laughter and, sometimes, refused even to feed him. Willard was also harried by importunities from Katherine to send her money with which to support herself and their daughter. In 1917, Willard was appointed literary editor for the NEW YORK EVENING MAIL. He compiled and edited, with an introduction, THE GREAT MODERN FRENCH STORIES: A CHRONOLOGICAL ANTHOLOGY (1917) for Boni and Liveright's Modern Library. He published a series of articles, more an exposé, on the eleventh edition of the ENCYCLOPEDIA BRITANNICA in REEDER'S MAGAZINE, which appeared in book form as MISINFORMING A NATION (1917); and he published a companion volume that same year, INFORMING A NATION (1917). Then the blow fell.

War hysteria was very high. The witch-hunting phenomenon so prevalent after the Second World War was no less true in the years 1917-1919. When Willard learned that his pro-German sympathies had made him a suspicious character, his zany sense of humor prompted him to dictate a wholly fictitious letter to the Washington correspondent of the EVENING MAIL concerned with projected sabotage for "our glorious Kaiser." Willard's secretary had been instructed by the Creel Press Bureau, which acted as a federal intelligence agency, to carbon all his letters. He surprised her doing it and actually chased her out of the building into the street, cornering her in a drug store. The incident received maximum publicity. Both Willard and the Washington correspondent lost their jobs. Mencken and Nathan blamed Willard as the cause of their friend losing his job and would have nothing further to do with him. Willard was effectively ostracized from most newspapers and periodicals. He had no choice but to return to California.

Once there, he was forced to write movie reviews for PHOTOPLAY and other magazines under various pen names. He even descended to copydesk work with long hours and low pay. Nervous fits returned and he relied increasingly on sedation and opium to quiet his agitated condition. In 1918, he managed to get a position as art and music critic for the San Francisco BULLETIN and this, combined with other hack work, tied him over while he worked furiously to complete THE FUTURE OF PAINTING (1923) and his *magnum opus*, PRINCIPLES OF AESTHETIC FORM AND ORGANIZATION, which he was never to finish and, finally, attributed to Philo Vance as one of the books the amateur sleuth had written. In late 1922, he was assigned the "Art of the Month" department for HEARST'S INTERNATIONAL. In 1923, his health broke down completely. He was a hopeless addict. He was sent to Paris by his mother to take a cure at a French clinic. He was kept in solitary confinement for six months. He had read detective fiction desultorily in the past, but at the clinic he began to read it voraciously, to study it as an art form. And, as had happened so many times to Stanford West in THE MAN OF PROMISE, dissolution and despair gave way to the desire to write. It was this which saved him. This, and meeting Claire Burke, a red-headed married woman temporarily estranged from her husband who began to support Willard after he returned to the United States. In THE MAN OF PROMISE, woman had been characterized as the destroyer of freedom and intellectual thought, essentially a Nietzschean idea. For Willard, as he later confessed to his daughter, Claire Burke was the only female in his life who was not, consciously or unconsciously, an intolerable incubus.

Willard assessed himself and his desperate financial condition. "My books," he recalled later, "had never brought me a sufficient income to live on. And all my literary life I had been compelled to eke out my royalties with magazine articles, stories, editorial work, translations, teaching, etc.,—the sort of things that tear an author's heart out of him and keep his nose to the grindstone day and night. The war had cut into my earnings deeply; my ebbing strength during 1921 and 1922 had curtailed my output; and the kind of books I wrote had little sale during the aftermath of the great world struggle. My collapse in 1923 had practically cut off all my income, and when, two and a half years later, I began to struggle back to life, with little more than skin, bones, viscera as my physical capital, my skies were black with discouragement. . . . 'Why,' I asked myself, 'if other writers, with far less experience and training than I have had, can achieve success at this kind of fiction, can't I? I've studied the detective novel, and I understand its rules and techniques. I know its needs, and have learned its pitfalls.' "[10]

Of course, Willard never admitted the real cause of his collapse and he pretended that he had discovered detective fiction during his recovery, claiming that it was the only kind of fiction his personal physician would allow him to read. It was all untrue, but it made for a romantic story. He wrote out three ten thousand word synopses of as many books. When he visited Maxwell E. Perkins of Charles Scribner's Sons, he admitted that another publisher had already turned them down. "He planned his campaign very carefully—," Perkins said later, "before he wrote his first story, he had outlined the plots of three. We took him up on the outline and paid advances. He was the kind of man who never did anything but that he did it thoroughly, thoughtfully, and well. He thought the first might sell very little but by the time the three came out he would be successful and then the other two would be picked up. As a matter of fact, even the first volume sold remarkably well for a detective story in those days and, by the time the third came, he'd reached 100,000 in the *original* edition. And he kept that up for several more. He gave the mystery novel a new twist and then had a lot of details that added interest, such as footnotes. People here disliked Philo Vance and his mannerisms and so I argued that matter with him, though I felt somewhat differently myself. He said the point was not whether people liked Vance but to make him distinctive, so that they could not forget him."[11] On another occasion Perkins reflected "that a detective story is necessarily relatively artificial and, if done by a skillful and scrupulous writer like Willard, should justify itself, even though he might not have a gift for fiction in general."[12]

A. Scott Berg in MAX PERKINS: EDITOR OF GENIUS (1978) was inclined to give much of the credit for the success of S. S. Van Dine to Perkins. "In a very few years S. S. Van Dine had become the best-known American mystery writer since Poe," he wrote, "and much of his success was as a result of Perkins' meticulous aid in the characterization of Philo Vance. Perkins brought to bear on his mystery writer the same keen intelligence and uncompromising standards that he lavished on Fitzgerald, Hemingway, and his other more clearly literary authors."[13] I believe this goes a bit too far. The Philo Vance novels were wholly Willard's own creation and he should not be denied it. When Perkins read the completed manuscript for THE GREEN MURDER CASE, he wrote to Willard, addressing him "Dear Wright: I think THE GREEN MURDER CASE magnificent. I did not suppose any story could keep me reading until 3:30 A.M., but this one did. There are two possible points that might be considered. More reasons could be easily given, I suppose, for Ada's adoption, about which the reader is left with a little curiosity. And I think it highly doubtful that one could count upon killing another instantly with a .32 caliber.

You often read of a suicide shooting himself in the head or heart with even a larger caliber, and not dying for hours or even days."[14] These are very valid objections and had Willard made the requisite changes in the story, which he did not, they would have made THE GREEN MURDER CASE a much more plausible detective story than it is. Had Willard, in fact, been at all willing to follow Perkins' advice on this and numerous other occasions he could have written even finer books than he did. What faults as well as what virtues are in them are due to Willard and no one else. Much of his seeming indifference is explained by why he wrote them.

His so-called "nervous breakdown" in the years 1923–1925 was brought on by his drug addiction and his despair at his own limitations. What followed was a vast, all-consuming cynicism. It was this cynicism which drove him to write detective stories, not in the spirit of trying his hand at a pursuit allowed by his doctor (which Willard alleged) but as a great gesture to "give the bastards what they want." He did not really want to be known only as the author of a best-selling series of detective novels and, when this did indeed happen, he spent the money he earned with an obscene urge as fast, and later faster, than he made it.

Willard chose S. S. Van Dine for his pen name, his *"nom de guerre,"* as he termed it. Publicly he claimed it was an old family name and the steam ship initials, but to his mother he confessed the truth, the steam ship initials symbolized his desire to travel and the dine was added because he hoped that at last the word would turn into a verb. He had, he said, lived so many years without having it in his vocabulary at all.

THE BENSON MURDER CASE sold out its first printing the week it appeared. THE "CANARY" MURDER CASE was serialized in SCRIBNER'S MAGAZINE and broke all publishing records for detective fiction, including those of Sir Arthur Conan Doyle at the time. From then on, it was for several years an uninterrupted ascent to wealth and fame. Under his own name, Willard edited THE WORLD'S GREAT DETECTIVE STORIES: A CHRONOLOGICAL ANTHOLOGY (1927). He wrote for it a highly literate introduction which surveyed the history of the entire genre until that time and set down the principles which he believed made the detective story unique. "There is no more stimulating activity than that of the mind," he opined, "and there is no more exciting adventure than that of the intellect."[15] It was this commitment to mental acumen which constituted Willard's justification of detective fiction as literature worthy of a degree of respect. He dedicated the anthology to Jacob Munter Lobsenz, his personal physician who would virtually move in with him during his last years to watch over him during his self-induced wake.

Willard moved from his apartment in a remodelled house to the penthouse of a new semi-art-deco apartment house on Central Park West. He lived plushly, ate lavishly, was seen at the best places, hob-nobbed with high society, and on a piece of property he had inherited in New Jersey he built a kennel at which he raised and bred Scottish terriors. Although he might hate them, he was one of them: *les nouveaux riches*. From 1926 to 1939, his work inspired twenty-seven motion pictures. The magazine serializations, book revenues, and reprints brought in a fortune.

In his "Twenty Rules for Writing Detective Stories," Willard summed up his views and his credo would have far-reaching effects on how detective stories were written for years to come, either in imitation of him or in violent contrast. He felt that a reader must have an equal opportunity with the detective to solve the mystery. No wilful tricks or deceptions should be played on the reader by the author. There must be no love interest. The detective must never be the culprit. The culprit's cupidity must be exposed strictly by means of logical deductions. There must always be a detective in the story. There must be a corpse. The problem must be solved "by naturalistic means."[16] In this, he was at one with Poe and Doyle. There must be but one detective. The culprit must turn out to be a character prominent in the story, and never a servant. There must be only one culprit and he cannot be either a professional criminal or a member of a secret society. "The method of murder, and the means of detecting it, must be rational and scientific."[17] The truth must at all times be apparent to the shrewd reader. There should be no long descriptions nor irrelevant conversations. The crime must never turn out to be an accident or a suicide. The motive must always be personal.

This was essentially what Willard had had to say in his introduction to THE WORLD'S GREAT DETECTIVE STORIES and so it was obvious that, while he did not publicize himself as S. S. Van Dine, he wanted to be found out and here was a very important clue. It was Harry Hansen, literary critic for THE NEW YORK WORLD, who first suggested in his column that S. S. Van Dine was no inexperienced novice but indeed an illustrious name with a sterling reputation. He proceeded to make a few guesses, mostly of people better known than Willard. The search was on and Scribner's got to take advantage of it. The nation became "detective" conscious. In those days, one could afford such pleasant diversions. Finally, Bruce Gould, a columnist for THE NEW YORK EVENING POST, wrote an article conclusively proving S. S. Van Dine to be Willard Huntington Wright. It was, I suspect, a put-up job. "We submit," Gould wrote after Willard had taken him to lunch at the exclusive Pierre's, "that no writer of cultural subjects, such as Mr. Wright is, could ever make enough money in America to lunch with friends at Pierre's. Therefore, we can only conclude that Mr. Wright has become very wealthy at the expense of his close friend, S. S. Van Dine."[18]

Once his identity was revealed, articles appeared about Willard in newspapers and magazines. He was interviewed on any number of subjects, for the press and over the radio. Two presidents of the United States declared him to be their favorite detective story writer. University bulletins were devoted to analyses of his novels and the novels themselves were translated into most foreign languages, including Croatian and Japanese. The Book-of-the-Month Club recommended "CANARY" and picked THE GREENE MURDER CASE as its first alternative. An ice cream sundae was named after the "CANARY" as was a rather potent cocktail. The "CANARY" MURDER CASE cocktail consists of ½ jigger dry gin, ½ jigger cognac, ½ jigger yellow vermouth, 1 jigger orange juice, 1 dash of orange bitters, all to be shaken well and served in a chilled glass.

Willard was interviewed by H. F. Manchester for an article which appeared in THE WRITER in September, 1931. " 'The writing of detective stories I consider the most strenuous form of literary activity,' " Willard is quoted as saying. " 'Once I thought it was an easy way to make money, but it is the hardest thing I could have picked on. Before writing a word of the final draft, I do a 30,000 word synopsis, and know precisely where each brick, each beam, and each bolt in the completed structure must go.' " So far, he was to be believed. But he didn't stop there. " 'When I start writing a story,' " he went on, " 'I cut myself off from the world and concentrate upon it. There are a great many little details to remember, and there must be no loose ends hanging when it is finished. If I go out for an evening, or see anyone, I find it takes me two days to get back where I was and pick up all the little ends. I get up every morning at seven and work until one o'clock the next morning, and keep this up for seven or eight months. It is the only way I can keep things balanced. During this time I take no coffee, no stimulants of any kind. People can keep going on stimulants for a short time, but unless I avoided them in my long ordeals, I would break down completely. Even as it is, I lose eight pounds every time I write a detective story. I go into a terrible state of depression, and when the story is finished, I shudder at the thought of ever writing another one.' " [19] Willard also persuaded Manchester to believe that he read in several languages and that he based his books on actual events in European criminal history.

Willard created Philo Vance to be what he wanted himself to be, an urbane intellectual with unlimited knowledge about every conceivable subject. In the beginning, he searched long and hard for all the erudite references which would contribute to this impression. For example, in a footnote in THE BISHOP MURDER CASE, Van Dine referred to a book which Professor Dillard, one of the characters, was at work upon titled THE ATOMIC STRUCTURE OF RADIANT ENERGY. According to Van Dine, this book "was a mathematical emendation of Planck's quantum theory refuting the classical axiom of the continuity of all physical processes, as contained in Maximus Tyrius' Οὐδὲ ἐνταῦθα ἡ φύσις μεταπηδᾷ ἀθρόως."[20] Maximus of Tyre was an obscure Neo-Platonist of the First Century A.D. who could not even correctly date the Peloponnesian War since he attributed the Athenian reversals in this conflict to their wickedness in putting Socrates to death when, in fact, he died some years after the war was over. He left behind some forty-one lectures, mostly on religious subjects. Willard obviously gleaned this quotation, totally out of context, from a secondary source and may not even have been able to translate it accurately since it reads literally, "Not even thither as nature jumps all of a piece from one place to another." Later, Willard listed this book as being among Philo Vance's publications, along with a treatise on Ming pottery, and publications on vowels in Egyptian hieroglyphics, fishing in Norwegian waters, and art and the criminal. It was because this is what he had once wanted and expected from himself; and despair came about when he realized how far short of his objective he had fallen. Vance was also restricted in the development of a human side to his personality. For all of his study of detective fiction, it had not occurred to Willard that the Sherlock Holmes stories were read as much, or more, because of an interest in Holmes than merely for the interest in one or another of his criminal problems. Vance also has unlimited funds, about as much a fantasy as his unlimited knowledge; and he is a bachelor with absolutely no private life. When Ogden Nash wrote that "Philo Vance needs a kick in the pance," it was a reference to the utter lack of a sense of humor. As Beverly Wright once put it about her father, wit he had, but humor not at all.

Christopher Ward did a parody of Van Dine's technique for THE SATURDAY REVIEW OF LITERATURE in 1929. Corey Ford went a step further and wrote a book-length parody of the Vance stories, THE JOHN RIDDELL MURDER CASE (1930), which Scribner's published. Van Dine was so taken with this book that he even contributed to it. Should this seem a rather bizarre happenstance, it must be remembered that the detective novels themselves were little removed from satire. Here is how THE SCARAB MURDER CASE (1930) opens:

"Scarlett almost dashed through the portières of the library when Currie had pulled back the sliding door for him to enter. Either the Courvoisier had added to his excitement or else Currie had woefully underrated the man's nervous state.

" 'Kyle has been murdered!' the newcomer blurted, leaning against the library table and staring at Vance with gaping eyes.

" 'Really, now! That's most distressin'.' Vance held out his cigarette-case. 'Do have one of my *Regies*. . . . And you'll find that chair beside you most comfortable. A Charles chair; I picked it up in London. . . . Beastly mess, people getting murdered, what? But it really can't be helped, don't y'know. The human race is so deuced blood-thirsty.' "[21]

Van Dine once gave Alex King a Scottie to tend while he went to Europe for a month. The dog was trained to squat whenever he heard the name "Alex." The Philo Vance stories are filled with this same wild and slightly cruel kind of witticism.

Yet for all his success, Willard lived, not dangerously as Nietzsche had instructed, but desperately. He chain-smoked his *Regies*. He substituted cognac for opium and became equally addicted. His pose was that of a product of an exhausted, waning culture, shortly before the deluge. Despair clung palpably to him. His attempts at aesthetics and poetry, main-stream fiction and literary criticism, his relationships with women, with friends, with his daughter—he felt it had all led nowhere. He wanted to die. He chose to chart his death scientifically as daily it stole upon him. He was obsessed with death and so he wrote about murder. Only when he quoted a Roman author directly could his Latin be trusted, as when Vance cited Horace, *"Eheu! fugaces, Postume, Postume, labuntur anni"* [Alas! O Postumus, Postumus, the years flow by rapidly].[22] But as his life ebbed, his books lost their magic, their passion, their luster. His eventual demise, so unexpected by many, was concisely planned. It even proved fortuitous since it preceded by only a few years the inevitable rejection of the kind of detective fiction Willard had written and the literary milieu he represented. I believe he had the prescience of mind to foresee this. Like so many of his murderers, he had gambled on a means to success; and when it came, when he had won all he had hoped for and more, he lost. It wasn't enough.

"Some day," Willard wrote in 1935, "I shall take a long vacation and rest. Will I make a walking tour through Norway, or live a *dolce-far-niente* life on some South Sea isle? Frankly, I don't know. All I know at present is that I'll go far away from crime, police departments, and circulating libraries, and imitate the lowly vegetable. Then, having bidden farewell to 'Philo Vance' and 'District Attorney Markham' and 'Sergeant Heath' I shall return to my other literary labors. Ah, but when will that be? Again, I frankly confess I do not know. Just now I crave nothing beyond a good *filet de sole marguery*, a bottle of 1904 Amontillado, and one of the later Beethoven sonatas."[23] He never did finish his scholarly books. He was working on detective stories right up to the day he died.

II

In his Introduction to THE WORLD'S GREAT DETECTIVE STORIES, Willard was quite adamant. " . . . It is significant," he wrote, "that the cinematograph has never been able to project a detective story. The detective story, in fact, is the only type of fiction that cannot be filmed. The test of popular fiction—namely, its presentation in visual pictures, or let us say, the visualizing of its word-pictures—goes to pieces when applied to detective stories. The difficulties confronting a motion-picture director in the screening of a detective tale are very much the same as those he would encounter if he strove to film a cross-word puzzle. The only serious attempt to transcribe a detective story onto the screen was the case of SHERLOCK HOLMES [Goldwyn, 1922]; and the effort was made possible only by reducing the actual detective elements to a minimum, and emphasizing all manner of irrelevant dramatic and adventurous factors; for there is neither drama nor adventure, in the conventional sense, in a good detective novel."[24]

This was written in 1927. If the year 1929 were to be judged in terms of its detective films on the basis of Paramount's THE RETURN OF SHERLOCK HOLMES, one would have to agree with Willard's contention of the unfilmability of a detective story. However, such was not the case.

E. C. Bentley published TRENT'S LAST CASE in 1913. In his Introduction Willard referred to Bentley's detective, Philip Trent, as a "somewhat baffled nemesis," but he found him "highly engaging" as a detective and the book, "though unconventional in conception, is, in its way, a masterpiece."[25] The Fox Film Corporation purchased screen rights to the property and Sol Wurtzel, in charge of production, assigned Howard Hawks to direct the photoplay in 1929.

Alfred A. Knopf re-issued the novel in 1930 to cash in on the added publicity afforded by the film. Then W. Somerset Maugham chose to include this novel in his anthology, TRAVELLER'S LIBRARY (1933), a collection of novels, short stories, poems, and essays. In a prefatory note, Maugham set down what he felt to be the principles of a good detective story. "The story," he wrote, "is the chief thing. The characters should be natural, but it is unnecessary to go into them in any detail. Their idiosyncracies are only of consequence if they are essential to the story. You do not want to know their opinions on art, life, or the immortality of the soul. Love-making is merely tiresome and the amorous attachment of one person to another is only opportune if it is a possible motive for an action. It is an insufficient, because too obvious, cause to lead to the unravelling of the mystery. The writing should be good, but the detective story is no place for elegances of style. Nothing should hold you up. The scene must be set, but you do not what to be bothered with descriptions of scenery. For my own part I think the detective story should deal with a murder."[26] There were more principles than these, but this should be adequate to illustrate how much what Maugham felt were the ingredients of a good detective story agreed with the Twenty Rules S. S. Van Dine had prescribed in his article for AMERICAN MAGAZINE in 1928. At the time, Bentley had not written any of the subsequent stories he would featuring Trent and so Maugham was correct when he commented that "it is the only detective story the author has written. I have often heard it lamented that he has never written another. My own opinion is that he has in this shown a singular wisdom, for when you have done a thing as perfectly as possible what on earth is the use of doing it again?"[27]

As a novel, I find TRENT'S LAST CASE dull reading and its plot preposterous. Sigsbee Manderson, in an effort to destroy his wife and her lover, plots his own murder and so construcs the evidence that the paramour will be convicted and executed. True, at the very end of the novel, it is suggested that Manderson only intended to wound himself before he is killed in a struggle with Mr. Cupples. Yet, his plot would not really have worked were there no body and this surmise is only a mincing rationalization. One might suppose Manderson to have been a lunatic to have come up with a scheme such as this; but this is not how Bentley explained it. Instead, he had Marlowe, Manderson's secretary, offer this solution: " 'I used to think that his strain of Indian blood, remote as it was, might have something to do with the cunning and ruthlessness of the man.' "[28] A little later, Marlowe adds that " 'my researches left me with the idea that there is a very great deal of aboriginal blood present in the genealogical make-up of the people of America, and that it is very widely spread.' "[29] Hence, we are to conclude that Manderson, and all others of a similar ilk, owe their nature to the amount of Native American blood flowing in their veins! Bentley also intended his detective to be something of a satire on Sherlock Holmes since Trent persistently makes the most elaborate deductions based on various clues only to be proven hopelessly wrong.

Hawks was not exactly pleased with being handed this property to film. He had signed in 1928 a six-picture contract with Fox after directing four pictures on a per picture basis for Sol Wurtzel. He was to be paid $30,000 each for the first three and $40,000 each for the second three. TRENT'S LAST CASE (Fox, 1929) was Hawks' fourth picture on the contract and, following it, he was fired. However unenthusiastic he may have been about making it, the film does have moments of exceptional brilliance and is capable of achieving precisely those results with a detective story which Willard thought impossible and which, surveying all of the silent detective films which survive, had been virtually unattainable by anyone else. The detective story, relying as it does so heavily on dialogue and interviews, would seemingly be adaptable primarily to the sound medium; Hawks demonstrated that it could be otherwise.

"A detective story depends on dialogue," Hawks once told me. "It is essential to it. When I made TRENT'S LAST CASE, we actually had a scenario for a talkie, but Fox couldn't get rights to make it as a talking picture. I had to shoot it as a silent."[30]

In the role of Sigsbee Manderson, Hawks cast Donald Crisp. Since all those who held Bentley's novel in such high esteem had had apparently no problem accepting its incredible premise, it was Sol Wurtzel's intention for it to be filmed as written. Hawks would not go along with this entirely. To him, it seemed totally ridiculous that through dialogue alone one might establish a believable character so vicious and lunatic to kill himself in order to frame his secretary. Scott Darling was assigned to the screenplay. Following Hawks' conception of the story, Sigsbee Manderson is very much a character and he is seen plotting and implementing his insane plan at every step of the way. In actually shooting the photoplay, Hawks quickened the pace considerably. Marceline Day, petite and charming, was cast as Manderson's long-suffering wife. The sophisticated silent comedian, Raymond Griffith, played Trent. This was an adept bit of casting insofar as Trent is bumbling and inept in the novel. Edgar Kennedy played Inspector Murch. At one point Murch and Trent collide, doing a double pratfall. Raymond Hatton portrayed Manderson's club-footed uncle, Mr. Cupples, a role which he carried off despite the fact that he was ten years Crisp's junior. He is shown in flashback interrupting Crisp during his elaborate preparations and, in the ensuing struggle, Crisp is shot. As in the novel, Trent arrives at the correct solution only when Mr. Cupples makes it known to him, right in the midst of Trent's attempt to pin the murder onto the innocent secretary.

Hawks was convinced that this material could only be handled in a light comic vein and that's one reason the film plays as well as it does. The photoplay managed to develop a number of interesting personality studies and the direction sustained an atmosphere of suspense at the same time as it never allowed excitement to flag. In this regard, TRENT'S LAST CASE anticipated the fast pacing typical of Hawksian comedies in succeeding decades. While he might not have been able to take the plot seriously, Hawks, notwithstanding, did demonstrate unsuspected possibilities in making a silent detective film where ratiocination, and not sheer action, remained predominant.

TRENT'S LAST CASE (Eagle-Lion, 1953) was remade, produced and directed by Herbert Wilcox. Margaret Lockwood, in her first important role in years, played Manderson's unfortunate wife. Just why she ever married him, considering how sweetly she is portrayed by both Marceline Day and Margaret Lockwood, is never adequately explained in either screenplay, as it is not in the original novel. Michael Wilding was cast as Trent, this time a newspaper reporter who rejects the inquest findings of suicide. Orson Welles, albeit only in flashbacks, portrayed the crazed Manderson. Pamela Bower's screenplay followed the book more closely and the case opens after Manderson is dead. The film fails, and it fails precisely because it is too garrulous. Everyone talks and talks. There is no action. Whereas Hawks' version moves at all times, be it from suspense to comedy, the sound remake is an embodiment of the notion that the essence of a detective story is the constant talking among characters rather than physical action. To find somehow an effective balance between dialogue and action has remained the great challenge, it would seem from the very beginning, for anyone seeking to film a detective story.

On 24 January 1928, Willard granted Paramount an option on his first Philo Vance novel, THE BENSON MURDER CASE, for $17,500 with a provision that should the studio exercise the option it could also purchase screen rights on both the "CANARY" and GREENE murder cases. Paramount acted quickly on all three once THE BISHOP MURDER CASE made the bestseller lists and stayed there for months. THE "CANARY" MURDER CASE went into production first.

For the role of Philo Vance, Paramount chose contract player William Powell. He was born in 1892 at Pittsburgh, the son of an accountant. When the family moved to Kansas City, Powell enrolled briefly at the University there but quit to go to work for the telephone company as a clerk. In view of how difficult he found acting throughout his career, it is curious that he should have been so taken with the prospect of it as to pack up his belongings and venture to New York where he enrolled at the American Academy of Dramatic Arts.

He gained experience doing one night stands. His New York debut came in 1912 in a play called NE'ER DO WELL. The next year he had a major role in WITHIN THE LAW and went on tour with the show for two years. A series of disappointments followed, stock companies, short-term contracts, innumerable plays, but always building up a repertory of parts which culminated in his initial Broadway success in 1920 in the play SPANISH LOVE. He was offered the role of Forman Wells in Samuel Goldwyn's production of SHERLOCK HOLMES on the basis of this success and the experience readily persuaded him that he preferred motion pictures to the legitimate stage. A number of roles in costume dramas followed. With ROMOLA (M-G-M, 1925) he started being cast in villainous parts. After appearing in DANGEROUS MONEY (Paramount, 1924) and TOO MANY KISSES (Paramount, 1925), Paramount placed him under contract. Powell starred in the studio's first all-talking picture, INTERFERENCE (Paramount, 1929), in which he played a murderer. The studio executives were pleased with how well his voice recorded and this perhaps most of all led to his being cast as Vance.

Malcolm St. Clair was slated to direct. THE "CANARY" MURDER CASE (Paramount, 1929) went into production as a silent but was changed at the last minute into a talkie. It seemed an obvious inference that a film with long sequences during which nothing happened other than interviewing suspects was best handled in the new medium. Louise Brooks was cast as the "Canary," a Broadway musical revue star who is portrayed on screen as even more of a tart than she is in the book, once married (according to the screenplay) to ex-convict Ned Sparks, and now systematically blackmailing the society men with whom she has gone to bed. Brooks left for Germany to appear as the slut Lulu in G. W. Pabst's production of PANDORAS BUCHSE [German, 1929]. This put Paramount in a bind. Margaret Livingston was called in to dub Brooks' voice in scenes that had been shot without sound. In its final release version, THE "CANARY" MURDER CASE was a curious hybrid product, some of it silent with sound intercuts for dialogue, or, in brief scenes, voices noticeably dubbed.

Willard was hired to work on dialogue at Paramount's Astoria studios in New York. Yet, this notwithstanding, the cinematic Philo Vance was nothing like his literary counterpart. The British accent, the posturing, the arcane and erudite references were replaced on screen by Powell's rather clipped, precise movements and mannerisms of speech. Eugene Pallette, cast as Sergeant Heath, took so well to the role that for many movie-goers he became inextricably associated with the part even when other studios began making Philo Vance films. St. Clair managed a moment of visual Expressionist poetry when he had Brooks, as the "Canary," swing out over her theatre audience, the camera focusing from the rafters on the distressed countenances of her blackmail victims watching her in somewhat lecherous awe from below. After screening the finished film, Willard changed his mind. "It is a much better picture than it was a book," he said. "At the risk of appearing as a very egotistical person, I am compelled to say that on the screen . . . it is the best mystery I have ever seen."[31]

Later, when Willard came out to Hollywood, he became instant friends with William Powell. Powell was by then under contract to Warner Bros., as was Willard, and Willard had the actor personally escort him to all the best baudy houses. Frank Tuttle, who directed the next two Paramount Philo Vance entries, also became a cohort of Willard's. He would gain a considerable reputation as a film director until the House UnAmerican Activities Committee branded him a subversive after the Second World War and he was henceforth confined to working as an art director.

Yet, I fear this has caused me to get ahead of myself. When THE BENSON MURDER CASE was published, it did not meet with a critical reception entirely commensurate with its commercial popularity. It was criticized for the naiveté of its plot; though, whatever its technical shortcomings, it did promulgate Van Dine's aesthetic and philosophic theories on how a crime, just as a work of art, bears the indelible imprint of its creator's personality and temperament. This methodology, eased by Van Dine's caricature of the police and deliberate blunting of their scientific routines, allowed Vance alone to identify the murderer while at the same time it permits a reader to experience an acute sense of pleasure when, suddenly, he perceives a generating line through the miasma of misleading information and conflicting evidence. Willard did not wholly desert his aesthetic proclivities when he became S. S. Van Dine; instead he wove them adroitly into a finely textured psychological fabric of crime and pursuit. The reader does not have to labor beneath the needless complexity of odd clues nor must he resort to endless fanciful speculations which ratiocination cannot really suggest but only confirm after the fact, as was so frequently the practice in the early and highly imitative Ellery Queen novels. Rather the crime or crimes, the web of circumstance and the generation of murder in a Van Dine novel are grasped quite suddenly as a unity. Our appreciation is aesthetic in character and the appeal is more to the sensibility than to merely deductive mental processes. Van Dine retained this formula through the first nine Philo Vance novels and, on this basis, I might almost agree with William Stanley Braithwaite that the imaginative as well as intellectual content of these novels lifted "the detective story onto the plane of a fine art."[32]

One of Van Dine's favorite means of reading personality was a man's relationship to gambling and, specifically, to poker. In THE BENSON MURDER CASE, in conversation with one of the suspects, Vance carefully analyzes the attitudes toward gambling true of each of the other suspects. In THE "CANARY" MURDER CASE, Van Dine took the theory a step farther and permitted Vance actually to engage the leading suspects in a poker game. The film techniques of the time, and the direction by St. Clair, were unable to make this episode particularly suspenseful when it was included in the photoplay. In both the novel and the film, this ploy was intended to allow the reader or viewer to construct a diagram of the murderer's personality and put it to the test.

One character, however, is sadly missing in all of the Philo Vance films, one so memorably evident in the books: the city of New York. Van Dine captured the city during one of its golden eras when it was the hub of American cultural and artistic expression. The ease and polish of life, the contrasts among the upper classes at the time Van Dine wrote, give almost as vivid an impression as we have of London in the Sherlock Holmes stories. The gallery showings, the concerts, the clubs and restaurants, the amusements, games, crafts, interests, and aesthetic passions of New York in the 'Twenties and 'Thirties, interlaced as they are with brokerage houses, Broadway shows, horse races, the parks, sights, buildings, reveal a mighty, exhausting tapestry of a city of endless riches and extravagances. That New York is gone, never to return. The fashions, sartorial displays, the tastes in tobacco, wine, and food of that period, the weather, sounds, and personalities of New York are as distant from us today as Vance's aesthetic ponderings on criminology—oh, perhaps only the weather is not too much changed. Yet, it is also a skewed, a distorted picture we have, as romantic in its way as Conan Doyle's London or Raymond Chandler's Los Angeles. Van Dine, even more than Conan Doyle, shows us only the rich, the well-to-do, the accomplished or unaccomplished, but the disengaged wealthy, those for whom life is essentially meaningless and whom we only see in terms of what they possess, their hobbies and enthusiasms. In this marvelous feeling for a great city you see only the lights of skyscrapers from a penthouse garden and never the people in the streets, the sordid, the lonely, the degenerate, the frustrated, the poor, the corrupt, the professional criminal. The occasional housebreaker or mobster is so highly stylized as to be preposterous.

Van Dine really believed that motive was fallacious as a tool in detection and so presented his cases as to make it irrelevant. In this fashion he further removed crime from any basis it might have in reality. Van Dine likened detective stories to puzzles, but he wrote not puzzles, rendering instead with *élan* paintings of personality, reduced detection not really to clues but to an instinctive sensitivity to temperament. For Van Dine human behavior really was inspired by caprice or perversity.

THE GREENE MURDER CASE was the third Philo Vance novel, but the second photoplay. Paramount rushed it into production right after THE "CANARY" MURDER CASE and it was released the same year. In the novel, Van Dine amused himself with the prospect of murdering a whole book of suspects and still to conceal the murderer's identity. A replica of the Greene mansion was built on a Paramount sound stage. Frank Tuttle in his direction managed effectively to create an atmosphere of suspicion and suspense.

Van Dine was enamored of the Cinderella fable, but with a variation: Cinderella as the most evil of the step sisters. This is the way Van Dine conceived Ada Greene in the novel and this is the way Jean Arthur played her on the screen. The compelling scene that brings the film to its climax is of the angelic Jean Arthur transformed into a fiend. She kicks and hacks at the second storey awning bar onto which Florence Eldridge as Sibella Greene is clinging for dear life until Vance can rescue her. Through a series of close-ups, Jean Arthur's face assumes a crazed frenzy that makes her perpetration of the murders believable, something not so convincingly portrayed in the novel.

Mark Larkin interviewed Van Dine for the April, 1929 issue of PHOTOPLAY magazine. No mention was made that the man pictured in the article with the Van Dyke beard, the moustache with the waxed tips (after the fashion of Kaiser Wilhelm II), and the monocle had once done hack work for that very magazine. Instead, what was written was Willard's story the way he wanted it told. "In addition to being a distinguished author," Larkin wrote, "Mr. Wright is also a worthy mathematician. Therein, perhaps, lies the secret of his great success as a deviser of mystery stories, for after all a mystery story is nothing more, he says, than an elaborate literary puzzle. Mr. Wright, like all who labor, has one consuming ambition. He hopes never to write another mystery story. Imagine that! Each book that he does means a small fortune, yet he hopes never to have to do another. He wants to write about biology and anthropology. And his crowning ambition is to complete the philology upon which he was working at the time he collapsed and became rich and famous."[33] Since the murderer in THE GREENE MURDER CASE was a woman, Willard also expressed himself on this subject. He had read enough criminology to know that women murderers are far fewer numerically than men. " 'They are the perfect murderers,' " Willard told Larkin. " 'But they are fewer. It is quite unusual for women to kill. Either that, or they cover their crimes so ingeniously that they are not caught. Women can be most disarming, you know, when they choose. I really believe, however, that the killer type is in the minority among them, as compared with the same percentage of murderers among men.' "[34]

Van Dine's detective stories embodied this viewpoint and this was probably another reason that they were so successfully challenged by the hard-boiled BLACK MASK school where women were most often murderers. There was a growing misogyny in the United States throughout the 'Thirties and, of course, it became predominant in the 'Forties.

Some years later Paramount remade THE GREENE MURDER CASE (Paramount, 1929) as A NIGHT OF MYSTERY (Paramount, 1937) with Grant Richards in the role of Vance. British Paramount had brought THE SCARAB MURDER CASE (1930) to the screen in 1936 in England and much of the talkiness of the foreign effort carried over to the American remake the next year. E. A. Dupont was assigned to direct. Malcolm St. Clair's Expressionist trapeze sequence in THE "CANARY" MURDER CASE had been compared by critics to similar sequences in Dupont's silent masterpiece, VARIETÉ (German, 1926), which Paramount had distributed in the United States. But Dupont's A NIGHT OF MYSTERY was no great achievement. It was produced on a very low budget and Grant Richards had to his credit little more than a minor role in the previous year's HOPALONG CASSIDY RETURNS (Paramount, 1936). In much of the publicity he was billed under loud-talking Roscoe Karns cast as Sergeant Heath. Rain was substituted for snow—the latter so intrinsic to the plot—in all but the one sheets. With customary German thoroughness, Dupont even purchased two hundred dead flies (not visible to the camera) for atmosphere in the scene where the long-sealed Greene library is searched. The sets had been used earlier that year in MURDER GOES TO COLLEGE (Paramount, 1937). Vance is a pipe-smoking dandy whose love for *haute cuisine* runs to beef stew (rather incredible when you reflect that Philo Vance's success permitted Willard to employ his own personal chef). Leonard Carey as Vance's valet is referred to as Lister in one part of the film and as Leslie in another. Primarily because Helen Burgess, cast as Ada Greene, died before the picture was completed, her exposure in the denouement was clumsily handled. Seeing that the jig is up, photographed in shadow, a double goes running down the hall after firing two shots, crashing and rolling down a flight of stairs, only to recover with a slight flesh wound. The well-lit A. E. Freudeman interiors prompted no terror and the film, hurriedly made, ended even more hurriedly.

THE BENSON MURDER CASE (Paramount, 1930) was based on the third and last of the three Van Dine novels on which the studio had an option. After an almost literal adherence to Van Dine's plots in both THE "CANARY" MURDER CASE and THE GREENE MURDER CASE, the plot of THE BENSON MURDER CASE was altered substantially from what it is in the novel. Alvin Benson, the victim in the novel, is changed to Anthony Benson in the film. Opening to a fine montage of descending values, margin desperation, sell-outs, and ruin at the stock exchange, a cast of curious suspects is assembled at Benson's river lodge. Paul Lukas, who would eventually play Philo Vance at M-G-M, was cast as a gigolo and a check forger. Probably one of the reasons that Paramount did not expend more effort on THE BENSON MURDER CASE was due to the fact that Van Dine had sold screen rights to his most popular book, THE BISHOP MURDER CASE, to M-G-M. It was announced in the trades that British character actor Basil Rathbone had been assigned the lead as Philo Vance.

S. S. Van Dine delighted in caricaturing his mother. Crazy, oppressive, stifling, eccentric mothers recur repeatedly in the novels. There's old Mrs. Greene and old Mrs. Drukker in THE BISHOP MURDER CASE, and later old Mrs. Stamm, old Mrs. Llewellyn, and old Mrs. Garden (poisoned with radioactive potassium). Most directors of the various Philo Vance films seemed to enjoy these characters best of all and in most cases went all out in their treatment of them in the respective photoplays. Nick Grindé directed THE BISHOP MURDER CASE (M-G-M, 1930). The studio pushed the picture through production so fast it actually beat THE BENSON MURDER CASE into theatres by three months. Regrettably, the cinematic techniques at Metro-Goldwyn-Mayer were even more stage-bound in filming a detective story than they were at Paramount. David Burton was selected to direct the actors and see to their elocution. Basil Rathbone had, as yet, only very limited experience before the camera and this picture did nothing for him. His delivery of dialogue was incredibly trying, albeit the visual effects were quite good and the various murders were handled with a flair for the grotesque. Roland Young was cast as Arnesson, the chief suspect; and he is about to be cornered by Vance when in a sudden *volte-face* gentle old Alec B. Francis is exposed as the murderer. Some changes, however, had to be made. Because Louis B. Mayer was in charge of production at M-G-M and since he felt motherhood to be sacred and that it must be honored in every film the studio released, old Mrs. Drukker could not be retained; she was written out of the screenplay and Drukker was given a sister instead. Also, at the end of the book, Vance deliberately poisons the murderer; such behavior was obviously deemed unacceptable in a detective hero and so this, too, was altered. Notwithstanding, THE BISHOP MURDER CASE opened to good reviews and, increasingly, motion picture companies were becoming convinced that detective stories were a wise investment. Because of their inherently static interrogatory scenes packed with little action and much dialogue, detective films were relatively cheap to manufacture in addition to utilizing fully the novelty of the sound medium. As the most popular living detective story author in 1930, S. S. Van Dine was in a charmed position to assume a dominant role in this medium as well.

Paramount did option THE SCARAB MURDER CASE while William Powell was still under contract. When he left, the property remained dormant until finally, with frozen funds, Paramount made the film in the United Kingdom. The plot of the novel relied on the device of the culprit deliberately fabricating such overwhelming evidence pointing to his own guilt as to divert suspicion. This could only really work in Van Dine's abstract and aesthetic fictional world. In reality, had Markham been a truly aggressive district attorney, he would have clapped this obvious suspect in jail and convicted him, innocent or guilty, at a spectacular trial. Paramount did make a Spanish language version of THE BENSON MURDER CASE titled EL CUERPO DEL DELITO released in Argentina in June, 1930, and in the promotional revue, PARAMOUNT ON PARADE (Paramount, 1930), William Powell and Eugene Pallette appeared in a short skit as Vance and Sergeant Heath. Warner Bros. then staged a raid on Paramount's contract players and directors. William Powell, who on 26 June 1931 married pert, outspoken Carole Lombard, was among those signed. Paramount, which was in financial trouble, no longer seemed the place to be. Accordingly, Jack L. Warner set about purchasing, before even they were written, screen rights to Van Dine's next two Philo Vance novels in which he intended to star Powell. Despite M-G-M's lone entry, in the popular mind William Powell was still intimately identified with the role. Next, Warner hired Van Dine and transported him to Hollywood to script twelve two-reel mystery short subjects for the studio's Vitaphone short subject series and to work on an original screen story for a feature film. Willard left New York in early spring, 1931, and did not return until late in summer. This interruption delayed progress on his sixth Philo Vance story, THE KENNEL MURDER CASE; but alone it did not account for its being two years in preparation. Willard had often commented that a detective story writer had only six good detective stories in him and any man so superstitious that he had to retain six letters in the titles of his books as a talisman to bring good fortune (because there were six letters in "Wright") could only view the publication of his sixth book as portentous. Maxwell Perkins asked Willard to suggest six detective novels which

Scribner's could reprint as the S. S. Van Dine Mystery Library. Willard's suggestions, seven in number, were still such, however, that two of the books, THE BIG BOW MYSTERY (1892) by Israel Zangwill and THE SIGN OF THE FOUR by Sir Arthur Conan Doyle, could be issued in the same volume and so keep the total number of volumes at six. Also, almost in desperation, Willard convinced Perkins to re-issue THE MAN OF PROMISE. H. L. Mencken's review of this book in 1916 in FORUM had the heading: "America Produces a Novelist." When it failed a second time, Willard's horizons again seemed dark, nay, darker, because now there was no possibility of resuming his past labors with any expectation of commercial success.

The Vitaphone shorts were not Philo Vance vehicles although Van Dine wrote all the stories. Many of them starred Donald Meek and were directed by Joseph Henabery who had once played Lincoln for D. W. Griffith in THE BIRTH OF A NATION (Epoch, 1915). Typical of these shorts is THE CAMPUS MYSTERY (Warner's, 1932) with Van Dine credited for the story and Burnet Hershey for the adaptation and dialogue. To Hershey, the short probably owes this interchange between John Hamilton as Inspector Carr and Harriet Hilliard as Wanda Terry:

CARR: Everyone's guilty until proven innocent, ma'am.
TERRY: Or influential.

Terry's father is dean of a college. He discovers discrepancies in the books of the Athletic Club and proposes to expose the culprit. Before he can, he is murdered. Willard drew the dean as a despicably moralistic stuffed-shirt and Wanda Terry as a perfectly willing co-ed, sufficiently liberated to educate her body as well as her mind. The crime is traced to a pole vaulter who uses a pole to jump into the second storey window of another student's room in order to steal his gun.

Willard had met Claire Delisle in 1929 and he fell in love for the last time in his life. He summarily instructed Katherine Boynton to divorce him. The decree became final on 26 October 1930 and Stanton suspected that Willard had jumped the gun by one day in marrying Claire. Willard had come to San Francisco in November, 1930 and visited with Katherine in the hotel where she had retreated. She asked him then if he had married again and he told her he had not, although he had. Claire shared Willard's extravagant tastes and was a spendthrift. When Stanton came to New York to visit, Claire did not get on at all with him. Stanton did not come again. Willard had just returned from Hollywood, having scripted the short subjects and having written an original story for the screen which he called THE BLUE MOON MURDER CASE. Willard had hoped that Walter Huston would be given the leading role. It was not to be. The story was filmed as GIRL MISSING (Warner's, 1933), directed by Robert Florey and starring Ben Lyon and Glenda Farrell. It was filmed in twelve days on a budget of $200,000. Willard disowned it.

Burton Rascoe came to see Willard. He was preparing an anthology of stories and articles which had appeared in THE SMART SET and he wanted to include a brief history of the magazine. When Wright had taken over as editor, he had included a short statement of what he considered the new policy of the magazine. "THE SMART SET magazine has no mission, social, religious or political, to perform," he had written. "But it must not be supposed that it has no purpose, no moving spirit. Behind it, animating all its pages and shaping all its activities there is a very Definite and Persistent Idea. Its Prime Purpose is to Provide Lively Entertainment for Minds That Are Not Primitive."[35] In his conversation with Rascoe, Willard related how Barry Benefield had come to him with a story after he had set in place his revolutionary new editorial program. "A shy, pale, wren-like creature," Rascoe wrote, "wearing a collar much too big for him, black string tie, and clothes that hung loosely upon his diminutive frame, with eyes peering from behind silver-rimmed glasses, timidly but amusedly, sat in a chair before Wright, handed over a smudged and much-handled manuscript and said, 'I think it is only fair to tell you that that story has been turned down by every magazine in the country—every single one.' Wright answered, 'That is the very best recommendation you can give it.' Benefield left and Wright read the story that night. Wright told me that next morning he was still trembling with the thrill of discovery over it and called Benefield up to tell him the story was sold, and asked him did he have any more that had been turned down by the leading magazines. Benefield replied he had six. Wright said he would take them all, sight unseen. And he did."[36]

Now, with what Nietzsche had called *"ein schlechtes Gewissen,"* a bad conscience, Willard found himself on a treadmill: the faster he made money, the faster he had to spend it, and the faster he had to grind out more material. "You have sensed his feelings of utter futility and despair during the last years of his life," Stanton once wrote to me. "Of course, you have known that his death was really a suicide. The last time I saw him—1932, I believe—he could think of nothing but the uselessness of human life, its aspirations and even its accomplishments. He would harangue me for hours on the subject, pointing out the idiocy of what I do . . . , the impermanency of everything and the stupidity of conceiving of anything as significant or important. My rejoinder that we had to act *as though* we knew something and accept the results as did Arjuna, he pooh-poohed with bitter irony, accusing me of a bourgeois faith. I would argue with him about his method of self-destruction and he would say I was as bad as Doc Lobsenz. He had his butler place a pony of Napoleon brandy at his side every half hour—he was playing for Bright's disease, but the other got him. . . . Need I say he was the perfect example of what the poets have said about the hope that one never achieves in one's age, the desires of one's youth?"[37]

THE KENNEL MURDER CASE ran serially in COSMOPOLITAN. All in all, the really fantastic element in the story is neither the Scottish terriers nor the Chinese porcelain about which Vance prattles. It is the incredible circumstance that the victim leaves the room in which he was fatally stabbed, enters his bedroom on the second floor where he expires, only to be murdered once dead by his brother who had also planned his murder. Since a conviction of the murderer could not be secured, Van Dine executed him by means of a Doberman Pinscher tearing out his throat. Vance could then calmly proceed to explain the mechanics of the crime. In the subsequent Warner Bros. photoplay, this incident was mitigated so that the murderer is instead frightened into confessing. William Powell played Vance and Michael Curtiz was assigned the direction. Robert N. Lee and Peter Milne were credited with the screenplay. The tendency in Warner Bros. detective films from this period to offer a reconstruction of the crime through flashbacks perpetrated one bit of absurdity due to the screenwriters' confusion over Van Dine's plot. Vance in the film was supposed to go into great detail in his reconstruction, even using miniature models of the Coe residence and the adjacent apartment house to demonstrate how the murderer must have seen Archer Coe enter his bedroom from a window in the apartment house. In the novel the murderer lives in an apartment in the adjacent building, so the explanation makes sense. In the film, he is living with Archer Coe, with his bedroom on the same floor as Coe's, only farther down the hall. Under these circumstances, it would have been unlikely for him to have been in an apartment house across the way observing Coe, nor is any alternative proposed to explain his presence there.

Jimmy Fidler, the Hollywood columnist, went drinking with William Powell and published the results of his conversation with him in PHOTOPLAY in October, 1932. Powell told Fidler that he was cursed with an inferiority complex; that he was afraid of strangers; that he was ill-at-ease in the company of women; that he was uncomfortable turning his back when leaving a crowded room; that he was a poor conversationalist and not the least bit witty; and that in real life he was anything but the *bon vivant* he played on screen. Notwithstanding Warner Bros. had felt his box-office attraction such that it had bribed him with a salary of $6,000 a week to get him away from Paramount. Then, when the studio went on a Depression economy drive, this was reduced to $4,000 a week. Powell was unhappy and insisted on more money. There are critics who feel THE KENNEL MURDER CASE (Warner's, 1933) to be the cinematic highwater mark of the Philo Vance films. Warner Bros. did not think so. The picture made nowhere near the kind of money that Powell's name as a drawing force was supposed to ensure. It was decided by mutual agreement that Powell should leave. Jack Warner announced to the trades the reason to be that Powell wanted to freelance, but in truth Warner just did not think Powell worth the money he was asking. Powell's agent entered into negotiations with Columbia Pictures and an agreement was reached whereby Powell would star for that studio in four pictures.

W. S. Van Dyke was directing MANHATTAN MELODRAMA (M-G-M, 1934) for Metro-Goldwyn-Mayer and he contacted Powell to play the best friend of Clark Gable in the film who, as governor, near the end of the picture places his political responsibilities above personal ties and permits Gable to be executed. Myrna Loy was cast as Powell's wife. These two, Powell and Loy, worked so spiritedly together that Van Dyke insisted on putting them right into THE THIN MAN (M-G-M, 1934). The studio had purchased screen rights to Dashiell Hammett's latest (and, as it turned out, last) novel. I will have more to say about this in a later chapter. But the two M-G-M pictures succeeded in making William Powell a bigger star than ever. M-G-M wanted him under contract so much that it bought up his Columbia contract and even project rights to a film about Florenz Ziegfeld that was in the planning stages at Universal and for which Powell had signed an option. Powell was immediately teamed again with Loy for EVELYN PRENTICE (M-G-M, 1934). But Powell was crafty this time. He refused to sign with Metro for more than two or three films at a time. The studio gave him the ultimate in star treatment. A series based on the Hammett characters, Nick and Nora Charles, was planned and inevitably S. S. Van Dine was contracted for his next two novels to be turned into photoplays with Powell in the lead as Philo Vance.

This left Warner Bros. holding the bag. The studio had purchased rights to THE DRAGON MURDER CASE which Van Dine had published later the same year as THE KENNEL MURDER CASE, but it no longer had William Powell. Hal B. Wallis who was in charge of production selected Warren William, a character actor from Warner Bros.'s roster, to play Vance. He next set about lining up a contract director to do the picture. He asked Michael Curtiz, who turned it down; then Archie Mayo, but it was no go; then Mervyn LeRoy, but it was still nothing doing; finally, in desperation, Wallis approached Alfred Green only to be rebuffed.

H. Bruce Humberstone, known to his intimates as "Lucky," had been an assistant director for over ten years. The first picture he directed was STRANGERS OF THE EVENING (Tiffany, 1931), a Poverty Row production which starred Zazu Pitts and Eugene Pallette. Pallette played a police sergeant in it, but, unlike his portrayal of Heath in the Philo Vance films, little of the comedy was at his expense. This was followed by THE CROOKED CIRCLE (WorldWide, 1932) which was a mystery-comedy with Ben Lyon, C. Henry Gordon, and James Gleason as a motorcycle cop. Gleason injected so much comedy that the haunted house theme receded into the background. After a brief stint at Paramount during which he worked on the George Raft segment of IF I HAD A MILLION (Paramount, 1933), Lucky was signed by Warner Bros. on a two-picture deal. Lucky's first film was MERRY WIVES OF RENO (Warner's, 1933), a comedy about divorce starring Margaret Lindsay. Wallis was impressed by what he aptly perceived as Humberstone's flair for visually interesting cinema with a high comic tone. He summoned Lucky to his office and gave him the screenplay of THE DRAGON MURDER CASE. "This is going to be your next picture," he told him confidently.[38]

Humberstone took the script home and read it. He showed up the next day and told Wallis, no. He knew that Curtiz, Mayo, LeRoy, Green, *et al.*, had turned down the picture; and, what is more, he knew why: it was a terrible story. He was just getting started in Hollywood. This kind of picture could be a disaster for a neophyte director. Humberstone vanished from the studio and went on a short vacation to Palm Springs. While resting in a hotel, Wallis called him. He said that the writers had gone to work on THE DRAGON MURDER CASE and had really improved it. Lucky should return to the lot at once. Humberstone did.

When he walked into Wallis' office, he was handed the same yellow-covered script he had been given before. "I won't do it," he protested, whereupon Wallis arranged for him to see Jack L. Warner personally. Ushered into Warner's office, Warner eyed the new director skeptically.

"How much are you making?" he asked.

"Seven hundred and fifty dollars a week," Humberstone replied.

"How old are you?" Warner asked.

"Twenty-nine."

"Do you know how much I was making when I was your age?" Warner asked. "Twenty bucks a week, selling meat." He paused for emphasis. "So, why don't you want to make this picture?"

"Because it's a lousy story," Humberstone responded.

"Listen," said Warner, "I don't care if it *is* a lousy story. You're going to make this picture. Do you think it matters that it's lousy? That picture, with my theatre chain, is going to make me fifty thousand dollars, good story or not. So, you're going to make it for me. Or," he paused again for emphasis, "or you're never going to direct another picture in this town."

Humberstone agreed to direct the picture.

Van Dine had long been a fancier of tropical fish, an even more exotic hobby than raising Scottish terriers. He had dedicated the book to his wife Claire and had used tropical fish as part of the setting. Rudolph Stamm, at whose estate the series of murders takes place, has a large collection of such fish. In one chapter Vance, Markham, and Heath are guided through the aquarium rooms and are shown many rare and unusual varieties brought back from dark, obscure parts of the globe. But in 1934 collecting tropical fish was almost unheard of in California. Humberstone searched far and wide, but no one could be found whose fish tanks and displays might be used as props. Being a stickler at details, Humberstone was resolved that fish had to be included. Then, as luck would have it, he came upon what could only be described as a fish "nut," a fellow working at the Weber Showcase Company in the Valley who not only collected tropical fish but had one of the most extensive arrays in the country. Humberstone worked out the arrangements for the studio to borrow the entire collection for use in the picture. Unfortunately neither Humberstone nor Van Dine anticipated the results of THE DRAGON MURDER CASE's impact on the public. Such was the popularity of the Philo Vance stories with the public and the concurrent photoplay series that a "fish craze" swept the nation. Shops started specializing in tropical fish displays and an entire industry sprang up.

Even Humberstone himself became an enthusiastic breeder of tropical fish for many years.

Eugene Pallette was back as Sergeant Heath and Robert Barrat, who had played Archer Coe in THE KENNEL MURDER CASE, played Stamm in this film. Etienne Giradot, although he might have infinite trouble with his lines and cost dozens of retakes, was again cast as Doctor Doremus, the Medical Examiner, and he was retained in the series as it traveled from studio to studio.

Whatever Jack L. Warner's cavalier attitude toward the picture, THE DRAGON MURDER CASE (First National, 1934) was still an "A" feature with a budget of $320,000. Van Dine fashioned the novel to challenge the theory of the perfect alibi. Humberstone changed the plot somewhat in the filming. In the novel, all of the suspects save Rudolph Stamm go swimming in the Dragon Pool on the Stamm estate. Sanford Montague dives into the water and does not come to the surface. Nearly a day later his mutilated body is discovered some distance from the estate in an ancient pothole. Presumably, Rudolph Stamm was too drunk to join the swimming party; but, since he is the only suspect with an opportunity to commit the murder, all the other suspects being constantly within sight of each other, his guilt is overly obvious. The photoplay removed one of the suspects from the vicinity of the Pool before Monty's fateful dive and the camera, combined with the direction, created so much confusion around the water's edge and, through adroit editing, within the Pool itself with the search for Montague, that some of this transparency was lost. Of all the Philo Vance films, THE DRAGON MURDER CASE remains the finest example of that intuitive experience Van Dine sought to achieve just before the denouement sections of his novels. At a certain point in the film the mechanics of the murder and the murderer's identity suddenly dawn upon the viewer almost as a revelation, and the entire plot becomes evident.

THE DRAGON MURDER CASE was the last book Van Dine wrote in precisely the style and according to the structure that had made him world-famous. Notwithstanding, the characters exude a loss of all significance. Willard might have a few more years to live, but a substantial part of him was already beyond reclaim. For Humberstone the film also proved a turning point. At the première he had his agent invite most of the noteworthy producers then in Hollywood. The film was extremely well-received. Jack L. Warner collared him afterwards, saying, "Don't sign with any of these guys. We want you." Yet a contract did not materialize, although a succession of assignments did at Twentieth Century-Fox which led to Humberstone's working extensively on the Charlie Chan series.

THE CASINO MURDER CASE (1934) may have adhered to the general format of previous novels but it lacked the intensity and conviction. No longer had Van Dine spent days looking up obscure trivia to illustrate Vance's mastery of everything from masonry to archery. Even the plot itself harked back to a device Van Dine had already used in THE GREENE MURDER CASE. Lynn

Llewellyn poisons himself, much as does Ada Greene, to cast suspicion onto another. Moments of visual brilliance can be found in the novel, such as the descriptions of Kincaid's gambling casino or Vance's surreptitious entrance into Kincaid's heavy water distillery housed in the cellar of his Closter hunting lodge. While the characters might still be vivid and the setting imaginative, the mechanics of the crimes and the emphasis on detection, which Willard felt to be so distinctive to the genre, became secondary to the dramatic overtones of the story.

M-G-M, rather than use William Powell, decided to cast Paul Lukas as Philo Vance. The thinking here was not that Powell was too valuable a property to appear in a detective film since on loan-out to RKO he would appear opposite Ginger Rogers as the detective in STAR OF MIDNIGHT (RKO, 1935), and he was slated to appear again as Nick Charles. Rather, it was the intention of the studio to try to build the same sort of screen rapport between Lukas and Rosalind Russell that existed between Powell and Loy. Donald Cook was cast as Lynn Llewellyn; Alison Skipworth played his mother; and Russell was cast as Skipworth's personal secretary. The fact that Lukas delivered his lines with a heavy Hungarian accent was apparently not deemed a problem. He was a romantic figure and the publicity for THE CASINO MURDER CASE (M-G-M, 1935) called it a successor to THE THIN MAN. Lucien Hubbard produced the film on a scale more lavish than that of any previous entry. Dimitri Tiomkin's musical arrangements, at times elaborate, provided smooth transitions between scenes while highlighting the drama.

There were problems, however. Ted Healy, under contract to M-G-M but now no longer appearing with the Three Stooges with whom he had first worked in films such as DANCING LADY (M-G-M, 1933), was totally miscast as Sergeant Heath. Louise Fazenda, married at the time to Hal B. Wallis, was added for inappropriate comic relief as the Llewellyn maid. In the original release prints, Edwin L. Marin, the director, included an actual "Vitali Test" to determine whether or not atropine had been the poison used to terminate Louise Henry's life. The sequence was filmed in Technicolor as a gimmick. It has since been removed from the negative. Louise Henry literally stole the picture. Perhaps that was what Van Dine had secretly intended. In the 'Thirties Henry was repeatedly cast in the role of a bitchy wife or mistress who was murdered. Van Dine claimed that he had used his wife Claire as his model.

Except for THE BENSON MURDER CASE, where the culprit is arrested in Markham's office after being exposed by Vance, a murderer never survived the end of the book. Many of these suicides and contrived deaths are the weakest parts of the narratives. In THE "CANARY" MURDER CASE, the murderer is permitted in the book to shoot himself, although in the film he dies in a railway accident. Ada Greene takes poison. Vance arranges the murderer's death in THE BISHOP MURDER CASE. In THE SCARAB MURDER CASE an Egyptian servant does in the murderer after he hears Vance's explanation. I have already told of the fate of the murderer in THE KENNEL MURDER

CASE. Stamm is arrested in the film, but in the book he is killed when a boulder falls on him. Lynn Llewellyn in THE CASINO MURDER CASE is shot by Kincaid in the book and Heath in the film. In THE GARDEN MURDER CASE (1935) the murderer jumps over a parapet, while in THE KIDNAP MURDER CASE (1936) the murderer shoots himself in full view of the remaining suspects. In THE GRACIE ALLEN MURDER CASE (1938), while in the film the murderer is arrested, in the novel he dies by smoking a poisoned cigarette given him by Vance. In THE WINTER MURDER CASE (1939) the murderer again takes poison. Ending a Philo Vance murder case with a suicide was definitely a convention with Van Dine. It gives one pause when recounting how Van Dine dealt with his creation as the 'Thirties, and with them Van Dine's life, came to a close.

III

Van Dine took to dictating his books. He engaged a secretary, Y. B. Garden, who took down his dictation and typed triple-spaced manuscript copies. While typing up her notes, Garden was free to interpolate her own ideas above the lines. "I was free to do this at any time," she recalled, "and of course he was free to accept or reject such suggestions."[39] The new system required an interpolation of a third draft. The first draft was now a ten thousand word synopsis, containing all of the events and summaries of all the conversations without any side-issues, literary and philosophical references, or any attempt at personality description. This first synopsis was then expanded to a thirty thousand word version which fleshed out the conversations and the characters. A final ten thousand words were then added to this second draft to amplify the plot, the characters, and the conversations, but without anything resembling the former scholarly apparatus. It would appear Willard no longer cared about erudition. He dedicated the first book written under this new arrangement, THE GARDEN MURDER CASE, to his mother.

Gambling fever spread in THE GARDEN MURDER CASE to include the race track. Consistent with the new tone of Van Dine's life Philo Vance was now a famous amateur sleuth, well-known at parties and in the best social circles for his interest in crime. Parker Bros. had just issued a popular parlour game called PHILO VANCE. It soon overtook BULLS AND BEARS in public demand and for a time rivaled MONOPOLY. "Up to that time I had never considered Vance a man of any deep personal emotion, except insofar as children and animals and his intimate masculine friendships were concerned," Van Dine found himself dictating in THE GARDEN MURDER CASE, and thus preparing to break his Third Rule for writing detective fiction which disparaged any romantic interest. "He had always impressed me as a man so highly mentalized, so cynical and impersonal in his attitude toward life, that an irrational human weakness like romance would be alien to his nature. But in the course of his deft inquiry into the murders in Professor Garden's penthouse, I saw, for the first time, another and softer side of his character. Vance was never a happy man in the conventional sense; but after the Garden murder case there were evidences of an even deeper loneliness in his sensitive nature."[40]

"Why did you marry Claire?" Stanton had asked Willard on the last visit they had had with one another. They were sitting in Willard's terrace garden, surrounded by potted trees and shrubs, high above New York's skyline and overlooking Central Park. They were sipping Napoleon brandy. Willard paused to light a *Regie* in an ebony holder. He was in a satin dressing gown. Behind them, lights burned in Willard's study with his kidney-shaped writing desk, his ceiling-high bookcases crammed with volumes in several languages, a gaudily decorated fireplace above which hung Stanton's painting titled NEW CHINA. Frank Tuttle, having met Stanton while directing the Paramount Vance films, purchased its companion, NEW JAPAN. Willard inhaled deeply. As Vance, he wore a monocle in his right eye. Fresh flowers in vases everywhere permeated the evening air.

"Because," he replied finally, "I liked her legs. We were aboard ship and the captain wouldn't stand for carryings-on between the passengers. I asked him to marry us at sea."

Of course, it was not true. When Stanton told me this anecdote many years later, he knew it was not true; but he had not known that at the time. Willard's cynical summation denied any real emotional commitment on his part.

THE GARDEN MURDER CASE (M-G-M, 1936) advanced the romance theme until it was almost more important than the mystery, with Virginia Bruce playing the Zalia Graem character of the novel opposite Edmund Lowe as a charming, debonair, albeit scarcely intellectual Philo Vance. Very little of the original plot was retained save for the general setting of horse racing. One of the minor characters in the novel was magnified into a major role enacted by Gene Lockhart. H. B. Warner, playing a fakir from the East not based on any character from the novel, inveigles Vance into a semi-hypnotic trance and instructs him to mount a parapet overlooking the city far below via rear-screen projection. Before he can persuade him to jump, Vance turns on him, not hypnotized at all, and exposes him as the murderer. Nat Pendleton as Sergeant Heath shoots Warner before he can lunge at Vance. The film ends with Vance and Zalia in a clinch. Benita Hume played Nurse Beeton in the film; in the novel, she was the murderer. Together with Frieda Inescort, Hume added feminine glamour to the already customary M-G-M polish.

By 1935, Willard realized that trends were changing in detective fiction. The hard-boiled writers, with their emphasis on professional criminals and mobsters, were having a definite impact on the changing tastes of the public. This alteration in perspective was reflected in THE KIDNAP MURDER CASE in which Vance and Heath match their acumen in a harrowing gun battle at the gangsters' hide-out. Although THE KIDNAP MURDER CASE was serialized in COSMOPOLITAN, beginning in the July, 1936 issue, it was not made into a motion picture, the only Philo Vance novel which was not. Van Dine had called personally on Max Perkins at Scribner's "to give notice" that he would be bringing in THE KIDNAP MURDER CASE by the first of August. "Good," Perkins had responded, "but why the ultimatum?" "Because," Van Dine had replied, "you said I was not punctual after I got married."

When Willard got his first royalty reports from Scribner's on THE KIDNAP MURDER CASE, he was appalled at how little money the book had earned. He wrote to Perkins to find out why. Perkins replied that Scribner's would publish the novels, but it could not induce the public to buy them. The real money was to be made in serial magazine rights and motion pictures. Willard's despair was only amplified. He sold off his kennel and his terriers. In an economy move, he gave up the penthouse apartment and moved to a more modest apartment in the same building.

President Roosevelt, an inveterate reader of detective stories, propounded a problem to Fulton Oursler, editor of the popular weekly, LIBERTY. Oursler invited a number of eminent detective story writers to contribute a chapter each to the story and S. S. Van Dine was among them. The mystery and its solution were subsequently published in book form and re-issued as recently as 1967 with a new conclusion for it written by Erle Stanley Gardner. Republic Pictures bought screen rights and filmed it as THE PRESIDENT'S MYSTERY (Republic, 1937).

Willard could not bring himself to write anything other than this. He was approached by the Modern Library in 1937 to edit a volume of the writings of Friedrich Nietzsche. At one time, he might have found this project a boon, perhaps translating the books to be contained in it himself, or at least writing an elaborate critical introduction. As it was, he did neither. His Introduction was brief, biographical and bibliographical, good journalism, but nothing more. He did, however, write also an Introduction to one of the five books included in the giant anthology, BEYOND GOOD AND EVIL (1886). "The Dionysian ideal, which underlies all the books that follow BEYOND GOOD AND EVIL, receives its first direct exposition and application," Willard concluded. "The hardier human traits, such as egotism, cruelty, arrogance, retaliation, and appropriation, are given ascendancy over the softer virtues, such as sympathy, charity, forgiveness, loyalty and humility, and are pronounced necessary constituents in the moral code of a natural aristocracy."[41] Such a summary would not indicate a very profound grasp of Nietzsche's thought and even the arrangement of the volume, with Nietzsche's first book placed last, did not really portend any notion of Nietzsche's philosophical development.

Willard toyed with ideas for another detective novel, but mostly he drank Courvoisier. Then, one evening in early January, 1938, a Paramount executive sat down to relax and tuned in the Burns and Allen radio program. In the episode, Gracie played a detective. The executive had an idea. The studio had recently released A NIGHT OF MYSTERY and THE SCARAB MURDER CASE had been made in the United Kingdom with Wilfred Hyde White as Vance on a supposed sojourn to England where Kathleen Kelly cast as Vance's secretary falls in love with Donald Scarlett played by John Robinson. Kathleen Kelly had received top billing. The idea the executive had was to combine Philo Vance and Gracie Allen.

Willard was contacted by Paramount. The studio requested that he prepare an outline approximately 3,000 words in length "to be used as the basis for the development of a detailed treatment, adaptation and/or continuity, with dialogue, suitable for reproduction as a motion picture photoplay of feature length in which Mr. George Burns and Miss Gracie Allen and/or Mr. John Barrymore properly could appear."[42] The title, THE GRACIE ALLEN MURDER CASE, was to remain the sole and absolute property of Paramount. Since Van Dine in THE BENSON MURDER CASE had described Vance as resembling most John Barrymore, the suggestion of including Barrymore presumably to play Vance (Barrymore was then under contract to the studio and appearing in various Paramount productions) must have pleased Van Dine; but he must have shuddered at having to break his reliance on the magical number of six in titling the story. By the time the contract was signed, Van Dine was guaranteed $25,000 for the project. Harold Ober, Willard's literary agent, negotiated the deal and the contract was signed between Willard and Neil F. Agnew, Paramount vice president, at Paramount's New York office on 11 February 1938.

For some reason, Willard was extremely paranoid about using the real names of George Burns and Gracie Allen in the novel. He met with them for lunch in early 1938 and got their verbal permission. "And that was all there was to it as far as we were concerned," Burns recalled. "He retained all the rights, and we took advantage of the publicity."[43] Still this was not enough. Willard insisted on calling the Gracie Allen character Lulu Tween in his first draft and told Paramount he must have written permission to the use of their names in the title and text of the book. Paramount sent Willard a letter indemnifying him, but that still was not enough. Finally, on 15 March 1938 Paramount got Burns and Allen to sign an agreement authorizing Wright to use the title THE GRACIE ALLEN MURDER CASE and to use them as characters in the novel. This was some time after Willard had turned in his first story outline to Paramount. The studio was quite pleased with the outline and gave Willard a green light to proceed to turn the outline into the prescribed novelette of 20,000 words. Willard began at once to dictate the book to Y. B. Garden.

It was the shortest Philo Vance story Van Dine had written to date. He could find no magazine interested in purchasing serial rights to it, although Scribner's would be publishing the book in August, 1938 and the film would likely engender interest. Critically, the novel proved a disaster and even staunch Van Dine fans condemned it. In the book, one of the suspects, "Owl" Owen, is dying of a cardiac disorder. In conversation with Vance, Owen becomes confidential. "Owen began speaking now of old books, of his days at Cambridge, of his cultural ambitions as a youth, of his early study of music," Van Dine wrote. "He was steeped in the lore of ancient civilizations and, to my astonishment, he dwelt with fanatical passion on the Tibetan BOOK OF THE

DEAD."[44] Elsewhere in the same conversation, Owen asks Vance: " 'You think that either of us willed this meeting? Man makes no choice. His choice is his temperament. . . . But why do I even bother, this shadow between two infinities? I can give only one answer: the obscene urge to eat well and live well—which, in turn, is an instinct and, therefore, a lie.' "[45] Willard had put his own despair into the mouth of a gangster. And why not? The novel drags, the murder scheme fails to sustain interest, and Gracie Allen is at best a somewhat irritating intrusion into what one had come to expect a serious business. Willard could not write comedy, so he wrote parody instead; and in doing so, he again broke many of his own rules. The murder, with which he prescribed every detective story should begin, does not occur until page 79 and the many coincidences make the whole affair preposterous. There is only "Owl" Owen whose crime is killing another gangster immersed in his philosophic ramblings, the setting of a gangland cafe, a poisoned cigarette as a murder weapon, and Gracie Allen as Vance's assistant to remind us how far we have come since 1926. " 'The goddesses of Zeus' Olympian ménage never harassed old Priam and Agamemnon with the éclat exhibited by Gracie Allen in harassing the recidivists of that highly scented affair,' " Philo Vance is made to remark. " 'Amazin'!"[46]

Even more amazing was THE GRACIE ALLEN MURDER CASE (Paramount, 1939), which Willard did not live to see. It was almost exclusively a vehicle for Gracie Allen. George Burns, whom Van Dine had included as a character, was replaced by Bill Brown, a role played by Kent Taylor. "It was a personal decision on our part for me not to appear," George Burns later remarked. "Gracie had always appeared with me, and we were anxious to see what the reaction would be if she appeared with another actor, and this seemed an appropriate time. It was the only time we were not together, except for once or twice with Jack Benny on his television show."[47] However, in an interview for the Washington EVENING STAR on 5 November 1941, Gracie stated that MR. AND MRS. NORTH (M-G-M, 1941), which she was then filming, was the first picture she had done without George's assistance. "I played without him in THE GRACIE ALLEN MURDER CASE," she said, "but he was around all the time to help me."[48] But, saddest of all is what happened to Philo Vance, if we remember how first he looked when William Powell projected him on the screen. Warren William was again given the part, but not the Warren William of THE DRAGON MURDER CASE, rather an older, wearier man with the signs of too much high living, totally indifferent to his characterization. Throughout the picture Gracie refers to him as "Fido" Vance and the satire is topped off when Markham and Heath, played respectively by Donald MacBride and William Demarest, in retrograde reference to Christopher Ward's parody of a decade before, arrest Vance as the murderer.

Van Dine had only just finished work on THE GRACIE ALLEN MURDER CASE when he received a letter from Julian Johnson. Johnson had been the editor of PHOTOPLAY when Willard was doing hack work for the magazine and all the hoopla in the trades about the Gracie Allen film had given Johnson, who was now head of the story department at Twentieth Century-Fox, a wonderful idea. "We have been discussing the possibility of your doing a story for Sonja Henie, along the familiar S. S. Van Dine mystery lines—say THE SONJA HENIE MYSTERY, if you wanted to call it that," Johnson wrote in his letter of 24 August 1938.[49] After much haggling back and forth about just how Willard would be paid $25,000—which was by then his asking price for an original motion picture story—the matter was finally reduced to a contract. Harry Joe Brown, an associate producer at Fox at the time, also liked the idea and at Johnson's instigation he wrote Van Dine a letter outlining Henie's capabilities. He suggested that Willard screen at the New York office two previous Henie vehicles, MY LUCKY STAR (20th-Fox, 1938) and THIN ICE (20th-Fox, 1937), for ideas as to characterization. "For your information," Brown pointed out, "we handle her with kid gloves because we consider her the present day Cinderella of the screen."[50]

Early in November, 1938, Van Dine viewed the two recommended Henie pictures. Afterwards he wrote Johnson that he wanted to create a story for Henie that would veer away from a musical comedy format and give her an opportunity, within her limitations, of expressing a depth of emotion that would move the audience as well as include her ice-skating technique and showmanship. In a questionnaire Van Dine sent to Johnson and Brown, he asked if there were any reservations about his including Philo Vance, District Attorney Markham, and Sergeant Heath in his story. Brown stated that he had no reservations, but stressed that the film would not be billed as a Philo Vance story.

Max Perkins came to visit Willard at his new apartment and perceived at once that he was in very poor health and extremely depressed. Staring into a snifter of Courvoisier, Willard reflected in a tone of resignation: " 'I'm so glad I've had all the brandy I've had. I've enjoyed the brandy. I only regret that I didn't drink more of it.' "[51]

Taking Brown's reference to Cinderella as his cue, Van Dine set about fashioning a modern Cinderella story with the character Sonja Henie was to play called Elaine Ash. In a cover letter to the studio, Van Dine explained his choice of this name. "The name Elaine Ash has a faint and not too definite indication of 'Cinderella,' " he commented, "and is used with a purpose. I wish to relate it lightly to the plot, but without any seeming fortuitousness or coincidence which might detract from the basic realism of the story. My idea is merely to point up the plot in its lighter moments of sentimental unraveling without any definite suggestion of fantasy. Whatever remote sense of fantasy may remain with the reader, according to his or her nature, will be merely the result of an intensification of the intimate actuality of the story itself, like clouds suddenly separating to show a vista of starlit sky. The name *Ash* has an association with *cinder*. The word for *cinder* is phonetically similar to 'ash' in the Scandinavian languages; and *cinder* in German is *Asche*, from which we undoubtedly get our American names like Ash, Asher, Ascher, etc. In fact, *Cinderella* in German is *Aschenputtel*, and *Elaine* is a distant hookup with *Ella*. Thus, the name 'Elaine Ash' while a commonplace enough English or American name without any particular significance, may have a vague association with the 'Cinderella' of the universal fairy tale."[52] For Elaine's lover, Van Dine selected the name Richard Rexon, who was to be the son of the owner of the Rexon estate where the whole group of characters would be gathered for the annual Ice Carnival. "Once again," Van Dine explained, "the name is chosen with the Cinderella idea in view. *Richard* etymologically signifies 'strong like a ruler'; and the name Rexon (which is, as far as I know, a manufactured name) might easily be broken down into 'the son of Rex,' to wit: the male offspring of a king—to wit: a prince. It would be too obvious to name him *Prince*, *Prinz*, *Printz*, *Principe*, or even *Königsohn*; but the name 'Richard Rexon' would escape attention as a symbol, avoid all fortuitousness, and yet carry on with the Cinderella layout when the time comes to point up the story as it unfolds in its structural development."[53] Philo Vance was to enact the role of the "Fairy Godmother" in the Cinderella story "on which has been superimposed a tale of suspense and mystery and modern human problems, without altering in any degree the fundamental and actuating Cinderella structure."[54] Van Dine proposed the following dialogue be used at the conclusion of the film:

"Vance, delighted, become whimsical again over the Cinderella idea and explains its implications.

VANCE (finishing): So you see, Mr. Rexon—or should I say Your Royal Highness—you really found Cinderella. And you found her at the royal ball—the Carnival, don't y'know.
RICHARD REXON: That's a clever and pretty fantasy, Mr. Vance. It lacks only the glass slipper.
VANCE: My word! You have something much lovelier and more appropriate than a mere glass slipper. What about Miss Ash's silver skates?
ELAINE: And I know! You, Mr. Vance—*you* are the Fairy Godmother.
VANCE: Heaven forbid!"[55]

This, then, was the story outline which Van Dine submitted to the studio at the end of December, 1938. There was a jewel robbery and a murder and Vance, in solving the crimes, would unite the lovers. That same month Willard came up to the fifth floor of Charles Scribner's Sons to see Perkins. He asked Perkins to be the executor of his estate. Perkins was several years older than Wright, but he could perceive Willard's deterioration and so he agreed.

The studio had all manner of suggested changes for Van Dine to make in the outline before he turned it into a novelette. Harry Joe Brown felt that Willard "has pulled his punches to a point where the story washes out to nothing much in the end" because he "didn't know how tough he could get with a Henie story or how shocking, so he wasn't tough or shocking at all . . . which is entirely wrong."[56] It was also stated that Van Dine's outline was too much a Philo Vance story and that it would need serious corrections to become a story for Sonja Henie. Brown wanted Henie to help Vance solve the mystery so that "when she goes on the ice the last time, she knows everything depends on that move."[57] Brown also insisted that "we should have more *amusement* out of Vance. Amusement and laughs. After all, here is a completely blasé man of the world thrown in among a lot of crazy cafe-society butterflies, whom he detests."[58] Finally, Brown wanted District Attorney Markham removed; he was "not, in our opinion, needed in this story at all. He only clutters things up."[59]

Willard must have seen that Philo Vance's days were numbered. The novels were not selling as once they did. He was being told to change his character, to make him a foil for Gracie Allen, and more amusing for Sonja Henie. He was doing hack work again. Gone were the days of his champion Scotty, Heather Reveller of Sporran, who had won many ribbons and trophies, and gone were the days of Philo Vance who by himself could carry a motion picture. Van Dine wrote the novelette to studio specifications because he quite desperately needed the money. A month before he completed this project, he suffered a heart attack. His recovery seemed assured. He completed the final draft. It was due at the studio on 1 May 1939. Van Dine finished it on 9 April and on 11 April he was dead from coronary thrombosis at the age of fifty-two. The studio paid the estate, but the project was shelved. When Scribner's published the 30,000 word text as THE WINTER MURDER CASE (1939), Perkins appended to it an unsigned Preface. "There were other influences at work on him perhaps," Perkins observed. "But no one who knew Willard and the purity of his perceptions in art, and his devotion to what he thought was the meaning of our civilization as expressed in the arts, can doubt that the shattering disillusionment and ruin of the war was what brought him at last to a nervous breakdown which incapacitated him for several years. He would never have explained it so, or any other way. He made no explanations, or excuses, ever, and his many apologies were out of the kindness of a heart so concealed by reticence that only a handful ever knew how gentle it really was. So at last all that he had done and aimed to do seemed to have come to ruin, and he himself too."[60]

Both Willard's daughter and Stanton were summoned to New York for a reading of Willard's will. They were shocked to learn that his estate amounted to only $13,000. In fact, they never believed it. However, they could not prove otherwise. I am inclined to accept this figure. Late in 1939, Claire sold off all of Willard's detective story library and his books on criminology, after she had catalogued them; then she set about cataloguing all of his other books. She moved to a more modest apartment, dressed simply, traveled nowhere, and saw very few people. She kept everything Willard had published and all the various editions of his books in a special place of honor. When she died, she left an estate of $124,000, plus her jewelry. It is entirely possible that these earnings came through astute investment of what royalties Willard's work continued to earn. Of course, had Willard wisely invested his money while he was making it, especially during the dark days of the Depression, he would have died many times a millionaire.

THE KENNEL MURDER CASE was remade as CALLING PHILO VANCE (Warner's, 1940); it was a comedy, although here the comedy was not altogether intentional as it had been in THE GRACIE ALLEN MURDER CASE. In the late 'Forties, Eagle-Lion negotiated screen rights to Philo Vance and three films were made. Alan Curtis was cast as Vance in PHILO VANCE'S SECRET MISSION (Eagle-Lion, 1947) and in PHILO VANCE'S GAMBLE (PRC, 1947); William Wright played Vance in the final entry, PHILO VANCE RETURNS (PRC, 1947). Vance in these films was more in the mold of the Falcon at RKO than anything that S. S. Van Dine had conceived. In PHILO VANCE'S SECRET MISSION, Vance married Sheila Ryan at the fade, but he was back as a bachelor in PHILO VANCE'S GAMBLE in order to trace the murders to his girl friend, Terry Austin. There was not, it would seem, even a value left in the name.

Once when I visited Stanton MacDonald-Wright at his home in the Pacific Palisades, I took note of the giant mural which covered the front of his house which he had designed at eighty-one. The only windows were in an enclosed court and in his studio which overlooked the ocean. I inquired about the absence of windows. He explained that many of his neighbors had binoculars and examined minutely each new acquisition as it was being moved inside. This way they could see nothing. The indoor furnishings were reminiscent of the many years of austerity he had spent living in a Buddhist monastery. He was well-to-do. His paintings were selling for tens of thousands of dollars. Having once surrounded himself with fine *objet d'art*, he was now obeying C. G. Jung's admonition to unload after forty and was selling off treasures from his collection. On the studio walls he kept several of his most powerful and provocative paintings, a flood of color and emotion—emotion necessarily detached from any particular for he had learned that abstract emotion must seek its own timbre and hue. He had a painting by Morgan Russell dating from their Synchronism period in Paris. It strongly attracted me. I asked him how much it cost. Stanton remarked that when Russell painted it, he had sold it for $500. It had cost Stanton $11,000 to buy it. Now perhaps it would fetch $13,000.

Stanton was smoking an American cigarette. When I remarked on it, he responded that it was he who had first introduced Willard to *Regie* cigarettes; but he no longer cared for them. The ocean could be heard in the courtyard and a dampness clung to the rocks and earth; yet here, in Stanton's studio, it was warm and very dry. The conversation lingered for a moment on Balzac's PEAU DE CHAGRIN (1831) and how analogous was its theme with Willard's life. Yet, as Stanton talked of Willard's peculiar romanticism and we sipped Courvoisier, I was reminded of Edna St. Vincent Millay's lines:

> My candle burns at both ends;
> It will not last the night;

> But ah, my foes, and oh, my friends—
> It gives a lovely light.[61]

Willard Huntington Wright was a sensitive soul, bewildered and frustrated, impeccably dressed, capable to a fault, cynical, confused, divided between the desire to live well and the desire to influence men's minds, and yet somehow cheated by life which held for him too much and too little. As S. S. Van Dine, he was what critics of the detective story term a traditionalist. With his emphasis on personality and temperament, he made way for a later generation of writers in whose methods he was at a loss. The philosophy of survival through character to be found in the BLACK MASK writers was not a feasible posture for him since he did not want to survive. He lived only long enough to murder Philo Vance. "This is not a creative, but a commercial age," he once wrote, "in which all ardent and conceptual ideas in the arts are dominated by a spirit subversive to their operation."[62] Yet, considering his desperate and guilt-ridden extravagances, I doubt very much that he would have lived otherwise no matter what had happened. He wore his financial success both flagrantly and dispiritedly. He lived, he was convinced, in keeping with his own temperament. He wrote detective stories with rare *élan*, certainly in the beginning, and he had excellent taste in detective fiction; his anthology is still a paradigm of its kind. His life, in the telling of it, much as his times, had such a zany and idiomatically American beginning only to come, almost in retrograde motion, to a rather fragile and thoughtful conclusion.

In terms of his impact on the history and future course of detective fiction, S. S. Van Dine's position will remain secure. In a few short years after he began, Van Dine had become the best known American writer of detective stories the world over; and, in Howard Haycraft's words, "he had rejuvenated and re-established the genre in his native land."[63] His initial success was owed to very tangible and admirable virtues. The plotting in the initial six novels was little less than brilliant and Willard's grasp of the English language was sufficiently extraordinary that he wrote what still may be considered some of the most literate detective stories produced by an American. His adept use of verisimilitude caused many naive readers to believe, at the outset anyway, that the murder cases had really occurred; and, as was also the case with Conan Doyle, while not an innovator himself, Van Dine perfected as he articulated the techniques of the puzzle, or so-called "classical," detective story from what they had been before he arrived on the scene. Beyond this, there were certain negative reasons for his sudden popularity. Haycraft perhaps said it best when he noted "the undeniable aura of pictured ostentation which . . . destined the stories for sure success in a decade which measured its own success in terms of yachts and silk shirts, as the case might be."[64] The erudition, however faulty it may be found to have been upon a close analysis, also gave the books a definite snob appeal; and, as a consequence, probably a different class of individuals read the Philo Vance stories than had formerly deigned to read detective stories. In the early books, the erudition was made intrinsic to the plot and its solution; and in the later books, it was by and large gratuitous and merely impeded the progress of the narrative.

Van Dine's influence on the history of the detective film was no less significant. To begin with, he really initiated the idea of a detective story author collaborating on the dialogue for photoplays based on his literary works and even providing original screen stories for cinematic detective stories. The upper class milieux of the Philo Vance films itself became a tradition in detective films of all kinds and many of the actors who rose to stardom playing Philo Vance—William Powell, Warren William, Basil Rathbone to name the three most important—went on to play in other detective series which made them even more famous and beloved by the viewing public. Finally, while totally lacking a sense of humor himself and therefore writing detective fiction singularly without humor, nonetheless Van Dine with THE GRACIE ALLEN MURDER CASE stood at the forefront of a trend in the detective film which would include liberal doses of comedy as an antidote to the more serious nature of an inquiry into murder.

3
The Master Detectives

Ellery Queen

I choose to close my mind to the human elements and treat it as a problem in mathematics. The fate of the murderer I leave to those who decide such things.

Ellery Queen[1]

The cousins who would later write under the pseudonym Ellery Queen were born in 1905 nine months and five blocks apart. They were both born into immigrant Jewish families in a crowded Brooklyn tenement district. Both later changed their family names. Daniel Nathan became Frederic Dannay and Manford Lepofsky became Manfred B. Lee. The year following his birth, Dannay's parents moved upstate to Elmira and remained there until 1917 at which time the family returned to New York City. Lee early discovered books and he claimed years later that he knew at eight that he would be a writer. His ambition, according to Francis M. Nevins in ROYAL BLOODLINE: ELLERY QUEEN, AUTHOR AND DETECTIVE (1974), was to be the Shakespeare of the Twentieth century. When Dannay returned to New York City he developed an abscess of the left ear which confined him to bed. While there, his aunt gave him a library book to read, Conan Doyle's THE ADVENTURES OF SHERLOCK HOLMES. For Dannay, in later years, this encounter took on the tones and hues of a religious conversion.

By the late'Twenties, both cousins were out of school. Dannay was working as a copywriter and art director for an advertising agency. Lee was writing publicity for a motion picture company. They met almost every day for lunch and they often discussed the possibility of writing a detective story together. What finally spurred them to action was the announcement of a $7,500 prize contest sponsored jointly by McCLURE'S magazine and the publishing house of Frederick A. Stokes. In arriving at the name for their detective, Ellery Queen, the cousins later claimed that they were too naive to recognize any homosexual connotation. The rules of the contest required that all authors assume a *nom de plume* and so it was decided to make the detective's name and the author's name the same. In this way, it would be less forgettable.

The book that resulted was THE ROMAN HAT MYSTERY (1929). The cousins were notified by McCLURE'S that their novel had won only for the magazine to be acquired by THE SMART SET which proceeded to pick a different winner. It was the first of what would become a long series of unexpected reversals in their lives. However, Stokes agreed to publish the book anyway. They had been tremendously influenced by S. S. Van Dine who was then at the height of his popularity. "He influenced us because he made so much money," Dannay later recalled, "and then, the kind of thing he did appealed to us in those days. It was complex, logical, deductive, almost entirely intellectual."[2]

Although the early Ellery Queen mysteries, in fact all the Ellery Queen novels the cousins would write, were written in the third person, the initial entries were supposedly set before the public by a characterless person known as J.J. McC. It was this J.J. McC who told readers of THE ROMAN HAT MYSTERY that Inspector Queen, formerly of the New York Police Department, his son Ellery, and their Gypsy houseboy Djuna had since retired to Italy, the same country where Van Dine claimed Philo Vance had gone to retire. Ellery Queen, as Philo Vance, is a pseudonym to conceal the real identity of the sleuth. Ellery, no less than Vance, prefers to use pompous literary allusions; but somehow they never come off as well as when Van Dine did it. For example, in THE ROMAN HAT MYSTERY, Ellery will casually comment to his father, casually and preposterously: " 'Please be logical, *M. le Gardien de la Paix*.' "[3] Or, rather obscurely, Ellery blurts out to the district attorney: " 'Exactly, Tacitus. . . . ' "[4] Nor did matters improve in subsequent books. *Ne quid nimis* was Terence's rendering of the Delphic Oracle's Μηδὲν ἄγαν [Nothing too much]. In THE GREEK COFFIN MYSTERY (1932) Ellery, explaining his reasoning, remarks: " 'You must have run across it in your readings, because a number of illustrious gentlemen have repeated it variously—La Fontaine, Terence, Coleridge, Cicero, Juvenal, Diogenes. It's an inscription on the Temple of Apollo at Delphi and has been attributed to Chilon of Sparta, Pythagoras, and Solon. In Latin it is: *Ne quis nimis*. In English it is: *Know thyself.*' "[5] Not only is the gender incorrect—changed from neuter: *quid* to masculine: *quis*, but the translation is wholly incorrect. Yet no effort was ever made to alter this intellectual *faux pas* in any of the subsequent editions of the novel; it stands as a reminder of just how superficial is Ellery's erudition. In THE EGYPTIAN CROSS MYSTERY (1932) we are to assume that for some reason Ellery memorized a passage from Plautus' MILES GLORIOSUS [THE SOLDIER BRAGGART] and has it—or at least part of it, with an incorrect participle—on the tip of his tongue: " 'As long as you're in a quotative mood,' smiled Ellery, stripping off his coat and flinging himself on the tesselated marble, 'you might consider the fact that *hospes nullus tam in amici hospitium diverti potest . . . odiosus siet.*' "[6] Vance became involved in crime detection through his friend Markham and Ellery's *entreé* is through his father's connection with the New York Police Department. The equivalent to Sergeant Heath is Sergeant Velie who refers to Ellery as Maestro and is suitably amazed at his deductions. The irate Medical Examiner, Dr. Doremus in the Philo Vance stories, is Dr. Samuel Prouty in the early Ellery Queen books. The equivalent of Vance's butler, Currie, is Djuna, named according to Danny after the novelist Djuna Barnes.

Yet, more significant than these similarities were the differences in plotting and structure between Van Dine and Ellery Queen. Van Dine was scrupulously honest in laying before his reader the vital clues necessary to solve the mystery; Ellery Queen was not. A brief sketch of the plot of THE ROMAN HAT MYSTERY will make the point. Monte Field, a blackmailer, is found poisoned in the back row of seats at the Roman Theatre. His top hat is missing. All persons in the theatre are checked as they leave to see that no one is without a top hat or has two top hats. The theatre is searched and no top hat is found. What of the poison used to kill Field who was drunk when he entered the theatre? Dr. Thaddeus Jones, in Ellery's words "New York City's Paracelsus and eminent Toxicologist,"[7] determines that the poison was tetra ethyl lead. " ' . . . As far as I know,' " he says, " 'tetra ethyl lead has never been used for criminal purposes!' "[8] When he is asked how long it would take tetra ethyl lead to kill someone, the toxicologist replies: " 'That's something I can't answer definitely, for the very good reason that to my knowledge no human being has ever died of its effects before.' "[9] It would appear, therefore, that the murderer must have had some very special familiarity with chemistry, but, since the man selected to be the murderer could not possibly have such knowledge, the issue is dealt with in this fashion. Ellery asks the toxicologist if this means of murder does not imply a man with laboratory experience. " 'No, it doesn't,' " the toxicologist responds. " 'Any man with a home-brew 'still' in his house could distill that poison without leaving a trace. The beauty of the process is that the tetra ethyl lead in the gasoline has a higher boiling point than any other of the fluid's constituents. All you have to do is distill everything out up to a certain temperature, and what's left is this poison.' "[10] Now this would seem to get the authors off the hook; they can name a person with no chemical or laboratory background, claim he merely overhead some conversation about how to distill tetra ethyl lead, and they are home free. However, this overlooks a very serious problem. According to Ellery, in his reconstruction of the crime, the murderer came to sit next to Field during the performance of the play, offered him a drink from his pocket flask, which Field accepted, after which he toppled over and died. This allowed the murderer to take Field's top hat, in which were concealed the blackmail documents and on the inner lining of which was written the murderer's name, and slip away in the darkness. The question which this explanation overlooks is this: if the effects of tetra ethyl lead are unknown, how could the murderer know how the poison would react? How quickly would Field die? Could he detect the poison in the alcohol he was offered to drink? Might he not cry out, or make some effort to attract attention? Since no human being has ever been killed by this poison before, why use this poison, as opposed to another poison the effects of which are known?

The method of murder is a serious flaw. However, no less serious, for me, is the fact that a map of the Roman Theatre is supplied at the beginning of the novel, again in the Van Dine tradition. When Ellery explains that the murderer, who is an actor in the play, by " 'hugging the wall, walking down the aisle as carefully and unobtrusively as possible, . . . gained the rear of the leftside boxes without anyone noticing him' "[11] and then " 'passed through the stage door,' "[12] the problem is that this stage door is not shown on the map. The map, as the "untraceable" poison, is what is termed a red herring, and scarcely fair to the reader. When no hat is found in the theatre, Ellery has a talk with the woman in charge of props and then disappears with her. The reader is not informed that he discovers one of the prop hats to be missing, therefore indicating that an actor removed it. It is a snap down top hat and so could be concealed under the murderer's clothing while he left wearing Field's hat—again, we have to assume that Field's hat fit the murderer and that this was just one of those fortunate accidents. Ellery and the inspector have the play staged for them and, again, the reader is not told that one of the principal actors was not on stage during the time when Field was murdered, another rather essential clue. This novel began the tradition in the early Ellery Queen books of interrupting the narrative with "A Challenge to the Reader" in which it is stated that "the solution—or enough of it to point unerringly to the guilty character—may be reached by a series of logical deductions and psychological observations. . . . "[13] With so much having been withheld from the reader, this is a gratuitous statement at best.

The matter of believable plotting did not improve over the intervening years. In fact, the plots remain the single most debilitating aspect of the Ellery Queen detective stories and one which is always destined to leave a reader dissatisfied. In THE EGYPTIAN CROSS MYSTERY, the reader is expected to believe that one of three brothers, in order to get a five thousand dollar inheritance due him, murders first a man who was a family enemy in the old country and leaves his crucified, beheaded body tied to a cross-road sign, fully expecting that this body will be identified as his. He then proceeds to murder one of his wealthy brothers in this same fashion. When his other brother returns and discovers that the rich one is dead but the poor one is still alive, he offers to give the poor brother five thousand dollars. This money offer the poor brother refuses. He goes ahead with a beheading crucifixion of the brother who has returned and then proceeds to behead and crucify his servant, whom he has been keeping a prisoner, expecting again that the servant's body, which shows no signs of confinement, will be mistaken for him. Ellery, in explaining this case, admits that he did not know the poor brother's motive and " 'I don't know it this minute. Actually, what difference does it make? A madman's motive—it may be as evanescent as air, as hard to crystallize as a pervert's. When I say madman, of course, I don't necessarily mean a raving maniac. Van, as you saw yourself, is apparently in full possession of his sanity. His mania is a quirk, a twist in his brain—in everything but one he is sane.' "[14]

One of the silliest and most far-fetched, albeit rather typical, examples of an Ellery Queen plot is that of THE CHINESE ORANGE MYSTERY (1934). The mystery is why is a man murdered and then all of his clothes put on backwards, all the furniture in the room turned upside down, and all the pictures turned toward the wall. The only clue given is that the man's tie is missing. The solution, according to the challenge to the reader to be arrived at through a use of logic, is that the murdered man was a cleric; wearing a Roman collar, the man had no tie to lose; and the murderer wanted to conceal this fact about the victim.

Dannay in later life explained that it was his intention in working out the Ellery Queen plots which he would hand over to Lee to flesh out with characterization and dialogue to create "a fantasy world: Ellery in Wonderland. It is a world different from the world outside, a world of its own, with its own rules and logic. It can't be a world that is existentialist or meaningless. Nevertheless, we can't leave Ellery there. He lives in a realistic world, so the solution of the case must be the exact opposite of fantasy; it will have none of the story's artificialities at all."[15] Theoretically, this sounds acceptable; but in practice the transition from Ellery in Wonderland to Ellery in the real world is never quite successful. In CAT OF MANY TAILS (1949), in terms of Lee's contribution of atmosphere and character one of the best-written Queen novels, the problem of motivation still remains, and it is motivation which so often makes the gulf between fantasy and reality unbridgeable. People unrelated in any way are being strangled to death, men with a blue cord, women with a pink cord. What is the solution? Why the physician who first brought them into the world has gone berserk and now wants to remove them from this world by means of strangulation!

THE ROMAN HAT MYSTERY and the books which followed featuring Ellery Queen and retaining geographical adjectives in their titles, another variation on Van Dine, did not sell as well as the cousins had expected. They were not purchased immediately for motion picture versions, nor were they sought after by the leading slick magazines. The cousins had quit their jobs in the hopes of making a living writing detective stories, but the success did not come. In an effort to make more money, they stepped up their production. In addition to two Ellery Queen mysteries a year, they also began a new series, under the pseudonym of Barnaby Ross, beginning with THE TRAGEDY OF X (1932), featuring an old Shakespearean actor as a detective. They opined that both series might become equally popular, but the Ross books met with an indifferent public and, after four entries, this series was dropped. For a time, the cousins went on tour, wearing masks, one of them pretending to be Ellery

Queen, the other Barnaby Ross, hoping to startle audiences with their ability to propound mysteries and solve them. It was not an altogether successful promotion; nor could they by this means, or any other, generate the interest in *who* was writing their detectives stories the way Willard Huntington Wright had. When the cousins revealed their indentities, it caused little sensation.

In an effort to equal Van Dine's success in the slick magazine market, the cousins' agent encouraged them to try writing a series of Ellery Queen short stories. The result was THE ADVENTURES OF ELLERY QUEEN (1934); but, as Nevins pointed out in ROYAL BLOODLINE, "Ellery's first short adventure wound up printed in a short-lived pulp (alongside stories by Dorothy Sayers, Earl Derr Biggers and Sax Rohmer) and paying a mere $35 which had to be shared by Dannay, Lee, and the agent."[16] However, it was in one of these short stories, "The Adventure of the Glass-Domed Clock" that Dannay introduced a plot innovation which would become an *idée fixe*. This was the plot with two solutions. First the circumstances of the crime would be presented, then Ellery would advance a solution which would seemingly solve the problem, only for it to be followed by a second solution which was the correct one. Of course, this gave those stories which employed this device a degree of artificiality beyond that even which they already had; but, if anything, the Ellery Queen mysteries were obsessed with plot any way. I think what appealed to Lee about writing was the opportunity to build interesting characters and create atmosphere. Dannay's plots, more times than not, were directly contradictory to these objectives. Consequently, the cousins quarreled, and quarreled frequently and vociferously.

Rand Lee, Manfred B. Lee's son, wrote a brief memoir of his father and uncle for TV GUIDE during the heyday of the second Ellery Queen television series. By that time, Lee lived in Connecticut and Dannay in Larchmont, New York. Rand scarcely ever saw his uncle. "Our conversations," he recalled, "on the phone were limited to 'Hello'; Cousin Fred would ask how I was and then ask to speak with Dad. I'd buzz Dad to alert him in the study and that would be that. It amazes me now that Dad and Cousin Fred could have produced so many Queen works. Their writing methods were unorthodox. All the time I was growing up they did their work over the telephone. Cousin Fred plotted all the novels and short stories, creating the characters and providing Dad with detailed skeletons that Dad fleshed out. Their talents determined this arrangement. I'm sure Dad could never have come up with the sort of plots Fred did. Dad and Fred's differences were not only professional. Often I would pick up the phone, hoping the line was free, and put down the receiver moments later with Dad's and Fred's arguing voices still ringing in my ears. On one occasion, Dad threw down a plot outline and exclaimed, 'He gives me the most ridiculous characters to work with and expects me to make them realistic!' Cousin Fred probably felt the same frustration with Dad's treatment of his plots."[17]

The lack of fairness to the reader in the novels became even more evident in these short stories and often Ellery solved the cases by clairvoyance; just as the murderers often required a similar clairvoyance in order to commit their crimes in the first place. With the failure of these stories to penetrate the slick magazine market, the cousins launched enthusiastically into a period of what can only be termed "hack" work. The first evident sign of the change was an alteration in the titles of the Ellery Queen novels. In the Foreward to HALF-WAY HOUSE (1936), Ellery points out to J.J. McC that the book might have been called THE SWEDISH MATCH MYSTERY; but it was not, and, altogether this novel preserves the subtitle of its predecessors, "A Problem in Deduction," it does mark the attempt to broaden the format of the Queen milieu to make it more attractive to motion picture companies. It was followed by THE DOOR BETWEEN (1937) which was an even more dramatic break with the past, with love interest stressed on every page. Obviously the revision in technique was working since this book appeared first in COSMOPOLITAN. The cousins had come to know S. S. Van Dine socially and, by rumor, Dannay learned enough about him to begin to base a number of characters and incidents on him. In THE DOOR BETWEEN, Nevins had this point to make: "John MacClure, worn out by years of search for a cancer cure, has come to treat money and fame and life with detached scientific aloofness. (Could Queen have modeled him on Van Dine?)"[18]

It was also during this period that the last of the books with a geographical title, THE SPANISH CAPE MYSTERY (1935), was sold to Hollywood. Nat Levine, who had founded Mascot Pictures in 1927, was a trail blazer in the low-budget field.[19] When Mascot merged in 1935 with Consolidated Film Industries to form Republic Pictures, Levine was put in charge of production. Already at Mascot he had introduced science fiction into the Western and he had initiated the singing Westerns with Gene Autry. At Republic, in the same year he introduced two detectives to the screen, the comic strip character Dick Tracy became the hero of a chapter play, always a Levine specialty, and Ellery Queen made his feature film debut in THE SPANISH CAPE MYSTERY (Republic, 1935). M.H. Hoffman, who had started out in the 'Thirties by setting up Allied Pictures to produce and distribute a series of Hoot Gibson specials, was the nominal producer on the film and Lewis D. Collins, who had worked primarily in low-budget Westerns and action films, was the director. Donald Cook was cast as Ellery Queen, the same year as he would portray the crazed murderer in THE CASINO MURDER CASE (M-G-M, 1935). Helen Twelvetrees played the heroine and the screenplay developed a romantic attachment between her and Ellery. It is perhaps worth noting that the production manager on this film was Rudolph C. Flothow who would later produce a number of detective film series at Columbia Pictures in the 'Forties.

In my opinion, THE SPANISH CAPE MYSTERY is the best of the early Ellery Queen books. It is legitimately plotted, which is to say that the reader is put in possession of a sufficient number of clues to solve the mystery by means of ratiocination as opposed to clairvoyance. Ellery and Judge Macklin head to the Atlantic seaboard on a vacation and become immediately involved in an abduction which occurs at Spanish Cape, the name given to a rocky abutment on which a millionaire has built a palatial estate keeping him and his family isolated from the outside world. Rosa Godfrey and her maternal uncle, David Kummer, are kidnapped by a sea-faring roustabout named Captain Kidd. Rosa is left tied up and unconscious in the cabin which Ellery and the judge are to occupy. Her uncle, who has been mistaken by Captain Kidd for gigolo John Marco, has been spirited away in a motor boat. At the family estate, on the landing just above the private bathing beach, the nude body of John Marco is found seated at a table, wearing only an opera cape. The book bears as a motto a brief quotation from Horace's CARMINA: *"Nudaque veritas."* Very shortly after THE ROMAN HAT MYSTERY, the cousins adopted Van Dine's formula of multiple murders to sustain reader interest. Another Van Dine ingredient, the presence at the scene of the murder of a secondary criminal whose actions are strictly adventitious but momentarily confusing to a clarification of just what happened first introduced in THE "CANARY" MURDER CASE, is also present in THE SPANISH CAPE MYSTERY. In fact, of all the early Queen novels written under the Van Dine aegis, this one is the closest and the most perfect. Inspector Moley, the local law official, is quite in the Sergeant Heath mode, jumping quickly to wrong conclusions; while Ellery is almost the equal of Philo Vance with the ready, if wildly inappropriate, classical quotation which somehow is not met with derision by characters such as Moley who, in real life, would have no understanding at all of what is being said. When Judge Macklin asks Ellery what he is driving at, Ellery responds, quoting Julius Caesar's DE BELLO GALLICO (III 18.6): " 'Inspector Moley, my dear Solon, believes with Caesar that *fere libenter homines id, quod volunt, credunt.* You find Mrs. Constable's suicide very convenient, don't you, Inspector?' "[20] In the best of the Van Dine books, as in this Queen novel, the notion of a clearly perceived causality in the Aristotelian sense is confused by what Aristotle termed accident. "Plans depend for success upon a multitude of factors which the planner relies upon to operate in perfect co-ordination," the authors explain in the third person; "this was especially true . . . in the plan of a murderer. Let one factor fail to function properly and the whole scheme was imperiled. The planner might patch it up on the instant, but a chain of circumstances over which he no longer had control would have been started. . . . It was here that the discordant note would creep in to muddle logic, to put the design off-balance, to spread a haze over the eyes of the investigator."[21] The intellectual pleasure one derives from the formal, deductive kind of detective story is quite the same, in theory, as the function of Greek drama: to explain, by means of motivation and transparent causality, what in real life appears capricious, even meaningless. Dannay's own problems with the Van Dine mode of detective fiction, perhaps to a degree unconsciously, had to do with his inner resistance to make order out of chaos, to abandon the world of Ellery in Wonderland to the rather bland world of reality. "Like poetry," Dannay once said, "the detective story makes order out of chaos. And order out of chaos is a sign of a stable, conservative society. We have always fought against that! I wish more people were aware of it.''[22]

For Van Dine, the rich were both his focal point and his point of reference. Philo Vance was independently wealthy. For Ellery Queen it was otherwise. When Ellery and Judge Macklin first come onto the Godfrey estate at Spanish cape, Ellery remarks to the judge: '' 'I invariably feel awed in the presence of riches . . . until I remember what Prud'hon said.' 'And what did Prud'hon say?' '' *'La propriété, c'est le vol.'* '' ' The judge grunted. 'And then I feel better. Humble as I am, I can still hold my own in the company of—er—thieves. Consequently, we may as well make ourselves at home.' ''[23] In contrast to Philo Vance, Ellery upholds a strictly middle-class orientation.

In the film, Guy Usher, usually a heavy, was cast as Inspector Queen, but he was only on screen briefly. Berton Churchill played Judge Macklin and the setting for the Spanish Cape was removed to California, a secluded area presumably overlooking the Pacific. Richard Cramer was cast in the role of Captain Kidd. He kidnaps Helen Twelvetrees' screen uncle, leaving her tied up in the cottage Ellery and the judge intend to occupy. From then on, in contrast to the novel, one member of her relation after another is murdered. Also, the first victim, instead of being nude when he is found, is provided with a pair of swimming trunks! The judge in one scene reads THE ADVENTURES OF ELLERY QUEEN. Harry Stubbs was cast as the loud-mouthed, quick-to-act sheriff.

THE SPANISH CAPE MYSTERY was not a very good film, but it was far better, in retrospect, than THE MANDARIN MYSTERY (Republic, 1936) which followed it, based on THE CHINESE ORANGE MYSTERY. What were the screenwriters to do with this plot? Obviously, the solution that seemed most practicable was to treat it as a comedy of the absurd. Charlotte Henry, who had played the title role in ALICE IN WONDERLAND (Paramount, 1933), arrives in New York with a postage stamp worth $50,000. She is at once implicated in a murder in which the victim's clothes have been turned backwards. Eddie Quillan, a former vaudevillian, was cast as Ellery and portrayed him as an idiot. Wade Boteler played Inspector Queen. The laughs, which were the whole *raison d'être* for the film, were of the cornball variety. After this picture, Republic lost interest in filming any more of the Queen stories.

The cousins had also collaborated with Lowell Bretano on a stage play which did not feature Ellery and which closed after a few nights in both Baltimore and Philadelphia. The plot concerns three playwrights who want to write a mystery play and end up discovering a corpse. When no one will believe them about the body, they solve the mystery themselves. This, too, was sold to Hollywood and was released as THE CRIME NOBODY SAW (Paramount, 1937) directed by Charles Barton and starring Lew Ayres, Benny Baker, and Eugene Pallette as the three playwrights.

The cousins, in the interim, produced three more Ellery Queen novels set in

Hollywood, THE DEVIL TO PAY (1938), THE FOUR OF HEARTS (1938), and THE DRAGON'S TEETH (1939), several more slick short stories which eventually appeared in THE NEW ADVENTURES OF ELLERY QUEEN (1942), and worked variously in Hollywood in the story departments of three different studios. Their first stint was at Columbia, and then later for Paramount and M-G-M. Their highly argumentative methods of working together caused friction with people in neighboring offices and, while the pay was lucrative, they did not manage to write anything which earned them a screen credit. By 1939, it was back to the East. Fred and his wife Mary took up suburban life in Great Neck, Long Island, while Manny, divorced from his first wife, lived with his two daughters in a spacious apartment on Park Avenue. Dannay continued to pursue his hobbies, collecting stamps and writing poetry, and added a new one which would have long-range consequences: he embarked on acquiring a copy of every book ever published devoted to crime and detective fiction. Lee played the violin and added to his sizable collection of classical record albums. They worked twelve hours a day at their respective homes and would meet once a week at a non-descript office which they rented under the name of Ellery Queen. Both men alternated between Pall Malls and pipes, with occasional cigars, so the atmosphere was heavy with tobacco smoke; and, however vague Ellery might be as a character, as Sherlock Holmes and Philo Vance, he is one of the great connoisseurs of tobacco in detective fiction. In THE FOUR OF HEARTS, Ellery is offered a Scotch by a film producer known as the Boy Wonder. " 'Brandy,' " Ellery says faintly. " 'Brandy!' The Boy Wonder looked pleased. 'Now there's a man with discriminating boozing habits. It gets your ticker after a while, but look at all the fun you have waiting for coronary thrombosis.' "[24] S.S. Van Dine was by now dead. He had not lived to see Philo Vance on the radio; that was still in the future. The cousins decided that it was here, rather than in Hollywood, they would concentrate their energy: Ellery Queen must have his own radio program.

George Zachary, a producer at CBS, wanted to produce and direct an hour-long detective series for the air which would challenge listeners to match wits with the detective and perhaps beat him to the solution of the crime. Other than the Sherlock Holmes series which had been on the air since 1930, there were no genuine detective series. He approached Dannay and Lee and proposed that Ellery Queen would be ideal for his purposes. His money offer, however, was not very encouraging: he proposed a weekly salary of $25 while the cousins were learning the ropes. Between them, the cousins had a wife, an ex-wife, and four children to support. THE DRAGON'S TEETH had not been sold to a slick magazine, the first Queen novel not to have done so since the duo had "gone Hollywood." At that, Ellery Queen short stories were being success-fully marketed to slick magazines such as BLUE BOOK. The attraction of radio was that it would reach literally millions of people who, otherwise, would never hear of Ellery Queen. After all, Ellery presented no real problems as a character. He had always been sufficiently vague that he had easily made the transition from being a Philo Vance clone to the Hollywood sleuth of the novels they had been writing lately.

The cousins accepted Zachary's offer. While the program format was being assembled, they set out to learn the fundamentals of radio scripting by writing scripts at minimal pay and without credit for two crime programs then being broadcast. The first was ALIAS JIMMY VALENTINE which was based remotely on an O. Henry short story and featured in the leading role Bert Lytell who had played the Lone Wolf in films. They also contributed to THE SHADOW. However, as Francis M. Nevins remarked in his book, THE SOUND OF DETECTION (1983), "when I asked Fred Dannay several years ago, he couldn't remember any episode titles he and Manny Lee had written, nor even whether The Shadow was being played by Orson Welles or his successor Bill Johnstone when the cousins' scripts were aired."[25]

Dannay and Lee also devised a radio venture which they sold to the Mutual network. It was titled AUTHOR! AUTHOR! and, during its short life, was hosted first by Ogden Nash and then by S. J. Perelman. Dannay and Lee were permanent panelists, billed respectively as "Mr. Ellery" and "Mr. Queen," and joined by various guest panelists which included such notables as Dorothy Parker, Heywood Broun, Moss Hart, George S. Kaufman, Erskine Caldwell, and Quentin Reynolds. Each week the announcer would propound some inexplicable event and the sponsor, B.F. Goodrich Rubber Co., offered $25 to any listener submitting an impossible plot which would be used on the air. An example employed on the first program was this: "A young man arrives for the reading of his uncle's will. The only heir, he is desperately in need of money to cover gambling debts. The will gives him a choice: Accept $10,000 in cash or the contents of an envelope. He opens the envelope, which is empty, with no stamps or writing on it. 'I will take the envelope,' he says."[26] The solution which Dannay proposed was that the young man had poisoned his uncle by means of a poison applied to the envelope and that his uncle, before dying, gave him the choice of destroying the evidence of his crime or to claim the money, for which he committed the crime, only to risk exposure. Panelists were supposed to devise this kind of solution on the spot, while being attacked by other panelists. This kind of mechanical approach to plotting obviously was especially appealing to Dannay who must have used a similar approach in plotting the Ellery Queen mysteries, but it did not appeal to listeners and it was cancelled at the end of the summer.

George Zachary had lined up actors for THE ADVENTURES OF ELLERY QUEEN. To play Ellery, Hugh Marlowe was cast, with Santos Ortega cast as Inspector Richard Queen, Howard Smith as Sergeant Velie, and Robert Strauss as Doc Prouty. To increase female interest, Ellery was given a secretary named Nikki Porter played by Marian Shockley, a former Wampus baby and heroine in "B" Westerns, who was married to Zachary at the time. The background music was arranged and conducted for the initial ten weeks by Bernard Herrmann who would go to Hollywood the next year to score Orson Welles' CIT-

IZEN KANE (RKO, 1941). In a variation on Queen's "Challenge to the Reader," Zachary would have the show stopped at a crucial point with a guest celebrity present to be asked to identify who had done it. Given the weirdness of a typical Dannay plot, I am not surprised that occasionally the celebrity would indulge in the facetious, such as naming Ellery as the murderer. When Zachary tried having members of the studio audience guess the wrong-doer, the results were not any more satisfactory. Zachary even withheld the solution from the actors until the final moments of the dress rehearsal so that the guilty party would not give away the answer by acting too innocent!

Dannay and Lee spent most of their writing time preparing the sixty-minute script needed each week for which, as Dannay observed much later, "we received the magnificent sum of $25. Imagine doing a one-hour original drama each week for $25! And we didn't really keep the money, because at the end of each show we'd take the cast out for coffee and cake—that's all we could afford, coffee and danish pastry—and blew the $25 each week."[27] On 28 April 1940, THE ADVENTURES OF ELLERY QUEEN finally found a sponsor. The program was trimmed to a half hour, but the cast was retained with the exception of Doc Prouty.

Larry Darmour now made his entrance. He had produced the Mickey McGuire short subjects with Mickey Rooney before he began producing features for release by Majestic Pictures. When Majestic was merged into Republic, Darmour switched his releasing to Columbia Pictures, beginning with a series of Ken Maynard Westerns made in the mid 'Thirties. In 1940 he commenced negotiations with the cousins. He wanted to bring Ellery Queen to the screen in a new series for Columbia release and he wanted the cousins to work on the screenplays. Darmour had been producing a series of Jack Holt pictures for Columbia and the studio agreed with him that Ellery Queen would be a good substitute, especially with the radio tie-in. The cousins would work on their broadcast scripts on the West Coast while also working on scripts for Darmour.

To portray Ellery, Darmour selected Ralph Bellamy. Bellamy had just appeared in a comedic role in Howard Hawks' HIS GIRL FRIDAY (Columbia, 1940). Darmour was convinced that the Ellery Queen role would build a new public image for him. The cousins were scheduled to begin work in August, 1940. The contract called for Darmour to produce three Ellery Queen pictures a year. Darmour was a native of Flushing, New York, born in 1895, and, despite his relative youth, he did not live out his contract with the cousins. He had been educated at Princeton University and he was sufficiently successful, particularly after he began independent production for Columbia release, that he acquired his own production facilities on Santa Monica Boulevard. Among his projects in the late 'Thirties was production of Columbia's chapter plays. While he wanted the cousins to work on the screenplays for the Ellery Queen series for their name value and possible approval of what was being done, he actually had very little real work for them to do. Their agent arranged for them to do a short stint at M-G-M, but nothing came of it, nor of their efforts at

Darmour's studio. Darmour wanted original story ideas from the cousins and what he got instead were a great many violent hassles. The upshot of it all was that the cousins were back in New York by November, 1940, having accomplished little more than a polish job on SHADOW OF THE THIN MAN (M-G-M, 1941) for which they received no screen credit.

Ralph Bellamy was born in Chicago in 1904. He was expelled from high school for smoking beneath the auditorium stage. He held various jobs from soda jerk, office clerk, and sheep pelt sorter to fruit picker. When his father fired him from a Chicago advertising company, Bellamy decided he would enter the theatre. He joined a stock company in Madison, Wisconsin. In the ensuing years, he was with nine different stock companies and played over 400 roles. He was well-received in TOWN BOY on Broadway in 1928, but the play opened on a Friday and closed after the Saturday matinee. Joseph Schenck of United Artists brought him to Hollywood in 1931, but the contract proved disagreeable and the two parted company. Bellamy free-lanced for the next several years until he was signed by Columbia Pictures. He liked to play tennis. In 1934, he and his good friend, Charles Farrell, went to Palm Springs. Few people lived there, most of them tuberculors; few had ever heard of it. Together the two bought a tract of land for $3,500. It amounted to some 53 acres. A short time later, they sold 40 acres for $5,000 and on the remaining land they hoped to build a tennis court for themselves. They ended up building several courts, adding a swimming pool, and before long they had made so many improvements they found themselves $78,000 in debt. The obvious solution was to open the Palm Springs Raquette Club. They sent out letters to 173 friends and acquaintances, offering single memberships at $50 each, family memberships at $75. The idea was to keep the price low and get everyone to join. No one joined. So they raised their prices. By the time the membership fee hit $650, there was a waiting list.

Bellamy was a gracious man who, as he aged, grew increasingly distinguished. He married four times. His third marriage to organist Ethel Smith made headlines when he sued her for desertion and she cross-filed for half his income. She was accustomed to locking their apartment door from the inside at 11:45 PM. If Bellamy was not home by that time, he did not get in; but she would heap abuse on his head from behind the door.

I once spoke to him about his role as Ellery Queen.

"They were such quickie pictures," he said. "We would shoot them in ten days, I guess. They didn't like retakes. It was on those pictures that I learned how to 'ruin' a take when I didn't like how a scene was going."

"You made four of them."

"I was signed to appear in four Ellery Queen pictures at $25,000 a picture. Larry Darmour was the producer, but he wasn't around very much. Rudolph Flothow—his family was associated with the Sells-Floto Circus—was always on the set. I had to go to New York to meet with Lee and Dannay. They took me around to different squad rooms so I would get the feel for what went on in one. Many years later, when I was starring in DETECTIVE STORY on Broadway, I went to squad rooms again to see what they were like. I spent six weeks in squad rooms. When Chester Morris was going to take the show on the road, I took him to squad rooms, the 52nd Precinct I guess it was. He had never been in one before.''

''You'd think he'd have known what they were like, since in every Boston Blackie picture he usually ended up in one.''

We laughed.

''A funny thing happened while we were there,'' Bellamy resumed. ''There were three blacks lined up along a counter who were being questioned about various things, with cops on the other side typing out reports, with two fingers, you know. The lieutenant had a little office off to one side. The sergeant was moving around between the three blacks. The window was open and a bat flew in through the wire mesh. You wouldn't believe the commotion. The sergeant pulled out his gun and was about to shoot at it. The lieutenant came out of his office and yelled, 'Not in here. You'll hit someone.' So all of them together, the sergeant, the lieutenant, the guy behind the desk, the three blacks, they're like a ballet moving around the squad room in unison, chasing this bat. Finally one of them stuns the bat with a broom. The lieutenant is aware again of where he is. 'All right, you guys,' he yells at the blacks. 'Get back over to the desk.' If you put that into a movie, nobody would believe it, how well they all worked together. When William Wyler was going to film the movie version of DETECTIVE STORY, I took him to a squad room. I've got pretty familiar with them.''

''The Ellery Queen films had good casts,'' I said, returning to the subject.

''Yes, they did. They had very good casts. The problem was the scripts. I was after Darmour to get better scripts, but he would listen to me and then come back that it wasn't in the budget. There were a lot of set-ups every day, and some location shooting. But Flothow was always there behind the director, a skinny fellow, what was his name?''

''James Hogan.''

''Yes, Hogan. He didn't have a chance to direct. The idea was just to get the picture finished.''

''Did you read the Ellery Queen novels before you worked in the pictures, to give you an idea of the character?''

''No,'' Bellamy said, ''not before the series came up. I read a lot of them later. I liked Erle Stanley Gardner. I knew him when he had that place in the desert. He raised horses out there, but he was afraid of them. He might feed them, when he walked up to the corral, but get on top of one, never! He didn't like telephones. He didn't have a telephone on the ranch. He didn't want to be disturbed. If you wanted to get hold of Gardner, you had to call a Standard station in Temecula. When one of Gardner's crew drove past the station, the attendant would flag him down and relay the message. If Gardner thought it important, he would come down to the station and make a call from the telephone there.''

"You also worked on WOMAN IN THE DARK [RKO, 1934], based on one of Dashiell Hammett's stories."

"I made that in New York," Bellamy replied, nodding.

"Did you meet Hammett? I understand he took quite an interest in the filming of his properties."

"Yes, I did. He was in New York with Lillian Hellman. They were with that Algonquin crowd. Dotty Parker, George Kaufman, that group. He was a nice, intellectual man, with a sharp, witty sense of humor. When I was the head of the Actors' Equity, I was responsible for setting up our guidelines concerning membership, you know, when there was the trouble. We were much more liberal than the other guilds. I sent out copies of the guidelines. I remember Bernard Baruch telephoned me. He said I should come out to his home at 7:30 in the morning. He lived on Long Island. I went out there. He was sitting behind his desk. 'I'm not afraid of many things,' he told me. 'But I'm very much afraid of Communism.' I didn't know what to say. He had been a liberal advisor for so many years. So I said nothing."

Ellery was flirtatious from the beginning in the movies, absurdly so with Eddie Quillan grinning into his bouquet of posies for a newspaper photograph. In ELLERY QUEEN, MASTER DETECTIVE (Columbia, 1940), the first entry in the Darmour series directed by Kurt Neumann, the amorous relationship between Ellery and Nikki Porter had more dignity than had been the case in the two previous films from Republic. Three versions were given in all as to how Ellery and Nikki first met. In ELLERY QUEEN, MASTER DETECTIVE, Nikki, played by Margaret Lindsay, is intent on becoming a mystery writer and so finds herself knee-deep in mayhem when the corpse of the head of a health-faddist empire is discovered. There is no weapon in the vicinity of the crime. Fred Niblo, who had directed the first BEN-HUR (M-G-M, 1926), played the murder victim. Inspector Queen, portrayed by Charley Grapewin, and James Burke as Sergeant Velie undertake the official investigation while both Ellery and Nikki pursue their own investigations. By the fade, Nikki is so impressed with Ellery's skill as a detective that she agrees to come to work for him, typing his manuscripts.

Eric Taylor had done the screenplay for ELLERY QUEEN, MASTER DETECTIVE and he had stressed comic elements to provide the film with a highly humorous tone. He ventured even farther in this direction for the next entry, ELLERY QUEEN'S PENTHOUSE MYSTERY (Columbia, 1941). James Hogan joined the series as the director and the four principals returned in their roles. The influence of the Thin Man series at M-G-M was apparent in reverse since Ellery and Nikki, obviously not married but in love with each other, spend most of their time together squabbling. Probably the biggest mystery in the film is how Ellery ever gets a book written since Nikki is constantly showing off her figure to Ellery, writing her own stories on his time, and conducting her own investigations. Given the period during which this film was made there was perhaps no choice but to maintain the relationship in these adolescent terms.

The plot involves two murders committed for possession of a valuable collection of jewels brought from China to be sold in the United States to help the Chinese war effort. This same plot was reworked some months hence to form the basis for a Lone Wolf feature.

In late November, 1940 Frederic Dannay was in an automobile accident which left him in critical condition with several broken ribs, severe internal injuries, and shock. On 15 January 1941, VARIETY reported that Dannay was on his way to Florida for a month's vacation during which time he hoped to recuperate. The cousins had started work on a new mystery novel and stayed in touch by telephone and wire. However, as it turned out, the proposed novel employed the same basic plot as Agatha Christie's AND THEN THERE WERE NONE (1939) and so it had to be scrapped. Desperate to continue publishing Ellery Queen books, the cousins agreed to have the plots for the first two motion pictures fictionalized in book form. Years later, Dannay might condemn the Columbia films, but he was not above passing off these plots as the work of Ellery Queen in 1941, nor again in the 1960s when he agreed to have these books re-issued as Ellery Queen novels in paperback editions. It was but one more instance when commercial exigencies—in Van Dine's words "the obscene urge to eat well and live well"[28]—were to be placed above all other considerations.

THE DEVIL TO PAY was made the basis for ELLERY QUEEN AND THE PERFECT CRIME (Columbia, 1941). Darmour's contract with the cousins permitted him to use any of their published stories as the basis for a photoplay. The film followed the novel rather closely, even to the identity of the murderer. However, it is precisely the plot where every Ellery Queen novel breaks down, in the denouement, in the mechanics and motivation for the murders. The reviews were nearly unanimous in stressing the fact that it was the explanation of the crime which removed much of the human interest built up for the various characters and their fates. Douglas Dumbrille played a nasty tycoon whose stock manipulations bring ruin to many, including his partner, adeptly played by H. B. Warner. In the novel the setting is the tycoon's guest house. This was changed in the film to the guest house of the tycoon's sister, played improbably in terms of the plot but entertainingly in terms of screen comedy by Spring Byington. Sidney Blackmer, appropriately menacing, played the tycoon's attorney and Byington's fiancé. The dialogue, typically, ran toward comedy, much of it the result of antics between the police portrayed by Charley Grapewin and James Burke, and, of course, Ellery and Nikki were at it again. The picture, had it been played straight and a different murderer substituted, might have been a compelling detective film; but, as it was, it is only disappointing.

ELLERY QUEEN AND THE MURDER RING (Columbia, 1941) was based on THE DUTCH SHOE MYSTERY (1931). It was Ralph Bellamy's fourth and last picture in the role, and James Hogan's third entry. Leon Ames was cast as the son of the rich Mrs. Stack who is strangled to death in her own hospital while undergoing an operation. I asked him what it was like to be on the set of an Ellery Queen film.

"You know," he said, "I'm glad you asked me that. I'll never forget that picture. Do you know why?"

I was not about to suggest that it had anything to do with artistic merit.

"No, Leon, why?"

"Because Ralph Bellamy was . . . how old? He was in his mid thirties at least and he didn't know how to tie a tie. I remember I had to teach him how."

The story was played strictly for slapstick laughs. The chief physician of Mrs. Stack's hospital is George Zucco who is a zany maniac with a heart condition which interrupts any conversation he might engage in with a spasm. Paul Hurst and Tom Dugan were cast as a pair of incompetent mobsters hired by Ames to get rid of his mother. They fail in their attempt to run her car off the road, although Hurst's leg is broken in the process. Hurst, with his leg in a giant cast, ends up in the same hospital where the old lady is actually croaked and Tom Dugan spends at least a fifth of the picture's running time in an effort to wheel Hurst out of the hospital. Then there is a comic switch in bodies. Hillary Brooke, using the screen name of Jean Fenwick, was cast as Ames' screen sister. In one scene, after engaging in some investigation, Ellery gets Nikki to come to his hospital room where he intends to continue dictation on his current novel. They are interrupted by Tom Dugan and then the hilarity begins anew.

The final episode of THE ADVENTURES OF ELLERY QUEEN broadcast on CBS, sponsored by Gulf, and starring Hugh Marlowe occurred on 22 September 1940. A fifteen-month hiatus followed during which the cousins returned to writing books. In view of the fact that Agatha Christie's novels were being serialized in THE SATURDAY EVENING POST and Erle Stanley Gardner's Doug Selby stories were appearing in THE COUNTRY GENTLEMAN, both Curtis publications which paid $25,000 for serial rights, the cousins thought they would alter the setting of the Ellery Queen stories to small-town America. The resulting novel was called CALAMITY TOWN (1942). According to Dannay, it was "the best book that we thought we had written up to that time. . . . It was submitted in the usual way to a national magazine, and it was turned down. And we couldn't understand it. So we set up a three-party telephone conversation, a telephone conference with the editor and our agent and Manny and me. And I asked the editor certain questions like: 'Didn't you like the book?' And he said: 'Oh, I like the book very much, in fact it's the best story you've sent to us.' So I said: 'Why didn't you publish it, why didn't you accept it?' And he said: 'I don't know.' So I said, 'May I probe?' And I said: 'Is it possible that our price has risen to the point where it's too high for your budget?' And he said: 'No.' And I said: 'Is it possible that you have too many stories in inventory and don't want to add to the inventory?' He said: 'No.' And I asked various other questions, and I finally wound up by saying: 'Why are you rejecting this manuscript?' And his answer was . . . . : 'I don't know.'

So Manny and I walked out of our agent's office where the conference took place, and I think it was I who said to Manny: 'We'd better find another basket for our eggs, because we can't keep all our eggs in the basket we thought we could keep them in. If you can be turned down with no reason apparent on the best book you've ever written, . . . then you've got to do something else.'" [29]

Dannay's interest in detective and crime short stories gave birth first to the Ellery Queen anthology, which he assembled and annotated himself without any assistance from Lee, 101 YEARS' ENTERTAINMENT (1941), published initially by Little, Brown and then later re-issued as part of the Modern Library by Random House. Dannay also convinced publisher Lawrence E. Spivak to launch ELLERY QUEEN'S MYSTERY MAGAZINE which Dannay was to edit from its first issue, in Fall, 1941, until shortly before his death in 1982. In time, Dannay so expanded these editorial activities that in the mid 1940s Spivak published nine distinct collections of Dashiell Hammett's short stories edited by Dannay under the Ellery Queen byline, which in turn were published in paperback format by Dell Books; and, in later years, Dannay would edit numerous pulp collections of stories published by Spivak in addition to hardbound anthologies which ranged from stories selected from the pages of ELLERY QUEEN'S MYSTERY MAGAZINE to so-called "classics" of the crime and detection genre. The cousins also committed themselves to a new radio series, once again titled THE ADVENTURES OF ELLERY QUEEN, which returned to the air in January, 1942 sponsored by Bromo-Seltzer. Carleton Young played Ellery, but the other cast members, Santos Ortega, Ted Corsia, and Marian Shockley, came along from the old series and George Zachary was the producer. The program was carried on NBC's Red Network. The cousins were back having to devise a new plot and script every week. Eventually the series was to return again to CBS and Dannay, heavily burdened with editorial activities, would be replaced by Anthony Boucher.

On 1 April 1942, Lee happened to visit the NBC studio during the rehearsal of that week's program, "The Black Syndicate," and while there he met a young radio actress, Kaye Brinker, who would become his second wife. Lee liked the money which came from writing for the radio and during the decade of the 'Forties, until the radio series left the air in 1948, the cousins produced only two novels, THERE WAS AN OLD WOMAN (1943) and THE MURDERER IS A FOX (1945) as well as a collection of short stories made up in part of fictionalized radio scripts.

When Ralph Bellamy left the Ellery Queen series at Columbia, he was replaced by William Gargan. James Hogan was firmly fixed as the director by this time, Eric Taylor as the chief scenarist, and, of course, Larry Darmour was still the producer. The emphasis was shifted in the Gargan films to accommodate an image of Ellery as somewhat more professional and serious. Instead of the comedy being generated by screwball characters and slap-stick antics, it was derived now more from situation and dialogue. CLOSE CALL FOR ELLERY QUEEN (Columbia, 1942) was Gargan's first entry. Ellery is shown to be primarily an investigator and only secondarily an author of detective fiction. Ralph Morgan, playing a retired, wealthy South Seas trader, is being blackmailed by some toughs. Ellery wants Nikki to stay out of the case while he goes out to Morgan's estate to nose around. Both of Morgan's daughters have been missing for some time, but one of them, played by Kay Linaker, shows up at Ellery's office and she and Nikki, pretending to be the other daughter, also go to Morgan's estate. The toughs are dispatched, but so is Morgan. Ellery is required to do some detecting without any dependence on the comic charades rampant in previous films.

Before DESPERATE CHANCE FOR ELLERY QUEEN (Columbia, 1942) could enter production, Larry Darmour died. His widow, Alice Darmour, announced in the trades that she intended to carry on production of the Columbia chapter play then in progress and the two Ellery Queen films scheduled for release that year. Although Dannay in his last decade condemned the Gargan films as much as those with Bellamy, at the time he and Lee were quite pleased with the series and even wanted the number of annual entries to be increased from three to four. Columbia balked at this demand and, following the two entries still to be filmed in 1942, closed down production altogether, replacing this series with The Crime Doctor about which I shall have more to say in a later chapter.

DESPERATE CHANCE FOR ELLERY QUEEN was at best a routine picture. When Ellery is planning a vacation, his itinerary is disrupted by Mrs. Hadley, played by Charlotte Winters, who consults him about her husband, long believed dead but who has been seen in San Francisco. Ellery and Nikki leave New York for San Francisco to get to the bottom of it. Nikki registers at a hotel as Mrs. Hadley who is there presumably to get married again. John Litel was cast as Mr. Hadley. When murder strikes, Hadley is the obvious suspect. Inspector Queen and Sergeant Velie arrive and Ellery even gets himself arrested by the San Francisco police before he is able to crack the case.

ENEMY AGENTS MEET ELLERY QUEEN (Columbia, 1942) involved Ellery in the war effort. Early in 1942, George Zachary had left the radio series to work for the Office of War Information and the cousins were asked by the OWI to include certain official propaganda motifs in their radio scripts. The same sort of thing was being done extensively in Hollywood. The cast for this last film in the Columbia series added to series regulars, Gargan, Lindsay, Grapewin, and Burke, a strong assortment of character actors: Gale Sondergaard, Gilbert Roland, Sig Rumann, and Minor Watson. The picture ended up being Gargan's best entry and perhaps the best in the entire series. What humor there is arises from legitimate situations. Velie is conked on the head and a murder suspect he is transporting to New York escapes. Ellery, in an attempt to save Velie's job, investigates and learns that some valuable diamonds have been smuggled out of Holland via a mummy case from Egypt. Nikki plays up to Gilbert Roland, cast as a Dutch refugee, but he avoids her advances, convinced that she is a disguised Nazi. Roland is then murdered. Ellery wants

Velie to receive credit for discovering Roland's body, only to be conked himself and the body to disappear while Velie is off getting the inspector. The plot culminates in a Turkish bath operated by Rumann who is the head of a spy ring.

In the years of transition between the demise of the radio series and Ellery's emergence on television, the cousins returned again to writing Ellery Queen novels. In terms of atmosphere and setting and characterization, these are among their finest books, albeit, as always, the improbable and fantastic plots prohibit any of them from being ultimately satisfying. One change that was of conscious design was for Ellery to become more human and more humane; he became personally involved with some of the characters in these stories and interacted with them. In TEN DAYS' WONDER (1948), it is Ellery's attachment for Howard Van Horn which brings him back to Wrightsville and implicates him in a family tragedy. Nevins in ROYAL BLOODLINE put his finger, I think, on what it was about CALAMITY TOWN that caused a slick magazine editor to have second thoughts about the book. "Several commentators on mystery fiction," he observed, "have written of CALAMITY TOWN as if it were a simple-minded tribute to the goodness of an unspoiled American community. Actually, however, Queen's Wrightsville is a fairly realistic microcosm of the United States, with plenty of rot and inhumanity and strife alongside all the grace and bucolic peace."[30] He also added, as a peculiarly insightful afterthought that "Queen is the most somber in world-view, except for Cornell Woolrich."[31] In TEN DAYS' WONDER, Howard Van Horn has had an affair with Sally, the young wife of his step-father. The objective for Dannay was to present only three characters, one of whom, Sally, is murdered, and one of whom, Howard, commits suicide (by shooting himself while hanging by his neck), and yet to leave the reader perplexed as to the identity of the murderer. It was an interesting experiment, but the plot has another ingredient: in order to drive his step-son to suicide as a fitting punishment for adultery, Diedrich Van Horn makes it appear as if Howard has broken each one of the Ten Commandments. Under the burden of this strain, Howard is driven into a frenzy of self-destruction! In DOUBLE, DOUBLE (1950), there was a return to Van Dine's serial murder plot of THE BISHOP MURDER CASE, only here people are being killed according to the nursery rhyme, "Doctor, lawyer, beggarman, thief. . . ."

THE ORIGIN OF EVIL (1951) represented a return to the Hollywood novel of the late 'Thirties, with Ellery back in the city of angels confronted by another convoluted murder plot. Two business partners begin to receive strange packages. Leander Hill, one of the partners, has a weak heart and he dies at once. Roger Priam, the other partner, and the incompetent businessman of the two, continues to receive the strange packages. Years before the two partners and a third man had found a buried treasure; the partners had left the third man, who was named Adam, behind them, came to California, and established their business, Hill & Priam. The solution to the mysterious objects is that they

represent the Darwinian descent of man. Priam is behind the whole thing and he has to continue to plague himself with the mysterious objects even after his intention has been attained—the death of Hill—so as to appear innocent. In reading this novel, a reader might ask: why would Priam seek to kill the man who has made Hill & Priam a success? But this is Ellery in Wonderland and such questions are irrelevant. " 'With Hill out of the way,' " Ellery tells Priam, " 'you would be undisputed master of the business. That you might run it into the ground probably never occurred to you. But if it did, I'm sure the danger didn't even make you hesitate. The big thing was to make everyone involved in or with Hill & Priam come crawling to you. The big thing was to be boss.' "[32]
In THE LAMP OF GOD (1935), a short novel included in THE NEW ADVENTURES OF ELLERY QUEEN, in order for the plot to work the reader has to accept as probable the circumstance that Ellery meets a woman when her ship docks, accompanies her on a drive onto Long Island, takes her to a house whereupon she walks upstairs to her room to freshen up. While she is upstairs, she is seized and another woman takes her place, walks downstairs, and neither Ellery nor anyone else notices the substitution! In THE ORIGIN OF EVIL, the reader is expected to accept the fact that Adam, the man supposedly left for dead years before, has in fact been working for Priam for years and was known also by Hill without either man recognizing him. In this way, Ellery can arrive at one solution that fits all the facts, only to discard it and arrive at another solution. This mechanical approach to plotting was always a problem, but it seems to have worsened as the years passed. As Julian Symons pointed out, "fantastic ingenuity takes over at the expense of characterization, as in TEN DAYS' WONDER . . . , where the crimes follow the Ten Commandments, or DOUBLE DOUBLE . . . , where the pattern of a nursery rhyme runs through a series of murders. One can admire the ingenuity, and yet sense that there is something wrong about the way in which Queen is turning back to Van Dine and abandoning the possibilities glimpsed in the first Wrightsville books."[33]

Symons also perceived another way in which the Queen formula failed to make the transition in the face of changing times. "Hammett," Symons wrote, "when introducing Ellery Queen to a lecture audience, began by asking: 'Mr. Queen, will you be good enough to explain your famous character's sex life, if any?' Such a question could not have been asked before World War II. Holmes could then be accepted as a misogynist, Poirot as an aging bachelor, Queen as a figure susceptible to feminine beauty but above or outside emotional entanglement; but with the acceptance during the 'Fifties and 'Sixties of the fact that everybody has some kind of real and/or fantasy sex life, such easy answers would no longer do. It now appeared suggestive of impotence to fall in love with lovely ladies in a purely platonic way like Ellery; there seemed something sexually ambiguous about the household of Nero Wolfe and Archie Goodwin. Without going into more details, it is clear that Hammett's question showed up sharply the totally mythical nature of the Great Detective. Queen's response was to say that a wife, mistress, or even physical love affair planted on Ellery after all these years would upset readers. This was no doubt true, but the difficulty remained, and was recognized."[34]

Michael R. Pitts noted that in 1949 Ellery Queen "came to television on the DuMont network with Richard Hart as Ellery Queen. The next year Lee Bowman took over the role and played it until 1954, when Hugh Marlowe (who had originated the part on radio) took over. The half-hour series ran until 1958 and was then moved to NBC where it became 'The Further Adventures of Ellery Queen' with George Nader and ran for sixty minutes. In 1959, for its final season, Lee Phillips played Ellery."[35] In Pitts' opinion, "Hugh Marlowe has been the most accurate purveyor of the sleuth in both the visual and audio media."[36] Whatever the case, the rather adolescent orientation of the Queen world-view became increasingly problematic for filmmakers, if not for readers. The property remained dormant for more than a decade before NBC purchased rights to CAT OF MANY TALES and made it as a TV movie as well as a pilot for a possible series. Peter Lawford was cast as Ellery and his characterization called for him to be more interested in women than in crime. For this film, made under the title ELLERY QUEEN: DON'T LOOK BEHIND YOU, Ellery was also a Britisher and Inspector Queen, played by Harry Morgan, was Ellery's American uncle, not his father. Viewer response was poor and nothing came of the projected series. Meanwhile, in France, Claude Chabrol, who had discovered Ellery Queen during the Occupation when he came upon a cache of Queen novels in an attic, brought to the screen TEN DAYS' WONDER (Levitt-Pickman, 1972), but Ellery was not even among the characters and the picture proved a failure both artistically and commercially. In 1975, MCA/Universal and NBC tried to resurrect the property by doing a stylish series with Jim Hutton as Ellery and David Wayne as his father. It was set circa 1947 with special guest stars as murder victims. "Despite these attractions," as Pitts has pointed out, "the series was not successful and ran for only one season, probably due partially to the miscasting of Jim Hutton as Ellery, since he played the sleuth in an intellectual-boyish manner."[37] But what else could be done with a character who, after all, does continue to live with his father long after he has reached his majority?

The novels that the cousins were producing in the late 'Fifties also revealed a frightful decline and inconsistency. In INSPECTOR QUEEN'S OWN CASE (1956), Richard Queen's age was given as 63. In view of the fact that the early books already had him retired and living in Italy with Ellery married, this was curious enough; but matters got worse. In what Dannay intended to be the final Ellery Queen novel, THE FINISHING STROKE (1958), most of the story occurs in 1929 with Ellery appearing as he appeared in the early novels; and, when the story is brought up to date, Richard Queen, two years later, is now a man in his eighties and the woman with whom he fell in love two years before is nowhere in evidence. In THE FINISHING STROKE, we have all the elements of the Van Dine plot which Queen had always so admired: the snow-bound house-party, the thirteenth guest, murder with an antique dagger, a séance, identical twins, mysterious clues which arrive daily from an unseen source and, of course, a knowledge of proofreader's symbols is necessary to solve the case—although, even at that, it takes Ellery twenty-seven years!

Whatever may have been Dannay's intention, it did not end there. The 'Sixties saw a few more lame novels and even a fictionalization of a Sherlock Holmes picture, A STUDY IN TERROR (1966), in which the cousins accepted the money offered by Columbia Pictures for what was essentially hack work and as a gratuity added Ellery Queen as a character in a spurious framing story. Nor did it stop there. Dannay had obviously run out of plots; it was only self-repetition. Lee had no more plots to fume about and claimed to have writer's block. Therefore, the cousins had their literary agent find hack writers who would be willing to produce Ellery Queen novels for a flat fee and without recognition anywhere in the published book, all royalties going to Ellery Queen. These books began appearing as paperback originals in 1961 at the rate of one or two a year. In addition to the novels contracted to others, the old novelizations of the Columbia films and of radio plays also appeared, numbering some twenty-seven titles by 1972 which have been discreetly ignored in reference tomes such as Steinbrunner and Penzler's ENCYCLOPEDIA OF MYSTERY AND DETECTION when it comes to a listing of the Ellery Queen books and Nevins avoided so much as mentioning them in ROYAL BLOODLINE. Yet, the pitiful fact remains that there are almost more Ellery Queen books written and published under this name that the cousins did nothing more than "edit" than there are books written by them.

Nevins told the following anecdote about his first meeting with Manny Lee. "When we were introduced to each other in the lounge of the Biltmore Hotel, a young man sitting nearby suddenly jumped up like a jack-in-the-box and whooped: 'Manfred B. Lee! I think you're the greatest writer that ever lived!' Lee peered owlishly at the intruder and quipped: 'That doesn't say much for your taste, does it?' "[38]

Lee died on 2 April 1971. For most of his life, Dannay had been a very shy man in public. This changed somewhat during the last decade of his life. He became increasingly concerned with posterity's view of his work. He put a stop to the spurious Ellery Queen novels, which he insisted had been Lee's idea; and, while he occasionally implied that he would write an Ellery Queen novel himself or find a new collaborator, he did neither. When he was given an honorary doctor of letters degree by Carrol College, he remarked at the informal convocation that "What I wanted to do, with all I knew about the detective story and all the experience Manny and I had in writing . . . , was to find a new form, a form that broke away from Edgar Allan Poe, a form that would be original, something altogether different and something so integral to the mainstream of the detective story that it would be part of it and yet absolutely new. I must confess to you I never found it."[39]

"In 1972, twenty-seven years after his first wife, Mary, had died of cancer,"

Francis M. Nevins observed of Dannay, "his second wife, Hilda, did likewise. And with her death Fred himself began dying by inches. Each time I visited him during the next few years he seemed to have shrunk in his chair a little more. A photograph of him taken by Santi Visalli in 1973 shows the empty, devastated face of a man waiting to die. The only thing that kept him functioning, he told me, was the inexorable work schedule demanded of him by ELLERY QUEEN'S MYSTERY MAGAZINE. I couldn't help feeling his days were numbered. And then he met the third woman in his life. At a dinner party he happened to be introduced to Rose Koppel, a recently widowed artist who worked at Manhattan's Ethical Culture School. In November, 1975 they were married, and Rose literally saved her seventy-year-old husband's life. He had always been a private person, so much so that after almost thirty years in the house on Byron Lane many of his closest neighbors still had no idea what he did for a living. Rose de-privatized him as no other person before her had ever succeeded in doing and made it possible for him to enjoy his role as elder statesman of mystery fiction that time and the deaths of more and more of his contemporaries had bestowed on him."[40]

Frederic Dannay died on Labor Day Weekend, 1982. If, ultimately, the juvenile perspective of Ellery in Wonderland contributed nothing to American literature, for the detective story it did mean that the so-called "classical" plot which S. S. Van Dine had pioneered was carried forward for yet another generation and a haven, a sinecure was created for those readers who wanted to believe, if only for a moment or two, that the complexities of modern life could be reduced to a mere problem in deduction.

PERRY MASON

> . . . Legal histories fairly swarm with instances in which circumstantial evidence has brought about convictions predicated upon a fortuitous chain of circumstances, circumstances which have subsequently been completely clarified and found to have no sinister significance whatever, yet circumstances which have, in the meantime, resulted in the conviction of an innocent person.
>
> Perry Mason[41]

Erle Stanley Gardner's tremendous popularity while he was alive—at one point his sales were twenty thousand copies a day—has tended to obscure his importance in the history of detective fiction and his rather extraordinary virtues as a man of American letters. He was born at Malden, Massachusetts on 17 July 1889. His father was a mining engineer and an expert in gold dredging which found Erle attending schools in Mississippi, Oregon, California, and in 1906 he spent several months in the Klondike. He completed high school in Palo Alto, California.

Erle was a youth of strong opinions and the temperament of a maverick. He was expelled from a school at Oroville for cartooning a long-chinned disciplinarian. It was also in Oroville that he fell in with "Swede" Meyerhoffer, a man who would eventually become known as a stunt flier and who would die in an airplane crash. Swede decided that he was going to turn Erle into a prize fighter. Meyerhoffer had founded the Butte Athletic Club in Oroville. One day, on his way to a contest with a contender imported by Meyerhoffer from Sacramento, Erle heard the clang of an ambulance and then saw a warm-up fighter who had been projected out of a window by the contender. Notwithstanding two black eyes and a cut-up face, Erle managed to stay the limit. The two went on to promote a number of unlicensed matches which got Erle in trouble with the district attorney's office. Following a lecture from a deputy district attorney on the consequences of what he was doing, Erle made up his mind to study the law. He enrolled at Valpariso University in Indiana, but he was expelled for slugging a professor.

Erle returned to California, this time to Oxnard, and assumed the position of clerk-typist with a law firm. After reading law for an average of fifty hours a week, Erle passed his bar examination in 1911 at the age of twenty-one. He joined I.W. Steward's law office in Oxnard that year and he made the acquaintance of Natalie Talbert, Stewart's young secretary. Nat, as she was known to her friends, had been raised by her mother's mother, had to work for a living, and had been hired by Stewart in 1910 when she was twenty-five. The two were drawn together by mutual attraction and Nat's legal knowledge put her in a position to talk intelligently with Gardner about his cases. On 9 April 1912, the two eloped—in order to avoid the pomp of a formal wedding so distasteful to Erle—and were married in San Diego. Although Nat was four years older than Erle, this presented no problem and their birthdays were such—Nat's was 16 July—that they celebrated them together until Nat's death in 1968.

In 1913 Erle was confronted by a particularly difficult case. A Los Angeles attorney had come to Oxnard and in a rather spectacular court hearing had managed to have acquitted a Chinese lottery-ticket seller, after which he had returned to Los Angeles leaving Erle with twenty other Chinese similarly charged. Presented with any serious intellectual problem, it was Erle's habit to pace the floor while thinking. Finally a solution occurred to him. Erle summoned a Chinese who was the unofficial "mayor" of Oxnard's Chinatown. He outlined his plan to the Chinese who agreed to put it into effect. The prosecutor intended to bring the twenty defendants to court at his leisure and hired an out-of-town detective to make the arrests. The first man arrested was booked as Ah Lee. An Oxnard deputy sheriff who was much admired for his ability to tell one Chinese from another informed the out-of-town detective that the man he arrested was not Ah Lee.

"That certainly is Ah Lee," the detective said. "I bought a ticket from him a week ago, and I just arrested him at Ah Lee's laundry."

"If that's Ah Lee, I'm your wife's grandmother," the deputy responded.

"I've known Ah Lee for ten years. He does my Sunday shirts. This is Wong Duck, the butcher."

"But I tell you he was running the laundry," the detective insisted. "He was bossing the others around. What would a butcher be doing running a laundry?"

The out-of-town detective then arrested another man from whom he said he had purchased a lottery ticket the previous week as Ho Ling, the grocer.

"He's Ong Hai Foo, the druggest," the deputy returned in a disgusted manner. "Ong's the biggest dealer in dried-lizard medicine in Southern California."

"But I tell you he was running Ho Ling's grocery when we arrested him," the out-of-town detective protested. "He was waiting on customers. Why would a druggist be selling vegetables?"

The deputy went to Chinatown to survey the situation for himself. He readily discovered that every Chinese shopkeeper was operating some other Chinese's business. When the prosecuting attorney heard what had happened, he knew he was licked.

"There's been a lot of monkey business going on here," he remarked, "but we can't get convictions when our witness starts by picking out the wrong men. All the cases will have to be dropped."

Erle's response was swift and wholly characteristic. "The authorities have no right to convict a man unless they can make an honest identification of him," he argued. "Their detective was identifying street addresses instead of human beings. All I did was to arrange a fair test of his ability to identify these defendants. It's not my fault that he flunked it."[42]

The Chinese were so impressed at Gardner's acumen that the "mayor" of Chinatown informed Erle that he had had him studied and that three incarnations back he had been Chinese. However, this did not improve Erle's standing with local officials. When Soo Hoo Yow was charged with selling a twenty-five cent lottery ticket, he was clearly guilty. This time the officials did not identify an address; rather the detective was able to recognize the defendant by sight. Erle, in his defense of Soo Hoo Yow, diverted the attention of the court from his client to Oxnard itself. He claimed he could produce a witness who had overheard a police official offer to let Chinatown run wide open if the Chinese would fire Erle and have a man plead guilty to lottery gambling at regular intervals so that the city could receive its share of the proceeds from the illicit business. The charge caused a sensation in the courtroom and resulted in a hung jury. At a second trial, Soo Hoo Yow was found guilty. Erle appealed his case. A California statute allowed cities to enact ordinances if they did not conflict with state law. Oxnard's gambling ordinance used the exact language of the state law. That, Erle pleaded, was the problem: Oxnard was trying to compete with the state and oust the state from proper jurisdiction. Erle's argument prevailed.

The city of Oxnard would strike back, of that Erle was certain. Before Soo

Hoo Yow could be re-arrested and tried under the state ordinance, Erle decided to use the twice-in-jeopardy defense. He could not invoke this defense merely on the basis of Soo Hoo Yow's having been tried on an unconstitutional ordinance. Instead, he drove the Chinese to Ventura and called upon Justice Knox, the local magistrate. Erle himself signed a complaint against Soo Hoo Yow. His explanation to the judge was that he had begun to feel pangs of conscience for having gotten his client off on a technicality. Soo Hoo Yow was guilty and some effort at restitution should be made. Justice Knox accepted the plea and fined the Chinese fifteen dollars.

Presently, back in Oxnard, Soo Hoo Yow was re-arrested and arraigned for trial. Erle's defense was once in jeopardy. This was just what the prosecutor had expected. He had with him a mass of authorities to prove that conviction under an unconstitutional ordinance could not be construed as constituting jeopardy. When Erle attempted to interrupt, the Oxnard judge told him to sit down and wait his turn. For an hour and a half the prosecutor cited his precedents. Finally, Erle was given a chance to speak.

"I didn't raise the question of once in jeopardy on that ground," he explained. "I raised it because the defendant has been tried, convicted, and fined under the state law."

"When, where, and before whom?" the prosecutor demanded.

"Before Justice Knox at Ventura on August 30, 1915."

"Who swore out the complaint?"

"I did."

"How much was he fined?"

"Fifteen dollars."[43]

The spectators went wild with amusement. Previously Erle had been called Chong Tzee T'oy which, because he was somewhat short in stature, means he was "the little lawyer." Now the Oxnard Chinese referred to him as Tai Chong Tzee which means "the great counselor."

Frank Orr, a leading young attorney in Ventura, then invited Erle to join him in a partnership. Besides the many advantages such a partnership would offer, Erle was also aware that he had so antagonized the officials in Oxnard that a change in venue would indeed be advisable. Orr was, according to Gardner, a walking encyclopedia when it came to bond issues, municipal law, and related matters. He and Gardner became lifelong friends and he remained Erle's family lawyer until his death. Many years later Orr reputedly gave an interview to a reporter from the NEW YORK TIMES. "In the courtroom Erle radiated self-confidence at all times. His voice was resonant and carried well. He was big, stocky, plain-looking. Erle didn't try for the dapper, slick-lawyer look. The jurors probably considered him as ordinary as themselves, which suited him just fine. His way with a hostile witness was plain wizardry. He could coax the fellow along, right into telling outright lies, or into confusion so complete the fellow would end up babbling and no jury could possibly take his testimony seriously. In behalf of his clients, he nosed about in forgotten statutes and cases to find just the right precedents to fit his needs. At the proper moment, he would spring the precedent on the judge and jury."[44]

Erle's and Nat's only child, a daughter named Grace, was born in 1913. It was not long after his association with Frank Orr that Erle met Agnes Walter. She was called Jean and was working as an assistant desk clerk and dining room hostess at the Pierpont Inn. Erle wanted her to come to work in the law office. Instead, Jean got her sister Peggy to join the firm as a secretary. However, Erle, as was his wont, remained persistent and within a year Jean also joined the firm and, shortly after that, her sister Honey. These three sisters would play an integral role in Erle's subsequent career as a writer.

In 1918 Joe Templeton, an old friend who was a manufacturers' agent in the automobile accessory business, convinced Erle that he should give up the law and try his hand at sales. Erle had always been a highly restless person, with tremendous energy. The detail work of the law bored him. It was only when in a courtroom that he found the profession exhilarating. The sales opportunity offered him certain definite advantages: he would be on the go a great deal, he would have an opportunity for far greater income, and he would not be hindered by paperwork. Erle was almost constantly on the road and for three years he literally lived out of a suitcase. The business prospered during the post-war boom and then, in 1921, it went into a slump. To his complete surprise some of Erle's former Chinese clients made anonymous deposits to his checking account to help tide him over. Although Frank Orr had added another partner, Louis Drapeau, he had kept Erle's office waiting for him. Erle did not want to be chained to an office or to a house. He had long been persuaded that, except for the independently wealthy, only writers could take their work with them and live independently, writers and owners of mail order businesses. He tried writing first. Since it was relatively easy to break into the pulp fiction field, that is where he began. "I say it was comparatively easy," he later reflected. "To my knowledge it has never been really easy for a writer to get started unless that writer had talent of an extraordinary nature . . . I didn't have an extraordinary talent. I didn't have any talent at all . . . I wrote and I typed and I purchased postage, and my stories came back . . . I collected an assorted drawerful of rejection slips. . . . Since my sales instinct told me that you could never sell a story while it was parked in a desk drawer, I sent out everything I wrote. As fast as it came back, I sent it bouncing out to collect more rejection slips."[45]

Erle became so discouraged with writing, and his lack of time to work at it due to the pressures of his law practice, that Nat counseled him by example. All one need do, she insisted, was to sit down and write a story. She did, and she sold it to the magazine section of the LOS ANGELES TIMES. Erle decided that what was needed was for him to study plotting. "I eventually became a pretty good plotter," he subsequently recalled, "although I certainly had to work up the hard way. I had to break down a plot to find out what it consisted of. I had to try to find out what people wanted to read, why they wanted to read, and how they read."[46] His study of organic plotting obviously paid off. There is perhaps no author of detective fiction who has been able to match Gardner for the ingenuity and the number of his plots. His stories began slowly to sell, but the income, compared with what he had earned either from the law or in sales, was disappointing. He decided to start a mail order business, selling lessons on the practice of law. The results with this idea were less than satisfying. "I hadn't as yet learned how to 'think on a typewriter,' " he later commented. "I had to write my stories laboriously in longhand on legal foolscap with a soft pencil; then copy the stories on a typewriter. . . ."[47]

When, in 1923, a story Gardner submitted to BLACK MASK magazine titled "The Shrieking Skeleton" was returned with the uncensored remarks of Phil Cody, one of the senior editors, the remarks were such that Gardner sat down, tore the story apart, and then laboriously began to rewrite it and rewrite it again. There were still a great number of rejections, but occasionally BLACK MASK would accept a story, or Erle would be counseled on how the story should be rewritten. Erle created assorted series characters for his pulp fiction markets. "It is no secret that many authors who have created series characters have come to hate their guts," he reflected. "This has never been the case with me. I fall in love with the guy and tackle each new story with renewed enthusiasm."[48] In time, he devised his plot wheel. It was a cardboard wheel with spokes radiating from the center. Some of the spokes would indicate characters or character types, some situations, some unexpected complications, some the lowest common denominators of reader interest. The wheel was so constructed that as the spokes revolved and stopped their points of contact would provide the nucleus of a plot. "If I couldn't get a plot within thirty seconds," Erle claimed, "I thought I was slipping and worked myself into a frenzy of activity."[49] I had occasion to see the plot wheel, reduced to a number of typed pages; it was an amazing device and the number of combinations which could be worked out was as extraordinary as the wheel was effective.

Erle's working habits were ambitious. Jean would come to his house after office hours and take dictation on matters connected with his writing. When she left, around ten o'clock, Erle would go to a typewriter and begin with his two-fingered system to work on a story. "I would work until one, one-thirty, or two o'clock in the morning when I would be so dog-tired that whenever I would stop to rest I would fall asleep in the chair and have nightmares, dreaming for the most part about the characters in the story, waking up a few seconds later all confused as to what was in the story and what had been in my dream," Erle recalled. "At that time I would go to bed. I would sleep about three hours a night, waking up around five or five-thirty in the morning. Then I would take a shower, shave, pull up my typewriter and write until it came time to go to the office. It's a wonder that I didn't kill myself with overwork. If I finished one story at twelve-thirty at night, I couldn't go to bed without starting another. For a period of several years I pounded out stories on the typewriter at the rate of a novelette every third day, and at the same time practiced law, much of it trying cases in front of juries, which I can testify is a very exhausting occupation."[50]

Gardner had begun to use a dictating machine when he was in sales work and he introduced the machine to the law office after his return. It was not too long before he tried to adapt the machine to his writing. He set himself a quota of one hundred thousand words a month divided into five thousand words a day. If he missed a day because of pressing trial work, he would double the quota for the next day. Even though she had become office manager and executive secretary to the firm, Jean continued to work after hours for Gardner. Once he sold "Three O'Clock in the Morning" to BLACK MASK, Erle became a fixture in that magazine. Although subsequently Captain Joseph T. Shaw, when he became editor of the magazine, would claim he had discovered the BLACK MASK headliners, the truth is that Dashiell Hammett, Carroll John Daly, and Erle Stanley Gardner had already been regular contributors for some time.

Phil Cody was still editing BLACK MASK in 1925. On a visit to the West Coast, Cody informed Gardner of an impending crisis. Supposedly Dashiell Hammett was unhappy with the magazine's rates and was threatening to stop writing for it unless he was paid more. The magazine needed Hammett's stories, but it could not afford to increase his pay. "I was practicing law and making enough money out of the practice of law so I didn't need to make money out of my writing in order to get by," Erle later commented. "On the other hand, BLACK MASK was my only regular market and if BLACK MASK couldn't keep on in business without Dashiell Hammett, which Cody felt was the case, I would suffer along with all the other writers. So I made Cody a business proposition. He could take a cent a word off my rate and add it to Hammett's rate. Cody thought that was most generous on my part, not recognizing the fact that I was making a business proposition from a business standpoint. Cody went back and told Eltinge Warner, the owner of the magazine, about my generous offer, and Warner never had much use for me afterwards. He said that was a perfectly cockeyed offer and no good businessman would have made it."[51] However, before Cody left for the East, he asked Gardner to accompany him to San Francisco to talk with Hammett about the rate problem. They went but they did not see Hammett. His wife met them at the door and, thinking perhaps they were bill collectors, she told them Hammett was out of town and she did not know when he would return. As it turned out, Hammett had found work writing advertising copy and retired for a time from writing for the pulps.

Eventually, Erle engaged a literary agent and, henceforth, although there would be problems and changes, he continued to work with an agent except for a very brief hiatus. What is most important about this decision is that Gardner's first agent, Robert Thomas Hardy, was responsible for encouraging Erle to try writing novels which would be suitable for sale to the slick magazines and thus to graduate from the pulp markets for which he was writing exclusively. In late 1932, Gardner wrote his first novel-length story which he titled REASONABLE DOUBT. Captain Shaw, by then editor of BLACK MASK, agreed with Hardy that the work merited more money than any pulp could pay. Hardy remarked to Gardner in a letter that the slick magazine business was changing. "You may remember," he wrote to Erle, "that not a great while ago SCRIBNER'S published a detective story by Van Dine. . . . What a strange thing this is, when one considers what SCRIBNER'S used to be."[52] Gardner wrote back to Hardy that he had already begun to dictate his second novel. Erle did not have a very high opinion of Van Dine. "I think," Erle commented, "his character, Philo Vance, was a pain in the neck, and that many of the readers also thought so. I think his plotting ability was exaggerated by himself to himself, and for that reason I don't think he knows why it was his stories had a success. Having now modestly placed myself in the position of knowing more about the stories than the guy who wrote them—and I only read one and skipped through the high spots of another—I will unblushingly state that I think his success came from his genius in depicting his subordinate characters. He had wonderful ability along those lines."[53] I do not know that too many others, familiar with Van Dine's stories, would agree that his subsidiary characters are more interesting than his plots. Notwithstanding, Erle also dismissed Van Dine's twenty rules. "I hate all forms of convention," he responded. "I believe a man can go further questioning fundamentals than conforming to them."[54]

Hardy, as he sent REASONABLE DOUBT to slick magazines, also submitted copies to book publishers. Clifton Fadiman at Simon and Schuster rejected it. When the manuscript was sent to Frederick A. Stokes, the publisher returned it. The editors there were of a mind that only two detective stories by any one author should be published in any given year, disliked the idea of any author writing under more than one name, and, as came out later, the house was committed to the Ellery Queen series it had just launched and did not want to compete with itself. Then Hardy tried Thayer Hobson at William Morrow and the book clicked. When Hobson learned that Gardner had already written a second novel, titled SILENT VERDICT, he wanted to see it as well. Hobson was profoundly instrumental in Gardner's success. He wanted the books retitled. Also, each book had a different lawyer-detective. Hobson wanted the two lawyers combined into one character and thus to begin a series. Erle agreed to rewrite REASONABLE DOUBT along these lines. A correspondence sprang up between him and Hobson. From this came a close working professional relationship and then an equally close personal friendship.

On his own, under the house name of Peter Field, Hobson wrote the first three in a series of hard-bound Western novels set in fictional Powder Valley featuring a trio of heroes, Pat Stevens, owner of the Lazy Mare ranch and sometimes sheriff of Powder Valley, Sam Sloan and Ezra, partners in the ES ranch and friends who help Pat out of the scrapes in which he finds himself. After the first three, Hobson hired a number of writers to contribute to the series, paying each a flat $500 for the novel without royalties. A number of Western writers contributed to this series, but so did Davis Dresser who would later create Mike Shayne. Hobson hoped to corner the Western market with the Peter Field series and the mystery market with the Perry Mason series. The names of the two lawyers in Gardner's first two novels were Stark and Keene respectively. As he was revising REASONABLE DOUBT, Gardner wrote Hobson that "I am making him into a new character, and since your editors apparently disapprove of both Stark and Keene as names, I am calling him Perry Mason, and the character I am trying to create for him is that of a fighter who is possessed of infinite patience."[55] Erle wanted to establish a style of swift motion in the Mason books that would be unrelenting from the start to the finish. "The Hemingway and Hammett style creates an illusion of fast motion," he wrote Hobson, "but when you analyze the plot and the motion you find that it's an illusion created through style rather than an event sequence which swoops breathlessly forward. . . ."[56]

Gardner had had good reason to study Hammett's technique. After THE MALTESE FALCON was serialized in BLACK MASK in 1930, Captain Shaw became an uninhibited worshipper at Hammett's shrine. It was ironic, in a way, since Hammett was able now to go on to other markets; so Shaw did the next best thing: he insisted his other authors attempt to imitate the Hammett style and technique. This Erle refused to do and, after that, he never received first-class treatment from the magazine. Some time later, in his essay, "The Case of the Early Beginning," which he wrote for Howard Haycraft's THE ART OF THE MYSTERY STORY (1946), Erle made a careful distinction. "Personally," he wrote, "I think it is a mistake to confuse the so-called 'hard-boiled' type of detective story with the action type of detective story. For very apparent reasons, the hard-boiled story is almost invariably told in the format of the action story; but the action story is not necessarily the hard-boiled story."[57] According to Erle, the action story has primarily to do with pacing and with activity. "In other words, the detective doesn't find a broken cuff link or a fragment of curved glass at the scene of the crime. Instead, one of the characters *does* something that turns out to be the significant clue."[58] As he was revising his first novel which became THE CASE OF THE VELVET CLAWS (1933), Erle was also analyzing what it was that made the book special. "The orthodox detective story is an arbitrary, intellectual puzzle," he wrote Hobson. "I believe there is an opening for a story of conflict in which the protagonist has to fight the forces of crime. Conflict is necessarily grim but it is passionately interesting. There is no love interest in a struggle between two football teams, but, nevertheless, that struggle commands huge financial returns. The first book is grim. It presents the character of a lawyer who is true to himself in that he fights for his client regardless of the fact that he is getting the double-cross from that client. The idea of a secretary was to show a contrast of feminine loyalty as opposed to the trickery of the other woman."[59]

It was Erle's idea to append to each title in the series the standard THE

CASE OF THE . . . , a notion which Hobson enthusiastically endorsed. Already in the first novel, Erle had his triad which would continue through all of the Perry Mason novels: Perry, his secretary Della Street, and Paul Drake of the Drake Detective Bureau (which became interchangeable with the Drake Detective Agency). Eva Griffin comes to Mason's office and wants to engage him as her attorney. There was an attempted hold-up the previous evening at the Beechwood Inn and, although she is married, she was present with another man, the political candidate, Harrison Burke. Frank Locke, who edits SPICY BITS, a scandal sheet, has learned of this and intends to run it unless, of course, he is bought off. Eva Griffin wants Mason to buy him off. Mason agrees to take her case. Once the client has left, Perry notices that she has made Della bristle. He asks Della why she hates Eva Griffin. Della tells him that she hates everything Eva Griffin stands for. " 'I never got a thing in life that I didn't work for. And lots of times I've worked for things and have had nothing in return. That woman is the type that has never worked for anything in her life! She doesn't give a damned thing in return for what she gets. Not even herself.' "[60] In the ensuing interchange, we learn that Della's family originally was wealthy but that it had lost its money. Della went to work. A lot of women would not have done that, Perry responds. Della demands to know what other women would have done, could have done. " 'They could,' " Perry tells her, " 'have married a man, and then gone out to the Beechwood Inn with some other man, got caught, and had to get a lawyer to get them out of a jam.' " Della's response is to turn toward the outer office, her eyes averted. "Those eyes were glowing. 'I started to talk about clients,' she observed, 'and you begin to talk about me.' "[61]

What an extraordinary innovation this was! There had been female detectives before 1933, but never before had a woman become an integral part of the masculine world of the action detective story. Perry Mason is no aloof misogynist as is Sherlock Holmes, no hopelessly single intellectual in whose life women were but a distraction as they are for Philo Vance or Ellery Queen, no super sleuth for whom women were an irrelevance as they are for Nero Wolfe or Hercule Poirot. Here were a man and a woman together in the business world, the very first manifestation in detective fiction of the new roles economic exigencies in the real world were bringing to the forefront. Behind Della's character we can perceive, perhaps, Nat as she was when Erle first encountered her as a legal secretary, and then the conglomerate posed by the Walter sisters.

It is something of a wonder that Erle was able to maintain the pretense of being a family man for more than twenty years, although even at that his absorption in his own work and his outdoor activities which included going off by himself or with friends, adventuring, camping, practicing archery precluded any deep involvement with his home life. His daughter Grace recalled that when her father was not involved in some sort of mental activity he could not sit still; he was up and about, seeking something physical to occupy him. In later years, Erle wrote Grace that he regretted not ever having gotten to know her better. "I suppose I had too much ambition and having decided I was going to be a writer," he confessed, "I subordinated every damn thing to being a writer, just as I had previously subordinated every damn thing to being a lawyer."[62] Erle went to China with Nat in the summer of 1931, but, when he was not sight-seeing, he was writing. That year he earned $20,525 from the pulp stories he wrote. Between the time of that trip and June, 1933, when Erle decided to put what he called the "Fiction Factory" on wheels, the breach between him and Nat was growing. He would live in a trailer he had bought and he purchased tents for the Walter sisters to live in while camping out at Podunking. Peggy brought along her husband, Ray Downs, and Ray would go off camping with Erle in the lower desert. Jean had also married Leslie Bethell. He came along as well, but, after the couple returned to Ventura, they separated. Erle had written to Nat that he thought they were finished in Ventura. If Nat were lonely because Grace was off at college, he could arrange for Peggy to stay with her. Nat opted instead to pay a visit to the camp. After that visit, Erle wrote to Nat that he did not think that the three Walter sisters would ever want "to go to Podunking again until things are straightened around so you're happy. . . . As far as I am concerned, I have had enough bickering to last a lifetime."[63]

Frank Orr was called East as an authority on bond issues and he needed a secretary familiar with the subject. Jean went East with him. Erle, Ray Downs, Peggy, and Honey moved to Laguna Beach in November, 1933. In December, Grace eloped to Reno to marry Alan Robert McKittrick to avoid a formal wedding. Thirteen years older than Grace and with a history of heart trouble, the marriage nonetheless lasted until McKittrick's death in 1962. Erle then moved everyone to New Orleans in December where they stayed until February, 1934. At that time Ray Downs was offered a job in San Francisco, so, rather than lose Peggy's services to the Fiction Factory, Erle decided to move his headquarters there, renting a studio apartment in the same building as Ray and Peggy had an apartment, while Honey found a place uptown and Nat took an apartment even farther uptown. When LIBERTY magazine signed an escalating contract with Erle for serial rights, in March, 1934, Erle asked Honey, who had taken over as his personal secretary from Jean who was still absent, to book them a six-week cruise to the South Seas. In June, Erle, Nat, Honey, and Peggy set sail. Honey's first marriage was being dissolved. On this cruise she met Walter Moore, whom she would later marry. In August, when they returned, Erle decided to move to Hollywood because production had begun on the Perry Mason films. Peggy's marriage was now being dissolved. She and Honey were put in charge of the actual move while Erle flew East with Nat. They were joined in New York by Jean whose job with Frank Orr had been completed and the three traveled back to California via the Panama Canal. Once he and Jean arrived in Los Angeles, Erle wrote to Hobson: "I have an apartment with Nat in San Francisco, a studio hideout in Hollywood, a trailer which is acclimated to the desert, with dictaphones and cylinders in all three places. Whenever anyone is looking for me in one place, I am always somewhere else. It makes a swell arrangement. I should be able to work."[64] His mailing address was the house in Hollywood where Honey and Peggy lived with the children from their marriages. Jean rented an apartment. All three Walter sisters were either separated or divorced.

Obviously Erle had a role in the personal life of each one of these women, although his intimate relationship would be with Jean. In 1935, Erle bought a house for Nat in Oakland. Erle bought another for himself in Los Angeles and set up housekeeping with two Filipino boys. Erle provided Nat with an allowance of $225 a month and, as his earnings increased, he added to it. He sent her more when she wanted to go to Europe. He was responsible for supporting himself, these various residences, his secretarial staff, and, until late in 1935, had even been sending Grace money to tide her over. It was an enormous burden. Similar extravagances might bring ruin to other writers, but not to Erle. He maintained his productivity with a single-mindedness bordering on obsession. He demanded of the women around him that they be completely professional and totally devoted in their loyalty. They were—and without them his success would have been impossible. It is this drama, somewhat stylized, which is played out between Perry Mason and Della Street in the first ten years of the Perry Mason saga, from THE CASE OF THE VELVET CLAWS to THE CASE OF THE DROWSY MOSQUITO (1943). It fascinated the three women who worked for him as it fascinated the women who worked at Morrow and who were charged with editing his books prior to publication and requiring that certain inconsistencies be cleared up by rewriting. Above all, it fascinated female readers, many of them forced into the labor market by the Depression and then by the World War.

In THE CASE OF THE VELVET CLAWS Perry remarks that "my clients aren't blameless. Many of them are crooks. Probably a lot of them are guilty. That's not for me to determine. That's for the jury to determine."[65] This was an attitude born from the free-wheeling morality found in the pulps. As Erle wanted more and more to break into the slick magazine market, he learned that he would have to alter the tone somewhat. Over the years, as he became more and more successful, Perry Mason became more and more conventional in his morality, although he retained his aggressive involvement with his cases, just as Erle, as he became more and more accepted by the Establishment, came more and more to identify with it. The solution to the VELVET CLAWS case depended on an accidental occurrence. It so happens that Eva Griffin's name is really Eva Belter. She is married to the man who secretly owns SPICY BITS for which Frank Locke is only a front. Living with Eva and her husband is Belter's nephew who stands to inherit his estate. In an argument with Belter, Eva fires a shot at him. The reader is supposed to believe that, having fired the shot, Eva became too rattled to find out if she had killed her husband. This is how Erle put it: "Woman-like, she supposed, of course, that because she had shot *at* a man, she had hit him."⁶⁶ So, running from the apparent scene of her crime, Eva believed she had killed Belter, whereas what really happened is that Belter was not even hit. The nephew then came into Belter's room, learned what happened, and realizing that Eva *thought* she had killed Belter he himself picked up the gun and murdered Belter. For a time, while Perry was the most deeply involved in the case, Della had lost faith in him. At the end, after a tearful embrace, she promises Perry that " 'never, never, never, so long as I live, will I ever doubt you again.' "⁶⁷

It was Hobson's idea that Erle should end each of the Perry Mason novels with a paragraph or two introducing the next case. In this way, while Perry wipes the lipstick off of his mouth from the kiss he has just enjoyed with Della and has a final few words with Eva Belter, Della informs him that a client is waiting in the outer office, a woman who is sulky. THE CASE OF THE SULKY GIRL (1933) begins with Fran Celine's being ushered into Perry's office by Della.

THE CASE OF THE VELVET CLAWS is flawed in having a rather implausible solution. THE CASE OF THE SULKY GIRL blatantly breaks Van Dine's twelfth rule: "There must be but one culprit, no matter how many murders are committed."⁶⁸ In order to succeed, the murdered man's partner and his secretary have to collaborate in his murder and in concocting false evidence which then appears to implicate Perry's client. It was, however, the first of the Mason novels in which the solution was arrived at during a courtroom trial. Erle began immediately to dictate his next Perry Mason novel, THE CASE OF THE HOWLING DOG (1934), in which the solution was also revealed during a trial sequence. Erle had some doubts, however, about the efficacy of this procedure. Referring to SULKY GIRL and HOWLING DOG, Erle told Hobson that "there's one technical defect in both of these. . . . and I don't know how to avoid it. The books show the facts leading up to the crime, and then the solution comes in the courtroom. In the first book the characters start from scratch and race breathlessly through to a finish. In the last two books, where the solution comes in the courtroom, it is necessary for a period of time to elapse which gives the reader an unconscious feeling of having lost his stride somewhere along the line. If the period of transition can be handled adroitly enough, and the reader is going fast enough when he hits it, he will simply coast from one period of emotional tension into another, but it's a technical defect, nevertheless. With books that are paced as rapidly as these are, there shouldn't be the interruption of action, but I see no way of avoiding it."⁶⁹ In the meantime, Erle had begun dictating THE CASE OF THE LUCKY LEGS (1934). It reverted to the formula of VELVET CLAWS and the solution came not in a courtroom but in Perry's office. Morrow, however, had serious editorial problems with HOWLING DOG and returned the manuscript to Gardner for substantial revisions. This meant that the end paragraphs had to be altered. Now THE CASE OF THE LUCKY LEGS would introduce THE CASE OF THE HOWLING DOG. THE CASE OF THE HOWLING DOG would introduce THE CASE OF THE

CURIOUS BRIDE (1934). Only editorial problems with THE CASE OF THE CURIOUS BRIDE caused its revision to be submitted after THE CASE OF THE COUNTERFEIT EYE (1935) which led to the curious circumstance that both HOWLING DOG *and* COUNTERFEIT EYE concluded with the entrance of the curious bride. This practice continued throughout the books published in the 1930s and was carried over into the early Pocket Books paper editions which began appearing in the 1940s. It was only in the later Pocket Books editions of these novels that the linking paragraphs were dropped. In fact, some of the subsequent Pocket Books editions were modified in other ways, mostly by way of eliminating some of the one sentence paragraphs of the originals.

" 'I always take risks,' " Perry tells the reporters gathered in his office at the conclusion of THE CASE OF THE LUCKY LEGS. " 'It's the way I play the game; I like it.' "[70] In the course of the story the reader learns that Della Street, as Perry Mason, smokes cigarettes. Perry appears to be almost clairvoyant when he hears that Marjorie Clune left her apartment at midnight and immediately "deduces" that she went to her secret destination by airplane. It is Perry's position that " 'you can't become an accessory by aiding a person who isn't guilty of anything. If your principal isn't guilty, you aren't guilty, no matter what you do.' "[71] Accordingly, Perry takes articles of bloodstained clothing from the apartment Marjorie Clune shares with Thelma Bell and has a cab driver check a hat box containing these items at Union Station. He also has Thelma dress in Marjorie's clothes so as to make the police think that she was the woman seen by a policeman outside the murdered man's apartment. However, the book is legitimately plotted with only one murderer and a sufficiency of well-placed clues so that a reader can arrive at the murderer's identity before Perry reveals it.

The same applies to THE CASE OF THE HOWLING DOG. In Conan Doyle's "Silver Blaze," there is that famous example of what Monsignor Ronald Knox termed "Sherlockismus" when Holmes remarks to Inspector Gregory that he would call his attention " 'to the curious incident of the dog in the night-time.' 'The dog did nothing in the night-time,' " Gregory responds. " 'That was the curious incident.' "[72] Because of Doyle's use of a dog in this story, Van Dine in his last rule felt it a sign of a lack in originality to use a "dog that does not bark and thereby reveals the fact that the intruder is familiar."[73] In Gardner's story it is a howling dog. " 'Sometimes,' " Perry remarks to Della Street, " 'I think I know why the dog howled, and then I can't figure why he quit howling,' "[74] It is only another variation on the idea of substitution which Erle had used in his law practice as long ago as the incident of the Chinese shopkeepers in Oxnard or as recently as THE CASE OF THE LUCKY LEGS when Thelma Bell substitutes for Marjorie Clune. In THE CASE OF THE HOWLING DOG, Perry hires an actress named Mae Sibley to impersonate Bessie Forbes and to approach the cab driver who drove Mrs. Forbes out to the home of her estranged husband and to claim as hers the handkerchief Mrs. Forbes left behind in the cab. By this means when Mrs. Forbes is put on trial at the end of the book and the cab driver identifies her by means of the perfume she wears Perry can produce Mae Sibley, totally confuse the cab driver, and have his testimony dismissed as unreliable. Perry also forges a confession supposedly written by a man he suspects was killed by Clinton Forbes and is buried together with his wife under an addition Forbes had built onto his garage. If, Mason argues in court, Clinton Forbes' dog was known and had loved Bessie Forbes, why would the dog have attacked Mrs. Forbes when she came to visit Forbes on the night he was murdered so that she would also have had to kill the dog? This is a cogent enough argument to have Mrs. Forbes acquitted. Yet the dog that howled and then stopped howling can only be explained by supposing that one dog had been substituted for the other dog, a dog that did not howl for the one that had. At the end of the book, Perry produces the real Prince, which Forbes had placed in a kennel, and he lovingly recognizes Bessie Forbes. Since the only possible culprit could have been Mrs. Forbes, as the wary reader suspects, this means in effect that Perry has defended a guilty client. " 'I have repeatedly told you,' " Perry says to Della, " 'that I am not a judge; nor am I a jury. On the other hand, I have never heard the story of Bessie Forbes; nor has any one else. It may have been that anything she did was done in self-defense. I feel certain that it was. She had to defend herself against a dog and a man. But I acted only as her lawyer.' "[75]

"Much against my wishes in this yarn," Erle wrote to Hobson about THE CASE OF THE COUNTERFEIT EYE, "my better judgment prompted me to tone down some of Perry Mason's so-called 'unscrupulous and unethical tactics,' in order to make it appear that he wouldn't defend a man and try to get him off if he thought that person was guilty of cold-blooded murder without any moral justification."[76] Erle was convinced that the burning question a criminal lawyer asks is whether or not a client can afford to pay his fee, not whether or not he is guilty of the crime with which he is charged. Yet, Erle wanted Perry to be bought by the movies and to make it into the slick magazine market and, therefore, had to indulge in hypocrisy. "Perry Mason confides to me," Erle continued, "that he's willing to turn respectable for a little while if I promise him that someday, after the magazines and the motion pictures get done with him, and the publisher finds he's not as much of a drawing card as he was, he can come out for one book with hypocrisy thrown to the winds and be just a damn good criminal attorney."[77] In THE CASE OF THE COUNTERFEIT EYE, Erle felt he had produced a "fast-moving story, an unusual plot development, a semblance of reality, and a touch of driving characterization."[78] All of the previous books had had an assortment of zealous and narrow-minded public prosecutors. This novel introduced Hamilton Burger as the recently elected Los Angeles district attorney who, in Perry's estimation, is " 'inclined to be a square-shooter. He wants to get convictions when he's certain he's prosecuting guilty people, but he doesn't want to convict innocent ones.' "[79]

Perry's client wears a glass eye. He has a number of different glass eyes for the various times of day and one that is blood-shot for when he is hung-over.

The blood-shot eye is stolen and a substitute of a cheaper kind is left in its place. When the unscrupulous money-lender, Hartley Basset, is found murdered, the missing glass eye is in his hand. An eye-witness claims to have seen a man run from the murder room, his face hidden by a make-shift mask consisting of a sheet of carbonpaper with two holes punched in it for the eyes. In one of the holes only an empty, gaping eye socket is visible. Now Perry's reasoning is quite apt: his client would have had to be a fool so to call attention to his malady, not merely leaving his glass eye behind but punching a hole in the carbonpaper so his blank socket would be visible! Therefore, as Perry explains in the course of the trial in the privacy of the judge's chambers, " 'if some other person in that household had an artificial eye and that fact was not suspected by any of the other persons in the house, he would have gone to great lengths to have made it appear that the crime was committed by a person who had only one eye. . . .' "[80] If we were, however, to submit this case to the modern calculus of probability, it cannot but stagger credulity.

For example, what is the probabilty that one could draw from an ordinary deck of playing cards two cards both of which would be red? If we use a formula in which "h" is equal to the datum that an ordinary deck consists of 26 red cards an 26 black cards and "p" stands for the equivalent that "the first card is red" and "q" for the equivalent that "the second card is red," then "$(p$ and $q)/h$" is the chance that both are red, "p/h" is the chance that the first is red, and "$q/(p$ and $h)$" is the chance that the second is red, given that the first is red. Thus "p/h" $= 1/2$, "$q/(p$ and $h)$" $= 25/51$. In terms of the calculus of probability, the chance that both would be red is $1/2 \times 25/51$. When this formula is applied to a structured card game such as poker, the calculus of probability indicates that one will be dealt at least one pair in every two hands, that one will receive two pair once in every twenty-one hands, and that one may expect to be dealt a straight flush once in every 65,000 hands. When it comes now to THE CASE OF THE COUNTERFEIT EYE, if, at the time the book was written, it was likely that out of a population of 70,000,000 American males there were as many as 100,000 who possessed glass eyes which fit perfectly due to 5% or less socket damage when the eye loss occurred, the reader can use this same formula to determine just what would be the chance of two such persons being involved in the same place at the same time. I bring up the point because Erle objected vociferously and repeatedly that too many detective stories were filled with utter improbabilities. When he saw that THE SATURDAY EVENING POST had purchased Agatha Christie's THE BODY IN THE LIBRARY (1942) to be serialized prior to book publication, he became "particularly interested in it because I saw she had got herself into such a position that, to my mind, there was no *logical* way out. But then she starts her chapter of explanation—oh, my God! But the point is the POST bought this story. More and more readers are reading Agatha Christie. The same is true of about half a dozen other writers whose stuff is full of improbabilities. Most of them get by with these things because they utterly ignore them."[81] It ought to be pointed out, however, in Gardner's behalf that improbability was never so great a problem in his fiction as it was with stories by Ellery Queen, Agatha Christie, and a good many others. Most often the improbabilities in his fiction had to do with time laws which Erle invariably subjected to the exigencies of fast pacing. "Erle violated time laws over and again—whenever he felt that hewing to the fact would slow down his story," Dorothy B. Hughes wrote in ERLE STANLEY GARDNER: THE CASE OF THE REAL PERRY MASON (1978). His editors, she added, never "let him get by with it, even if, as a usual thing, he ignored their findings."[82] Perhaps the most typical example of a problematic time-table can be found in the first book Erle wrote under the pseudonym A. A. Fair. He submitted the novel to Morrow as if it were written by a new author, but his style and approach were readily recognized. The book features a private detective, Bertha Cool, and her assistant, a disbarred lawyer named Donald Lam. It was the first in what would prove to be a long-running series. It is titled THE BIGGER THEY COME (1939). In an incredible time sequence, Donald Lam listens to Alma Hunter's story at the agency office. He then goes to lunch with Alma, after which they go together to Sandra Birks' apartment. Donald has a talk with Sandra's brother Bleetie (who turns out to be the missing man Donald has been hired to find, only in disguise). Donald then talks to Sandra and gets some photographs from her before he returns to the office. Upon his arrival at the office, he notes the time, because Bertha is out to lunch. All of this has occurred in fifty-five minutes! Even in 1939, it was not possible to get around Los Angeles that quickly.

In THE CASE OF THE COUNTERFEIT EYE, Perry makes it quite clear to Hamilton Burger where he stands on the question of homicide: *he* will decide whether or not his client is morally justified. " ' . . . If I should find one of my clients was really guilty of murder and wasn't morally or legally justified,' " he informs Burger, " 'I'd make that client plead guilty and trust to the mercy of the Court.' "[83] In THE CASE OF THE CURIOUS BRIDE Perry has no doubts. " 'I know that Moxley needed killing,' " he comments about the murder victim, " 'if ever a man needed killing.' "[84] It is this conviction which inspires him to tamper with evidence and, while exonerating his client, prompts him to make no effort to reveal the murderer's identity to the authorities. Moxley's apartment house has four bells in the four apartments. Following Moxley's murder, Perry takes a lease on the entire building. In the dark of night, he changes all of the door bells to buzzers. Then he rents the murdered man's apartment to an electrician and instructs the electrician to change the buzzers to bells. During the trial when the jury is taken out to the scene of the crime, the sound of the door bells is distinctly audible. However, when the electrician gets on the stand and testifies that he changed the buzzers and substituted bells, the prosecution's case, which has been built on testimony having to do with bells and not buzzers, is seen to collapse.

There is a second murder in THE CASE OF THE COUNTERFEIT EYE but, generally, there is only one murder in the Perry Mason mysteries which permitted Erle to stress the multiple perspectives which are made possible where conviction depends upon circumstantial evidence that can be variously interpreted. It is construed in one way for the prosecution to obtain a guilty verdict and it must be interpreted in another, even more convincing fashion by the defense. In THE CASE OF THE CARETAKER'S CAT (1935), Perry takes as a client an old man named Ashton who is a caretaker and whose right to maintain his cat Clinker was guaranteed by the terms of Peter Laxter's will. Now that Samuel C. Laxter has control of the estate, he wants to force Ashton to get rid of the cat. When Ashton is found murdered and there are cat tracks on the bedding, it would seem from this evidence possible to set the time of death and identify the guilty person on the basis of opportunity. In the trial sequence, Perry is called to the stand by the prosecution. " 'Keene was undoubtedly in Ashton's room, where the body was subsequently found, at ten thirty,' " Perry testifies. " 'There were cat tracks on the counterpane. The police jumped to the conclusion those tracks were made by Clinker. But Keene said he had left the house shortly after eleven, taken Clinker with him, and, at the time he left, Ashton's body was most certainly not in the room. In place of following the reasoning of the police and acting on the assumption Keene was lying, I decided to act upon the assumption Keene might be telling the truth. In that event, the cat tracks could not have been those of Clinker; in that event Ashton could not have been at the place where his body was found at ten thirty. Yet, since he was undoubtedly killed at ten thirty, it becomes very apparent that he must have been killed at some place other than that in which his body was found. In that event, the cat tracks must have been made by some cat other than Clinker.' "[85] In the best of the Perry Mason books, this multiple shifting of perspectives is at once fascinating to a reader and totally legitimate so that a shrewd reader is able to anticipate how the evidence might be variously interpreted and who the real culprit is. Since Perry does occasionally defend a guilty client, it is not actually possible to exclude his client automatically as a possibility.

In THE CASE OF THE SULKY GIRL, Della Street's age is given as twenty-seven. In THE CASE OF THE CARETAKER'S CAT, the implication is made that Perry is fifteen years Della's senior. Part of the plot in this novel requires Della to pretend to be a new bride with Perry in the role of the groom calling himself Watson Clammert. Perry tells Della that she will have to practice her best honeymoon manners and to quit calling him Chief. " 'Okay,' she said . . . 'Darling,' and, leaning forward, pressed her mouth close to his surprised lips. Then, before he could move, she had shot back the clutch, stepped on the throttle and whizzed away from the curb like a bullet, leaving Perry Mason standing on the curb blinking with surprise, lipstick showing on his lips."[86] In THE CASE OF THE CURIOUS BRIDE, the reader learns that "between Della Street and Perry Mason was that peculiar bond which comes to exist between persons of the opposite sex who have spent years together in an exacting work where success can only be obtained by perfect co-ordination of effort. All personal relations are subordinated to the task of achievement, which brings about a more perfect companionship than where companionship is consciously sought."[87] In THE CASE OF THE SLEEPWALKER'S NIECE (1936) Paul Drake knocks on the corridor door of Perry's private office while he and Della are kissing passionately. Della becomes somewhat flustered. Perry protests. " 'He'd be a hell of a detective if he didn't know a busy executive kissed his secretary once in awhile.' "[88] In the same book, the reader is told that Della has "the carefree laugh of a woman who is sallying forth in life to encounter adventure side by side with a man to whom she has given her loyalty."[89] In THE CASE OF THE LAME CANARY (1937), Perry proposes to Della. She asks him if, as his wife, she would still be his secretary. Perry tells her that would not work, that he could not give her orders since it would not sit well with clients, but that she would not have to work and she would have her own car. " 'That's what I thought,' " she interrupts him. " 'We're getting along swell the way it is. You'd establish me in a home somewhere as your wife. Then you'd get a secretary to help you with your work. The first thing you knew, you'd be sharing excitement and experiences with the secretary and I'd be entirely out of your life. No, Mr. Perry Mason, you aren't the marrying kind. You live at too high speed. You're too wrapped up in mysteries. I'd rather share in your life than in your bank roll.' "[90] At the conclusion of THE CASE OF THE SUBSTITUTE FACE (1938), Della has much the same response when she warns Perry not to become too sentimental. " 'You don't want a wife,' " she tells him. " 'But you do need a secretary who can take chances with you. . . .' "[91] Perry tries for the last time to propose in THE CASE OF THE DROWSY MOSQUITO. " 'We're happy now,' " Della says. " 'You can't tell what marriage would do to us. We'd have a home. I'd be a housekeeper. You'd need a new secretary. . . . You don't want a home. I don't want you to have a new secretary.' "[92]

It would be misleading to attribute these romantic scenes between Della and Perry solely to Erle's view of an ideal relationship between a man and a woman. Mostly they had to do with the fact that Erle wanted the Perry Mason stories to be serialized in the major slick magazines and, because of a broad female readership, romance was a requisite. When Thayer Hobson encouraged Erle to go yet farther in depicting the private lives of Perry and Della, Erle recoiled. It might exasperate readers to keep the two at arms' length, but to marry them would destroy Perry's sex appeal. "How little you know of human nature," Erle wrote to Hobson. "Those who want Della to sleep with her boss are the ones who are afraid she isn't, and those who think she shouldn't are the ones who are certain she is."[93] Yet, the whole situation was not without its personal stamp. Erle preferred to maintain this fictional ambiguity in his own private life. People might speculate all they wanted, he would give them no basis for gossip. However tender and intimate Erle's relationship may have been with Jean Bethell all the years she was his secretary, when they traveled on business he always made it a point that he and Jean had separate rooms on different floors of the same hotel.

Once Erle's books began being reprinted by Pocket Books, it occurred to him that the Perry Mason mysteries might have far greater longevity than he had at first suspected. Henceforth he tried to remove from the books anything which might tend to date them, so that conceivably a person in 1950 might read a book written in 1940 and not be aware that the events of the story had occurred a full decade before. On a short-term basis it was a prudent decision; but what Erle could not foresee, as most could not, was the so-called "sexual" revolution of the 1960s. To a later generation, the fact that Perry and Della *seem* to have no sex life was deemed ridiculous, whereas to an earlier generation to have shown explicitly that they had might have been regarded as offensive.

The primary reason Erle had made his headquarters in Hollywood was his intention to sell his stories to the movies and perhaps even write for the various studios. A short novel titled FUGITIVE GOLD had been serialized in THIS WEEK from 26 May until 7 July 1935. It was purchased by RKO to serve as the basis for a programmer which starred Richard Dix as the central character, an Eastern criminal lawyer who goes West to avenge himself on the gang who murdered his younger brother. In the process, he falls in love with the sister of the gang's leader. In the film, which was retitled SPECIAL INVESTIGATOR (RKO, 1936) upon release, Margaret Callahan was cast as the heroine. Louis King directed. It would also appear that Erle's novel, THIS IS MURDER (1935) published by Morrow under the pseudonym Charles J. Kenny, was placed under an option and Honey included it as a film on the master bibliography she compiled of Erle's literary work for use by Dorothy B. Hughes in writing her biography. However, the Academy of Motion Picture Arts and Sciences Library has no record of such a film ever having been made or released. The novel itself is of interest primarily for the contrast it provides with Dashiell Hammett's THE GLASS KEY (1931). In the Gardner book, a nameless city is variously run by two corrupt political bosses, depending on which party sweeps local elections. The protagonist is Sam Moraine who runs an advertising agency and who is a good friend of the incumbent district attorney. Sam solves two murders with the help of his secretary, Natalie Rice, and the exposure occurs during a hearing before the grand jury. The district attorney divorces himself from corruption by the end of the book and goes about prosecuting the forces of organized crime. To say the least, this was an optimistic view both of American politics and due process. The book so impressed the editors of AMERICAN MAGAZINE that Gardner was asked to follow it up with a thirty-thousand-word short novel featuring the same characters which appeared in magazine form under the title COME-ON GIRL (1936).

The most promising motion picture contract was that with Warner Bros. for film rights to the Perry Mason books. It called for $10,000 to be paid for the first book, $15,000 for the second and third, $20,000 for the fourth and fifth, and $25,000 for the sixth. After that, the contract would have to be renegotiated. These payments were to be made one third upon acceptance, one third in sixty days, and the final third after another thirty days. THE CASE OF THE HOWLING DOG (Warner's, 1935) was the first film to be made. Warren William, who had just appeared as Philo Vance in THE DRAGON MURDER CASE, was cast as Perry Mason. The thinking at Warner Bros. was that now that M-G-M had both William Powell and Philo Vance, a Perry Mason series could supply a viable alternative. Warren William Krech was born in 1896 at Aitkin, Minnesota. After seeing service in a field artillery unit in France, he went on stage with a troupe touring Army camps. After the war, he returned to Minnesota and tried newspaper work. He returned to acting when he secured a role in the road company of I LOVE YOU, a stage success with Richard Dix in the lead. William then landed a position with a stock company in Erie, Pennsylvania. He made his Broadway debut in EXPRESSING WILLIE. Harry Warner signed him as a Warner Bros. contract player after seeing him on stage in New York in 1931. Having had to struggle, William tended to be frugal. When the Warner Bros. salary cuts went into effect, unlike William Powell who quit or James Cagney who, as William, was cut from $1,250 to $1,000 a week and went on strike with Ann Dvorak who was cut from $250 a week to $210, William stayed put. No doubt he agreed with Edward G. Robinson whose response to being cut from $2,500 a week to $1,975 was that somehow he could survive on that reduced salary.

Alan Crosland directed THE CASE OF THE HOWLING DOG. Allan Jenkins was cast as Sergeant Holcolm and Helen Trenholme played Della Street. Mary Astor was assigned the role of Mason's client, Bessie Foley. The scenarist, Ben Markson, did not know how to handle the Paul Drake role, so it was dropped. In variance with the novel, Mason has a large law practice with several attorneys and numerous secretaries. However, the essential plot of the book was retained. Bessie Foley is accused of murdering her husband. At one point Perry has Della impersonate Bessie Foley and Helen Trenholme does it surprisingly well. The implication that Bessie Foley is guilty is the same at the conclusion of the film as in the novel. One difference is Perry's romantic attachment to Della, which is stressed, and they are kissing at the fade.

THE CASE OF THE CURIOUS BRIDE (Warner's, 1935) followed. It was subtitled "A Crime Club Picture" and was directed by Michael Curtiz with more *élan* and polish than had been true of even his highly praised screen version of THE KENNEL MURDER CASE. Margaret Lindsay was cast as Rhoda and Claire Dodd played Della Street. Donald Woods had a supporting role and Allen Jenkins returned, not as the irascible Sergeant Holcolm but instead as Spudsy, a side-kick of Mason's obviously modeled loosely on Paul Drake. Errol Flynn appeared, albeit only briefly and only in flashback, as the murder victim. Perry is a gourmet and his persona, as portrayed by Warren William, differs dramatically from the rough and tumble Perry Mason of the novels. While Perry is preparing crabs à la Newberg at an Italian restaurant, Margaret Lindsay seeks him out. She is in trouble and wants his help. Mason is planning a trip to the Orient. "I wish I was going to China with you, Perry," the coroner is heard to remark. "You would," Jenkins quips, referring to Della Street, "if you were blonde and could take shorthand." Della calls Perry "darling" and is shrewishly jealous of other women in his life. The setting is not Los Angeles, but San Francisco. This time Perry has a one-man office. Barton MacLane was cast as the homicide detective. The comedy routines get so absurd that in one scene Perry and Spudsy sob into their handkerchiefs under the influence of tear gas. Perry maintains a walk-in bar in his office. There is no trial sequence, as there is in the novel; rather, Perry exposes the culprit during an informal cocktail party at his home. As was customary, Curtiz retained the technique of the detailed reconstruction, illustrated by means of elaborate flashbacks, which he had employed to such good effect in THE KENNEL MURDER CASE.

Gardner was displeased with what Warner Bros. was doing to his characters and he complained. But Warren William was playing Perry Mason after his own heart and was enjoying himself. He remarked in the trades that he was once a chicken farmer and had wanted to train a Rhode Island red as an actor. He went through thirty of them. He felt they were the dumbest of the dumb animals, totally devoid of any of the finer instincts. Hal Wallis was happy with his performances and offered him a new contract with an increase in salary and the promise that his first picture under the new agreement would be to play Perry Mason in THE CASE OF THE LUCKY LEGS (Warner's, 1935). Flush with his newly found success, William bought an estate which soon became a show place for guided tours past the homes of the stars. William liked to invent contraptions and even went so far as to patent a lawn suction device.

Brown Holmes, who had worked on the screenplay of THE CASE OF THE CURIOUS BRIDE, joined Ben Markson in scripting THE CASE OF THE LUCKY LEGS. The picture opens with Perry wrapped up and asleep in a carpet behind his desk. Porter Hall wants to hire him, but Perry is sadly quite hung over. He staggers over to his gigantic liquor cabinet and pours himself a healthy eye-opener. Notwithstanding, Hall persists, explaining that it is a complicated case. "Good," Perry quips. "I was afraid it was going to be so simple I couldn't swing any more of a fee out of it." At no point in the film is Perry sufficiently self-possessed to get his client's name right and he has his personal physician come in to give him an examination while Hall is narrating to him his woes. Della Street, for her part, stays in the office playing solitaire and drinking while Perry goes out to investigate. THE CASE OF THE LUCKY LEGS was one of Gardner's most effective early novels, legitimately plotted, with a breath-taking pace; and yet one would never know this from the film. While interrogating two female suspects, Perry raids their refrigerator. For the final explanation, he calls everybody into his office. The physician is there again to give him another physical examination. Perry continues his explanation, reconstructing the crime for the police headed by Barton MacLane, as everyone accompanies him to the doctor's office so he can have some x-rays run.

"I have no temperament to speak of," Gardner wrote to his agent, "I don't want the motion pictures to follow a book slavishly, and I recognize that when they have purchased something, they can do what they damn please with it, but good business demands that when they have ruined a character, we should make plans to protect our own interests in the future."[94] Warner Bros. had also indicated that it was considering a reduction in the rising scale of prices as agreed to in the contract with Gardner. "I made a living before I ever saw Hollywood and I can do it again."[95]

THE CASE OF THE VELVET CLAWS (Warner's, 1936) opens to Warren William as Perry and Claire Dodd as Della getting married. Della has insisted that, in order to be a truly devoted husband, Perry must give up his law practice. Perry brings Della to his apartment where a woman climbs in his bedroom window and, at gunpoint, forces him to accept her as a client. Della becomes so outraged that she lights a cigarette with the $5,000 retainer. The woman is being blackmailed by SPICY BITS, a gossip magazine, because she was seen in the company of a man who is not her husband. Perry leaves Della with his chum, Spudsy Drake, played in this film by Eddie Acuff, who shares his apartment with him. The woman's husband, a millionaire, turns out to be the secret owner of the magazine. This ingredient was taken over from the novel. However, the low attempt at comedy was not. Mason has a head cold which finds him sneezing all through the picture. When the millionaire is murdered, his widow implicates Mason and he is wanted for the commission of the crime. At the denouement, the entire cast presumably has caught Mason's cold and, amid everyone's sneezing, Mason reconstructs the crime and reveals the murderer. The fade finds Della suing Mason for divorce. William Clemens directed the fiasco.

Shortly after Natalie died and two years before his own death, Erle married Jean Bethell. When I visited with her, the subject of the Warner Bros.' films inevitably came up.

"Oh," she said, horrified, "they were just awful. Erle would get so mad at what they were doing to his characters. He thought the pictures would turn readers away, not attract them."

I made reference to all the memoranda Erle had supplied the writers on the subsequent television series on how his characters were to be treated when the plots were not based on any of his books.

"He had control on the television series," Jean Bethell Gardner said. "He could say nothing at all about the Warner Bros. movies, except to continue complaining—which he did."

With somewhat more prescience than the fabled Belshazzar, Erle could see the writing on the wall. His agent sold THE CASE OF THE LAME CANARY to the SATURDAY EVENING POST for $15,000 with an option on his next book for $17,500. In the meantime, Ben Hibbs, editor of THE COUNTRY GENTLEMAN, contacted Gardner through Morrow, requesting that he create a new character for a mystery serial to be run in that magazine. The result was THE D.A. CALLS IT MURDER (1937), featuring Doug Selby, district attorney in Madison City, a small town some one hundred miles distant from Los Angeles. The serial sold for $10,000 and launched a new series both in serial and book form.

Warren William left Warner Bros. for Columbia Pictures where he was slated to star as the Lone Wolf in a series about which I shall have more to say in a later chapter. He was replaced as Perry Mason by Ricardo Cortez in THE CASE OF THE BLACK CAT (Warner's, 1936) based on THE CASE OF THE CARETAKER'S CAT. June Travis was cast as Della Street. William McGann directed from a screenplay by F. Hugh Herbert. Bill Elliott, who had been cast as the drunken nephew of the owner of SPICY BITS in the previous entry, was cast as Sam Laxter. Perry is seated behind his desk calmly working a crossword puzzle despite the fact that his office is filled with people. The notice on his door indicates that Mason is both an attorney and a private investigator. Paul Drake was a character, but his responsibilities seem to be confined to supplying Perry with new crossword puzzles. Guy Usher was cast as Hamilton Burger. The film ends with a courtroom scene, with Perry providing a rather poorly staged reconstruction of the crime via flashbacks. THE CASE OF THE STUTTERING BISHOP (Warner's, 1937) followed, based on the 1936 novel of the same title. Donald Woods, who had been a minor character in the cast of THE CASE OF THE CURIOUS BRIDE, was now cast as Mason with Ann Dvorak playing Della Street, probably the best of all the actresses who had essayed the role. William Clemens directed. Woods wore a moustache. Ann Dvorak kept her remarks appropriately sardonic. A French pronunciation is given to the district attorney's name; in this picture he is Hamilton Bergere. Joseph Crehan, a familiar heavy, was miscast as Paul Drake. The plot of this novel is extremely complex and Perry arrives at the correct solution only through clairvoyance. Nor did it film well. There is a preliminary hearing in the picture, but it proves slow and repetitious.

Left without an attractive actor to play Perry Mason, Warner Bros. decided with this film to drop the series. According to the studio's agreement with Gardner, he could not sell character rights to another producing company for a period of three years. The studio retained screen rights to THE CASE OF THE DANGEROUS DOWAGER (1937), but when it did finally release it the film had nothing to do with Perry Mason. It was titled GRANNY GET YOUR GUN (Warner's, 1940).

Gardner began to have second thoughts about Perry Mason and even considered shelving the character entirely. Thayer Hobson called an editorial meeting at Morrow to discuss the possibility and the result was he advised Erle that perhaps the idea of ending the Mason series with a trip to the Orient for the lawyer and his secretary was a good one, especially since Erle lacked conviction about the character's endurance with the public. Much of Erle's frustration, beyond the collapse of the motion picture deal, was due to THE CASE OF THE LAME CANARY which he did not like. "From THE CASE OF THE SLEEPWALKER'S NIECE on," Gardner wrote to Hobson, "the plots have been weird murder mystery plots like my esteemed contemporaries are trying to do, only with the Gardner touch they became complicated like a Chinese puzzle. HOWLING DOG was about the best of the bunch except for VELVET CLAWS, simply because in those cases the character of Perry Mason was the thing which was in the foreground all the time. I'm going back to the first Mason formulae and write a last story which is going to be simple in plot but strong in characterization and action. I don't know the answer yet, but I do know that when a lawyer gets tangled up in cases with lame canaries and moving vans and silenced rifles and firebugs and trick garages and substituted amnesia victims and what the hell have we, that I'm writing the same old murder yarn under a diffferent tag. No real life lawyer would ever have been mixed in a mess like that."[96] My own objections to THE CASE OF THE LAME CANARY are more succinct. In it there is the corpse of a man who is unrecognizable due to excessive battering. The almost invariable rule of thumb with such a plot ingredient is this: an unrecognizable corpse = substitution of one character for another. Perry's arrival at the correct solution comes about not through logical reasoning, but through clairvoyance—which would continue to be a flaw that would plague Gardner's detective stories. Having devised a baffling plot, he often did not know how to present it so that the reader had a chance of solving it before Mason would reveal the solution. Above all, there are two murderers in THE CASE OF THE LAME CANARY.

However, when THE CASE OF THE LAME CANARY was sold to the SATURDAY EVENING POST, Erle began to have second thoughts about his second thoughts. It occurred to him that, if he could continue to write Mason mysteries which sold to the POST, he would have a viable source of income to replace the loss incurred from Warner Bros.'s decision to drop the Mason series. He wrote THE CASE OF THE SUBSTITUTE FACE. The novel opens on a boat with Perry and Della returning from the trip to the Orient on which they had embarked at the conclusion of THE CASE OF THE LAME CANARY. Erle was "absolutely convinced it was not only the best Mason I'd written, but the best I could write."[97] In this, he was perhaps accurate. It is a legitimately plotted novel, albeit the plot again hinges on a character substitution. Mason's personality is toned down somewhat for the intended slick market. He and Paul Drake do break and enter, but, as Perry explains, " 'for the purpose of leaving a choice assortment of fingerprints.' "[98] Della Street vanishes voluntarily because she fears, if she is served with a subpoena, she will have to give testimony damaging to Perry's client. When he locates her, Perry shows more emotion than had hitherto been his wont. " 'Don't ever leave me like that again, Della,' he said, his voice choking. 'I need you.' "[99] Once again, Mason's fighting character is in the foreground, as when he explains to his law clerk, Jackson, " 'when you start fighting, never try to hit the other man where he's expecting the punch. And when you once start a fight, never give up until the other man's licked. If you can't do it by hook, do it by crook.' "[100] The story actually finds Mason insisting at one point to Paul Drake that the only way a certain character can be smoked out into the open is for them to frame him. The overall pacing, the imagery of the storm at sea, the variety of locations on board ship and in the San Francisco area, plus the inclusion of a romance between two of the secondary characters who are brought together by the end were all effective ingredients which combine to make it a better book and more desirable to the slick magazine market. Unfortunately, the SATURDAY EVENING POST rejected it.

Gardner fired his literary agent and found another one. In 1938, Erle wrote to Hobson that it was costing him $2,500 a month to keep up with his expenses which included "my payments to the wife by way of allowance, the property I am buying for the wife, my salaries here, my insurance, income tax, etc."[101] This notwithstanding, Erle purchased a thousand-acre ranch near Temecula and renamed it Rancho del Paisano. Originally this desert home consisted of a large general room where he could have his secretaries type and file and Jean would cook. Gardner continued to dictate his stories, using first one dictaphone and then another. He had erected a giant windmill to supply power for the installation. In time he had a number of guest cottages built and loved, best of all, to entertain his friends there. He was hired by M-G-M at $1,500 a week to work on a story for the Nick Carter series which the studio had begun with Walter Pigeon in the title role. He had six weeks at this salary to come up with a story which, if the studio accepted it, would bring him another $6,000. He ended up being paid for the six weeks, but his story outline was scrapped. After THE CASE OF THE LAME CANARY, Erle did not make another sale to the SATURDAY EVENING POST until 1941, and then only some short stories featuring a character named Pete Quint. The next Perry Mason serial to be purchased by the magazine was THE CASE OF THE CARELESS KITTEN (1942). In THE CASE OF THE SILENT PARTNER (1940) he introduced the sophisticated Lieutenant Arthur Tragg who came, increasingly, to replace the obnoxious and pugnacious Sergeant Holcolm. This upgrading of the image of the police was calculated to make the Mason stories more appealing, more suitable for the slick magazine market than the perpetual images of corrupt policeman which continued to populate pulp detective fiction. In this, too, Gardner was ahead of his time, and certainly ahead of motion picture representations of policemen.

Erle did manage to have a Doug Selby D.A. story serialized in COUNTRY GENTLEMAN in 1938 and another in 1940. After the SATURDAY EVENING POST ran THE CASE OF THE CARELESS KITTEN, Erle began seriously to court the magazine's editors. Prior to this, he had tried to structure the Mason novels in such a way as to make them appealing to the POST's editors. It had not mattered. The stories had not been accepted. As Erle observed, "with [THE CASE OF THE] DROWSY MOSQUITO I decided to forget the POST requirements, and I think it's an infinitely better story because of that."[102] Much of the story takes place in the desert and Gardner is nearly as eloquent in his descriptions of the Mojave as were Dane Coolidge and Zane Grey in a different genre. At one point Tragg analyzes Della Street's relationship to her employer. " 'She's made being your secretary her life's work,' " Tragg says to Mason. " 'Lord knows all the things she's had to put up with, too. I imagine that with your nervous temperament you're not the easiest man in the world to get along with. I used to think it was a loyalty to you personally that kept her at it, but now I guess it's a loyalty to the job and what it stands for.' "[103] The characterizations are also somewhat more vivid than had been the case in the last several books. What ultimately disappoints is the plot. There are two variations of what were Van Dine plot ingredients. There is a man who is literally murdered twice as occurs in THE KENNEL MURDER CASE—from which arises the interesting legal point: who can be convicted?—and, as in THE GREENE MURDER CASE, two of the prospective murderers simulate being poisoned in order to cast suspicion elsewhere. Of the three people technically guilty of murder, Mason arrives at the identification of the culprits once again by means of clairvoyance. It simply did not concern Gardner in the majority of his books to make the solutions to the plots accessible to the reader. Instead, as he stated in 1941, he wanted to work out "a technique by which loose threads can be tied up as we go along, leaving only one loose thread to be hooked up to bring the whole cloth into a recognizable pattern."[104]

What definitely assisted in easing Erle's pressing financial needs was the start of the Perry Mason series on radio in October, 1943 as a daytime serial broadcast Monday through Friday sponsored by Proctor and Gamble and initially featuring John Larkin as Perry Mason and Joan Alexander as Della Street. For the twelve years that the program was on the air, Gardner was unceasing in his monitoring of it. No matter what else might be going on at the ranch, he would customarily retire alone to his study for that half hour and compile notes, usually objecting to what was being done until Irving Vendig took over as the chief writer, after which all proceeded smoothly.

Gardner was of the opinion that "actually you become friendly with an editor because he buys your material, learns to like it, and finally meets you and then learns to like you."[105] This is what happened eventually with the SATURDAY EVENING POST. With increasingly greater regularity, and especially in the years before its demise, Erle's new Perry Mason novels were serialized in the POST. In the end, he would write eighty-two full-length Mason novels. There was a gradual decline in quality throughout the 'Forties and 'Fifties which became dramatically pronounced in the books written in the 'Sixties. Descriptions and characterization were cut back constantly until they were virtually non-existent. Fairness to the reader became no consideration at all. In THE CASE OF THE SUNBATHER'S DIARY (1955), Mason reveals as the murderer a character not even introduced to the reader except by reference to hi name. On the other hand, in THE CASE OF THE DEMURE DEFENDANT (1956), the story *is* legitimately plotted and an observant reader is provided with the essential clue identifying the murderer. By the time he came to write THE CASE OF THE DARING DIVORCEE (1964), a book of 172 pages in its original Morrow edition, the murderer is not introduced until page 102 and he is not heard of again until Mason pulls him out of a hat through clairvoyance in the final chapter. In THE CASE OF THE FABULOUS FAKE (1969), the last Perry Mason novel to be published, the text is confined almost completely to dialogue and Mason's methodology remains the sheerest legerdemain. It is interesting to note, however, that although Mason manages to secure a sizeable fee for his participation in the case it is also mentioned in the narrative that "Mason was in court all day defending a young Negro lad who had been accused of robbing a pawnshop." [106]

In the late 'Thirties, Hobson set up the Jefferson House division of Morrow to publish the Peter Field books and had Gardner write new introductions to all of the titles which were re-issued by Pocket Books. Each of these editions meant that Gardner's name was on another book in addition to his own and only served to increase his familiarity with the book-buying public. In paperback reprint, Gardner's sales continued to soar.

Cornwell Jackson, who functioned as Gardner's Hollywood agent, was married to Gail Patrick in 1955 when the transition was made to television. Erle put Gail in charge of production on the television series. Casting, I told her when we spoke in her Los Angeles home, had been the key to success in the Perry Mason television series.

"Yes," she agreed, "but I had an angel on my shoulder."

Originally, Bill Hopper, Hedda Hopper's son, was supposed to play Perry Mason and Raymond Burr was to be tested for the role of Hamilton Burger.

"Ray lost a hundred and twenty pounds so he could try out for the Perry Mason part," Gail said. "We tested him in some trial sequences. We knew at once that we had the right man."

Gail wanted Barbara Hale for the part of Della Street. When Barbara's husband, Bill Williams, heard of the offer, he suggested she take it. Barbara objected that the role would be very demanding.

"That's just it," Williams had told her. "No television series has ever gone for one hour week after week about one person. It can't possibly succeed. Sign the contract for its full term. It won't last more than ten weeks."

Nine years later, Barbara Hale was still playing Della Street.

In the beginning, each episode cost $85,000. By the final year, episodes were running $185,000. Raymond Burr was receiving a million dollars a year. Gardner read all the scripts and supervised how the characters and plots were to be treated.

"Erle was concerned," Gail said, "that the courtroom scenes be kept authentic. So we had the same judges, bailiffs, and so on, so the viewers could concentrate on the proceedings."

CBS wanted the new shows to be done in color but the network was unwilling adequately to finance them. In the final episode, Gail had one line of dialogue and Erle Stanley Gardner himself portrayed the judge on the bench.

"You became close friends with Erle Stanley Gardner over the years," I said. "What kind of man was he?"

"His loyalty to his friends was boundless," Gail replied. "He always wanted people to be happy, it seemed. He was sentimental and he loved the outdoors and animals. He was a short man, five feet seven, and he lived in his own world. If he knew he was right in an argument, he still wouldn't push the point. When you visited him, he was constantly trying to feed you. But you ended up doing more eating that he did, since he talked so much. Near the end, when he knew he was dying, of cancer, he never let you know it. You kept silent because you knew he was going to go on right to the end living just as he had always wanted to live, enjoying the things he enjoyed, until, suddenly, it stopped, and that was it."

Raymond Chandler became a visitor at Rancho del Paisano. "He's a terrible talker," Chandler recalled about Gardner, "just wears you out, but he is not a dull talker. He just talks too loud and too much. Years of yapping into a dictaphone machine have destroyed the quality of his voice, which now has all the delicate chiaroscuro of a French taxi horn. His production methods amaze me (he can write a whole book in ten days easily) and once in a while he does something pretty good."[107]

Chandler was, it would appear, a better correspondent than a raconteur and his letters to Gardner were oftentimes an attempt to rate Gardner critically. For example, he once wrote Erle that "I found out that the trickiest part of your technique was the ability to put over situations which verged on the implausible but which in the reading seemed quite real. I hope you understand that I mean this as a compliment. I have never come even near to doing it myself."[108] Chandler was obsessed with the notion that detective fiction at its best ought to be regarded as literature and he told Gardner that, in his view, "when a book, any sort of book, reaches a certain intensity of artistic performance, it becomes literature."[109] He liked the A.A. Fair stories, "especially the first ones, but they have in the end the same defect as the Nero Wolfe stories have: an eccentric character wears out its welcome. The character that lasts is an ordinary guy with some extraordinary qualities. Perry Mason is the perfect detective because he has the intellectual approach of the juridical mind and at the same time the restless quality of the adventurer who won't stay put. I think he is just about perfect. So let's not have any more of that phooey about 'as literature my stuff stinks.' Who says so—William Dean Howells?"[110] This may have been comforting to Gardner, but I do not feel it to be altogether accurate. After all, the greatest characters in literature have always been unusual or eccentric, from Odysseus and Æneas to Don Quixote; and what makes DAVID COPPERFIELD a masterpiece is not its rather insipid hero but all the extravagantly eccentric and fantastical characters with which he is surrounded. Chandler wa slumming and refused to admit it. Gardner, without such pretensions, was the more honest.

In 1946 Alva Johnston interviewed Erle Stanley Gardner for a lengthy article which appeared in the SATURDAY EVENING POST and which was published in a little chapbook in cloth binding the next year by Morrow under the same title, THE CASE OF ERLE STANLEY GARDNER (1947). "One source of Gardner's popularity is undoubtedly the average American's fondness for legal problems," Johnston wrote. "Erle has a nation of amateur lawyers from whom to draw his public. We love nothing so much as the law, except seeing it beaten. The county courthouse is the original center of mass entertainment in America. The big trial lawyers are among the most fascinating peacetime heroes. Belasco said that nothing on the stage ever equalled the drama of a murder trial. Crime is best, but the civil law is also fascinating at every turn."[111] Johnston adduced that "in the Perry Mason stories, Gardner has a formula within a formula. Not only must there be a surprise solution at the end, but that solution must be brought about by Perry's cross-examination of witnesses in a courtroom. It is also practically a statutory requirement that Perry, in his unparalleled services for his clients, should get himself in dire peril of being arrested as an accessory after the fact and of being hauled up before the grievance committee of the Bar Association."[112]

Johnston's article helped further to establish Gardner as a POST writer. It also presented Gardner as a champion of the underdog and this image appealed to a wide assortment of people. "All I know for sure," Erle later reflected, "is that many, many million people read that I was the champion of the underdog. I was therefore literally deluged with underdogs who needed championing."[113] One case which was brought to Gardner's attention was that of William Marvin Lindley who had been arrested for a sex murder, adjudged insane, and then sent to a state hospital where, after spending about a year, he was pronounced sane, returned for trial, convicted in the first degree, and sentenced to death. The date of execution was at hand. Gardner was sent a transcript of the trial by the defense attorney. There was an impending deadline for a Perry Mason radio script, a Perry Mason novel, and the beginning of an excursion to Baja California which would form the basis for one of the travel and adventure books he had started to produce as an adjunct to his fiction. After studying the transcript, Gardner realized that the wrong man had been convicted and that there was sufficient evidence pointing to the actual culprit, notwithstanding the circumstantial evidence, the positive identification by witnesses, and the victim having apparently accused the convicted man. Gardner sent letters to the governor's office and each member of the state supreme court, indicating his reasons for believing that an innocent man was about to be executed. Governor Warren commuted the sentence to life imprisonment in order that a new investigation could be made. In due course, Lindley was proven innocent.

This situation indicated to Gardner the necessity of setting up a Court of Last

Resort which would seek to further the ends of justice. On the trip to Baja, he took along Harry Steeger, publisher of ARGOSY, and together they agreed that Gardner was to present dubious cases to the public and the magazine would stand behind him. A Board of Investigators was to be organized which would assist in the gathering and analysis of evidence. As Dorothy B. Hughes observed, "Erle did not neglect his writing for his work with the Court, he simply added on the extra hours. How, only he could explain. But for some ten years, according to his own figuring, the activities of the Court took up approximately eighty percent of his time. It led to many 'interrelated activities' concerning justice and law enforcement, led him to speaking dates throughout the country before law organizations and law enforcement officials, and to receiving many honors in the legal field."[114] In 1952 Gardner published in detail many of the cases which had been handled by the Court in his book, THE COURT OF LAST RESORT. It was re-issued in 1954 in an augmented edition by Pocket Books and served, for a brief period, as the basis of a television series. When the Court became involved with the infamous Caryl Chessman case, Gardner became disgruntled and felt it was being used for political, not juridical, purposes. ARGOSY also began to lose interest because enthusiasm among readers seemed to be waning. Notwithstanding, it cannot be denied, as Dorothy B. Hughes pointed out, that Gardner must be credited "with helping bring about the Supreme Court ruling that a man on trial, and without funds for legal help, is entitled to a lawyer paid for by the state. And that the accused is also entitled to expert witnesses and to independent experts, and to study the prosecution's pathology and fingerprint reports . . . all at the expense of the state."[115]

It would be impossible to reconstruct from the Perry Mason books a consistent view of Mason's life outside of a particular case. In THE CASE OF THE LAME CANARY, Perry lives in a flat; in THE CASE OF THE SHOPLIFTER'S SHOE (1938), published the next year, Perry lives in an apartment hotel. Della, too, lives in a flat in THE CASE OF THE COUNTERFEIT EYE, but in THE CASE OF THE DANGEROUS DOWAGER she lives in an apartment. What does remain the same is her weight: it is given as one hundred and twelve pounds in THE CASE OF THE SHOPLIFTER'S SHOE and that is what it remains in THE CASE OF THE SUNBATHER'S DIARY. From the latter we also learn that her height is five feet two and one-half inches. By the time Gardner wrote THE CASE OF THE PERJURED PARROT (1939), he could have Perry remark, in contrast to earlier books, that "I never take a case unless I am convinced my client was incapable of committing the crime charged."

Out of one hundred and fifty-one mystery books published in the years 1895 to 1965 which sold more than a million copies, ninety-one of them were written by Erle Stanley Gardner, either under his own name or as A. A. Fair. Because of his efforts in behalf of justice, and in view of the number of competently plotted and dramatically paced detective stories which he wrote, I have no problem at all being persuaded that Gardner deserves to be ranked as one of the most important authors of detective fiction in the Twentieth century. His Perry Mason novels are sober and concerned with the interpretation of circumstantial evidence; his A. A. Fair books are filled with delightful humor; and his Doug Selby stories successfully capture the atmosphere of a small town in the middle decades of this century. If he had a failing, and I believe it to have been a serious one, he never could create memorable characters the way Rex Stout could, so that his books could be read with continued pleasure for a reason beyond and other than the plot. Because the old television series persisted in having an extraordinary success in syndication, it was thought in 1973 to revive the property and so THE NEW PERRY MASON series of hour-long programs went into production with Monte Markham in the title role and Sharon Acker as Della Street. The new format permitted lawyer and secretary to be seen in social situations outside of the office.

"They thought they had to update the characters," Jean Bethell Gardner told me.

"I can understand that," I said, recalling how Barbara Hale had regarded me with a wry smile when I reminded her that never once had Perry so much as patted her shoulder, much less any other part of her anatomy.

"I guess we've changed too much for it to be the way Erle wrote about the relationship," Jean sighed.

Yet the new series was not a success. Perhaps the change had gone deeper than a matter of character; perhaps enthusiasm for revenge and bloodshed had outdistanced real concern about justice. If true, in the long run this would be a far more dismal effect than Perry's and Della's loss of innocence.

However, on 1 December 1985 on NBC a made-for-television movie was run titled PERRY MASON RETURNS. It starred Raymond Burr again in the role of Perry, this time an appellate judge who steps down to defend his former secretary, Della Street, played by Barbara Hale, on a charge of murder. Barbara's son, William Katt, was cast as Paul Drake's son, a private detective working out of Paul's old office (William Hopper died in 1970). It was an extremely well-done enterprise, with sufficient time for development of an intricate plot worthy of Gardner. More of these special films followed. Since this is the case, it could mean that a new generation of readers will have an opportunity to discover Gardner's novels and share his intense commitment to the rightful administration of justice.

HERCULE POIROT AND JANE MARPLE

It is always wise to suspect everybody until you can prove logically, and to your own satisfaction, that they are innocent.
Hercule Poirot[116]

It is really very dangerous to believe people. *I* never have for years.
Jane Marple[117]

While they were still alive, Erle Stanley Gardner's publishers and Agatha Christie's publishers used to compete with each other in claims regarding world wide sales figures and how each was the world's best selling author of detective stories. Yet, posthumously, Agatha Christie's books have virtually all remained in print, while Gardner's have not. Her popularity seems not to have suffered in the least by her death. According to Janet Morgan in AGATHA CHRISTIE: A BIOGRAPHY (1985), "the complexities of the Christie estate make it impossible to establish the total income from her work or to estimate trends. The figures that are available do show, however, that the popularity of her work continues to grow."[118] Through the 1980s, the income from Christie copyrights has been yielding at least a million pounds a year.

In WATTEAU'S SHEPHERDS: THE DETECTIVE NOVEL IN BRITAIN 1914-1940 (1979), LeRoy Lad Panek asked: "Why do people read her books? The novels lack any sort of stylistic distinction, as she would have admitted, her characters are vapid or superficial, hardly any scene setting or atmosphere comes into her novels, and the consideration of moral or social issues is banal. Readers for fifty years have forgotten or overlooked this and identified Christie with Hercule Poirot's idiosyncratic character, and the pace of the action in her plots. Her reputation and popularity [rest] on these things, and Christie knew it; she used Poirot in thirty-five novels between 1920 and 1975, and prided herself on the fresh surprises provided by the least likely character routine."[119] Janet Morgan in her book addressed the same question and concluded that while some "criticize Agatha's work for the flatness of her writing and its lack of emotional and topographical color . . . , her admirers regard this as part of her strength; they defend her work because it appeals to pure reason. Agatha Christie's fascination . . . lies not in appeasing the reader's appetite for sensation or emotion but in satisfying curiosity."[120] In this, Morgan and Panek would seem to disagree. As far as Panek was concerned, Agatha Christie never wrote straight detective novels in the accepted sense, but "camouflaged thrillers. Thriller characters and techniques seep into all of her novels despite protests to the contrary."[121] In Panek's view, "Christie's consistent purpose in her thrillers as well as her detective novels was to shock the readers with the denouement. 'The least likely suspect' formula with which Christie has been tagged is really 'the most surprising solution' formula. She continuously worked out solutions which would surprise, and, because they infuriated many people who hollered about 'playing fair,' shock. When one of the detectives commits the murder, when the narrator is the murderer, when the 'victim' is the one, when everyone in the plot has bashed, stabbed, or shot the corpse, the reader must be surprised and in most cases shocked—in a more emphatic way than one is shocked in the thriller. In thrillers we expect it, for the whole fictional world is hostile to the hero struggling toward his goal. Detective stories supposedly have more normal values, where crimes occur because of explainable, domesticated motives."[122] My own suspicion is that both Morgan and Panek are correct. Agatha Christie's unique ingenuity, and the basis for much of her popularity, is to be found in her ability to persuade a reader that the most surprising solution is at the same time the product of pure reason.

Agatha Christie was born Agatha Miller on 15 September 1890 at Torquay, in Devonshire. Her father, an American, died when she was very young and she was raised together with an older sister by her widowed mother. She was very reclusive as a child and had no formal schooling. What her childhood did afford her was the conviction that there is a sense of order in life. "Meals, punctually served, were benchmarks in the day and the ceremonies of presenting and consuming food were fascinating, especially since she was orderly and fond of ritual," Janet Morgan wrote. "Throughout her life she served formal meals as they were composed in her childhood, with silver and glasses correctly placed, flowers arranged, napkins folded, course succeeding course. A meal was a celebration. Liking the way things were arranged, Agatha was also interested in the way people were ordered."[123] She remained wedded to the British class system all her life.

Agatha learned idiomatic French from a servant who spoke no English. When she became a teenager and her mother sent her to a succession of *pensions* at which she boarded in Paris, she could never master French grammar nor could she take dictation in French; she had learned the language by ear and that is how she spoke it. Later she made Poirot a Belgian. "Of course," Panek pointed out, "Poirot is not really Belgian—he is supposed to be but he is not. He may insist that he is a Belgian to people who mistake him for a Frenchman, but he is wrong. Poirot is really French . . . Christie, I think, . . . regretted making Poirot Belgian since she knew little of Belgians, and because Belgians do not, after all, have a national identity which is well-enough established to provide attitudes which can be successfully burlesqued. . . . What we find in Poirot is a stage Frenchman with quaint attitudes toward life, women, food, *le bon Dieu*, rationality, and everything else."[124]

Agatha had been very imaginative throughout childhood and her mother constantly had encouraged her to write. During the Great War, she worked as a dispenser for the Red Cross at Torquay and between times, on a challenge from her sister, Madge, began writing a detective story. When it was completed, she called it THE MYSTERIOUS AFFAIR AT STYLES (1921). It was sent off to various publishers and John Lane, after sitting on the manuscript for almost a year, offered to publish it. Agatha was to receive "a ten percent royalty on any English sales over two thousand copies and on American sales exceeding one thousand copies, together with half of anything the book earned from serial or dramatic rights," according to Janet Morgan. "The Bodley Head was to have an option, at only a slightly increased rate of royalty, on her next five books. In later years, when Agatha knew her work was popular and her name valuable, she would feel that John Lane had taken advantage of her inexperience—as indeed he had."[125]

THE MYSTERIOUS AFFAIR AT STYLES introduced Hercule Poirot to the world. He is, to be sure, less flamboyant and his mannerisms less eccentric and exaggerated than they would become. "Poirot was an extraordinary looking little man," readers are told by John Hastings who would continue intermittently as a first person narrator until POIROT LOSES A CLIENT (1937), after which he vanished entirely except for his encore appearance in CURTAIN (1975). "He was hardly more than five feet, four inches, but carried himself with great dignity. His head was exactly the shape of an egg, and he always perched it a little on one side. His moustache was very stiff and military. The neatness of his attire was almost incredible. I believe a speck of dust would have caused him more pain than a bullet wound. Yet this quaint dandified little man who, I was sorry to see, now limped badly, had been in his time one of the most celebrated members of the Belgian police."[126] It became a matter of some regret later that Poirot had made his debut as a man already old since he had decades of novels and stories yet before him. This novel was also but the first of a number of Agatha Christie detective stories in which the crime was the result of a joint effort on the part of the murderer and his accomplice. When S. S. Van Dine came subsequently to insist that "there must be one culprit, no matter how many murders are committed,"[127] he probably had had Agatha Christie in mind. As Panek observed, "most writers of the period used accomplices sparingly since using them was too much like the old thriller technique of plotting by pulling rabbits out of hats; the use of an accomplice means that anyone can be the criminal. Christie, however, often depends on pairs of people in her legitimate detective works. Accomplices do their dirty work in THE MYSTERIOUS AFFAIR AT STYLES, THE MYSTERY OF THE BLUE TRAIN [1928], THIRTEEN AT DINNER [1933], MURDER AT THE VICARAGE [1930], MURDER ON THE CALAIS COACH [1934] in which there is a gang of sorts, THE BOOMERANG CLUE [1934], DEATH IN THE AIR [1935], and DEATH ON THE NILE [1937]. Of course it helps the plotting to have gangs—or accomplices. They function as ready and easy ways to unravel plots, and more complicated plots can be produced with an accomplice than with a single murderer."[128] THE MYSTERIOUS AFFAIR AT STYLES had a sufficient success that Agatha could easily follow it with the remaining books called for in her contract with The Bodley Head, some featuring Poirot, some definitely in the straight thriller category.

In 1912, Agatha had been engaged to Archibald Christie who went on to become a colonel in the Royal Flying Corps during the Great War. It was not exactly the marriage her mother had hoped for her, but the two were presumably very much in love and were married on Christmas Eve in 1914. After the war, Archie began civilian life in business and took up golf as a hobby. On weekends, the Christies would travel from their flat in London to the golf links at East Croydon. It was Archie's enthusiasm for the game which prompted Agatha to dedicate her third novel and second Poirot book, MURDER ON THE LINKS (1923), "To my husband." However, Agatha eventually became somewhat disillusioned with the game, not being a very good player herself. "After a while," she recalled, "we seemed to go *every* weekend to East Croydon:

Little by little I was becoming that well-known figure of a golf widow. . . . I did not really mind, but . . . in the end that choice of recreation was to make a big difference in our lives.''[129] In MURDER ON THE LINKS, Agatha took great pains to distinguish her detective from Sherlock Holmes, although the novel is still narrated by Captain Hastings, who is even more dim-witted than Watson at his most bumbling.

"He had a certain disdain for tangible evidence, such as footprints and cigarette ash, and would maintain that, taken by themselves, they would never enable a detective to solve a problem," Hastings informs the reader about Poirot. "Then he would tap his egg-shaped head with absurd complacency, and remark with great satisfaction, 'The true work, it is done from *within. The little gray cells*—remember always the little gray cells, *mon ami!*' "[130] Poirot was even given a foil, a French detective named Giraud in the Sherlock Holmes mode. While Giraud is collecting physical clues, Poirot points out: " 'Here we have a true clue—a psychological clue. You may know all about cigarettes and match ends, M. Giraud, but I, Hercule Poirot, know the mind of man!' "[131] Yet, at the denouement, it is a physical clue—a dagger—which Poirot indicates to be the one essential clue which led him to the solution. Notwithstanding, the novel is more fairly plotted than THE MYSTERIOUS AFFAIR AT STYLES and the reader does not have to contend with an accomplice.

In 1926, the stress in Agatha's personal life reached a high point. Her mother had died and she discovered that Archie had fallen in love with another woman, Nancy Neele, and he wanted a divorce. THE MURDER OF ROGER ACKROYD (1926) had just been published. In AN AUTOBIOGRAPHY (1977), Agatha declared that it was due to a suggestion of her brother-in-law, James Watts, that she had decided to write a detective story in which the narrator was the culprit. In addition, as she later acknowledged, Lord Louis Mountbatten, who did not know her personally, wrote her a letter suggesting that she should write a story in which the Watsonian narrator was the murderer. Both of these claims may have some validity. However, as Panek wrote, "THE MAN IN THE BROWN SUIT [1924] contains a mixture of third person narrative, Anne's narration of her adventures, and extracts from the diary of Sir Eustace Pedler, M.P., a nice enough old codger who is delivering some papers from the Government to South Africa. Only Pedler is the Master Crook, and Christie fools the reader by giving innocent snatches from his diary worked in with other kinds of narration. Here is the germ of THE MURDER OF ROGER ACKROYD, Christie's best known deception, written in a thriller fully two years before the publication of the straight detective story."[132] Dr. James Shepherd, a country doctor, is the narrator. To strengthen the impression that the reader is to accept Shepherd as Captain Hastings' replacement, Poirot has a conversation with Shepherd in which he remarks that Hastings now " 'lives and flourishes—but on the other side of the world. He is now in the Argentine.' "[133] To this he adds the misleading remark that in Shepherd " 'I have made the acquaintance of a man who in some ways resembles my far-off friend.' "[134]

Critical reaction was mixed, some readers having been delighted, some outraged. Among this latter group was S. S. Van Dine. THE MURDER OF ROGER ACKROYD, however, did prove to be Agatha Christie's most popular book so far and one reason for this, certainly, was that soon after its publication she left her Berkshire home and disappeared. The car she had been driving was found abandoned in a field, after having been pushed down a hill. Her coat was on the seat. The episode was soon taken up by the newspapers and three days after her disappearance Archie went to Scotland Yard to seek its assistance. A national search for her was mounted and both Dorothy L. Sayers and Sir Arthur Conan Doyle were asked to lend a hand in helping to determine her whereabouts.

She was located eventually at a resort in Yorkshire registered under the name Theresa Neele. Years later, after consultations with specialists, all that Agatha could determine about the origin of this name was that Theresa was the name of a woman who lived in Torquay and that Neele was the name of the woman Archie loved. Agatha herself at the time had no memory of what had occurred. It was purported to have been amnesia, although Janet Morgan came up with an alternative explanation. "A rarer and more complex manifestation of this anaesthetizing process is the sudden loss of memory known as an 'hysterical fugue,' in which a person experiencing great stress flees from intolerable strain by utterly forgetting his or her own identity. Some psychiatric experts believe this probably happened in Agatha's case."[135] It can be stated with some certitude, I believe, that the disappearance was *not* a publicity stunt; such an action would be entirely out of character at any time for a woman who so loathed publicity. Archibald Christie was granted his wish for a divorce. He remarried and this second marriage proved lasting. Agatha retained his name for her *nom de plume*. She continued to write books and traveled as much as she could, especially to the Near East. Two years after her divorce, her wanderings brought her to southern Iraq where C. Leonard Woolley, the noted archeologist, was head of a joint expedition organized by the British Museum and the Museum of the University of Pennsylvania, engaged in excavations at the site of the prehistoric city of Ur. Agatha had a letter of introduction to Professor Woolley. He entertained her and she was introduced to his assistant, a man of twenty-six years, Max Mallowan. The two of them, in one of those unpredictable occurrences, fell in love, or at least found their personalities sufficiently compatible that they were married in September, 1930. The difference in age mattered little—as, in actual fact, it seems rarely to do. Mallowan was deeply involved in his archeological work and quite content to encourage his wife to pursue her vocation as—to use her word—an authoress. Agatha's second marriage also lasted.

Max was inclined constantly to recommend books for Agatha to read, the Greek and Latin classics and books which dealt with his interests. He was fond of smoking cigarettes and was a connoisseur of wine. On the whole, Agatha loathed the taste of alcohol and disliked its effect. She is known only once in her adult life to have ordered alcohol, as a consequence of a Fundamentalist who came to lunch and condemned the evils of drink with such zealotry that Agatha cheerfully demanded a bottle of beer! She and Max did try to have a child, but the attempt ended in a miscarriage. Later they slept in separate beds, but in the same room. Agatha liked almost best of all to sit in the bathtub, eating apples, and thinking up plots for books. Agatha's mother had always stressed to her that men require constant encouragement and companionship, an example which, except for the interruption of the Second World War, she followed in her marriage to Max and which advice she passed on to younger women.

Following her disappearance, Agatha found herself in the unenviable position of owing her publishers a book and she did not have one. "Fifteen years later, when she asked her agent to hold a manuscript in reserve, she remembered that time," Janet Morgan wrote. " 'I have been, once, in a position where I *wanted* to write just for the sake of money coming in . . . and when I felt I *couldn't*—it is a nerve-racking feeling. If I had had one MS then "up my sleeve" it would have made a big difference. That was the time I had to produce that rotten book THE BIG FOUR [1927] and had to force myself in THE MYSTERY OF THE BLUE TRAIN [1928].' "[136] THE BIG FOUR was a patch-work, consisting of twelve Poirot stories which had appeared in the magazine, SKETCH. As Panek wrote, "the adventure begins with a secret service agent stumbling into Poirot's flat and dying, leaving an enigmatic clue— comparable to what happens to Hannay at the beginning of THE THIRTY NINE STEPS [1915]. Conan Doyle comes in too. One simply cannot see Poirot's invention of a smarter brother, Archille, as anything but a laugh about Mycroft. How could it be serious imitation? And Fu Manchu plays a large role too. In the persons of the Big Four, Christie simply split Fu Manchu up into his constituent parts. One villain is a vastly intellectual Chinaman, another is a master of disguise, and a third is a scientist who perverts science from its pure course."[137] For Panek, the book is a burlesque. Perhaps, in part, it is; but it also indicates that Agatha had read widely in the field of detective and thriller fiction. Poirot, as Holmes, is even given a very special woman, the Countess Vera Rossakoff. "She was, he was wont to declare in moments of enthusiasm, a woman in a thousand."[138] Captain Hastings is back as the narrator, having lived for a year and a half in the Argentine with his new bride. His involvement in this case keeps him in England for more than six months, something that not even Watson's wives had had to tolerate.

One of the authors Agatha Christie read was S. S. Van Dine. He had learned some things from her himself, such as his penchant for drawings and floor plans, which he refined. On the other hand, he preferred unity of place, and, following THE MYSTERY OF THE BLUE TRAIN, this became a characteristic of the detective novels Agatha Christie began to produce in the 'Thirties. THE MURDER AT THE VICARAGE (1930) and PERIL AT END HOUSE (1932) have the strictest unity of place. The latter, in fact, employs rather the same device Van Dine did in THE GREENE MURDER CASE wherein the supposed victim of a murderer is herself the murderer. THE ABC MURDERS (1936) was Agatha Christie's first experiment with the serial murder pattern which was so typical of Van Dine's most popular Philo Vance novels and CARDS ON THE TABLE (1936) used bridge in the solution of the case much as Van Dine used poker in THE "CANARY" MURDER CASE. In his Introduction to THE GREAT DETECTIVE STORIES, Van Dine had written that "Poirot is more fantastic and far less credible than his brother criminologists of the syllogistic fraternity, Dr. Priestley, Father Brown, and Reginald Fortune; and the stories in which he figures are often so artificial, and their problems so far fetched, that all sense of reality is lost, and consequently the interest in the solution is vitiated."[139] Van Dine, in that same Introduction, also had occasion to quote G. K. Chesterton's comments on a detective story by Walter S. Masterman where he said, among other things, " 'He does not introduce about six people in succession to do little bits of the same small murder, one man to bring the dagger, and another to point it, and another to stick it in properly.' "[140] It was precisely this plot which Agatha Christie employed in MURDER ON THE ORIENT EXPRESS (1934). As Raymond Chandler put it in his essay, "The Simple Art of Murder" (1944), "there is a scheme of Agatha Christie's featuring M. Hercule Poirot, that ingenious Belgian who talks in a literal translation of school-boy French. By duly messing around with his 'little gray cells' M. Poirot decides that since nobody on a certain through sleeper could have done the murder alone, everybody did it together, breaking the process down into a series of simple operations like assembling an egg beater. This is the type that is guaranteed to knock the keenest mind for a loop. Only a half wit could guess it."[141]

Already in THE MURDER OF ROGER ACKROYD, Agatha had managed to introduce a character that would have a history and popularity second only among her creations to that of Poirot himself. It is Caroline Shepherd, the sister of the narrator who knows everything that is going on in the village. " 'I was able to set M. Poirot right upon several points,' " she says to her brother. " 'He was very grateful to me. He said I had the makings of a born detective in me—and a wonderful psychological instinct into human nature.' "[142] In THE MYSTERY OF THE BLUE TRAIN, one of the characters, Katherine Grey, comes from a small village about which she can say, " 'You know, things don't happen in St. Mary Mead.' "[143] When the character did finally emerge she was Miss Jane Marple of St. Mary Mead. The year was 1928. "I wrote a series of six stories for a magazine," Agatha recalled, "and chose six people whom I thought might meet once a week in a small village and describe some unsolved crime. I started with Miss Jane Marple, the sort of old lady who would have been rather like some of my grandmother's Ealing cronies—old ladies whom I have met in so many villages where I have gone to stay as a girl."[144] Miss Marple first appeared in novel form in THE MURDER AT THE VICARAGE. It is an illegitimately plotted story in that there is a dual murderer, but the setting has charm and Miss Marple is a remarkable character. The novel is narrated in the first person by the vicar and Miss Marple remarks to him at one point that " 'I'm afraid that, observing human nature for as long as I have done, one gets not to expect very much from it.' "[145] Miss Marple also quotes her Great Aunt Fanny who used to say, " 'The young people think the old people are fools—but the old people *know* the young people are fools!' "[146]

THE MURDER AT THE VICARAGE is dedicated to Rosalind, Agatha's only child from her marriage to Archie, and the two remained close over the years. In the short story, "The Tuesday Night Club" (1928), which marked Miss Marple's first appearance in print, she "wore a black brocade dress, very much pinched in round the waist. Mechlin lace was arranged in a cascade down the front of the bodice. She had on black lace mittens, and a black lace cap surmounted the piled-up masses of her snowy hair. She was knitting—something white and soft and fleecy. Her faded blue eyes benignant and kindly, surveyed her nephew and her nephew's guests with gentle pleasure."[147] In SLEEPING MURDER (1976), the last Miss Marple novel to be published although it was actually written shortly after the Second World War, Miss Marple was described as "an attractive old lady, tall and thin, with pink cheeks and blue eyes, and a gentle, rather fussy manner. Her blue eyes often had a little twinkle in them."[148]

After THE MURDER AT THE VICARAGE and the Miss Marple story collection, THE TUESDAY CLUB MURDERS (1932), she did not appear in another novel until 1942 in THE BODY IN THE LIBRARY. One reason for this was that by 1942 Agatha had become definitely alienated from Poirot and, after all, it was during this period that she wrote the novel in which he died at the end. Beyond this, however, Dennis Sanders and Len Lovallo in THE AGATHA CHRISTIE COMPANION (1984) have suggested, rightly perhaps, that it was "only with the approach of her own middle age that Christie began to appreciate fully the possibilities and appeal of an elderly female detective."[149]

Agatha Christie's second novel was a thriller titled THE SECRET ADVERSARY (1922) in which she introduced the couple, Tommy Beresford and Tuppence Cowley. The Fox Film Corporation in Germany produced a film based on this book called DIE ABENTEUER G.m.b.H. (Fox, 1928). Although *Abenteuer*, which means "adventure," is a neuter noun and should have the definite article "*das*," every reference to the film makes it a feminine noun. The G.m.b.H. is merely the German abbreviation for a corporation with limited liability. No prints appear to survive of this film, but it was the first cinematic adaptation of a Christie story. The same year saw the British release of THE PASSING OF MR. QUIN (Strand, 1928) which was based on the short story, "The Coming of Mr. Quin," which was published in magazine form before it was collected in THE MYSTERIOUS MR. QUINN (1930). The film title added an extra "n" to the character's name. Trilby Clark starred as Mrs. Appleby, Ursula Jeans as the maid, and Stewart Rome was the doctor and the leading protagonist. The plot has to do with the innocence or guilt of a tramp suspected of having murdered a woman's first husband. The picture met with an unexciting box office.

As early as 1928 Michael Morton adapted THE MURDER OF ROGER ACKROYD for the stage, retitling it ALIBI. It opened on 15 May 1928 with Charles Laughton in the role of Poirot. It proved a huge critical and commercial success and marked the beginning of Agatha Christie's equally successful career as a playwright, eventually having to her credit in THE MOUSE TRAP the longest-running stage play in British theatrical history. Laughton came to New York in 1932 in the play, now titled FATAL ALIBI, supported by a young Jane Wyatt. It closed after only twenty-four performances. According to contemporary British accounts, Laughton gave a stunning performance, his Belgian accent flawless, his cross-examinations of suspects deadly, and his exposure of the murderer electrifying. It was on the basis of this success that it was brought to the screen as ALIBI (Twickenham, 1931) with Austin Trevor in the role of Poirot. Unfortunately, not only was Trevor clean-shaven and without any accent whatsoever, but everywhere the film suffered from those qualities so common to the British cinema of that era: lethargic pacing and a lack of any solid or engaging characterization. Leslie Hiscott was the director and the film was produced on a budget of $50,000.

Hard on the stage success of ALIBI, Agatha herself wrote an original Poirot play titled BLACK COFFEE which opened at the Embassy on 8 December 1930 with Francis L. Sullivan as Poirot. Twickenham, which had decided to alternate their Sherlock Holmes releases with Hercule Poirot films, again cast Austin Trevor as Poirot, with Richard Cooper as Captain Hastings and Melville Cooper as Inspector Japp. The plot concerns a scientist who is murdered at a house party after his papers have been stolen.

The two Poirot films did well enough, particularly in the American market, that a third was made, LORD EDGWARE DIES (Real-Art, 1934), based on an adaptation of THIRTEEN AT DINNER (1933) under its British title. Austin Trevor was retained as Poirot, although John Turnbull was substituted to play Inspector Japp. The film somewhat followed the plot of the novel, except that the actress/impersonator did not die. It did very poorly at the box office and Poirot remained off the screen until THE ALPHABET MURDERS (M-G-M, 1966). When THE ABC MURDERS (1936) first appeared, M-G-M actually bought the title, but no film based on it was made for thirty years, and when it was made it was on a different contract.

Frank Vosper adapted the short story, "Philomel Cottage" (1934), for the stage. The play opened at Wyndhams in London on 2 February 1936 with Vosper himself in the lead. As in the case of ALIBI, a short New York run followed. It was filmed twice. LOVE FROM A STRANGER (United Artists, 1937), as it was titled upon release, was directed by Rowland V. Lee. It was filmed in England and starred Ann Harding and Basil Rathbone. The original film is vastly superior in all departments to the remake, LOVE FROM A

STRANGER (Eagle-Lion, 1947) directed by Richard Whorf, which starred Sylvia Sydney and John Hodiak. The plot concerns a young woman who marries a man only to discover that he is a maniac and that he has murdered his previous wives.

Agatha published AND THEN THERE WERE NONE (1939) originally titled TEN LITTLE NIGGERS. The novel, in which ten people are mysteriously summoned to an island, all of them presumably murderers and all of them murdered themselves one by one, proved a sensational success. The idea to bring it to the British stage occurred during the Second World War and in this case Agatha wanted to do the adaptation herself. In the novel, the judge is able to kill the other nine before committing suicide. It is a highly improbable plot and only a number of coincidences and a phenomenal good fortune permits the judge to bring it off. Before he kills himself, the judge writes a confession, places it in a bottle, and it is this which is later found. The police sum it up. " 'We do know *why*, more or less. Some fanatic with a bee in his bonnet about justice. He was out to get people who were beyond the reach of the law. He picked ten people—whether they were really guilty or not doesn't matter. . . . ' "[150] Since the poem had an alternative termination, "He got married and then there were none," Agatha proposed that for the stage version Lombard and Vera, the last two to die in the novel, might live and turn the tables on the judge. This was considered to be good theatre and it was the ending adopted in the stage play and in the film version, AND THEN THERE WERE NONE (20th-Fox, 1945), directed by Rene Clair. Louis Hayward was cast as Lombard, viewed now as a man summoned by mistake; June Duprez was Vera and Barry Fitzgerald was cast as the judge.

George Pollack, who had directed all the Miss Marple pictures, directed the remake, TEN LITTLE INDIANS (Seven Arts, 1965), financed abroad and filmed in Ireland with a setting elaborated by uncredited second unit work shot in the Austrian Alps. This version could in no way compare with Clair's masterpiece, probably the best film made so far based on a work by Agatha Christie; but it was a workmanlike job with a few moments of suspense. Shirley Eaton was the romantic interest for Hugh O'Brien who had the Lombard role. Fabian got killed off with a poisoned cocktail early in the action while Wilfred Hyde-White, who had once played a British Philo Vance, was given the role of the murderer. A gimmick was introduced near the denouement. The film was supposed to be stopped in order to ask the audience to identify the person behind the murders. As disappointing as this remake might be, it is nowhere near the disaster of TEN LITTLE INDIANS (Avco-Embassy, 1975) directed by Peter Collinson. This film had an international cast with much dubbing. The setting was changed to an isolated hotel in the Iranian desert because Iran was among the financial backers.

It is to Billy Wilder that is owed the only film which approaches Rene Clair's AND THEN THERE WERE NONE, namely WITNESS FOR THE PROSECUTION (United Artists, 1957). The short story, written in 1933, is improbable and it was vastly improved at the time Agatha adapted it herself for the stage, opening in London's West End on 28 October 1953 with Patricia Jessel and David Horne as the leads. Patricia Jessel came to New York for the American production, joined by Francis L. Sullivan. It was voted the Best Foreign Play of the season and ran for 645 performances. Agatha sold the film rights for £116,000. Billy Wilder and Harry Kurnitz did the screenplay.

"Arthur Hornblow was the producer on the film," Wilder told me. "He had given me my first chance to direct. We both agreed that we wanted Marlene Dietrich and Charles Laughton for the film version. Laughton was very easy for me to work with. He was, in fact, the best single actor I have ever worked with. You can see from the picture how deeply involved he became with the part. We only changed a few things from the original, such as Elsa Lanchester's role as the barrister's nurse."

On his bulletin board at the time I visited with him, Wilder still had after all the years a clipping of the London review of the picture's premiere. Laughton's performance during the trial sequence made the critics ecstatic and it is still one of his most powerful deliveries, especially when he has Marlene Dietrich in the box and his voice, starting at a whisper, rises to a shaking accusation that she is "a liar," the word reverberating for several seconds.

Margaret Rutherford was born in London in 1892. She became a singing and elocution teacher and in 1924 she attended the Old Vic School of Acting. She made her stage debut at thirty-three as the fairy with the long nose in a pantomime play, LITTLE JACK HORNER. She met Stringer Davis in 1931 when he was a leading man at the Oxford Repertory Company. Although they were apparently in love, they did not marry until 1945. In the course of their consummately happy marriage, they adopted four children. One of them, George Langley Hall, when he was thirty-eight in 1968, underwent a sex change operation and assumed the name of Dawn Hall. The next year Dawn married a twenty-five-year-old Black male. When queried, Margaret Rutherford said she approved of the marriage except for the fact that the groom was a Baptist. Rutherford's motion picture debut was in DUSTY ERMINE (British, 1936). On stage in 1939 she permanently established herself in the role of Miss Prism in Sir John Gielgud's production of THE IMPORTANCE OF BEING EARNEST. She went to New York with the company in 1947. She loved reading poetry and all her life gave recitations in churches and manors. When M-G-M approached her to play the role of Miss Marple in a projected series of photoplays to be filmed at the rate of two a year, she rejected the idea. However, after giving the matter further thought, she changed her mind.

MURDER SHE SAID (M-G-M, 1962) was the first in the series. "I see her as a dear spinster lady," Dame Rutherford remarked of the Miss Marple character, "very much like myself to look at, living in a small country town, who is able to apply her knowledge of human nature to any conceivable crime and come up with a solution, always just one jump ahead of the police. She is eccentric but her passion for justice is very real." She was seventy-one when she began in the role. Stringer Davis, who customarily would help her remember her lines (her eyesight increasingly was failing), was cast in the picture as Mr. Stringer, the local librarian, a role he retained throughout the series. On the set Dame Rutherford would walk purposefully to the mark under the lights and, adjusting a wayward fold in her dress, would nod to George Pollack, the director, and tell him that she was ready when he was. Stringer Davis recalled in the pressbook issued with the film that when they had first met she had been a bit player and he had been the leading man. Now, she was the star and he was lucky if newspaper columnists spelled his name correctly. When they were working, he would rise at five in the morning, glad of the fact that his wife was somewhat deaf so that the alarm did not wake her and he was able to bring her a cup of tea. Although seven years her junior, Davis was completely devoted to her. They would go over her lines before she got out of bed. He would see to it that she had a constant supply of her favorite ginger chocolates or peppermint creams. He would order her lunch, usually soup and cheese and biscuits, and see that it was sent to her dressing room. He would even answer all her fan mail because she believed that if people are kind enough to write they deserve the courtesy of a reply.

Agatha Christie visited the set of MURDER SHE SAID. Afterwards, when interviewers would ask her if she knew Dame Christie, Margaret Rutherford would recall that visit and add, "She's eighty-one, you know. Hers is the world of observation and the pen. Mine—well, it's speech. As I get older, I find I'm slower to pick up contemporary doings. I don't do a great deal of reading any more."

The screenplay by David Pursall and Jack Seddon was based on the Miss Marple novel, 4:50 FROM PADDINGTON (1957). Miss Marple boards a train at Victoria Station. When another train passes the one she is on, she sees a man struggling with a woman, choking her. She reports the incident to the police. She is disbelieved because no body is found. Investigating on her own with the help of Mr. Stringer, Miss Marple comes to suspect that the body is hidden somewhere in the grounds of an estate alongside the railroad track. She hires on at the estate as a cook. A touching human relationship develops between her and Master Alexander, played by Ronnie Raymond, one of the few instances in detective films where there is such a rapport between an old person and a youth. But then, among her special interests, Margaret Rutherford was a parent-confessor at a boys' reformatory, as was Stringer Davis. Six murders occur before Miss Marple solves the case.

By the time M-G-M came to make MURDER AT THE GALLOP (M-G-M, 1963), the studio held exclusive contracts with Agatha Christie, entitling it to screen rights on eighty books and some 400 short stories. Margaret Rutherford was also under contract. While making this film, Dame Rutherford was invited to Buckingham Palace to receive the Order of the British Empire from Queen Elizabeth. "I have no desire to sit back and write my memoirs," she said, once she returned to the set. "I like to make people laugh. I want to make them forget their troubles and it's what I can do best. After all, it's so easy to laugh at an old gal like me, isn't it?" She would frequently cause the cast to break up by dancing a jig and when it came time for her to dance in the film she declined the waltz George Pollack had in mind and insisted on doing the twist.

MURDER AT THE GALLOP was based on the Poirot novel, AFTER THE FUNERAL (1953), with a screenplay by James P. Cavanagh, David Pursall, and Jack Seddon. While making a charity collection at a manor, Miss Marple and Mr. Stringer find the owner dying. They also find a cat, which is curious because the owner of the manor was deathly afraid of cats. Inspector Craddock is played by Charles Tingwell who makes a valiant effort to keep Miss Marple off the case, but to no avail. "Have we ever read a thriller that stops with a single killing?" she asks Mr. Stringer, and proceeds to rent a room at Robert Morley's inn to observe the various heirs. She does eventually expose the murderer. That same year Margaret Rutherford appeared in the V.I.P.S. (M-G-M, 1963) with Elizabeth Taylor and Richard Burton, for which she won an Academy Award.

MURDER MOST FOUL (M-G-M, 1964) was based on the Poirot novel, MRS. McGINTY'S DEAD (1952). David Pursall and Jack Seddon did the screenplay and George Pollack again directed. Miss Marple is on a jury. The police are certain of a conviction. Craddock, still played by Charles Tingwell, has had a promotion to Chief Inspector. It is a hung jury because of Miss Marple. She decides to investigate the murder on her own. A playbill among the murdered Mrs. McGinty's effects prompts Miss Marple to join a small touring repertory company. One of the company is also murdered. "While it must irritate you, Inspector," Miss Marple tells Craddock, "women do sometimes have superior minds." She traps the culprit during the performance of a play they all are in.

MURDER AHOY (M-G-M, 1964) was fourth in the series, but the M-G-M sales department thought it better than MURDER MOST FOUL. Consequently, it was third into release. Since the picture culminates in a sword fight between Miss Marple and the murderer, Margaret Rutherford was given fencing lessons by an expert. David Pursall and Jack Seddon for this picture came up with a wholly original screenplay again directed by George Pollack. Miss Marple becomes a trustee on a board which trains youngsters in seamanship on an old sailing vessel. Most of the action takes place on the ship, exteriors being filmed aboard an actual training vessel on the Thames. In this entry, as in the others, the police are not so much stupid as unimaginative.

" 'Frankly, it's pretty poor!' " Janet Morgan quoted Agatha Christie after seeing MURDER SHE SAID. " 'I thought so that evening in London, but I couldn't say so before Margaret Rutherford. The truth is there's no sustained interest—it's muddling with a lot of brothers turning up in the middle, and *no* kind of suspense, no feeling of things happening.' She had wondered from the start why M-G-M had chosen that particular book, a difficult one, she thought.

Even so, she added, 'I do think it a bad script (*I* could have made it more exciting).' . . . Agatha concluded, 'I have been spared a good deal by keeping aloof from films etc. TEN LITTLE NIGGERS was bad. SPIDER'S WEB [British, 1960] moderate. Only WITNESS was good.' . . . 'Don't think I'm upset by MURDER SHE SAID. I'm not! It's more or less what I expected all along.' "[151] After the third and fourth films appeared, she gave out an interview which was even more negative. "I kept off films for years because I thought they'd give me too many heartaches. Then I sold the rights to M-G-M, hoping they'd use them for television. But they chose films. It was too awful. They did things like taking a Poirot book and putting Miss Marple in it. And all the climaxes were so poor, you could see them coming. I get an unregenerate pleasure when I think they're not being a success. They wrote their own script for the last one—nothing to do with me at all. MURDER AHOY, one of the silliest things you ever saw! It got very bad reviews, I'm delighted to say."[152]

M-G-M wanted Margaret Rutherford to come to Hollywood in January, 1964 to appear in a picture. She refused to go. The next Miss Marple picture scheduled was THE BODY IN THE LIBRARY based on the Miss Marple novel. M-G-M executives scrapped plans for making it when Dame Rutherford would not come to Hollywood and her option was not renewed. Beyond their pique, the M-G-M executives were also aware that the Miss Marple pictures had not been as successful with American audiences as had originally been hoped.

This suited Margaret Rutherford. She and Stringer Davis lived in their fifth home since their marriage, Elm Close, and on the surrounding lawns the couple built a bird sanctuary. It was their intention to have an open air theatre. In 1968, Dame Rutherford tripped over a rug and broke her leg while filming in Italy. Two hip fractures finally led to complications. She died on 22 May 1972. "Old age?" she had once said. "That's nothing to be ashamed of. I'm beginning to be rather proud of it." It was in her old age that she won international recognition.

THE ALPHABET MURDERS was based on a screenplay by David Pursall and Jack Seddon. It was directed by Frank Tashlin. No one knew, apparently, quite how to deal with Hercule Poirot. Consequently the film was done in a camp humor style. Tony Randall with a hairpiece played the aging Poirot who has had to give up smoking and who is followed every step of the way by Robert Morley who is connected with the Home Office and has been assigned to look after Poirot's safety. The plot is complex and involuted, done in the continental manner where, if one should lose the story line, it really should not matter because the story is not important anyway. There is some good comedy in it. When Poirot is being released from jail, Margaret Rutherford and Stringer Davis make a cameo appearance as Miss Marple and Mr. Stringer. Some of the effects are also enterprising, such as the use of mirrors when Morley and Randall first talk to each other. Yet, as a detective film, it is a dismal failure.

M-G-M next proposed to film MURDER ON THE ORIENT EXPRESS. This

Agatha Christie found wholly unacceptable. She told her agent that the book had taken "a lot of careful planning and technique and to have it possibly transformed into a rollicking farce with Miss Marple injected into it and probably acting as the engine driver, though great fun, no doubt, would be *somewhat* harmful to *my* reputation!"[153] The M-G-M contract ended and it was several years before the novel was brought to the screen. Albert Finney was cast as Poirot in MURDER ON THE ORIENT EXPRESS (Paramount, 1974), produced by EMI in Great Britain and directed by Sidney Lumet. The stellar array of suspects included Lauren Bacall, Ingrid Bergman, Jacqueline Bisset, Sean Connery, Sir John Gielgud, Anthony Perkins, Vanessa Redgrave, Michael York, and as the murder victim Richard Widmark. Ingrid Bergman won an Academy Award for her portrayal. "The only other Poirot I have ever met was Charles Laughton," Finney commented later, "who introduced me to Agatha Christie when he played the Belgian detective on the stage. Being portly himself, Laughton was the right shape for the role, but in order to get the short, solid look I needed as Agatha Christie's elder statesman of criminologists, I wore body padding, a T-shirt draped with cotton wool. I also had to have padded thighs to make me look wide so that my height appeared less. Facially the transformation was achieved with a false nose and padded cheeks to achieve the egg-shaped look. By far the most important part of the make-up was the gleaming black hair and the meticulously trimmed, trained, and waxed period moustache."

At the London premiere, Dame Christie was greeted by Queen Elizabeth. Pictures were taken. The film did splendid business everywhere, so much so that EMI decided to continue making Poirot films. DEATH ON THE NILE (Paramount, 1978) directed by John Guillermin and EVIL UNDER THE SUN (EMI, 1982) directed by Guy Hamilton both starred Peter Ustinov as Poirot. Neither is the equal of MURDER ON THE ORIENT EXPRESS in sophistication and effective filmmaking, but each has its virtues. The box-office receipts, however, declined with each film, as well with THE MIRROR CRACK'D (EMI, 1980) with Angela Lansbury as Miss Marple and another star-studded cast which included Elizabeth Taylor, Kim Novak, and Rock Hudson.

Yet, whatever effect changing life-styles may have on the viability of filming Agatha Christie's stories, her world-view was already old-fashioned when the first talking films were made featuring Hercule Poirot. George Grella perhaps said it best in his essay, "Murder and Manners: The Formal Detective Novel" (1976), when he observed that "finding a meaning in the tiniest clue enables the detective to know the truth; thus, his universe seems explainable, the typical cosmos of English fiction, unlike the extravagant and grotesque realities of the American novel. . . . The detective novels of the Golden Age never mention the tensions and dangers that threatened the precarious stability of the 'Twenties and 'Thirties. They say nothing of the Depression, the social, economic, and political unrest of that time, but choose to remain within the genteel luxury of an aristocratic world, suffering the intrusions of the police and the initially suspected nameless vagabond before the detective hero turns suspicion on society. Except for these brief intrusions, themselves conventional, the great concern of the detective novel is centripetal; it is a formal minuet leading to an inescapable conclusion, as mannered and unreal as the masque, the sonnet, or the drawing room farce."[154]

This was the world in which Agatha Christie lived spiritually and, at her various homes but especially at Greenway, the way of life she continued to live. At Greenway there were long grassy slopes, top gardens, a boathouse, servants, and a full-dress Sunday luncheon and full-dress dinners. "Their style is not graceful or magical," Janet Morgan wrote about Agatha Christie's detective stories, "their characters are stereotypes, the plots often implausible, but her work is sincere and, for all its contrivance, spontaneous. Agatha minded greatly about the way people should treat one another; she had firm views about good and evil, justice and mercy, innocence, cruelty and revenge. She said what she felt in her books and, increasingly as she grew older, her plays."[155] She once told an interviewer that she was of the same opinion as Dorothy Sayers "that the detective story is the direct successor of the old Morality Play. It is the triumph of good over evil—the deliverance of the innocent from the aggressor—that is what makes it exciting."[156]

Agatha Christie died peacefully on 12 January 1976. In her eighties, as captured in photographs by Lord Snowden, she had attained an attractiveness denied her in earlier years by that curiosity of nature which sometimes rights in older age what it neglected to do in youth. She requested that these lines of Edmund Spenser be quoted at her funeral service:

> Is not short pain well borne, that brings long ease,
> And layes the soule to sleepe in quiet grave?
> Sleepe after toyle, port after stormie seas,
> Ease after war, death after life does greatly please.

She had lived all her life in a world created by her own imagination and in her last years her books and plays were earning her $10,000 a week in royalties, more money than she literally knew what to do with and from which she often provided generously for others. When asked to contrast the modern world with the Victorian Age in which she had been nurtured, she concluded that there were few advantages to the earlier period but there was one of special significance: "Leisure. Our greatest loss. The one really valuable thing in life—a possession that is yours to do what you like with. Without it, where are you?"[157]

4

Oriental Detectives

I seek to win reputation as philosopher, not as fortuneteller.

Charlie Chan[1]

I

It is somewhat a pity that Earl Derr Biggers did not live long enough to realize the full measure of fame and bounty earned by his creation of Charlie Chan. Biggers was born in 1884 at Warren, Ohio. He graduated from Harvard in 1907. Apparently his professors were shocked by his irreverence for the English literary classics. He preferred such story-tellers as Rudyard Kipling and Richard Harding Davis to Oliver Goldsmith. His affinity for the poetry of Franklin P. Adams prompted his classmates to request he leave the room when, at twilight, they elected to read Keats to one another. Biggers secured employment writing a humorous column for the BOSTON TRAVELER, but he did not care much about it. He was promoted to drama critic. He offended so many readers with his devastating critiques of plays he did not like that he was eventually fired. He tried his hand at a novel which he titled SEVEN KEYS TO BALDPATE (1913). It was set at a deserted summer resort in the midst of winter and concerned the secrets of several individuals who suddenly show up and meet under mysterious circumstances at the resort. Billy Magee is the romantic hero, an author of romances who wants to write serious fiction. He has come to the deserted resort on Baldpate to be alone, but in the course of the story he meets a young woman who turns out to be a newspaper reporter. They fall in love at the end, much as Biggers fell in love with Eleanor Ladd, who also worked for the BOSTON TRAVELER, and whom he married. The novel enjoyed a success with the reading public and that same year it was adapted for the stage by George M. Cohan who starred in the production. Subsequently, it served as the basis for no less than five motion picture adaptations, the most recent released by RKO in 1947.

Biggers had found his metier in its combination of romance and melodrama. He followed it with another successful novel, LOVE INSURANCE (1914), and then a short novel which stressed mystery, THE AGONY COLUMN (1916), which was serialized in THE SATURDAY EVENING POST. Biggers' association with the POST continued over the years and all six of his novels featuring Charlie Chan were serialized in its pages prior to book appearance. Following publication of SEVEN KEYS TO BALDPATE and his marriage, Biggers moved with his wife to New York. Many years after his death, Eleanor Biggers commented that her husband employed no secretaries, notes, or research files; and he never kept copies of his work. In view of the success of his first novel as a stage play, Biggers turned his immediate attention to writing plays, among them INSIDE THE LINES (1915), A CURE FOR CURABLES (1917), THREE'S A CROWD (1919), and SEE-SAW (1919) based on LOVE INSURANCE but with a musical format. These stage plays enjoyed a varying reception, but all in all Biggers' sentiments were well in keeping with the inclinations of the times which seemed to have a penchant for mystery and romance. After the Great War, in search of a more temperate climate, Biggers moved to Pasadena, California.

FIFTY CANDLES (1926) was serialized in THE SATURDAY EVENING POST. The short novel was a romance; but, more than that, it was set for the most part in San Francisco and concerned a murder. Among the characters are two Chinese, one of them a wealthy businessman, the other a manservant who has been attached to the victim. In order to escape deportation from Honolulu years before, the manservant had indentured himself to the victim, Henry Drew. When, however, the manservant, who goes by the name Hung Chin-chung, fell in love, Drew and his partner, Dr. Su Yen Hun, prevented the marriage by forcing the girl to marry the partner. Drew and Su are murdered on the same night, by Hung Chin-chung who plans then to escape with Su's widow. Rather than face imprisonment, Hung commits suicide with a knife originally stolen from the narrator. "He was at the end of the path at last, that Chinese boy born near Queen Emma's yard, on the beach at Waikiki. Looking down at him I was conscious of a feeling of pity—until I recalled the knife he had taken from my luggage. Then for the first time I realized all I had escaped. And quicker than the tule-fog lifting from San Francisco all gloomy apprehension vanished from my heart."[2] The narrator is now able to declare his intentions to the heroine with whom he fell in love at first sight.

A year prior to the publication of FIFTY CANDLES, Biggers had already decided to write a detective story featuring a Chinese detective. "Sinister and wicked Chinese are old stuff," Biggers once remarked, "but an amiable Chinese on the side of law and order had never been used."[3] The result was THE HOUSE WITHOUT A KEY (1925), the first of the novels to feature Charlie Chan. It was serialized in THE SATURDAY EVENING POST. While he was at work on it, Biggers had perused several Honolulu newspapers and had come across a reference to a police case effectively solved by two Oriental policemen named Chang Apana and Lee Fook. He used them as a model for Detective-Sergeant Chan. Charlie is scarcely a central character in this book; in fact, he did not even make his appearance in the first POST installment which appeared on 24 September 1925. The major theme of the novel, other than who killed Dan Winterslip one night as he slept on his lanai, is just how the easy-going life of the islands will affect John Quincey Winterslip who has arrived from Boston and who falls in love with a girl who has been schooled on the mainland but who grew up in Honolulu. Given John Quincey's background, much of the tension is caused by the clash of his Boston values with the mode of life to be found in Hawaii. The murderer is exposed at the end, but the structure is not such that his exposure is to be seen as a challenge to the reader. Charlie believes in what is termed "the essential clue," in this case a wrist watch which glows in the dark.

Whatever his minor status in the book, it was Charlie Chan who immediately captured the public's fancy and Biggers rapidly produced a sequel in THE CHINESE PARROT (1926). This novel opens in San Francisco but soon changes its location to the California desert which Biggers had been introduced to by Senator Charles C. Cook of Connecticut. For most of the story, Charlie is disguised as a Chinese cook who speaks pidgin English. The solution to the mystery is so obvious that the plot appears to move at a snail's pace and even when it comes to the denouement it is handled by means of that creaky old device of having one criminal expose another criminal since any real proof of wrong-doing is absent. However, near the end of the novel, Biggers had occasion to describe a movie company on location. It was rather prophetic for Charlie who is playing a role most of the time. That same year Pathé had purchased screen rights for THE HOUSE WITHOUT A KEY and adapted it for the screen as a chapter play in ten episodes.

Allene Ray and Walter Miller were a tremendously popular serial team. Pathé evidently thought Biggers' tale an ideal property for an action/mystery adventure film. Frank Leon Smith, chief scenarist for the Pathé serials, did the screen adaptation and Spencer Gordon Bennet directed. George K. Kuwa, billed twelfth in the credits, was cast as Chan. The existence of evidence of treachery contained in a chest, a minor plot ingredient in the novel, was magnified in significance in the film to the point where Walter Miller spent most of his time in its pursuit. Frank Lackteen, who almost invariably menaced Allene Ray in Pathé serials, played the villain.

"No prints of THE HOUSE WITHOUT A KEY [Pathé, 1926] are known to survive," I once remarked to Spencer Gordon Bennet as we spoke in an office at the old Columbia Pictures lot on Gower Street. "I guess I am going to have to rely on your memory."

"Well, I can tell you this," Bennet responded. "It was no Charlie Chan picture. Chan was just a detective. He wasn't that involved in the action. In fact, we were a couple of chapters into the story before he even made an appearance."

"Warner Oland didn't suggest himself to you for the role?"

"Not to me, no." Bennet shook his head. "Of course, he specialized in playing Orientals, usually villains. I was at Pathé in New York when he worked in THE YELLOW ARM [Pathé, 1921]. I remember I was given the job of finding him when he disappeared. Warner was a heavy drinker and might vanish for days on end. I spent nearly a week going through every bar on Third Avenue before I finally found him. We were then able to sober him up and shoot his scenes. He was a splendid actor. The part in THE HOUSE WITHOUT A KEY would have been too small for him, even if somebody had suggested he be cast for it."

George K. Kuwa was a Japanese. When Universal Pictures bought screen rights to THE CHINESE PARROT, the studio cast another Japanese actor, Kamiyama Sojin, as Chan. J. Grubb Alexander did the screenplay. Paul Leni, the German director, was given this picture as his second directorial assignment in Hollywood. There was some tinkering with the plot—the string of pearls, kept by Charlie on his person in the novel, is as much an object for pursuit in this film as the chest is in THE HOUSE WITHOUT A KEY—but Chan is a major character and Sojin's performance was generally praised in the trades.

BEHIND THAT CURTAIN (1928) was Biggers' third Chan novel and probably his best. Charlie's character was becoming amplified and he began now to come up with pithy sayings which were later termed Chanograms. "Falling hurts least those who fly low," Charlie remarks on one occasion.[4] There are definite impossibilities in the plot, not merely improbabilities, such as when the assistant district attorney claims that she will arrange with the postal authorities to have the mail sent to one of the suspects routed through her office. The victim is Sir Frederic Bruce and the solution to his murder is to be found in two events, seemingly unrelated, which happened many years in the past. Charlie, who had nine children in THE HOUSE WITHOUT A KEY, now has eleven, the most recent being a young son. The heroine in THE CHINESE PARROT was a very independent woman and Miss Morrow, the assistant district attorney, is no less so in this novel. Biggers dedicated the book to his wife, Eleanor, calling her "the only critic whom I love."[5] It was an accepted part of THE SATURDAY EVENING POST's editorial policy for serials that there be a romance in the story so as to keep female readers interested. There is such a romance at the center of all the Chan novels. In BEHIND THAT CURTAIN, it is between Barry Kirk, at whose apartment the murder occurs, and Miss Morrow. Miss Morrow is assigned to the case, but she and Chan are a fit subject for ridicule by Captain Flannery of the police. " 'A woman and a Chinaman,' " he remarks. " 'Hell, I'll be the joke of the force.' "[6] Predictably, of course, it is Chan, and not Captain Flannery, who solves the case. Another ingredient which was to become standard fare in the film versions is that the culprit is shown to be the least suspicious character. "Charlie looked grimly at Flannery. 'Now the truth arrives,' he said. 'That you once listened to a Chinaman is, after all, no lasting disgrace.' "[7] Although the plot was substantially changed, BEHIND THAT CURTAIN (Fox, 1929) was the first Chan film to be produced by the Fox Film Corporation. Irving Cummings directed with E. L. Park, billed last, in the role of Charlie Chan.

The fourth Chan novel was THE BLACK CAMEL (1929), its title having been inspired by an old Eastern maxim, "Death is the black camel that kneels unbid at every gate." By this time, Chan had been made an inspector with the Honolulu Police and, as with THE HOUSE WITHOUT A KEY, the setting is Hawaii. The plot involves the fatal stabbing of movie star Shelah Fane in her pavilion. Behind her death is the unsolved murder of a Hollywood actor three years before, a murder which bears an intentional resemblance to the circumstances surrounding the death of film director William Desmond Taylor. Chan has his share of prejudice against the Japanese, the equivalent to Anglo-American bias against Orientals in general, and, in an attempt at humor, he is given a Japanese assistant named Kashimo. The character is important since it obviously was the prototype for the roles assigned to Charlie's various offspring in subsequent Chan films.

THE BLACK CAMEL was not brought to the screen at once. Instead, it was Biggers' fifth novel, CHARLIE CHAN CARRIES ON (1930), which was filmed next. Henry Raleigh illustrated it for THE SATURDAY EVENING POST and his drawings showed Chan to be fatter than had previous artists, his eyebrows more dramatically sloped, and for the first time he sports a moustache. Perhaps Warner Oland had served unconsciously as the model. At any rate, Fox in an inspired bit of casting chose Oland for the role. Oland was born in 1880 in Umea, Sweden. He came to the United States when he was thirteen, making his stage debut with Sarah Bernhardt's company. Following a season with Nazimova, Oland lost all he had saved producing his own productions at the Hudson Theatre in New York. He drifted into films, beginning with JEWELS OF THE MADONNA (Fox, 1909) which starred Theda Bara. While he worked for several companies in varying roles, much of his movie work during the silent era was for Fox. He was cast as the Satanic devil doctor in THE MYSTERIOUS DR. FU MANCHU (Paramount, 1929), starred in THE RETURN OF DR. FU MANCHU (Paramount, 1930), and did a cameo as Fu Manchu in PARAMOUNT ON PARADE (Paramount, 1930).

CHARLIE CHAN CARRIES ON (Fox, 1931) follows the novel to the extent that Charlie does not appear until midway through the story—the murder victim being Inspector Duff of Scotland Yard, a character first introduced in BEHIND THAT CURTAIN. Warner Oland was credited third. Marguerite Churchill was the headliner. William Holden and George Brent both had roles. The series of murders on a world cruise is perpetrated by C. Henry Gordon in an effort to avenge himself on Jason Robards because many years before the story opens Robards stole the affections of Gordon's wife. Biggers liked to find the solutions to his mysteries in events in the past. This ingredient was one of the first to go when Fox began producing original screenplays. Chanograms were already present in abundance. At one point, Charlie declares "only a very brave mouse will make its nest in a cat's ear." Later he asserts that "he who feeds the chicken deserves the egg" and that "only a very sly man can shoot off a cannon quietly." The reviewer for the NEW YORK TIMES remarked that the audience was so charmed by the Chanograms that it could have listened to Charlie Chan for another hour. At the end, in a gesture so typical of Oland's approach to the role, Chan takes the audience into his confidence. He says of the young hero and heroine, "Pam and Mark are to be one—more later."

Hamilton MacFadden directed CHARLIE CHAN CARRIES ON. The film was such a success that Fox immediately purchased rights to THE BLACK CAMEL and adapted it for the screen with Chan as the central character. Dorothy Revier was cast in the role of Shelah Fane. However, Warner Oland's characterization dominated the picture with Bela Lugosi's portrayal of the psychic, Tarnaverro, being the only really competitive role. In making Shelah the murderer of the celebrated actor in the book, changed to a film director in the photoplay, it would seem that both Biggers and the Fox screenwriters may have been suggesting that Mabel Normand was at the bottom of the Taylor affair, as rumors had it in Hollywood at the time. Mabel Normand died in 1930. C. Henry Gordon returned as a red herring in THE BLACK CAMEL (Fox, 1931).

THE KEEPER OF THE KEYS (1932) was Biggers' last novel. Charlie Chan made his appearance on the second page. The story is set at Lake Tahoe during the winter. Chan's penchant for aphorisms seems to have increased with his creator's exposure to Warner Oland's screen portrayal. One of the subsidiary themes is evoked by Chan's interaction with Sing, a Chinese servant who works for Dudley Ward who has invited all the former husbands of opera star, Ellen Landini, to his isolated lake-side home. Sing speaks pidgin English and has little respect for Charlie. " 'I traveled with the current,' " Charlie explains. " 'I was ambitious. I sought success. For what I have won, I paid the price. Am I an American? No. Am I, then, Chinese? Not in the eyes of Ah Sing.' "[8] When Landini is murdered, Charlie helps the local sheriff find the culprit. One of the more interesting characters is the current sheriff's father, a man now blind, who was for many years himself sheriff of the district. A fatalism has crept into Charlie's outlook. As he puts it to one character, " 'I am sorry to remind you that, though we walk a thousand miles along the way with a friend, moment of good-by is still inevitable.' "[9] By the end of the story, the case is solved and the young sheriff has found himself a wife. " 'Three things the wise man does not do,' " Charlie counsels him. " 'He does not plow the sky. He does not paint pictures on the water. And he does not argue with a woman.' "[10]

The book was adapted for the legitimate stage, although it ran only three weeks before closing. Curiously, it was the only Charlie Chan novel not ever to be filmed. Shortly after its publication, Biggers died of heart disease. Warner Oland, who had recently appeared as an Austrian officer opposite Marlene Dietrich in SHANGHAI EXPRESS (Paramount, 1932), expressed his sincere regret that he had not met Biggers. Yet, for Oland, the Chan role was becoming so much a part of his intrinsic personality that he began increasingly to limit his screen work to Chan films. Biggers himself had been no less enchanted with the character. He went so far as to inscribe his books with Charlie's signature, very different from his own. On his Charlie Chan New Year's card, he told friends: "For the New Year I warmly wish you plenty rice—since even the sunrise is without beauty to the hungry; plenty health—since even the road down hill is hard for the sick; and plenty peace of mind—since trouble follows the restless like flies in the fifth month."

Biggers was still alive when CHARLIE CHAN'S CHANCE (Fox, 1932) directed by John Blystone was released. It was a remake of BEHIND THAT CURTAIN. There was a lot of talk and little suspense. H. B. Warner played the retired Scotland Yard inspector and Marion Nixon was cast as a masked dancer. More than ever, it was Oland's portrayal which made the picture work.

Fox acquired rights to THE HOUSE WITHOUT A KEY and it formed the basis for the only entry the next year, CHARLIE CHAN'S GREATEST CASE (Fox, 1933). As in the novel and the former photoplay, Chan was introduced late in the film. However, the trades, by this time alert to Oland's popularity, recommended exhibitors stress his presence in the film. CHARLIE CHAN'S COURAGE (Fox, 1934) followed, based on THE CHINESE PARROT, Fox having bought screen rights from Universal. With this entry, John Stone was appointed associate producer for the series by Sol Wurtzel. Stone was born in New York in 1888 and he began in the industry as a screenwriter for Fox, specializing in Westerns. Stone as much as anyone was constantly thinking up Chanograms. Seton Miller, the scenarist on CHARLIE CHAN'S COURAGE, followed the novel and Oland varied his performance during those sequences when he had to play a Chinese cook.

Production under Stone was increased to three Chan films a year. Fox had originally intended to make only four Chan pictures. Oland was supposed to be paid $10,000 a picture. He got $10,000 for his first. The popular response prompted him to ask for $12,500 for the second one. He wanted $20,000 for the third, but the studio kept him at $12,500 an entry until CHARLIE CHAN AT THE CIRCUS (20th-Fox, 1936), at which time he contracted to do three Chan films at $20,000 a picture. When his option was picked up again, he signed for his last three Chan films at $30,000 a picture.

Now that the original stories were exhausted, Stone came up with the idea of starting Charlie on a round the world trip of murder investigations. CHARLIE CHAN IN LONDON (Fox, 1934) was the first stop. Eugene Forde directed it. E. E. Clive appeared as a Scotland Yard inspector and a young Ray Milland was among the suspects. It was the longest film in the series, with a running time of eighty minutes. While it was slow-moving at times, it introduced several new ingredients to the formula. Instead of Charlie tricking the guilty party through a ruse or physical action, the suspects were now gathered together for a reconstruction of the crime. Charlie's presentation of the evidence would conclude with the verbal confrontation: "You . . . are . . . murderer." A love interest between two of the characters, so much a staple of the novels, became secondary and eventually unimportant. One reason for this was the appearance of a new character in CHARLIE CHAN IN PARIS (Fox, 1935).

Keye Luke was born near Canton in 1904. He was thirty-one years old when he appeared as Charlie's son, Lee Chan, in CHARLIE CHAN IN PARIS; he looked twenty. He had as yet no desire to be a detective. He was not yet Charlie's Number One son. He referred to Charlie as Dad, not as Pop. Instead of stealing his father's collar button, as he would later do in CHARLIE CHAN ON BROADWAY (20th-Fox, 1937), in one scene he bent down to take off Charlie's shoes. Keye was almost seventy when I visited him at his Hollywood apartment. He was surrounded by his books on art and on the walls were hung examples of his meticulous pen drawings. He had begun with Fox as an artist and, later, moved on to RKO in the same capacity. He had once studied under Stanton MacDonald-Wright when the latter was artist-in-residence at the University of Southern California. At RKO, Luke was made a technical advisor on Chinese films and was even cast in two-reelers. He had appeared in THE PAINTED VEIL (M-G-M, 1934) with Herbert Marshall and Greta Garbo before John Stone selected him for the role of Lee Chan. Once he joined the series, the story line was tightened up. Charlie uttered fewer aphorisms, but they were more to the point. Philip MacDonald, the detective story writer, did the screenplay for CHARLIE CHAN IN PARIS. No one apparently remarked on the potential charm of the relationship between Oland and Luke until after the film was released. CHARLIE CHAN IN EGYPT (Fox, 1935), next in the series, was made without Keye Luke. But once Stone became aware of the popular reaction, Keye was immediately put under contract and was cast in all but one of the remaining Oland films. CHARLIE CHAN IN EGYPT was also the last film in the series before the merger between Twentieth Century and Fox Film Corporation. After the merger, Darryl F. Zanuck was in charge of "A" picture production, Sol Wurtzel of the "B" unit.

Despite Keye Luke's absence, CHARLIE CHAN IN EGYPT is, in my opinion, the best Chan film Oland was to make. Comic relief was supplied by Lincoln Perry under his screen name of Stepin Fetchit. It was by a curious linking of a Chinese, a Black, a Jew, and an Egyptian with several Europeans that a rather unusual commentary on life, death, and racism emerged. The plot of this film had a complicated origin, but it is worth recounting because of the light it sheds on the tremendous social impact of the cinematic detective in the 'Thirties. Throughout the second half of the Nineteenth century, interest had run high in the discoveries being made in Egypt and the preparation of a consistent history of ancient Egypt which continued excavations by European-sponsored expeditions made possible. This interest became so consuming that, variously, Great Britain and France exercised powerful political influence over modern Egypt culminating in its being annexed to the British Empire as a

Crown Protectorate. In the 'Twenties, thinking among Egyptologists agreed that most of the tomb treasures had been exhausted; political control lessened with the ceasing of hostilities on the continent while foreign museums were glutted with their plundered shares of the great finds.

Howard Carter first came to Egypt while still in his teens apprenticed to P. E. Newberry, the famous Egyptologist. He served as an assistant to Petrie in 1892 and, under Maspero's second tenure as the director of antiquities, began his first excavations in the Valley of the Kings. An American, Theodore Davis, who held the excavation concession in 1914, went on record declaring the Valley to be definitely exhausted of tombs. The concession was duly passed on to George Herbert, the fifth Earl of Carnarvon. Carter managed to convince the Earl, based on several minor finds he had made while employed by Davis, that a tomb was not accounted for, that of Tutankhamen, a young king of the Eighteenth Dynasty whose life and times, in the wake of heretic king Amenhotep IV, better known as Akhenaton, remained in shadow. By 1921, with no result, the Earl was tempted to withdraw his support. He was persuaded to persist only when Carter himself offered to finance another expedition, if the Earl did not. Scarcely a week after re-opening the campaign, on 28 October 1922, a flight of steps was laid bare. It was not until 1928, amid world-wide publicity and talk of ancient curses, that Carter finally penetrated to the pharaoh's sarcophagus and succeeded in opening to the light, after four thousand years, the tomb of solid gold. It has become the best known of all the Egyptian discoveries.

"Slowly, desperately slowly it seemed to us as we watched," Carter described the dramatic scene, "the remains of passage debris that encumbered the lower part of the doorway were removed, until at last we had the whole door clear before us. The decisive moment had arrived. With trembling hands I made a tiny breach in the upper left-hand corner. Darkness and blank space, as far as the iron testing-rod could reach, showed that whatever lay beyond was empty, and not filled like the passage we had just cleared. Candle tests were applied as a precaution against possible foul gases, and then, widening the hole a little, I inserted the candle and peered in, Lord Carnarvon, Lady Evelyn, and Callender standing anxiously beside me to hear the verdict. At first, I could see nothing, the hot air escaping from the chamber causing the candle flame to flicker, but presently, as my eyes grew accustomed to the light, details of the room within emerged slowly from the mist, strange animals, statues, and gold—everywhere the glint of gold. For the moment—an eternity it must have seemed to the others standing by—I was struck dumb with amazement, and when Lord Carnarvon, unable to stand the suspense any longer, inquired anxiously, 'Can you see anything?' it was all I could do to get out the words, 'Yes, wonderful things.' Then widening the hole a little further, so that we both could see, we inserted the electric torch."[11]

CHARLIE CHAN IN EGYPT called on Carter's book relating these experiences. Reproduced almost exactly at the opening of the picture is the joy of discovery, the electric torch illumining a room of long-buried treasure and everywhere gold sparkling in the shadows. Robert Ellis and Helen Logan, who worked on the screenplay and would successfully collaborate on subsequent entries, also borrowed from R. Austin Freeman's THE EYE OF OSIRIS (1911), one of the six volumes picked for reprint in the S. S. Van Dine Mystery Library. The story is concerned with the disappearance of an Egyptologist of independent means named John Bellingham. Dr. Thorndyke, Freeman's scientific investigator, brings his search for the missing man to a small chamber off the fourth Egyptian room at the British Museum. It is here that, with the aid of a gigantic x-ray apparatus, Thorndyke demonstrates conclusively to the Museum officials and the police that the body wrapped in a mummy case presented to the museum by Bellingham, far from being that of Sebek-Hotep, is in fact the dessicated remains of none other than Bellingham himself. While the ancient Egyptians were familiar with dentistry in a primitive fashion, not only fillings but even an artificial tooth show up on the x-ray. Metal sutures in the victim's kneecaps, the result of a serious injury, also show up. Ellis and Logan snatched this moment for CHARLIE CHAN IN EGYPT.

Van Dine was equally taken with Egyptology. He introduced it as a setting for THE SCARAB MURDER CASE in which a man named Kyle is found dead in the Bliss Museum in New York, his head crushed beneath a statue of Sakhmet, the god who protects the Egyptian dead. Ellis and Logan borrowed this element so that in the film Professor Arnold's son is permanently crippled when a tomb wall guarded by a statue of Sakhmet collapses on his leg.

Once this film was in release, Warner Oland took a trip to the Orient. He was mobbed when his ship disembarked at Shanghai. The Chinese mayor of the city invited him to a celebration in his honor, attended by all the luminaries of the international quarter. "Am so happy," he commented in his after dinner speech, "to be once again in the land of honorable ancestors." Fox publicity was sufficiently impressed by Oland's reception in China to write this scene into his next film, CHARLIE CHAN IN SHANGHAI (20th-Fox, 1935). Oland lavished all his talent on his role as Chan and created an idealized human being: sensitive, wise, cautious, humorous, and gentle. Charle Chan on screen neither drank nor smoked, although the character did both occasionally in the novels and Warner Oland certainly did both. That Chan was a Chinese detective helped immensely to transform the image of the Oriental in the eyes of viewers, in the States as well as throughout the world. One has to remember that at the time Oland visited Shanghai, the British policed the international quarter and there was a sign hanging over Shanghai Park stating:"Neither Chinese nor dogs allowed." Many decades later, Chinese-American critics would condemn the Charlie Chan films for portraying Orientals as essentially passive and acquiescent.

In CHARLIE CHAN IN EGYPT, when Oland and Tommy Beck, playing an American Egyptologist, are inspecting the inner chamber to the high-priest Ameti's tomb, Charlie asks what the hieroglyphics on the walls mean. Tommy explains that the lines around the top represent Ameti's prayer to Sakhmet for protection and the others are the alternating symbols for life and death. Charlie traces the symbols, muttering, "Story of man very simple . . . life, death, life, death." Then he straddles the two symbols with his arms, turning to face Tommy. "Am reminded of ancient sage, Confucius, who say: 'From life to death is reach of man.' " Later on, he tells a different character, "Theory like mist on eyeglasses—obscures facts." On one level CHARLIE CHAN IN EGYPT may be regarded as a racial analogue, for it is a plodding Chinese and a seemingly inept Black who are the true heroes of the film. The Europeans are arrogant, self-assured, in a sense wasting their time digging up treasures of an ancient civilization primarily for material gain rather than for any cultural or spiritual enrichment. The lives they lead are without real reason or purpose while Tommy Beck, the American, is innocent, headstrong, handsome, but a somewhat simple-minded scholar who can translate Egyptian hieroglyphics yet remain insensitive to their meaning. The murders are committed for possession of a treasure that, by rights, should belong to the Egyptians, but about which they, embodied in a brilliant characterization by Nigel de Brulier, care very little except to keep it out of the hands of others. Charlie Chan and Stepin Fetchit, whose traditions meet on an inverse plane, the one with an ancient history, the other with no history at all, are united by their lack of greed and their interest in truth and justice. Both Chan and Stepin Fetchit are parodying on screen the white man's postures and conceits toward the non-white races. A Jewish guide in the film is constantly trying to get Stepin Fetchit to give him money so he can excavate the remains of the latter's great, great, great, great, great grandfather. Stepin Fetchit tells Chan that according to a fortuneteller in Mississippi his ancestors came from Egypt. They may have been Nubian kings, but the implication is more likely they were slaves. Somehow Stepin Fetchit cannot become as enthusiastic about ancestry and the discovery of remains as the Europeans are, financing great and expensive expeditions. Just as Chan can make wise sayings, so Stepin Fetchit can make pithy comments as when he tells a Black Egyptian girlfriend: "Come back to Mississippi with me. You don't have to worry about no job dere. Ah knows a lot of white folks that'll keep you working." Chan, Stepin Fetchit, and the whites comprise three different attitudes toward the ancient Egyptians, Chan alike only in his respect for the past, Stepin Fetchit baffled by the passion of the whites, and the whites anxious to unearth hidden wealth. At the conclusion of the film, which was so ably directed by Louis King, Stepin Fetchit chooses to follow Charlie Chan, for the expedition has brought only murder, sadness, and ultimate frustration to the white men. Chan is wiser. He is following the life force which, as a feather, floats on the water and follows the current.

The role of Lee Chan was much expanded in CHARLIE CHAN IN SHANGHAI. Edward T. Lowe and Gerald Fairlie, the latter then currently carrying on the Bulldog Drummond stories, wrote the screenplay. In a charming opening scene, Oland is aboard ship *en route* to Shanghai. He sings a Chinese song about "Ming Loh Fuei" with a reference to the Emperor Fu Manchu. He reflects, once he concludes, his facial expression and intonation adding significantly to the words, that he is "sixty summers young, sixty winters old." At a reception—ostensibly in Shanghai—Oland recites an address in Chinese which he had rehearsed beforehand with Keye Luke, An inquisitive reporter asks another what all that means. "Thank you so much" is the response. Keye Luke got a chance to draw a sketch in the context of the story and there were many pleasant interchanges between the two of them. The culprit, of course, is still the least suspected person. Charlie resorts to a trap to flush him out.

Robert Ellis and Helen Logan were back for the screenplay to CHARLIE CHAN'S SECRET (20th-Fox, 1936). Keye Luke was not in the cast. The plot was altered somewhat from the by now customary story line with Chan's being engaged to find a missing heir. At the Lowell family estate, amid eerie goings-on, Charlie has an opportunity to expose a couple of phony mediums after a spooky séance. The suspects are gathered together at the end for an explanation.

Faith Service, a columnist, wrote a long biographical article on Warner Oland which appeared in the July, 1937 issue of MODERN SCREEN. She began her story by lunching with Oland at the Fox commissary where they had Mandarin Chicken Chow Mein and yellow tomato juice. Commenting on his reticence to give interviews, Oland remarked, " 'Don't talk too much. Words like sunbeams. The more they are condensed the more they burn.' "[12] The columnist was astonished at how much Oland was into his part as Charlie Chan so that he even spoke in Chanograms. Oland was married to Edith Shearn. She was ten years his senior. They had met in New York when Oland was playing in Ibsen's PEER GYNT at the Keith and Proctor Theatre. Edith Shearn was a well-known portrait painter who had written a one-act play. According to what they both told Faith Service, it was upon meeting as if they had known each other all their lives. Edith was so impressed with Warner's modesty, his humility and sincerity, that she cancelled all of her appointments just to talk. " 'It is a marriage,' " Warner said, speaking objectively as Charlie Chan, " 'which is enduring because it is joined by the treasures of the mind which neither rust nor corrupt. They are as much married in their tastes and interests as in their affections.' "[13] Oland was coming increasingly to look upon everything, himself included, as Charlie Chan would. " 'He has habit, for instance,' " Warner continued, still speaking as Charlie Chan about some third person, " 'of putting his lighted cigarettes—at all times he resembles a lighted chimney rather than a portly gentleman of some 200 pounds—on desks, tables, ancient books, choice prints. Accidents occur. I would like to tell him that he should pay attention to detail. Insignificant molehill sometimes more worthy of notice than conspicuous mountain. He does the same with wet fountain pen. Mrs. Oland does not believe in Occidental wifely habit of nagging. As Oriental wife, she bears and forebears; she permits him to blot and burn.' "[14] The Olands at the time lived quietly on their ranch in the Carpenteria Valley near Santa Barbara in a farm house facing the sea on one side, the Santa Barbara hills on the other.

They also had a farm house in Southboro, Massachusetts and a seven thousand acre ranch on the wild Mexican island of Palmetto de la Virgin. " 'Now and then he does some gardening himself. But he is an indolent fellow, this Oland,' " Charlie summed up the Warner Oland side of his personality. " 'He spends much time walking by the sea and in the hills. He calls this "refreshing his soul." He also sits before the fire, meditating and reading Chinese philosophies. As the years go by, he is becoming more and more steeped in Oriental literature and the ancient wisdoms. But he says, sadly, that not all his reading will "capture the sea of literature in the thimble of man's brief span of time." ' "[15]

Oland's drinking was becoming a very serious problem. "Pop imbibed immoderately," Keye Luke put it. "Sometimes he was really lit. It made him benign, with a perpetual grin on his face. You couldn't help but love him." Yet the studio and Mrs. Oland were concerned. While he was filming CHARLIE CHAN AT THE CIRCUS (20th-Fox, 1936), a private nurse was assigned to see to it that he did not drink. Oland started bringing his lunch in a metal lunchbox. He would eat with Keye Luke. He took out two thermos bottles. "For Number One son," he said, "good split pea soup." Then, looking over his shoulder to make sure the coast was clear, he poured out a martini from the second thermos. "For honorable father, tiger tea."

CHARLIE CHAN AT THE CIRCUS is a consistently entertaining picture, written by Robert Ellis and Helen Logan and directed by Harry Lachman. Lachman could be both engaging and personable, but he was a taskmaster on the set. A real circus was used. J. Carrol Naish, who much later would portray Charlie Chan in an abortive television series, was cast as a snake charmer. He commits the murders while dressed in an ape suit. All twelve of Charlie's children and Mrs. Chan were in attendance at the circus. Much was added to the grace and interest of the picture by the skilful inclusion of the capable midgets, George and Olive Brasno. Lackman liked to ride them on the set. Keye Luke reproved Lachman only for Lachman to call Sol Wurtzel and complain about Keye. But these episodes were incidental. Charlie's interplay with the midgets was quite touching.

At this point, Lucky Humberstone entered upon the scene. Sol Wurtzel had first engaged Humberstone some six months after the release of THE DRAGON MURDER CASE (First National, 1934) to direct LADIES LOVE DANGER (Fox, 1935), a detective film which starred Gilbert Roland as an amateur sleuth. Now he engaged Humberstone to direct CHARLIE CHAN AT THE RACETRACK (20th-Fox, 1936).

While shooting the exteriors for the racing sequence at the Santa Anita track, Oland disappeared and the entire crew set out to find him. He was in a deep sleep in the track restaurant. Humberstone wanted to intercut a shot of Chan supposedly watching the horse race, but Oland kept dozing off. Humberstone solved the problem by having extras around Oland to bolster him up.

"I know you can't see anything," Humberstone told Oland, "but just turn your head with the sound."

It worked.

Yet, for all that, Humberstone was a devil's advocate. He encouraged Oland to drink before doing his scenes. After screening rushes, Oland had to agree with Humberstone that alcohol improved his characterization. As fine an actor as he might be sober, he recited his lines too quickly; alcohol fogged his memory and it seemed, on screen at least, as if the Oriental detective were grappling with a difficult, alien language when, in fact, the Swedish actor was only groping for his line. Humberstone also started casting Jimmy Flavin regularly as a cop in his films, regarding the brassy-voiced Irishman as a good luck charm. CHARLIE CHAN AT THE RACETRACK was well received as Wurtzel retained Humberstone to direct CHARLIE CHAN AT THE OPERA (20th-Fox, 1937).

It was Humberstone's idea to cast Boris Karloff as an amnesiac opera singer. Sol Wurtzel initially resisted the notion because of the additional expense. Karloff had gained a considerable reputation since his earlier appearance in THE BLACK CAMEL, but Humberstone won out. A subtitle to the picture read "Warner Oland vs. Boris Karloff." Oscar Levant composed an undistinguished opera sequence titled "Carnival." In the actual production, Humberstone utilized several of the elaborate sets Zanuck had had built for E. H. Griffith's CAFE METROPOLE (20th-Fox, 1937). Griffith had shot most of his scenes in extreme close-up. When Zanuck saw the production value the sets brought to CHARLIE CHAN AT THE OPERA, he remarked to Wurtzel, "This son-of-a-bitch Humberstone is making my 'A' directors look sick turning out a 'B' that looks like this. Put him under contract." Wurtzel, too, made a contribution to the completed film. After seeing rushes of Nedda Harrigan as an opera singer, he emerged from the projection room.

"Humberstone," he said in his thick Jewish accent, "tell me something. Does a *lady* fuck?"

"What?"

"You heard me, Humberstone. Does a *lady* fuck?"

"I suppose she does."

"Well, this one doesn't look like she does. Shoot it again."

Humberstone directed CHARLIE CHAN AT THE OLYMPICS (20th-Fox, 1937) which featured Layne Tom, Jr., as Charlie's Number Two son. It is an interesting film because of its various locales and expert use of stock footage interpolations of everything from the Zepplin Von Hindenberg to the Olympic games in Germany in 1936. Only Keye Luke's performance, calling for him incessantly to spout Chanograms, seems a little heavy-handed.

The Chan films were being shot in four weeks with an extra week for retakes. Budgeted between $250,000 and $275,000, they were each netting a million dollars upon release. Oland rented a bungalow at the Beverly Hills Hotel while in production. Shortly after the MODERN SCREEN story about the marital bliss of the Olands appeared, Edith Oland sued Warner for separate maintenance. She could not take the drinking. The nurse was not much help. Keye Luke would visit Oland in his dressing room and Warner would tiptoe to the closet where he kept a bottle hidden.

"Nurse smart," he would say, "but honorable father smarter."

Oland's mind was deteriorating. While Humberstone found the fumbling words an asset to the characterization, it might require a dozen takes to get out a single line. In CHARLIE CHAN'S SECRET—a rather appropriate title under the circumstances—Henrietta Crosman and Oland did a scene in which Warner had to trudge up a flight of steps, speak his line, and she would answer with hers. Henrietta always got her line. Oland always blew his. On the twenty-third take, Oland finally got it right; but Henrietta, so shocked that he had, blew hers! Oland would resort to excuses, "Honorable father not in marks" or "Honorable father picked up wrong object."

After the separation, Oland moved into the Beverly Hills home of his agent. The nurse went along. Keye Luke visited him on New Year's Day to find him waltzing to music from the radio during a broadcast of the Rose Bowl game. "We had a grand visit," Keye recalled, "and it was good to see Pop in such good 'spirits.' Everyone loved him. He had a crowd around him whenever he went out. Once he called me up. 'Honorable father invite Number One son to go for ride.' Sure enough, he stopped out front in his limousine. We rode around the Hollywood hills. When we came to the Oriental Gardens, Pop had the car stop. 'Must pay respects,' he said, getting out. People began to notice us. When a crowd started in our direction, Pop turned toward a bush. 'Try make yourself inconspicuous,' he said. But," Keye added, laughing, "he loved it. He was mobbed everywhere. 'Charlie Chan,' people would say, 'it's Charlie Chan.' "

William Demarest had played an anti-Chinese cop in CHARLIE CHAN AT THE OPERA. Early in the film he exclaimed to his superior, "You're not going to call in Chop Suey, are you?" Harold Huber played a less biased cop in CHARLIE CHAN ON BROADWAY which also brought director Eugene Forde back to the series. Huber did a lot of talking, so much talking in fact that Oland's dialogue could be kept at a minimum even in the denouement. Joan Marsh played a pert and curvaceous free-lance photographer. Leon Ames played a sophisticated gangster. Louise Henry, the glamorous murder victim in THE CASINO MURDER CASE (M-G-M, 1935), was done in once more. When Charlie Chan's boat docks in New York, Huber, not knowing the Chinese national anthem, has the police band play "Chinatown, My Chinatown" by way of a greeting—forgetting that Charlie is an American.

CHARLIE CHAN AT MONTE CARLO (20th-Fox, 1938) was Oland's last Charlie Chan film. The trades declared it his greatest success to date. At least a third of the dialogue was in French, but it actually added polish to the exposition of the plot. Eugene Forde directed and Huber, cast here as a French prefect, handled most of the interrogations.

CHARLIE CHAN AT THE RINGSIDE went into production on 10 January 1938. Oland's condition had worsened considerably. He had been found in the early hours of the morning wandering aimlessly far from Hollywood and unable to say who he was. It was seventy-seven degrees in the shade when Oland insisted it was too drafty on sound stage 6 at the Fox lot on Western Avenue.

The number on the stage was changed. Oland was not fooled. He walked off the picture. When he quit on director James Tinling for the fourth time on 17 January, Darryl Zanuck scrapped the picture, partially completed at a cost of $100,000. Oland was put on suspension. The rest of the cast was paid off. Although Keye Luke had been tested for a series tentatively titled "Son of Chan" in case of an emergency, Fox executives now agreed that Oland was too closely identified with the role for any substitution to be made.

Oland was reportedly suffering from a nervous breakdown. The collapse of his marriage certainly had affected him deeply. It made national headlines when a photograph was taken of him sitting on the running board of his limousine throwing away his shoes.

"Honorable father must go to Europe," he told Keye Luke. "Must see once more the chestnut trees of Florence."

Oland was hospitalized in February. By March, he was released. He signed a new contract with Darryl Zanuck to make three more Charlie Chan films for the 1938-1939 season. Zanuck agreed that an ocean voyage might be a good idea before resuming work. Warner and Edith talked of reconciliation prior to his sailing. It was not to be. On an excursion to Stockholm, Oland fell ill with bronchial pneumonia.

"Life," Warner had once said as Charlie Chan, "like piece of delicate jade, difficult to create, easy to destroy."

Sol Wurtzel was three days into production on the first Chan film under the new contract when the news came. He had previously cabled Oland to return at once so the picture could stay on schedule. But on 6 August 1938 wire services around the globe carried the message that Warner Oland was dead. He had passed away quietly, reposing in his mother's bed. "Life, death, life death," he had said as Charlie Chan. Now at fifty-seven his life had reached its span. Wurtzel gave the crew the rest of the day off. Edith long survived him. She died in 1968, fully expectant to make it to a hundred. "No use to hurry," Warner had once said on screen, "unless sure of catching right train."

II

Of all the authors I have mentioned so far, and of all those that I shall mention, John P. Marquand is the only one who was not known primarily as the creator of a particular detective. When he was alive, Marquand was an extraordinarily popular writer, his books selling in the millions, although today that popularity has diminished to a surprising degree. Leo Gurko in an essay in the AMERICAN SCHOLAR, published in 1952, claimed that Marquand's novels, on which the claim for his being a serious novelist was based, are actually "almost exactly alike. They deal with a fixed problem, and pass through identical stages in the course of working it out. Marquand's technical skill conceals this fact for a time, creating the illusion of variety and change. But when it becomes plain, one realizes that here is the restricting element that has kept Marquand—and will probably always keep him—from reaching the level of his great predecessors."[16]

John Gross, on the other hand, in his book on Marquand's fiction rallied to his defense and insisted that "what looks like formula is . . . more properly a stubborn reiteration of convictions and principles that are continually reasserted. If the restatement of Kafka's compulsion in his work is a formula, then so is Marquand's. The real point is that Marquand, like any other moralist or like any novelist with a particular view of life, should not be judged adversely because he restates in succeeding novels his basic convictions and beliefs or his ideas, but because these ideas in themselves are limited."[17] Gross, in making his case for Marquand, speculated that perhaps it was the Mr. Moto stories, along with Marquand's other slick magazine fiction, which prompted his critics to be less than kindly, and yet, he concluded, "the Moto stories are deserving of respect."[18] Other than this isolated comment, however, he found no other occasion in his book to mention the Moto novels.

John P. Marquand was born at Wilmington, Delaware in 1893. He married too young; but he compounded his error. According to one of his biographers, Stephen Birmingham in THE LATE JOHN MARQUAND (1972), after receiving a divorce from one impossible woman, Christina, he married another, even worse for him. From early childhood evidently, Marquand's values were distorted by the peculiar New England emotional climate in which he was raised. Attending Harvard certainly did not help. He secured employment with the J. Walter Thompson advertising agency, but proved unsuited to a business career. By then it no longer mattered. He was selling short stories to THE SATURDAY EVENING POST. He was a naturally gifted stylist with a vividly melodramatic imagination who also, as Earl Derr Biggers, happened to be wholly in tune with the popular sentiments of his time. He was in the military during the Great War and was repelled by the wanton slaughter he witnessed while in the trenches in France.

Marquand discovered that he could dictate his stories to a stenographer. He also tended, to the irritation of both of his wives, to fall in love with his stenographers. On a number of occasions Marquand remarked on the loneliness which writing imposed on him and perhaps this was one of the reasons behind his preference for writing by dictation. Since, for me, of all the activities I might do, writing is the one in which I am most intensely alive, I found Marquand's attitude sufficiently baffling to mention it once in conversation with Ross Macdonald. He agreed with Marquand.

"Writing is painfully lonely," he said, and then paused. "But I make sure I'm not alone the rest of the time."

Marquand spent the better part of his life trying to prove himself, first to his fellows at Harvard, then to his first wife's parents, then to Christina whom he did finally marry after a prolonged courtship, then to the critics. Had this not been the dynamic of his personality, he might well have written very different kinds of novels from those he did write. Whatever anguish his marriage to Christina may have caused him, it is to her that we own the Mr. Moto stories.

Interest in the Far East unquestionably ran high among Americans between the wars. Ray Long, editor of COSMOPOLITAN, negotiated a very lucrative contract with W. Somerset Maugham to write short stories with a Far Eastern setting. George Horace Lorimer, editor of THE SATURDAY EVENING POST, had much the same close working relationship with Marquand that Long had with Maugham. Almost every month there was at least one story by Marquand in the POST. Marquand was an optative writer in the POST. He could publish a story in 1934 in the POST titled "Winner Take All" less than a year after Hemingway had published a collection of his short fiction with the comment that "unlike all other forms of butte or combat, the conditions are that the winner shall take nothing; neither his ease, nor his pleasure, nor any notions of glory, nor, if he win far enough, shall there be any reward within himself."[19]

When Earl Derr Biggers died, Lorimer wanted to continue the by now traditional annual POST serial with an Oriental setting and, ideally, an Oriental detective. Hearing about Marquand's marital problems with Christina, he proposed a long holiday in the East without her, with the POST picking up all the expenses. Lorimer even went so far as to suggest that while Marquand was there he should put his mind to inventing a successor to Charlie Chan. It proved a worthwhile investment. Marquand's first Mr. Moto novel, NO HERO (1935), began its serialization in the POST under the title "Mr. Moto Takes a Hand" in the 30 March 1935 issue. Marquand's creation of the dapper, intelligent, obsequious Japanese secret service agent was an immediate success with POST readers.

The image of the Orient in NO HERO is that of a world in which anything might happen and usually does. It is a first person narrative by K. C. Lee, an airplane pilot who first received his training during the war and now is an adventurer. It was a period in which Japan was extending its political influence and Lee, responding to Mr. Moto, reflected that "I have an idea that he would agree with me heartily in wishing for perpetual amity between Japan and the United States, as long as that amity did not interfere with what he and his own political faction conceive to be his nation's divine mission to establish a hegemony in the East. Distance sometimes makes it difficult to remember that the Japanese are capable people, sensitive and intelligent. Still, although it sometimes seems incredible that our two nations should ever go to war, there is always the thought of war behind the scenes in every nation."[20] The convention of the major emphasis being on the young hero and the heroine whom he meets and with whom he falls in requited love was carried over from the Charlie Chan novels and is to be found in all four of the Moto stories Marquand published in the POST before the Second World War. Sonya Karaloff is the heroine, a Russian who asks Lee a most prescient question. " ' . . . Think of a great country,' " she says, " 'which is always moving forward—taking. The United States is moving toward Asia—her hand has reached out over Hawaii, over Guam, over the Philippines. Where is she going to stop?' "[21] It would not be until the seventh decade of this century that that question could be answered. Lee himself makes a remark that would resound ironically only many years later in the sixth and final Moto novel: "Men die for their faith who have never been inside a church, and men die for their country, although they may have spent their lives criticizing all its works. The amazing thing about it is that they are probably surprised by their irrational willingness to die."[22]

Marquand had an awkward tendency, even in his best fiction, toward melodramatic overstatement. It was no different, really, in the Moto stories, except it is probably more acceptable there. NO HERO was dictated to Carol Brandt, the wife of Marquand's literary agent. In one of those strange relationships which when you encounter them in life are so commonplace and so preposterous when you encounter them in fiction Marquand eventually began a long-term affair with Mrs. Brandt that was only mildly disapproved by her husband. The trip to the Orient had yet another effect. Marquand had met the heiress, Adelaide Ferry Hooker, with whom he did not get along and whom, once he was divorced from Christina, he married. The rest of his life, almost, was spent trying finally to get clear of Adelaide.

Marquand was a heavy drinker. Dictation would begin in the morning and would last for about four hours. Then a tray of martinis would arrive. Woe be to the stenographer who would not join Marquand for a cocktail break, although the afternoon had to be spent editing material already transcribed. THANK YOU, MR. MOTO (1936) came next. It, too, is filled with careful and interesting observations about China, where it is set. It is, however, a third person narrative, as the remainder of the Moto books are. "Those sounds," Marquand observes, "all came together into an endless wave of sound, peaceful, enveloping, the noise of China where men lived and died according to fixed etiquette, where nothing mattered very much, except perhaps tranquility."[23] In comparing the English with the Americans in the Far East, Marquand discovered that "the pleasing impersonality of the well-bred Englishman enabled him to remain a complete stranger, an impossibility for an American after a few hours' acquaintance."[24] In THINK FAST, MR. MOTO (1937), which is set for the most part in Hawaii, Marquand extended this comparison even further. Wilson Hitchings, the hero, sees "that institution, the filling station, with its pumps all lighted, exactly as they were at home, and an all night lunchroom and a drugstore. America had come to those islands, leaving as definite an impression of ideas of living as England invariably left on the outposts of the British Empire. It amused Wilson to think that the lighter ideals of his own country were stronger and more in tune with the present than those of the older nation. He recalled jazz orchestras in the Orient, each a conscientious imitation of Broadway; and the Wild West motion pictures in Tokyo, and the baseball in Japan, and the amusement parks of Shanghai. The genius of his own nation was in them all—tawdry, superficial, but somehow strong and appealing."[25] By the time he came to publish the fourth in the series, MR. MOTO IS SO SORRY (1938), Moto himself gives his position. " 'Excuse me,' " Moto says,

" 'your own great country has taken territory. The British Empire has taken nearly half the globe. Why should not Japan? It is the manifest destiny of the stronger nations. Nevertheless, we do not wish to grab. We only desire a partnership, a cordial co-operation, an understanding with the Chinese. We wish to advise and to help them, to develop their resources. I am sure that you are clever enough to understand.' "[26]

After Marquand completed MR. MOTO IS SO SORRY, Adelaide began to meddle in his work, an intrusion that quixotically even led to her sharing copyright notices on four books. She felt the Moto stories were beneath him. Marquand was not decided in his own mind. He wanted to write what he considered serious fiction, and he did; but he returned twice more to the little Japanese over the years which saw him publish novels such as H. M. PULLMAN, ESQUIRE (1941) and WOMEN AND THOMAS HARROW (1958). LAST LAUGH, MR. MOTO (1942) was run serially in COLLIER'S, not the POST, after the war with Japan had begun. Consistent with the anti-Japanese sentiment of the time, Moto is constantly being outwitted, an entirely different experience for him than that of the first four novels.

Marquand had been inspired to create the secret service agent as a result of his time in Japan. While there, he had been shadowed everywhere by a polite little Japanese detective. It was on this person that he based Mr. Moto. Yet, whatever his origin, Mr. Moto in the novels remains at all times as shadowy and one-dimensional as his prototype seems to have been. This was by design. Marquand wanted to stress the lives and interrelationships of his main characters with Moto only darting in and out of the narrative at strategic points. Biggers had done this with Charlie Chan in at least two of the novels; but, however brief his appearances, Charlie Chan's personality had more substance than Moto's which is probably why he went on to remain an American box-office hero for many years longer than Moto did.

With the death of Warner Oland, Twentieth Century-Fox Film Corporation was up against the same dilemma the POST had been when Biggers had died. The company solved the problem in the same way, by deciding to replace the Chan film series by stepping up production of the Mr. Moto film series which starred Peter Lorre. Lorre was born in 1904, at Rosenberg, Hungary, the eldest of the four sons of Alois and Elvira Lorre. Alois made a living selling wood off the land he owned until that played out and his wife died. He moved with his family to Vienna and eventually became a manager for the Steyr automobile company. Alois did not approve of his son's desire to become an actor. He was so adamant that Peter ran away shortly after the Armistice. It was his exophthalmic eyes, diminutive stature, and delicate voice which became his most memorable attributes as an actor. He was also, apparently from a very early age, peculiar emotionally. All of this he turned to his advantage when he began playing psychopathic roles, but initially it must have been something of a handicap.

During the Inflation in the early 'Twenties in Germany, Lorre took to sleeping on park benches at night and looking for work during the day. He tried one-man performances, readings illustrated by pantomime. For a brief time he got into banking, but he was soon terminated for being irresponsible. He landed a small job in a stock company in Breslau which was directed by Mitler, later a film director. He got acting jobs in Zurich and Vienna and finally ended up at the *Volksbühne* in Berlin. He played a sex fiend and the adolescent Moritz Stiefel in Franz Wedekind's FRÜHLINGS ERWACHEN who commits suicide when he finds himself unable to deal with his sexual urges. Fritz Lang saw him in the latter role and went backstage to ask Lorre how he would like to be in pictures. Reflecting on his physical endowments and the role he was playing on stage, Lorre was perplexed by the question. Yet, Lang was right. Lorre was rehearsing in Berthold Brecht's MANN IST MANN at the Berlin Staatstheatre when Lang offered him the starring role of a psychopathic killer in MÖRDERER UNTER UNS (Nerofilm, 1931), released in this country as M. While the picture was in production, Lorre commuted between the make-shift studio outside Berlin to the Staatstheatre and back again. Brecht was personally directing his play. It opened and closed after two days. M found a wider audience. It became a classic of the Weimar cinema and its reputation spread abroad, typecasting Lorre as an unbalanced and haunting screen personality. UFA in Germany signed Lorre to a contract. He preferred comedy roles and his contract afforded him the opportunity to appear in both humorous and villainous roles.

The rise of National Socialism interrupted Lorre's stage and screen career. He was convinced that his name was on the lists of persons the Nazis intended to eliminate. He fled to Vienna three days before the Reichstag fire. Notwithstanding, as long as they were broadcast, he seldom missed Hitler's radio speeches. Sam Spiegel who was the Universal Pictures representative in Germany placed Lorre in a bad program picture that persuaded him he ought best to seek his fortune in Paris where he ended up living in a boarding house with other emigrés, including Billy Wilder, Franz Waxman, and Paul Lukas. Despite his impossible French, Lorre landed a job dubbing Lukas' voice on a French sound track. Times were bad and got worse before Lorre emigrated to England, having no money and speaking no English. Sidney Bernstein, a producer, introduced Lorre to Alfred Hitchcock who had once been an assistant director at UFA. Hitchcock cast him as an anarchist in THE MAN WHO KNEW TOO MUCH (Gaumont, 1934). Cecilia Lvovsky, whom Lorre had first met in Berlin, played a Russian aristocrat in the film. They were married.

Lorre years later in an interview recalled his initial meeting with Hitchcock. "Hitch talked," he said, "and I leaned forward looking intelligent but not understanding a word. By following his gestures, I'd guess when he was coming to the gag-line and I'd laugh out loud. I got the role and it was two weeks before Hitch found out I spoke no English. I must say he got a big kick out of it."

When I visited Alfred Hitchcock at his office on the Universal lot, his last film, THE FAMILY PLOT (Universal, 1976), had just been released.

"Photographs are forbidden in here," he said.

Since I was not carrying a camera, his first words to me were rather perplexing. But he was genial and the conversation turned almost at once to Peter Lorre. I repeated Lorre's version of their first meeting.

"I had no idea at all," Hitchcock drawled, "that Lorre was Hungarian, so, when we met, I spoke to him in German. I had to learn German when I worked in Germany as an art director ten years earlier."

Josef von Sternberg in Hollywood decided to cast Lorre as Raskolnikov in the film version of Dostoyevsky's CRIME AND PUNISHMENT (Columbia, 1935), another psychopathic role which Lorre accepted with alacrity and departed from England for the States. Before production began, Lorre was loaned out to Metro to play a bald maniac in MAD LOVE (M-G-M, 1935) directed by Karl Freund, a remake of the 1924 film ORLACS HÄNDE which had originally featured Conrad Veidt. When, in 1936, Hitchcock decided to film THE SECRET AGENT (Gaumont, 1936), based on W. Somerset Maugham's Ashenden stories, he cast Lorre as a curly haired killer, inspired oddly enough by the rather unpleasant hairless Mexican in the literary source. Lorre considered the whole business of his having curly hair in this role an inside joke. He later remarked that, as a prank, upon departing England for the States for a second time he purchased an entire pet shop of canaries and had them shipped to Hitchcock's home. According to Lorre, Hitchcock had his revenge. He began cabling Lorre aboard ship every fifteen minutes, night and day, telling him how he had named each of the canaries and providing him with a moment-by-moment description of what each of the canaries was doing. It was so incessant that Lorre was unable to sleep.

I asked Hitchcock if that, indeed, had ever happened.

"No," he said.

We talked of other things. Finally, our meeting nearly over, I let out a sigh. Hitchcock looked at me with curiosity.

"I wish the story about the canaries had been true," I confessed. "It makes such a fine anecdote."

Hitchcock smiled quietly. "Why don't you say," he drawled, "my memory is bad, for it is sometimes. Let's just say, I don't remember it as having happened."

Lorre was put on a three-year contract with Twentieth Century-Fox and had appeared in two non-descript films before he found himself in the midst of Sol Wurtzel's brainstorm to bring Mr. Moto to the screen. Lorre was one part of the package. Norman Foster was another. Foster had been married and divorced from Claudette Colbert and in 1936 was married to Sally Blane, Loretta Young's older sister. Sally had been working on the Fox lot and was now pregnant. She and Norman Foster had decided to go to New York to look for acting jobs when Wurtzel intervened.

My first contact with Norman Foster was by telephone when he was suffering from laryngitis. Sally handled the call, relaying my questions and Foster's answers.

"Sol really did us a favor," Sally said. "He asked Norm, 'How does Sally feel about going to New York with a baby?' 'She doesn't like it,' Norm told him. Sol suggested Norm become a director at Fox and Norm took him up on it. He started for $350 a week, when he had been getting $2,000 a week as an actor."

"Lorre complained toward the end of his life that the Moto characterization did nothing for him," I said.

"Well," Sally said, "he didn't talk that way so much when he was making the pictures. Peter and his wife were frequently our guests. He was a gentle. . . . What was that, Norm?"

There was a pause.

"Oh, yes," Sally resumed, "Peter did once say to Norm, after their first couple of pictures together, that 'we're like a husband and wife who have been living together for too long.' "

"Did Norm have any trouble directing him?"

Sally put the question to Foster who croaked his response.

"Not," Sally relayed, "if you take into account that he was an actor with a German accent playing an Oriental. Sometimes he would get temperamental and have a complete breakdown, sobbing and totally unable to work."

"He would just start sobbing?"

"Yes." Sally paused. "What was that, Norm?" There was another pause while Sally listened. "Norm says you have to remember that Peter was in a rest home at the time Sol cast him, recovering from drug addition. When they began filming, he had a dressing room on the set where a doctor would come daily to give him a shot. He was very thin and frail then compared to later years. He had suffered from malnutrition when he was small, and his teeth were rotten."

"How much did Lorre really contribute to the characterization?"

"I don't know. Norm had a lot to do with it. He talked over the character with John Marquand and, besides directing, he worked on the screenplays."

"Sally, I suspect Wurtzel originally started the Moto series to keep Warner Oland in line, the way he once promoted Buck Jones to act as a brake on Tom Mix' salary demands. Then he increased production when Oland died. But why did he drop the series?"

"Originally it wasn't supposed to be a series, but the first picture was such a success that Sol kept making them. I guess he got angry at Peter. . . . "

"Or Lorre at the part," I interrupted.

"Maybe both. Sol just stopped. He was like that. He was a wonderful man. But if he became angry at someone, that was it. He just stopped. Norm always blamed it on horse racing. Sol would sit in his office, feet up on his desk getting a haircut, manicure, and shoe shine while talking on the 'phone to his bookie."

Foster directed FAIR WARNING (20th-Fox, 1937) for Wurtzel and was then assigned to direct THINK FAST, MR. MOTO (20th-Fox, 1937), the first Moto film based on Marquand's third novel. Fox publicity dreamed up a logo to promote Lorre in the film, terming Lorre "Europe's One Man Chamber of Horrors." Yet the script did not reveal Lorre to be a ghoul. He was soft-spoken, wily, very much the enchanting little character of the stories. Possibly Lorre proved so apt for the role precisely because he left the personality of Moto quite unaffected. The plot of the book was changed somewhat. The setting was altered from a gambling house in Honolulu as a blind to sneak Chinese money into the Japanese colony of Manchukuo to smuggling in general. Although the picture opened in San Francisco, much of the action took place in Shanghai. Tommy Beck and Virginia Field supplied the love interest.

While MR. MOTO TAKES A CHANCE (20th-Fox, 1938) was fourth to be released, it was second in order of production. It was previewed under its working title of LOOK OUT, MR. MOTO. Lou Breslow and John Patrick did the screenplay based on an original story by Willis Cooper and Norman Foster and Foster directed. The setting was the Cambodian jungle. Robert Kent and Chick Chandler were cast as two newsreel photographers who stumble upon the crashed plane of aviatrix Rochelle Hudson. The natives take them all prisoner. Prospects for escape are dim until Moto, disguised as a religious recluse, frees a captive French secret service agent and sets matters aright.

Third in order of production and second into release was THANK YOU, MR. MOTO (20th-Fox, 1937). The screenplay by Willis Cooper and Norman Foster was based on the Marquand novel of the same title. Again the plot was altered. Instead of stealing Chinese art treasures as in the novel, seven scrolls are supposed to give the whereabouts, when pieced together, of Genghis Khan's hidden wealth. After much intrigue, Moto gets the scrolls and burns them, thus leaving the Khan's booty undisturbed.

Fourth in production, but third into release, was MR. MOTO'S GAMBLE (20th-Fox, 1938) which had begun as the Charlie Chan picture in production at the time of Warner Oland's death. James Tinling, who had been assigned to direct CHARLIE CHAN AT THE RINGSIDE, stayed on as the director. Since so much footage had been shot of Keye Luke, Sol Wurtzel told the writers to give him a role. John Stone remained the associate producer, although he had not previously been involved in the Moto series. When a fighter is poisoned in the ring, Moto investigates with Keye Luke as Lee Chan and Harold Huber playing a New York policeman as his comic assistants. By necessity, the Chan formula was crossed with the Moto formula in this picture. Wurtzel was pleased with the results.

Norman Foster and Philip MacDonald contributed to the screenplay and Foster directed the fifth entry, MYSTERIOUS MR. MOTO (20th-Fox, 1938). It was one of the most ambitious films of the series, opening to the escape of two criminals from Devil's Island, Leon Ames and Peter Lorre as Moto. Moto becomes Ames' houseboy in London where Ames attaches himself to Harold Huber's assassination ring. Henry Wilcoxen is their next victim, cast as a Czech industrialist who plays Chopin at the piano while dictating business letters to his secretary with whom he is in love. Moto foils the plot and exposes the identity of the ring's secret leader.

I had already spoken in person with Norman Foster and Lloyd Nolan when I met Leon Ames at the Brown Derby in Hollywood. Ames and Nolan had been best friends for years.

"Thank God for Lloyd Nolan," I said to Leon Ames as he joined me.

"Why for Nolan?"

"I got your 'phone number from his wife because he's out of town. I tried for days to get to you through your agent but with no luck. When I had talked with Lloyd, he had asked me if I wanted your number. So, in desperation, I called, got his wife, and here we are."

"Well," said Ames, laughing cordially, "that's because I told my agent I didn't want to be interviewed. Someone from a Valley newspaper interviewed me a short time ago and misquoted me about a great many people. I didn't want that again. But I certainly am glad I came." He paused and dropped his voice. "I want you to know, though, that I'm going to give Noly a helluva hard time about this. I'm going to tell him how outrageous he was in offering you my telephone number."

"I talked with Norman Foster on the 'phone and then visited him. He told me Peter Lorre would listen to Hitler's speeches in his dressing room and then come racing out with an insane look on his face, nose running, saliva coming from his mouth, shouting, 'How can you want me to make pictures when the world is falling apart?' "

"He was quite a character," Ames conceded, smiling. "He had the foulest breath because of his teeth. He later had them taken out. But he was fond, when we worked on those Moto pictures, of going up to girls and saying, 'Could you get used to my body, you think?' He relished being gnome-like. And he was an expert at matching scenes. When we'd stop shooting and then begin again, he knew exactly what he had been doing, where he was standing, and how he was holding his body."

"Do you have any idea why the series was dropped? Was it Sol Wurtzel?"

"Actually," Ames replied, "there were four Wurtzels working on that lot when I came to Fox. I remember it was a studio joke that there was a girl under contract for the last three years who had yet to make a picture because she was sleeping with the wrong Wurtzel."

A waiter came with drinks.

"I don't know," Ames continued. "I think the pictures just got boring. I recall when we were doing that Devil's Island sequence together, Lorre and I had to go through the swamps at night in order to escape. It was shot on the Fox back lot. We were wading in mud up to our necks. There was a tiger in a tree, supposedly chained. But when we got close to it, I saw there wasn't anything like a chain around him, not even a small rope. We then had to crawl into a small boat and we get shot at. Foster had sharp-shooters out there, using real bullets. That's when I rebelled. I told them to stop everything. The tiger had been bad enough, but I wasn't going to get shot at for the sake of any picture."

"Norman Foster told me that he met Peter Lorre many years later and that Peter Lorre looked at him and commented wryly that it was too bad Norman didn't know him now." Ames smiled knowingly.

Philip MacDonald collaborated with Norman Foster on the screenplay for MR. MOTO'S LAST WARNING (20th-Fox, 1939) and Foster directed. When Warner Oland had had his nervous breakdown during the 1937-1938 season, Wurtzel had reduced the number of Chan releases from three to two and had increased Moto production from three to four pictures a year. Even when production resumed on the Chan films for the 1938-1939 season, Wurtzel kept them at two a year, the Motos at four. The setting of MR. MOTO'S LAST WARNING is Port Said and the plot involves an attempt to sabotage the French fleet. Moto saves the day. George Sanders was in the picture, but did not want to be. He took it out on Foster by running up large restaurant bills and charging them to Foster's account. One night, when they were shooting late, it was Foster's birthday and the script girls had gotten together and bought him a quart of expensive bonded whiskey. Sanders had a scene to do. He found the bottle first and drank all of it. Foster was so angry he shot the sequence with Sanders in his inebriated condition. Sanders just smirked. The next day the footage had to be scrapped.

Next into production, although last in release, was MR. MOTO TAKES A VACATION (20th-Fox, 1939). MacDonald and Foster again did the screenplay and Foster directed. The casting was strong with Joseph Schildkraut, Lionel Atwill, and Virginia Field in major roles. The trades at the time were agreed on Norman Foster's capable direction but faulted the screenplay. The story still does not make sense at this late date. Schildkraut finances an expedition to find the crown of the Queen of Sheba. Moto watches over the crown all the way back to San Francisco. It is rumored that a famous criminal, long thought dead, will steal the crown. This criminal turns out to be none other than Schildkraut who scarcely would have had to resort to theft to possess the crown.

Because of the cutback in Chan production, John Stone had another Moto picture added to his complement of pictures for the next season. The picture, MR. MOTO IN DANGER ISLAND (20th-Fox, 1939), remains a tribute to him. Although released three months before MR. MOTO TAKES A VACATION and produced three months after it, MR. MOTO IN DANGER ISLAND may well be the best picture in the series. Herbert I. Leeds directed it and Jean Hersholt, Warren Hymer, Leon Ames, and Douglas Dumbrille were all prominently in the cast. Moto is called in to solve diamond smuggling in Puerto Rico, with Warren Hymer playing his dumb sidekick. In one effective scene, a servant drawing a bath for Moto at the hotel is electrocuted because the tub was been wired to get Moto out of the way. Unfortunately the character played by Jean Hersholt had never gone to the movies. Moto exposes him by means of the hospital ruse where a man already dead is said to be alive but in a coma, thus encouraging an attempt on his life before he can talk. Hersholt is apprehended in making the attempt.

From February, 1937 until December, 1938 Peter Lorre appeared in eight Moto pictures. He deported himself very much as the Moto of the stories and he spoke his characteristic dialogue well, "I am so very, very happy," or "Not ever again, I am thinking," or "You must not make a sound, please." The films were so well mounted with casts of such entertaining and polished players and stories filled with intrigue and action that you do not notice how insignificant the Moto character is until you compare it with Warner Oland's projection of Charlie Chan in that series. Lorre did not want to make any more Moto pictures and he rebelled. Sol Wurtzel shut down production. Lorre was idle for three months before he asked to be released from his Fox contract. Wurtzel dropped the three Motos scheduled for the 1939-1940 season with the same indifference he had responded to Lorre's checking off the Fox lot. Between Lorre and Oland, Wurtzel had certainly had his hands full with distraught actors playing Orientals.

Shortly before his death, John P. Marquand returned to the Moto character in STOPOVER: TOKYO (1956) which was also run serially in THE SATURDAY EVENING POST. The story is set in post-war Japan. Jack Rhyce and Ruth Bogart are American secret service agents sent to Tokyo to foil a Communist plot. They fall in love with each other. But there the similarity ends. It is a darker time, and Marquand's view of the world had become darker. By the end of the novel, Ruth is dead, a victim of the Communists, and Jack is determined to keep his word to her and quit the service. Mr. Moto is the same, although older, still in the service of his country. " 'I am not anti-American,' " Moto says to Rhyce. " 'I hope so very much that you are not anti-Japanese. . . . ' "[27] In the same conversation, Moto observes, rather poignantly, " 'Americans are always so very sentimental when they are not using flamethrowers and napalm.' "[28] Twentieth Century-Fox purchased screen rights to the book, but the Moto character was deleted by the time STOPOVER: TOKYO (20th-Fox, 1957) went into production with Robert Wagner and Joan Collins. When, finally, an attempt was made to resurrect the character, in THE RETURN OF MR. MOTO (20th-Fox, 1965) directed by Ernest Morris, Henry Silva appeared as Moto against a cast of unknowns. The plot had to do with the murder of an oil magnate and an effort to seize the leases he held on fields in the Persian Gulf. At one point, Moto is thrown into the Thames in a weighted sack. He cuts himself loose, much as Peter Lorre had in a similar scrape; but there the similarity ended. A new era had found new heroes and James Bond better articulated the fantasy of an international secret service agent.

Marquand did not live to see this film. One summer morning in July, 1960 Marquand's houseman brought him his breakfast. He opened the bedroom curtains. He dropped the tray when he realized that John Marquand would not be waking up. Marquand's son, Lonnie, who was staying with him rushed to his side. It was too late. He had died in his sleep. He may have been all written out, but he had written a last book he had wanted to write sheerly for his own amusement. He had divested himself of Adelaide. He was sixty-six years old. Lonnie, who was his youngest son, had thought nothing of it when Marquand the previous night over dinner had remarked that he thought he would have another heart attack. He had patted the boy on the head and retired early. He was living alone and sleeping alone and, as his biographer Stephen Birmingham noted rather cruelly, he died alone.

III

Some four days after Warner Oland's death, VARIETY reported that Twentieth Century-Fox was canvassing exhibitors concerning possible replacements in the Charlie Chan role. A total of thirty-four actors were tested before a final choice was announced on 18 October 1938. Sidney Toler, who was awarded the part, was born at Warrensburg, Missouri in 1875. He was nearly sixty when he started in the role. He had begun in films with MADAME X (M-G-M, 1929) after working on the stage. Production on CHARLIE CHAN IN HONOLULU (20th-Fox, 1938) was scheduled to begin on 24 October. Sol Wurtzel had once commented to Keye Luke that "with this team, there's one smart one and one dumb one. You're the dumb one." Luke asked to be excused from his role in the Chan pictures and he was released from his contract. He did not feel that anyone could really replace Oland and he resented the pay cut he had received when Oland had died. Wurtzel cast Victor Sen Young as Charlie Chan's Number Two son, Jimmy Chan, the screenplay for CHARLIE CHAN IN HONOLULU explaining that elder son Lee was away at art school. Sen Young, whose real name was Sen Yew Cheung, had been a chemical salesman who thought he might like to be in pictures. Lucky Humberstone was assigned to direct CHARLIE CHAN IN HONOLULU. After the first few days of shooting, he found Toler's performance awkward and wooden. Flaring at Sen Young's inexperience, he would rage: "Get Keye Luke back!" For Toler he had more practical advice.

"I knew Sidney was a heavy drinker," Humberstone confided to me. "I told him I wanted him to take a few stiff belts before he started work the next morning. Sidney could hardly believe his ears, but he did it. He loosened up and gave a better characterization."

John Stone opined correctly that the only way to compensate in the long run for Toler's shortcomings was to devise scripts of strong intrigue and unusual interest. As a consequence, most of the plots of the Toler films are superior to those of Oland's films. CHARLIE CHAN IN HONOLULU was no exception. The film opens with Charlie Chan at table with his wife and twelve children. A murder aboard ship in the harbor and its solution are set against the tension of the delivery of Charlie's first grandchild. George Zucco was cast as an eccentric psychologist who pretends to be hard of hearing and who carries about with him the brain of a Chinese criminal which he keeps alive in a chemical concoction. Because Humberstone was directing, much in the picture was played for comic effect, such as Oscar, a tame lion on the ship, that gets involved in several humorous situations.

CHARLIE CHAN IN RENO (20th-Fox, 1939) was based on a novel by Philip Wylie and Norman Foster directed. Louise Henry was back as a bitchy divorcée who is murdered. Slim Summerville was cast as a rustic sheriff, assisting Charlie in the investigation. The film proved such a popular success that the studio almost outdid itself with the next entry, CHARLIE CHAN AT TREASURE ISLAND (20th-Fox, 1939). Edward Kaufman, who had just joined Fox as an associate producer after leaving Warner Bros., was the producer and Norman Foster directed. Cesar Romero was in the cast as was Douglas Dumbrille. The previous year Toler had appeared as Dumbrille's sidekick in Harry Sherman's production of Zane Grey's THE MYSTERIOUS RIDER (Paramount, 1938). Toler liked Dumbrille and, hence, it is not surprising that Dumbrille worked in several more of Toler's Chan films. The plot is concerned with a phony medium who uses his guise as a psychic consultant to blackmail his clients.

John Stone returned as associate producer for CHARLIE CHAN IN THE CITY OF DARKNESS (20th-Fox, 1939) with a screenplay by Robert Ellis and Helen Logan. Herbert I. Leeds directed. Set in Paris, the city is in darkness due to blackouts and the investigations are intermittently disrupted by the terrible drone of fighter planes flying overhead. The coming of a far greater catastrophe is nearly palpable in the oppressive opening to the film featuring newsreel footage of the Czech crisis. Douglas Dumbrille attempts to seduce Lynn Bari, playing the wife of his male secretary, before he is murdered. Victor Sen Young is absent but his presence is compensated for by Harold Huber cast as the prefect's assistant. This time his French was kept at a minimum. "Have not prepared for emergency," Charlie Chan comments at one point, "like man who buys suit with only one pair of pants." Nor did the quality of the Chanograms improve in later entries.

Two illegal Charlie Chan films were made by the Hsin Hwa Motion Picture Company in Shanghai, CHARLIE CHAN IN HOMELAND and CHARLIE CHAN IN RADIO STATION. Hsu Hsin-yuan was cast in the role of Chan. The pictures were done in Chinese but were never distributed beyond the borders of the war-torn mainland.

CHARLIE CHAN IN PANAMA (20th-Fox, 1940) was directed by Norman Foster. Espionage was the theme with Charlie working as an undercover agent sent to Central America to protect the Panama Canal and the U.S. fleet. It was the first film in the series produced with the idea of courting the Latin American market, in anticipation that Europe would be cut off because of war.

Robertson White and Lester Ziffren returned to Biggers' original novel, CHARLIE CHAN CARRIES ON, for the next entry, a remake titled CHARLIE CHAN'S MURDER CRUISE (20th-Fox, 1940). This time, however, Charlie was in the picture almost from the beginning. Inspector Duff comes to Charlie's office in Honolulu just prior to his being murdered. Layne Tom, Jr., who had played Charlie's Number Two son in CHARLIE CHAN AT THE OLYMPICS was cast in this film as Charlie's seventh son with Victor Sen Young in the role of Number Two. Although well directed by Eugene Forde, Sol Wurtzel announced after release of CHARLIE CHAN'S MURDER CRUISE that it was Fox' intention to drop the series from the production schedule for the 1940-1941 season. A sudden change of heart led to a new contract with both Toler and Sen Young that called for three new Chan films a year, definitely for the next season and with a renewable option for succeeding seasons.

CHARLIE CHAN AT THE WAX MUSEUM (20th-Fox, 1940) was the first of the three new Chans. C. Henry Gordon was cast as a crooked doctor who uses his crime museum as a hide-out where he performs plastic surgery on escaped criminals. Sen Young's Jimmy Chan was supposedly a law student. He was a chemistry student in MURDER OVER NEW YORK (20th-Fox, 1940), the next entry, actually the third cinematic version of Biggers' BEHIND THAT CURTAIN. The idea of poison gas in a glass sphere, so unique in CHARLIE CHAN IN EGYPT, was now again the means of murder, and this well after such a device had been used in MR. WONG, DETECTIVE (Monogram, 1938), a rival series to which I shall return; nor was it even the last time it would be used in the Chan series. Toler's Charlie Chan at his wittiest introduces "favorite son, Jimmy, without whose assistance many cases would have been solved much sooner."

Harry Lachman, who directed DEAD MEN TELL (20th-Fox, 1941), intensified his use of lighting, shadows, and close-ups to gain eerie effects, and to these he added sound. A group of suspects, the map to the location of a treasure divided among them, are invited to search for it aboard a pirate sailing ship. The sonic accompaniments are a parrot's screeching voice and the thumping of old Black Hook's wooden leg. Of course, it is the murderer who has donned this outfit, first to frighten one victim to death and then to menace Charlie on the deserted dock.

The war in Europe and the Far East continued to take its toll on the foreign market. The Chan films depended for their profitability on world-wide grosses. Sol Wurtzel, in a further effort to open a new market, made a tour of South America, returning to Hollywood the same month DEAD MEN TELL was released. He gave out a press release that the next Charlie Chan film would be set in Rio de Janeiro, but the screenwriters did not knock themselves out for CHARLIE CHAN IN RIO (20th-Fox, 1941). It was, in fact, a remake of THE BLACK CAMEL, this time with Victor Jory in the old Bela Lugosi role. Harold Huber played a Spanish-speaking policeman. Harry Lachman directed it, as he did CASTLE IN THE DESERT (20th-Fox, 1942). As Toler aged, his performance was becoming increasingly lifeless and inflexible. Lachman tried to make up for this by an economical yet interesting choice of sets: the Fox Western town set and the mansion that had housed Alan Mowbray's estate in

CHARLIE CHAN IN LONDON and had also served as Baskerville Hall in THE HOUND OF THE BASKERVILLES (20th-Fox, 1939). The story was a loose remake of THE CHINESE PARROT with Douglas Dumbrille in a major role. Lachman hoped that these other ingredients would carry the show, which they did: but not to South America. Sol Wurtzel cancelled the Charlie Chan series with this entry and turned his attention to producing a series with Laurel and Hardy. In all, he had supervised production of twenty-six Charlie Chan pictures. When Toler learned of Wurtzel's decision, he immediately negotiated screen rights with Biggers' widow, now remarried. It was his intention to find financing and let Twentieth Century-Fox distribute. Nothing went according to plan.

THE MYSTERIOUS MR. WONG (Monogram, 1935) starred Bela Lugosi as a surrogate Dr. Fu Manchu. The film is worth mentioning only to distinguish it from the later series of Mr. Wong films produced and released by Monogram. This series was based on a group of short stories written by Hugh Wiley and published in COLLIER'S. William Nigh directed all five of the Wong films which starred Boris Karloff in the role. Karloff must have been bored since he made no effort at a memorable characterization. The only thing Chinese about him, other than the name of the character and the fact that he drank tea, was his execrable make-up which was dropped in later entries. MR. WONG, DETECTIVE was the first film. Grant Withers, cast as the brow-beating, overbearing Captain Street, is grilling John St. Polis at police headquarters because St. Polis' business partners, who stole his formula for the manufacture of poison gas, are being systematically gassed to death. While the interrogation is taking place, the surviving partner has barricaded himself in his library and calls Captain Street on the 'phone. Street races to his home, sirens blaring, only to discover the man is dead. He races back and continues to brow-beat St. Polis. It takes Mr. Wong to show Street that the gas that killed the victims was placed in glass spheres which would burst only when a siren sounds outside. Luckily for St. Polis' mad scheme, Street's siren is the only one to be heard in the vicinities of the victims for several days.

Matters did not improve with THE MYSTERY OF MR. WONG (Monogram, 1939). It depended on dialogue such as that of the boyfriend of the intended murder victim's wife shouting into the camera: "I won't stand by and watch the woman I love torn to pieces." I had occasion to watch outtakes from this picture. Maybe they should have been left in. In one scene in the released version, Wong opens the victim's safe to extract a letter written before he died which states the name of his murderer.

"The door is open," Karloff observes, opening the safe door. In the outtakes, Karloff walks over to the safe.

"The door is open," he observes. He tugs at the door. He tugs some more. Then he turns to the director.

"The goddamned door won't open!" He resumes tugging. William Nigh calls: "Cut!"

MR. WONG IN CHINATOWN (Monogram, 1939) added Marjorie Reynolds to the series as news reporter, Bobbie Logan. Her one beat, apparently, is Captain Street's office. She sits on his desk, rides in his car, listens to all the conversations he has, and 'phones in to her paper to report every expletive. The plot concerns a Chinese princess, her maid, and a grotesque dwarf, all of whom are shot in the neck by a hand-operated Chinese bamboo blow gun loaded with giant-sized poison darts. Once a banker is introduced as a suspect and you learn the princess had a million dollars on deposit at his bank, it follows, especially at Monogram, that his bank is short of funds. Yet just why the banker should resort to such a clumsy death apparatus is not explained when Wong confronts him with his culpability. The banker jumps off the ship they are on and splashes about two inches away from the side of the vessel before Grant Withers' double plunges directly on top of him for a split-second arrest.

My first reaction, upon seeing these films, was that Monogram's producers must have cringed at the thought of the scathing reviews, that what the series needed was to be upgraded with more plausible plots. That was not the case. Indeed, once Monogram was producing the Charlie Chan series, these Wong scripts were remade as Charlie Chan vehicles!

DOOMED TO DIE (Monogram, 1940) opens to stock footage of a freighter burning. The shot has the ship move from right to left. It is an extremely short shot, so the clip was reversed and the ship is seen to burn some more, this time moving from left to right. An entire scene between Karloff and Richard Loo from MR. WONG IN CHINATOWN was lifted and interpolated into this film. One character is arguing with another character. The murderer opens the office door, shoots one of the characters, throws in the gun, and the other character is so shocked he fails to look in the direction of the door in order to see the murderer. In this way, the case can only be solved by Mr. Wong. Midway through the picture, Kenneth Harlan, cast as a chauffeur, is caught prowling on a fire escape in broad daylight.

"It's a pleasure to meet you," Wong comments.

"The pleasure is all yours," Harlan replies.

"What were you doing on the fire escape?" Street demands.

"Parking the car."

Of course, Harlan is the guilty one. He had a secret deal going with a powerful tong and feared exposure.

THE FATAL HOUR (Monogram, 1940) was the nadir. It would have been over early in the game if Jason Robards, Sr., had had a chance to talk. He is sitting in Street's waiting room. Although the room is very crowded, the murderer enters, steals a long, metal fingernail file from the desk sergeant, and plunges it into Robards' neck. Robards does not cry out and so the murder goes undiscovered until Wong enters the room. At Monogram, rather than avoid scenes likely to be expensive to create for the camera, screenwriters seemed to take perverse delight in including them. Two characters go out to dine at a supposedly swank night club. There is no orchestra, not even a juke box. The tables are made of bamboo with postage stamp table cloths. When the script needed to establish that there was gambling going on upstairs, to save on costs one character simply remarked to another: "A little gambling, eh? I can hear the poker chips." No one botherred to insert such a sound on the track.

Karloff did not care. His Monogram contract ran out before the final Mr. Wong picture could be rushed into production. Scott Dunlap, in charge of production, pleaded with Karloff, but to no avail. Karloff was happy to be done with the series. Monogram had presold three Wong pictures for 1940. What to do? The solution was obvious. What was always done in the 'Forties, for whatever the reason, when a producer needed a Chinese actor fast? The answer was inevitably Keye Luke.

There was no phantom in PHANTOM OF CHINATOWN (Monogram, 1940) and Keye Luke was scarcely suited to the Mr. Wong role and even with a moustache looked too young. Grant Withers as Captain Street is unacquainted with him until a third of the way into the picture. When they do get together, it is to expose the culprit by means of the old hospital routine where Keye is confined to his bed and catches the murderer when he tries to sneak into his room.

It was the last Wong picture. And so it happened that Monogram was looking for a replacement series when Toler was searching around for a production outlet. Scott Dunlap, on behalf of Monogram, agreed in May, 1943 to finance and release the Charlie Chan series. Dunlap figured that by lowering the budgets from $200,000 to $75,000 and with the return of the world market following the war, the studio stood a good chance of showing a profit. Toler, however, was even more aged. He literally shuffled through most of his scenes in the first entry, CHARLIE CHAN IN THE SECRET SERVICE (Monogram, 1944). Benson Fong, who would quit pictures to go into the restaurant business, was cast as Charlie's Number Three son, Tommy; Marianne Quon was his daughter, Iris Chan; and because Monogram had strong distribution in the South Mantan Moreland was cast as Birmingham, Charlie's Negro chauffeur. Moreland's contribution to the series consisted primarily of rolling his eyes and acting absurdly frightened at the sight of a corpse. After the initial murder, the murderer takes an occasional pot shot at Charlie, which causes Charlie to reassemble the entire cast again and again for questioning. In THE BIRTH OF A NATION (Epoch, 1915), D. W. Griffith included a close-up of Raoul Walsh's eye just before, as Booth, he shoots Lincoln. Phil Rosen was evidently so impressed with this device that he used it repeatedly in the Chan films he directed, presuming perhaps that a close-up of an unknown murderer's eye could only enhance the viewer's suspense.

THE CHINESE CAT (Monogram, 1944) was little better. Phil Rosen directed and Benson Fong was the only Chan offspring in the cast. Mantan Moreland was now a taxi driver. Jewel thieves are holed up in an abandoned fun house and the last two reels of the picture are played for laughs with the gang chasing Chan and Moreland around the fun house.

It is Moreland who gets Charlie enmeshed in murder in MEETING AT MIDNIGHT (Monogram, 1944) when he takes a job as a butler in the home of a crooked medium. The picture was also issued under the title BLACK MAGIC; but, under whatever title you might see it, the plot with its notion of frozen blood bullets carried in a refrigerator cigar case is patently ridiculous. Frances Chan played one of Charlie's daughters. Neither she nor Benson Fong, apparently, was available for THE JADE MASK (Monogram, 1945), so Edwin Luke, Keye Luke's brother, was drafted for the role of Charlie's Number Four son, Eddie. Since the beginning of the series, Charlie was working for the government. In this picture, he is promoted to an inspector. The murderer uses a rubber mask to make him look like one of the other suspects while his puppeteer wife has corpses dance around on steel wires so as to appear alive after they have been murdered.

THE SCARLET CLUE (Monogram, 1945) is set for the most part in a radio station with Charlie, Benson Fong, and Mantan Moreland wandering around interviewing suspects between murders. The murder weapon is a poison gas hidden in a microphone which kills when mixed in the air with cigarette smoke. The gimmick for THE SHANGHAI COBRA (Monogram, 1945) is stranger still. Cobra poison is rubbed on a needle beneath the selection knob of a juke box which punctures the victim's finger tip. While Mantan Moreland is absent from THE RED DRAGON (Monogram, 1946), Willie Best as Chattanooga supplied the necessary low Negro humor. Although the picture is presumably set in Mexico City, a shot of the neon signs of night spots are all of the Los Angeles clubs of the period. The best Charlie can do for a Chanogram is to remark somewhat pathetically: "Confucius could give answer to that. Unfortunately, Confucius not here at the moment."

I can readily sympathize should a reader become irritated at this point if I dwell on plots of pictures that, in all probability, one would have avoided seeing in the first place. Notwithstanding, they got worse. DARK ALIBI (Monogram, 1946) is about a love-sick prison guard who uses phony fingerprints to convict his beloved's father. SHADOWS OVER CHINATOWN (Monogram, 1946) was sustained, if unintentional, comedy, with Victor Sen Young returning to the series to replace Benson Fong, appearing first as Jimmy Chan and then changing, suddenly, into Chan's Number Three son, Tommy. Sidney Toler was deteriorating rapidly. He dragged himself doggedly through THE TRAP (Monogram, 1946) which, for story and direction, hit an all time low. The picture was released on 30 November 1946. On 12 February 1947, Sidney Toler died.

Monogram was hard pressed to find a replacement quickly. Roland Winternitz was born in Boston in 1904. His father was a concert violinist. "I was restless when I was young," Winters recalled in an interview, "and was always looking for something exciting to do. I decided to become a sailor as a teenager and shipped out with the United Fruit lines for two summer trips, one to Central America and the other to the West Indies. When I was sixteen, a friend of mine got me interested in one of Boston's little theatre groups. This led me to working with many stock companies and eventually to Broadway in 1924. A classmate of my brother's was producing THE FIREBRAND and so I landed a part in the play. The cast was loaded with other actors who, like myself, were to come into their own later on. Joseph Schildkraut, Edward G. Robinson, Allyn Joslyn, and Frank Morgan were the type of unknowns I worked with back then." He began in radio in 1931 and made his film debut in 13 RUE MADELINE (20th-Fox, 1947). On the basis of this appearance, he was tested by Monogram to play Charlie Chan and was given the role. THE CHINESE RING (Monogram, 1947), Winters' first Chan film, was a remake of MR. WONG IN CHINATOWN. The blow gun was switched to a European air rifle. The Grant Withers role was played by Warren Douglas with Louise Currie as the obnoxious female reporter. Even several of the sets were the same. Victor Sen Young and Mantan Moreland were Charlie's assistants. The lines were still bad and the acting no better.

The murder mechanism for the next Chan, DOCKS OF NEW ORLEANS (Monogram, 1948), was changed from what it had been in MR. WONG, DETECTIVE to poison gas hidden in radio tubes which was only released when the mad inventor could get his prospective victims to tune in to a program featuring his wife singing operatic arias, her high-pitched voice bursting the tubes! The Monogram executives were so pleased at how well Winters was doing in the role that Oliver Drake was hired to do the screenplays for subsequent entries. Drake was a veteran screenwriter for Westerns and he had an unfortunate penchant for re-using his previous material. Beginning with THE SHANGHAI CHEST (Monogram, 1948), Drake began adapting Three Mesquiteer and other Western properties he had worked on in the 'Thirties. THE GOLDEN EYE (Monogram, 1948) even kept the Western setting with Chan going to Arizona to get to the bottom of a phony gold mine racket.

For THE FEATHERED SERPENT (Monogram, 1948), Drake used his script from THE RIDERS OF THE WHISTLING SKULL (Republic, 1937). By a fluke of casting, Robert Livingston who had starred as Stony Brooke in the Three Mesquiteer picture turns out to be the culprit Chan exposes at the end. Keye Luke also rejoined the series in this film, at the very twilight of the series, playing one of Chan's sons while Sen Young played another and Mantan Moreland, staying on as Charlie's servant, was about equivalent to Max Terhune's dummy Elmer in the Mesquiteer Westerns.

The Chan unit was one of the very last to be working on the nearly deserted Monogram lot. In a move toward expansion and refinancing, the studio was soon absorbed into Allied Artists. Keye Luke appeared alone with Winters in the sixth and last Chan film of his series, SKY DRAGON (Monogram, 1949) which was directed by Lesley Selander. When I met Selander once for breakfast, I handed him a copy of his screen credits. As he paged through it, I told him that I just visited again with Keye Luke and that after the ill-fated Charlie Chan television series with J. Carrol Naish Keye had finally had an opportunity to play Chan—or, at least, his voice—in the equally short-lived Hanna-Barbera cartoon series.

"He did the characterization the way Warner Oland had," I said. "He recalled for me, laughing, how Oland had responded when Philip Morris approached him to sponsor a Charlie Chan radio program: 'Honorable father doesn't want to work that hard.' "

Instead Walter Connolly, Ed Begley, and Santos Ortega played the Oriental sleuth on radio. Selander continued to glance through his screen credits.

"You directed SKY DRAGON, the last theatrical Chan picture. Elena Verdugo was an airline stewardess and the murderer. When it completed the picture, Monogram was going to shoot a couple of Chans out of frozen funds in England. The deal fell through. Elena was cast in the lead in the MEET MILLIE television series with Roland Winters as her boss."

Selander was still paging through his filmography.

"What year was that?" he asked.

"Nineteen Forty-Nine. A funny thing. Keye Luke, who remembers so much about working with Warner Oland, couldn't really be of much help when it came to SKY DRAGON."

"Are you sure of that title?" he asked, his forehead furrowed in concentration.

"Here it is," I said, going over my copy of his credits. "It's listed under its working title, MURDER IN THE AIR."

He looked sheepishly at me. There was a silence.

"I certainly wish I could help you out," he said then, "but to be perfectly honest I can't even remember having directed that picture."

For better or worse, when now Charlie Chan in the movies is recalled, it is Warner Oland who comes to mind, with his soft, persuasive reassurance to the viewer, "Not very good detective . . . just lucky old Chinaman."

5
The Song of the Thin Man

I don't like eloquence; if it isn't effective enough to pierce your hide, it's tiresome; and if it is effective enough, then it muddles your thoughts.

The Continental Op[1]

I

In his book DASHIELL HAMMETT (1984) Dennis Dooley prefaced his study of Hammett's fiction with the observation that "as a writer he had asked important questions, and ventured some bold answers . . . and showed us things about our society and our very language—the way we talk and think about our lives—that have become a permanent part of what we know. But perhaps the most remarkable thing of all about Dashiell Hammett is that he managed to accomplish all of these things in the course of turning out some of the best detective stories anybody ever wrote."[2] Yet, in the final analysis, Hammett's so-called "realistic" characters actually resolve themselves into simplified, objectified human motives and are not characters in the fuller human sense at all. They are embodiments of varying attitudes toward life and central among them is that of the detective himself. Hammett, it seems to me, in creating his various detectives sought to articulate for himself a persona with which to face the world and that persona was perhaps most successfully and effectively projected in the personality of Sam Spade as he appears in THE MALTESE FALCON (1930).

Samuel Dashiell Hammett was born on 27 May 1894 in St. Mary's County, Maryland, the son of Richard Thomas Hammett and Annie Bond Hammett. His youth was spent in Baltimore and Philadelphia. He was twenty when he applied to an advertisement and was hired as a Pinkerton operative. He worked in a number of Pinkerton offices around the country assigned to a multitude of cases before he enlisted in June, 1918 in the Army and found himself in the Motor Ambulance Corps. He was stationed only twenty miles from his family home in Baltimore. According to William F. Nolan, "Hammett tried to make the best of his situation, but he was never comfortable behind the wheel of the awkward, top-heavy ambulance he'd been assigned to drive. While he was transporting some patients from the hospital, his ambulance struck a rock in the roadway, overturned, and dumped the startled patients into the dirt. This accident, for which he took full blame, was traumatic; he swore he would never drive again. And there is no evidence that, once he was out of the service, he ever did."[3]

When he fell victim to the wave of influenza which swept over the world, it was discovered that he had tuberculosis. This was the beginning of a lifelong battle with various types of lung disease. Hammett was transferred to a veteran's hospital in Tacoma. While a patient there, he met a floor nurse, Josephine Dolan. As his condition improved, they went out on dates to restaurants or walked together in parks. Hammett was again transferred, this time to the veteran's hospital in San Diego. Jose, as she was called, was transferred to the Cheyenne Hospital in Helena, Montana. She was pregnant. Once Hammett was released from the hospital in San Diego, he went to San Francisco and reapplied to the Pinkerton agency. After he was rehired, he wrote to Josephine and asked that she join him.

The couple was married at St. Mary's Cathedral on Van Ness. They were driven there in a taxi. Hammett gave Josephine a bouquet of flowers. They rented a furnished apartment on Eddy Street for $45 a month. There was a living room in front, a small room with a folding bed, more an interconnecting hall, and a kitchen. When Hammett began to write, he wrote at the kitchen table. The apartment had steam heat. The landlady was a bootlegger. The police were among her customers. Hammett frequently did the cooking. He preferred hamburger, when they could afford it. He rolled his own cigarettes. Pinkerton detectives were paid $6 a day, every day of the year; but work was irregular. Hammett might have off two or three days and then be out on a job for a week.

The San Francisco agency was run by a man named Phil Geaque who once had been a bodyguard for Theodore Roosevelt. He was short, bald-headed, and as Hammett's Continental Op preferred Fatima cigarettes. Hammett worked for a time on the Fatty Arbuckle case and for a time tailed Fanny Brice, hoping to locate her second husband who was wanted for theft. Hammett was particularly expert at shadowing and was usually given this kind of assignment. He found in his everyday experience that drinking was unrelated to trustworthiness in bonding a man, that fingerprints are generally useless, that burglary provides so poor a living that most burglers end up living off their women, and that the best way to beat a rap is to deny everything. San Francisco is a damp, fog-laden city. Hammett's shadowing jobs kept him outdoors and, frequently, near the docks. He started to hemorrhage again. He would not complain. He might say that he had had a nasty day. Then he would not eat at all. He would stay in bed and just sit there, night and day, night and day. He would drink to ease the pain of recurrent coughing and the irritation of excessive smoking.

When the Pinkerton agency was retained by the mining companies in an attempt to suppress labor unions, Hammett was sent to Butte, Montana to participate in strike-breaking. He later confessed to his elder daughter, Mary Jane, that he did not care if his clients were bums, he was strictly out to do his job— an attitude which his fictional detectives often retained. Life was hard and there was seldom much money. Hammett would take Mary Jane with him to speakeasies and let her drink sparkling water in a champagne glass. During his days off, he used to sit with her on his lap and read to her. When there was time, he would also go in the afternoons to the Public Library and read. He discovered pulp magazines at the library. He told Mary Jane, after reading some of these pulp stories, that he could write better than that. At Christmas, he would spend hours with Mary Jane decorating the tree. He wanted to be a poet and so he wrote in his spare time. He also tried to write fiction.

Hammett's first short story, "The Barber and His Wife," appeared in the December, 1922 issue of BRIEF STORIES at the same time as his first story for BLACK MASK appeared in the December issue of that magazine. Both were signed "Peter Collinson." Hammett took the name from Peter Collins, slang for a nobody. Hammett's somewhat brief career as an author of detective fiction was inextricably bound up with BLACK MASK magazine. It had been founded in 1920 by H. L. Mencken and George Jean Nathan as a moneymaking pulp to subsidize their efforts on behalf of THE SMART SET to which they were deeply committed. After less than six months, they sold BLACK MASK for $12,500 to Eugene Crowe and Eltinge Warner, owners and publishers of THE SMART SET. The new owners appointed Francis M. Osborne to edit BLACK MASK. He was succeeded by George Sutton, Jr., who edited the magazine from October, 1922 to March, 1924 with his associate editor, Harry North, who was with BLACK MASK from October, 1922 to September, 1925. In 1923, still writing under the pseudonym Peter Collinson, Hammett submitted the first two of his stories featuring the nameless operative working for the Continental Detective Agency, "Arson Plus" which was published in the 1 October 1923 issue and "Slippery Fingers" which was published in the 15 October 1923 issue. The latter also carried an Op story titled "Crooked Souls," which Hammett did sign with his new *nom de plume*, Dashiell Hammett. Only when he went to New York in late 1929 and to Hollywood in late 1930, where he was not known, did people call him and did he call himself Dash Hammett. In San Francisco, he was still simply Sam Hammett. Concerning the Op, Hammett commented in a letter to the editor that "I didn't deliberately keep him nameless, but he got through 'Slippery Fingers' and 'Arson Plus' without needing one, so I suppose I may well let him run along that way. I'm not sure he's entitled to a name, anyhow. He's more or less of a type: the private detective who oftenest is successful. . . ."[4]

Hammett resigned from the Pinkerton agency on 15 February 1922 in order to concentrate on writing. Hammett's physical condition had also worsened. When Josephine gave birth to their second daughter, medical advice was that the family should split up until Hammett's tuberculosis improved. After living apart for a time, in 1925 Hammett shipped Josephine and the two girls to Montana where they stayed for six months with relatives. Hammett was convinced that he could cure himself of lung disease by making a success of it as a writer and by drinking large doses of Scotch whiskey. Hammett would write all night. He gave up sleeping, but it told on him. He had rented a cheap room on Pine Street. He would line up chairs from the bed to the bathroom so he could support himself on the way to the toilet. He made the acquaintance of a girl across the hall and would sleep with her when he was up to it. He found another girl on Grant Street to fill in when the girl across the hall was otherwise engaged. If he ate at all, he ate cheap food. Mostly he lived on soup, coffee, Scotch, and cigarettes. He was constantly trying to have his disability pension increased. A penny a word was not a living wage when one wrote the way Hammett did, at a typewriter, writing over and over and over again. Yet, in the years 1924–1925, following this regimen, Hammett wrote twenty-three short stories, mostly published in BLACK MASK. If fact, he even called his writing "Blackmasking."

Frequently, Hammett would emphasize his personal experience as a private detective in order to claim that this gave a special verisimilitude to his fiction. When it came to the Op's motivation, Hammett remarked that "I see in him a little man going forward day after day through mud and blood and death and deceit—as callous and brutal and cynical as necessary—towards a dim goal, with nothing to push or pull him towards it except he's been hired to reach it."[5] Hammett's achievement in these early stories, according to A. Alvarez, was "to have evolved a prose in which the most grotesque or shocking details are handled as though they were matters of routine, part of the job."[6]

Hammett's view of society is that it is universally corrupt. This is a constant motif in all of his detective fiction, but nowhere perhaps is it better articulated than in "Women, Politics, and Murder," published in the September, 1924 issue of BLACK MASK. The Op is sent by the agency to talk with Mrs. Gilmore. It seems her husband was found on Pine Street, shot to death. The only curious thing about the death is the angle of the bullet which apparently penetrated the body when it was already in a prostrate position. Mrs. Gilmore tells the Op that her husband had a string of women over the years, but his latest mistress is Cara Kendall whose apartment is very near where her husband's body was found. The Op goes to question the Kendall woman and learns nothing. He talks to his friend on the police force, Sergeant O'Gar, who tells him about the body being first discovered by a beat cop named Kelly. O'Gar draws no conclusions because he is not paid to think. The Op goes back to talk to Mrs. Gilmore. She is out, but the Gilmore maid tells the Op that Mrs. Gilmore followed her husband the night he left the house and was killed.

When Mrs. Gilmore returns, the Op confronts her with this information without revealing his source. Mrs. Gilmore admits that she did follow her husband but insists that she did not kill him. She also admits she tried to telephone Cara Kendall about the time of the murder and that she did not answer her 'phone. The Op goes back to interview Cara Kendall. This time she admits that Gilmore had called off their relationship. The Op does not get any further because Stanley Tennant arrives, using his own key in the front door. Tennant is an assistant city engineer. He does not like the case the Op appears to be building against Cara who is now *his* mistress, so he pulls a gun on the Op. With the Op watching, he rips Cara's clothing and belts her in the face. He then tells Cara to call the police. She is to back his story that the Op tried to assault her with intent to rape while questioning her. With the pull he has in city hall, he is convinced that he can get the Op sent up. The Op tries to fight his way out of this frame, but Cara gets hold of Tennant's gun and taps him a couple of times on the head. At headquarters, the police are readily convinced by Tennant's story, backed up by Cara's testimony; even O'Gar is wavering toward believing it. And why not? Here's an easy conviction in court. The Gilmore killing is not likely to be solved. The Op is about to be railroaded when he demands to see Kelly, the beat cop who discovered Gilmore's body. He accuses him of the murder. Kelly confesses that it was an accident. He saw Gilmore's shadow in a building archway, told him to stop, and pulled out his gun. He tripped. The gun went off. Gilmore was shot. The charges against the Op are dropped. Tennant wants to give the Op some money as they leave the station house. The Op is willing not to make trouble for Tennant because he does not want more trouble for himself, but still he is not up to this. He slugs Tennant and feels good about it.

There is physical action all through this story, but the emphasis is not so much on it as on the closing circle of the legal, political, and judicial system in which the characters live. The tension is not created by concern over who committed the murder so much as by the reader's instinctive knowledge that society is ever ready to nail a fall guy. Truth and justice have nothing to do with anything. The narrative is economical. Much is handled by means of dialogue. Description, as in Hammett generally, is at a minimum. The plot has a fine, inevitable precision. The Op saves himself at the last possible moment, but it is too close a call for him not to be shaken by it, and the reader with him. Many years later, one of the students from the writing class that Hammett taught at the Jefferson School of Social Science in New York put it this way: 'He taught us that tempo is the vital thing in fiction, that you've got to keep things moving, and that character can be drawn *within* the action. . . . ''[7]

Hammett once confessed that he was a heavy drinker because he was "confused by the fact that people's feelings and talk and actions didn't have much to do with one another.''[8] Motives in fiction in general and especially in detective fiction are made to coincide with the preconcluded course the plot will follow. Because of this convention, we are invariably led to believe that we understand why characters behave as they do. Yet, in life we actually know next to nothing about motive. Indeed, in life motives are known to change both suddenly and unaccountably. Hammett tried to solve this difficulty in his fiction by means of describing truthfully what his characters said and did, without ever taking a reader inside of them to speculate on *why* they did it. Because he was able to do this, and do it so well, his detective fiction is certainly unconventional.

One of Hammett's pervasive themes, alongside the vision of a corrupt society, is the way in which women customarily use sexual temptation as a method of catching a man off guard. This theme is central to the non-Op story, "The Man Who Killed Dan Odams," which appeared in the 15 January 1924 issue, in the Op stories, "The Girl with the Silver Eyes" from the June, 1924 issue, "The Whosis Kid" from the March, 1925 issue, "The Gutting of Couffignal" from the December, 1925 issue, the two Op novels, both of which ran serially in BLACK MASK before book publication, RED HARVEST (1929) and THE DAIN CURSE (1929), as well as THE MALTESE FALCON. In fact, when the Op turns down the Princess Zhukovski in "The Gutting of Couffignal" it is only a rehearsal for the scene where Sam Spade tells Brigid O'Shaughnessy his reasons for sending her over. After telling the princess why he must turn down her money bribe—he likes being a detective, likes the work: " 'You can't weigh that against any sum of money,' "[9]—he shoots her in the calf of her left leg. "I had never shot a woman before," the Op reflects. "I felt queer about it. 'You ought to have known I'd do it!' My voice sounded harsh and savage and like a stranger's in my ears. 'Didn't I steal a crutch from a cripple?' "[10] Nor, in retrospect, was this practice of rehearsing themes unusual for Hammett. He did so often in his short stories, each time further refining and perfecting how a particular theme was handled.

"Nightmare Town," a long short story which appeared in ARGOSY ALL-STORY in the 27 December 1924 issue, was a rehearsal for RED HARVEST. The protagonist, Steve Threefall, arrives in Izzard, a town in the desert. He is plunged into an immediate awareness of widespread corruption, but it is not until the end of the story that he learns that the entire town is a fake, a front for a bootlegging operation. Almost at once, Steve is put on trial for disturbing the peace and his fine is every last cent he has: "That, he knew, was the way of justice everywhere with the stranger. . . . "[11] He finds a friend in Kamp, who turns out to be an undercover agent and is killed. In a poker game it is observed that "not one of the six—except Steve, and perhaps Kamp—would have hesitated to favor himself at the expense of honesty had the opportunity come to him; but where knowledge of trickery is evenly distributed honesty not infrequently prevails."[12] In a fight, Steve is able to defend himself admirably with a weighted stick for "behind his stick that had become a living part of him, Steve Threefall knew happiness—that rare happiness which only the expert ever finds—the joy in doing a thing that he can do supremely well. Blows he took—blows that shook him, staggered him—but he scarcely noticed them. His whole consciousness was in his right arm and the stick it spun."[13]

It was the same kind of physical exhilaration in battle that the Op would experience in a later story, "The Big Knockover," which appeared in the February, 1927 issue of BLACK MASK. "It was a swell bag of nails," the Op remarks in that story. "Swing right, swing left, kick, swing right, swing left, kick. Don't hesitate, don't look for targets. God will see that there's always a mug there for your gun or blackjack to sock, a belly for your foot. A bottle came through and found my forehead. My hat saved me some, but the crack didn't do me any good. I swayed and broke a nose where I should have smashed a skull."[14]

But to return to "Nightmare Town." Larry Ormsby, a gangster, remarks, " 'that a man is moved to protect what he *thinks* belongs to him,' " to which Steve responds, " 'Maybe you're right . . . but I've never had enough experience with property to know how I'd feel about being deprived of it.' "[15] Steve is gripped by what is nearly akin to existentialist *Angst*—a combination of dread and nausea—as he witnesses the butchery that begins to happen. "He had the sensation of being caught in a monstrous net—a net without beginning or end, and whose meshes were slimy with blood. Nausea—spiritual and physical—gripped him, held him impotent."[16] The bootleggers begin to prey upon each other, driven into a frenzy by their greed. " 'God, there never was a bigger game!' " Ormsby tells Steve. " 'It couldn't flop—unless we spoiled it for ourselves. And that's what we've done. It was too big for us! There was too much money in it—it went to our heads! At first we played square with the syndicate. We made booze and shipped it out—shipped it in carload lots, in trucks, did everything but pipe it out, and we made money for the syndicate and for ourselves. Then we got the real idea—the big one! We kept on making the hooch, but we got the big idea of going for our own profit.' "[17] It is Ormsby who sounds the death knell for Izzard and its inhabitants. " 'The game has blown up! It was too rich for us. Everybody is trying to slit everybody else's throat.' "[18] The notion that criminals, as humans in general inspired by greed, will destroy each other is another one of Hammett's pervasive themes. In RED HARVEST, the Op chooses to treat violence with violence, only to recognize in the end that it was a mistake. "This damn burg's getting to me," he reflects. "If I don't get away soon, I'll be going blood-simple like the natives. There's been . . . a dozen and a half murders since I've been here. . . . I've arranged a killing or two in my time, when it's necessary. But this is the first time I've ever got the fever. It's this damn burg. You can't go straight here. . . ."[19]

In "The Scorched Face," an Op story published in the May, 1925 issue of BLACK MASK, the Op is hired to trace two young women who are missing. There is a cop named Pat Reddy who is married to a wealthy woman but works hard at his police job anyway. They join forces on the case and, compiling a list of criminal activities in the city in the past year, the feeling of universal corruption is made to seem almost comic. "Its size would have embarrassed the Chamber of Commerce. It looked like a hunk of the telephone book. Things happened in a city in a year. The section devoted to strayed wives and daughters was the largest; suicides next; and even the smallest division—murders—wasn't any too short."[20] The scam is a phony religious cult which gets women into compromising situations, takes photographs of them, then blackmails them, with many of the women as a result committing suicide or vanishing. The only morality which exists is the pretense of upright behavior and, at bottom, that is only another lie. The Op who is not above arranging a murder when he feels it is necessary—as he confesses in RED HARVEST—is also not above a cover-up. He persuades Pat to join him in covering up for one of the girls whom he has been tracing and who shoots the leader of the phony religious cult. The Op offers him credit for the bust. "My idea," he reflects, "was that if Pat took the credit, he couldn't very well ease himself out afterward, no matter what happened. Pat's a right guy, and I'd trust him anywhere—but you can trust a man just as easily if you have him sewed up."[21] Ironically, Pat is a double winner for going along with the Op. "The sixth photograph in the stack," the Op says of the evidence that Pat lets him destroy, "had been of his wife—the coffee importer's reckless, hot-eyed daughter."[22]

I think it is interesting to note that it is wives and daughters and girlfriends who wander in the Op stories. When Hammett did include an anecdote about a wandering male—as, for example, the Flitcraft story in THE MALTESE FALCON, a man who abandons his comfortable middle-class life when a beam nearly smashes him and he realizes the fragility of existence—the male usually has a profound psychological reason for what he does. Women, to the contrary, usually do not; usually they are covering up for some sexual indiscretion or destructive passion.

Jose was opposed to Hammett's writing because it did not earn him very much money. In the latter part of 1925, Hammett's tubercular condition was declared "cured," by which it was meant that the virulent progress of his illness had been arrested. He was far from really cured. In fact, in 1927 he would be termed totally disabled by it and thus entitled to the maximum pension. He was reunited with his family and making two thousand dollars a year from his writing when, in March, 1926, he put an advertisement in the SAN FRANCISCO CHRONICLE in the "position wanted" columns. He was hired as advertising manager by Albert S. Samuels, a local jeweler who owned four stores and preferred to use large, story advertisements in the newspaper as opposed to handbills. He needed a writer to turn out copy for him. Hammett did well at the job and got on well with Samuels. Hammett had an affair with Peggy O'Toole, his assistant. Jose lived in one apartment with the girls while Hammett also maintained a separate studio apartment for himself on Turk Street where he would write. Hammett became increasingly fond of his youngest daughter, also named Josephine. Hammett called her Jo. He was earning $350 a month working for Samuels and Jose was able to keep ahead of the bills. But in late July, less than five months after he had begun, Hammett collapsed on the floor of his office, hemorrhaging from the lungs. It took him eight weeks to recover. He realized that he could not work full time at anything. His health would not permit it. He rented a different apartment for Jose and the children and moved to a small, two-room flat for himself. As far as he was concerned, he had retired from writing fiction. Now he would be a free-lance advertising man. And so it might have remained had Captain Joseph T. Shaw not bought a financial interest in BLACK MASK in 1927 and become its editor.

In the Introduction to his anthology, THE HARD-BOILED OMNIBUS: EARLY STORIES FROM BLACK MASK (1946), Shaw himself tended to take much of the credit for having developed the hard-boiled detective story, claiming that "we meditated on the possibility of creating a new type of detective story differing from . . . the deductive type, the cross-word puzzle sort, lacking—deliberately—all other human emotional values."[23] Shaw further claimed that he went through back numbers of the magazine and decided Dashiell Hammett's stories came closest to what he had in mind. "The formula or pattern" which Shaw wanted "emphasizes character and the problems inherent in human behavior over crime solution. In other words, in this new pattern, character conflict is the main theme; the ensuing crime, or its threat, is incidental."[24] It is also probably worth mentioning that Richard Layman in SHADOW MAN: THE LIFE OF DASHIELL HAMMETT (1981), while noting the discrepancies in this claim, was willing to credit Shaw with being "as important as he claims to have been in the development of the hard-boiled detective story, because he was a promoter. By August, 1929 he had increased circulation to 92,000 copies per issue. His editorial judgment was often questionable, and he seems to have done little by way of offering helpful editorial advice to his authors; but he took an active interest in the careers of his best authors and used contacts he had established in the New York publishing world to get his elite group of BLACK MASK writers book publication and even publication in other magazines. Moreover, he raised the rates he paid for good stories. By the end of the 1920s, Shaw was paying as much as six cents a word for stories (that is $720 for a twelve-thousand-word story), though his normal rate was two cents a word."[25]

Shaw's encouragement, financial and otherwise, decided Hammett to resume writing for the magazine and to try his hand at longer fictions. Two long Op short stories, "The Big Knockover" and "$106,000 Blood Money," the latter running in the May, 1927 issue of BLACK MASK, were actually parts of the same story and were combined in 1943 into a single story titled BLOOD MONEY. By the end of 1927 BLACK MASK began running the first of four installments of what became RED HARVEST and in November, 1928 the first of four installments of what became THE DAIN CURSE. Usually, BLOOD MONEY is not counted as being among Hammett's five novels and, of those that are, THE DAIN CURSE is surely the weakest. It is a poorly structured story with far too many characters and a wholly improbable plot, but it does illustrate, rather nicely, how committed Hammett was to Gothic plot ingredients.

In "Part One: The Dains," Mrs. Leggett, née Alice Dain, is blamed for the murder of her sister, Lily Dain, the first Mrs. Leggett, although by the end of the novel it is not made quite clear if she did this murder herself or manipulated Lily's daughter and her stepdaughter, Gabrielle, to do it. She did, however, murder two blackmailers, Upton and Ruppert, and her husband, Leggett. Fitzstephan, an unsuccessful novelist who is insane and is actually behind most of the twelve murders in the novel (down from the twenty-five murders in RED HARVEST), calls Alice Leggett "a serene sane soul" in describing her to the Op whom he has known for a number of years, but once the Op exposes her he observes about her that "the housewife—Fitzstephan's serene sane soul—was suddenly gone. This was a blonde woman whose body was rounded, not with the plumpness of contented, well-cared-for middle age, but with the cushioned, soft-sheathed muscles of the hunting cats, whether in jungle or alley."[26] She tries to make a getaway and, in the struggle with the Op and Fitzstephan, the gun she is holding plugs her in the throat. Before she attempts her escape, she tells Gabrielle: " ' . . . You're cursed with the same black soul and rotten blood that she [Lily] and I and all the Dains have had. . . . ' "[27]

The Op dismisses this curse as " 'words in an angry woman's mouth.' "[28] But it is very real to Gabrielle who is addicted to morphine which does not help her mental condition. Fitzstephan is in love with Gabrielle but she rejects him; so he proceeds to murder all those who are close to her. "Part Two: The Temple" deals with Gabrielle's adventures in the Temple of the Holy Grail, a fake religion secretly set up by Fitzstephan and operated by the Haldorns. The tone of much of the narration borders on the comic because the events are so preposterous. Eric Collinson is Gabrielle's fiancé. The Op is sent to watch over Gabrielle while she is supposedly recuperating at the Temple. He is drugged. When he comes to, he finds that Gabrielle has left her room. Collinson is at the front door.

"Eric Collinson was there, wild-eyed, white-faced, and frantic.

" 'Where's Gaby?' he gasped.

" 'God damn you,' I said and hit him in the face with the gun. He drooped, bending forward, stopped himself with hands on the vestibule's opposite walls, hung there a moment, and slowly pulled himself upright again. Blood leaked from a corner of his mouth.

" 'Where's Gaby?' he repeated doggedly."[29]

Peter Wolfe remarked in BEAMS FALLING: THE ART OF DASHIELL HAMMETT (1980) that "the religious coloring that seeps through Part Two of THE DAIN CURSE hearkens back to the convents and monasteries used by Gothic writers 250 years earlier. The corpse that slides in and out of view, the dark corridors, staircases, and rooms, the strange noises, and the unworldly apparition of the mechanical ghost [the] Op fights in Chapter 11 refer just as pointedly to Gothic romance. Like an Ann Radcliffe or a 'Monk' Lewis novel, THE DAIN CURSE asks us to suspend rational disbelief in order to savor the marvelous.''[30] However, THE DAIN CURSE does not break faith with the materialism indigenous to the *Weltanschauung* of detective fiction: all of the mysterious phenomena have a natural, albeit exotic and far-fetched, explanation. Hammett apparently had an abiding interest in tales of terror and the supernatural since he edited a collection of them titled CREEPS BY NIGHT (1931). In his Introduction to it, Hammett commented that "the effectiveness of the sort of stories that we are here concerned with depends on the reader's believing that certain things cannot happen and on the writer's making him feel—if not actually believe—that they can but should not happen.''[31] Hammett often said that he was most influenced by Henry James and while elsewhere in his fiction he experimented with combining the Gothic and seemingly supernatural with the narrative structures of detective fiction perhaps nowhere did he do so more than in THE DAIN CURSE.

In the third part of this novel, "Quesada," the Op undertakes to help Gabrielle cure herself of her morphine addiction. A Mexican servant removes some packets of morphine from the Op's pocket while he is ostensibly sleeping. He says nothing about it at the time. Later the next day, Gabrielle confesses to the Op that she has had the packets ever since the Mexican servant slipped them to her, but she did not use them. The Op tells her that he knew she had them. " 'You knew?' " she remarks with emotion. " 'You trusted me that much—to go away and leave me with them?' " The Op, true to his persona, comments to the reader: "Nobody but an idiot would have confessed that for two days the folded papers had held powdered sugar instead of the original morphine.''[32] Ultimately, to be effective, the Op dares trust no one and leaves nothing to chance.

Fitzstephan has his right arm and his right leg blown off, indeed he loses an eye, an ear, half his face in a bomb explosion; notwithstanding, he survives and is put on trial. In his defense he claims that he plotted so many murders because "he looked on Gabrielle . . . as his property, bought with the deaths he had caused. Each death had increased her price, her value to him.''[33] In short, he pleads innocence by virtue of insanity. After a year in an asylum, he is released, a battered wreck. In a reversal of Edna Ferber's code wherein men are hopeless dreamers and women practical realists, in Hammett's fiction men are capable of being realists through great effort, women are romantic dreamers. Aaronia Haldorn, an extremely attractive woman whose husband was killed by the Op, had been Fitzstephan's mistress, but he had thrown her over in his pursuit of Gabrielle and even tried to have her killed. In a typical example—for Hammett—of female romanticism Aaronia carries Fitzstephan off to an island in Puget Sound. And yet is this ending really so very different from the conclusion of Charlotte Brontë's JANE EYRE (1847)? "Healthy sexuality is absent from Hammett's work . . . ,'' Richard Layman pointed out, although he also argued that it can be found in THE THIN MAN (1934) where, actually, it is avoided almost entirely.[34] For me, the matter is far more thorough-going. The great object lesson in all of Hammett's fiction is that one must never be a "sap"—to use Sam Spade's graphic term—for either sex or money if one is to survive with his personality intact and uncorrupted.

Lillian Hellman, with whom Hammett would live on and off for thirty years, told a revealing anecdote about him. "I think Hammett was the only person I ever met who really didn't care about money, made no complaints and had no regrets when it was gone," she wrote. He had long wanted a crossbow. It was expensive and, when he did buy it, it meant going without other things. On the day he got it—he was living with Hellman at the time—some friends arrived with a ten-year-old boy. Hammett spent the afternoon with the boy playing with the crossbow. When it came time to leave, Hammett put the crossbow into the car with the boy and hurried into the house, despite protestations. Hellman remonstrated with him afterwards, considering how much he had originally wanted the crossbow for himself. " 'The kid wanted it more,' " Hammett responded. " 'Things belong to people who want them most.' "[35]

Some critics—Peter Wolfe among them—presume that Hammett's Marxist leanings hold the key to his view of American society. I do not. Nor, do I believe, would anyone well versed in Marxist thought. In "Zigzags of Treachery," an Op story which appeared in the 1 March 1924 issue of BLACK MASK, Hammett had the Op reflect: "I'm not what you'd call a brilliant thinker—such results as I get are usually the fruits of patience, industry, and unimaginative plugging, helped out now and then, maybe, by a little luck—but I do have my flashes of intelligence."[36] I think what appealed to Hammett about Marxism was its disapproval of capitalistic society and, on the most superficial level, its seeming attitude about money and the accumulation of money.

"If this book had been written with the help of an outline or notes or even a clearly defined plot-idea in my head I might now be able to say how it came to be written and why it took the shape it did," Hammett wrote in his Introduction to the Modern Library edition of THE MALTESE FALCON, "but all I can remember about its invention is that somewhere I had read of the peculiar rental agreement between Charles V and the Order of the Hospital of Saint John of Jerusalem, that in a short story called 'The Whosis Kid' I had failed to make the most of a situation I liked, that in another called 'The Gutting of Couffignal' I had been equally unfortunate with an equally promising denouement, and that I thought I might have better luck with these two failures if I combined them with the Maltese lease in a longer story."[37] After citing this passage, Richard Layman felt constrained to add that "Hammett failed to mention that Brigid O'Shaughnessy, the villainess of THE MALTESE FALCON, was the epitome of the beautiful, dangerous woman he had been developing in his stories since spring, 1924."[38] This prototypical character was what Dennis Dooley termed the "Dark Lady" of the Op stories who "symbolizes in a way another side of himself he is afraid to know or to acknowledge—but to which he is forever and relentlessly drawn. To be able to trust this character completely would be to realize the fulness of his humanity, finally to be whole; but having seen too much of the evil of the world, he does not dare let down his guard. So he has learned instead to act a role that will keep him safe, though it is to accept a kind of death."[39]

In a way, THE MALTESE FALCON is a repudiation of the familiar Gothic theme of a damsel in distress. Brigid is no Gabrielle. " 'How bad a hole are you actually in' " Spade asks her. " 'As bad,' " she tells him, " 'as could be.' "

" 'Physical danger?'

" 'I'm not heroic. I don't think there's anything worse than death.'

" 'Then it's that?'

" 'It's that as surely as we're sitting here'—she shivered—'unless you help me.' "[40]

It is not too long before Spade begins to penetrate behind her facade and the miasma of lies which surrounds her and colors everything she says. When Brigid again pleads with him to trust her, Spade is moved to tell her: " 'You told me that this afternoon in the same words, same tone. It's a speech you've practiced.' "[41]

There is a stage-bound quality to virtually every scene in the novel. The objective style, keeping the reader outside of the characters, intensifies the impression of set speeches, of pretending, of play-acting. Robert I. Edenbaum in his essay, "The Poetics of the Private-Eye: The Novels of Dashiell Hammett" (1968), has, in my opinion, understood what Hammett was about in his fiction better than anyone else I have read. His perception of THE MALTESE FALCON is that in it Hammett was "less concerned with the intricacies of the detective story plot than with the combat between a villain(ess) who is a woman of sentiment, and who thrives on the sentiment of others, and a hero who has none and survives because he has none."[42] Edenbaum also felt that he had to qualify the word "combat," "for there can be only unequal combat when one antagonist holds all the cards and the other is always a victim; when the one manipulates and the other is deceived; when the actions of the one are unpredictable and the responses of the other stock. These terms would seem to describe the villain and his victim in Gothic fiction from THE MYSTERIES OF UDOLPHO to THE LIME TWIG. But Hammett, in THE MALTESE FALCON, reverses the roles. Brigid O'Shaughnessy, the murderer of Sam Spade's partner Miles Archer, is the manipulated, the deceived, the predictable, finally, in a very real sense, the victim."[43]

"Only the most courageous amongst us," Friedrich Nietzsche admonished in DIE GÖTZENDÄMMERUNG [THE TWILIGHT OF THE IDOLS] (1888), "has the rare courage to admit what he really *knows*. . . . "[44] I agree with Edenbaum—albeit changing his terminology just slightly—that Spade lives according to the vision of the Flitcraft story, as one who *really* knows. The story is a parable illustrating what Martin Luther meant by the school for character. Spade has overcome—or, rather, overcomes by the end of the story—the temptations of a close relationship with a woman and excessive, obsessional avarice. He is enabled to do so, in part, because he has overcome his fear of death and, therefore, the threat of death is meaningless to him. He warns Gutman that no amount of persuasion can be effective unless it carries the threat of death and, if one is immune to this threat, he is incapable of being intimidated. Gutman values objects—in particular the Maltese falcon—above people, and, therefore, he can agree to let Spade have Wilmer as a fall guy; he can inflict injury on his daughter in order to make the lie she is to tell Spade more credible to him. Spade, no less than Brigid, Cairo, Wilmer, Gutman, is breathing heavily as the falcon is unwrapped, but, when it proves a fake, he is released from his greed, whereas the others are still victims to their obsessions and passions. Spade's repudiation of sentimentality, sentiment, romance, and romanticism leaves him isolated from women and from money. He turns over the thousand dollar bill he conned from Gutman to the police when he turns over Brigid to them. " 'You had Thursby hooked and you knew it,' " he tells Brigid. " 'He was a sucker for women. His record shows that—the only falls he took were over women. And once a chump, always a chump.' "[45] Spade will not let her do it to him, will not let her make him play the sap for her, will not, he says, because everything inside of him wants to and, because, she had counted on that with him as she had with all the others.

It is possible to complain that this premise for living is as ultimately unsatisfying and futile as obsessive greed. But Spade would not argue that. It is the way he must live and the way he wants to live. I attach little significance to Effie Perine's momentary rejection of Spade at the end of the novel because she prefers to cherish for yet a while longer her romantic illusions. Hammett went on to include Spade and Effie in three short stories after publication of THE MALTESE FALCON. They are weak stories—two are, in fact, rewrites of earlier stories—but they do show Spade and Effie as friends. Professional friendship was the one option open to Spade, as perhaps to Hammett, when marital and romantic commitment to a woman were avenues that had to be closed in order to retain one's sense of integrity. "Spade had no original," Hammett observed. "He is a dream man in the sense that he is what most of the private detectives I worked with would like to have been and what quite a few of them in their cockier moments thought they approached. For your private detective does not—or did not ten years ago when he was my colleague—want to be an erudite solver of riddles in the Sherlock Holmes manner; he wants to be a hard and shifty fellow, able to take care of himself in any situation, able to get the best of anybody he comes in contact with, whether criminal, innocent bystander, or client."[46]

Hammett anticipated that THE MALTESE FALCON would be published in book form by Knopf and so, unlike his first two novels, he kept all the violence *in camera*. It was published first in BLACK MASK and Shaw checked the manuscript carefully. "Sex was a problem," as William F. Nolan pointed out. "Brigid's line 'I'm not ashamed to be naked before you' was dropped, as was a line from Cairo directed to her regarding a boy she had failed to seduce ('The one you couldn't make'). A *damn* or a *hell* was permitted, but outright swearing was not. (Hammett got around this neatly, losing none of the intended impact: 'The boy spoke two words, the first a short guttural verb, the second "you" ') Hammett's line from Spade 'How long have you been off the gooseberry lay, son?' was changed to 'How long have you been off the lay?' since Shaw was certain Hammett had something gamy in mind. He was mistaken. A 'gooseberry lay' was crook slang for stealing wash from a clothesline. However, Shaw did not touch the line 'Keep that gunsel away from me. . . . ' He assumed the word 'gunsel' meant gunman. Actually, it was a homosexual term meaning a 'kept boy.' Homosexuality, in fact, was not censored nearly as much as heterosexuality during those early pulp days. In the published book version, when Spade questions a house detective about Joel Cairo, the man answers with a leer, 'Oh, that one.' The original magazine version was bolder: 'Oh, her!' " [47]

The conviction that nothing can last, that there can be no sustaining relationships permeates THE GLASS KEY which was also serialized in BLACK MASK. Hammett had begun the book in San Francisco, but he left that city for New York with Nell Martin to whom it is dedicated. In it, Hammett tried to write a novel in which the characters are driven by motives other than greed, by loyalty and love. It was his favorite among his books. Yet, in this intention he failed, because his objective style reduced everything to mechanical pretense. Hammett could not shake himself free from the vision he had had, although it also proved enervating. John G. Cawelti may well have been right when he wrote in ADVENTURE, MYSTERY, AND ROMANCE: FORMULA STORIES AS ART AND POPULAR CULTURE (1976) that Hammett's "stories are essentially about the discovery that the comforting pieties of the past—belief in a benevolent universe, in progress, in romantic love—are illusions and that man is alone in a meaningless universe." [48] If he was not another Flitcraft, somehow to forget the vision of a meaningless universe and the character he felt one had to develop in order to cope with it successfully, there was nothing left but steadfast retreat, waiting for the end. Ironically, the waiting would not be weeks or even years, but more than three decades.

THE GLASS KEY is set in Baltimore, although the city is unnamed. Ned Beaumont has been there for fifteen months, right hand to political boss, Paul Madvig. Madvig is supporting Senator Henry for re-election because he is in love with his daughter, Janet Henry. Janet has only contempt for Paul which turns to hatred when her brother is murdered in the street and Janet believes Paul killed him. Paul's daughter, Opal, was Taylor Henry's mistress, only one of the women with whom the senator's son was having an affair. She, too, comes to hate Paul. Ned puts it this way: " 'That's splendid! Paul's daughter and his sweetheart both trying to steer him to the electric chair. He certainly has a lot of luck with women.' " [49] Ned takes a terrific beating from Jeff, an apish man who works for gangster Shad O'Rory. Ned ends up in the hospital and Janet comes to visit him. " 'You're his best friend,' " Janet tells Ned. "She paused, then added: 'He thinks so.' 'What do you think?' he asked with incomplete seriousness. 'I think you are,' she said gravely, 'or you would not be here now. You would not have gone through that for him.' "[50] By the end of the story, Beaumont exposes Senator Henry as the culprit. The senator asks Ned for the return of his revolver and five minutes alone in a room. In an S. S. Van Dine novel, this would have been the conclusion. But Hammett had been reviewing detective fiction for THE SATURDAY REVIEW OF LITERATURE and he detested what he considered the fantasies in Van Dine's novels. Ned Beaumont tells the senator, no: " 'You'll take what's coming to you.' "[51] He does this even though he knows what the senator will get will be a manslaughter conviction and a sentence that is set aside or suspended. All that is left for Ned is to leave Paul, to leave town, to go somewhere else. Janet wants to come with him. He makes no commitment to her, but he is willing to let her accompany him. He has to leave Paul because Paul has too many romantic illusions, he has been a fall guy, a sap for women, and Ned can no longer respect him.

For Robert I. Edenbaum, THE GLASS KEY is Hammett's least successful book because it ignores motivation. Notwithstanding, that is its novelty. Hammett himself did not understand motivation, probably did not even believe in it, and did not live his life as if it had any significance. Peter Wolfe was repelled by Beaumont. "His neglect of the poor, the sick, and the jobless make him, along with his free spending, an unlikely Depression hero. Beaumont has sold out to the machine. A believer in the spoils system, he hands out bribes, sinecures, and patronage jobs in return for political favors."[52] This implies that Hammett wanted somehow to create heroes. I do not think he did. He wanted, instead, to devise a persona with which a man could face a meaningless universe, in which each person was ultimately completely alone, and by means of which a man might hope to survive without compromising. Diane Johnson said it best in DASHIELL HAMMETT: A LIFE (1983): "In Ned Beaumont—principled, forlorn, afflicted with an uneasy worldliness and the ability to understand the meaner motives and ambitions of his friends, and tubercular—Hammett produced his nearest self-portrait."[53]

"You could feel that Papa was at home in San Francisco . . . ," Mary Jane said about her father. "He belonged. Some places, you can live in and never belong. But he belonged in San Francisco."[54] His last apartment in San Francisco had been at 1155 Leavenworth. In New York, he lived in an apartment at 133 East 38th Street. He completed THE GLASS KEY there and began the first draft of THE THIN MAN which he would put aside and start over once he met Lillian Hellman. Hammett got a job as a book reviewer for the NEW YORK EVENING POST. He was doing a lot of drinking and socializing. He was in constant need of money. He went one day to the editorial offices of DETECTIVE FICTION WEEKLY and presented the editor with a story he had written, in haste, and signed as by Samuel Dashiell and titled "The Diamond

Wager." He asked the editor to read it while he sat there in his office. When the editor finished it, he informed Hammett that he would accept it. Hammett said that since the periodical paid upon acceptance he wanted a check at once. However, the editor wanted some changes made. Hammett agreed to the changes and left with the check and the manuscript, insisting that he would make the changes himself. He proceeded to go on a long bender. The editor grew increasingly nervous as the publication date approached with the story featured on the cover and no Hammett. At almost the last minute, a taxi driver appeared with the altered manuscript. Hammett, in speakeasy, had made the corrections and dispatched the cabbie to make delivery. Lillian Hellman, when she heard Hammett relate this story, tried the same approach when attempting to get her first play produced, and it worked as well for her.

Paramount Pictures purchased screen rights from Knopf for RED HARVEST. The terms were not very lucrative for Hammett but he used the purchase to negotiate a job for himself in the Paramount writing department. ROADHOUSE NIGHTS (Paramount, 1930), as the film was titled upon release, was directed by Hobart Henley with the screen adaptation by Ben Hecht who had started the gangster film cycle with his script for Josef von Sternberg's UNDERWORLD (Paramount, 1927). Fred Kohler, Sr., is the rackets boss in a small town, using a roadhouse as the headquarters for his bootlegging activities. A big city newspaper, seeking to expose him, sends in a reporter to get the goods, but Kohler has him bumped. Charles Ruggles is then sent in by the same paper, assuming more or less the role the Continental Op has in the novel. Helen Morgan, making her debut as a film star, was cast as a singer in the roadhouse and Kohler's mistress. Jimmy Durante, as Daffy, is her piano accompanist. Ruggles and Morgan turn out to be old sweethearts. With help from Daffy and the Coast Guard, Ruggles and Morgan have Kohler brought to justice. It was not a very good picture and it was also not Hammett's story.

Hammett's original screen story for Paramount was released as CITY STREETS (Paramount, 1931) directed by Rouben Mamoulian. Clara Bow was originally to have starred, but Sylvia Sydney replaced her at the last minute. Sydney was cast as Guy Kibbee's step-daughter. Kibbee works for bootlegger William "Stage" Boyd. Sydney falls in love with Gary Cooper and urges him to chuck his carnival job to join the rackets. Cooper does not welcome the idea. Kibbee knocks off Stanley Fields so that Boyd can get Fields' girlfriend played by Wynne Gibson. Boyd covers for Kibbee. When Sydney refuses to finger Kibbee, the law railroads her to prison on a phony charge. That does it. Cooper joins the rackets to find enough evidence to spring her. Once Sydney gets out of stir, she cannot convince Cooper to quit the rackets. She goes to Boyd for help but Wynne Gibson knocks him off and blames Sydney for it. Sydney is taken for a ride, but Cooper comes to her rescue. Despite its subject matter, the film managed to be both touching and melodramatic.

When Warner Bros. purchased screen rights to THE MALTESE FALCON, Hammett felt he had arrived. He sent for Josephine and the children to join him, setting them up in a place in Los Angeles. He did not live with his family, but he did like to spend time visiting with his daughters. His carousing and womanizing intensified, all part of an ultimately futile effort to escape the sense of physical imprisonment and mental claustrophobia from which he seemed chronically to suffer. "From the day I met Hammett," screenwriter Nunnally Johnson recalled, "in the late 'Twenties, his behavior could be accounted for only by an assumption that he had no expectation of being alive much beyond Thursday. He had had a severe case of tuberculosis and he told me that he now had but one lung. Once this assumption was accepted, Hammett's way of life made a form of sense. Even allowing for exuberance and the headiness of the certain approach of success, not to mention the daffiness of the 'Twenties, no one could have spent himself and his money with such recklessness who expected to be alive much longer. For once in my life I knew a man who was clearly convinced that there would never be a tomorrow. . . . I suppose that by the time he came to realize that he would in all likelihood be here not only next Thursday but for many Thursdays to come it was too late to sit down at the typewriter again with much confidence. When the end approached, it was thirty years later than he expected it, and Death owed him a genuine apology when it eventually made its tardy appearance."[55] The persona Hammett had developed and his defiant life-style finished him first as the foremost author of hard-boiled detective fiction. Then it finished him with the studios. Finally, albeit a very long finally, it finished him altogether.

II

When THE MALTESE FALCON (Warner's, 1931) was filmed the first time in Hollywood, the nation was starving. Colonel Robert R. McCormick in his CHICAGO TRIBUNE called on every citizen to pay his taxes and declared his own taxable income to be only $25,250 against which he was levied $1,515. Louis Florsheim, the shoe magnate, was worse off; he paid only $90 in income tax. J. P. Morgan called upon his employees to contribute from their wages to the national relief and himself paid no income tax in 1930, 1931, or 1932. A march of the unemployed on the Henry Ford plant in Detroit was met first with tear gas, then freezing water from fire hoses, then gunfire from revolvers, finally with fire from machine guns. A group of Russian technicians, visiting the plant to learn Ford's production methods, observed the demonstration from the windows over Gate Four.

"I followed Gutman's original in Washington," Hammett recalled, "and I never remember shadowing a man who bored me so much. He was not after a jeweled falcon, of course; but he *was* suspected of being a German spy. . . . I worked with Dundy's prototype in a North Carolina railroad yard. The Cairo character I picked up on a forgery charge in 1920. Effie, the good girl, once asked me to go into the narcotic smuggling business with her in San Diego. Wilmer, the gunman, was picked up in Stockton, California, a neat small smooth-aced quiet boy of perhaps 21. He was serenely proud of the name the papers gave him—The Midget Bandit. He'd robbed a Stockton filling station the previous week—and had been annoyed by the description the station proprietor had given of him and by the proprietor's statement of what he would do to that little runt if he ever laid eyes on him again. So he'd stolen a car and returned to stick the guy up again and see what he wanted to do about it. That's when we nabbed him.''[56]

Roy Del Ruth directed the film. Ricardo Cortez, in retrospect, seems no more at home in the role of Sam Spade than he was later in the role of Perry Mason. Walter Long, a familiar heavy, was cast as Archer. Bebe Daniels played Ruth Wonderly, the Brigid character. Dudley Digges was cast as Gutman, Una Merkel as Effie, Otto Matieson as Cairo, Dwight Frye as Wilmer, Robert Elliott as Dundy, and Thelma Todd as Iva Archer, the woman with whom Spade continues to carry on an affair after Archer is murdered. This last was especially poor casting in a picture where casting was weak throughout. Thelma Todd could not stop playing the comedienne. She was too young. Four years later she might have known what it was all about. Divorced from the good-looking Pat Di Cicco, she shared a roadhouse apartment on the same floor as film director Roland West, her partner in the joint venture of Thelma Todd's Sidewalk Cafe. A week before her death, she had been slugged in the mouth by West. She was getting threatening letters demanding money and pressure was on her to include gambling in the new addition being added to her cafe. Roland West told her to be home by two o'clock in the morning from a party Ida Lupino's family was throwing for her. Todd was flippant. When her body was found, she had been slugged again in the face, the blow smashing a false front tooth and drawing blood from her nose and mouth. She had been left in her car in a closed garage with the motor running. She was thirty years old. The case was never officially solved, although it was well known that West objected to Todd's promiscuity, particularly since he had set her up in business. When she could not get into her apartment early that Sunday morning, she had rebelled. She liked her independence, but it may have cost her life. West was subsequently compelled to give up his career as a director and retired to running the cafe. In the screenplay Spade is rewarded for sending over the murderess by being given a position in the district attorney's office.

THE MALTESE FALCON was remade as SATAN MET A LADY (Warner's, 1936), a vehicle for Warren William and Bette Davis directed by William Dieterle. It was the loosest kind of remake with William cast as a detective named Ted Shayne and Gutman changed to a woman played by Alison Skipworth. Effie became Murgetroyd played by Marie Wilson.

John Huston, who had been a screenwriter, when he was to direct his first picture for Jack L. Warner wanted to remake it again, THE MALTESE FALCON (Warner's, 1941). Howard Hawks, talking to Huston about the project, suggested that if the picture was to be done at all it ought to follow the plot in the novel exactly. This, wisely, was the course Huston followed. He had to humanize the Sam Spade role somewhat—Hollywood was not quite ready for the idea of a dubious protagonist who was as corrupt in a small way as the other characters were in a big way—but, otherwise, Huston could and did follow the novel with only minor changes. The film is probably more familiar than any other detective vehicle of the decade. Sidney Greenstreet, who had specialized in playing butlers on Broadway, was imported to portray Gutman. His being teamed with Peter Lorre as Cairo proved sufficiently popular that the two went on to appear in a number of films, to paraphrase Lorre sort of a Laurel and Hardy of villainy. Huston wanted Geraldine Fitzgerald to play Brigid but the front office vetoed that idea in favor of Mary Astor. Huston's father, Walter, appeared in a cameo role, to bring his son luck. Huston had Mary Astor run around the set several times before he shot her scenes, to give her perpetual lying a breathless quality and to keep her nerves tensed.

"You originally wanted George Raft as Sam Spade?" I once asked Huston.

"Yes," he said, "I did. I thought Raft would be perfect as Spade. If," and Huston leered, "the lines didn't prove too long for him. George liked his lines short. But he turned it down because it was my first picture as a director. So I took Bogart."

"Edward Dmytryk told me that when he directed Bogart, he would have to wait for ten minutes before each of Bogart's scenes so he could cough his lungs out on one side of the camera. Bogart didn't want to cough in the middle of a scene."

"Now," said Huston, smiling, "I wouldn't know about that." He inhaled deeply on his cigar. "Because I was probably on the other side of the camera, coughing."

If THE MALTESE FALCON is not Bogart's best picture, it is certainly one of his most memorable. It can be viewed repeatedly. The outcome is not important. Huston managed to achieve in film what Hammett had achieved in detective fiction: to make us more interested in the characters than in the plot.

It was George Raft who once said to me in conversation: "The underworld taught me that you could buy anything you want—cops, lawyers, judges, politicians—if you paid enough." He was born in 1895 in a family tenement building on Forty-first Street between Ninth and Tenth Avenues in New York City. The area, because of rampant lawlessness, was known as "Hell's Kitchen." Raft grew up in the streets. He became a member of the Gophers, the reigning street gang. Shortly after a youth named Owen Madden from the slums of England moved into the neighborhood he met Georgie Ranft as Raft was then known, and the two became fast friends. Madden worked his way up in the Gophers until he became one of its leaders. In 1914 Madden, by then called Owney the Killer, was sentenced to Sing Sing for ten to twenty years for the murder of one Patsy Doyle. Over the years until his release in 1923, Georgie Ranft was one of Madden's most frequent visitors. When Madden got out, he found a different world. Prohibition had done what probably nothing else could have done: it had organized the gangs into a network, first controlling sections of cities, then entire cities, and before long vast parts of the country.

Georgie had changed his name to Raft and was pursuing a career as a hoofer in New York night clubs. Nearly all the night clubs were speakeasies and most of them were owned by gangsters. Being a gangster was fashionable. The Volstead Act existed to be broken. Owney Madden formed a partnership with Larry Fay. They paid police protection for their brewery and when it could not supply enough beer they resorted to hijacking. In his off hours, Georgie drove reconnaissance for Madden's liquor shipments which were delivered to Dutch Schultz or one of his mob. Madden started financing Broadway and off-Broadway shows and got Raft parts where he could; he also got him increased exposure in night clubs. Madden owned 50% of Mae West's DIAMOND LIL which opened at the Royal Theatre in New York for 323 performances before it went on the road. Raft was Madden's messenger and would appear nightly to pick up Madden's split of the box office. George met the play's star, Mae West.

Madden and Fay eventually split, Fay leaving for Miami with the woman who had been the main attraction at his El Fey night club, "Texas" Guinan. They tried to force Raft to go with them, but he got out of it. Madden formed a new alliance with "Big Frenchy" de Mange. Between the two of them, they controlled the Parody, El Fey, the Stork Club, and the Cotton Club in Harlem which King Oliver and Duke Ellington were making famous. "Texas" came back after a time and engaged in a torrid affair with Madden. Warner Bros. proposed she come to Hollywood to make a musical based on New York cabaret life. Madden sent Raft along to watch over her. He even got a role in the production which was titled QUEEN OF THE NIGHT CLUBS (Warner's, 1929).

Raft was back in New York in 1930 at the time "Mad Dog" Coll quit Dutch Schultz' gang and, with a group of ruffians, set himself up to challenge the others. He kidnapped "Big Frenchy" de Mange and demanded a ransom from Madden. Madden got "Big Frenchy" back, but he could see trouble brewing, possibly an all-out gang war. He and George went to California on vacation. Madden was intent on seeing his pal in pictures. He felt he had talent, and looks, and he deserved a chance. Once he hit town, he registered at the Beverly Hills Hotel under an alias and made a number of calls on George's behalf to people he had met at his various clubs. Raft was at the Mark Twain Hotel in Hollywood. When Madden went back East, he bankrolled George. One of the calls paid off. Rowland Brown showed up at the Brown Derby one day when George was there and offered him a part as a gangster in a picture he was to direct, QUICK MILLIONS (Fox, 1931). Raft seemed presently to be on his way. Another role as a gang member followed in HUSH MONEY (Fox, 1931) and then a comic role in PALMY DAYS (United Artists, 1931).

Howard Hawks was preparing a screenplay, together with Ben Hecht, titled SCARFACE, and he was anxious to meet any gangsters who might be in town.

He ran into Madden and Raft one night at the fights. Madden had promoted Primo Carnera into a wholly fraudulent championship and was about to start the fighter on a national tour. Madden offered Raft a job with the tour but Hawks was interested in having Raft appear in SCARFACE. Raft, who did not drink, went back to his hotel, while Hawks and Madden went to Madden's suite to drink and talk. The next day Hawks invited Raft to come over to the General Service Studio. He asked Raft how he would like to work in the picture. Raft said he already had a job with Madden and would be leaving for Miami soon, so the offer would have to be definite or not at all.

"How's this?" Hawks queried. "You're on the payroll as of right now."

Hawks suggested to Raft that he flip a nickel in all of his scenes. Raft practiced it for days until he could look at another actor without his hand pausing in the flipping action. Raft also found that Hawks and Hecht were constantly pumping him for information. Raft had met Al Capone on several occasions in New York at the crap game in the back room of the El Fey Club.

While Hawks was still in production, several of Capone's associates came to the studio asking to preview the film. Hawks told them to relay to Capone that when the picture came out Al could buy a ticket. Capone's associates did not like that answer. Under pressure, Hawks screened a rough cut for them. Capone's associates thought it was great and related their sentiments to Al. Hawks was invited to Chicago to meet Capone.

"They met me at the train," Hawks told me. "They were late. One of the fellows said, 'There was a killing last night and we had to go to the funeral.' I said, 'Do I have to ride with you if there was a killing last night?' They said I could ride in a different car. When we went into a cafe, they would sit with their backs to the wall and I had my back to the door. We had some damned good-looking girls with us, a bit brassy but very pretty. When I saw Capone, we had tea and he was dressed in a morning coat, striped trousers. I was with him for two or three hours."

When the film opened in Chicago, Raft appeared there as part of a promotional tour. Capone had sent Hawks a miniature machine gun as a trophy. Now he sent for Raft. George was escorted to the gangster's headquarters at the Lexington Hotel on Michigan Avenue. Capone sat behind a big mahogany desk and conducted most of the conversation as if it were an interrogation. Raft recalled the conversation for his biographer, Lewis Yablonsky.

" 'Georgie, so you been playin' my bodyguard, Frank Rio, in this SCARFACE pitcher.'

" 'Yes, I did, Al,' I said. 'But it's nothing personal. Actors do what they're told.'

"Capone rubbed the long scar on his face. Then, kidding on the square, said, 'Well, you tell them guys in Hollywood that they don't know Al Capone. They bumped me off in the end and nobody's bumpin' Al off while he's running Chicago. Yeah, you tell 'em that.'

"We talked a while longer about people we had known in New York and this and that. I was anxious to leave and finally figured the interview was over. When I said good-bye, and started to walk out, Capone stopped me. 'Wait a minute, Georgie, I see you tossin' a coin all through the pitcher.'

" 'Just a little theatrical touch.'

" 'A four-bit piece, yeah?'

" 'No, it was a nickel.'

" 'That's worse. You tell 'em that if any of my boys are tossin' coins, they'll be twenty-dollar gold pieces.'

"I wasn't sure if he was kidding or meant it, but I promised to convey the message to Hollywood. 'You like the picture, Al?' I asked. By now, he was flattered with the attention the movie had brought him, with the name SCARFACE on marquees across the country. 'Yeah, I liked it,' he said."[57]

George Raft was in demand. When he signed a long-term contract with Paramount, he became a top box-office personality. He brought Mae West to Hollywood to work with him in NIGHT AFTER NIGHT (Paramount, 1932). He had millions of fans, thousands of acquaintances, hundreds of co-workers who liked him. When his mother died in 1937, however, right in the midst of plans to bring her to Hollywood from New York, none of his Hollywood or New York friends came to the funeral. Yet, sitting in the front row paying their respects, were Owney Madden and "Big Frenchy" de Mange. Raft never forgot their loyalty.

Madden got sent back to prison for violating his parole. When he was released, the syndicate in New York gave him a no-options offer: to take what money he had and move to Hot Springs, Arkansas. Once there, he would be given control of that state's gambling. Eventually Madden became a most highly respected citizen in Hot Springs and he lived there comfortably until he died from emphysema in 1965 at the age of seventy-three.

Hammett was still very much a Hollywood favorite when THE GLASS KEY (Paramount, 1935) was brought to the screen for the first time. THE THIN MAN (M-G-M, 1934) had been successfully filmed the previous year and his short novel had also been filmed under its title, WOMAN IN THE DARK (RKO, 1934). He had provided an original screen story for MISTER DYNAMITE (Universal, 1935) which, however bleak it may have been in Hammett's original conception, was a witty and satirical detective film upon its release. THE GLASS KEY was directed by Frank Tuttle with George Raft cast as Ed Beaumont, a man who could believe in nothing but his friend, the political boss Paul Madvig played by Edward Arnold; and, when he could no longer believe even in him, he was left with nothing. The *néant* of *film noir* was only beginning to be felt. Almost all of the interconnecting links between politics and the underworld were toned down or removed. The plot was subtly altered so that Paul Madvig comes out more a reformer than a city boss who picks the candidates for whom the electorate is to vote. The romance between Madvig and Janet Henry, played by Claire Dodd, does not have the complexity it does in the novel, nor is she attracted to Beaumont. Instead, there is a romantic spark between Beaumont and Opal Madvig played by Rosalind Keith. Beaumont breaks up the affair between Opal and Taylor Henry, played by Ray Milland, and even if the murder and its perpetrator remain the same they mean so much less in this context. Guinn "Big Boy" Williams was effectively cast as the brutal and sadistic Jeff and the scene of Beaumont's terrible beating, while being held prisoner by Jeff, was not diluted nor the scene where Jeff chokes to death Shad O'Rory played by Robert Gleckler.

Raft proved attractive to women from the beginning. While at work on SCARFACE, Howard Hawks had given a party to which Raft came accompanied by Ann Dvorak. She wanted Raft to dance with her. When he refused, she came over to him in her low-cut gown and did a sensuous, enticing sexual number which so impressed Hawks that he put it in the picture. Several of Raft's affairs in Hollywood in the early days were well publicized, but the succession of hookers at the rate of two a day, every day, did not begin until after he broke up with Betty Grable. Virginia Pine, with whom he carried on a relationship for years, taught him refinement; Norma Shearer, Irving Thalberg's widow, taught him about the arts. George used as his excuse the hasty marriage he had had to Grace Mulrooney in 1923, claiming that she would not give him a divorce. After being separated for nearly twenty years, Raft could have forced a divorce, but he never did. Being alone proved preferable to binding attachments. He might go places with women; he might sleep with women; he did not live with a woman. He had as a consequence more than a little in common with the Ned Beaumont character and even more with that character's creator. After coming to Hollywood, Hammett, too, entertained himself with a constant succession of hookers which, when combined with his alcoholism and his bouts with gonorrhea, led to periods of impotence. Raft had more luck. He did not drink and he seems to have avoided venereal disease.

Sitting across from him for the first time at his favorite table at the Brown Derby in Beverly Hills, he did not look to be a man of eighty. He had undergone aneurysmatic surgery early in 1976. Combined with his emphysema, his physical condition had been weakened.

"You could never tell it by looking at you," I said.

"Yeah. I asked my doctor if I was looking pretty good. 'Yeah,' he said, 'but not as good as you looked thirty years ago.' "

Raft was dressed in a dark polo shirt with a long collar and a pink, white, and blue checked sport jacket. Although his hair was thinning, his face retained its smoothness and his eyes were alive, watching the young women walk past our table or studying the faces of various patrons. As we talked, a man in a neighboring booth kept watching us.

"I think we're being watched," I said.

George smiled. "When I had my trouble in England, I was watched by the F.B.I. I invited the guy into my apartment. I was doing the morning dishes. 'You're going to have a dull job,' I told him. 'I stay inside most of the time. I go out to eat. That's about all.' "

"Did you meet Hammett while you were making THE GLASS KEY?"

"Yeah. He came on the set once. I didn't know much about him. I've never been much of a reader. I like horse racing, sports, that king of thing. I wasn't very well educated. I didn't know very much. What education I got was in a Catholic school. You know what that's like. Hammett was a very distinguished man. I told him I hoped the picture turned out."

"How did you get on with the director, Frank Tuttle?"

"He was a great guy. I think he was afraid of me. He thought I was the tough guy I portrayed on the screen. I nearly got in trouble on that picture."

"How's that?"

"Tuttle's wife was a Communist. So was Frank. She was always selling tickets to Communist meetings. They were like benefits. I'd buy tickets from her. Why not? But I'd never go. What did I know about politics?"

Raft had turned down the lead role in DEAD END (United Artists, 1937) because he felt the gangster to be unsympathetic. He turned down the lead in HIGH SIERRA (Warner's, 1941) because he did not want to get shot again and die in another picture.

"Why did you turn down the part of Sam Spade in THE MALTESE FALCON?"

"I listened to my agent, Myron Selznick. Maybe I shouldn't have listened to him so much. But, like I say, I didn't know much, so I listened to guys who were supposed to know something. Selznick said the three women in the picture weren't that hot. So I said, no. Besides, it was John Huston's first picture. He was untried. 'An inexperienced director and three babes like this,' Selznick said. 'Turn it down.' It was a low budget picture."

Raoul Walsh directed BACKGROUND TO DANGER (Warner's 1943) based on a novel by Eric Ambler with a screenplay by W. R. Burnett.

"You got your chance to work with Peter Lorre and Sidney Greenstreet in BACKGROUND TO DANGER."

"Yeah."

"How did you like Lorre?"

"I didn't."

"Oh?"

"Yeah. He stole my hat."

"He stole your hat?"

"Yeah. We all had our own prop wardrobe. I checked mine out. My hat was there. When I went back to get it, it was gone."

"How did you know Lorre stole it?"

"I saw him wearing it."

"What did you do?"

"I let him wear it."

"And for that reason you disliked him?"

"No. I had this scene where I enter a room and look around. I get hit on the head. I wanted to come back to that room when I search the place a second time. The director said, no. He had me tied up. Lorre was sitting on a table in front of me. He was a mean little guy. Lorre blew cigarette smoke in my face. I didn't like it. Lorre grinned. We had retake after retake. Lorre kept blowing smoke in my face. He kept getting closer and closer to my eyes with that cigarette. 'Untie me,' I said before the next retake. I grabbed Lorre. 'You keep that cigarette out of my face,' I said. Lorre ran away and locked himself in his dressing room. When they had me tied up again, he comes prancing out. He sits on the table. He blows smoke in my face. And he flicks the cigarette around, real close to my eyes. When I got untied, I slugged him. I told him he was a German spy. That upset him. But he didn't blow smoke at me again.''

''And Greenstreet?''

''Bad at dialogue. He'd get it down two or three days ahead of time and then would never change a word of it. But he got along with Lorre.''

''I liked JOHNNY ALLEGRO.'' It was released by Columbia Pictures in 1948.

''Yeah?''

''Yeah. You played an ex-con hired by the Treasury Department to get to the bottom of some counterfeiting.''

''Yeah, I remember.''

''It was set in Florida. Did you shoot it on location?''

''No. We shot some of it on Catalina.''

''At the end, did George MacCreedy really fire those arrows at you?''

''No actor fires arrows at George Raft.''

''Did you have an expert?''

''Yeah. We had to. I did my own stunting, as long as I could.''

''I also liked you in RED LIGHT.'' It was released by United Artists in 1949. ''When your brother, who's a priest, gets murdered, you set out to find who did it. It was on the order of JOHNNY ANGEL [RKO, 1945] where you were hunting down the murderer of your father, J. Farrell MacDonald.''

''Yeah.'' George smiled. ''Pictures in those days were too much alike.''

''In RED LIGHT, Raymond Burr was a vicious killer. In one scene he knocks a semi truck down on top of Gene Lockhart.''

''I thought Burr had a lot of talent. He did a good job in that picture. But I didn't like the title. I thought it should be something else. It's like the dialogue I had in JOHNNY ALLEGRO. I tell this government man that the racket is counterfeiting. He says, 'We know.' I tell him MacCreedy is behind it. He says, 'We know.' I tell him they're using old Nazi plates. He says, 'We know.' I asked our director on that picture, Ted Tetslaff: 'If he knows all this stuff, why make me repeat it all for him?' It was too much dialogue. I should have fought harder. They left it in the picture.''

I had along a copy of THE GEORGE RAFT FILE (1973) because of its filmography. The book was written by James Robert Parish with Steven Whitney. Raft gestured toward it.

''That's not my official biography. I was going to fight that book, but my attorneys advised me that fighting it would only draw attention to it. And that's something I definitely didn't want."

I told him that Parish claimed he did not smoke.

"I don't like that book. Well, he's wrong. I don't drink. I used to smoke four packs of Lucky Strikes a day, all my life, until a couple of years ago. It's the smog, here. It irritates my emphysema. They should have let me stay in England. I wasn't bothered by it at all over there. Maybe it was the dampness."

"I thought dampness was bad for emphysema. I thought dryness best, like in the desert. Dashiell Hammett tried drinking. It kept his body dehydrated."

"Yeah." Raft smiled. "But I don't drink."

"What about that England business?"

"It was unfair. Sure, I knew people in the underworld. A lot of them took on my mannerisms. Like Bugsy Siegel. I loaned that guy a hundred grand, and I never saw it again. It was guilt by association. They still won't give me a hearing."

Raft was correct. He had been victimized because syndicate gambling interests had invested in the George Raft Colony Club in London. The British had objected.

The man at the neighboring table finally got up the courage to come over. He introduced himself.

"Can I have your autograph, Mr. Raft?"

He pulled a card out of his card case and placed it on the table. Raft signed it.

"I'm a Federal judge," he said. "And I've always loved your movies."

He pulled out another card.

"Let me know if there is ever anything I can do for you."

George laughed.

"Where were you when I needed you?" he asked.

Then we all laughed.

III

While Hammett worked in the Paramount story department, he would occasionally attend a Hollywood party given by a fellow writer or some studio luminary. He talked very little at these affairs and would mostly stand around, drinking. Midway through the party likely as not he was to be found in the kitchen, still drinking and having an animated discussion with a servant about detective fiction or world literature. Not a man to make friends easily, he never felt sufficiently drawn to most of the people he met at these parties to want to engage them in even small talk. He had a drinking booth at Musso & Frank's on Hollywood Boulevard where he would invariably sit for hours on end. He liked to dine at the Hollywood Brown Derby. He met S. J. and Laura Perelman while working at Paramount and he also met and became almost as friendly with Arthur Kober. Kober, an Austrian emigrant, had made a name for himself in New York theatrical circles as a press agent. He was hired by Paramount in 1931 to come to Hollywood to write original screenplays and supervise screen adaptations. Kober had married Lillian Hellman in 1925 when she was working for Boni & Liveright in New York. She drank heavily and was convinced that it was her destiny to be a writer.

Hammett was plagued only by an occasional cough and was recovering from a five-day drunk when he first met Hellman at a Hollywood restaurant. Lillian had followed Kober to the West Coast. She had urged him to move out of the small apartment he had been renting; he could afford it on $450 a week, she had said. Kober had been reluctant because he was not at all sure that such easy money was going to last. By the time they had moved into a large house in the hills above Hollywood Boulevard, Lillian was spending her days in a leather chair reading and her nights drinking. She had finally persuaded Kober to help her find a job. She had gone to work for Metro-Goldwyn-Mayer as a manuscript reader. She was unhappy with her marriage and unhappy with herself. She was not a particularly attractive woman, but Hammett, whose preference in women ran to Oriental and Black prostitutes, must have found her intellectual conversation stimulating and he may have been charmed by her unabashed admiration for him.

Hammett was still on the party circuit. That summer he had gone to Turkey Hill with Ben Hecht and Charles MacArthur. It was a wooden castle perched on a Hollywood hill. MacArthur and Hecht lived there with an agent, Leland Howard. It got its name from the two hundred and fifty turkeys which roamed the grounds. The partying was continuous. Around the bar, one would find gathered an assortment which included Jean Harlow, blazing sex to match her hair, holding hands with Paul Bern who would commit suicide when he found that he could not perform adequately in bed with her after they were married. John Gilbert, whose career was already fading, was glued to the bar with three whores he had rented for the night. He would spend the final years of his life literally passed out. He was married for a brief time to Virginia Bruce who would bring him along to social events. Gilbert would ask where the nearest bedroom was, if he could speak at all; usually he just wandered around until he found a bed and then fell into an alcoholic slumber until Virginia would wake him because it was time to go. Gilbert did insist on driving everywhere they went. Harpo Marx might be there, playing craps with Ernst Lubitsch. Howard Hawks, sad-eyed, with a drink in his hand, would listen to a scarcely sober George Anthiel rendering a melody at the piano. Myron Selznick was accustomed to drop in to look over new starlets who might be in need of management. He soon delegated most of the work at his agency to his employees and devoted himself exclusively to drinking, unless summoned by one of his clients who was concerned about whether or not to take a part in a proposed film project. Hammett might have based more than one novel or story on this world. He did not. He was mostly too drunk even to work on screenplays. It was left to Nathanael

West, Laura Perelman's brother, to render Hollywood as it was in the 'Thirties in his satires.

Hammett was quite taken with Lillian's rejection of Hollywood. The season was passing now into winter which, back then, without smog, meant sunlight and frequent rain. He had recently lost a damage suit filed by Elise de Viane who alleged that Hammett had taken her to his apartment, ostensibly for a couple of drinks, and then had tried to rape her. Many women, apparently, were quite willing. Perhaps he had liked the challenge of one who was not. Increasingly Hammett and Hellman spent their time together, talking and drinking. Kober seemed to have no real objection. He liked Hammett personally and probably realized that his union with Lillian ultimately could not last. Hammett had a Black homosexual couple for manservants. He spent most of his money, as George Raft did, on a succession of women. They taught him nothing, but, as alcohol, perhaps they did deaden the sheer pain of existence. When his lungs would bother him, he would take his temperature and count the number of times he went to the toilet.

Lillian, longing for the stability of New York, agreed to go East with the Perelmans and Nathanael West. Hammett wrote her letters. "So you're not coming home, eh? I suppose it doesn't make any difference if I have to go on practically masturbating!"[58] In conversations with Hellman, Hammett would make a distinction between real love and sleeping around which, for him, meant "practically masturbating." She did not buy it. His perpetual, compulsive womanizing tended to make her jealous and miserable.

The Perelmans returned to Hollywood. Hammett ran into them in the company of Arthur Kober at the Brown Derby. "I ran into Arthur, Sid and Laura in the Brown Doiby night before last . . . ," he wrote to Hellman, "and tried to pump Laura about your conduct in New York, but she was so circumspect, gave you such a respectable tint, that I'd have suspected you of the loosest sort of conduct even if I hadn't previously received reports about you. Ts! Ts! Ts! Just a she-Hammett!"[59] Hammett was obviously compelled to view all women as hopelessly promiscuous, all that is except for his daughter, Mary Jane. When he learned years later that she was as wild as he had been, he blackened both of her eyes.

When Alfred Knopf sent Hammett a telegram to inform him that THE GLASS KEY was getting a good reception, Hammett, who was currently unemployed, pressured him into coming across with a thousand dollars. He even went on the wagon with the intention of resuming work on THE THIN MAN, the novel he had begun in 1930. The fragment from his false start survives and perhaps William F. Nolan summed up best the impression that John Guild, the detective in the story, gives to a reader: "Guild trusts no one, believes nothing until it becomes proven fact. Hammett stripped him of all emotion; he is machine-like, coldly efficient, more robot than man. . . . Even Sam Spade seems warm and outgoing in comparison. Guild would never allow himself to love Brigid; he would 'send her over' without a qualm. There would be no 'sleepless nights' for John Guild.''[60] The novel had been the last thing Hammett had been working on before he went to Hollywood to work for Paramount. The fragment ran sixty-five pages and was postponed originally because Knopf had delayed publication of THE GLASS KEY for eight months. Looking over the manuscript now, Hammett was dissatisfied and decided he would have to start it over from the beginning.

When Lillian Hellman returned to Hollywood, she had made up her mind to divorce Arthur Kober. He was amicable. His attorney represented her while another attorney in the same firm represented him. At the hearing, Hellman had difficulty suppressing her laughter when she heard the grounds read as cruelty. Hammett and Kober remained friends. In future years Kober held Hellman's opinion so highly that he had her approve decorations in an apartment he intended to lease in New York and even asked her to pass judgment on his fiancée, Margaret Frohnknecht. Lillian was matron of honor at his wedding in 1941.

After the divorce, Lillian and Hammett moved back to New York. The Perelmans had bought a home in Bucks County. Nathanael West was the manager of the Sutton Hotel in New York. When Hammett ran out of money, he and Lillian moved into the Sutton. The quarters were downright dingy and the food nearly inedible, but the two of them were obviously very much in love and found it all extremely exciting. In Hollywood friends had noticed that when they were together they could not keep their hands off each other. Now they were sequestered away from the world and Hammett was working. "I had never seen anybody work that way: the care for every word, the pride in the neatness of the typed page itself, the refusal . . . to go out for a walk for fear something would be lost," Hellman would later recall.[61] Hammett, who dedicated the novel to Lillian, decided he would update his detective to his new circumstances. Nick Charles, a former employee of the Trans-American Detective Agency, is temporarily in New York for the holidays. However tough Nick may once have been, he has mellowed now and refuses to take anything seriously, quite in keeping with the frivolous tone Hammett associated with Lillian and her Eastern friends. He is married to Nora and has retired from his profession in order to manage her business interests. Their life together is one of unceasing drinking and partying. Nick does not want to work, but Nora gets him into a situation where he must. The book has its share of characters definitely out of the Hammett milieu, starting with Nick's old flame Mimi Jorgensen who lies as persistently as Brigid O'Shaughnessy, the wacky Dorothy Wynant who is Mimi's daughter, Herbert Macauley, a crooked lawyer intent on pretending that the missing Wynant is still alive for his personal gain, and Shep Morelli, a nervous gangster. " 'I love you, Nicky,' " Nora tells him, " 'because you smell nice and know such fascinating people.' "[62] Nora's rejection of Nicky's off-color playmates would not emerge until the late 'Thirties in the screenplays for the Thin Man films with which Hammett had nothing to do.

Hammett based his Nick and Nora on himself and Hellman, so much that Lillian later commented that she recognized their word-for-word dialogue in several scenes. Yet, something was missing, and it was unnoticed by critics when the book was published. The plot itself is really a short story, expanded by means of padding and dialogue to the length of a novel. Only recently have critics recognized the empty center in the book's characters. "A direct line can be traced," William F. Nolan wrote, "from the reluctantly heroic Continental Op, through the more cynical Sam Spade, to the final emptiness of Beaumont and Nick Charles."[63] Dennis Dooley went even farther when he noted that "not even New Year's Eve or the coming of the New Year will evoke any quickening of the spirit in the strangely deadened lives of this superficially charming couple, will prove no occasion at all except for another bout of silly partying and still more drinking. Indeed, there are so many references to . . . drinking and hangovers in the first pages of the book that by the beginning of Chapter 4 drinking has become almost a subtheme."[64]

After delivering the manuscript to Knopf, Hammett and Hellman spent days and nights drinking and partying. The Perelmans invited them to their farm in Bucks County. Hammett became friends with William Faulkner and they would frequently drink all through the night until, by morning, the two men would rejuvenate themselves, with or without breakfast, by means of another bottle. A recurrent theme was Hammett's disbelief that Faulkner could possibly have written SANCTUARY (1931) just for the money. It was a silly argument in view of the fact that Hammett had his New York literary agent circulate THE THIN MAN (1934) to a number of slick magazines for a prepublication sale. Edwin Balmer of REDBOOK bought it but he deleted the bit of dialogue in which Nora asks Nick if, when he was wrestling with Mimi, he had an erection and Nick answers, " 'Oh, a little.' "[65] Knopf thought enough of the line to make it the basis for his advertising campaign for the book. When Hammett received his money from REDBOOK, he went with Lillian to the Florida Keys where they spent their time in splendid isolation. He was happier there than he had been in New York. He took great interest in encouraging Lillian to write plays and for the rest of his life her work became a surrogate for his own writing, as he would help her with construction, character, and even dialogue. He was finished already, but he did not know it. He was finished because meaning had evaporated from life and he never could find a way to restore it.

Metro-Goldwyn-Mayer negotiated screen rights for THE THIN MAN. The book had proven a runaway success. Almost every one seemed to be delighted with the idea of a detective who thinks it is too early for breakfast but not too early for a drink, a perfect antidote to Depression blues. But who would play Nick and Nora? That was the question.

Myrna Loy was born Myrna Williams in 1905 near Helena, Montana. Her family moved to California while she was still in high school. She was intent on a theatrical career and worked in several of the prologues which were customary at Grauman's Chinese Theatre. She made an impression on Rudolph

Valentino's wife who undertook to see that she got work in pictures. Loy had a bit part in PRETTY LADIES (M-G-M, 1925) and continued, for the rest of the silent era, to take character parts. These parts varied. In ROGUE OF THE RIO GRANDE (Sono-Art, 1930), for example, she played a Mexican dancer who did little more than wiggle her torso seductively in a costume dress. While she was working on ARROWSMITH (United Artists, 1931), she met Arthur Hornblow, Jr. Hornblow was Samuel Goldwyn's right-hand man. According to Loy, it was love at first sight. She told Hornblow of her ambitions. He helped in getting her a contract with M-G-M where her first role was in EMMA (M-G-M, 1932). Her roles varied, but they were mostly villainous. In THE MASK OF FU MANCHU (M-G-M, 1932), she played Fa Lo Suee opposite Boris Karloff as the devil doctor. She might have been stuck in such roles indefinitely had Woody Van Dyke not cast her to play with Warner Baxter in a screwball comedy titled PENTHOUSE (M-G-M, 1933). Next Van Dyke cast her opposite William Powell in MANHATTAN MELODRAMA (M-G-M, 1934). The trades announced that Van Dyke had been taken off the THIN MAN project in order to get MANHATTAN MELODRAMA made. Van Dyke became convinced that Powell and Loy had precisely the rapport he wanted to bring Nick and Nora to the screen. Louis B. Mayer was not at all certain. He felt Loy worked best as an Oriental and the studio wanted Powell to star in THE CASINO MURDER CASE. Van Dyke, who was able to shoot pictures with a staggering rapidity, assured Mayer he could have the film in the can in twelve days. Myron Selznick was still negotiating Powell's contract with M-G-M. Mayer thought no harm could come of it, provided Van Dyke could finish the film that quickly. Edward Ellis, whom the studio had originally slated for the Nick Charles role, was retained in the cast as Clyde Wynant, the actual "thin man" of the novel. Edward Brophy played the gangster, Joe Morelli, for comedy, and Nat Pendleton played Lieutenant John Guild, the character who had been the private detective in Hammett's first draft and who was retained, albeit transformed into a policeman. Porter Hall was cast as the crafty attorney, Macauley, and Minna Gombell was Mimi Wynant. Albert Hackett and Frances Goodrich did the screenplay in three weeks.

Van Dyke did not complete the film in twelve days, but he did it in eighteen. He would have one set-up behind the camera and one in front of it. As soon as he finished shooting the scene in front of the camera, he would have the crew turn around and the cast change positions and shoot until that scene was finished while the other stage was being readied for yet the next scene. The picture was brought in for only $231,000. Upon release, it earned a profit of $729,000. MANHATTAN MELODRAMA had required twenty-four days to shoot, had cost $335,000, and made a profit of $415,000. M-G-M knew that it had a winner in the team of Powell and Loy.

Powell's contract terms were met. It was reported in the trades that his first picture under the contract would be THE CASINO MURDER CASE, but the continuing popularity of THE THIN MAN caused M-G-M to shelve that idea in favor of putting Powell in another picture with Loy. Much of the initial success of THE THIN MAN probably had to do with the fact that Powell really loved the role. For one thing, as a steady drinker (at his home in Palm Springs he was rarely without a glass in his hand), he could be entirely natural. The dialogue made the film sparkle and obscured the rather routine plot. When Nora asks Nick if he has her drink, he asks her what she's drinking. She responds rye. He guzzles the drink and quips, "Yes, yes. It's yours." Nick teases Nora about her financial status.

NORA: I think it's a dirty trick to bring me all the way to New York just to make a widow out of me.

NICK: You wouldn't be a widow long.

NORA: You bet I wouldn't.

NICK: Not with all your money.

Absent was any hint of Hammett's objective style and the kind of helplessness to be found in the novel, as when Nick remarks: " 'I just tell what happens; I don't explain it.' "

EVELYN PRENTICE (M-G-M, 1934) was the next film made by Powell and Loy, again as a married couple. M-G-M knew that it had an extremely saleable property in THE THIN MAN, so it did what no other studio had the wisdom to do: it decided to space out the pictures over the years, thus limiting exposure and keeping the property current. VARIETY announced that M-G-M was planning to star Powell and Loy in THE CASINO MURDER CASE, but Powell objected. He had had enough of Philo Vance, with or without Loy. Instead he starred with Joan Crawford in RECKLESS (M-G-M, 1935) and then went on loan-out, permitted by his contract, to make STAR OF MIDNIGHT (RKO, 1935). Dodging the Philo Vance film, Powell nonetheless got his chance to play opposite Rosalind Russell in RENDEZVOUS (M-G-M, 1935). He was nominated for an Academy Award for THE THIN MAN, but lost out to Clark Gable for IT HAPPENED ONE NIGHT (Columbia, 1934). Powell was convinced that it would come to him once he appeared in THE GREAT ZIEGFELD (M-G-M, 1936). It did not turn out that way, but the public loved the film and Myrna Loy was cast in it as Billie Burke.

The second picture on the two-picture loan-out deal to RKO was THE EX-MRS. BRADFORD (RKO, 1936) which cast Powell as a Los Angeles surgeon whose ex-wife wants him back and comically embroils him in a race track murder. It was played in the THIN MAN vein and proved popular. Another picture on loan-out followed, MY MAN GODFREY (Universal, 1936), which co-starred Powell with his real ex-wife, Carole Lombard. Having always been a retiring man, Powell had admired her vivacity. While they were married, Lombard had dragged him to every kind of party. Although he dressed well, Powell did not like to dress until the latest possible moment. He preferred staying in bed and even had an extra large bed specially built. Powell had not been in the least bitter about the divorce, claiming that marriage to him had allowed Carole to spread her wings. She had a wicked sense of humor, however, and insisted on calling him Philo off-screen all through the picture, knowing how much Powell hated the reference. Powell was then quickly co-starred again with Loy in LIBELLED LADY (M-G-M, 1936) while the second THIN MAN picture was in preproduction. The fan magazines felt that the two made such a perfect couple on screen that they should marry in private life. This was highly unlikely. Arthur Hornblow had succeeded finally in getting a divorce so he and Loy could marry and Powell had fallen in love with Jean Harlow.

Dashiell Hammett was once more in Hollywood. M-G-M hired him to provide the original story from which Albert Hackett and Frances Goodwin would do the screenplay. Hammett installed himself in a beautiful house in Bel Air with his two Black manservants. The studio provided him with a secretary who would come each day for dictation. She would sit on a sofa, a notebook on her knees, waiting. Sometimes Hammett did not come down at all and at five o'clock the studio limousine would simply take her back without having seen him. Sometimes Hammett would come down and sit across from her and remain silent all day long. Sometimes he would work crossword puzzles and so would she and the only conversation that would pass between them would be when they would ask each other words. Sometimes he would call her to come upstairs. She would lie on the bed with him. Nothing would happen. He would just hold her in silence. Sometimes he would take her out to expensive restaurants or to gambling casinos where he would spend large quantities of money. Sometimes, many times women from Madame Lee Francis' brothel would come down the stairs in the morning, usually Black or Oriental women, always someone different. Sometimes Hammett would do very strange things, such as stopping at a florist shop and sending all the flowers in the store to her flat which would annoy her husband. On those days when she did not work, she wondered if Hammett had bothered to get up or was he just lying there in his darkened room.

Occasionally Hammett would throw a party. Albert Hackett recalled the time that "there was this hooker in his bathroom, a call girl altogether nude up there—it was a practical joke against Sid Perelman . . . and Sid went to the bathroom and gee, he was gone a long time, and then Laura Perelman and whoever went up there and caught them flagrante delicto. That was a story. It ended with Laura going off to San Francisco with Hammett . . . they were gone for days, and there was hell to pay all around."[66] Mostly, though, women were put off by the whores Hammett always had around him. "I'm still surprised at the fuss the 'Thin Man' made out here," Hammett wrote to Lillian in New York. "People bring the Joan Crawfords and Gables over to meet me instead of the usual vice versa! Hot-cha!"[67] With Hammett's help and encouragement, Hellman had written her first play, THE CHILDREN'S HOUR. She insisted Herman Shumlin read it. She had met him through Arthur Kober. Shumlin read the play while Hellman flipped through a magazine. When he finished, he said he would produce it. She had only $55 in her bank account. The play would earn her $125,000. In its initial New York engagement, it would run for 691 performances. After the performance opening night, Hellman telephoned Hammett. She was startled when a woman answered the 'phone, claiming to be Hammett's secretary and saying that he was asleep and could not be disturbed. She became so angry that she flew to Los Angeles, went to Hammett's rented house and smashed the ice-cream parlor in the basement, and then, without seeing him, took the next flight to New York.

All of these distractions notwithstanding, Hammett did manage to complete his original screen story for AFTER THE THIN MAN (M-G-M, 1936). It opens with Nick and Nora returning to San Francisco. Asta becomes the father of pups. Nora again is the one who gets Nick involved in a case, this time trying to find out what happened to her cousin Selma's husband. The cast included James Stewart, Joseph Calleia, Jessie Ralph, and Penny Singleton. George Zucco was on hand as a zany psychiatrist. Although Nick and Nora are always pictured sleeping discreetly separately in twin beds, much of the bedroom dialogue is the best in the picture and at the end it is announced that Nora will have a baby. Detection was secondary even to chasing Asta around the house.

It would be three years before the third entry was released. In the interim, Powell and Loy starred in DOUBLE WEDDING (M-G-M, 1937), a slap-stick comedy. Powell married Harlow, her third, his second. In 1937, Harlow was strickened with an inflamed gall bladder. Uremic poisoning followed and she died in June at the age of twenty-six. Powell was overwhelmed by grief. He wept uncontrollably at her funeral. After the funeral, Powell spent a month on Ronald Colman's yacht and then went to Europe. Shortly after he returned, it was discovered that he had cancer of the rectum. He underwent a colon bypass operation attended by radium treatments. M-G-M reported to the trades that in view of Powell's difficulties the next THIN MAN picture would star a new team: Virginia Bruce and Melvyn Douglas. Ever since THE CASINO MURDER CASE which teamed Paul Lukas and Rosalind Russell, the studio had been looking for a second team that would click the way Powell and Loy did. Not only was there concern about Powell's living long enough to make another picture, but Loy herself, who was quite difficult to get along with and anything but the model wife off-screen, wanted the studio to give her the kind of star build-up which it had to Crawford and Garbo.

Hammett had found a new source of income by writing commentary for a comic strip titled SECRET AGENT X-9. Here again, however, his constant drinking began to take its toll. His physical condition became considerably weakened. He wanted to be regarded as a serious novelist and even signed a contract with Random House for an advance of $5,000 to write a book to be called THERE WAS A YOUNG MAN. Hammett had had a falling out with Knopf. " 'Go ahead,' " Knopf had told Bennett Cerf, " 'but you'll have nothing but trouble with Hammett. He's a terrible man.' " Cerf did not agree. "Dash was *not* a terrible man," he recalled in AT RANDOM (1977). "One of the reasons I remember him with particular fondness is that we gave him a five-thousand-dollar advance for a book, and after about two years he offered to give us back the money. That doesn't happen very often. I didn't want to take it. I said, 'I think you'll do the book someday, Dash.' But he said, 'No. I'm afraid I'll never write it. I'm petering out.' He knew he was getting sicker all the time. . . . It was the fine gesture of a man with integrity."[68]

William Powell recovered fully and M-G-M again approached Hammett to supply an original screen story. "It was as if he had abdicated life: he wrote nothing, and was troubled by sexual impotence, that most dreaded symptom and punishment," Diane Johnson wrote. "He left his hotel rooms less and less. His hotel bill grew huge, and was left unpaid. He looked gaunt and white. His absences were noticed, his friends grew worried."[69] As early as 1937, M-G-M wanted insurance about the THIN MAN property and had purchased screen rights to Nick and Nora from Hammett. "Maybe there are better writers in the world," Hammett wrote to Hellman, "but nobody ever invented a more insufferably smug pair of characters. They can't take that away from me, even for $40,000."[70] Hammett finished his final 144-page screen outline for ANOTHER THIN MAN on 13 May 1938. It was in the form of a short novel, opening with Nora on the telephone, and ending with the beautiful but deadly female murderer being somewhat more philosophical than Brigid O'Shaughnessy had been: "Oh, well, all you can do is try to play the breaks as far as you get them."[71]

Hammett gambled away all the money he had made. Albert Hackett and his wife Frances Goodrich who had done the screenplay were so alarmed they wanted Hammett to see a doctor. He was not only broke, but his physical condition had deteriorated to the point where he could only smile at them feebly, mutely. They paid his eight thousand dollar hotel bill at the Beverly Wilshire and got him on a plane to New York where he was met by Lillian. She took him in an ambulance to Lenox Hill Hospital. He was impotent and terrified of insanity.

While he had been in Hollywood, besides the drinking, Hammett had become a political radical and had joined or supported a number of left-wing and Communist organizations. He was also one of the prime movers in organizing the Screen Writers Guild. The F. B. I. had begun to watch him. ANOTHER THIN MAN was his last screen effort in writing a detective story, although he would later create a new detective character.

Woody Van Dyke directed ANOTHER THIN MAN (M-G-M, 1939). The film opens in New York with Nick, Nora, Nick, Jr., a baby, and Asta all checking into a hotel. C. Aubrey Smith invites them for the week-end to Long Island. On the way, they see a corpse in the road which disappears. Once there, Smith locks the liquor cabinet, but Nora picks his pocket. Nora's father was Smith's partner. Sheldon Leonard shows up, claiming that he has spent ten years in jail for doing Smith's dirty work. When Smith is murdered and with Nat Pendleton and Edward Gargan representing the police, Nick has no choice but to investigate. As in the two previous entries and all the Philo Vance films, Powell gloried in his long speech at the conclusion, indentifying the culprit. Loy was growing more and more resentful, however. She did not like her role as Nora nor did she like the fact that Powell got so many more scenes than she did. As early as 1935 in her lawsuit against M-G-M to break her contract, she had alleged that the way the studio was handling her had brought her to the brink of a nervous breakdown. The press mentioned none of this. The fan magazines carried instead reams of copy about the marvelous rapport between Powell and Loy on the set. The studio continued to star the two together, in I LOVE YOU AGAIN (M-G-M, 1940) and in LOVE CRAZY (M-G-M, 1941). When SHADOW OF THE THIN MAN (M-G-M, 1941) was announced, it would be their fourth time as Nick and Nora. Hammett had nothing to do with the plot, which was just as well.

Harry Kurnitz, who had worked on other M-G-M husband and wife mystery films, worked on the screenplay of SHADOW OF THE THIN MAN as did Irving Brecher, who was credited, and Manfred B. Lee and Frederic Dannay, who were not. Woody Van Dyke again directed. It was with this film that the studio made as much a soap opera out of this series as it had of its Andy Hardy films. Dickie Hall was cast as Nick, Jr. Most of the film was given over to Nick and Nora going to a wrestling match where Nora becomes too animated and to Nick taking a little Nick, who is supposed to be four, to an amusement park. Contract players such as Donna Reed and Barry Nelson carried much of the plot line which was rather thin. Nick refuses to be involved in an investigation surrounding a murdered jockey until one reporter is murdered and another is suspected wrongly of having done it. Only then does Nick come once more out of retirement.

If the THIN MAN films were keeping viewers updated on what was happening within the Charles family, the principals were also carrying on their personal lives. Between ANOTHER THIN MAN and SHADOW OF THE THIN MAN, William Powell met Diana Lewis at Chasen's. She was a twenty-one-year-old contract player at M-G-M. When they went upstairs together, Mousie, as she was called, sang from a collection of old songs. Powell could not believe that a youngster went for the old songs. A couple of nights later the couple eloped. After this marriage, Powell spent almost all of his spare time in Palm Springs. It proved to be a lasting marriage. Powell's son from an earlier marriage, William, Jr., entered the service and had a fine war record. He later turned to screenwriting. In his forty-third year he stabbed himself to death with a paring knife.

Myrna Loy was also active. She divorced Arthur Hornblow in 1942 and a week later married John Hertz, Jr., a wealthy heir and advertising man. She quit pictures, disgusted at the treatment she had been accorded in Hollywood, and went to New York. M-G-M released her from her contract provided she would continue to play Nora whenever a THIN MAN picture was scheduled. She divorced Hertz in 1944 on the grounds of mental cruelty and in little over a year married Gene Markey, a screenwriter and producer whose star seemed on the rise. She confided to the press that in this case it was definitely love at first sight.

Between marriages, Loy did have time for THE THIN MAN GOES HOME (M-G-M, 1944). Robert Riskin and Harry Kurnitz did the screenplay and Richard Thorpe directed. Nowhere before had there been any indication that Nick had a family. In this film, however, Harry Davenport was cast as Dr. Charles and Lucile Watson played Nick's mother. They live in Judge Hardy's house on the M-G-M back lot. Nick has gone on the wagon and finds murder in his home town when Leon Ames wants a painting that an art dealer played by Donald Meek sold to Nora. Nora is convinced that the murderer is Edward Brophy, a friend of Nick's who is posing as a greeting card salesman. The comedy reaches its high point when Nora shadows Brophy while Ames shadows Nora. Nick becomes so exasperated with her that he paddles her derrière with a newspaper. Loy objected to it because it was undignified but went through with it. Years later, she turned down a role in MURDER BY DEATH (Columbia, 1976) because she felt it would ruin her image as Nora Charles to have her seventy-one-year-old bottom pinched by David Niven! On the whole, THE THIN MAN GOES HOME was a superior comedy to the previous two entries, if it did not score very highly as a detective story. Loy did not help the picture much when she complained in the trades that what had once been camaraderie between her and Nick had now disintegrated into little more than a string of wise-cracks. She felt murder was no longer to be treated in a comic vein. She blamed the problems on the fact that Dash Hammett had not been involved and that Woody Van Dyke was dead. Louis B. Mayer, on the other hand, loved this new family atmosphere in the THIN MAN films.

After the success of her play, THE LITTLE FOXES, Lillian Hellman bought a farm outside Pleasantville. Hammett frequently stayed there with her. Hellman called it Hardscrabble, after the road which it bordered. THE ADVENTURES OF THE THIN MAN began regular broadcasts in 1941 on NBC with Lester Damon and Claudia Morgan as Nick and Nora. It would continue to earn Hammett a large weekly salary throughout the decade although he contributed nothing to the radio stories. In future years, THE ADVENTURES OF SAM SPADE would also go on the air. "My sole duty in regard to these programs is to look in the mail for a check once a week," Hammett remarked. "I don't even listen to them. If I did, I'd complain about how they were being handled, and then I'd fall into the trap of being asked to come down and help. I don't want to have anything to do with the radio. It's a dizzy world—makes the movies seem highly intellectual."[72]

In AN UNFINISHED WOMAN (1969), Hellman recalled an angry speech she had made one night: "it had to do with injustice, his carelessness, his insistence that he get his way, his sharpness with me but not with himself.

was drunk, but he was drunker, and when my strides around the room carried me close to the chair where he was sitting, I stared in disbelief at what I saw. He was grinding a burning cigarette into his cheek.

"I said, 'What are you doing?'

" 'Keeping myself from doing it to you,' he said.

"The mark on his cheek was ugly for a few weeks, but in time it faded into the scar that remained for the rest of his life. We never again spoke of that night because, I think, he was ashamed of the angry gesture that made him once again the winner in the game that men and women play against each other, and I was ashamed that I caused myself to lose so often.''[73]

Hammett would spend his week-ends at Hardscrabble and his weeks in an apartment he rented in New York, making the rounds to his favorite clubs. One night, as Lillian was driving him back, he was more drunk than usual. He began to paw her and to leer. When he suggested they make love, Lillian refused him. "She had never said no before to any of his demands or sexual whims," Diane Johnson wrote. "Tonight, simply, no. This surprised him, sobered him, shocked him. That was it, then. He loved Lily, would always love her. But he decided he would never make love to her again, and he never did, and never spoke of it."[74] It was shortly after this that Paramount announced its intention to remake THE GLASS KEY (Paramount, 1942). Hammett decided, since now war had been declared, that he would enlist. Despite his age and the tuberculosis which still showed on his x-rays, he was accepted. He was stationed several places but spent most of the war in the Aleutians. He appeared to like the discipline of military life, working with much younger men editing the base newspaper. From all indications, he seemed happier than he had ever been in Hollywood or New York.

SONG OF THE THIN MAN (M-G-M, 1947) was the final entry. Leon Ames was in the cast as was Patricia Morison, playing Ames' wife, Dean Stockwell as Nick, Jr., Keenan Wynn, Gloria Grahame, Jayne Meadows, Tom Dugan, and Jimmy Flavin as a cop. Edward Buzzell was the director.

"Bill Powell was bored with his role," Ames told me, "but that was nothing. Here was America's happiest couple. For years the public had believed that. And they never talked. Except when they were in front of the camera. I'm surprised that they talked even then. Some of the time, they talked to the camera alone and the film was edited together later."

M-G-M's publicity department stressed the fact that Asta, who had died in 1946, had been replaced by Asta, Jr., and was doubled by his brother, Zip. As was the case with M-G-M's other canine star, Lassie, Asta, Jr., was given his own dressing room. Myrna Loy was clearly fed up with being cast as the perfect wife. The dialogue was very poor. When Nick finds a razor blade in the murder room, he reflects for a moment, saying, "Somerset Maugham? No, it couldn't have been." Nick takes the case and Asta is more a companion to him than Nora who is busy in their ultra-modern apartment being a non-drinking mother. The apartment is so contemporary in its furnishings that it even has a television set! At the finish, Patricia Morison drills Leon Ames until her gun is empty.

Myrna Loy did have a brief cameo appearance as Powell's wife in THE SENATOR WAS INDISCREET (Universal, 1947). In the autumn of 1950 she divorced Gene Markey in Mexico although she herself was not present. Her grounds were mental cruelty. In 1951 she married Howland H. Sargeant, a Deputy Assistant Secretary of State. They were divorced in 1955. William Powell spent his declining years on the screen in a series of minor vehicles and character roles until his permanent retirement in 1955. Increasing deafness made him disinclined to give interviews, although he liked quiet parties with friends, golf outings, and sitting in front of the television set he had installed in his bedroom in his Palm Springs home. Powell, when he was younger, used to comment that people are born with one of two temperaments, happy or melancholy, and that he was somewhere between them. During his final years in Palm Springs, surrounded by the incessant heat and the seclusion, with his television and Mousie and the drink in his hand and the occasional cigarette, even hardness of hearing did not interfere with his sense of philosophical tranquility.

It was to be otherwise for Dashiell Hammett. He loved his country as few writers and the Aleutians were as far as he ever ventured beyond its continental borders. His attraction to Marxism, if more radical than Lillian Hellman's, was also more internal. He was convinced that American politics were hopelessly corrupt but uncertain that any other system would be preferable. Although Hammett and Jose were divorced in 1937, they both continued to consider themselves married. When it came to Lillian Hellman, "he received an immense amount of satisfaction in working with [her]," as William F. Nolan observed, "sublimating his own creative drive in furthering her expanding theatrical career. Lillian Hellman's success was, in a way, his own. Each of her plays benefited from Hammett's tough, unrelenting criticism, and she often commented on this: 'Nobody ever gave more aid to anybody than he gave to me. . . . It was more than friendship. It was the care and sacrifice of a scholarly, warm-hearted man who knew about writing, who wanted it to be good, and who was generous enough to help. . . . He was generous to all writers who came to him—because writing was something he respected very deeply.' "[75]

Why did Hammett quit writing after THE THIN MAN? Well, he did not really. He just did not want to repeat himself and write another detective story. Over a twenty-year period, he progressed through a half dozen attempts to write a novel, from THERE WAS A YOUNG MAN (1938) MY BROTHER FELIX (1939), THE VALLEY SHEEP ARE FATTER (1944-1946), THE HUNTING BOY (1949–1950), DECEMBER 1 (1950), until finally TULIP (1952–1954). When he had completed THE THIN MAN, as Nolan pointed out, "ill health had brought him close to death, and detective work had revealed its dark face to him many times. Cynicism had been replaced by bitterness; troubling visions of a meaningless universe possessed him—and his method of dealing with such visions was to write about them. Balanced against this bleakness of spirit was the soul of a poet, a romantic."[76] Hammett would try to write. He would play tricks on himself, writing in longhand to get started, or buying himself a new typewriter, having a drink of whiskey before sitting down to write, not having a drink until after he had written something, walking, but no strategy worked. "He could not write," Diane Johnson concluded, " . . . because he had nothing to write about. His life, in some sense, had ended when he left San Francisco and obscurity, and his work and family, and the social class to which he owed allegiance but was uncomfortable in. He could no longer make any sense of his life, but he also couldn't bring himself to put an end to it more directly than by drinking."[77]

Hammett did the screen adaptation of Hellman's WATCH ON THE RHINE (Warner's, 1943) for which he was nominated for an Academy Award. Once he quit the service because, again, he had begun drinking in excess, he returned to civilian life in New York. Both the THIN MAN and SAM SPADE radio programs were still on the air, although Warner Bros. joined by Knopf had instituted a lawsuit against him, claiming that the studio owned all rights to the character when it purchased screen rights. The suit was ultimately settled in Hammett's favor, but by that time SAM SPADE had been taken off the air. ABC with Hammett's help developed a radio series based loosely on the Continental Op featuring a detective named Brad Runyon. The program was titled THE FAT MAN. As each program began, Runyon would step on a scale and inform his listeners that his weight was 237 pounds and that his fortune was danger. J. Scott Smart was cast in the role in THE FAT MAN (Universal-International, 1951) directed by William Castle. Julie London, Rock Hudson in his first screen appearance, and Jayne Meadows were also in the cast. Emmett Kelly, the pantomime clown, was notable as the villain, but otherwise the film was not remarkable and a series did not result.

Hammett was already in trouble with the authorities when William Wyler hired him to do the screen adaptation for DETECTIVE STORY (Paramount, 1951). He paid Hammett a large advance, rented a suite of rooms for him at the Beverly-Wilshire, and told him he was confident he could do it. Wyler would visit Hammett every two or three days to see how the script was coming. Hammett would talk with him but became evasive about his progress. He had been at it for three weeks when, one day, he met Wyler at the door to his suite. He had a cashier's check in the amount of the advance. He handed it to the stunned director.

"I can't do it," he said simply. "I just can't do it any more." He paused for a moment. "I'm sorry."

A couple of years earlier, when his youngest daughter was to be married, Hammett had returned to Los Angeles and moved into the house he had bought Jose. "It ought to have been a happy time, with the family together again, but it was not," Diane Johnson wrote. "Hammett, who had never been cruel to Jose, not, anyway, in little ways, was cruel now. He made caustic remarks and unreasonable demands, to which she always acceded. 'See how I've got your mother trained,' he'd say. He went unshaven for days; his daughters had never seen him like this. And he wept, when he was drunk, and regretted that he had no sons and made dreadful scenes, so that Jo was happy that she was getting married and out of there. But he was lovely at the wedding, so handsome and famous and charming to everyone."[78]

In New York at this time, Hammett was virtually alone. Only Rose Evans, his housekeeper, came every day to look after things. Lillian now refused to see him. He had no secretary. Ed Rosenberg, the producer of the SAM SPADE radio shows, would drop by only to find Hammett in bed and usually drunk. In fact, Hammett stayed in bed, drinking, scarcely able to make it to the bathroom. Rose became so alarmed that she insisted Lillian come over. The end result was that Hammett was finally admitted to a hospital and informed that if he did not stop drinking he would be dead in a month or two. He promised to stop drinking, and he kept the promise.

In April, 1951, Hammett was therefore sober when he was called before Federal Justice Sylvester Ryan. He did not know the names of the contributors to the bail-bond fund of the Civil Rights Congress. The fund had permitted several convicted Communist sympathizers to elude the law. Hammett was, however, defiant. He was not going to be dictated to by any judge. So he went to prison for six months on a charge of contempt of court. He was first confined to the Federal House of Detention on West Street in New York and then was transferred to the Federal Correctional Institution near Ashland, Kentucky. Included among his duties while in prison was washing out the latrines.

When Hammett was released, he was called before the McCarthy Committee. The senator was investigating, among other things, the infiltration of books by Communist sympathizers into what was issued by the U.S. Information Service. "Mr. Hammett," McCarthy asked him, "if you were spending, as we are, over $100,000 a year on an information program allegedly for the purpose of fighting Communism, and if you were in charge of that program to fight Communism, would you purchase the works of some 75 Communist authors and distribute their works throughout the world, placing our official stamp of approval on those works?" Hammett's reply was direct. "Well, I think—of course, I don't know—if I were fighting Communism I don't think I would give people any books at all."[79]

The Treasury Department filed notice of a tax lien against Hammett for $100,629.03. The lien permitted the seizure of all royalties from his books, radio, and motion picture residuals for the rest of his life. Most of this claim seems to have been penalties and interest, but as the Treasury Department pointed out "it was the first such action taken against any one involved in an investigation of subversive activity."[80] Hammett continued to live alone as long as he could, supported by Lillian. When his health began to fail to the extent that he felt he could no longer take care of himself and wanted to check into a veterans' hospital, Lillian persuaded him instead to move in with her

" . . . I keep from myself even now the possible meaning of a night, very late, a short time before his death," Lillian wrote later. "I came into his room and for the only time in the years I knew him, there were tears in his eyes and the book was lying unread. I sat down beside him and waited a long time before I could say, 'Do you want to talk about it?' He said, almost with anger, 'No. My only chance is not to talk about it.' And he never did. His patience, his courage, his dignity in those suffering months were very great. It was as if all that makes a man's life had come together to prove itself: suffering was a private matter and there was to be no invasion of it."[81]

In December, 1960 Hammett had to be taken to the hospital. It hurt Lillian for the rest of her life that as the medical attendants were putting Hammett on a stretcher in the elevator, he opened his eyes and asked in what seemed evident surprise if she were coming, as if he thought that were the last thing she would do. He came out of the hospital and then went back in again. For years he had been plagued by emphysema, but that condition had become complicated by cancer. Lillian shouted at him when he was slipping into the coma in which two days later he would die, shouted at him, brought him back for only a moment it seemed, long enough for him to look at her with a startled expression, an expression she felt of profound terror. He died 10 January 1961.

As a veteran of two wars, Hammett could be buried as he wanted, in Arlington National Cemetery. In its obituary, the NEW YORK TIMES said of him that "his prose was clean and entirely unique. His characters were as sharply and economically defined as any in American fiction. His stories were as consistent as mathematics and as intricate as psychology . . . the Latin scholar responded to the classic precision of his language and the comic strip reader to the excitment of his plots."[82] Lillian Hellman, in her funeral address, spoke more of the man she had known: "He believed in man's right to dignity and never in all the years did he play anybody's game but his own—he never lied, he never faked, he never stooped."[83]

The primary cause of Hammett's death was a cancerous tumor in the right lung which had been complicated by emphysema and pneumonia as well as disease of the heart, liver, kidneys, spleen, and the prostate gland. It was as if his body had simply given out all at once from the years and years of abuse, and illness, and suppressed emotion. Lillian Hellman was named executrix for Hammett's estate and it was in this capacity that she was finally able to free his copyrights by achieving a compromise with the government. Hellman selected which works of his would remain in print and which ones would not be reprinted when, in view of how well his stories continue to sell even to this day and the interest which continues in him, all of his fiction deserves to be kept in print. It is reputed that the CBS network paid $250,000 to adapt THE DAIN CURSE in 1978. After more than five years in production, the film HAMMETT, directed mostly by Wim Wenders, produced by Francis Ford Coppola, and based on Joe Gores' book, HAMMETT (1975), was finally released to poor notices. Yet what is so often overlooked in critical assessments of Hammett and what is absent from virtually all of the films based on his work is the tenuousness of reality. It is this which is his great contribution to the detective story. As Dennis Dooley put it, "any one person's reality is only a version of the truth, a subjective interpretation of people and events based on what he has experienced, been told or surmised, and on what he wants to believe. A detective is concerned not only with ferreting out the truth, but with his own survival as well. Cast adrift on a sea of unknowns, he must be skeptical not only of everybody else's version of reality, but his own, too."[84] This was the way in which Hammett had approached life and he succeeded in capturing it in his fiction.

1. John Barrymore on location overlooking the Thames while filming SHERLOCK HOLMES (Goldwyn, 1922). Photo courtesy of the British Film Institute.

2. Basil Rathbone and Nigel Bruce in period costume as they appeared in THE HOUND OF THE BASKERVILLES (20th-Fox, 1939). Photo courtesy of Twentieth Century-Fox Film Corporation.

3. Nicholas Rowe (l.) and Alan Cox as a young Sherlock Holmes and John Watson in YOUNG SHERLOCK HOLMES (Paramount, 1985). Photo courtesy of Paramount Pictures Corporation Publicity.

4. Willard Huntington Wright in his Central Park West Apartment during his halcyon days as S. S. Van Dine. Photo courtesy of Stanton MacDonald-Wright.

5. Robert Wace (extreme l.), Eugene Pallette and Warren William in the foreground, Robert Barrat in knickers, as the police are about to enter the Dragon Pool in THE DRAGON MURDER CASE (Warner's-First National, 1934). Photo courtesy of VIEWS & REVIEWS Magazine.

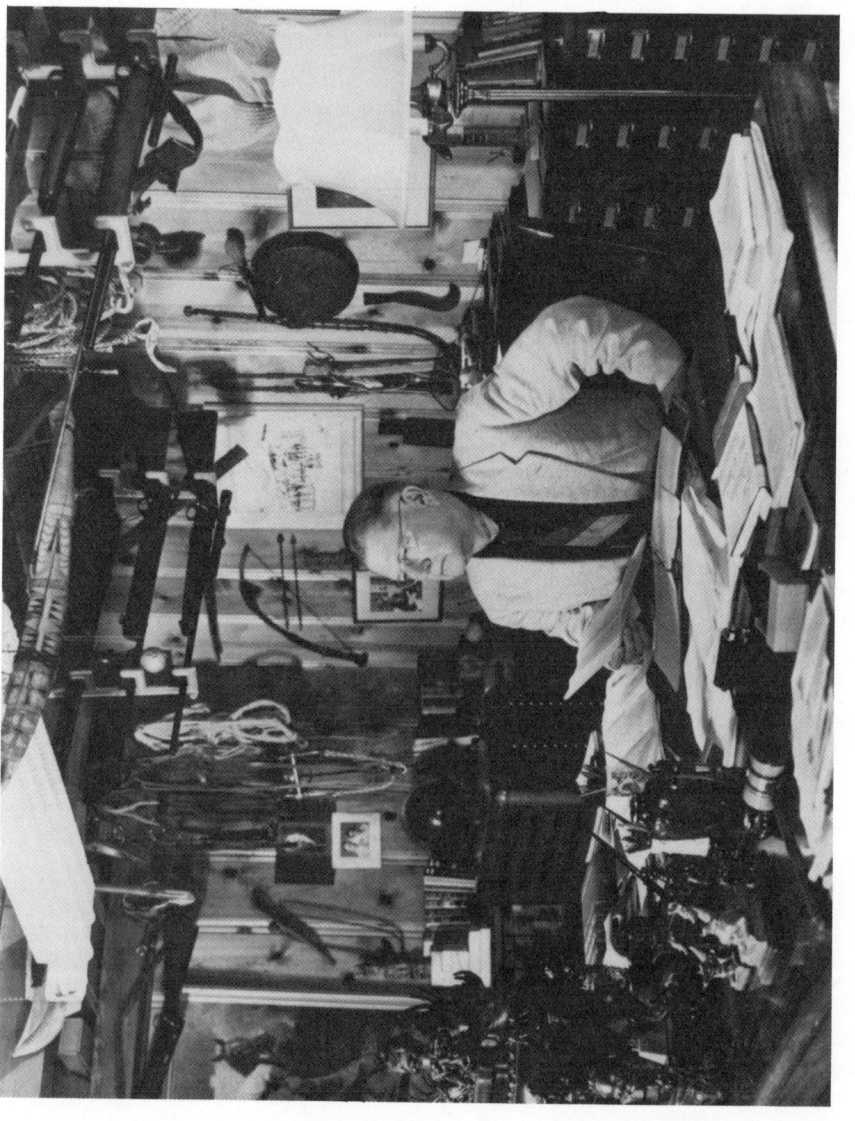

6. Erle Stanley Gardner in his study at his desert ranch. Photo courtesy of Jean Gardner.

7. The only way Winifred Shaw can get Warren William as Perry Mason to represent her and leave the shrewish Della "Mason," played by Claire Dodd is to hold a gun on him in THE CASE OF THE VELVET CLAWS (Warner's, 1936). Eddie Acuff played Spudsy Drake. Photo courtesy of United Artists Television.

8. Publicity poster for the first Ralph Bellamy/Ellery Queen film. Photo courtesy of Columbia Pictures Industries.

9. Margaret Rutherford as Miss Marple in MURDER SHE SAID (M-G-M, 1962). Photo courtesy of Metro-Goldwyn-Mayer.

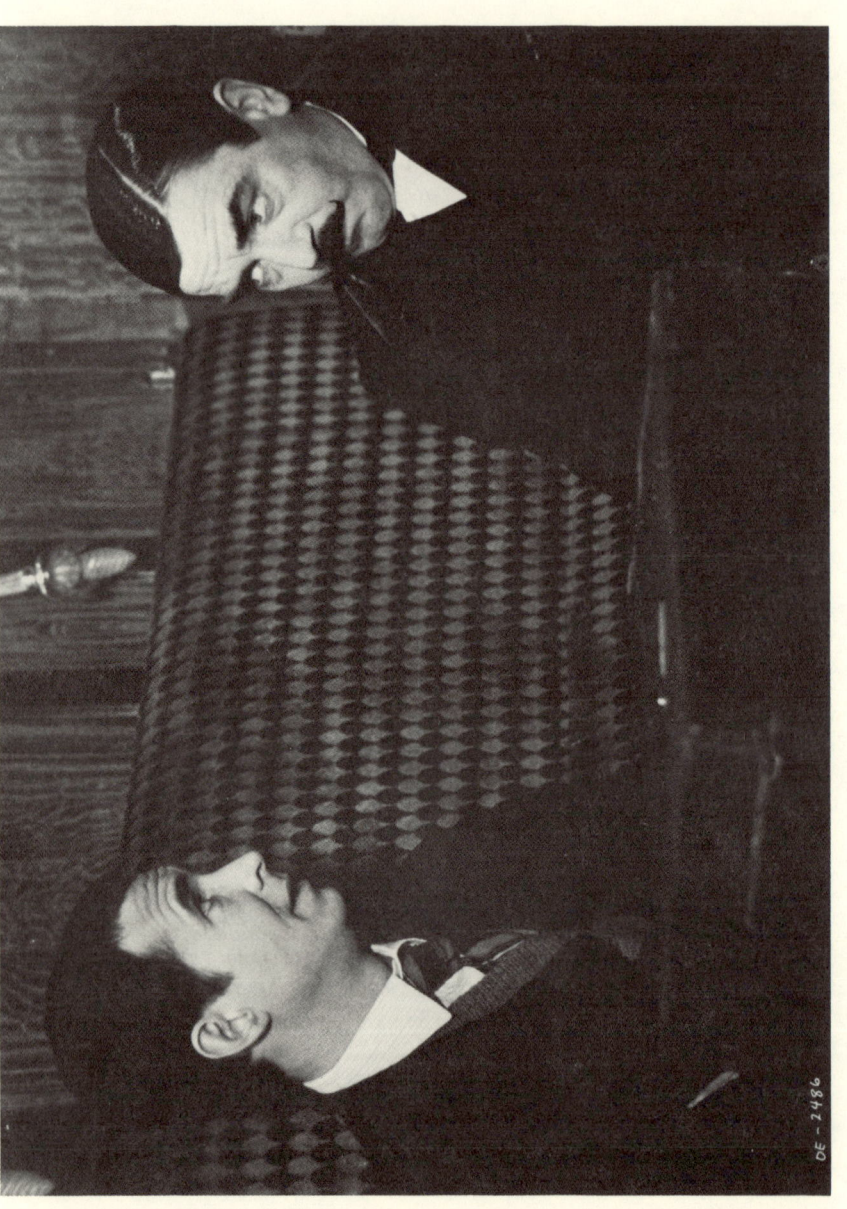

10. Albert Finney (r.) as Hercule Poirot interrogating Anthony Perkins in MURDER ON THE ORIENT EXPRESS (Paramount, 1974). Photo courtesy of Paramount Pictures Corporation Publicity.

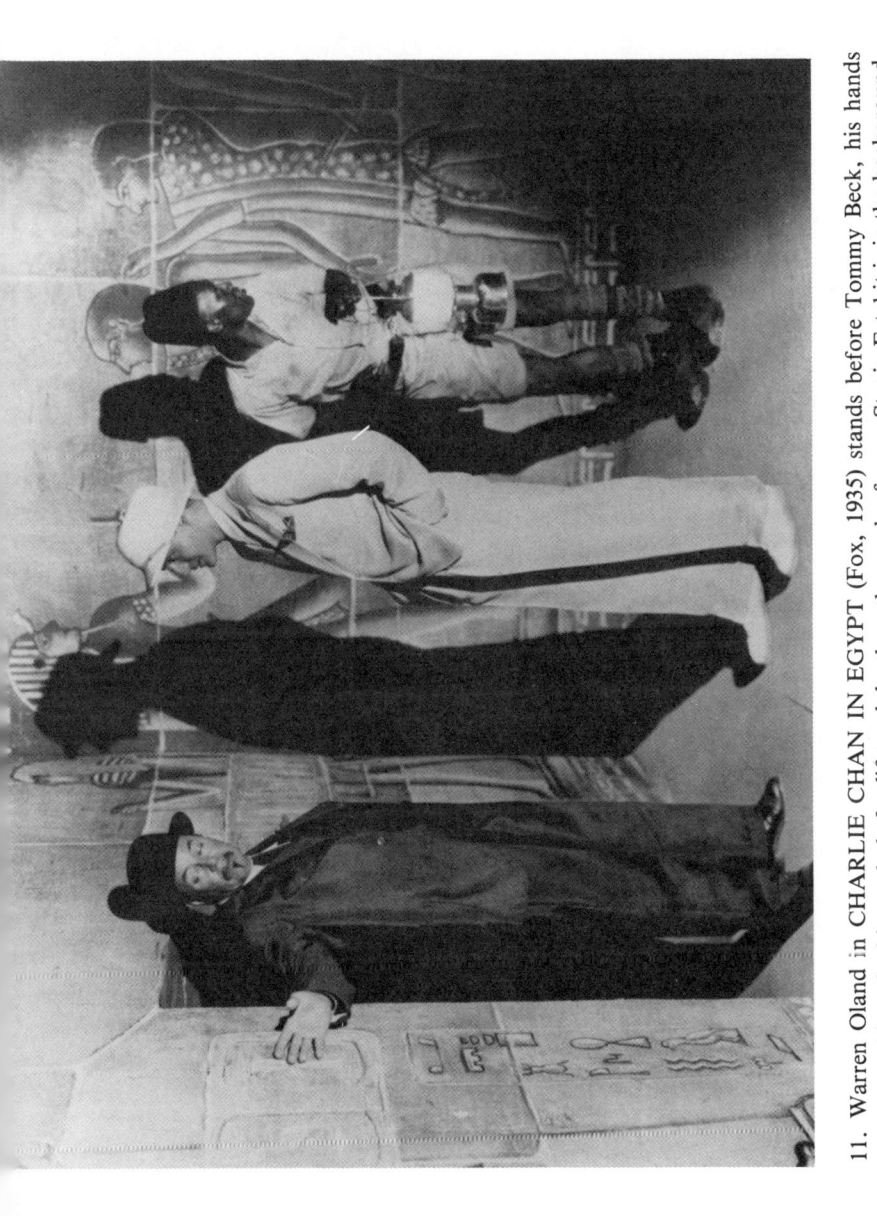

11. Warren Oland in CHARLIE CHAN IN EGYPT (Fox, 1935) stands before Tommy Beck, his hands joining the hieroglyphic symbols for life and death as the reach of man. Stepin Fetchit is in the background. Photo courtesy of Twentieth Century-Fox Film Corporation.

12. Warner Oland and H. Bruce Humberstone on the set of CHARLIE CHAN AT THE RACE TRACK. Photo courtesy of H. Bruce Humberstone.

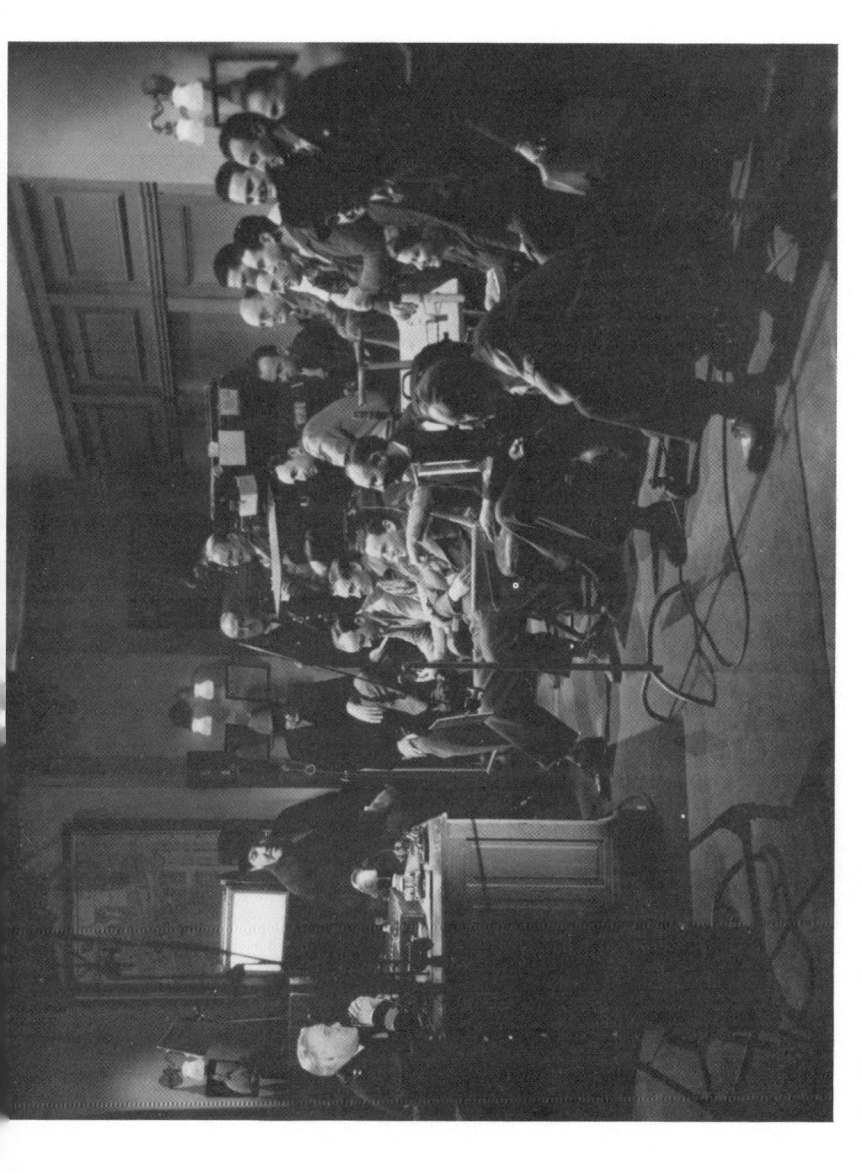

13. Norman Foster (with his arm over the chair) directing a scene from CHARLIE CHAN IN RENO (20th-Fox, 1939) with the crew and some of the cast. Photo courtesy of Norman Foster.

14. Boris Karloff as Mr. Wong talking to a frustrated Grant Withers in MR. WONG IN CHINATOWN (Monogram, 1939). Photo courtesy of the National Film Archive.

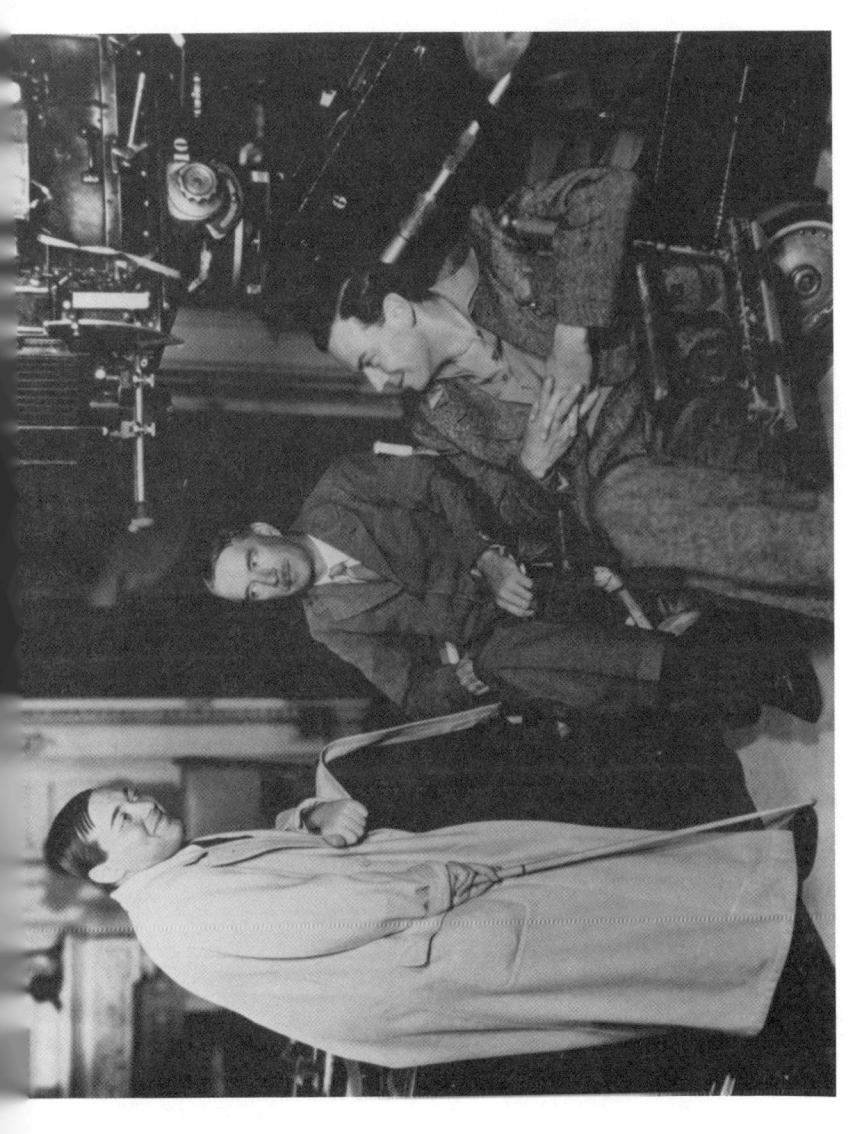

15. John P. Marquand (center) joins Norman Foster and Peter Lorre on the set of a Mr. Moto film. Photo courtesy of Norman Foster.

16. Keye Luke, Harold Huber, and Peter Lorre in MR. MOTO'S GAMBLE (20th-Fox, 1938). Photo courtesy of Twentieth Century-Fox Film Corporation.

17. William Powell (l.) with white-haired Dashiell Hammett and director W. S. "Woody" Van Dyke during the production of THE THIN MAN (M-G-M, 1934). Photo courtesy of the National Film Archive.

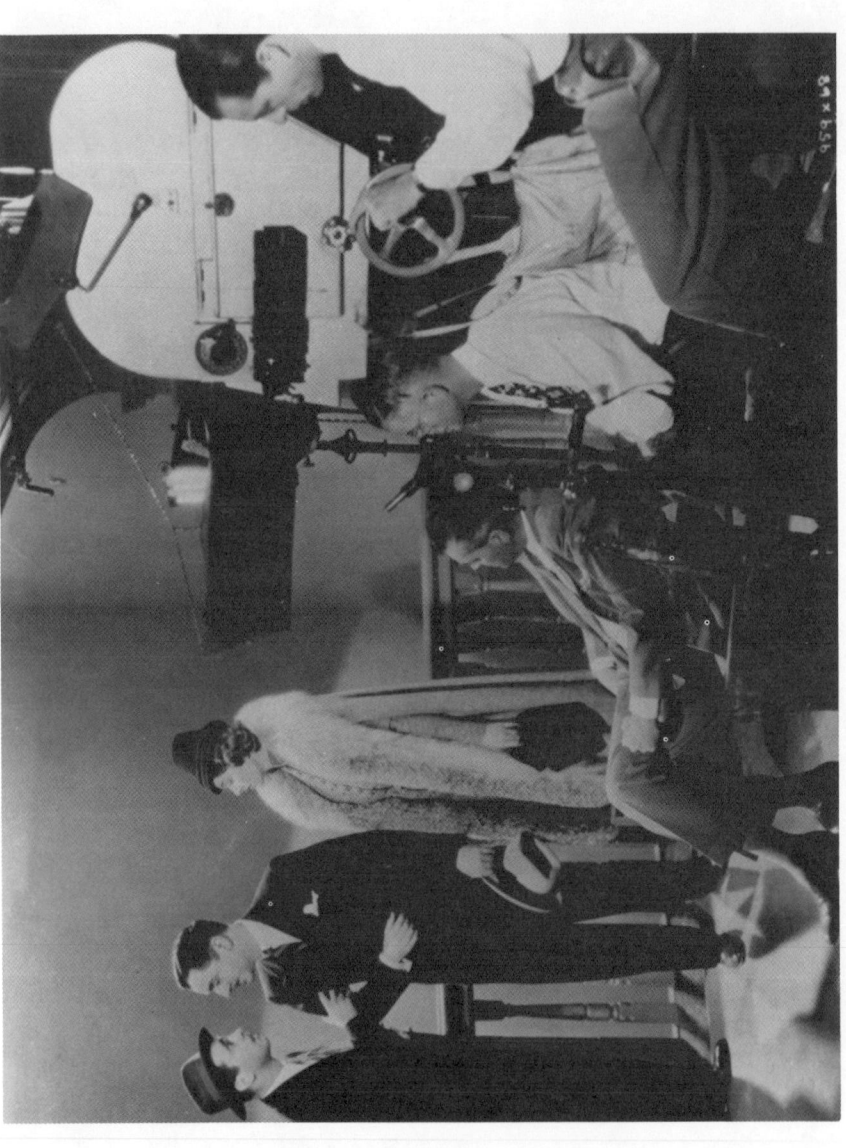

18. W. S. Van Dyke directing William Powell, Myrna Loy, and Sam Levine in a scene from AFTER THE THIN MAN (M.G.M., 1936). Photo courtesy of the National Film Archive.

19. Peter Lorre was supposed to be menacing George Raft in BACKGROUND TO DANGER (Warner's, 1943), but off-camera it was a different story. Photo courtesy of the National Film Archive.

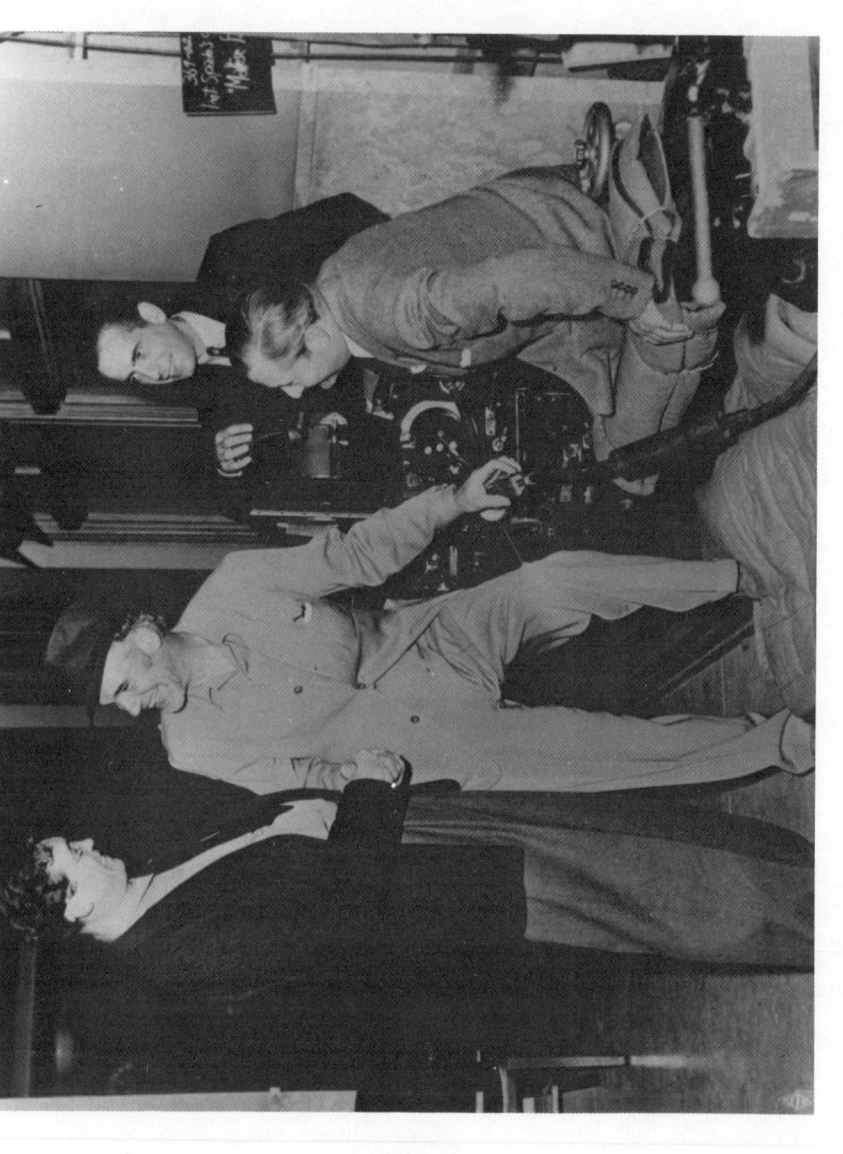

20. Director John Huston shaking hands with his father, Walter Huston, with Humphrey Bogart and the cinematographer on the set of THE MALTESE FALCON (Warner's, 1941). Photo courtesy of the

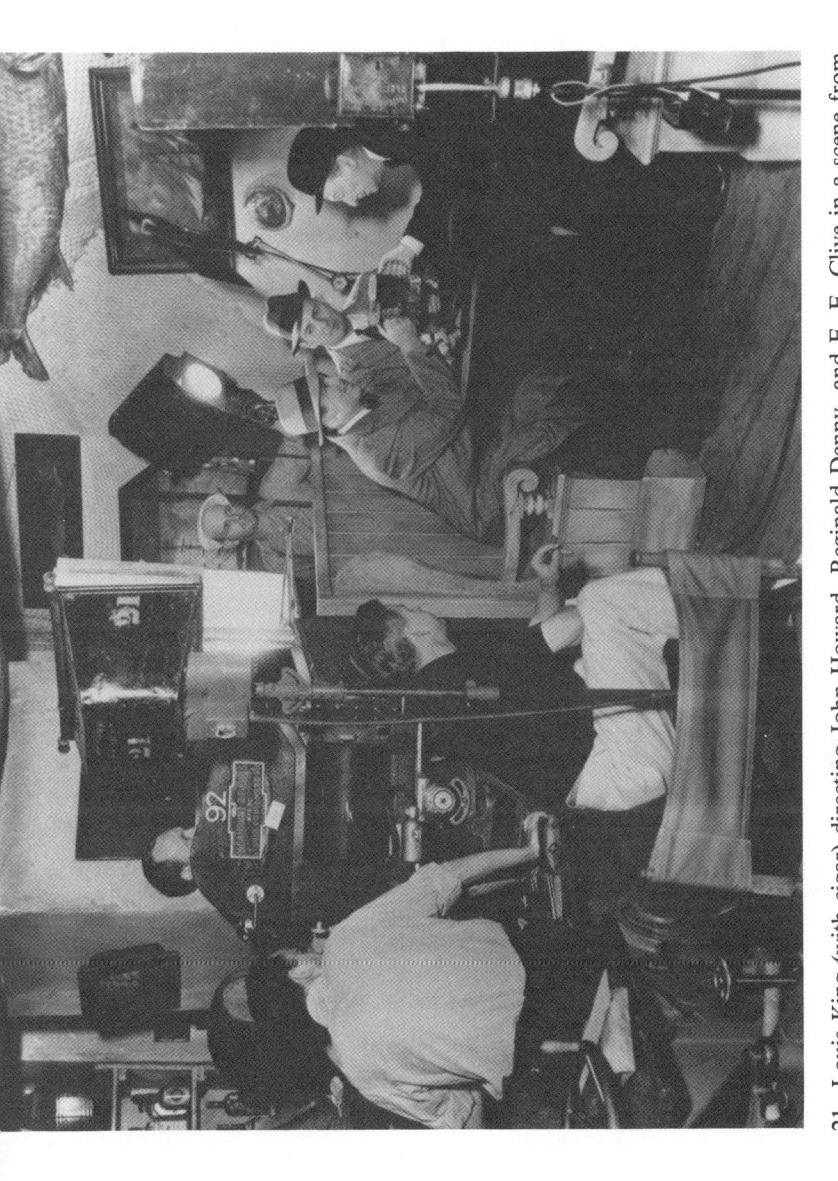

21. Louis King (with cigar) directing John Howard, Reginald Denny, and E. E. Clive in a scene from BULLDOG DRUMMOND COMES BACK (Paramount, 1937). Photo courtesy of the National Film Archive.

22. Warren William and Eric Blore make a getaway while Fred Kelsey (in the derby) and Thurston Hall are searching for them in a typical scene from a Lone Wolf film. Photo courtesy of Columbia Pictures Industries.

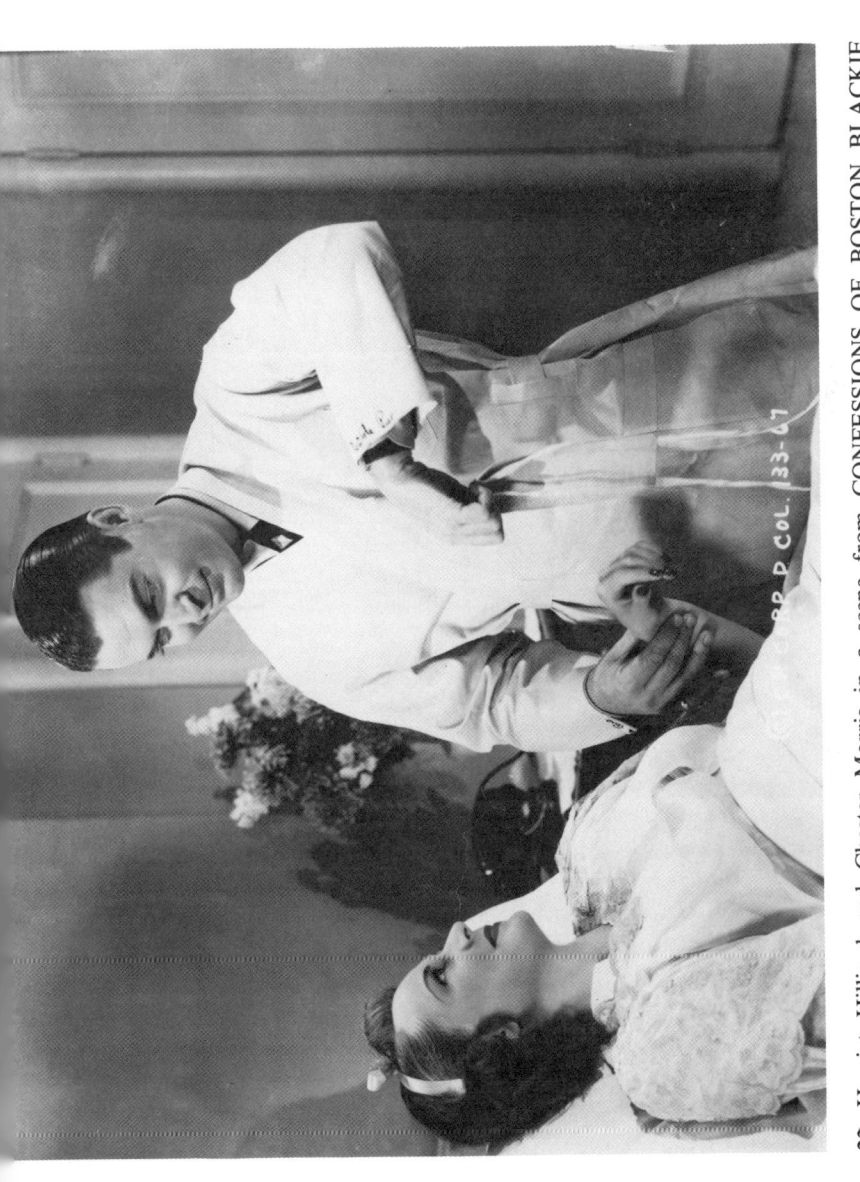

23. Harriet Hilliard and Chester Morris in a scene from CONFESSIONS OF BOSTON BLACKIE (Columbia, 1941). Photo courtesy of Columbia Pictures Industries.

24. George Sanders and Wendy Barrie in a scene from THE GAY FALCON (RKO, 1941). Photo

25. Barbara Hale looks on as Sheldon Leonard holds a gun on Tom Conway in THE FALCON IN HOLLYWOOD (RKO, 1944). Photo courtesy of RKO General.

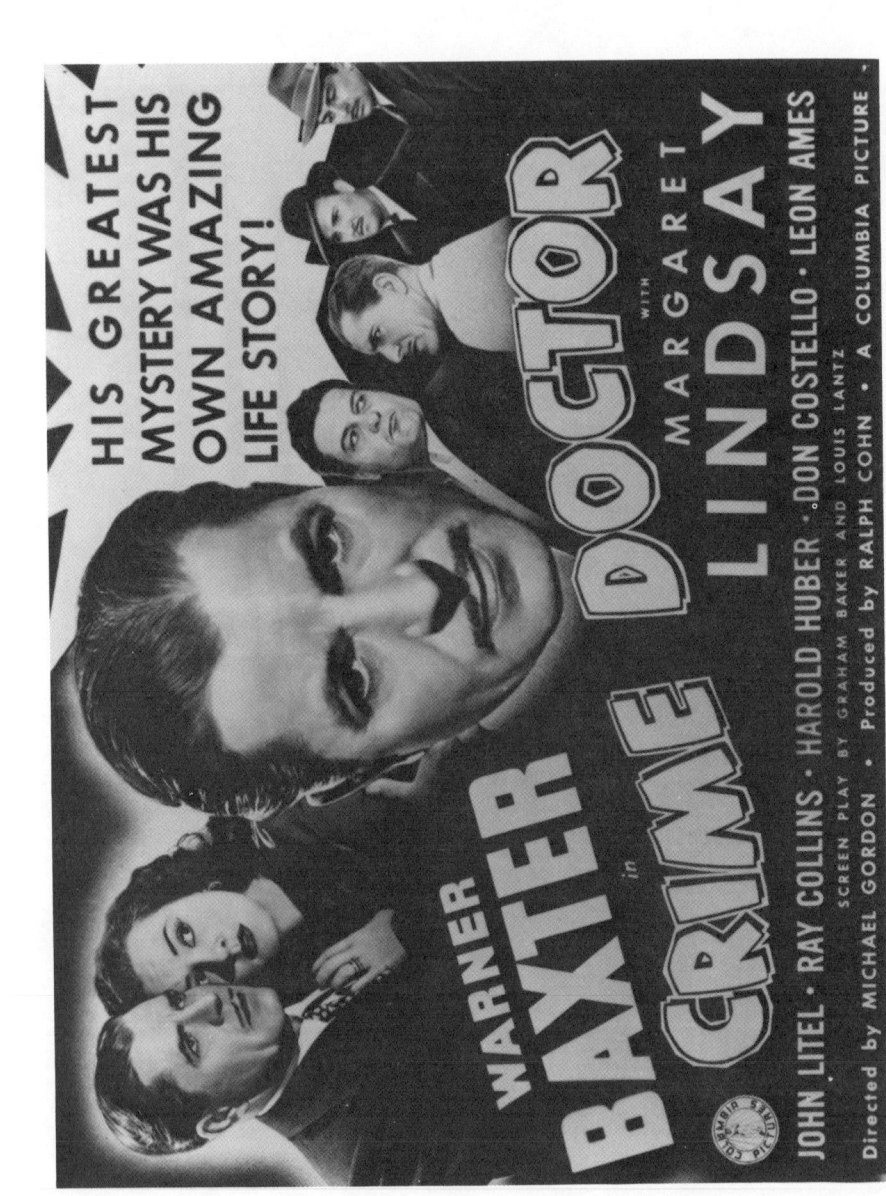

27. Lloyd Nolan and Marjorie Weaver in MICHAEL SHAYNE, PRIVATE DETECTIVE (20th-Fox, 1940). Photo courtesy of Twentieth Century-Fox Film Corporation.

28. Lizabeth Scott, Marvin Miller, and Humphrey Bogart in DEAD RECKONING (Columbia, 1946). Photo

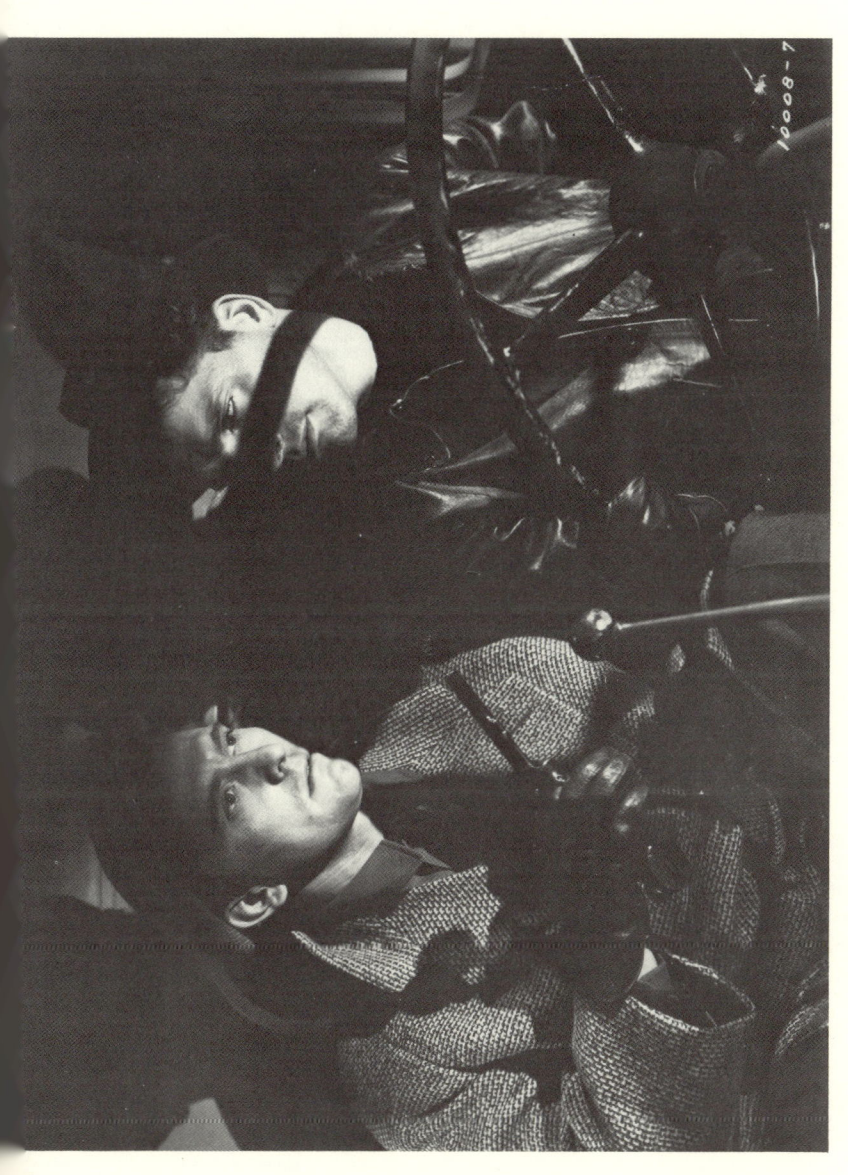

29. Kirk Douglas and Burt Lancaster amid the *film noir* lighting of I WALK ALONE (Paramount, 1947). Photo courtesy of VIEWS & REVIEWS Magazine.

30. Billy Wilder directing Barbara Stanwyck and Fred MacMurray in DOUBLE INDEMNITY (Paramount,

31. Raymond Chandler on a Los Angeles street. Photo courtesy of the UCLA Archive.

32. Edward Dmytryk directing Claire Trevor in MURDER, MY SWEET (RKO, 1944). Photo courtesy of Edward Dmytryk.

33. Robert Montgomery (in director's chair) directing Lloyd Nolan in LADY IN THE LAKE (M-G-M, 1946). Photo courtesy of the National Film Archive.

34. A script conference on THE BIG SLEEP (Warner's, 1946) with (l. to r.) Howard Hawks, Sonia Darwin, Margaret Cunningham (Hawks' secretary), Lauren Bacall, Humphrey Bogart, and Louis Jean

35. Robert Altman directing Nina van Pallandt and Elliott Gould in THE LONG GOODBYE (United Artists, 1969). Photo courtesy of the National Film Archive.

36. The detective as an avenger. Clint Eastwood in DIRTY HARRY (Warner's, 1971). Photo courtesy of Warner Bros.

6
Adventurers and Thieves

BULLDOG DRUMMOND

There are many things, we know, which are wrong in this jolly old country of ours; but given time and the right methods I am sufficiently optimistic to believe that they could be put right.

Bulldog Drummond[1]

Herman Cyril McNeile, the son of Captain Malcolm McNeile of the Royal Navy, was born in 1888 and educated at the Royal Military Academy. At 19 he joined the Royal Engineers and served for twelve years until he retired in 1919 with the rank of lieutenant colonel. He began writing adventure stories while in the service and, since it was not permitted for him to use his own name, signed them simply "Sapper," which was British slang for an engineer. His decision to retire was so that he might devote all of his time to writing. He had a restless and excited imagination and a penchant for the wildly improbable, all of which characterized his first novel, BULLDOG DRUMMOND (1920), and the many novels which followed.

McNeile was somewhat indebted to R. Austin Freeman's inverted detective stories and Sax Rohmer's melodramas about Dr. Fu Manchu for his technique and structure. Already in BULLDOG DRUMMOND, McNeile permitted the reader to witness the criminals' plotting before ever Captain Hugh Drummond, D. S. O., M. C., late of His Majesty's Royal Loamshires, was introduced as a character. This technique allowed the reader both to know what really was going on and to watch how Drummond learned about the plot in order to foil it. Slightly under six feet, Drummond's "best friend would not have called him good-looking, but he was the fortunate possessor of that cheerful type of ugliness which inspires immediate confidence in its owner."[2] Drummond is a man of action and "having once made up his mind to go through with a thing, he was in the habit of going and looking neither to the right nor to the left."[3] The master villain is Carl Peterson in BULLDOG DRUMMOND and in several sequels, until he is finally killed off in THE FINAL COUNT (1926); after which time his daughter, Irma Peterson, takes over heading up various nefarious schemes with assorted recusants in THE FEMALE OF THE SPECIES (1928) and for several more novels. Here, again, McNeile was only following in the footsteps of Sax Rohmer who gave his evil devil doctor a daughter, Fah Lo Suee, also known as Madame Ingomar. In BULLDOG DRUMMOND RETURNS (1932), Irma is known as Madame Saumur. However, he was not as inventive as Rohmer who frequently used Fu Manchu's daughter to contravene her father's plans and thus compelled his protagonist, Sir Denis Nayland Smith, to wage battle against both a plot and a counter-plot. When Peterson was first introduced, the reader is told of him "that his scheme would bring ruin, perhaps death, to thousands of innocent men and women caused him no qualm: he was a supreme egoist. All that appealed to him was that he had seen the opportunity that existed, and that he had the nerve and the brain to turn that opportunity to his own advantage."[4]

Peterson's initial plot is to subvert Great Britain by a socialist revolution similar to what had recently occurred within the Soviet Union and thus permit wealthy capitalists in other countries to benefit from the situation. Peterson's price for this service is a million pounds. His minions include an actual Bolshevik who is provided with this kind of dialogue: " 'Have you ever seen men killed with the knotted rope; burned almost to death and then set free, charred and mutilated wrecks? But what does it matter provided only freedom comes, as it has in Russia. Tomorrow it will be England: in a week the world. . . . Even if we have to wade through rivers of blood up to our throats, nevertheless it will come. And in the end we shall have a new earth.' "[5] He is quickly dispatched by Hugh, killed in a death trap intended for Drummond, who reflects that "the world would not be appreciably poorer for his sudden decease."[6] There are numerous other stereotypes, already in the first novel. There is a German minion who gets his in the chapter titled "The Hun Nation Decreases By One." He is given a strange pseudo-German manner of speaking: " 'They will not shout twice,' he said in his guttural voice. 'The dirty Boche to it himself will see.' "[7] If McNeile was to go to these lengths, he might at least have portrayed German syntax accurately: "The dirty Boche himself will to it see."

No doubt Professor Moriarty was the prototype for Peterson and, at one point, a surrogate Andamanese Islander is sent to kill Hugh. "Lying on the floor by the window was one of the smallest men he had ever seen. He was a native of sorts, and Hugh turned him over with his foot."[8] This is an image right out of THE SIGN OF THE FOUR.

Drummond and his friends who go to battle against Peterson and his gang are all from the upper class. As such, their education would have included a grounding in Latin, possibly Greek, and fluent French. Yet Hugh, who has been at the front in France, notwithstanding cannot speak French at all well and, when trying to explain to a gendarme how the airplane he was in crashed into a field, his French comes out in a garbled manner meant to be humorous: " *'Mais vous comprenez que nous avons crashé dans un* field *des* turnipes— *non; des rognons . . . ,'* " which comes out meaning, "But you understand that we have spit into a field of kidneys!" [9]

A persistent flaw in all the novels is that, having created such efficient and cruel villains, McNeile never permits them to be ruthless with regard to Drummond. Repeatedly, he falls into their hands only, predictably, to be spared for some future torture which allows him to escape. In BULLDOG DRUMMOND, in an effort to get an American millionaire to back him, Peterson has his secretary killed and destroys one of the man's thumbs with a thumb-screw. Yet, when Hugh is drugged, Lackington, Peterson's right-hand man, decides not to take advantage of the situation and kill Hugh then and there. Later, when once again Hugh is captured, Peterson tells Hugh that they are going to drive him mad because " 'the disposal of corpses, even in these days of advanced science, presents certain difficulties—not insuperable—but a nuisance' " [10]; only for Hugh in the very next scene to witness how Lackington submerges the dead Bolshevik in a vat of acid and to see his remains vanish completely! In TEMPLE TOWER (1929), Irma kidnaps Phyllis, Hugh's wife, in order to revenge herself on Hugh for the death of her father. In BULLDOG DRUMMOND RETURNS, Phyllis is visiting in America. Hugh is lured by Irma and her minions into a subterranean room where he is locked in with what purports to be a time bomb. Irma's voice on a gramophone recording informs Hugh that he will now die, only for the bomb to fizzle; the villains come into the room to tell Hugh that he is to take this experience as a warning and keep his distance from them!

Phyllis and Hugh meet in BULLDOG DRUMMOND. Hugh has just been mustered out of the service and is bored with civilian life. He runs a personal in the newspaper offering his services. Phyllis responds to the personal and asks him to assist her in getting her father away from Peterson and his gang. They fall in love and, henceforth, most of the time she is involved in his future encounters with Peterson and then with Irma. Many of Hugh's upper-class friends who join forces with him in the novels, such as Peter Darrell and Ted Jerningham, rarely made it to the screen, although Algy Longworth generally did. When Paramount began its Bulldog Drummond series, Denny, Hugh's valet, was included in the cast, albeit with his name changed to Tenny because Reginald Denny had been cast as Algy. The Phyllis Benton character also had her name changed to Phyllis Clavering in the Paramount series. While she and Hugh were married in the 1920 novel, it took a lot longer for this to happen in the film series.

I suspect that originally McNeile had not anticipated writing a series of books about Hugh Drummond. The novel was in its way a transition book, keeping alive the wartime spirit of camaraderie of British Tommies after the Great War coupled with the emphasis on melodrama which had preoccupied British writers since Conan Doyle. However, as early as 1921 BULLDOG DRUMMOND was brought to the London stage with Sir Gerald du Maurier in the title role. Its extraordinary success led to a Broadway production later that year with A. E. Matthews in the role and then an American tour of the play with H. B. Warner cast as Drummond. The next year the first photoplay was produced, BULLDOG DRUMMOND (Hodkinson, 1922), starring Carlyle Blackwell as Drummond and Evelyn Greely as Phyllis Benton. This immediate success no doubt induced McNeile to turn the prototype into a series. When Ronald Colman appeared for the first time in the role in 1929, the character became truly popular with Americans. George H. Doran, McNeile's American publisher, merged with Doubleday in 1934 and in conjunction with Colman's second cinematic adventure in the role the newly combined firm published all the McNeile books, those with Drummond and those featuring other characters such as Jim Maitland, in a matched set. Nevertheless, it is worth noting that Doran in his memoirs, CHRONICLES OF BARABBAS, neither in the 1935 edition nor in the expanded 1952 edition so much as mentioned McNeile, although he did provide portraits of virtually every other author with whom he had been associated.

This ought not be too puzzling. Despite his popularity on both sides of the Atlantic, Bulldog Drummond is not really a very savory character. C. Day Lewis, the English poet who translated Virgil's AENEID, wrote detective fiction under the pseudonym Nicholas Blake. He remarked in an essay, "The Detective Story—Why?," that "the detective story's clientele are relatively prosperous persons, who have a stake in the social system and must, therefore, even in fantasy, see the ultimate triumph of their particular social values ensured. It is significant that even the 'thrillers' most popular with the ruling classes usually represent their hero as being on the side of law and order—the bourgeois conception of law and order, of course (that unspeakable public school bully and neurotic exhibitionist, Bulldog Drummond, is a case in point), or as a reformed criminal. . . . "[11] It is for precisely this reason that Drummond belongs with the "reformed" thieves, from Arsène Lupin to Simon Templar. Taking his cue from Blake's cogent observation, Julian Symons concluded that "in terms of the early thriller writers, no Hun, and later no Red, was likely to be an honorable man, and this was particularly true of Reds, whose allegiance to some abstract impractical theory led them to behave in an unsporting and ungentlemanly way. They were quite the opposite of Bulldog Drummond, about whom Sapper said: 'He lives clean, loves sport, and fights hard. I don't think he's ever done anything dirty; I can assure you he never will.' Drummond sometimes seems to be a sporting tough parodying an English gentleman, but the rule about the wickedness of radicals was hardly ever broken. Raffles was only an acceptable character as a gentleman burglar because he was good at cricket and died fighting for his country against the Boers. In France, Arsène Lupin atoned for his criminal career by joining the Foreign Legion. On the social level, then, what crime literature offered to its readers for half a century from 1890 onward was a reassuring world in which those who tried to disturb the established order were always discovered and punished."[12]

This may seem innocuous in its way, but George Orwell saw clearly the sinister political and psychological implications of this kind of propaganda masquerading as entertainment fiction. "To what extent people draw their ideas from fiction is disputable," he wrote. "Personally I believe that most people are influenced far more than they would care to admit by novels, serial stories, films and so forth, and that from this point of view the worst books are often the most important, because they are usually the ones that are read earliest in life. It is probable that many people who could consider themselves extremely sophisticated and 'advanced' are actually carrying through life an imaginative background which they acquired in childhood from (for instance) Sapper. . . . "[13] Behind such figures as Drummond, and that legion of reformed thieves who preceded and followed him in challenging master criminals, Orwell perceived what was the real drama being played out. "Their whole theme is the struggle for power and the triumph of the strong over the weak. The big gangsters wipe out the little ones as mercilessly as a pike gobbling up the little fish in a pond; the police kill off the criminals as cruelly as the angler kills the pike. If ultimately one sides with the police against the gangsters, it is merely because they are better organized and more powerful, because, in fact, the law is a bigger racket than crime. Might is right: *vae victis*."[14]

In BULLDOG DRUMMOND RETURNS, Drummond and his friends rescue millionaire Edward Greatorex from the hands of the villains led by Irma Peterson. The plot would have permitted the kidnappers to accumulate a fortune at Greatorex' expense through stock market manipulations. At the end, the reader is supposed to be amused when Greatorex sends Hugh a letter in which he comments: "I feel sure you would like to have your chauffeur's insolent behavior brought to your notice. We stopped on the way up to London for an early lunch, and to my pained amazement I found on receiving the bill an item of eightpence for beer was included. I at once demanded an explanation, and on discovering that your man had drunk it, I struck it out and told the waiter to obtain the money from him. It is a matter of principle with me never to pay for alcohol consumed by servants."[15] It is precisely because the kinds of people Drummond tended to rescue tend to be themselves somewhat despicable that the emergence of a protagonist such as Simon Templar, the Saint, was almost inevitable, where he would outwit criminals seemingly more powerful than himself while foiling the police. In this new milieu, a character such as Greatorex is no better than his abductors—but that is perhaps to anticipate. In the novels, Drummond prefers to work independently from the police for the most part, although Colonel Neilson of Scotland Yard was introduced as a minor character. It was in the films that his character was amplified to major status by way of reassuring viewers that Drummond was firmly allied with the existing social order.

The plot of the first film, BULLDOG DRUMMOND, altered certain aspects of the story as they are presented in the novel. Drummond is not a man of independent means, but rather an employee of an advertising agency bored with his job. Evelyn Greely as Phyllis hires Drummond to find her father who has been kidnapped by Peterson and his gang. Toward the end of the decade, Carlyle Blackwell, cast here as Drummond, would play Sherlock Holmes in the UFA film THE HOUND OF THE BASKERVILLES (German, 1929).

McNeile published his second Bulldog Drummond novel the same year as this film was released, titled THE BLACK GANG (1922). Subsequently, Drummond summed up this adventure. "Years ago," he said, "we had an amusing little show rounding up Communists and other unwashed people of that type. We called ourselves the Black Gang, and it was great sport while it lasted."[16] Here McNeile's model seems to have been Edgar Wallace's THE FOUR JUST MEN (1905) in which four men take it upon themselves to prevent certain events from occurring through murdering potential wrong-doers. They are justified in the murders because of the uprightness of their cause. The four, although in reality only three since one dies before they begin in earnest, are determined to see justice done where the law cannot, or will not, do anything about it. If you combine Wallace's just men, or McNeile's Black Gang, into one, you come up with a prototype that would eventually emerge and become embodied in such diverse figures as Ian Fleming's James Bond or Mickey Spillane's Mike Hammer.

THE THIRD ROUND (1925) was the third Bulldog Drummond novel and it was filmed the same year it was published as BULLDOG DRUMMOND'S THIRD ROUND (Astra-National, 1925) with Jack Buchanan cast as Drummond. Buchanan, as Drummond did in the novels, donned a number of disguises while attempting to foil Peterson's attempt to steal a formula for manufacturing synthetic diamonds.

Samuel Goldwyn made the first sound Drummond film and the first American production featuring the British adventurer. Originally Goldwyn wanted a talking film that would be suitable for Ronald Colman who was under contract to him. Arthur Hornblow, Goldwyn's story editor, went to New York to locate a stage play since the Hollywood theory at the time was that audiences for sound pictures wanted talking and plenty of it. Hornblow became enamored of the stage version of BULLDOG DRUMMOND and, upon inquiry, learned that rights were available for a sound film. Next he engaged Sidney Howard to do the screen treatment; Howard had had two extravagant Broadway successes in the 'Twenties and he was personally an admirer of Colman. Voice tests done on Colman proved to be excellent. Goldwyn was especially enthusiastic because BULLDOG DRUMMOND (United Artists, 1929) would be made so as to combine talking *and* action.

Goldwyn also instituted an innovation which would become *de rigueur* in manufacturing talking pictures: he insisted that the film's director, F. Richard Jones, hold exhaustive rehearsals *prior* to filming on the elaborate sets he had had built. Screening rushes one day, according to Arthur Marx in GOLDWYN: A BIOGRAPHY OF THE MAN BEHIND THE MYTH (1976), Goldwyn "complained to Richard Jones that he thought he heard the word *din*. Was that true? Jones corroborated that. 'What does this word *din* mean?' asked Sam, contorting his face in puzzlement. 'It means noise,' replied Jones. 'Then why didn't the writer say *noise*?' demanded Sam. And he ordered Jones to reshoot the scene, substituting the word *noise*. Since the set had to be rebuilt and the actors rehired, this involved considerable expense—approximately $20,000 more. But in the end, Sam must have felt that all the care and attention he lavished on BULLDOG DRUMMOND were well worth every extra penny. For both the public and critics were delighted with the final product, which starred, in addition to Ronald Colman, Joan Bennett, in her first screen role, and Lilyan Tashman, one of the great beauties of the day."[17]

The plot followed the book somewhat more closely than the previous effort. Colman's Hugh Drummond is a man bored with civilian life and in quest of adventure. He runs an advertisement in the papers and meets Phyllis, played by Joan Bennett. Here, however, the plot again veered away from its source: Phyllis' uncle is being held against his will in an asylum by Lawrence Grant as Peterson and an assortment of unscrupulous heavies. Perhaps it was felt inappropriate to include the figure of Phyllis' weak and frequently drunken father, as is the case in the novel. Claude Allister played Algy Longworth. When the film opened at the Apollo Theatre in New York, Colman made a personal appearance and was literally mobbed by the audience which had fallen in love with his voice as it had, in the silent era, with his eyes. Colman infused such a light-hearted tone into his manner and delivery that apparently no one objected to lines such as, "If you hurt but one hair on her head, I'll kill you," or, "We'll see who laughs last, Bulldog Drummond," to which Colman quietly smiles. If the film doesn't stand up today, that may have more to do with the overstatement of its plot and what now appear to be clumsy cinematic techniques, although even at the time I doubt if many viewers could take this story seriously. Colman was nominated for an Oscar for his portrayal here and in CONDEMNED (United Artists, 1929) from the same year.

The Fox Film Corporation lost no time in trying to duplicate Goldwyn's success. The company purchased rights to McNeile's latest novel, TEMPLE TOWER (1929), and filmed it under the same title, TEMPLE TOWER (Fox, 1930). Kenneth MacKenna was cast as Drummond, Marceline Day as the fearful heroine in distress, and Cyril Chadwick, cast as Peter Darrell, played the role for sheer comedy. Henry B. Walthall was cast as the principal villain and proved himself the most able performer. When this follow-up picture proved a disastrous failure, studio executives comforted themselves with the notion that only Ronald Colman could play Drummond effectively.

Certainly this was Darryl Zanuck's reasoning when his newly formed Twentieth Century Pictures signed Ronald Colman to a contract. Zanuck's films were also distributed by United Artists, so all the change-over required of Colman was a switch of dressing rooms on the same lot. Zanuck cast Loretta Young as the heroine in BULLDOG DRUMMOND STRIKES BACK (20th, 1934), Nunnally Johnson's script ignoring the earlier pictures and Drummond's marriage to Phyllis. C. Aubrey Smith was cast as Inspector Neilson and Warner Oland performed slyly as Prince Achmen, the Oriental villain who would smuggle precious furs off a steamer infested with cholera. The action was almost subverted by Charles Butterworth, cast as Algy, who had just married Gwen, played by Una Merkel, but who cannot consummate their union because he is being constantly called away by Drummond. Everytime Drummond produces a witness to Achmen's skullduggery, the witness disappears before Scotland Yard can take over the questioning. The film proved to be only the first of a series of successes for Colman during his association with Zanuck.

Ralph Richardson was the first to appear as Drummond in the initial talking Drummond film produced in the United Kingdom, THE RETURN OF BULLDOG DRUMMOND (British-Wardour, 1934), based on McNeile's novel, THE BLACK GANG. Drummond and his friends, calling themselves the Black Gang, make a crusade against wrongdoers and warmongers, without, however, the political and ethnic stereotypes being quite so pronounced as in the book. The events, particularly the race by the Gang to save Drummond at the end, were rather similar to a matinee serial. Ann Todd was cast as Drummond's wife, Phyllis. BULLDOG JACK (British-Gaumont, 1935) appeared close on the heels of THE RETURN OF BULLDOG DRUMMOND, only it was a satire of the Bulldog Drummond character and the melodramatic escapades in which he found himself. Atholl Fleming played Drummond but, early in the picture, he is laid up and Jack Hurlbert, a popular British comedy star at the time, impersonates him. Ralph Richardson was back, only this time playing the master villain who kidnaps Cyril Smith and his screen daughter played by Fay Wray. For American release, the film was retitled ALIAS BULLDOG DRUMMOND, but under whatever title it was a wretchedly mounted picture.

Paramount then negotiated a contract with McNeile for a ten-year license to film all of his previously published books and any new ones he might write. McNeile died soon after signing this agreement. With the approval of the estate, Gerard Fairlie, a fellow writer and a close friend of McNeile's, was asked to continue the fictional adventures. BULLDOG DRUMMOND ESCAPES (Paramount, 1937), the first entry in the new film series, was based on BULLDOG DRUMMOND HITS OUT, a 1936 stage play on which Fairlie had collaborated with McNeile, and on screen Fairlie was given joint credit with McNeile for the "Sapper" stories. Ray Milland was cast as Drummond and Heather Angel as Phyllis Clavering. Phyllis is being held prisoner on her estate by Porter Hall and his accomplices. Hall is her guardian and he is printing up a phony bond issue in the basement. Reginald Denny, known mostly as a comedian, played the role of Algy for laughs and Sir Guy Standing was cast as the Yard inspector who prefers to be known by his military title, Colonel Neilson. Borrowing from the earlier BULLDOG DRUMMOND STRIKES BACK, Algy is anxiety-ridden over the baby Gwen is about to have, but he is constantly dragged off by Drummond in an effort to rescue Phyllis. James Hogan directed and Edward T. Lowe wrote the screenplay.

John Howard was born on 14 April 1913 at Cleveland, Ohio. He was signed to a long-term contract by Paramount while he was still a student at Western Reserve University. Once he began working, he moved his mother and father to Brentwood and lived with them, along with a collection of 500 model ducks. Perhaps it was Frank Capra's decision to cast Ronald Colman and John Howard as brothers in LOST HORIZON (Columbia, 1937) which was the impetus behind the idea, but at any rate Paramount hoped to build him into a major box-office property by starring him as Bulldog Drummond in what remained of the series. For the Drummond role, Howard had to affect a slight British accent. E. E. Clive who in BULLDOG DRUMMOND ESCAPES had played Dobbs, Drummond's valet, returned in the same role with the name change already mentioned in Howard's first picture, BULLDOG DRUMMOND COMES BACK (Paramount, 1937). John Barrymore, however, received top billing, cast as Colonel Neilson. Phyllis was played by Louise Campbell who had a certain physical resemblance to Heather Angel. Algy was still played by Reginald Denny. Henry King's brother, Louis King, directed. Edward T. Lowe was credited with the script. J. Carrol Naish played the master villain, operating in consort with Helen Freeman, wife of a man Drummond once convicted. Tenny, Algy, and Phyllis are all kidnapped, but only Phyllis is retained by the gang. Drummond is provided with phonograph recordings which take him from one location to another in a desperate search to find Phyllis and free her. Barrymore, joining into the spirit of the game, dons several disguises so he can shadow Drummond and watch over him. His disguises are outlandish, but he obviously dissolved himself into these various identities with enthusiasm. The trail finally leads to a lonely dungeon where the villains introduce poison gas into the death chamber, but it all ends with Hugh holding the winning hand. The reviews at the time singled out Barrymore's performance as notable but otherwise did not find this picture up to the standards set by earlier Bulldog Drummond films. A contemporary viewer, however, might well be inclined to find BULLDOG DRUMMOND COMES BACK superior to BULLDOG DRUMMOND ESCAPES and perhaps all of the previous entries.

John Barrymore, although he had fewer scenes in it, continued to dominate BULLDOG DRUMMOND'S REVENGE (Paramount, 1937). Since he was no longer able to remember even the briefest dialogue, it is always interesting to see how, with perfect timing, he will have it right on the button by looking at a paper on his desk or glancing quite naturally off in another direction. He was under contract to Paramount and the studio felt his name would not only establish the series but also give added class to the pictures. Howard, Denny, Louise

Campbell, and Clive all kept their customary roles. But, by this time, Howard's understated approach to the Drummond character took command. Hugh and Phyllis are off to Switzerland to be married when the pilot of a plane carrying the inventor of a new explosive kills the inventor and bails out. Hugh is drawn into the case. Phyllis in what was to become a shrewish cliché concerning girlfriends of detectives in the late 'Thirties and the 'Forties wants Hugh to try some other line of endeavor. At one point, she packs up and threatens to leave him for good, but of course she doesn't. Barrymore and Howard together apprehend the pilot.

BULLDOG DRUMMOND'S PERIL (Paramount, 1938) was directed by James Hogan. Stuart Palmer did the screenplay, basing it on McNeile's THE THIRD ROUND. As the picture opens, Hugh and Phyllis are definitely getting married; the announcements have been printed. Algy in a bit of inside humor gives Hugh a penguin as a wedding present, no doubt a reference to Palmer's THE PENGUIN POOL MURDER (1931). Gwen Longworth, played by Nydia Westman, gives Phyllis one of the diamonds created by her father using a new synthetic process. The diamond is stolen and Hugh takes off after the thieves. There are two rival gangs in this case, with Porter Hall, cast as a scientist, heading up the smarter gang. Edward Dmytryk was the film editor on this picture and James Hogan permitted him to be continuously on the set to see how the picture played so he would best know how to cut it. He would often engage in word games with Barrymore, Howard, and Hogan, consulting an unabridged dictionary.

"Barrymore was excellent," Dmytryk recalled. "He had a huge vocabulary. Yet, strange thing, Barrymore had an unbelievably dirty collar. He didn't seem to care about things like that. After 6:00 PM, Jack was usually drunk. Hogan would have to have someone watch him if he wanted to use Jack after that time. There was a dialogue director hanging around. Dialogue directors did nothing. Barrymore was drunk. It was after six. He told the dialogue director to hold the idiot card higher. He kept saying, 'Higher, higher.' An apple box was brought for him to stand on. 'Higher,' Barrymore ordered. Hogan finally had to call it quits that day since Barrymore was too drunk to continue." It would be the last time he appeared in the series.

McNeile, at the time of his death, had earned a reputed $400,000 from the Bulldog Drummond property. Paramount was so pleased with the success of the series that, negotiating with the widow, the studio extended its option, which had been limited to four photoplays, to an additional three photoplays in the same ten-year term. This was a cogent move. BULLDOG DRUMMOND STRIKES BACK had cost $514,152.95 to make. It earned $714,651.76 in the United States and had a foreign gross of $591,432 which included revenue from the United Kingdom of $378,243. This meant that the pictures were generally grossing more than twice what they were costing to produce.

Barrymore was replaced by H. B. Warner in the role of Colonel Neilson for BULLDOG DRUMMOND IN AFRICA (Paramount, 1938). Heather Angel returned to the series in the role of Phyllis. J. Carrol Naish was also back as the master villain, leader of an international spy ring who kidnaps Colonel Neilson and spirits him off to Morocco. Hugh, Phyllis, Algy, and Tenny come to his rescue. The screenplay was by Garnett Weston. Louis King directed.

Heather Angel was retained in the role of Phyllis, along with other cast regulars, until the demise of the Paramount series. BULLDOG DRUMMOND'S SECRET POLICE (Paramount, 1939) had a screenplay by Garnett Weston based on TEMPLE TOWER. As the film opens, somewhat wearily by this time, Hugh and Phyllis are about to marry when Hugh learns of a fabulous treasure hidden beneath his castle. The treasure is coveted by murderer Leo G. Carroll. The principals find themselves in an underground chamber of horrors before finally Carroll is apprehended.

BULLDOG DRUMMOND'S BRIDE (Paramount, 1939) was attributed to a book which neither McNeile nor Fairlie wrote, titled BULLDOG DRUMMOND AND THE ORIENTAL MIND. Stuart Palmer and Garnett Weston collaborated on this screenplay which is mistitled since Hugh and Phyllis are not really wed, not yet. Hugh is lured away to help Colonel Neilson in the capture of an elusive bank robber played by Eduardo Cianelli. Stuart Palmer alone was credited for the screenplay for the final entry, ARREST BULLDOG DRUMMOND (Paramount, 1939), directed by James Hogan. Based on THE FINAL COUNT (1926), this time Hugh and Phyllis are married, but not before Hugh, joined by Algy and Tenny, pursues and captures George Zucco who has stolen a death ray machine and blamed the theft on Hugh. It was a disappointing film, as were most of the entries after John Barrymore left the series; but it should be evident how much the Drummond character was modified, even in the Barrymore entries, from what he is in the Sapper books. He was refashioned, made into simply an adventurer, an all-American hero; and so it is not surprising that, following ARREST BULLDOG DRUMMOND, the character should appear in a radio series broadcast by the Mutual Network beginning in 1941. "Out of the fog . . . out of the night . . . and into his American adventures . . . comes . . . Bulldog Drummond!" This is how the weekly radio series began and in its run it had three different actors portray the roving champion of noble causes.

Drummond did not return to the screen until Columbia Pictures resurrected the property when it became apparent to the studio that Gerald Mohr would not be a success cast in the role of the Lone Wolf. Ron Randell starred in BULLDOG DRUMMOND AT BAY (Columbia, 1947). It had a screenplay by Frank Gruber based on the McNeile book by the same title published in 1935. Drummond is assisted by his old friend, Algy Longworth, played by Pat O'Moore and a cub reporter, Seymour, played by Terence Kilburn. Holmes Herbert was cast as Inspector Melvar of Scotland Yard. The plot found Drummond, recently discharged from the British Army, in pursuit of a murderer with a loot of diamonds. These same cast members also appeared in BULLDOG DRUMMOND STRIKES BACK (Columbia, 1947). In the latter, Hugh is hired by a rich heiress to find the woman who is impersonating her and claiming her fortune. Both of these books had been filmed previously and in versions that more closely resembled the novels on which they were based. These Columbia efforts were low-grade "B" productions and, following release, Ron Randell retired from the role, only to surface in the last Lone Wolf entry from the same studio, THE LONE WOLF AND HIS LADY (Columbia, 1949).

Bernard Small was the co-producer on the two Columbia films and he next took the Bulldog Drummond property to Twentieth Century-Fox for a brace of films starring Tom Conway in the role of Drummond. Conway, of course, had replaced George Sanders as The Falcon at RKO Radio until that studio dropped the series in 1946. He was also familiar to radio listeners as Basil Rathbone's replacement as Sherlock Holmes and as The Saint. These films, THE CHALLENGE (20th-Fox, 1948) and 13 LEAD SOLDIERS (20th-Fox, 1948), were financed and released by Twentieth Century-Fox but produced by Reliance Pictures, an independent company controlled by Small. John Newland was cast as Algy Longworth while Terence Kilburn was retained from the Columbia films in the role of Seymour. THE CHALLENGE found this trio solving a series of murders associated with a search for a casket of gold whereas in 13 LEAD SOLDIERS the toy soldiers hold the combination for a hidden treasure which has caused three murders. Perhaps the only interesting aspect of THE CHALLENGE was the variation on Agatha Christie's plot for MURDER ON THE ORIENT EXPRESS in which Drummond finds everyone guilty except the heroine, played by June Vincent. Reliance Pictures was a subsidiary of Edward Small Productions, but the quality of these Drummond films is almost an embarrassment when compared with most of the company's previous efforts filming literary properties. Tom Conway played Drummond just the way he had The Falcon, which meant that the Drummond character was totally diluted to nothing more than a low-budget screen detective.

There were two subsequent, albeit similarly unsuccessful, attempts to resurrect the Bulldog Drummond property. The most ambitious, surely, was CALLING BULLDOG DRUMMOND (M-G-M, 1951), filmed in the United Kingdom out of frozen funds. In the late 1930s, M-G-M had announced that it had purchased screen rights to some 1,100 stories written about the fictional sleuth, Nick Carter, who had begun his long and not very illustrious career in a series of adventures written by his creator, John R. Coryell, in 1884 for the NEW YORK WEEKLY. The character was carried on by other writers. Despite this imposing purchase, when M-G-M brought the character to the screen in NICK CARTER—MASTER DETECTIVE (M-G-M, 1939), the plot called on none of the 1,100 sources but was instead fashioned especially for the film. Walter Pidgeon starred as Nick Carter and the studio hoped to use this series as a springboard to build him into a leading male player. PHANTOM RAIDERS (M-G-M, 1940) and SKY MURDER (M-G-M, 1940) followed and then the series was dropped. Pidgeon began in that series of pictures with Greer Garson which led to his nomination for an Academy Award for his performance in

MRS. MINIVER (M-G-M, 1942). In 1951, his career was again on the wane and so he was selected to portray an older version of Hugh Drummond in CALLING BULLDOG DRUMMOND, coming out of retirement to assist a police woman, played by Margaret Leighton, in apprehending a criminal gang in London. Gerard Fairlie co-authored the screenplay, based on his novel of the same title which appeared that year, and all in all it was a slick, glossy, fast-paced product, but with no special quality beyond this. The only off-shoot was that Robert Beatty, who had played the villain Guns in the film, was cast as Drummond in a series made by British television.

A hiatus of sixteen years ensued before the J. Arthur Rank Company in the United Kingdom sought to revamp the character and bring him back to the screen in two films released in the United States by Universal. In DEADLIER THAN THE MALE (Universal, 1967) and SOME GIRLS DO (Universal, 1969), Richard Johnson was cast as Drummond, but he bore no relationship to the character in the novels or the earlier films; he was quite clearly a surrogate James Bond and the stress was now on sex and sadism. In DEADLIER THAN THE MALE, Nigel Green was cast as a maniacal tycoon who employs very titillating female assistants to kill off his competitors, only to be foiled at the end by Drummond. The master villain in SOME GIRLS DO, played by James Villiers, also employs two deadly female assistants, played by Daliah Lavi and Beba Loncar, and a number of female robots who presumably have "artificial brains." Villiers' character name is Carl Peterson, but that is his only relationship to McNeile's creation. These films were intended as spoofs of the Bond films, but for the most part they not only are not funny, they are actually boring.

As was the case again and again in detective film series, attempts at updating the principal character, or changing the character to be something other than what he was originally, reduced itself in the end to a hollow stereotype with only the name to identify him with his literary source. Low budgets, poor scripts, indifferent direction and performances did the rest.

RAFFLES

Why should I work when I could steal? Why settle down to some humdrum uncongenial billet, when excitement, romance, danger, and a decent living were all going begging together?

Raffles[18]

Ernest William Hornung was born in Middlesbrough, Yorkshire in 1866. He suffered from poor health and, as a result, moved to Australia when he was eighteen. He remained in that country less than three years but he absorbed enough of its terrain and atmosphere for it to appear frequently as a setting in his later fiction. After his return to England, he met and eventually married

Constance Doyle, sister of Sir Arthur Conan Doyle. Because the British had used Australia as a penal colony and given his own fascination with crime and criminals, Hornung tended to focus on stories and novels concerned with convicts and bushrangers (escaped convicts living in the bush). He managed in his Australian fiction to achieve a high degree of verisimilitude and some critics have tended to single out this aspect of his work as his best.

Hornung's most notable creation, however, would still seem to be A. J. Raffles, the amateur cracksman who began appearing in a series of short stories collected under the title THE AMATEUR CRACKSMAN (1899). The collection was dedicated to his brother-in-law, "To ACD This Form of Flattery." Hornung, it may be recalled, arrived at his character's name from Conan Doyle's short story, "The Doings of Raffles Haw." Conan Doyle was seven years Hornung's senior. "He is one of the sweetest-natured and most delicate-minded men I ever knew," he said of him after Hornung died in 1921. Already when Hornung was twenty-six, Conan Doyle had felt that he was "an author certainly standing much higher than I did at his age."[19] In MEMORIES AND ADVENTURES, Conan Doyle confided that Hornung remained among his most vivid memories and that "his famous character Raffles was a kind of inversion of Sherlock Holmes, Bunny playing Watson. He admits as much in his kindly dedication. I think there are few finer examples of short-story writing in our language than these, though I confess they are rather dangerous in their suggestion. I told him so before he put pen to paper, and the result has, I fear, borne me out. You must not make the criminal a hero."[20]

In his critical essay, "Raffles and Miss Blandish" (1944), George Orwell contrasted the Raffles stories with what was then a contemporary crime novel. He approached this genre of fiction from a standpoint opposed to the antihumanitarian values to be found in it. "Since 1918 . . . ," he declared, "a detective story not containing a murder has been a great rarity, and the most disgusting details of dismemberment and exhumation are commonly exploited. . . . The Raffles stories, written from the angle of the criminal, are much less anti-social than many modern stories written from the angle of the detective."[21] It was Orwell's conviction that Americans had a cultural tolerance for crime and even an admiration for the criminal and it was because of these aberrations that it was possible for "crime to flourish" on a very wide scale in the United States.[22]

In my collection of Western stories, THE AMERICAN WEST IN FICTION (1982), I included that section from Mark Twain's ROUGHING IT (1872) concerned with Jack Slade. I was careful to point out, however, that what Twain wrote was only the most exaggerated frontier hyperbole. Slade is, in fact, known only to have killed one man, a horse thief named Jules Reni who had put five bullets into Slade in a street fight before their final showdown a year later near Cold Springs, Colorado. Orwell, in citing Twain's narrative, accepted what Twain had said about Slade at face value. Yet, knowing the facts as Orwell did not, does not really allow one to escape from his moral indictment of Twain for "adopting much the same attitude towards the disgusting bandit Slade, hero of twenty-eight murders, and towards Western desperadoes generally. They were successful, they 'made good,' therefore he admired them."[23] For Orwell, such a posture in the end could only reduce itself to "worshipping power and successful cruelty. It is important to notice that the cult of power tends to be mixed up with a love of cruelty and wickedness *for their own sakes.*"[24] More incisively, he lamented the change in adventure stories characteristic of the English-speaking peoples wherein the fundamental hero has been one who has had to fight against all odds. This is the kind of hero that one encounters all the way from the tales of Robin Hood to the story of Jack the Giant Killer, "but to be brought up to date this should be renamed Jack the Dwarf-Killer, and there already exists a considerable literature which teaches, either overtly or implicitly, that one should side with the big man against the little man."[25]

Unquestionably this alteration in perspective has been as true of the detective film as it has been of detective and crime fiction. But there is perhaps a dimension which Orwell overlooked. It was Nietzsche who, in DIE GÖTZENDÄMMERUNG [THE TWILIGHT OF THE IDOLS], scorned the English for their naive presumption that the tenets of Christian morality could survive the loss of belief in the Christian God. "Christianity is a system," Nietzsche wrote, "a consistently thought out and *complete* view of things. If a fundamental notion as the belief in God is broken off from it, the whole is shattered into pieces: of necessity one loses his grasp on everything. Christianity assumes that man knows nothing—is able to know nothing—of what is good for him, what evil; he believes in God who alone knows. Christian morality is a commandment; its origin is transcendent; it is beyond criticism, beyond even the right to criticize; it has truth insofar as God is truth—it stands or falls with the belief in God. If as the English believe, that they know 'intuitively' what is good and evil, if consequently they believe it is not necessary to have Christianity as a guarantee of morality, that this morality is merely a *consequence* of the tradition of Christian value-judgments and an expression of the *strength* and *depth* of this tradition: so that the origin of English morality has been forgotten, so that the very conditionality of its right to exist can no longer be felt. For the English morality is still no problem. . . ."[26]

For Orwell, "Raffles . . . has no real moral code, no religion, certainly no social consciousness. All he has is a set of reflexes—the nervous system, as it were, of a gentleman. Give him a sharp tap on this reflex or that (they are called 'sport,' 'pal,' 'woman,' 'king and country' and so forth), and you get a predictable reaction."[27] Orwell recognized that according to the English public school code to which both Raffles and Bunny subscribe "there is only one means of rehabilitation: death in battle. Raffles dies fighting the Boers (a practised reader would foresee this from the start), and in the eyes of both Bunny and his creator this cancels his crimes."[28] However, precisely because Raffles has no religion, because all he has is a certain snobbishness which must substitute for Christianity, Orwell concludes that "one is driven to feel that snobbishness, like hypocrisy, is a check upon behavior whose value from a social point of view has been underrated."[29] This, apparently, was the philosophical dilemma in which Orwell was placed when attempting to champion the "immorality" of the Raffles stories—in his view Raffles was "still one of the best-known characters in English fiction"[30]—with the violent and brutal "immorality" of James Hadley Chase's NO ORCHIDS FOR MISS BLANDISH (1939). Of course, by contemporary standards, the violence and worship of naked power of the latter are rather mild, even bland.

I am not going to attempt to argue this question further, except to say that Nietzsche was quite prescient of the moral issues involved and that the only viable substitute the modern world could find for medieval morality has been materialism. Orwell himself subscribed to a variation of it in his interpretation of Marxism. The problem with materialism as a substitute for a non-material morality is that there are no boundaries or limits. How far does one go in the worship of power, success, and material possessions? What are the extremes beyond which one ought not venture? Raffles was only the first in a line of gentlemen thieves. Of the lot, he is the most hampered by his English "reflexes," as Orwell termed them. When he first makes Bunny's acquaintance after the years of separation following their time together in school, Raffles saves Bunny from suicide over embarrassment due to indebtedness. His own solution, which he proposes for Bunny, is simply to steal. " 'Of course, it's very wrong,' " he reflects, " 'but we can't all be moralists, and the distribution of wealth is very wrong to begin with. Besides, you're not at it all the time.' " To some, this may sound to be very much what the British psychoanalyst Ernest Jones coined rationalization, but it is the heart and soul of Raffles' philosophy and, no doubt, its outrageousness to Victorian readers accounted for the amateur cracksman's success with the reading public. Bunny undertakes to record their adventures. In "The Gift of the Emperor," the final story included in THE AMATEUR CRACKSMAN, Bunny summarizes Raffles' perspective. "Human nature was a board of chequers; why not reconcile one's self to alternate black and white? Why desire to be all one thing or all the other, like our forefathers on the stage or in the old-fashioned fiction? For his part, he enjoyed himself on all squares of the board, and liked the light the better for the shade."[31]

In toto, Hornung published three collections of short stories and one novel about Raffles. THE AMATEUR CRACKSMAN ends with Raffles overboard from a vessel sailing among the islands from Genoa to Naples and ostensibly drowned. When Raffles reappears in THE BLACK MASK (1901), he must live clandestinely as a fugitive. Always a master of disguises, as is Sherlock Holmes, and as later would be Arsène Lupin and Carl Peterson, Raffles must now perpetually conceal his true identity. The final story in this collection, "The Knees of the Gods," narrates how Raffles loses his life during the Boer War but not before he exposes a spy in the British ranks. The tone, as well might be imagined, has altered somewhat from the first collection. In THE

AMATEUR CRACKSMAN, when Raffles was scheming to murder a fence who threatens to expose his identity, he blithely informs Bunny: " 'You don't suppose I prefer foul play to fair, do you? But die he must, by one or the other, or it's a long stretch for you and me.' "[32] This story is titled "Wilful Murder" and, while Raffles is saved from committing the deed by a propitious turn of circumstance, he nonetheless can utter this outrageous sentiment: " 'I've told you before that the biggest man alive is the man who's committed a murder, and not yet been found out; at least he ought to be, but he so very seldom has the soul to appreciate himself. Just think of it! Think of coming here and talking to the men, very likely about the murder itself; and knowing you've done it; and wondering how they'd look if they knew.' "[33] In contrast, here is the kind of dialogue one finds in "The Knees of the Gods."

" 'I have had a good time, Bunny.'

"Yes, his voice was sad; but that was all; the vibration must have been in me.

" 'I know you have, old chap,' said I.

" 'I am grateful to the General for giving me today. It may be the last. Then I can only say it's been the best—by Jove!' "[34]

The entire drama of the Raffles saga is really played out against this kind of adolescent naiveté. As a thief, Raffles has his failures and his successes; and his crimes, whatever they might be, are expiated by his sacrifice of his life. It was Horace who wrote, *"Dulce et decorum est pro patria mori"* [It is sweet and gracefully fitting to die for your country]; but, as Edith Hamilton observed in THE GREEK WAY (1930), "the Greeks never said it was sweet to die for anything. They had no vital lies."[35] What keeps Raffles going, not only in his final hours but throughout the saga, are the vital lies to which he subscribes; and it is perhaps for this reason that the stories seem so painfully dated to many contemporary readers.

Hornung's third collection of stories was titled A THIEF IN THE NIGHT (1905) and these stories were flashbacks to earlier times, when Raffles lived at the Albany and plied his trade among the rich. Hornung published last his novel about Raffles' adventures, MR. JUSTICE RAFFLES (1909).

Around the turn of the century, Hornung collaborated with Eugene Presbrey to adapt his first story collection for the stage. RAFFLES, THE AMATEUR CRACKSMAN: A PLAY IN FOUR ACTS was successfully produced in London with Sir Gerald du Maurier in the title role. In 1903 the play was brought to the United States with matinee idol Kyrle Bellew cast as Raffles. The character made his motion picture debut in a short American film in 1905 and in 1911 he was featured in an Italian chapter play. The first major production was RAFFLES, THE AMATEUR CRACKSMAN (Hiller-Wilk, 1917) in which John Barrymore was cast in the role. Not quite a decade later House Peters starred as Raffles in a film with the same title, RAFFLES, THE AMATEUR CRACKSMAN (Universal, 1925). The plot of this latter film is interesting insofar as the character, as portrayed, is strictly revisionist. Raffles attends a house party. A criminologist named Captain Bedford, played by Frederick Esmelton, is on hand to guarantee that a string of pearls will not be stolen. Predictably, Raffles steals the pearls. Bedford lays a trap for him but Raffles is saved by Lady Gwendolyn, with whom he has fallen in love. He escapes from the trap and flees with her to London. The are married and Raffles returns the pearls, vowing that he will reform.

Samuel Goldwyn produced the first sound film based on the Raffles stories, titled simply RAFFLES (United Artists, 1930). It was intended as another vehicle for Ronald Colman and a fitting followup to his appearance, the previous year, as Bulldog Drummond. Bette Davis made a screen test for the role of Lady Gwendolyn. When Goldwyn's casting director ran the test for him, Goldwyn jumped out of his chair when it was over. "What are you guys trying to do to me?" he shouted angrily. He detested her pop-eyed looks and her clipped speech. Yet, Bette Davis had her revenge. When, a decade later, Goldwyn wanted her for a picture, she held out for the unheard of price of $385,000, all of which was to be paid to her and no part to Warner Bros. where she was under contract. She got it. Kay Francis was awarded the role of Gwen and Bunny, who had been only a minor character in the previous Universal release, was played by Bramwell Fletcher who received third billing.

The plot for RAFFLES was a refinement of the earlier film. Raffles is in love with Lady Gwen and has promised to reform. However, when Bunny attempts suicide in financial desperation, Raffles decides to commit a final robbery for the sake of his friend. He has his eye on a diamond necklace owned by Lady Melrose. At the fade, Raffles eludes the police and he and Gwen plan to have a rendezvous in Paris. Harry D'Abbadie D'Arrast and George Fitzmaurice shared credit for the direction.

RAFFLES was scarcely a highpoint in filmmaking, but henceforth the films only declined further. In THE RETURN OF RAFFLES (British, 1932) directed by Mansfield Markham, George Barraud had the title role. At a house party, a gang steals a necklace and frames Raffles for the deed. The tension of the plot is that he must capture the gang, restore the merchandise, and prove his own innocence.

Sam Goldwyn had a second try with the remake, RAFFLES (United Artists, 1940) directed by Sam Wood. Tony Thomas in his career study of Sam Wood for THE HOLLYWOOD PROFESSIONALS: VOLUME TWO (1974) noted that the film "gave David Niven one of his first starring roles, as the gentlemanly, circumspect jewel thief whose attitude toward crime in high society circles is tongue-in-cheek rather than malicious, a light-fingered Lothario who likes to foil Scotland Yard for the fun of it." Obviously, Goldwyn thought the remake a good idea because of the concurrent success the Lone Wolf was having at Columbia and the Saint at RKO, but the box office proved disappointing.

The 1940 film is the last screen appearance Raffles would make. However, in 1932, Barry Perowne, pseudonym for Philip Atkey, worked out an agreement with the Hornung estate whereby he could revive the character as an adventurer whose exploits take place in a modern (circa 1932) setting. These escapades were featured in THE THRILLER, a British version of an American pulp magazine. The Second World War interrupted both Perowne's writing and publication of THE THRILLER. When Perowne returned to writing Raffles stories after the war, the character was again in his Victorian setting. Raffles is still a hedonist, but his crimes, as those of the Saint, are committed primarily to right injustice and profit is at best a secondary motive. These short stories appeared in ELLERY QUEEN'S MYSTERY MAGAZINE and were subsequently collected in book form in RAFFLES REVISITED: NEW ADVENTURES OF A FAMOUS GENTLEMAN CROOK (1974).

ARSÈNE LUPIN

I wonder why more people do not adopt the profitable and pleasant occupation of burglar. With a little care and reflection, it becomes a most delightful profession. Not too quiet and monotonous, of course, as it would then become wearisome.

Arsène Lupin[36]

Maurice Leblanc was born in 1864 at Rouen in France. He was educated in France and also studied in Berlin and Manchester. He read at the law before he became a crime reporter for various French periodicals. His sister was Georgette Leblanc who was mistress to the playwright, Maurice Maeterlinck. This family liaison may have been beneficial to Leblanc since his stage plays are commonly regarded as his most polished literary productions.

There seems to be no dispute regarding the fact that Leblanc created his flamboyant thief, Arsène Lupin, in 1906 when he was asked to write a short story for a new French periodical. Where the dispute arises is when, presumably, Leblanc died. Willard Huntington Wright in THE WORLD'S GREAT DETECTIVE STORIES, in which he included an English translation of *"Des pas sur la neige"* ["Footprints in the Snow"], claimed that Leblanc "died in Paris in 1926." Jacques Barzun and Wendell Hertig Taylor in A CATALOGUE OF CRIME represented his *terminus ad quem* as 1925. The truth of the matter is that he lived until 6 November 1941.

The creation of Arsène Lupin immediately made Leblanc popular in France and, very soon, throughout Western Europe and the United States. The earliest short stories were as daring and innovative when it came to technique as is the central character. They were collected in ARSÈNE LUPIN: GENTLEMAN-CAMBRIOLEUR (1907) which was titled in the United States THE EXPLOITS OF ARSÈNE LUPIN. Until the final paragraph, "The Arrest of Arsène Lupin" is narrated in the first person; only at the end do we learn that the narrator is himself the notorious thief, Lupin, who is being sought aboard a ship bound for the United States. Other stories are narrated in the third person; while "The Seven of Hearts" presumably tells how Leblanc came to know

Lupin and how he was selected to be his memoirist. The last story was titled "Holmlock Shears Arrives Too Late." It concludes with Shears' commenting that "the world is too small—we will meet—we must meet—and then—."[37] Leblanc next published ARSÈNE LUPIN CONTRE HERLOCK SHOLMES (1908). By the time his first story collection was re-issued in the United States as THE EXTRAORDINARY ADVENTURES OF ARSÈNE LUPIN, GENTLEMAN-BURGLAR in 1910, Leblanc had received permission from Sir Arthur Conan Doyle to identify the character properly and in that edition, published by M. A. Donahue & Co., of Chicago, the last story was titled "Sherlock Holmes Arrives Too Late." Leblanc described Holmes as "a man about fifty years of age, tall, smooth-shaven, and wearing clothes of a foreign cut. He carried a heavy cane, and a small satchel was strapped across his shoulder."[38] Lupin, unknown to the English detective by sight at this time, informs him that "'Sherlock Holmes has no more ardent admirer than . . . myself.' There was a touch of irony in his voice that he quickly regretted, for Sherlock Holmes scrutinized him from head to foot with such a keen, penetrating eye that Arsène Lupin experienced the sensation of being seized, imprisoned, and registered by that look more thoroughly and precisely than he had ever been by a camera. 'My negative is taken now,' he thought, 'and it will be useless to use a disguise with that man. He would look right through it. But, I wonder, has he recognized me?'"[39]

In only one of the stories in that first collection is Lupin unsuccessful, but the tale narrates events very early in his career. Invariably, he is triumphant except when his path crosses that of Miss Nelly Underdown. It is his infatuation with Miss Nelly which brings about his initial arrest by Ganimard, the detective who is Lupin's would-be nemesis, although at all other times Ganimard is foiled. In "Sherlock Holmes Arrives Too Late," Lupin returns all of his plunder only to impress Miss Nelly, thus leaving Holmes nothing to solve. As the saga progressed, Lupin would often resort to the deductive activities of a detective, but usually for the purpose of self-enrichment and, somewhat secondarily, aiding thereby the police. In 813 (1910) Lupin, in disguise as a prefecture of police, leads a murder investigation in order to exonerate himself. The short story, "Footprints in the Snow," is from the collection THE EIGHT STROKES OF THE CLOCK (1922) and in it Lupin solves a case of insurance fraud and apparent murder without recompense. His later activities as a reformed criminal pursuing the profession of a detective are, among critics, the least enchanting of all of his adventures. When Frederic Dannay selected "The Red Silk Scarf" for inclusion in 101 YEARS' ENTERTAINMENT, he made the justifiable assertion that this was the only short story Leblanc wrote in which Lupin functions *both* as a thief and a detective. With his customary grandiloquent verve, he boasts to Ganimard: "'You thought that, in the domain of police deductions, such feats as those were prohibited to outsiders! Wrong, sir! Lupin juggles with inferences and deductions for all the world like a detective in a novel. My proofs are dazzling and absolutely simple.'"[40] Of course, as early as "The Black Pearl" in the first collection of stories, Lupin disguised himself as a police inspector in order to extort the plunder referred to in the title from the man who was acquitted for the murder by which he had obtained it; but what distinguishes the later story from the earlier one is that in "The Red Silk Scarf" Lupin actually shares with the reader the deductive reasoning by which means he identifies the culprit.

Raffles is not of the landed gentry. He is welcomed into their homes only because of his reputation at cricket. " 'As a general rule,' " he tells Bunny at one point, " 'nothing would induce me to abuse my position as a guest. I've never done it, Bunny. But in this case we're engaged like the waiters and the band, and by heaven we'll take our toll!' "[41] I think what is especially charming about Lupin is that he has no such scruples. If he shows up anywhere at a party, he will be disguised and his reason for being there is to steal. In the Raffles stories, perhaps because Bunny is the narrator, Raffles is always the central character and the hero-worshipping Bunny keeps the focus on him. In the Lupin stories, the focus is on the location, the situation, the characters, and Lupin moves in and out of the story in mysterious ways. We learn virtually nothing of how or where Lupin lives. We know that he has a gang of ruffians and street urchins at his command, but they are almost always invisible. Whatever the sentimentality in connection with Miss Nelly, there is a worldly cynicism in the way Leblanc writes which is refreshing when compared to Hornung's rather straight-laced Victorianism.

ARSÈNE LUPIN (Greater Film Company, 1917) marked Lupin's cinematic debut in the United States. THE TEETH OF THE TIGER (Paramount, 1919) featured David Powell in the role, a film steeped with the sinister excitement of chapter play melodramas. Wedgewood Newell was Lupin in 813 (Robertson-Cole, 1920) where, as in the novel on which it was based, Lupin leads the investigation to clear himself of a murder charge.

ARSÈNE LUPIN (M-G-M, 1932) was directed by Jack Conway. It marked Lupin's talking-picture debut with John Barrymore, who had once played Raffles, in the title role. Carey Wilson based his screenplay on the stories in Leblanc's first collection. Lionel Barrymore was cast in the role of Lupin's adversary, Ganimard. The picture served as a showcase for the brothers to try and outdo each other for the camera and steal each scene from the other. It opens to a house being robbed. Ganimard arrests Lupin, but he has to let him go. Lupin in this version is a duke without money, rather similar to the larcenous baron Barrymore would play in GRAND HOTEL (M-G-M, 1932) where he breaks into Greta Garbo's room, intent on her jewels, only to fall in love with her instead. The remainder of the film has to do with Lupin's stated intention to make off with all the valuable *objets d'art* of a nobleman. In the short story from which this plot ingredient was taken, "Arsène Lupin in Prison," he is successful. In the film, no doubt because of the injunction of the Hays Office that crime could not be shown to pay, Lupin is foiled by the police. In fact, Lupin is even denied his flamboyant escape from prison, which Leblanc recounted; instead, it is Ganimard who gratuitously sets him free.

Nothing was done further with the character until ARSÈNE LUPIN RE-

TURNS (M-G-M, 1938). Melvyn Douglas, earlier in the decade, had given a fine account playing the Lone Wolf for Columbia and so, since he was now under contract to M-G-M, the studio thought he might do as well playing Lupin. George Fitzmaurice was put in charge of direction and the screenplay was prepared by James Kevin McGuiness with the help of BLACK MASK detective story writer, George Harmon Coxe, among others. In this photoplay, Lupin has retired and is believed by all the world to be dead. He has secluded himself at a rustic estate where he raises pigs and terriers and is pursuing a romance with Virginia Bruce. E. E. Clive, cast as an English crook, and Nat Pendleton, a bumptious American, are Lupin's confederates and are responsible for much of the comedy in the film. Warren William, who was about to become the Lone Wolf, was cast as an American detective in search of a necklace stolen in New York. George Zucco was on hand to play the prefect of police which role he handled about as adroitly as Bela Lugosi the next year was to play a Soviet commissar in NINOTCHKA (M-G-M, 1939). Monte Woolley was also after the emerald neck piece. With a cast such as this, the film really could not miss being entertaining, albeit scarcely faithful to its source. If anything, Douglas was even more suave and polished than when he had played the Lone Wolf. Jonathan Hale, a staple cast member in the Saint films at RKO, was cast as a special agent for the F. B. I. Perplexity as to who is behind the theft is better handled than in many detective films and the suspicion which shrouds Lupin is more effectively projected than it is in the majority of Lone Wolf and Saint films, only intensifying the suspense created as both Douglas and William vie for Virginia Bruce's attention.

Although he would continue as a character in French films until the 'Fifties, Lupin's final appearance in an American film was in ENTER ARSÈNE LUPIN (Universal, 1944) which was obviously intended to initiate a series which never materialized. It was originally intended also as a vehicle to gain additional exposure for Ella Raines, Howard Hawks' discovery whom the studio was in the process of building into a star. Ford Beebe, a graduate from Universal chapter plays, was the director. Charles Kovin was cast as Lupin who is intent on stealing an emerald from Raines only to regret his action once he perceives how beautiful she is and that she is also in danger for her life and her estate from an unscrupulous aunt and uncle. J. Carrol Naish, Miles Mander, and Gale Sondergaard, staples in Universal thriller pictures of this sort, rounded out the cast in what remains an average programmer.

BOSTON BLACKIE

I never forget a friend or a favor.

Boston Blackie[42]

Most of what we know of Jack Boyle, who created the character Boston Blackie, we owe to Edward D. Hoch in his Introduction to the reissue of BOS

TON BLACKIE (1919) by the Gregg Press in 1979. We do not know when he was born, only that it was prior to 1880 and that he grew up in Chicago. He was in San Francisco around the turn of the century, working as a newspaper journalist. It was here that he became addicted to opium. When he lost his newspaper job, he still had a habit which cost him four dollars a day. He passed a bad check in a bookstore and, when he tried to cash a second bad check, he was apprehended and sentenced to a year in prison. He continued his habit while behind bars. Upon his release, in need of money, he and a companion lured a man to a hotel room and robbed him of diamonds and cash at gunpoint. Boyle was identified by the victim from a mug shot and this time was sent to San Quentin. It was while in San Quentin that he began to write and completed four stories about Boston Blackie which he titled "Around the Opium Lamp." These stories were mainly narrated by Blackie to his men as they smoked opium following a successful theft. Boyle sent these stories to THE AMERICAN MAGAZINE. The editor was impressed with them, bought all four, and asked Boyle to write in addition a short biographical essay about himself to preface the stories. Boyle complied, signing the article as he did the stories, No. 6606, which was his prison number.

"Five years ago," he wrote, "I was the editor and manager of a metropolitan daily newspaper. Today I am a convict serving my second penitentiary sentence—'two-time loser' in the language of the underworld, my world now. Between these extremes is a single cause—*opium*. For five years I have been a smoker of opium. For five years there has not been a day, scarcely an hour, during which my mind and body have not been under the influence of the most subtle and insidious of drugs. And now, after weeks of agony in a prison where an honest warden has made it impossible to secure the drug, I am myself again, a normal-minded man, able to look back critically and impartially over the ruinous past."[43]

The first Boston Blackie story began running in THE AMERICAN MAGAZINE in July, 1914. It was titled "The Price of Principle" and in it Blackie was described as "gray-haired, stern-faced, laconic and efficient."[44] His nickname is said to have come about as a result of his "piercing black eyes and New England birthplace."[45] Blackie has an assistant named "The Cushions Kid." All the stories are strongly drug-related and the fourth one for certain is set in Chicago. These were establishing stories. Although Boyle would continue to write tales about Boston Blackie, never again in any of these stories would he include any description of his physical appearance.

Ray Long, then editor of THE RED BOOK, was impressed with these stories and wrote to No. 6606 in care of THE AMERICAN and suggested he submit some stories to THE RED BOOK. Boyle did not answer Long's letter but a couple of years later he visited him in his office in Chicago. Long later wrote in the Introduction to a 1932 anthology that Boyle had apparently served a brief third term in prison in Colorado. Long described Boyle as "a tall, handsome chap" and "a hard drinking man if ever there was one."[46] Long convinced Boyle to resume writing and his stories began to appear in THE

RED BOOK in 1917. Boyle even revived the character of Boston Blackie, but somewhat modified him. In these new stories he was not an opium addict. The Cushions Kid had been replaced by Blackie's wife, Mary—she is called Boston Blackie's Mary—and we learn about her that her father had done time and that so had she because she would not rat on a criminal associate although she was innocent. She is Blackie's best pal and sole confidant. Perhaps the finest story from this period is "Boston Blackie's Mary" which ran in the November, 1917 issue and which was widely reprinted in anthologies, including one by James M. Cain, and Rex Stout included it in his short-lived mystery magazine. Boyle's long suit was not characterization or style, although he did introduce some underworld argot long before it became fashionable in the pages of BLACK MASK. What he could do superbly was create unusual dramatic situations and sustain tension. When he wrote about life in prison, as he did in "Boston Blackie's Mary," the realism is unquestionable. Because he had been part of the underworld, he understood better than E. W. Hornung and Maurice Leblanc before him and Louis Joseph Vance and Leslie Charteris after him the unbridgeable gap of antagonism which separates the criminal from the bourgeois society around him; and he also anticipated the BLACK MASK writers in recognizing that society is as corrupt in different ways as is the criminal element. There is a patina of sentiment, often bordering on sentimentality, in the Boston Blackie stories that seems old-fashioned and dated today, but there is also psychological tensity which retains all its sting and fascination.

In the June, 1918 issue of THE RED BOOK, Boyle's story "The Baby and the Burglar" was featured. It was purchased by Metro Pictures and served as the basis for BOSTON BLACKIE'S LITTLE PAL (Metro, 1918). Bert Lytell, who had played the Lone Wolf the previous year, was cast as Boston Blackie. Instead of being only his wife, Mary, played by Rhea Mitchell, is also Blackie's assistant whom he plants in the home of an unhappily married couple to reconnoiter the safe. As in the story, Blackie overhears a conversation between the unhappy wife and her would-be lover at the end of which she gives the suitor her jewels. Also as in the story, Blackie relieves the suitor of the jewels and is responsible for bringing the couple back together. Prior to the commission of this theft, he befriended the small boy in the couple's home before trying to open the safe himself only to be interrupted by the return of the wife and her suitor. In the story, Blackie pockets the jewels. In the film, the matter is left more nebulous, with a title card asking viewers if, indeed, Blackie did not deserve the gems for having saved the couple's marriage.

Metro immediately followed this film with BOSTON BLACKIE'S REDEMPTION (Metro, 1919) which was based on "Boston Blackie's Mary." In the film version, Blackie and Mary are not married, only contemplating marriage, when Blackie is framed and sent to prison. He escapes, is confronted by the warden who traces him to his hide-out but is allowed to escape by the warden when he cannot bring himself to shoot the prison official. Blackie then learns that the man who framed him is planning a robbery at a lumber company. He causes the man to be captured, is exonerated, and sets sail with his new bride for Honolulu. Bert Lytell was again cast as Blackie.

The story is far superior insofar as Blackie remains what he is and the deputy warden remains what he is, albeit both have to admit the virtues which exist in the other. The story concerns a conflict of wills. When Blackie, who is framed for a crime he did not commit and is convicted by a jury for other crimes which he undoubtedly did commit, is sent to prison, he comes up against Martin Sherwood, the deputy warden. Blackie leads a successful prison revolt against bad food and excessive punishment. Sherwood waits his chance and, at last, he has the excuse to put Blackie in the straightjacket. "Fully tightened," Boyle wrote, "the jacket shuts off blood circulation throughout the body almost completely. For the first five minutes, oppressed breathing is the only inconvenience felt. Then the stagnating blood commences to cause the most excruciating torture—a thousand pains as if white-hot needles are being passed through the flesh run through the body. The feet and limbs swell and turn black. Irresistible weights seem to be crushing the brain. Four hours in the jacket made one convict a paralytic for life. Some men have endured it for a half or three-quarters of an hour without crying out, but only a few. Boston Blackie had been in the jacket for an hour and five minutes, and as yet Martin Sherwood had waited in vain for groans and pleas for release."[47] This is the contest around which the story revolves. No one has ever escaped from Sherwood's prison, but Blackie does. When Sherwood finally traces Blackie to his hideout, he refuses to shoot it out with Sherwood. Blackie is a thief, not a killer, and he breaks down finally when the other will not allow him to beat him in a fair fight. It is Blackie's breaking down which brings about Sherwood's change of heart to the degree that he permits him to escape. Nowhere is it hinted that Blackie will reform. It was in the films, and not in Boyle's stories, where the idea of a reformed thief turned detective was born.

When, in 1919, Ray Long became editor of COSMOPOLITAN, he convinced Boyle to come along and virtually every issue carried a Boyle story or article. Based on the success of the magazine stories and the first two films, H. K. Fly, a small New York publisher, decided to bring out a novel titled BOSTON BLACKIE (1919). What Boyle did for this book—a common practice at the time—was slightly to rewrite several of his short stories to give them the coherence of at least a picaresque novel. The volume began with "Boston Blackie's Little Pal" and ended with "Boston Blackie's Mary." This was the only book Boyle would ever publish.

In the meantime, Famous Players-Lasky released MISSING MILLIONS (Paramount, 1922) which combined two of THE RED BOOK short stories (which had also appeared in the novel) with David Powell, who had earlier played Arsène Lupin for the same company, in the role of Blackie. The role of Boston Blackie's Mary was replaced by a character named May who is a pal of Blackie's. In the sequence of stories, Blackie engineers a heist of one hundred and fifty pounds of gold bars from several tons which are in a ship's stronghold. The Chief of Police, a man named Rentor, decides to frame the ship's purser, an innocent young man who had fallen in love with Mary on the voyage. Mary goes to Judge Garber and asks him to defend the purser. " 'So this rat Rentor, who is getting rich on the graft he is collecting from gambling houses and red light dens, thinks he'll make a reputation by railroading to prison a boy whose only crime is that he is too decent to ruin a girl's reputation!' " Garber exclaims after Mary tells him all that has happened. " 'He won't succeed as long as I keep my Southern blood and remain a member of the Seattle bar.' "[48] In the film, as in the story, one of Blackie's reasons for undertaking the crime is that the man who owns the gold framed Mary's father for a crime he did not commit. In the story, Mary proposes to give the gold back if the charges are dropped and Blackie, when he hears of her offer, endorses it. In the film, there is an interesting alteration. While Blackie does give back the gold, the owner of it commits suicide, thinking he is destitute! Boyle might indulge in sentiment in the story to the extent of reflecting that "the smile of happiness in Mary's eyes just then was worth more to Boston Blackie than all the gold the *Humboldt* ever carried."[49] But he would not ever have been guilty of the unrealistic sentimentality of the photoplay.

Although Boyle continued to sell fiction to THE RED BOOK after Long had left the magazine, his new Boston Blackie stories appeared exclusively in COSMOPOLITAN. Boyle's Blackie story, "The Face in the Fog," which ran in the May, 1920 issue was purchased for the screen by Paramount and Boyle was asked to come to Hollywood to help write the screenplay. This was the only picture on which he would collaborate that featured his most famous character. THE FACE IN THE FOG (Paramount, 1922) cast Lionel Barrymore in the role of Blackie. The basic event of the story is one of those situations where Blackie sees a chance to do a good turn. Blackie is given the surname of Dawson. A grand duchess from Russia and her lover try to smuggle the Romanov jewels into the United States. On their trail is a gang of thieves led by a crooked count. The United States government is also after the jewels. Blackie's strategy manages at once to foil the thieves and to substitute paste imitations for the real jewels sufficient to fool the government men. The real jewels are restored to the grand duchess and she flees the country with her lover.

Boyle remained for some time in Hollywood, working on various film projects and contributing at least six original stories for film melodramas which had nothing to do with Boston Blackie. At the same time films continued to be made based on Boston Blackie stories Boyle had written earlier. BOSTON BLACKIE (Fox, 1923) was adapted from the story "The Water Cross," which had appeared in COSMOPOLITAN in 1919, although, once again, the film version was lacking in the realism of the original. Blackie is shown being released from prison. He promises the warden, played by Frank Brownlee, that he is going to lose his job because he uses the water-cross torture on his prisoners. Before Blackie can make good on his words, he is framed and sent back to prison. Eva Novak, cast as Mary Carter, Blackie's girlfriend, helps him to escape and it is she who goes to the governor and secures a pardon for Blackie. The warden is removed. The view of political administration may have been unduly naive, but the film did reflect Boyle's continuing concern with the abuse of prison inmates.

CROOKED ALLEY (Universal, 1923) was based on an original screen story by Boyle. It was by all accounts an inferior film. Blackie appears as a reformed thief who wants revenge on a judge who refused a pardon to a dying friend. He schemes to have the dead friend's daughter strike up a romance with the judge's son and then has the boy arrested after he steals money from his father. Blackie's plan fails because the two actually do fall in love. Thomas Carrigan was cast as Blackie.

THROUGH THE DARK (Cosmopolitan, 1924) also seems to have been based on an original story by Boyle. Its account of how Blackie and Mary met certainly does not agree with earlier published accounts. Margaret Seddon was cast as Mother McGinn who runs a hide-out for criminals on the lam and is able to send her daughter, Mary McGinn played by Colleen Moore, to a fashionable girls' school. Mary does not know that her father died in prison in this story. When Boston Blackie, played by Forrest Stanley, breaks out of San Quentin during a prison riot, Mary assists him in avoiding the police. Mary is expelled from the school when the police inform the administrators of her background. She returns to live with her mother, encounters Blackie again whom she has come to love, and she persuades him to return to prison with the promise that she will be waiting for him when he is released. So much had the character and personality of Boston Blackie's Mary been changed by the "moral" exigencies of motion pictures, to say nothing of Blackie himself.

Rin Tin Tin had proved a box-office sensation with his debut in 1923. Every studio was of a mind that it had to have a competing canine star. One of Boyle's earliest successes in Hollywood was to write an original screen story which featured his dog creation Peter the Great and a new canine celebrity came upon the scene when it was filmed as THE SILENT ACCUSER (M-G-M, 1924). The story has Peter the Great the sole witness to a murder for which his master is unjustly imprisoned. Peter helps his master to escape and to trail the real murderer to Mexico where he is brought to justice. THE RETURN OF BOSTON BLACKIE (First Division, 1927), based loosely on a Boyle story which had appeared in COSMOPOLITAN, is distinguished by the fact that Blackie's assistant in the film is Strongheart, the only real competition to Rin Tin Tin during the 'Twenties. Raymond Glenn was cast as Blackie. Subsequently Glenn changed his screen name to Bob Custer, but his woeful incompetence before the camera did not lessen; and, hence, the addition of Strongheart to the cast is comprehensible as almost a necessity. Blackie has gone straight and decides to help reform a blonde woman who is trying to steal a necklace from a cabaret dancer. When Blackie learns that the cabaret dancer acquired the necklace from the woman's philandering father, he does the right thing: he restores the necklace to its original owner.

Boyle appears to have wearied of living in Los Angeles sometime in 1926. The last story he submitted to COSMOPOLITAN in 1926 indicates that he was still living at Hermosa Beach, near Hollywood; but by the time he sold his final story to THE RED BOOK, in 1927, his address had changed to Greenwich Village. All indications are that he died in 1928.

The Boston Blackie property remained dormant until MEET BOSTON BLACKIE (Columbia, 1941). The studio's Lone Wolf series had proved a box-office staple and it was felt that another series about a reformed thief turned detective might also do well. Chester Morris was cast in the role. He had been born in New York City in 1901 and had been a contract player with Columbia Pictures since 1936. He had come from a theatrical family. After several years on the stage, he began his motion picture career with ALIBI (United Artists, 1929) for which he was nominated for an Oscar. In 1926, he married actress Suzanne Kilbourne; they were divorced in 1938. In 1940, Morris married Lillian Kenton Barker, the original Chesterfield Girl from the "They Satisfy" advertisements. I suspect Morris felt his career was slipping and he took the role initially because he could retain his starring status. I met Chester Morris but once, when he was touring with the popular Broadway play, based on Allen Drury's novel of the same title, ADVISE AND CONSENT. He was to appear at the Pabst Theatre in Milwaukee, Wisconsin where I lived at the time. Had I talked to him prior to the performance, I could have told him that it was a mistake, in Milwaukee, to announce to reporters as he had that "politics is a dirty business." Political leaders in the city had been given free tickets to the play. One of them called a press conference. He claimed that it would be unthinkable for him to attend the play after a person of Chester Morris' standing in the theatre had so calumniously indicted politicians without taking into account the careers of so many men totally devoted to public service who thanklessly pursue this end all of their lives without unjust enrichment.

"Maybe you took the Boston Blackie character too seriously," I suggested.

"Maybe I take America *too* seriously," he snapped back.

We were in the star dressing room back stage. The first article I had ever written was propaganda to save the Pabst Theatre from demolition. That had been while I was still a student at Marquette University and working for a classical music station. In this room I had first interviewed Leopold Stokowski, Fritz Reiner, and other conductors who appeared with the Chicago Symphony.

"This is a cold city," Morris remarked, lighting a cigarette. He looked still much as he had in the Blackie films at Columbia, his straight black hair slicked back from the temples, his ready grin, his harsh-toned voice. "And I don't mean the temperature outside."

I recalled that Sir Thomas Beecham, when he conducted the Chicago Symphony, had commented to me that Milwaukee "was more bleak than Berlin." Pierre Monteux, when he had come, had been more laconic. "*Je vais maintenant à Chicago. Comme on dit en anglais?*: 'Whew!' "

"I wanted to talk to you about the Boston Blackie films at Columbia," I said.

"What about them?"

"That's what I want to know. What about them?"

Morris chuckled.

"I was signed by Columbia to make those pictures. At the time, I thought it was a great contract. But those pictures nearly ruined my career. We could shoot one in 12 days. And then it would be four or five months before we'd start another. I nearly went to pieces just finding something to occupy my time. All the Blackie pictures were 'B' films. They didn't do a thing for my career."

"Why didn't you star in the television series?"

Morris inhaled from his cigarette.

"I didn't want to. I had been Boston Blackie on the radio, you know. And I was in all the movies. They were always playing on television in those days. How typecast can an actor get? I wanted to do something else."

The something else in 1951 was DETECTIVE STORY at the Ivar Theatre in Hollywood. Morris starred with Allen Jenkins and Marvin Miller in support. That began nearly two decades of Broadway and road work in theatrical productions.

"Didn't you think Blackie's relationship to the Runt was peculiar?" I asked. "In the television series with Kent Taylor, the Runt was replaced by a dog."

Morris threw his head back and laughed.

"No, not really," he replied. "Georgie Stone. I won't ever forget. He was the delay on those pictures. He could never remember his lines. Everyone was held up by him. But he was perfect for the role. And a real sweet guy. Besides, the Runt was in a story by Jack Boyle on which the whole thing was based. He was as important to the pictures as Farraday."

"I've got another question," I said.

"What's that?" Morris asked, lighting another cigarette.

"It has to do with your remarks about politics."

"What about them?"

"What's wrong?"

"Now that's a very good question." He leaned back in his chair. "It isn't so much what's wrong with politics. Everything's wrong with politics in this country. What's really wrong is that we hide from it. We don't like to admit that it's a dirty game played by dirty men for their advantage. That's what's wrong, and I wonder how long it's going to be before we have the backbone to wake up and see it. I'll tell you this. We'd better wake up soon, because if we don't, it'll be too late. Then it won't much matter, will it?"

It was nearly a decade later that Chester Morris was staying at a motel in New Hope, Pennsylvania. He was starring at the Bucks County Playhouse in THE CAINE MUTINY COURT-MARTIAL. He was 69. He talked to cast members and seemed happy the morning of 11 September 1970. He had a luncheon appointment he had said on the telephone that he intended to keep. Those closest to him knew that Morris was suffering from an extremely rare and incurable ailment that had reduced his weight to under a hundred pounds and which prevented him from drinking and eating most foods. His memory was so shattered by the malady that he lived in perpetual terror of forgetting his lines. His weakened and hopeless condition brought him frequently into a state of despair. The coroner refused to inform the press whether or not the overdose had been accidental.

Ralph Cohn was the producer on MEET BOSTON BLACKIE and Robert Florey directed. The plot finds Blackie returning from a trip to Europe. He is met while still on the boat by Inspector Farraday played by Richard Lane in all the films. When a corpse is found in Blackie's stateroom, Farraday jumps to the obvious conclusion. Blackie has to escape in order to clear himself and this became the basic formula for nearly all the entries. They were, however, played for comedy and Chester Morris was perfectly suited to the role with his brash, airy manner. Blackie's sidekick in the series was the Runt, played in this first film by Charles Wagenheim. With Rochelle Hudson's assistance, Blackie discovers that the murder was the work of a spy ring after government secrets and using an oceanside carnival as a blind.

CONFESSIONS OF BOSTON BLACKIE (Columbia, 1941) was perhaps the best film in the series. George E. Stone was aptly cast as the Runt and he remained in that role until the last picture. Lloyd Corrigan, himself a director, was cast as Blackie's wealthy, if feather-brained, friend Arthur Manleder. Walter Sande, who had played an uniformed cop in MEET BOSTON BLACKIE, was promoted to the role of Sergeant Matthews, Farraday's dim-witted assistant, thus making the police again a comic duo. Harriet Hilliard played the feminine lead. A gang of swindlers is selling phony art objects. When Harriet gets too close to the truth, she is shot by one of the gang. Blackie is suspected. Joan Woodbury played Blackie's girlfriend who, in a fit of jealous rage, smashes up Blackie's apartment. Corrigan got most of the laughs, but he played against an excellent cast. Edward Dmytryk directed the film.

"Of course," Dmytryk said, "it was easy to work with Chester Morris, even though he didn't particularly like the role. He did what he had to do. But he didn't like stunt work and refused to do anything strenuous, even so much as stand on a box. Chet was an amateur magician and he was always carrying a deck of cards around with him doing tricks. I knew it was a comedy, but I tried to introduce a sort of gallows humor into it." He added, with a sly smile, "It was so well liked that I was rewarded with two Lone Wolf pictures."

ALIAS BOSTON BLACKIE (Columbia, 1942) was directed by Lew Landers and kept the same basic cast. Cy Kendall was added to the roster as Jumbo Madigan, a pawn broker who comes to Blackie's assistance. Larry Parks, later famous for his portrayal of Al Jolson, played Joe Trilby who escapes from prison while Blackie is putting on a magic show for the inmates. He wants to prove his innocence. Blackie is suspected of having helped him to escape, but he vindicates both himself and Parks by the end.

BOSTON BLACKIE GOES HOLLYWOOD (Columbia, 1942) directed by Michael Gordon is quite possibly the funniest film in the series other than CONFESSIONS OF BOSTON BLACKIE. Arthur Manleder gets himself into trouble with a gang of hoodlums led by Blackie's old cellmate, William Wright. In MEET BOSTON BLACKIE, Farraday makes quite a to-do about getting Blackie's fingerprints, but by this time it is established that Blackie has a prison record, so the character was undergoing *some* changes. Jumbo Madigan provides Blackie and the Runt with disguises, the Runt decked out in junior togs playing Blackie's child. The height of hilarity is reached when Blackie dumps an ant colony on Farraday and Matthews while they are trying to do an undercover tail job.

Lew Landers was back to direct AFTER MIDNIGHT WITH BOSTON BLACKIE (Columbia, 1943). This time Cy Kendall was cast as a night club owner and a crook. When Walter Baldwin is released from prison, he wants his daughter, played by Ann Savage, to have his cache of diamonds. Kendall wants the diamonds and shoots Baldwin to get them. Blackie is suspected of being at the bottom of it. In the meantime, the Runt is about to be married at Arthur Manleder's apartment. Johnny Bond, the Country and Western singer, was on the set at Columbia when this film was being made. Once when I was a guest in his home, he showed me the color footage he had shot with his hand-operated camera while Chester Morris' double was jumping from the top of a building for a scene. Morris was on the sidelines in a powder blue suit, smoking and laughing. It made me regret that at least one of the Blackie films had not been made in color.

William Castle was assigned to direct CHANCE OF A LIFETIME (Columbia, 1943). "Chester Morris, a fine actor, played the lead," he wrote in his autobiography. "He tried to breathe some life into a part that had died at birth. Jeanne Bates hopelessly tried to play the *femme fatale*. Every day I viewed the rushes, and my assistants told me what a great job I was doing. Irving Briskin remained silent as long as I didn't change a word of dialogue. Finally I started to believe I was getting a good picture, and I plowed ahead, completing the picture in 12 days. I saw the final cut with Irving Briskin. When the lights came up he turned to me and uttered the not unexpected. 'It's a piece of shit!' "[50] Briskin was in charge of Columbia's "B" department. Rather despairingly Castle observed that "to help me correct the 'piece of shit,' Briskin took the end of the picture and put it at the beginning, then spliced a section of Reel Four into Reel Two, a section of Two into Four, and some of Five into Six. Reel Seven he took out entirely. Eight, he trimmed, and Nine, he left alone. After his glowing contribution, CHANCE OF A LIFETIME became even more muddled and screwed up than it had been originally, if that was possible."[51] Not having seen the original script, I cannot verify what changes Briskin made; but the beginning of the picture could not have come at the end, except for a shot or two. The story concerns Blackie's scheme to get a group of convicts released from prison to work in Arthur Manleder's machine shop making war materials. One of them has the loot from a robbery and Douglas Fowley and his partner want it. Blackie is in hot water for a time, but the other convicts, staying at Blackie's apartment, make Fowley confess and all ends well with Blackie getting yet another batch of convicts for his rehabilitation program.

ONE MYSTERIOUS NIGHT (Columbia, 1944) is interesting only because Oscar Boetticher, Jr., who would later direct a series of memorable Westerns as Budd Boetticher, directed it; otherwise it is not. Blackie actually becomes a special agent of the New York Police Department to recover the Blue Star of the Nile diamond which was stolen from a War Relief exhibit. BOSTON BLACKIE BOOKED ON SUSPICION (Columbia, 1945) directed by Arthur Dreifuss marked Lloyd Corrigan's last portrayal of Manleder. Walter Sande was replaced by Frank Sully in the Sergeant Matthews role. Manleder purchases a rare book shop. When the manager falls ill, Blackie agrees to impersonate him at a forthcoming auction. Lynn Merrick, who works in the shop, is the typical ruthless blonde *femme fatale* of the 'Forties, keeping Steve Cochrane, her escaped convict husband, in her apartment. She plots a fraud, a phony original edition of Charles Dickens' THE PICKWICK PAPERS, and then shoots her accomplice. Blackie is the one Farraday suspects, but Merrick is caught by the fade.

Nina Foch was given the female lead in BOSTON BLACKIE'S RENDEZ-VOUS (Columbia, 1945). Harry Hayden was rather inadequately cast as Manleder and, after this entry, the character was dropped. Steve Cochrane was back, this time as an escaped lunatic, a nephew of Manleder's, who strangles two women before he corners Nina Foch. Farraday is so busy chasing Blackie that Cochrane almost gets away with it. At one point, running from Farraday, Blackie and Runt get themselves up in black face and play a couple of colored chamber maids. When questioned by a passing cop about Boston Blackie, they reply, "We'se from Adaho."

John Stone, long associated with some of the better Charlie Chan entries at Fox, took over as the producer on CLOSE CALL FOR BOSTON BLACKIE (Columbia, 1946) which Lew Landers directed. Farraday warns Blackie off women at the beginning. Then Lynn Merrick, now an old flame, shows up and claims to have had a baby by her convict husband. The husband is shot and Blackie is suspected by Farraday. It all proves to be a scam to get money out of the baby's supposed grandfather. Blackie proves the baby a fake and Merrick a crook. Both Blackie and Runt get a chance to disguise themselves, this time with the Runt pretending to be a female nurse. THE PHANTOM THIEF (Columbia, 1946) was directed by D. Ross Lederman with Marvin Miller cast as a fake medium who, together with Jeff Donnell's husband, has been swindling her out of money. After the obligatory scenes with Farraday suspecting Blackie, the two join forces to expose the hoax.

BOSTON BLACKIE AND THE LAW (Columbia, 1946) directed by Ted Richmond provided Chester Morris ample opportunity to perform magic tricks, while the script was a reworking of ALIAS BOSTON BLACKIE. This time Blackie is giving a magic show at a women's prison when one of the inmates escapes. Farraday is after Blackie. The girl was once a partner in crime with a famous magician. Blackie impersonates the magician. The magician's assistant proves to be the one behind the murders. The film depended on stock footage of such things as the face of a giant clock from SHERLOCK HOLMES FACES DEATH (Universal, 1943) and the interior shot of a bank from Frank Capra's YOU CAN'T TAKE IT WITH YOU (Columbia, 1938). Yet the series was not really winding down to a slow-paced finish as had so many other detective series. The next entry, TRAPPED BY BOSTON BLACKIE (Columbia, 1948), came after a year's hiatus. It was produced by Rudolph C. Flothow who was no longer able to work on the Crime Doctor series due to Warner Baxter's illness and was directed by Seymour Friedman. When a detective is killed in a car crash, Blackie and Runt agree to help his widow save his detective agency. They offer to guard a pearl necklace at a society party. When the necklace is stolen, Farraday goes after Blackie. Notwithstanding, the picture was tightly plotted and had Blackie again indulge in the art of disguise.

BOSTON BLACKIE'S CHINESE VENTURE (Columbia, 1949) was the final entry, produced by Flothow and directed by Friedman, with George E. Stone regrettably replaced by Sid Tomack. When a murder occurs in Chinatown, Farraday immediately accuses Blackie. Blackie and Runt manage before the conclusion to catch the real culprit.

"Friend to those who have no friends; enemy to those who make him an enemy" was the way Boston Blackie was introduced on the radio. All in all, it was a characterization that, over the air at least, brought out Chester Morris' personality, although he remained starring in the films longer than he remained with the radio series. I would not do the man justice were I not to say of him, in parting, that he was a most committed actor. He might be so sick he could hardly function, as he was near the end; he might miss his lines because he could not remember due to illness. Yet, invariably, he gave of himself, and he kept trying long after most men would have given up.

THE LONE WOLF

If I fail, then, it will be because I'm unfit—and I'll go under, and never be heard of again. . . . But I shan't fail. It seems to me the very fact that I want to go straight is proof enough that I've something inherently decent in me to build on.

The Lone Wolf[52]

What possibly inspired Louis Joseph Vance most to become an author of popular fiction was the suspense of being in debt. It is not the same thing as poverty. Those in debt never have a moment's peace from the importunities of creditors.

Vance was born in New York in 1879, the son of Wilson Vance, a newspaperman and novelist. He attended the Brooklyn Polytechnic Institute. He married Elizabeth Hodges at nineteen and he was already in debt. Marriage only added to his financial woes. Vance attended the Art Students League in hope of becoming a commercial illustrator, but it did not work out. He worked at various jobs during the day and wrote six hours every night. The first story he wrote was universally rejected. His second story he sold for $25.

Thus reassured, Vance continued to write prolifically, turning out any kind of prose he could sell. When THE BRASS BOWL (1907) became a bestseller, his career took a turn for the better. Vance followed it with one popular romance after another. Eventually all he did was write. He worked at night. It was his custom to plot out his books to the last detail before committing anything to paper. He typed his manuscripts and could turn out a 100,000 word book in the space of two months. He did a lot of rewriting. Some chapters he would rework up to forty times.

His novel, THE LONE WOLF (1914), was scarcely based on a new idea. True, Hornung had given up writing about Raffles, but Boston Blackie was popular with American readers and Vance was not unaware of Arsène Lupin. In fact, in THE LONE WOLF, Lucy Shannon, with whom the Lone Wolf falls in love, remarks: " 'I think . . . that you're very like the other lone wolf, the fictitious one—Lupin, you know—a bit of a blagueur.' "[53] What made the Lone Wolf adventure different from its predecessors is that from his debut Michael Lanyard wants to correct the errors of his ways because of the love he has for a woman. This kind of sentimentality occurred only once to Lupin and the condition was scarcely lasting—in Raffles it would have been unthinkable. After the fashion of the good bad man played by William S. Hart in films such as THE RETURN OF DRAW EGAN (Triangle, 1916), Lanyard sees a woman, falls in love with her at first sight, and decides he must reform.

Lanyard, at a young age, is left an orphan to be raised at Troyon's, a somewhat disreputable hotel in Paris. He has a suspicion that he may be American, but he grows up speaking French. He tries to steal from a professional thief who is staying there, a man named Bourke. He is called Michael Troyon, his surname taken from the establishment. Bourke apprentices Michael and teaches him all the skills he will need to become a master criminal. Michael eventually changes his surname to Lanyard and goes forth into the world armed with Bourke's wisdom summarized in three basic principles: to know one's "ground thoroughly before venturing upon it; to strike and retreat with the swift precision of a hawk; to be friendless. And the last of these was the greatest."[54]

An aged American named Bannon is in Paris attempting to organize an international crime ring. In the meantime, a group known as The Pack, consisting of an Englishman named Wertheimer who heads up English crime, a man named

Popinot who leads the Parisian Apaches, Mr. Goodenough Smith who represents New York gunmen, and the Count De Morbihan try to force Lanyard to join their group and to pay them a percentage of his take. Lanyard refuses and so they set out to destroy him. Added to this group is a German named Ekstrom who also is an enemy of Lanyard's who managed to steal some plans for submarine manufacture; Ekstrom wants these plans for the German government and Lanyard turns them over to the French Minister of War. In the course of the novel, Lanyard succeeds in removing most of these obstacles, except for Ekstrom. Lucy Shannon is traveling with Bannon and Lanyard rescues her. " 'Oh,' " he tells her, " 'I've said it a dozen different ways of indirection, but I may as well say it squarely now: I love you; it's love of you makes me want to go straight—the hope that when I've proved myself you'll maybe let me ask you to marry me.' "[55] Wertheimer turns out to be a secret serviceman in disguise. In a final airplane chase across the English Channel, Wertheimer is flying a plane with Lanyard and Lucy as passengers when they are presumably pursued by Ekstrom who is sent crashing to his death.

However, Ekstrom was not in the pursuit plane, as readers learn in the next Lone Wolf book, THE FALSE FACES (1918). He is now heading up the Prussian spy system and Lanyard has become his sworn adversary. Lanyard puts it this way. " 'Ekstrom had accompanied the army of invasion, had seen and recognized Lucy in passing through Louvain. Therefore she and my son were among the first to be sacrificed. . . . When I stood over her grave I dedicated my life to the extermination of Ekstrom and all his breed. I have since done things I do not like to think about. But the Prussian spy system is the weaker for my work. . . . ' "[56] THE FALSE FACES has a much better plot than THE LONE WOLF, opening aboard a ship bound for the United States. In exchange for his assistance, the British have given Lanyard a false identity and he intends to continue his pursuit of Ekstrom to New York where he has organized a Prussian spy ring. During the voyage, the United States enters the war on the side of the Allies. Lanyard is thrown from the ship but, rather improbably, is saved when the German submarine which torpedoes it surfaces beneath him and he is taken prisoner. He is able, finally, to sink the submarine while it is docked at a secret cove near Martha's Vineyard and makes his way to New York. He settles with Ekstrom in due course, although he does not kill him, rather permitting his own men to do it. He rescues Cecelia Brooke from Ekstrom's clutches and finds, at the close, that he is in love with her. Cecelia is an English woman and her presence allowed Vance to retain the traditional structure of the romance at the heart of an adventure story.

The war gave pith and moment to Lanyard's activities. Unfortunately, this focus was lost with the Armistice. Although he remained in the secret service, his exploits had to become more mundane, such as recovering stolen jewelry in ALIAS THE LONE WOLF (1921) or fighting Communist plotters in RED MASQUERADE (1921). In THE LONE WOLF RETURNS (1923), he fell in love again, and once more for the sake of a woman he promises to change his ways. Henceforth Lanyard would become an unconventional family man and, after the hiatus of almost a decade, THE LONE WOLF'S SON (1931) shows him as an aging parent. Over a span of twenty years, there were only eight Lone Wolf novels, of which THE LONE WOLF'S LAST PROWL (1934) was published posthumously. Close to Christmas, 1933, Vance died in his apartment, ostensibly as a result of falling asleep while smoking a cigar. He was found lying on the floor of the apartment, his head and right shoulder resting on the seat of a blazing upholstered armchair. The unclothed upper part of his body was severely burned.

The Lone Wolf was brought to the screen very early in his career and perhaps without this inducement Vance would not have continued with the character in a series of books. THE LONE WOLF (Selznick, 1917) was purchased for the screen by Lewis J. Selznick, the father of David O. Selznick. Bert Lytell was given the starring role, largely on the basis of his good looks and dashing mien. Henry B. Walthall next played the role in the film based on the second novel, THE FALSE FACES (Paramount, 1919). Vance did not introduce the Lone Wolf's motherless daughter into his novels until RED MASQUERADE, but she was already a character in the film THE LONE WOLF'S DAUGHTER (Paramount, 1919).

Throughout the decade of the 'Twenties, a good many of Vance's romances were brought to the screen and he scarcely had to depend on the Lone Wolf for one of his books to be a bestseller or for a film to be based on it. Jack Holt, who had starred in Universal chapter plays and Paramount Westerns, was next given the role in THE LONE WOLF (Associated Exhibitors, 1924). This was actually a remake of the Selznick picture, although the plot was updated. Dorothy Dalton was cast as Lucy Shannon, actually a secret service agent intent upon regaining plans for a stolen defense apparatus. The Lone Wolf agrees to help her provided he is granted asylum from "The Pack" in the United States. The thrilling escape in an airplane was too good to pass up and the picture made use of it as well as the confusing array of master criminals with whom the Lone Wolf has to battle in the original novel.

Columbia Pictures then purchased exclusive screen rights to the property and for the next two decades kept resurrecting the Lone Wolf. THE LONE WOLF RETURNS (Columbia, 1926), based on the novel by the same title, was the first entry in the Columbia series. Ralph Ince, who had been under contract to Selznick when the first Lone Wolf film was made, directed and again cast Bert Lytell in the lead. The picture opens to Lanyard robbing a safe when he hears the approach of the police. He hides a necklace in his cigarette case and retires quickly to a nearby house where a masked ball is taking place. Billie Dove, a stunningly attractive belle, falls in love with the Lone Wolf. She seeks to protect him when all the guests, by order of the police, are compelled to unmask and Lanyard's presence is discovered. Nor does she say anything when she observes Lanyard replacing her own jewels which he stole while the ball was in progress. Inspector Crane is played by Alphonse Ethier who deports himself well in his portrayal, something not so true of later actors in the role. The real imbeciles are some thieves whom Lanyard, with Billie Dove's assistance, brings to justice.

In all of these early pictures, while Lanyard may commit a burglary or two, he is definitely on his way to reform; and the films certainly retained Vance's romantic notion that the cause of the Lone Wolf's reformation is the discovery of requited love. He is capable, however, of violence, something the fictional Lone Wolf would not countenance. When Lanyard confronts Ekstrom in THE FALSE FACES, the man who murdered his wife and child and now the man who has kidnapped Cecelia Brooke, he cannot shoot him unless Ekstrom should take the offensive. "The instincts of a killer were not his," the reader is told. " . . . He gulped convulsively, swallowing what had almost been a sob."[57]

ALIAS THE LONE WOLF (Columbia, 1927) came next. Bert Lytell was back in the role, but Billie Dove was replaced by a new heroine played by Lois Wilson. Popinot—the French criminal Vance introduced and dispatched in the first novel—and his cohorts are aboard ship with Lois Wilson and the Lone Wolf. Lois Wilson has a valuable jewel she hopes to smuggle into the United States and needs the money from its sale to liberate her brother who is imprisoned. Lanyard pretends to work with the thieves, but he tricks them. They avenge their cause by stealing the jewel and Lanyard is arrested. He escapes and brings the actual thieves to justice. Lois Wilson, for a time estranged to Lanyard, is won to him forever once she learns that he is working for the American secret service. E. H. Griffith directed the film and his sense of pacing was so sure and the scenes so well conceived that the film won critical endorsement at the same time as it proved popular with audiences. Louella Parsons in her column singled out the picture as a prime example of how Columbia had capably upgraded its feature photoplay product from the quickie films for which the studio had formerly been known.

Columbia decided, for the next entry, to remake THE LONE WOLF'S DAUGHTER (Columbia, 1929). The novelty was not the plot, but rather the addition of sound in the first reel. The sound, however, was not very good. Reviewers in New York hastened to remind their readers that simultaneously with the release of this picture Bert Lytell was appearing on stage in that city in the play BROTHERS. This was because Lytell, as the Lone Wolf in the employ of Scotland Yard to catch a band of thieves, seemed to lisp on screen. He says "Inthpector" and talks of "vithiting" and "thoforth." According to the screenplay, Lanyard wants to keep his former identity a secret so that his adopted daughter, Adrienne, played by Florence Allen, can have a successful society wedding to Donald Keith. He performs his official police task so adeptly that he wins the love of Gertrude Olmstead who is the heroine. Primarily because he wants to conceal his identity, Lanyard is forced by the Count and Countess Polinac, international jewel thieves, to open the safe of the Crenshaws at Adrienne's engagement party. By the end of the film, Lanyard gets the goods on them.

Bert Lytell's final appearance as the Lone Wolf was in the first all-talking film in the series, LAST OF THE LONE WOLF (Columbia, 1930). It was also Lytell's worst Lone Wolf film. His voice was much improved due to better recording techniques. However, the plot is far-fetched and the picture drags. Lanyard is being held prisoner in a mythical Balkan country called Saxonia. The king orders a ring he gave the queen and which she gave an admirer restored from its current possessor, the Count von Rimpau played by Henry Daniell. Lanyard is offered his liberty in exchange for retrieving the ring. After various adventures including falling in love with the queen's lady-in-waiting played by Patsy Ruth Miller, Lanyard succeeds.

The Lone Wolf was off the screen for a couple of years and during this hiatus, when he did make a brief appearance, it was in the only non-Columbia entry of the sound era, CHEATERS AT PLAY (Fox, 1932). Thomas Meighan starred as Michael Lanyard who, according to the screenplay, had once been known as "Lone" Lanyard. The plot concerns Charlotte Greenwood, an old favorite of Lanyard's, who is aboard ship bound for New York with a collection of emeralds which has come to her as a result of her opportune marriage. Also on board is James Kirkwood as Crane, a retired detective rather than the American secret service agent he was in the books. William Bakewell was cast as the Lone Wolf's son who is unaware of his father's presence aboard ship. Lanyard sets him on the right path at the same time as he brings a band of jewel thieves plotting to steal the emeralds to the bar of justice.

THE LONE WOLF RETURNS (Columbia, 1936), while a remake of the Bert Lytell picture of a decade earlier, remains to my mind the best of the Lone Wolf films. Melvyn Douglas played Lanyard and gave the role both the romance and the sophistication it demanded, much as he did when later he played Arsène Lupin. Gail Patrick played the heroine, Marcia Stewart, whose aunt has a prized emerald collection. Roy William Neill, who would direct most of the Universal Sherlock Holmes films with Basil Rathbone, was the director. Thurston Hall made his first appearance in the role of Crane, still a retired detective, this time called back into service from his farm in upper state New York to match wits with the Lone Wolf. The picture opens to Lanyard cracking a safe and hiding the pearls he finds in his cigarette case. To escape the police, he crashes Marcia's party and the two fall in love. The romance is adroitly handled in its understatement. The emphasis is shifted from the rapid pacing of events to the human concerns of the characters. Raymond Walburn performs aptly as Lanyard's valet, Jenkins. Because of his love for Marcia, Lanyard decides to reform. Douglas Dumbrille, appropriately nasty as the mastermind of a jewel theft ring, is a credible adversary. Lanyard is framed but exonerates himself by the end. The direction is so subtle and sensitive that the viewer can bear Lanyard's indiscretions with equanimity and even sympathy while, at the same time, being induced to condemn the more vulgar and determined chicanery of Dumbrille and his gang. This is an interesting use of the persuasiveness of film to present an ethical perspective that, in other circumstances, might not be acceptable to a viewer. The lighting invests the picture with that romantic sheen so typical of the glamour, polish, and sparkle of the cinema in the 'Thirties. Nor is comedy neglected in THE LONE WOLF RETURNS. Dumbrille, who paid a lot of money for two of his minions to go to Europe to lay the groundwork for the heist, complains to Crane as he is being carted off, "Every time I get ready to go to Europe, I end up going back to jail." Memorable scenes are to be found in the way Crane worries about the flowers he raises, in Lanyard's gentle embarrassment about his past life, and in Marcia's caution about loving anyone so completely.

THE LONE WOLF IN PARIS (Columbia, 1938) is not a good picture, and yet it should have been. Lucien Ballard was the cinematographer and Albert Rogell directed. But Francis Lederer as "Michel" Lanyard and Frances Drake as the Princess Thania simply could not make convincing this weird combination of THE LONE WOLF RETURNS and THE PRISONER OF ZENDA (United Artists, 1937). Michel is permitted to occupy a hotel room in Paris only because he can produce letters from detective bureaus in all the major capitals testifying to his reformation. He sets out to help the princess retrieve the crown jewels of her vest-pocket kingdom stolen by three unsavory nobles. The film indicates nothing so much as a high-budget idea victimized by too much "B" picture corner-cutting.

Columbia Pictures committed itself the next year to the concept of a series, a new series with a new Lone Wolf. Joseph Sistrom, brother of William Sistrom then at RKO and involved in the production of the Saint series, was made associate producer for the first entry. Warren William, who had bought up his Warner Bros. contract before it expired so he could free-lance in films such as THE GRACIE ALLEN MURDER CASE (Paramount, 1939), was signed to play the lead and became in due course a Columbia contract player. If casting for THE LONE WOLF SPY HUNT (Columbia, 1939) was weak with Don Beddoe as Inspector Thomas and Leonard Carey as Laynard's valet, it was somewhat off-set by featuring Ida Lupino in the role of the Lone Wolf's outspoken, aggressive girlfriend Val Carson and Rita Hayworth as Karen, consort to the principal heavy played by Ralph Morgan.

THE LONE WOLF IN PARIS had actually been a pale remake of LAST OF THE LONE WOLF. THE LONE WOLF SPY HUNT started with the old script for THE LONE WOLF'S DAUGHTER. Fortunately, Jonathan Latimer, who would later work on THE GLASS KEY (Paramount, 1942) and who was one of Raymond Chandler's few friends in La Jolla, was assigned to the screenplay. Latimer had followed in Dashiell Hammett's footsteps in creating a hard-boiled detective named Bill Crane who made his debut in MURDER IN THE MADHOUSE (1934), the first of a series of books. Preston Foster was given the role in three Universal films based on Latimer's fiction. Crane, in the books, is a hard drinker who knows as much about the different kinds of alcohol as Sherlock Holmes knows about the varieties of tobacco. The old script, doubtless, hindered Latimer somewhat, but he did manage in the course of the film to create interesting female characters. Jack Norton, whose screen career consisted exclusively of playing drunks, was given a strong part in the screenplay, totally consonant with Latimer's penchant for boozey types. When THE LONE WOLF SPY HUNT turned out to be a success, Columbia settled down to the comfortable formula of a popular series.

The screen name of Lanyard's valet was changed from Jenkins to Jameson for THE LONE WOLF SPY HUNT. In the next entry, THE LONE WOLF STRIKES (Columbia, 1940), the spelling of the name was changed to Jamison and by an adroit bit of casting Eric Blore was assigned the role. He had played Philo Vance's valet in THE CASINO MURDER CASE (M-G-M, 1936) and he brought to his characterization of Jamison an outlandish sense of humor tempered by British understatement which played rather well opposite Warren William's sober and sophisticated Lone Wolf. Joan Perry, who would marry Columbia production chief Harry Cohn, was given the female lead and comedy player Fred Kelsey was cast as Sergeant Dickens. The screenplay was by Dalton Trumbo who would become one of the Hollywood Ten. Lanyard has retired to a New York apartment where he now collects tropical fish, an enthusiasm the reader may recall Warren William had when he portrayed Philo Vance in THE DRAGON MURDER CASE (First National, 1934). Addison Richards involves Lanyard in trying to regain possession of a pearl necklace stolen from his business partner and which supposedly led to the partner's death. The police naturally suspect Lanyard to such an extent that they close their minds to any other possible interpretation of the evidence. This, then, became the dominant *leit-motif* in the series. Henceforth, the plots became so standardized that while the Lone Wolf customarily would help someone in distress, the police invariably blamed him—as they did Boston Blackie in *that* series—and he was constantly being handcuffed by Kelsey or arrested for the crime at issue. From year to year I do not suppose this greatly mattered, but were one to watch these pictures one after another it does become repetitious and irritating.

Thurston Hall returned as Inspector Crane for THE LONE WOLF MEETS A LADY (Columbia, 1940) with Fred Kelsey as his assistant. The film was highly entertaining with some very good sequences in Lanyard's New York apartment and in the scene where Kelsey trails Lanyard. THE LONE WOLF TAKES A CHANCE (Columbia, 1941) was only slightly less so. The plot had June Storey in love with Lloyd Bridges who has invented a safe car for the transportation of engraving plates from the Treasury. Evalyn Knapp, a heroine in Westerns in the 'Thirties, played one of the gang conspiring to steal the plates. This fact might not be notable except that the footage of the Lone Wolf overtaking a speeding train with the safe car attached to it was lifted directly from SPEED WINGS (Columbia, 1934), a film in which Evalyn Knapp was the heroine opposite Tim McCoy.

Ralph Cohn became the producer on THE LONE WOLF TAKES A CHANCE and he remained for the next entry, THE LONE WOLF KEEPS A DATE (Columbia, 1941). Don Beddoe, who had been playing cops so far in the series, was miscast as a mobster in the latter entry and at the bottom of a kidnapping attempt which is foiled by the Lone Wolf. The setting is Florida, but that did not matter. Hall and Kelsey are called in to assist the Florida police and, at once, blame the whole thing on Lanyard.

Edward Dmytryk who would also become one of the Hollywood Ten was signed to direct SECRETS OF THE LONE WOLF (Columbia, 1941) and COUNTER-ESPIONAGE (Columbia, 1942). SECRETS OF THE LONE WOLF opens to Hall and Kelsey asking the Lone Wolf's advice as how best to protect the newly arrived Napoleon jewel collection and then, when the collection is stolen, they accuse him of having done it. As in CONFESSIONS OF BOSTON BLACKIE (Columbia, 1941), which Dmytryk had previously directed, he stressed the comic elements in the script. There is an episode which, were it not played in a comic vein would not have worked at all, when the ring of jewel thieves mistakes Jamison for Lanyard and seeks to make him their leader. COUNTER-ESPIONAGE was a transition film in which the Lone Wolf, as was also the case with Boston Blackie and Ellery Queen, entered the war effort on the side of the Allies. The setting is London during the height of the Battle of Britain. Dmytryk vividly evoked the atmosphere of an air raid shelter and the ghastly sound effects during a blitz. Hillary Brooke was in the cast as a worker in the shelter while Forrest Tucker played a Nazi spy. The Lone Wolf's mission is to hinder Tucker's success. Unfortunately neither Scotland Yard nor the American police are aware of the patriotic sympathies inspiring Lanyard's activities.

Hillary Brooke thought Warren William splendid to work with and she noted how much he seemed to like the comic aspects of the screenplay. Edward Dmytryk felt otherwise. "Warren William was a nice guy," he told me, "not at all like the sophisticated role he was playing. He had a Shakespearean manner, though, and, of course, a Barrymore profile. I couldn't get to him. Mostly it was because Warren had such a negative attitude toward making cheap pictures and the Lone Wolf pictures were medium-budget films. He had fixed up a truck into a mobile dressing room. He parked it near the sound stage where we were shooting. He never hung around the set. He always hid out in his dressing room. He never had a twinkle in his eye . . . unless a broad walked past. But he loved to do his own stunts. All that running around on steam pipes in SECRETS OF THE LONE WOLF he did himself."

William's weariness with the role and perhaps his boredom with low-budget pictures to which his career now seemed permanently condemned after it had once held such promise in the early 'Thirties began really to tell on his characterization in ONE DANGEROUS NIGHT (Columbia, 1943). The plot opens with Lanyard and Jamison stopping to assist Marguerite Chapman with a flat tire. This brings them into contact with a blackmail racket masterminded by Gerald Mohr. When Mohr is killed, Hall and Kelsey, rather than suspecting any of the many women Mohr had been blackmailing for their jewelry, pounce immediately on the Lone Wolf.

William had become so dissatisfied in the role by the time he made his ninth entry in the series, PASSPORT TO SUEZ (Columbia, 1943), that I even doubt it would have amused him had he known that Gerald Mohr was to succeed him as the Lone Wolf. John Stone, who was under contract and who had also been called in on the Boston Blackie series, wrote the screenplay and Andre de Toth directed. Notwithstanding, the picture could not be saved. Sheldon Leonard had an off-beat role as a cafe owner in Constantinople which was derivative of Humphrey Bogart's Rick in CASABLANCA (Warner's, 1942). Lanyard is working for the British government in an attempt to prevent a Nazi seizure of the Suez canal. Perhaps the effects of his terminal illness were already beginning to be felt. PASSPORT TO SUEZ was William's last Lone Wolf picture. He died in 1948, after appearances in very low-budget and even embarrassing films such as FEAR (Monogram, 1946) which was an attempt to film Dostoyevsky's CRIME AND PUNISHMENT. He suffered from multiple myeloma, a rare blood disease. Eric Blore and Thurston Hall, who had become close friends during the series, were in attendance at his funeral. William's ashes were scattered in the Long Island Sound. His wife, Helen Nelson William, who had contracted a heart ailment, did not survive him by very long.

With William's quitting Columbia at the end of his contract, a hiatus in production of the Lone Wolf films ensued. THE NOTORIOUS LONE WOLF (Columbia, 1946) sought to resurrect the series with Gerald Mohr in the leading role. Only Eric Blore's Jamison gave this new effort any life. William Davidson was cast as Crane. The dialogue was less than scintillating. Mohr observes at one point, "If you find the ice cubes fuzzy, it's because these modern rugs are constantly linting." Lanyard's absence from the screen is explained by his having been in the military service. D. Ross Lederman directed this film in a sluggish fashion. When a sapphire is stolen, Lanyard is suspected; although, true to form, he eventually identifies the guilty party.

THE LONE WOLF IN MEXICO (Columbia, 1947) was also directed by Lederman and nothing improved. The Mexican casino milieu was shot on strictly indoor sets. Lanyard becomes involved in retrieving Sheila Ryan's jewels from a casino safe, only for them to turn out to be paste. When Ryan is murdered, Lanyard, to the police if not to the audience, is the most likely suspect. THE LONE WOLF IN LONDON (Columbia, 1947) was even a worse picture with Lanyard in the British capital researching a book he is writing on famous gems. When a gem collector asks his help in disposing of his collection, matters become complicated after the most priceless jewels are stolen.

If the series was to be saved, something had to be done. Rudolph C. Flothow was called in to produce THE LONE WOLF AND HIS LADY (Columbia, 1949) with a new Michael Lanyard, Ron Randell, number nine to be exact. Alan Mowbray was cast as Jamison and William Frawley as Inspector Crane. Since Randell had played Bulldog Drummond in previous films, it was hoped he might breathe new life into the tired property; but, if such was the thinking, it was defeated by the script which called for Lanyard to be hired by a newspaper to cover the public exhibit of a famous diamond only to be the chief suspect when it is stolen. He has to elude the police while in pursuit of the real thieves.

The Lone Wolf was on the radio briefly in 1949 on the Mutual Network with Walter Coy in the title role. His television debut was delayed until 1954 with Louis Hayward, who had played the Saint twice on the screen, most recently that same year, in the role of the Lone Wolf. Sadly, the smirking and glib Hayward was no better as Michael Lanyard than he had been as Simon Templar.

THE SAINT

> The man Fritz spun round with an oath and stepped towards him, and with a feeling akin to holy joy the Saint shot him in the stomach and watched him crumple to the floor. Then he faced round. "I should keep very still, if I were you, Rudolf. . . . Otherwise you might go the same way home."
> Simon Templar[58]

Leslie Charteris was born Leslie Charles Bowyer Yin in 1907 in Singapore when it was part of the Federated Malay States and the largest seaport in the world. His mother was English and his father Chinese, a physician. According to Charteris when he was very young, he began typing out his own magazine. He wrote everything in it, articles, stories, poems, serial installments, and even a comic strip. Charteris claimed that he was not very good as an artist and rather lazy, so his cartoons consisted of stick figures. He later varied one of these to become the symbol of his chief literary creation, Simon Templar, alias the Saint. It was his parents' idea that he venture to England for his higher education. He preferred writing. When his first book, written during his freshman year at Cambridge, was accepted, he quit school and hoped to embark on a writing career. He continued to turn out adventure stories, but his earnings took some time to catch up with him. He worked at various jobs from shipping out on a freighter to a stint as a bartender at a country inn. Before his first novel was published, X ESQUIRE (1927), he had already legally changed his name to Leslie Charteris, based apparently on admiration for a certain Colonel Francis Charteris who was a bit of a romantic bounder.

Simon Templar was introduced in Charteris' third book, MEET THE TIGER (1928). In a special introduction to a re-issue of the book under the title THE SAINT MEETS THE TIGER (1980), Charteris noted that, being only twenty-one and "cleverly judging that no adult reader would accept a swashbuckling hero of my own age, I started the Saint out at 25, giving him a head start on myself which would forever haunt me."[59] The mechanics of the plot follow the structure established for adventure fiction as far back as THE ODYSSEY which requires the reader to follow one character until he finds himself in a harrowing situation only to cut away then to another character and to follow that character until he, too, finds himself in a harrowing situation whereupon the first situation again becomes the focus until it leads once more to another harrowing situation. Finally, near the end, the two characters are linked and the story concludes. At stake is a fortune in gold bars which a master criminal known only as The Tiger has looted from a Chicago bank and is now trying to smuggle out of England. Simon has reached an agreement with the bank that if he can restore the gold he will get twenty per cent of it as a commission. He is accompanied by his manservant, Orace, a former Marine who speaks in a heavy Cockney accent. It is during this adventure that Simon meets and falls in love with Patricia Holm who would become a regular in the Saint books and stories for a number of years. Patricia is as game as Simon. She joins forces with him and, when she believes he is dead, carries on by herself because "it was the sort of reckless dare-devil thing that people did in books and films, the forlorn hope that always materialized in time to provide a happy ending. She could think of no precedent for it in real life, and therefore the only thing to go by was the standard of fiction—according to which it was bound to succeed."[60] Charteris had obviously studied Edgar Wallace's technique, as well as the Bulldog Drummond books and the Raffles type. As for the identity of The Tiger, it is rather obvious to the seasoned reader and perhaps even to a novice when, in the second chapter, Algernon de Breton Lomas-Coper is introduced as "one of the genial Algys made famous by Mr. P. G. Wodehouse, and accordingly he often ejaculated 'What? What?' to show that he could hardly believe his own brilliance; but now he ejaculated 'What? What?' to show that he could hardly believe his own ears."[61]

Ward Lock was Charteris' publisher for his early books and two books not featuring the Saint followed before he switched to Hodder & Stoughton, after which all the books Charteris wrote, with two exceptions, a novel published by Heinemann's and a book titled SPANISH FOR FUN (1964), were either novels or story collections about Simon Templar. His first novel for Hodder & Stoughton was titled THE LAST HERO (1930). Taking another leaf from the Bulldog Drummond stories, the Saint was now surrounded by a number of young Englishmen who had joined cause with him to go up against organized crime in the United Kingdom and to foil it, charging ten per cent for the effort and usually leaving the criminals either dead or in the hands of the law. To accomplish these ends, this group of "Saints" would often have to resort to illegal or extra-legal means. In contrast to Phyllis in the McNeile books, Patricia was no damsel in distress, even when she might be kidnapped by the villains. "She was a law unto herself. She was of a mettle so utterly different to that of any girl he had ever dreamed of, a mettle so much finer and fiercer, that if she had not been so paradoxically feminine with it he would have sworn that she ought to have been a man."[62] A mad scientist has invented a futuristic war machine and Simon resolves that " 'the invention must cease to be . . . and the brain that conceived it, which could recreate it—that also must cease to be. It is expedient that one man should die for many people. . . . ' "[63] There is a three-way conflict. Scotland Yard, embodied in Claud Eustace Teal, wants to protect the scientist and his invention for the sake of Great Britain. Dr. Rayt Marius and Crown Prince Rudolf want the device for the interests which they represent. The Saint and his group are opposed to war and wish to destroy it and its inventor for humanitarian purposes.

Norman Kent, one of the Saint's group, loses his life in the skirmish, the "last hero" of the title. In his next book, ENTER THE SAINT (1930), Charteris included a brief Foreword in which he explained that these were earlier exploits of the Saint "which are also the stories of Archie Sheridan, Roger Conway, Dicky Tremayne, and Norman Kent, who were with him in all his misdeeds. And if it be thought that there is too little of Norman Kent in these stories, it should be remembered that in the end he did that which may yet set him above them all."[64] Even this early, however, inconsistencies were apparent. Teal is seen to know that Simon Templar is the Saint whereas he did not know it in THE LAST HERO, although set at a later time. The reader is also told that Simon has had "eight years of gay buccaneering"[65] and that the Saint in these stories, which pre-date MEET THE TIGER, "was then nearly twenty-eight."[66] The book consists of three short novels and, in truth, Charteris never did prove adept at writing fiction of novel length, being more at ease in stories of briefer duration. ENTER THE SAINT is dedicated to P. M. Haydon. Haydon was the controlling editor of the THRILLER, and it was in this pulp publication that Charteris' stories and short novels began to appear with great regularity. W. O. G. Lofts and Derek Adley in THE SAINT AND LESLIE CHARTERIS (1970) pointed out that Monty Haydon gave Charteris "help on practically every story he wrote for the THRILLER, and if Leslie was ever at a loss for an idea, Monty could always toss out something stimulating. If Leslie got 'stuck' as he went along, Monty could usually suggest a way out of the impasse. They regularly kicked ideas around together over innumerable three-hour lunches, usually at the Press Club. Over the years the association developed into a close personal friendship. . . . "[67]

The format Charteris adopted for the THRILLER was that of the short novel and, as the years passed, he would collect three of these short novels and publish them in book form at the rate of two or three a year. Charteris was certainly no notable stylist and the prose in which he couched the Saint's adventures is pompous at times, self-conscious, occasionally conceited, and almost always jejune. Where he was often extraordinary, and what may account for the popularity of the stories, was in his ability to devise plots and counter-plots, schemes for the villains and stratagems by which the Saint could foil them. Pacing is not to be found in the rather cumbrous prose, but rather in the sudden twists in narrative structure, sudden confrontations, surprises, revelations.

In 1932, Charteris left London and came to the United States. He found the markets for fiction more lucrative than they had been in England, although he seems not really to have broken into any major American magazines. What he ended up doing was going to work in the story department at Paramount Pictures where he contributed to a number of screenplays and presumably provided the original screenplay for MIDNIGHT CLUB (Paramount, 1933) which starred George Raft as a detective out to get Clive Brook. He did manage to establish a relationship with Doubleday as his American publisher and THE SAINT IN NEW YORK (1935) ran first as a serial in the AMERICAN MAGAZINE before it was issued as a book or appeared as a magazine serial in the THRILLER. Eighteen months after his departure, Charteris was again in the United Kingdom. THE MISFORTUNES OF MR. TEAL (1934) consists of three short novels, the first of which is "The Simon Templar Foundation," one of the better adventures of the Saint and one which would seem to embody Charteris' perspectives on society and war in rather a comprehensive fashion. Simon has succeeded in putting Rayt Marius out of the way, but what he has inherited from the man who was one of the conspirators in THE LAST HERO is a book identifying a number of men eminent and powerful in the British government and British industry who made fortunes illegally during the war. He organizes the Simon Templar Foundation which is to be capitalized at a million pounds contributed in five equal shares by the five men who figure most prominently in Marius' book. "The Foundation," as Simon explains in his letter to the contributors, "will be devoted to the care and comfort of men maimed and crippled in war, to helping the wives and children of men killed in war, and to the endowment of any cause which has a chance of doing something to promote peace in the future."[68] This was a bold step and a new kind of criminal for the Saint to tackle. It is pointed out that Simon "knew how utterly false to human psychology were the ranting villains who committed the murders in fiction and films. Murder was so rarely done like that. It was done by heavy, grandiose, flabby, frightened men—like Lord Iveldown or the Honourable Leo Farwill or Mr. Neville Yorkland, M. P."[69] The Honourable Leo Farwill is in fact the Home Secretary for the United Kingdom. In the early novels the Saint has eschewed firearms in favor of knives which he kept concealed on his person. As he prospered—he is thirty-two in these stories—he was more and more willing to use a gun to solve the problem of human obstacles in his path. Indeed, in the third story in this collection, "The Art of Alibi," Chief Inspector Teal observed, " 'I know that all the men you've robbed and . . . ' the somnolent eyes steadied themselves deliberately for a moment—'and killed,' he said, 'they've deserved it—in a way. But I also know that, technically, you're the most dangerous and persistent criminal outside of prison.' "[70] Surely one of the sources of the popularity of the Saint stories was precisely this alienation from the established social order, rife with political corruption. The police are not themselves corrupt in Charteris' books, only ineffectual.

In 1936 Charteris founded The Saint Club. Subscriptions and donations, after deduction of minimal running expenses, were turned over to the Invalid and Crippled Children's Hospital in the East End of London where, for several years, an eight-bed "Saint Ward" was maintained. After the Second World War when British hospitals were nationalized, this support was transferred to the Arbour Youth Centre in Stepney and, even throughout the 1980s, this activity was still ongoing. Charteris himself wrote up the rules and members were provided with a membership card on the back of which was a notice to the police that "the bearer of this card is probably a person of hideous antecedents and low moral character, and upon apprehension for any cause, should be immediately released in order to save other prisoners from contamination."[71]

The humanitarianism of this organization as well as the antiwar sentiments of much of his fiction were one side of Charteris' muse. There was another side. In GETAWAY (1932), Simon was in Germany with Patricia Holm and Monty Hayward, the character in the early stories based on Monty Haydon. Aboard a passenger train, Simon's "roving eye" surveys the passengers, "excrescences upon the cosmos roosted at regular intervals in their upholstered pens, each tending his own little candle of witness to God's patronage of the almost human race. Simon looked at them all, and felt his share of the milk of human kindness curdling under the strain."[72] It is in this novel that Crown Prince Rudolf is finally dispatched.

RKO Radio Pictures purchased screen rights to THE SAINT IN NEW YORK and put William Sistrom, who had been born at Lincolnshire, England in 1886, in charge of the production. To play Inspector Fernack, Simon Templar's foil on the New York Police Department, Jonathan Hale was cast, while Louis Hayward was selected to portray the Saint. Hayward, born at Johannesburg, South Africa in 1909, was a slight man, five feet ten, dark brown hair, blue eyes, and to agent and producer Edward Small at least the embodiment of Louis XIV and the Count of Monte Cristo. Having first begun in the British film industry, Hayward had come to Hollywood to play foppish lovers at Warner Bros. before he was cast as the Saint and went on to star in Small's historical melodramas. The screenplay by Charles Kaufman and Mortimer Offner followed the novel somewhat closely. New York is laid low by a crime wave. Right thinking citizens and the police despair of the judicial system and the Crime Commission, of its own accord, decides to call in the Saint. It knows his reputation and, if judges will not serve the cause of justice, perhaps the Saint will. Simon is charged with bringing six gangsters to justice or, barring that, eliminating them. Kay Sutton provided the love interest. Patricia Holm had been left behind in London when the Saint in the novel set out for New York and from that point on she played an increasingly minor role until she vanished from the stories altogether. However, Charteris did not forget about her completely; he named his only daughter after her. The film's dialogue was good and the pacing was swift. The Saint, disguised as a nun, shoots a gangster in one scene just as he is about to plug a policeman. These individual episodes of mayhem are linked together by a search for the Big Fellow. As is always the case in films of this ilk, the hero dispatches all the underlings until at last he is confronted with the Big Fellow himself who, almost as inevitably, turns out to be the most upstanding character in the story, in this case the man who first hired the Saint.

THE SAINT IN NEW YORK (RKO, 1938) proved a success and the studio decided to begin a series. Since Louis Hayward had gone on to starring vehicles, George Sanders, on loan-out from Twentieth Century-Fox, was cast in the role. Doubtless, one inducement for him to play the part was the hope that it would do for his career what it had done for Hayward's. Sanders was born in 1906 in St. Petersburg, Russia. His parents were of Scottish descent. When the Russian Revolution broke out, the family fled across the icy wastes of Finland, finally settling in England. George thought little of English schools and his masters, apparently, thought even less of him for he later recalled that he left school with the conviction that he was too stupid to cope with life. He tried working in a textile factory only to emigrate to Argentina where he found employment with a cigarette manufacturing company. He worked in market research and enjoyed the position. However, he was chucked out after a time, only to find similar employment with a tobacco company in Chile. This job terminated when he found himself jailed for fighting a duel with the fiancé of the woman with whom he was sleeping. He finally was able to return to England where he found work at an advertising agency in which Greer Garson was the head of the market research department. She encouraged him to join an amateur theatrical group. He appeared in a number of plays before being signed by British and Dominion Studios. From there he went to Hollywood where Twentieth Century-Fox cast him in a character role in LLOYDS OF LONDON (20th-Fox, 1936).

THE SAINT STRIKES BACK (RKO, 1939), in addition to Sanders in the lead, cast Wendy Barrie, herself later an intimate of mobster Benny Siegel, as a gang leader. Based on Charteris' SHE WAS A LADY (1931) set in London, the screenplay changed the location to San Francisco. Robert Sisk replaced Sistrom as the producer and John Farrow succeeded Ben Holmes who had directed the first film. Inspector Fernack is being sent from New York to San Francisco to protect that community from the Saint. Simon joins him in New York and they make the trip together. The Saint is searching for a master criminal named Waldman and, in the process, proves that Wendy Barrie's deceased father, a policeman, had actually been framed.

George Sanders had next to go to England to make a picture and RKO thought the situation presented a ready opportunity to make another Saint film, this time on location. William Sistrom returned to produce THE SAINT IN LONDON (RKO, 1939) directed by John Paddy Carstairs. Lynn Root and Frank Fenton, a writing team which had recently joined RKO and whom Charteris himself would parody in THE SAINT GOES WEST (1942), prepared the screenplay based on the short novel, "The Million Pound Day," contained in THE HOLY TERROR (1932). Simon, back in London after having cleaned up New York, declares open war on Bruno Lang, an underworld lord. Gordon McLeod was cast as Inspector Teal, eternally suspicious of the Saint. Sally Gray played Penny Parker, the female accompanying the Saint on his exploits, and David Burns was Dugan, an American pickpocket who is the Saint's sidekick. The film probably represents Sanders' best performance in the role.

Yet, whatever the public enthusiasm or the positive critical response, Charteris did not like THE SAINT IN LONDON. He felt Sanders at six foot three was better cast physically than Louis Hayward, but that was where his approval stopped and his grousing began. Charteris would have preferred Cary Grant or Ronald Colman. Unfortunately those actors were not under contract to RKO and it is doubtful if either would have accepted the role even if it had been offered to him. Jack Hively who was assigned to direct the next entry in the series, THE SAINT'S DOUBLE TROUBLE (RKO, 1940), once suggested to me that Charteris' constant complaining about the casting of the role may have concealed a frustrated desire to play the part himself. Certainly Charteris closely identified with his character and even went so far upon occasion as to declare that he might be considered an inferior brother to the Saint. Hively dismissed Charteris as an eccentric.

"My objections to what RKO 'did with' the Saint," Charteris insisted to me, "did not arise from a frustrated desire to star in the part myself. Much as I should have enjoyed this, a glance in the mirror was quite enough to show me that it just wasn't in the cards. However, this did not make me any happier about what I considered the gross miscasting. I hardly think that this concern for good casting makes me 'eccentric.' If the adjective is meant to refer to any other of my idiosyncracies, it rather surprises me. I have always thought that I was regarded, personally, as rather a square. Even more than casting, I objected to RKO's treatment of character and story lines. Here, of course, I was fighting the well-known producer syndrome which automatically makes any film executive a genius who knows how much better a character could be portrayed and a plot developed than the stupid original creator. THE SAINT OVERBOARD [1936] was an incidental case in point. It was one of the books which RKO bought, but by the time the studio wizards had got through with it, there was absolutely nothing left of the original except the title, and that was by then totally irrelevant. I therefore prevailed on them to give me back the title, and thus preserved my property intact for possible future use."

It is a commonplace that what works in one medium may not in another. Charteris had his own ideas about his character, granted, but they were not necessarily commercially viable. RKO was making what the studio considered a successful product and the capable personnel they had working on the films did not particularly appreciate Charteris' outspoken and volatile interference. THE SAINT'S DOUBLE TROUBLE had George Sanders cast in a dual role, as the Saint and as Duke Plato, a gangster. On Charteris' behalf, it must be admitted that it was a bit difficult for a viewer to distinguish between Sanders' two portrayals since he was obviously bored with both characters. The picture opened with what was now identified as "the Saint's tune" being whistled over the credits and showing the stick drawing monogram. The plot begins in Cairo with Bela Lugosi cast as a jewel thief shipping a mummy to a professor in Philadelphia. Inspector Fernack, played by Jonathan Hale, happens to be visiting the professor when, presently, Simon Templar shows up. A couple of murders are committed by the Saint's double who leaves behind Simon's calling card. The look-alike aspect did produce some rather amusing routines only, in the end, for Simon to trick his alter-ego into getting shot. With this picture, Cliff Reid who had produced such films as THE LOST PATROL (RKO, 1934) and THE INFORMER (RKO, 1935), both directed by John Ford, and Howard Hawks' BRINGING UP BABY (RKO, 1938) took over as the producer. The studio obviously regarded the series as important. None of this fazed Charteris. He reviled RKO for what he felt to be George Sanders' sneering attitude and the lack of dependence on a literal translation of his character and plots to the screen. In a placating move, RKO replaced Reid with Lee Marcus who had formerly been in distribution and was a past president of the RKO subsidiary, Pathé Pictures. Marcus made the concession to Charteris that he could tinker with the screenplay for the next entry, THE SAINT TAKES OVER (RKO, 1940), which was written by Frank Fenton and Lynn Root. He was even credited on the publicity with having made script revisions.

Yet, despite all of this, the plot was not extensively different. Wendy Barrie was back, this time as the murderer. Paul Guilfoyle was cast as Purley Gates, the Saint's sidekick, and Jack Hively directed. When Jonathan Hale as Inspector Fernack is to be kicked off the force due to scheming by organized crime, the Saint sets out to help his ambivalent friend. One after another the members of the underworld conspiracy are killed off; and, although Barrie confesses, it is not enough to save her. One curious alteration is the Saint's insistence all through the picture that whatever he does must be done by legally acceptable means.

On 27 October 1940, George Sanders married for the first time, to Elsie M. Poole who worked in pictures under the professional name of Susan Larson. Even then George was a somewhat contemplative and retiring man who liked to spend his time reading and sleeping. He insisted that the only thing he was good at was a life of idleness. When, years later, he came to write his autobiography, MEMOIRS OF A PROFESSIONAL CAD (1960), he produced a book which had a fascinating beginning only to drop off as if, after the first few chapters, he had become bored even with retelling the story of his life. He did manage, however, to quote enough arcane literature to indicate rather far-flung reading.

THE SAINT IN PALM SPRINGS (RKO, 1941) directed by Jack Hively and produced by Howard Benedict was George Sanders' last appearance as the Saint. Jerry Cady, who had collaborated at Twentieth Century-Fox on such detective films as MR. MOTO'S GAMBLE (20th-Fox, 1938), wrote the screenplay based on a story outline provided personally by Charteris. Jonathan Hale as Fernack asks the Saint to protect a friend of his who is going to Palm

Springs with postage stamps worth $200,000 on his person. When this man is shot, Simon holds onto the postage stamps and intends to turn them over to the man's niece, played predictably by Wendy Barrie, now as much a cast regular as Paul Guilfoyle as Purley. Wendy's part builds all through the second half of the picture as does the emphasis on the Saint's roving eye for feminine pulchritude. By the end of the film, the Saint has both exposed the murderer and saved the stamps with a minimum of location shooting.

RKO made the decision to have George Sanders star in a new detective series, playing a character called The Falcon. In the meantime, the Saint films would continue to be produced in the United Kingdom, financed with frozen funds. Hugh Sinclair was cast in the role of the Saint and the other players were British actors. Two such films were made, the first of which was THE SAINT'S VACATION (RKO, 1941) based on THE SAINT'S GETAWAY with Charteris credited along with Jeffrey Dell for the screenplay. William Sistrom, who had begun with the series, was the producer on both of these entries. Arthur MacRae was cast as Monty Hayward and his portrayal was almost a parody of Louis Hayward's acting style. Sally Gray follows Simon and Monty on vacation and they see a man murdered. All the excitement is over a music box in which are hidden plans for a coveted sound detector. The same train that Alfred Hitchcock used for THE LADY VANISHES (Gaumont, 1938) is used and Cecil Parker, who played a stuffy coward in Hitchcock's earlier thriller, was cast as the master villain in THE SAINT'S VACATION. Hugh Sinclair was no George Sanders; in fact, he was not even fair in the role of the Saint. Audiences knew it and the picture died. Charteris, of course, had been saying all along that Cary Grant ought to be cast in the lead.

There was also an epilogue of sorts. Hugh Sinclair made a second Saint film for RKO in 1941 based on Charteris' first novel, THE SAINT MEETS THE TIGER (Republic, 1943). Release was delayed due to yet another squabble with Charteris, about which more will be said presently.

The Saint was off the screen for some years. Charteris was hired to write scripts for the Sherlock Holmes radio series starring Basil Rathbone. In 1944, the Saint began himself to appear in a regular radio series and over the next five years he was variously portrayed by Edgar Barrier, Brian Aherne, Barry Sullivan, Vincent Price, and Tom Conway. On 27 July 1946 Charteris became an American citizen. During the 'Forties he turned out few books and stories. For one thing, there was the Saint radio program; and, for another, there was the Saint syndicated comic strip for which Charteris wrote the continuity. He would winter in California and during the summer he would travel about the United States with a trailer of his own design.

There was a comic strip quality in the Saint stories already in the late 'Thirties. In the short novel, "The Higher Finance," in THE MISFORTUNES OF MR. TEAL, Simon Templar, after disposing of the evil Ivar Nordsten, arranges for his brother to step into his persona and carry on Ivar's life. In the short story, "The Man Who Liked Ants," included in THE HAPPY HIGHWAY-

MAN (1939), false Ivar returns. Simon, while visiting with him, encounters a mad scientist who is breeding giant ants with the ambition of loosing the ants on the world, to kill or enslave the human race. This story is no allegory for the rise of fascism, although there may some day be an enterprising critic who will try to project such a fantasy into it. Basically, it is a mixture of science fantasy and adventure story. At the end, after Simon has wiped out the scientist and a very pregnant giant queen ant, Nordsten comments that he thought the Saint disliked the human race. " 'Taken in the mass,' " Simon responds, " 'it will probably go on nauseating me. But it isn't my job to alter it. If Sardon was right, Nature will find her own remedy. But the world has millions of years left, and I think evolution can afford to wait.' "[73] Actually, there was this kind of blending of science fantasy as early as THE LAST HERO. The transition from this type of fiction to a comic strip must have been relatively easy.

The only significant change that did occur in the Saint books that were published in the 'Forties is that he most often appeared in the guise not of a thief and bounder but as a detective. In THE SAINT GOES WEST, there are two short novels in both of which Simon functions as a detective. In the first, titled "Palm Springs," Simon is hired by Freddie Pellman to get to the bottom of who is behind a series of attempts on his life. Obviously, Charteris was well aware of the conventions set up by S. S. Van Dine and others since he remarks in the text that "the mysterious murderer just doesn't turn out to be the cook or the butler any more. That was worked to death twenty years ago. So of course no cook or butler in real life would ever dream of murdering anyone any more, because they'd know it was just too corny."[74] In the second story, "Hollywood," Charteris provided his view of the motion picture industry. Simon is hired to star in a film about his life only for the producer who hired him to be murdered. Simon arrives at the correct solution before the police do, but as in "Palm Springs" it is not the truth which comes out. " 'I like to see puzzles worked out to the right solution,' " he tells the murderer. " 'I don't mean the correct solution. That's dull pedantic stuff. I mean the right one. Which means the right one for all concerned, as well as I can see it. Don't try to put too many haloes on me.' "[75] Such an ending to a detective story is more in keeping with the hard-boiled American tradition than with the classical English detective story plot. The explanation given to the public is one which seems to fit the facts, although it is not the real explanation; the real explanation is something to be concealed and the truth something to be manipulated according to the whim of the private detective. If the Saint feels that the person murdered deserved to die, his murderer is to be protected. This, for him, is the "right" solution. It is an interesting contrast to the image of the Saint projected in the films where, as has been mentioned, pains were taken to show that all that the Saint might do was done within the law.

The movies were not prepared to deal with this image in the early films, nor did the situation change greatly when the Saint returned to the screen in THE

SAINT'S GIRL FRIDAY (RKO, 1954). This film was made by Royal Productions in London and was produced by Julian Lesser, son of Sol Lesser, a low-budget producer of Poverty Row Hollywood films in the 'Thirties. Charteris had a financial interest in the picture as well as apparently no objection this time around to Louis Hayward again appearing in the title role. When a wealthy lady, a friend of an older, wearier Simon Templar, dies in an auto crash, the Saint investigates only to uncover an illegal gambling casino on a river barge and a gang of criminals behind the death.

Two French efforts were made to film the Saint's adventures, LE SAINT MENE LA DANCE (Films du Cyclope, 1961) with Felix Marten in the role and LE SAINT PREND L'AFFUT (SNC/Intermonida, 1966). Charteris thought so little of the first film that he refused to allow it to be released in any English-speaking country. In the case of the later film, which featured Jean Marais in the role, Charteris was so outraged that he refused the producers a license to make any more Saint films. He was happiest, it would appear, with the British television series which began in 1962 and continued for six years with Roger Moore in the role of the Saint. Even here, he had not really changed. When the producers altered the locations of his stories, or plot elements to bring a story up to date, he balked, complained, and took his right of script approval quite seriously. What finished the series, which was also seen in the United States, was Roger Moore's resolve not to appear in any more episodes. "I really mean it," Moore said at the time. "I am becoming lazy in my work because I have a set character. I have been playing the Saint non-stop for six years and have made 120 complete stories, and now I need a change of face." [76]

One by-product of the Saint television series was that Charteris began to use some of what he considered the better stories as the basis for fictionalization and had these published as further adventures of the Saint. As early as 1953, THE SAINT MYSTERY MAGAZINE began to appear and in its pages he recycled all of the Saint short stories and some of the short novels he had written previously. Charteris' original contribution to each issue was a brief editorial column. Publication was suspended in 1967. In fiction that Charteris himself wrote, the Saint returned to fleecing swindlers rather than acting as a detective. When Charteris was working on the Sherlock Holmes radio broadcasts, his job was to come up with plots which were then dramatized; and it was no different when he was contributing plots to the SECRET AGENT X-9 comic strip in the years 1934–1936—originally the creation of Dashiell Hammett—and his own Saint comic strip which ran for almost a decade. He was always able to devise interesting plots. When and where he did err was occasionally on the side of probability. In the short novel, "The Unsaintly Santa," contained in COUNT ON THE SAINT (1980), the reader is expected to believe that the bursar of one of the colleges in Cambridge University would dress up in a monk's cowl, the equivalent of the British Santa Claus, and kill off financial backers in a matter of a few days in order not to be exposed for embezzlement. In a sense, it was a return to the days when the Saint functioned as a detective; but it is also a story with only a pallid reflection of the Saint as he had once been, without any of his flamboyance or derring-do. Simon Templar could not age after the 1930s and he did not. Yet, one cannot escape the feeling, when reading a book such as COUNT ON THE SAINT—the first short novel, "The Pastor's Problem," is more traditional fare—that the Saint is something of an anachronism. He belongs to an earlier time when crime was less sophisticated than it has become; and, of course, there never was an awareness of external political events in the stories, an omission which fostered the pleasant unreality of pure escapism, only later to make them somehow seem adolescent and irrelevant.

Julian Symons wrote that the Saint "might be called an unsadistic Bulldog Drummond with the looks of a prewar matinee idol. The stories about him occasionally have a pleasant double twist of ingenuity, as in THE SAINT IN NEW YORK, in which he disposes of a number of the city's nastier gangsters only to find that he has been doing so with the help of the biggest gangster of all. They are too often written with the sort of rodomontade that makes Charteris say that somebody has 'a weakness for the stuff that maketh glad the heart of man' when he means that he is slightly tight. For those, however, who can endure the Saint's total invincibility and self-satisfaction, his adventures are lively and marked by some touches of humor."[77] Whatever has been the Saint's appeal to the popular imagination, it is probable that readers saw him otherwise than in the droll, sophisticated, but bored image consistently projected by George Sanders.

THE FALCON

The sophisticated adventurer . . . was the only American series detective to die on the screen—in order to advance the career of George Sanders, who felt limited by the continuing role of the debonair semiscoundrel.
ENCYCLOPEDIA OF MYSTERY AND DETECTION[78]

It was so cool in the courtyard that, glancing for a moment at the swimming pool, I almost forgot that I was in Palm Springs. Maurice Geraghty had admitted me through the wrought-iron gate and led me past several doors of the sloping house. He told me that he preferred to divide his time between living in England and living here in the desert. As we entered the living room, he showed me a painting done by his sister, the late Carmelita Geraghty, who had been a leading lady in early sound Westerns. Over glasses of sassafras, we got down to business. With the exception of John Houseman who filed each year's correspondence and memoranda in letter boxes placed in chronological order on the walls of his study and who had obviously planned writing in advance of his series of autobiographical accounts, Geraghty was the most well organized person in the film industry with whom I have spoken.

"You know, your records are extraordinary," I said, indicating the budget sheets with which he had supplied me on every Falcon picture he had produced. "Howard Benedict started the series, didn't he?"

"He did," Geraghty agreed. "He produced the first three, before he went over to Universal to work on their Sherlock Holmes series."

In view of the many problems the studio was having with Leslie Charteris, it developed a new formula for a detective series. George Sanders, of course, would continue to star. The new detective was based on a character from a short story by Michael Arlen titled "Gay Falcon." Arlen was born at Rustchuk, Bulgaria, in 1895 and christened Dikran Kuyumjian. His parents were Armenian. As a boy he went to England and in 1922 he became a naturalized British subject. He was educated at Malvern College and, in 1928, he married the Countess Atalanta Mercanti. Until the outbreak of the Second World War, the couple lived at Cannes. Arlen made his splash in the literary world writing a novel in English called THE GREEN HAT (1924). It earned him better than a half million in royalties. Yet, try as he might, he could not duplicate this success. The explanation rests perhaps in the fact that Arlen concerned himself with a social order that was obsolete even as he wrote about it. Intimates described him as alert, vain, friendly, a man who relished his acclaim and pursued unabashedly the acquisition of wealth. Apparently his superficial sophistication concealed an incredible naiveté. Arlen was not very ambitious. He worked briefly in Hollywood as a screen writer once the war had begun in Europe and produced exactly nothing. But then, why should he have? His pseudo-hard-boiled short story was sold to RKO for $5,490. The picture, THE GAY FALCON (RKO, 1941), for which the leading character's name was changed from Gay Stanhope Falcon to Gay Laurence, proved a success upon release and generated a series from which Arlen collected royalties. Arlen had commented, following a brief stint at M-G-M, that he was too indolent for screenwriting, too much of a loller, and more than a bit of his personality crept into Gay Laurence's screen characterization. However, despite this quality of lackadaisicalness, as far as Charteris was concerned George Sanders did not attempt to project an image sufficiently different from when he had been playing the Saint.

"RKO's switch to the Falcon was not, in my opinion, due to my discontent," Charteris told me, "which I credit them with a completely pachydermatous ability to have survived. Simply and practically, RKO discovered that by attributing their formula to the Michael Arlen character, they were able to save a huge percentage of the price they were paying me. Indeed, their promotion of the Falcon was so shamelessly liable as to allow many dull-witted audiences to think they were still getting the Saint. I brought a suit against them for 'unfair competition.' "

RKO had agreed to film the Hugh Sinclair Saint films in England as a means of placating Charteris. The strategy obviously did not work. THE SAINT MEETS THE TIGER had been produced but had not yet been released when this latest flare-up with Charteris occurred. It is a very dull and slow picture with substantial changes in the plot from the way Charteris had written it. The Tiger in the film is a mystery man disguising himself as a photo journalist. The object of his scheming is to steal a million pounds from a London bank. Paul Stein directed. Disgusted by the law suit, RKO decided to sell the film to Republic rather than distribute it and to settle with Charteris out of court. It was such a smart deal that RKO received enough not only to recoup its investment in the picture but even enough to pay off Charteris. Eventually, however, distribution rights did revert to RKO.

THE GAY FALCON actually preceded THE SAINT MEETS THE TIGER into production. Preproduction began in March, 1941 and shooting commenced in June, 1941, lasting into July. THE SAINT MEETS THE TIGER began in production at RKO-British studios in late June, 1941. The studio was relieved to be rid of Charteris, but probably no more so than he was to be quits of RKO. The working title for THE GAY FALCON—possibly as a result of attempting to keep the whole business a secret—had been MEET THE VIKING!

In all fairness to RKO, the studio evidently felt what it had to sell the public was George Sanders and not the Saint. The closer the films had come to Charteris' character as presented in his Saint stories, the less popular the films had proved. Gay Laurence in THE GAY FALCON is a rich playboy engaged to Anne Hunter who insists that, if he is to marry her, he must give up his interest in crime and other women. Neither is easy, especially since Wendy Barrie was back as the girl in distress who inveigles the Falcon to help her. Adept casting made Allen Jenkins the Falcon's assistant and he played very well opposite Sanders, particularly when it is remembered how miscast he had been in the Paul Drake role in the Perry Mason films. His advice to Barrie, when she first approaches the Falcon, is to "try Ellery Queen." Barrie persists and the Falcon ends up exposing a high class ring of jewel thieves. Arthur Shields was cast as the police captain with Ed Brophy and Eddie Dunn teaming up as a dumb duo assigned to keep tabs on the Falcon. Irving Reis directed the film and the studio executives liked it. A DATE WITH THE FALCON (RKO, 1942) went into production in late August, 1941.

Lynn Root and Frank Fenton did the screenplay for this second film in the series. They had worked together in the story department at Twentieth Century-Fox and they had done the screenplay for WHILE NEW YORK SLEEPS (20th-Fox, 1939) in which Cliff Clark and Edward Gargan, elder brother of William Gargan, were cast as a dumb cop duo. This notion surfaced again in A DATE WITH THE FALCON, no doubt because Root and Fenton had brought the idea along with them when they switched studios, with James Gleason as Captain Mike O'Hara and Edward Gargan as his rather stupid assistant. Here is some typical dialogue. Bates is sent by O'Hara to pick up Waldo Sampson, a noted scientist working on a formula to manufacture synthetic diamonds inexpensively. Bates finds Sampson gone and calls O'Hara.

BATES: This is Bates, Chief. Sampson ain't here. —How do I know where he went? Well, after making a thorough examination, I deduced the following facts. First, he must have forgotten the combination to his safe. —What do you mean, how do I know? A guy don't blow his safe open if he remembers the numbers.

O'HARA: That's great!

BATES: He must have forgotten where he put something 'cause he wrecked the place trying to find it before he left. But I come right over and he ain't here. Yuh got nothing to worry about, Chief. I'll get right on his trail.

O'HARA: (yelling) And when it runs out, meet me in front of the employment office on Sixth Avenue.

Under the circumstances, O'Hara is forced to involve his friend, the Falcon. Sanders in the role was, if anything, even more sardonic than when he was playing the Saint. At one point he is kidnapped by the gang of thugs after the diamond formula. When the car is stopped at an intersection, Sanders sticks out his tongue at two patrolmen in a police car. They make an issue of it. Sanders pretends he is drunk and slaps one of the officers. That does it. He is arrested and in this way eludes his captors. Sanders especially enjoyed scenes such as this because they permitted him to respond naturally.

THE FALCON TAKES OVER (RKO, 1942) was the third entry. Wendy Barrie, who had been in the first two pictures, was dropped and was replaced by Lynn Bari. Arlen was paid $2,250 for the use of his character and Root and Fenton received $7,000 for their screenplay based on Raymond Chandler's novel, FAREWELL, MY LOVELY (1940). This was the final Falcon film produced by Howard Benedict and Irving Reis directed it as he had the previous entries. Chandler's dark, misogynistic plot could not really be translated to the screen as a crime comedy, although Sanders did have his moments. After he finishes questioning the alcoholic widow of a deceased tavern keeper, she throws a whiskey bottle at him and it smashes against the door. Sanders sticks his head around the corner and comments, "Tch, tch, now you won't get your deposit back." The interaction between Allen Jenkins as Goldy with Ward Bond as Moose Malloy and the antics of Gleason and Gargan reduced the proceedings to farce.

Sanders had a split contract with Twentieth Century-Fox and RKO Radio Pictures. He felt he was being typecast in the Falcon films and did not want to make any more. Opportunities which came his way, such as playing Charles Strickland in David L. Loew's adaptation of W. Somerset Maugham's THE MOON AND SIXPENCE (United Artists, 1942), reaffirmed his conviction.

"RKO was very anxious to have Sanders continue in the Falcon series," Geraghty explained. "But their pleading fell on deaf ears. Then one of the bright front-office executives got the idea of offering to co-star Geroge's brother, Tom Conway, just to get another picture out of George. They gave George a glowing picture of how it would make a star of his brother, but, actually, they had no such intentions. They just wanted another picture from George. So it was astonishing to them when Tom Conway caught on right away and carried the series on, even outgrossing the pictures George had made."

Sanders had long ago wearied of supporting his family. He had been instrumental in securing Tom a job as a contract player at RKO. Although Tom also had been born in St. Petersburg, and had gone to Brighton with George, in fact had once got them both expelled from a school for holding a loaded gun on a master, he was more withdrawn than George, more saturnine, with a quiet suavity nourished by heavy drinking. George had seen to it that Tom changed his last name from Sanders to Conway before he was signed at RKO. Tom had begun acting in 1933 in Manchester, slightly before George had, and was signed first by M-G-M when Sanders had refused to attend a luncheon with Louis B. Mayer. Why not let Tom have the role of the Falcon now that he had tired of it?

THE FALCON'S BROTHER (RKO, 1942) cost only $114,965.73 compared to $140,315.70 for THE FALCON TAKES OVER and it was filmed in fourteen days compared to twenty for the earlier film. The reason for this was that Maurice Geraghty had been promoted to produce the series. He had been born at Rushville, Indiana on 29 September 1908, two years after his brother Gerald. The brothers attended Princeton. Gerald early began contributing fiction to pulp magazines and he ended up coming to Hollywood and going to work for Mascot Pictures. The company housed its staff in offices located above a cement factory just across Santa Monica Boulevard from the Hollywood Cemetery. Maurice soon joined Gerald at Mascot. The first picture the two collaborated on was the feature version of the twelve chapter serial THE PHANTOM EMPIRE (Mascot, 1935) which was released as RADIO RANCH. They stayed on when Mascot was merged into Republic Pictures, working on numerous "B" Westerns with Gene Autry and the Three Mesquiteers. Both also worked for Harry Sherman on the screenplays for the Hopalong Cassidy series released by Paramount. Maurice signed with M-G-M for a short stint in the writing department before joining RKO.

Production on THE FALCON'S BROTHER began on 25 June 1942. Earl Fenton, Frank's brother, was paid $1,400, working until 1 June. Frank Fenton and Lynn Root each got $500 working to completion. Craig Rice got $875, working until 6 June, and Stuart Palmer was paid $1,750, working until 13 June. Craig Rice and Stuart Palmer received screen credit.

"The picture was made in the days when the studios had total control of screen credits," Geraghty told me, "and arbitrarily decided who got credit. Thus, for example, when I started writing screenplays I was left off of credit and naturally objected. I was told it was not studio policy to give credit to a writer on his first few screenplays. After I had written a few more, they said I would get credit. The Writers Guild now determines credits which is more fair, but not entirely. I inherited Root and Fenton who had written all the previous scripts before I was hired. It seems that someone had promised them they would be the producers of the Falcon series after Benedict left. I came in with no knowledge of this and found there was a certain lack of communication between Root and Fenton and myself. I thought they had done a fine job on the series and wanted them, but couldn't get anywhere. So they left and I got other writers. Their charges on the budget do not necessarily reflect what they were paid on THE FALCON'S BROTHER. Craig Rice and Stuart Palmer were both top mystery-detective writers. The accountants juggled around the charges since Palmer and Rice were writing on other scripts, and their charges were no doubt all plunked into THE FALCON'S BROTHER because the studio expected the series to fold."

George Sanders was paid $14,000 for his last entry. Tom Conway got only his contract salary.

"What were they like?" I asked.

"Oh," Geraghty responded, "George had personality. He was extravagant. He loved parties on yachts. He had a certain giggle."

"George once said he sold his yacht because he preferred being a guest to being a host."

"That was George," Geraghty agreed. "Tom was different. He was one-dimensional, but full of overtones and undertones. He was self-conscious, shy. But when the series became more and more popular, it went to his head. He thought *he* was the series and the only reason for its success."

The spelling of the Falcon's surname was changed for the picture. Consistent with the war themes of the time, both Gay and Tom Lawrence are battling Nazi spies who use magazine covers to relay messages. The plot is to assassinate Dr. DeSola. Cliff Clark replaced James Gleason opposite Edward Gargan, so now the dumb duo from WHILE NEW YORK SLEEPS was together again. In a gallant act, Gay sacrifices his life, taking a bullet intended for DeSola. Tom swears to carry on his memory. Throughout the film, Sanders is humdrum. He has none of the wit and amusement he had had earlier. It probably was not deliberate, but it did tend to accentuate Tom Conway's performance.

Edward Dmytryk was signed to direct the next entry, Tom Conway's first starring vehicle, THE FALCON STRIKES BACK (RKO, 1943). Dmytryk and Maurice Geraghty had gone to Hollywood High together and had both been on the football team, Geraghty right end, Dmytryk left end. I once asked Dmytryk about George Sanders.

"He was a lot like Warren William," Dmytryk reflected. "You know, a do-it-yourselfer. He built a telescope. He loved math. We would exchange difficult math problems when we were both at RKO, but he was a very unhappy man, very insecure. Like Warren William, too, George began early in his career to make poor pictures. He was always being forced to make pictures he didn't want to make. A man has to adjust to this sort of thing, and it isn't easy. Men become so vain, worried about how they look. Women actually dominate them because they are so worried about getting old and not being attractive to them.

Sanders was like a rebelling teenager. You have to understand actors. They need a lot of encouragement. I always try to build up their confidence. I take time to try and figure them out. George would be rude one day and the next day he would apologize. But he would compound his problem, because he would become even more rude when he was apologizing."

"Tom Conway wasn't at all like that?" I interjected.

"No, he wasn't. He took a nice walk through a picture. He couldn't really give anything to a part."

"Was it because you had used Harriet Hilliard before that you cast her in the Falcon picture?"

"Yes. But I must tell you that for some reason I simply don't remember much about that particular picture."

I mentioned this circumstance to Maurice Geraghty as we talked.

"Eddie was one of the finest directors who ever worked in pictures. I didn't know then anything about his being a Marxist, and, if I had, I wouldn't have cared."

I nodded. But I remember Eddie with his melancholy eyes and lined, solemn face sitting across from me, his expression unfathomable.

"People used to come to Hollywood with such enthusiasm," Dmytryk said. "Some became rich and famous, only to find themselves not any the happier for it."

"And you?"

"I was an idealist. When you're young, you think you're doing something so important. You think you can change everything. You really believe in what you're doing."

"You believed enough in what you thought to go to prison for it."

Eddie gazed at me in silence for a long time. Then he sighed.

"Yes, and all of a sudden you look around. And you're an old man. Don't forget that. You're just an old man. And you've wasted a lot of your life believing you could change things, only to learn that all that's changed is yourself, you're older."

Eddie and I kept in touch over the intervening years and, once he began teaching film direction first at the University of Texas at Austin and then at the University of Southern California and after the success of his autobiography, IT'S A HELL OF A LIFE, BUT NOT A BAD LIVING (1978), he no longer believed that he was just an old man. The most he would concede is that, while things may not change for the better, we must at least try to prevent them from becoming worse. He began to look younger, to feel younger. He had married Jean Porter in 1948, his second marriage on the eve of his troubles with the House UnAmerican Activities Committee. Jean had given him a new lease on life then, amid the tensions and blacklisting of those times; and she would again and again. What we think is too often a consequence of the way we feel for human thought on any subject to be ever entirely reliable.

Dmytryk was paid $500 a week for five weeks to direct THE FALCON

STRIKES BACK. Tom Conway got his stock company salary. The screenplay was by Edward Dein and Gerald Geraghty, who received credit and Craig Rice, Stuart Palmer, and Maurice Geraghty who did not. Early in the 'Forties Craig Rice, who was born Georgiana Ann Randolph in Chicago in 1908, ghosted two detective novels for stripper Gypsy Rose Lee. She now took some time off to ghost a novel called CRIME ON MY HANDS (1944) with George Sanders credited as the author. Sanders played himself by name and went about solving a series of murders at a film studio. It was Sanders' swan song to the detective genre. Edgar Kennedy, who was starring in a series of short comedies for RKO, was given the part of a crazed puppeteer. The biggest surprise, however, was doubtless Wynne Gibson, probably best known for her role of Iris Dawn in NIGHT AFTER NIGHT (Paramount, 1932) with George Raft and Mae West. She was thirty-five but looked fifty, and that is how Dmytryk played it in the picture.

Cliff Clark's character name was changed to Donovan in THE FALCON STRIKES BACK, to distinguish him from the two previous Mike O'Haras. He was back with Edward Gargan again for THE FALCON IN DANGER (RKO, 1943) which took twenty-two days to complete and was brought in for $127,542.85. Three Falcon pictures a year earned RKO just over a million dollars. William Clemens directed this film and the next two in the series. The story had Clarence Kolb faking his own kidnapping only to be shot at the end by the Falcon.

Clemens had directed the Nancy Drew pictures at Warner Bros. in the 'Thirties, starring Bonita Granville, and he had one Torchy Blane film to his credit as well as CALLING PHILO VANCE (Warner's, 1940). He did so well on THE FALCON IN DANGER that Geraghty wanted him again for THE FALCON AND THE CO-EDS (RKO, 1943). Murder at an exclusive girls' school combined with an atmospheric use of the ocean waves pounding on the beach maintain a high level of suspense. In addition to the attractive Jean Brooks playing a drama coach and Rita Corday as a campus psychic, Isobel Jewel was cast as a retiring music teacher, not at all someone to flirt with the Falcon but capable of devising a sinister series of crimes. The Falcon has no sidekick in this picture and his presence is not missed; Donovan and Bates provide the required humor.

THE FALCON OUT WEST (RKO, 1945) was shot in just over three weeks. Both Joan Barclay and Barbara Hale are among the attractive suspects the Falcon meets in the course of his investigation. Thurston Hall was originally cast as Dave Colby but, at the last minute, he was replaced by Minor Watson. Watson had played exactly the same character, even to having the identical character name, in HIDDEN GOLD (Paramount, 1939), an entry in the Hopalong Cassidy series which the Geraghtys had worked on. Barbara Hale was an RKO contract player who had previously appeared with Tom Conway in Val Lewton's THE SEVENTH VICTIM (RKO, 1943). She was born in DeKalb, Illinois on 18 April 1921 and had been signed by an RKO talent scout as a result of her work as a model in Chicago. It is perhaps interesting to contrast her attitude toward marriage with that of Tom Conway. Conway married Lillian Eggers, a model, in 1941. When she sued him for divorce in 1953, she was forced, since the marriage had been childless, to accept as a property settlement their Beverly Hills home and $5,000 which was all Conway had in the way of liquid assets. She told the judge that Conway had insisted that actors are a class apart and that their careers must come before all else, that an actor should be permitted to live as a bachelor even if he might have a wife. When she disagreed with these sentiments, Conway had told her, she alleged, that she had middle-class ideas and simply was not sophisticated enough for Hollywood. Barbara Hale was another case entirely. She met Bill Williams at RKO. They worked together on the Zane Grey Western WEST OF THE PECOS (RKO, 1945) which starred Robert Mitchum. When Barbara married Bill Williams, her career became secondary to making her marriage work.

Once, when I lived in Los Angeles, we breakfasted together and I told her that the only thing of any substance that had been written about her had been the career study of her in THE RKO GALS (1974). She knew the book. The author, James Robert Parish, had stressed what he presumed to be marital discord and how she had always downgraded her own career opportunities to preserve the continuity of her role as a wife and mother.

"The author of that book never even talked to me," she said. "How can he say those things about me when he doesn't even know me?"

"That's the easiest way to be able to say them."

"I wept when I read what he wrote."

She had tears in her eyes.

"Listen, you played Della Street, the consummate professional secretary, for too many years to take anything so seriously. I know what we should do. Let's watch THE FALCON OUT WEST together."

"But I was so young when I made that picture. I so much want to help you, but I don't know if I can remember anything. I know that Tom Conway was just as charming on the set as he was in the pictures he made. He helped new actors. He had a real feeling for their problems. I remember once in THE FALCON OUT WEST we had a scene where I was on top of a horse. I forgot to take the reins. He didn't stop the take. He picked up the reins and handed them to me, and said, 'Haven't you forgotten something?' I had to laugh because I had. I had forgotten my reins. But they left it in like that and no one noticed."

I had Barbara and Bill Williams over to my apartment to screen THE FALCON OUT WEST. Of course, women I knew in Hollywood, on second, third, or fourth marriages had told me that Barbara Hale had been a fool, but she had wanted a successful marriage more than anything else, and she had that as well as a career. Bill was very distinguished with his silver-blond hair. When the film was over, Barbara collapsed on the couch in simulated fear.

"I think you're going to kill me," she said.

"Why?"

"Can you understand this? It was all so very long ago that I don't remember having said those lines, or having stood in those places. I know the locations, at General Service Studio and at Corriganville for exteriors. And Tom, he was a dear. When I was supposed to ride alongside the stagecoach, one of the stunt men slapped my horse on the rump and I flew down the hill. The horse raced all the way back to the barn and into his stall, with me on top. We had to shoot the whole thing over again. That's why Tom is smiling at me when I climb onto the stage beside him. He was quiet and gentle in all that he did." She paused. "Do you know what happened to him?"

"Don't you?"

"No," she replied. "I really don't."

THE FALCON IN MEXICO (RKO, 1944) saw Conway graduating from stock. He was paid $3,262 for his work on the picture, more than he had been getting but quite a distance from the $14,000 George had been paid. William Berke was the director. Because of its Mexican setting, a number of Spanish-American actors were used. Lorraine Gauguin was among them. She was the daughter of Mexican character actor, Julian Rivero. In her later years, Lorraine became a columnist and she was a regular contributor to VIEWS & REVIEWS Magazine when I was publishing it.

"I was a Mexican waitress in THE FALCON IN MEXICO," she once told me.

"What was Tom Conway like to work with?"

"He was very shy, especially around women. He never made any advances at all toward the many girls who were in the picture with him."

Lorraine was doing a series of articles for PHOTOPLAY and she was busy with research, books piled all around her living room. She was renting a house in North Hollywood. We made a date to screen THE FALCON IN MEXICO. Lorraine never made the screening. Her house was broken into by vandals. She was raped and then beaten to death. Gasoline was poured over her and then ignited, the house burning down around her corpse. No arrest was ever made—but then, this was real life and not a movie.

Emory Parnell, cast as the murderer in THE FALCON IN MEXICO, was back as a police officer in THE FALCON IN HOLLYWOOD (RKO, 1944) with Frank Jenks as his dumb assistant. Sheldon Leonard was cast as a mobster in love with a rising young star played by Barbara Hale. Veda Ann Borg was cast as a garrulous taxi driver. Rita Corday and Jean Brooks decorated the film as potential suspects. Conway was paid $5,500 for walking through the picture and solving the series of murders, a facile task in view of police stupidity (with Parnell and Jenks arresting various characters in virtually every scene).

THE FALCON IN SAN FRANCISCO (RKO, 1945) was the last entry in the series produced by Maurice Geraghty. Sid Rogell, brother of film director Albert Rogell, was put in charge of studio operations. RKO's fortunes were flagging. Only the Falcon series and the Tim Holt program Westerns were making money. Rogell immediately involved himself in all the studio's productions.

Tom Conway was paid $7,333.34 for his role. Ed Brophy, who had played Bates in George Sanders' first Falcon picture, was given the part of Goldie. He had a rapport with Tom Conway that was as evident on the screen in its way as the balance had been between George Sanders and Allen Jenkins.

"I felt THE FALCON IN SAN FRANCISCO was a strong picture, with location shooting," Maurice Geraghty summed it up. "But Rogell agreed with Tom Conway that what the Falcon pictures had to offer was Tom Conway. The budgets should be cut. As far as he was concerned, the films were being overproduced. Budgets could be cut. Production values could be sacrificed. We didn't agree, and I left the series."

William Berke, the director of THE FALCON IN MEXICO, was made the new producer. Ray McCarey was engaged to direct THE FALCON'S ALIBI (RKO, 1946), the first film to incorporate the Rogell economy measures. It was filmed completely on indoor sets. Rogell was also chopping contract players which reduced the availability of attractive character actors. No care was taken with the script and the identity of the murderer is transparent from the beginning. There were hints in the plot of THE FALCON'S ALIBI that the screenplay was an adroit reworking of THE GAY FALCON. Such hints were even more obvious in THE FALCON'S ADVENTURE (RKO, 1946) which William Berke himself directed and which was in fact a remake of A DATE WITH THE FALCON. The Geraghty films had had as many as 15,000 bookings. Bookings fell off after Geraghty left the series. Rogell attributed this to a change in public taste. He offered the Falcon property for sale. It was purchased by Philip N. Krasne who was an independent producer during the 'Forties and who had acquired both the Charlie Chan and Cisco Kid properties when Twentieth Century-Fox decided to abandon production on those series. He had been partners with Sidney Toler.

The new Falcon series, produced by Krasne, was based on the radio series which had begun on the Mutual Network in 1945. The Falcon's name was changed to Michael Waring, as it was on the radio. John Calvert was given the role. DEVIL's CARGO (Film Classics, 1948) was the first entry. It was filmed in ten days and looks it. The budget was further cut for the next picture, APPOINTMENT WITH MURDER (Film Classics, 1948), shot in eight days. SEARCH FOR DANGER (Film Classics, 1949) was the end of it. The notion of continuing the series was scrapped.

Tom Conway's contract at RKO was not renewed. He took to freelancing. What lay ahead for RKO was a gradual diminishing of efforts on all fronts, a closing down of facilities, and finally the sale of all assets to the General Tire Company. Howard Hughes, who had seized control of the company in the 'Forties, lost any interest he may ever have had in filmmaking. Sid Rogell went on to a successful career in banking.

Conway tried marriage a second time, to Queenie Lord, but it ended in divorce in 1962. He played Bulldog Drummond in the two pictures produced by Edward Small for Twentieth Century-Fox and, briefly, starred as a detective in the television series, MARK SABRE. His last role was in a Perry Mason episode in 1963. How different it was to look across a desk at Raymond Burr and Barbara Hale, both of whom he had known at RKO. On 14 September 1965 Conway celebrated his sixty-first birthday. He was living in a two-dollar-a-day room at the Charles Hotel at 23½ Winward Avenue in Venice, California. Gene Youngblood of the LOS ANGELES HERALD-EXAMINER interviewed him. An operation for cataracts had left him nearly blind. He had been the Saint and Sherlock Holmes on the radio, but no one remembered. He told Youngblood, as he reclined in the glare of a naked bulb taped to the headboard of the bed, that he had lost his last $15,000 in a lumber swindle. His features were worn, his hands trembled from years of alcoholism. A welfare worker had refused his application for relief and he was refused bus fare for transportation to a camp for the indigent. The interview gained him a certain notoriety. He was telephoned by many who had seen him as the Falcon wishing him well, but an offer of free room and board in West Hollywood fell through. His physical condition was such that he could not work. Soon after he entered a hospital and underwent intensive treatment for cirrhosis of the liver from which condition he expired on 22 April 1967. His brother, with whom he had not spoken for years, made arrangements for the body to be shipped back to England.

George Sanders, younger by two years, fared much better. His marriage to Zsa Zsa Gabor in 1949 ended in divorce in 1954 after he had wearied, in his words, of being a paying guest at Zsa Zsa's Bel-Air home and moved into his own house. Sanders had consulted a number of psychoanalysts before he tried Zsa Zsa's. This one cured him, he said later, of his compulsion to be self-destructive, above all by being married to Zsa Zsa. Good fortune led Sanders to find happiness at last in his marriage to Benita Hume, Ronald Colman's widow, whom he married in 1959. To many, it seemed a strange, even an inexplicable combination, but for Sanders it worked. He had prudently begun playing character roles and his career prospered. He got into difficulties through an investment in a food processing plant in Scotland which, after consuming better than a quarter of a million of his savings, led him to declare bankruptcy rather than to continue to remain what he regarded as the dupe of court injustice and creditors' malice. Yet happiness, outside of the movies, is seldom permanent. When Benita died in 1967, Sanders knew that it was over for him. He had once remarked about Tyrone Power that the actor had spent his money freely on a yacht, a private airplane, lavish parties, and especially on women who, in his opinion, were more expensive than yachts and airplanes and who found ways of spending Power's money when he had run out of ideas. Power had not seemed to mind, perhaps because he had had a premonition that he would not need to save for his old age. When Rex Reed interviewed Sanders in 1969, he accused him of having liked Tyrone Power. To this, Sanders objected. He said of the actor who had died on the set of SOLOMON AND SHEBA (United Artists, 1959) that Tyrone Power had just been someone he had known, as one knew a lot of people. He compared making a film to an ocean voyage during which you swear you will meet each other again, but that you never do. He claimed that he had no friends, no relatives, no family, that everyone was dead and that he intended to die, too. It was not entirely the truth. George had one surviving relative, a sister in England. He left a note in Spanish instructing that his body should be sent to her care. The $1,500 in cash in his hotel room in Casteldelfels, near Barcelona, would be enough to get him there. The note he left in English said something else.

Sanders' last role was as a transvestite in THE KREMLIN LETTER (20th-Fox, 1970). He had been signed to play a homosexual in his next picture. He had once felt that playing the Saint had been the nadir of his career, but no doubt he felt now that he had reached a new nadir. He had sold his home to Charles Boyer who would also commit suicide after his wife died. He had lived in many places and found them all wanting. His suicide note in English said that he was bored and that he felt that he had lived long enough. Unlike Charles Strickland, whom he had once played so well, Sanders did not feel it was his lot to leave behind any work of art which would justify his existence. And, after all, no one survives old age. Edward Dmytryk understood George Sanders, as he understood so many of the players he directed. An actor needs constant encouragement. When the world no longer had that to offer George Sanders, he decided to make his final exit, which he did by means of an overdose of veronal.

7

The Detective Film in Transition

THE CRIME DOCTOR

He made his debut just when psychiatry was enjoying its first important vogue as a dramatic device, and he was ready to solve any problems with glib Freudian generalities, some of them extremely suspect.
ENCYCLOPEDIA OF MYSTERY AND DETECTION[1]

I have already mentioned that Willard Huntington Wright chose Israel Zangwill's THE BIG BOW MYSTERY to be included in THE S. S. Van Dine Detective Library issued in six volumes by Scribner's in 1929. If Poe had introduced the idea of a locked-room murder to detective fiction, Zangwill was the first to use this device in a short novel. He wrote the story in a matter of two weeks as a serial for the LONDON STAR in 1891 and it was published in book form the following year. Although it was intended to be something of a parody, the book was to be profoundly influential, particularly during the period between the wars when, in retrograde motion to the carnage the world had witnessed and would soon witness again, murder came for a time to be a strictly *private* affair where the emphasis could be placed on how the crime might possibly have been committed rather than on the crime itself. S. S. Van Dine produced a locked-room murder in THE "CANARY" MURDER CASE, and his lead was followed by Ellery Queen, Dorothy Sayers, and others; John Dickson Carr, under his own name and the pseudonym Carter Dickson, became a specialist in plotting "impossible" crimes.

In Zangwill's story, when Arthur Constant refuses to be awakened by his landlady's knocking on his door, she becomes convinced that he has been murdered. She runs across the street to the residence of the celebrated ex-detective Grodman. He soon joins her outside the lodger's door and proceeds to break in. Arthur Constant is found with his throat cut and, as in A. A. Milne's subsequent THE RED HOUSE MYSTERY (1922), no murder weapon is to be found. In his Twenty Rules, S. S. Van Dine barred from further use the plot contrivance in this story, namely "the commission of the murder in a locked room after the police have actually broken in."[2] Technically, George Grodman is no longer of the official police, that role now being filled by Edward Wimp of Scotland Yard who would seek to rival Grodman's reputation as a sleuth. It isn't until Wimp is being applauded for arresting an innocent man who is convicted and sentenced to hang that Grodman finally comes forward and admits that he murdered Constant to prove that the "perfect crime" could be committed. Unquestionably THE BIG BOW MYSTERY suggested the plot structure to Gaston Leroux for his LE MYSTÈRE DE LA CHAMBRE JAUNE (1907) which was translated into English as THE MYSTERY OF THE YELLOW ROOM (1908) and also included in The S. S. Van Dine Detective Library. Here Leroux' young police reporter, Joseph Rouletabille, undertook to solve an impossible crime. Van Dine had no problem insofar as Rouletabille traces the murder to the official investigator assigned to the case (perhaps since he is not the point-of-view detective); whereas in THE MURDER OF ROGER ACKROYD, as was noted, he objected to the book's narrator being the culprit, albeit he is not the detective's point-of-view (merely the detective's amanuensis and hence the reader's point-of-view).

Zangwill's story was brought to the screen for the first time as THE PERFECT CRIME (F.B.O., 1928) directed by Bert Glennon and starring Clive Brook. I would not have brought up the subject at all, save it was filmed again as THE CRIME DOCTOR (RKO, 1934) by Film Booking Office's successor. John Robertson was the director. The plot was altered somewhat from Zangwill's original conception, but the essential ingredients remained the same. Otto Kruger was cast as Dan Gifford, a noted criminologist. When he learns that his wife, played by Karen Morley, is hopelessly in love with Nils Asther, he undertakes to murder Judith Wood, who has been blackmailing Asther, and cleverly plants evidence which leads to Asther's capture and conviction. William Frawley was cast as the homicide detective, Fred Kelsey as a dim-witted flatfoot (his usual role), and Donald Crisp played the district attorney. R. Austin Freeman had ably demonstrated with his "inverted" detective stories that witnessing the commission of a crime and then following its detection can be just as fascinating as its solution when the identity of the perpetrator is withheld. The viewer knows from the start that Kruger has plotted the whole thing, but Robertson's direction was sufficiently suspenseful that one is intrigued watching due process glibly and enthusiastically convict the wrong man and prepare to execute him. Due process itself, even when uncorrupted by special interest or judicial incompetence, is seen as infinitely fallible and this precisely because of the situation so often dramatized by Erle Stanley Gardner: circumstantial evidence can be variously and convincingly argued and construed. Kruger discovers, to his own dismay but no doubt to the satisfaction of the Hays Office, that even the conviction of his wife's lover will not bring her back to him; so he does the right thing. He confesses and then does away with himself. Had the fade been five minutes sooner, THE CRIME DOCTOR would have been a powerful and compelling indictment. As it was, it had to settle for being an entertainment.

Max Marcin, who was born at Posen (then in Germany, now in Poland) in 1879, came to the United States when he was a child. It was he who devised the half-hour radio show titled CRIME DOCTOR which kept eleven million listeners faithfully tuned to CBS every Tuesday night. The psychiatrist-detective known as the Crime Doctor was Dr. Robert Ordway. Ray Collins was first to be featured in the role on radio. Once the Ellery Queen series came to a close, Ralph Cohn at Columbia Pictures was put in charge of developing a new detective film series for the next season. He decided upon CRIME DOCTOR, since it had the same kind of radio tie-in Ellery Queen had had. Fortunately veteran Warner Baxter was selected for the title role. Michael R. Pitts felt in FAMOUS MOVIE DETECTIVES that "if any one reason can be given for the continued popularity of the Crime Doctor series (outside the fact it was the cinema counterpart of a popular radio program), it would be the fact that the title role in all ten films was played by Warner Baxter. The Academy Award-winning star gave the part a classy interpretation and his ability to portray the strengths of a middle-age detective in a time of debonair and much younger sleuths greatly contributed to the success of the . . . series."[3]

Baxter, who was born at Columbus, Ohio in 1893, entered films in 1922. His had not been an easy childhood. When he was nine, he moved with his widowed mother to San Francisco. The family was wiped out by the disastrous earthquake. "For two weeks," Baxter later recalled, "we lived in a tent, in mortal terror of the fire. I can remember a young woman, almost naked, hysterically rubbing her head into the ground. And the countless thousands frantically searching for their kin."[4] Baxter had begun his career in vaudeville and, except for brief periods when he worked in sales to tide him over, he kept to the stage with touring companies and then finally Broadway before entering pictures. He was established as a star with IN OLD ARIZONA (Fox, 1929), the first talking Western. He played the Cisco Kid. Henceforth, his career continued to fluctuate. "I was a failure and a success three times in Hollywood," he said later. "I have even had trouble paying my rent. . . . My three depressions were suddenly ended by three pictures, each of which boosted me higher than I had ever been. IN OLD ARIZONA ended a two-year slump. THE CISCO KID [Fox, 1931] brought me back into popular favor after a series of bad stories. And 42nd STREET [Warner's 1933] revived me after THE CISCO KID had worn off. Like most actors, I wanted to cling to juvenility to the bitter end. But after I repeated 42nd STREET several times, it occurred to me that actors, drugged by pride, can make first-class asses of themselves."[5] THE RETURN OF THE CISCO KID (20th-Fox, 1939) marked Baxter's third time in the role. He made the fewest films of all the screen's Cisco Kids, but he seems to be better remembered in the role than anyone else. Baxter's contract with Twentieth Century-Fox was about to expire when he suffered a nervous breakdown and subsequently underwent psychoanalysis. He was in his late forties and the Cisco Kid could not do it for him a third time. He had to resign himself, it would appear, to playing character roles.

Columbia Pictures was not at all certain that a series would result from CRIME DOCTOR (Columbia, 1943), so the studio gave Baxter a love interest in the film in the form of Margaret Lindsay. If the film proved a success, the studio reasoned, Baxter and Lindsay might take over where Gargan and Lindsay had left off in the Ellery Queen series. However, it did not work out that way. CRIME DOCTOR was a success, but Lindsay's contract came up for renewal and it was decided to drop her. She worked in some programmers for Monogram and Producers Releasing Corporation before turning to character roles. Warner Baxter, on the other hand, for what was left of the 'Forties had found a home.

Graham Baker and Louis Lantz did the screenplay for CRIME DOCTOR as adapted from the radio program by Jerome Odlum and directed by Michael Gordon. Ray Collins appeared in the film as Dr. Carey, the physician who takes in Baxter after an automobile crash has left him a helpless amnesiac. While trying to discover his real identity, Baxter assumes the name of the man who founded the hospital where he is staying, Dr. Robert Ordway, and pursues the study of medicine. Once he is graduated, Ordway goes to work for an insane asylum as a staff psychiatrist where he meets Margaret Lindsay who is on the parole board. A touching love affair develops, one of Margaret Lindsay's best performances. Leon Ames was cast as a hardened criminal. I asked him about Warner Baxter.

"Nervous breakdown?" he inquired. "You couldn't prove it by me. He looked perfectly all right. He was always a pleasant man, very charming when we were on the set. He had lots of outside interests. While we were making that picture, I remember I was invited to a party at his home. It was held on the tennis court. Baxter was sponsoring a new comedian and he wanted everyone in Hollywood to see the man perform. It was Sid Caesar. We had a good time, I can tell you that. Caesar had everyone in stitches."

The sub-plot of CRIME DOCTOR is the fact that, in his former life, Ordway was a criminal. John Litel and Harold Huber, trying very hard to play tough hoodlums, haunt Ordway, thinking his amnesia is a pretense and that he can really lead them to a stash of money. They end up getting jailed. Ordway brings his case before a jury and he is acquitted. The idea at the fade is that now Baxter and Lindsay can put the past behind them and settle down to connubial bliss. THE CRIME DOCTOR'S STRANGEST CASE (Columbia, 1943) went immediately into production, but Ordway was a bachelor in it and such he remained throughout the remainder of the series. This gave young love a chance to bloom by way of a sub-plot. Constance Worth was cast as Ordway's nurse in the film and, at times, the role seemed to be patterned on that of Nikki

Porter, but the notion did not last beyond this entry. Lloyd Bridges and Lynn Merrick played a young couple very much in love. They come to Ordway, seeking his advice. Bridges was acquitted of poisoning his former employer only after a new trial which Ordway had arranged. Now the couple want to marry. Their intention is frustrated when Bridges' current employer is poisoned and Barton MacLane as the police detective assigned to the case tags Bridges as the obvious culprit. Ordway's solution to the crime entails uncovering a thirty-year-old murder. It is an adroitly plotted mystery with a screenplay by Eric Taylor and direction by Eugene Forde. With this picture Rudolph C. Flothow became the producer for the series. He was born at Frankfurt, Germany in 1895 and had entered the industry at the age of twenty working for Paramount. At Columbia he had charge of the Crime Doctor series and the Whistler films. Baxter's contract with Columbia called for him to appear in only two pictures a year. This was consistent with what Columbia wanted from the Crime Doctor series and what, of course, the studio had been unable to get from Ellery Queen while making the Ellery Queen series.

Baxter made only one Crime Doctor film in 1944 because he was given a strong supporting role in LADY IN THE DARK (Columbia, 1944), a lavish production based on Kurt Weill's music and a story heavily laden with psychoanalytic themes. The title song for the film gained some stature when Leopold Stokowski recorded it the next year with the Hollywood Bowl Symphony. SHADOWS OF THE NIGHT (Columbia, 1944) was by far the best entry in the series. Opening on an appropriately stormy night, a youthful Nina Foch shows up at Ordway's home. She is troubled by recurring suicidal nightmares. When Ordway learns that their conversation has been overheard (by that lovable sub-criminal, Ben Weldon), he decides to accept Nina's invitation and come for the week-end to her oceanside home. George Zucco was cast as Nina's slightly unbalanced uncle who is engaged in chemical experiments to create a wholly new synthetic fabric. He becomes a major suspect when Ordway discovers that Nina's nightmares are induced by a hypnotic gas piped into her bedroom. Eugene Forde again directed and Eric Taylor once more provided the original screenplay.

George Sherman joined the Flothow-Taylor team as the director of CRIME DOCTOR'S COURAGE (Columbia, 1945). A man has been married twice and both times his new bride has come to a tragic death on their honeymoon. Now it is Hillary Brooke's turn. Consistent with the kind of casting she got at Columbia (she confided to me that it was due to the fact that she would not permit Harry Cohn to pat her bottom), she is marrying the man, played by Stephen Crane, only for his money. Dr. Ordway, on vacation at the Beverly Hills Hotel titled for this picture the Hotel Royale, is not involved in the case for very long before Crane is shot, an apparent suicide which Ordway reveals to have been murder. Anthony Caruso and Lupita Tovar, a dance team, are the obvious suspects. Their lives are surrounded by mystery and they live in Bela Lugosi's former estate (which Lugosi had difficulties maintaining after times became lean); and, since they are never seen in the daylight, the obvious inference is that they are vampires. Yet this proves a red herring, only a publicly stunt created for the dancers by Jerome Cowan. Ordway, with the help of Emory Parnell cast as a police detective, finally cracks the case.

If you pause to consider that Eric Taylor did the original screenplay and William Castle directed CRIME DOCTOR'S WARNING (Columbia, 1945), the year's second entry in the series, you might well expect it to be a better picture than it was. John Lytell returned, this time cast as a police inspector seeking Ordway's assistance. A model has been murdered and the artist painting her, who has lapses in memory, is the ready suspect. However, there is more to it than this, as Ordway soon discovers. He traces the crime to an art dealer, played by Miles Mander, who once more (as was so often the case with him) was cast as a man married to a much younger woman. When confronted by her threat to leave him, the situation offers only one solution. Then, to keep his crime a secret, he has to murder two models who were her friends.

Leigh Brackett, who had worked so effectively on Howard Hawks' production of TO HAVE AND HAVE NOT (Warner's, 1944) and THE BIG SLEEP (Warner's, 1946), did the screenplay for CRIME DOCTOR'S MANHUNT (Columbia, 1946) and William Castle directed. It might have been a very good picture, but was not, perhaps because of Castle's relative indifference. Ellen Drew had the challenging role of playing a schizophrenic in both of her personality manifestations. William Frawley, cast as a police inspector, introduced too much humor into a film that might have consisted of the same kind of wrenching suspense William Castle achieved in the best of his Whistler films.

JUST BEFORE DAWN (Columbia, 1946) also had about it elements for a more extraordinary picture than it turned out to be. Eric Taylor did the screenplay and William Castle directed. Martin Kosleck and Marvin Miller devise a phony insulin kit. Ordway accidentally injects a victim with the solution. When the victim dies, the police ask Ordway to participate in the investigation. The gang is headquartered in a mortuary, made rather eerie by Castle's experimental lighting. Ordway pretends that he is blinded by a bullet and resorts to a disguise in order to expose the gang.

George Archainbaud, who had been directing Gene Autry Westerns at Columbia, took over the direction for THE MILLERSON CASE (Columbia, 1947) with most of his action, not altogether unexpectedly, occurring in a rural community situated on the Columbia ranch town set in Burbank. Ordway is on vacation when he encounters a typhoid epidemic. In all the confusion, the town barber, played by Trevor Bardette, is poisoned and Ordway heads up the investigation. The charm of the film resides in the excellent character actors playing the town's more notable citizens, especially Clem Bevans as the sheriff and Addison Richards as a country doctor. An amusing sub-plot is the boredom of most of the town's housewives which prompts them to carry on affairs with Bardette; his amorous inclinations proved to be his nemesis. Ordway, after much trial and error, arrives at the identity of the murderer.

William Castle returned to the series to direct CRIME DOCTOR'S GAMBLE (Columbia, 1947), but his enthusiasm had waned considerably since JUST BEFORE DAWN. Ordway, on a visit to Paris, is invited by the police to assist them in determining who murdered a noted art dealer. The picture was so bad that the trades began to warn Columbia that it had better do something to save the series from becoming poison at the box office.

The problem may have been due, in part, to Warner Baxter's arthritis which was becoming increasingly crippling. His condition was so serious in 1948 that no entries were filmed that year. When he made his last film in the series, CRIME DOCTOR'S DIARY (Columbia, 1949), he was off camera most of the time. The plot concerned a man released from prison who sets out to find the person who really committed the crime for which he was imprisoned. When his chief suspect is murdered, the man is again pursued by the police. Ordway, however, proves that the culprit was actually the man's girlfriend who is shot at the end.

Baxter's last film role was that of a prisoner trying to escape in STATE PENITENTIARY (Columbia, 1950). Off-screen, Baxter agreed to submit to a partial lobotomy in an effort to ease the pain of the arthritis. He did not survive the operation. Yet, he was a suave and gentle man, whatever the encroaching brittleness of his portrayals, and in the best of the Crime Doctor films projected an ease and charm in his characterization that occasionally belied the limited budgets. "Most actors object to typing," he once commented. "I don't. In the first place, it is the public who types an actor, not the studio. If an actor is so good in a certain character, he can afford to submerge his urge to portray many parts in favor of a neat financial return."[6]

THE WHISTLER

> I've had to cut down on the booze, and no more big action stuff for yours truly. But the industry's been very good to me, and I'll keep going as long as they want me.
>
> Richard Dix[7]

William Castle made his initial impact as a director of highly special gifts, not in the Crime Doctor series, but in connection with The Whistler films. CHANCE OF A LIFETIME (Columbia, 1943) in the Boston Blackie series was Castle's first solo credit as a director. The film opened to generally bad reviews, but it made money. Harry Cohn summoned Castle to his office on the Columbia lot. He handed the director the script for his next picture.

"Read it," he told Castle, "and when you've finished, call me at home and let me know how you like it. The switchboard'll put you through."[8]

Cohn demanded of Castle that he be honest in his appraisal. The script was titled THE WHISTLER and it was based on the popular radio program originating from the West Coast studio of the Columbia Broadcasting System. Castle commented in his autobiography that he read the script three times before he telephoned Cohn. He relayed his enthusiasm about the proposed production a little after midnight. The screenplay had been written by Eric Taylor and was based on a story idea supplied by J. Donald Wilson who scripted the radio series.

"I tried every effort I could dream up to create a mood of terror: low-key lighting, wide-angle lenses to give an eerie feeling, and a hand-held camera in many of the important scenes to give a sense of reality to the horror," Castle recalled. "To achieve a mood of desperation, I insisted that [Richard] Dix give up smoking and go on a diet. This made him nervous and irritable, particularly when I gave him early morning calls and kept him waiting on the set—sometimes for an entire day before using him in a scene. He was constantly off-center, restless, fidgety, and nervous as a cat. When I finally used him in a scene, I'd make him do it over and over until he was ready to explode. It achieved the desired effect—that of a man haunted by fear and trying to keep from being murdered."[9]

Richard Dix was cast as a small industrialist who is so distraught by the loss of his wife, for which he feels partially to blame, that he hires an assassin to murder him. The go-between whom Dix contacts is killed by the police soon after he talks to Dix. The contract passes on, however, to J. Carrol Naish whose business it is to kill Dix. In the meantime, Dix learns that his wife is not dead, that she is being held prisoner in a Japanese internment camp, and so now he wants to stop the terrible machinery he has started only to discover that he cannot. The suspense mounts as Naish decides, rather than shooting Dix, he will try to frighten him to death. Gloria Stuart, cast as Dix' secretary, finally comes to his rescue. THE WHISTLER (Columbia, 1944) won rave reviews from the critics.

Richard Dix' career as a leading man until this time had been primarily the result of appearing in Westerns. On 4 April 1944 it was announced in the trades that he had signed a contract with Columbia Pictures to appear in The Whistler series. Rudolph C. Flothow was slated to produce the films. Dix' reason for agreeing to do the series, he confided in an interview, was because of his health. He suffered from high blood pressure and was generally red of face and short of breath. He had long been a heavy drinker and, while he earnestly intended to cut down, he was not altogether successful. Throughout the 'Thirties, in fact, he would almost invariably show up for work hung over. The most unfortunate aspect of this situation was that during his recuperation process Dix was subject to fits of hiccups. One never knew when the hiccups might begin, so whoever the director would be, he would have to rush him before the camera. Usually then the hiccups would start in the middle of a scene. The other players would try to cover them, but nothing really could be done. Dix would have to rest until noon, by which time the hiccups had generally subsided. THE WHISTLER was filmed at the Darmour lot on Santa

Monica Boulevard and thanks to Castle's careful direction, even though the first picture was budgeted at $75,000, it won ready acceptance from audiences.

Both Dix and Flothow wanted William Castle to direct the next entry, THE MARK OF THE WHISTLER (Columbia, 1944); and, if anything, it proved even better than the first picture. The original story was by Cornell Woolrich whose tales of suspense would have a tremendous effect on *film noir* in the 'Forties. Dix was cast as a down-and-out hobo sitting on a park bench who sees a notice in a newspaper that a bank is seeking to locate heirs for various accounts it is holding. Dix determines that he can successfully pretend to be one of the account holders. After much anxious worry, he manages to establish his claim for an account totaling $99,010. Instead of leaving town with his booty, he checks into a high class hotel only to find to his dismay that now a man is intent on killing him, believing him to be the man he is pretending to be. Paul Guilfoyle, cast as Limpy, a beggar selling pencils, and Janis Carter, a reporter, befriend Dix who finally, with their help, liberates himself from his difficulties, but not without having to confess the fraud.

Kate Cameron in the NEW YORK DAILY NEWS remarked that "William Castle has made another exciting picture based on the adventures of The Whistler. The latter is a radio character known only on the West Coast and I, for one, am grateful to Columbia Pictures for selecting the mysterious Whistler for a series of thrilling adventure films and thus introducing him to the country at large. The Whistler may be Fate, or he may be the voice of conscience signaling a warning to a person about to take his first plunge into crime. We see him in THE MARK OF THE WHISTLER . . . merely as a shadow accompanied by an eerily whistled refrain. In the first picture of the series, THE WHISTLER, Richard Dix played the part of a man whose footsteps were dogged by the shadow and whose ears were filled with the notes of warning as he went about the breathless business of trying to throw a killer off his trail. In the new adventure, Dix appears in the role of a hunted man."[10]

Surely, the emotional and psychological climate of the detective film, under the aegis of *film noir* or parallel to it, was in the process of a dramatic change. Lew Landers replaced William Castle as the director of the third entry, THE POWER OF THE WHISTLER (Columbia, 1945). Dorothy Masters, reviewing the new release for the NEW YORK DAILY NEWS, noted the decline, commenting that "it was director William Castle, who produced a 'sleeper' (low budget film of exceptional merit and appeal) in THE WHISTLER, and while Lew Landers maintains considerable suspense and some control over the players, his picture doesn't quite rate a three-star par."[11] Aubrey Wisberg did the original screenplay which found Richard Dix suffering from temporary amnesia after receiving a glancing blow from an automobile. He meets Janis Carter, who tries to help him discover his identity from certain objects he finds in his pockets. The emphasis in the first two-thirds of the film is strictly on detection as Dix, Carter, and Carter's sister, played by Jeff Donnell, pursue the various clues. Then, of a sudden, Dix becomes aware of his identity: he has escaped from an asylum with one object in mind, to murder the administrator of the asylum and the judge who placed him there. This is foreshadowed by the deaths of assorted creatures with which Dix has come into contact, a canary in the girls' apartment, a kitten with which a child is playing, a squirrel in a park. Janis Carter, once she learns his identity, is in danger of her life.

William Castle might have made it a far more suspenseful film than it was and, for this reason, was doubtless back to direct THE VOICE OF THE WHISTLER (Columbia, 1945). Lynn Merrick, perhaps the actress most capable of playing *femmes fatales* in the Columbia "B" unit, renders a performance which nearly qualifies the picture to be considered a *film noir*. Dix, cast as an ailing industrialist, lonely, dissatisfied, with only a short time to live, takes a vacation and hopes to lose his identity. He is befriended by Rhys Williams, a prize fighter who now has retired from the ring to drive a cab in Chicago. This friendship theme generates an uncommon degree of sympathy. Before leaving to live an isolated life in a lighthouse on the ocean, Dix proposes marriage to Lynn Merrick, a nurse engaged to a young intern, offering her all of his wealth. Turning hard against the prospect of poverty and struggle facing her otherwise, Merrick agrees. When, sometime later, Dix does not die but instead falls in love with Merrick whose former fiancé arrives for a visit, both men plot murder. Dix succeeds, but he loses his freedom; and Merrick, who wanted wealth and loved people, is shown at the end living quite alone in the lighthouse.

MYSTERIOUS INTRUDER (Columbia, 1946) directed by William Castle from a screenplay by Eric Taylor is perhaps the best entry in the series. Don Miller in an article titled "Private Eyes" (1975) thought that Dix' role in this film constituted "perhaps the best of the non-Chandler private eyes of the period" and that "the Eric Taylor original had a fine gimmick, the quest for some rare Jenny Lind recordings, and some unforgettable characters, such as Mike Mazurki's brutish killer without a word of dialogue. Most haunting of all was the sleuth, Don Gale, as played by Richard Dix. 'I'm an unusual kind of detective,' says Dix early in the film, which is pure understatement. Dix had played a madman in a Val Lewton film a few years previously, but compared to the maniacal intensity of his Don Gale, it was a performance of placid calm. . . . There is always the possibility that part of this characterization is attributable to Dix rather than the script, but in either case the effect is unsettling yet fascinating."[12] William Castle in his direction had certainly been influenced by what Edward Dmytryk had achieved in MURDER, MY SWEET (RKO, 1944). The sets are musty old shops or a dilapidated house where Mazurki is sleeping off a drunk. All of the important action takes place in fitful lighting and heavy shadows. Gale is motivated by greed, as are most of the other characters. He proves himself smarter, however, although, ironically, in his haste, he makes a fatal mistake. I would even suggest that MYSTERIOUS INTRUDER may be the best film Castle made while he was under contract to Columbia.

THE SECRET OF THE WHISTLER (Columbia, 1947) was unquestionably a let-down. None of the characters is sympathetic and there was no imagination in either the acting or the direction by George Sherman. Richard Dix was cast as an artist who must depend on his ailing wife for his bounty. When his wife, played by Mary Carrier, overhears Dix making love to his model, portrayed by Leslie Brooks, she informs Dix that she intends to disinherit him. Dix tries to poison her. His wife makes a note of the occurrence in her diary. Then she dies of a heart attack. Dix, believing he murdered her, cremates the body. He marries the model who turns out to be a spiteful golddigger. To get her hands on Dix' fortune, she plots to get evidence against him. She finds the diary but, before she can show it to the police, Dix strangles her. The police arrive with proof that Dix did not murder his wife only by now it is too late to save him from a murder charge.

THE THIRTEENTH HOUR (Columbia, 1947) was not an improvement. It has Karen Morley as Dix' girlfriend. If anything, the two of them carry the picture, but it was not enough to overcome William Clemens' lackluster direction. The plot has Dix running a trucking company. He stops to see Karen Morley and has a drink. When he is involved in an accident, the liquor on his breath causes his license to be suspended. During the six months when he is not supposed to drive, he attempts to run anyway. He is ambushed by a mysterious figure and a highway patrolman is murdered. Dix is suspected and hounded by the police. He manages to expose the culprit by the end, but by that time the story had become tedious.

Dix' health began seriously to fail. THE THIRTEENTH HOUR proved to be his final film. In October, 1948, he suffered a massive heart attack and was placed for a time in a sanitarium. He sold his Santa Monica ranch and with his wife set sail for Europe. While aboard ship at Cherbourg in August, 1949, he had a second, nearly fatal heart attack. He was kept alive, with lengthy stays in New York and Chicago, until he made it back to California. He died on 20 September 1949 at the Presbyterian Hospital in Hollywood.

Columbia Pictures thought it might save the series by revamping it completely. Instead of relying on a single star, such as Richard Dix, the new series would concentrate on stories. RETURN OF THE WHISTLER (Columbia, 1949) was the first entry without Dix. It was directed by an indifferent veteran, D. Ross Lederman, from an original story by Cornell Woolrich. A man intends to marry a French woman he has known for only a few weeks. His state of love is rather trying on a viewer's patience. When the girl unaccountably disappears, the man, played by Michael Duane, frantically searches for her. Richard Lane was cast as a private detective but his portrayal was very much in the vein of his appearances as Inspector Farraday in the Boston Blackie series. The denouement is in an insane asylum where the girl, played by Leonore Aubert, is being held against her will. The Woolrich story had stressed the crushing autocracy of asylum administration and its bending medical practice to serve whoever is paying the bill. None of this was in the film, save in the most fleeting insinuations. Reviewers almost unanimously lamented the loss of William Castle to the series and, so, with this picture, The Whistler took his last bow.

MICHAEL SHAYNE

A snort of brandy puts me in touch with the cosmic forces.
Michael Shayne[13]

Brett Halliday was born Davis Dresser in Chicago in 1904. He made every effort, in later years, to obscure his past and he constantly tried to create the impression that his most famous creation, Michael Shayne, was a real person. It is known that he spent his childhood in Texas and that he ran away from home at the age of fourteen to join the U.S. Army. He was sent to serve at Fort Bliss in El Paso on the Mexican border. He was eventually discovered and was discharged at sixteen for being under age. He returned to finish high school and then sought work as a rough-neck in the oil fields from Burkburnett in Texas to Signal Hill in California. He attended the Tri-State College in Indiana long enough to get a certificate in civil engineering. It was at this profession that he worked while attempting to write pulp fiction under all manner of pseudonyms. His efforts increased, especially during the Depression, when economic conditions made it difficult to find engineering and surveying assignments.

Near the end of the decade of the 1930s, the opportunity came to enter a mystery contest, which Davis did. His entry did not win, but he managed to find a publisher for it. It was narrated in the first person by Asa Baker, the pseudonym under which it was written, and it was set in El Paso, an area which Dresser knew well. Baker, much as Dresser himself, tells the reader that he is an author of Western fiction who has decided to try his hand at a detective story. "I felt," Baker wrote, "as though I'd go gaga if I had to turn out another range-war, cattle-rustler, crooked-foreman thriller."[14] The title of the book was MUM'S THE WORD FOR MURDER (1938) and for his detective Dresser created a character named Jerry Burke, a singularly dull and uninteresting man who was supposedly the co-ordinator of all the law-enforcement agencies in El Paso. It is filled with the wildest improbabilities. One suspect, who is not guilty of the series murders, becomes so nervous when being interrogated that he jumps out of a sixth storey window. Burke shrugs off this behavior. " 'Look at it from this angle: Even though Gray *didn't* murder her, the papers can make out a powerful case against him. Disgrace and possible conviction are all he can see. What more natural than to step out of a window?' "[15] The only characteristic Burke shares with Mike Shayne is that drinking brandy, far from impairing his faculties, tends to make him "keener and more alert with every drink."[16] The most obvious suspect in each of the three unrelated murders had an iron-clad alibi. This is because the three have gotten together and agreed to murder people whom they do not know but whom one of the others wants out of the way. At the end, Baker notes that "we stood by the table and watched them drag the three murderers out."[17]

This is such a poorly plotted book that it is difficult for me to accept Dresser's claim that the first Mike Shayne mystery, DIVIDEND ON DEATH (1939), was written four years prior to it only to meet with constant rejection. The only thing that can be said on behalf of MUM'S THE WORD FOR MURDER is that Patricia Highsmith used a variation of this plot for the novel which Alfred Hitchcock later filmed very effectively, STRANGERS ON A TRAIN (Warner's, 1951). The plot of DIVIDEND ON DEATH is extremely convoluted, but its unravelment is at least probable and Shayne is a far more attractive detective than Burke. The story opens with Shayne's being consulted by Phyllis Brighton whose mother has recently remarried and who is under a psychiatrist's care because she supposedly harbors murderous impulses toward her mother. Phyllis has also been made to suspect that she is a Lesbian and, at one point, she offers herself sexually to Shayne. " 'The books say normal men can tell and won't have anything to do with girls like that. If you can't—if you won't—if you don't want me, I'll *know*. And I'll kill myself.' "[18] Shayne gets himself out of this tight spot by explaining that he is old enough to be Phyllis' father. That ploy is not very successful and Phyllis is in bed waiting for him when he is "saved" by the arrival of Will Gentry, chief of the Miami Police, and Peter Painter, chief of the Miami Beach Police. These two were to become regular characters in the series and one or both of them would be involved in all of Mike's future cases set in Miami.

One receives the impression from reading DIVIDEND ON DEATH that Dresser was familiar with Miami in only the most cursory fashion, although this shortcoming would be remedied in future books. Dresser would never evoke the sense of place the way Raymond Chandler could, but his familiarity with Miami and its environs would certainly equal Hammett's deft acquaintance with the appointments of San Francisco in his Continental Op stories. In fact, it is to Hammett that Dresser owed his orientation in detective fiction and in many ways Mike Shayne is the primary successor to Sam Spade. As Spade, he is a former operative with an inter-state agency. He is worldly, an habitual drinker, and in the early novels, at least, frequently brutalized by the lackeys of mobsters in scenes reminiscent of THE GLASS KEY. Where he differs from Spade is that he is never above extracting a large fee from a case and he will collect wherever he can. Peter Painter is his arch-enemy and, if Shayne is involved in any murder case, he is always ready to suspect and arrest Shayne first without regard to the evidence. In the second entry, THE PRIVATE PRACTICE OF MIKE SHAYNE (1940), Phyllis Brighton has now come into her estate and he is surrounded by criminal leaches and gigolos who want to seize her inherited wealth. " 'I don't need you to look after me,' " she tells Shayne contemptuously, but his response is glib and typical: " 'You're going to be looked after whether you like it or not, Angel.' "[19] In DIVIDEND ON DEATH, Shayne destroyed evidence which was part of a frame-up and he made the police go along with it. In THE PRIVATE PRACTICE OF MIKE SHAYNE, Shayne switches gun barrels so that his automatic, planted next to a corpse, will not be found to be the murder weapon only to discover that, in making the switch, the substitute barrel in his automatic now does make it the murder weapon. This creates quite a quandary, since the police would "never believe him if he told his story of exchanging pistol barrels—and if they did believe him, he'd be indicted for planting evidence in a homicide."[20] To expose the murderer, Shayne has actually to forge evidence, but it works. The situation with Phyllis has also progressed to the point where Shayne is aware that he is in love with her and, of course, she has been in love with him since they first met. For the next five books, Shayne must operate as a hard-boiled detective in the Sam Spade tradition but, as Nick Charles, one who is also married to a woman who wants to be involved in his cases and his adventures.

In point of fact, marrying Mike Shayne and Phyllis Brighton was a mistake and it left Dresser in something of a literary dilemma. For one thing, Phyllis did not share Shayne's addiction to hard drinking and she was obviously too intent on a "normal" married life to adjust readily or satisfactorily to the violent criminal world in which Shayne had to function. In THE UNCOMPLAINING CORPSES (1940), TICKETS FOR DEATH (1941), BODIES ARE WHERE YOU FIND THEM (1941), THE CORPSE CAME CALLING (1942), and MURDER WEARS A MUMMER'S MASK (1943) Mike conducts his cases with Phyllis uncomfortably on his hands most of the time. This is not to say that Dresser did not try to make the best of the situation or that he did not create wholly new and innovative scenes because of it. In TICKETS FOR DEATH, when Mike is retained to get to the bottom of a racket at the dog racing track in Cocopalm, he tells Phyllis, " 'I always begin a case by suspecting everybody. . . . ' "[21] He conveniently leaves her in their hotel room while he goes down the hall to the room of the man who sent for him only to run into two gunmen whom he kills. When Chief of Police Boyle would hinder his efforts to investigate, Mike is ready to wade into him, but Phyllis intervenes. " 'You could avoid all sorts of complications if you would just leave a man like that a little corner to back into. He's sort of pathetic. . . . ' "[22] The strategy works. Shayne backs off and ends the scene by confessing to Phyllis that he does not understand how he has been able to get along for so many years without her. The story concludes with Shayne arriving at the correct solution, but it is such that it must, at least as far as the public is concerned, result in a cover-up which the police actively endorse.

In THE CORPSE CAME CALLING, Phyllis sets herself up as Mike's secretary, but his job still depresses her. " 'I mean the danger,' " she informs him. " 'Pitting yourself against murderous forces. That's what you really like about it, Michael.' She shuddered again. He was thoughtfully silent for a time.

'Maybe so, Phyl. I never put it into words before.' His voice roughened. 'I'm sorry if it's tough on you, but you knew my business before you married me.' 'I'm not kicking,' she disclaimed quickly. She sat up straighter, reached over, and got two cigarettes from a pack in his shirt pocket. She lit them both, inserted one between his lips. 'Let it be a short life and a merry one,' she went on with mock bravado. 'Only—it *is* fun being married to you, darling. I'd like to have it last another month or so.' 'I lasted a lot of years before I had you to worry about me. And you'd better be glad,' he went on, 'that I'm not flying a bomber or riding a submarine tonight. Bucking a couple of New York gunsels isn't half so dangerous as taking a whack at the Nazis.' "[23]

Perhaps the most interesting of the novels with Phyllis is MURDER WEARS A MUMMER'S MASK which is set in Central City, Colorado, a former mining town in a Western setting where Mike and Phyllis have gone on vacation. Yet, more than ever, Mike is becoming irritated with Phyllis. When Shayne wants to make a man talk, the woman with the man warns Mike that he cannot hit a man when he is down. " 'I can kick his face to a pulp if he doesn't start talking,' " Mike rebuts.[24] Phyllis is upset by this behavior. " 'Do you have to brawl, Michael—and on our vacation?' " she wails. " 'Couldn't you ever, just once, solve a case with your brains instead of your fists?' Shayne regarded her intently, then said in a sour tone, 'I'll always wonder whether that guy would have come clean if I had kicked him in the face. That's your doing, Phyl. Marriage has softened me. Next thing I know, I'll be starting, by God, a fund for indigent murderers.' "[25] Evidence is withheld from the reader, however, which if he were to have it would have allowed him to arrive at the solution before Shayne reveals it. Obviously what to do about the Phyllis character had become serious enough that it had to be addressed.

BLOOD ON THE BLACK MARKET (1943) opens with Shayne's phone ringing while he is asleep. "He couldn't reach out and lift it from the night table any more," the reader is told. "That was in the other apartment one flight up where he had lived with Phyllis before her death. Remembering sent a surge of pain through Shayne and cleared his sleep-drugged mind."[26] The only other reference to Phyllis is a rather cryptic one and it is not until much later on, in BLOOD ON BISCAYNE BAY (1946), that the reader learns for certain that Phyllis died in childbirth, as did the child. BLOOD ON THE BLACK MARKET is about traffic in gasoline which is being rationed due to the war. Much in the plot is preposterous, but nothing so much as Shayne's having Will Gentry bring an extraordinary assortment of suspects to the home of one of the characters so he can hold a dramatic denouement. After the death of Phyllis, Timothy Rourke, a journalist on the MIAMI NEWS and a secondary character, comes into increasing prominence in the stories as Mike's friend and drinking companion. He is, in fact, Mike's one friend, although they do upon occasion have misunderstandings.

When BODIES ARE WHERE YOU FIND THEM was issued in paperback by Dell Books, Dresser included an essay titled, "Michael Shayne As I Know

Him,'' signed "by Brett Halliday." It is written, of course, as if Mike Shayne were a real person, only that not being his name and his place of business not being in Miami. According to Dresser, it was as a young man during his second night ashore with a group of sailors that he ended up in a tough waterfront bar filled with Mexicans who did not like gringos. The only other American in the bar was a redheaded Irishman who was sitting alone at a table in the rear, a bottle of tequila and a glass of ice water in front of him. A fight inevitably broke out. Halliday was slugged and fell to the floor. The Mexicans were armed with knives. The Irishman, surveying the odds, rose from his table in the rear and, fists swinging, entered the fracas. He had the glint of battle in his eyes. He knocked the natives this way and that, clearing a path to the doorway through which the sailors expeditiously could make their hurried retreat. In one of the incredible coincidences in life, some years later Halliday was in New Orleans and strolled into a Rampart Street bar one evening looking for story material. He saw the redheaded Irishman again. He was sitting alone at a table, a bottle of cognac in front of him this time, and a glass of ice water. Halliday went over and introduced himself. The man smiled when Halliday recounted how he had first seen him in Tampico. He confided that he was a private detective in New Orleans on a case. Halliday was sitting with his back to the door. He saw the Irishman stiffen in his chair. His eyes narrowed to bleak, gray slits. Scarcely moving his lips, the man told Halliday to get out of the saloon fast and to forget he had ever seen him. Halliday got to his feet slowly. The man's eyes commanded the situation. Two men had come through the entrance. As Halliday headed out the door, he saw the men approaching the Irishman's table. Lingering outside, the redhead emerged after a time with the two men, one on either side with bulging pockets. It was that night that Halliday decided he would write a mystery novel featuring a redheaded, two-fisted, cognac-drinking Irish detective as its hero.

"I noted a subtle change in Mike's inner character after Phyllis' death," Halliday continued in the same vein, after having explained how he and the redhead eventually became such good friends that he was given the opportunity to narrate all of his cases. "In some ways he became more ruthless and driving and demanding of himself, but the hard outer shell of assumed cynicism was cracked, and for the first time in his life he wasn't afraid to let traces of gentleness and pity shine through."[27] In the many novels following BLOOD ON THE BLACK MARKET, this is true to a certain extent, which is what makes Mike Shayne so different from the other post-Hammett developments in the private eye genre, those such as Mike Hammer and Travis McGee, although, unlike Philip Marlowe, Shayne was never permitted to become sentimental. The idea of Shayne's being a real person even extended to a book in the series, SHE WOKE TO DARKNESS (1954), where Halliday is in New York to attend a Mystery Writers of America awards dinner only to find himself a murder suspect. Mike Shayne comes from Miami to find the murderer and exonerate the man who narrates his adventures. Even the fact that Mike Shayne was an adopted name was later dropped so that one of the characters in THE CORPSE THAT NEVER WAS (1963) compares real-life detecting to the way it was presented " 'on TeeVee when your program was running.' "[28]

But before television, before radio even, there came the motion pictures. In 1941, due to problems already narrated which had to do with Peter Lorre, Twentieth Century-Fox Film Corporation was looking for a detective series character to replace Mr. Moto. Sol Wurtzel was assigned the task of bringing Mike Shayne to the screen. It was a one-picture deal with Lloyd Nolan slated to play Shayne, but when the film clicked at the box office Nolan was placed under contract to the studio. Once the Shayne series began, Dresser was only in the process of publishing his fourth Michael Shayne novel and so, after the first entry which was based on THE PRIVATE PRACTICE OF MICHAEL SHAYNE, the studio sought out other story ideas upon which to base the photoplays. Perhaps for this reason, coupled with Nolan's fine, albeit idiosyncratic, approach to the role, the character on screen was substantially different from the one Dresser had created. It is also worth noting that during the same period as the Nolan series of Shayne films was being made Dresser was signed by Thayer Hobson at Morrow to continue writing novels in the Peter Field series of Powder Valley Westerns which, for the previous three years, veteran Harry Sinclair Drago had been writing. Dresser wrote all the Peter Field entries at the rate of two a year from 1941 to THE SMOKING IRON (1944). By that time, Michael Shayne was well enough established that Dresser could concentrate on books in the Shayne series.

MICHAEL SHAYNE, PRIVATE DETECTIVE (20th-Fox, 1941) was directed by Eugene Forde. Clarence Kolb hires Shayne to keep an eye on his wayward daughter, played by Marjorie Weaver. Douglas Dumbrille was cast as a gambling casino owner. Walter Abel was the owner of a race horse who manages a substitution at the track which brings him a lot of money on a long shot. Donald MacBride, whom Lloyd Nolan once described to me as a "bottle baby," played Captain Painter, Shayne's protagonist in the stories, with Adrian Morris, Chester Morris' brother, filling in as his assistant to make for the dumb cop duo which was a requisite of detective films in the 'Forties. The unique element in the picture was Elizabeth Patterson, cast as Marjorie Weaver's aunt. She is fascinated by detective stories and tells Shayne at one point that she has read and solved most of the Ellery Queen novels. She is constantly relating complex and artificial detective story plots to Mike, expecting him to solve them. It was sort of a back-handed slap at the kind of detective fiction Ellery Queen was writing and the more realistic fiction presumably Hammett and Halliday had come to represent. Charles Coleman played Ponsley, the butler who together with Patterson keeps elaborate files on the detective fiction they have read, much in the fashion of the later Miss Marple movies.

Lloyd Nolan bought a house in Brentwood for $13,000 on the strength of his new contract at Twentieth Century-Fox which was worth two and a half million dollars when I first visited him in 1976. He always had a bad memory.

Once, years before, he had gotten into a car with some friends and gave them lengthy instructions on how to find his home when they were only half a block away. One of the things Lloyd forgot for all of his career, since it could be found virtually nowhere, was his age, but he was born in 1903. He was a voracious reader of books on art and history. He was raised in San Francisco, where his father owned a shoe factory. Lloyd wanted no part of the family business. For five years, he attended the Santa Clara Academy and went out for theatricals. He entered Stanford University but was so busy with the University players that he flunked out after his first year. With a fraternity brother, he shipped out on a freighter. The ship burned up in New York harbor and Lloyd had to send home for money in order to return. By 1927, he was working at the Pasadena Playhouse, for nothing, supporting himself out of money his father had left him. He went to New York a year later, while he still had the fare to get there. He worked in New York, at Cape Cod, and in stock. In 1933 he married Mel Efrid while they were appearing together in minor roles in a play called SWEET STRANGER. His break on the stage did not come until he won the part of Biff Grimes in ONE SUNDAY AFTERNOON which had a forty-three week run on Broadway. He was tested by Paramount in 1934 and decided to accept the contract the studio offered him. He came to Hollywood and, after sitting around doing nothing for six months, he was cast in STOLEN HARMONY (Paramount, 1935). The star of the film was George Raft.

"I'm really worried about this memory business," I told him at our initial meeting.

"Well," he said, pulling out a red folder with a number of pages of typescript inside of it, "maybe this will help. It's a list of all my film appearances that a fan made up and sent to me. Those with the stars after them are titles of pictures he has prints of."

I took the folder and opened it.

"He's got you starting in STOLEN HARMONY. So far, so good."

"That was a George Raft picture. George was a bad actor. He always wanted his lines shortened. He didn't like dialogue. But, for playing such a hard guy all the time, he didn't drink and was a very devout Catholic."

"You've always played both heavies *and* good guys."

"About fifty-fifty. My first break came because Chester Morris only wanted to play heroes and leads. He was offered the part of the main heavy in TEXAS RANGERS [Paramount, 1936] and he turned it down. I took the part."

"You knew Morris?"

"Oh, yeah. And I knew him when he was playing Boston Blackie. How he hated that role. I thought about that myself when I told them I didn't want to play Mike Shayne any more. I didn't want to get channeled into playing only one character. I was getting to be another king of the 'B' pictures, and I didn't like it."

"Can you remember anything that happened on the set during the seven Mike Shayne pictures you did make?"

Lloyd laughed, that infectious laughter of his which always came across so well on screen.

"Now you're asking me to remember," he said. He paused to think. "No," he said finally, "nothing really. Except I liked the role. I liked the Mike Shayne character, the kind of guy he was."

"Do you remember anything about the first picture, MICHAEL SHAYNE, PRIVATE DETECTIVE?"

"I don't even remember the part I had in the Ellery Queen television episode," he confessed, work which he had done about a month prior to my visit.

"Nothing? Nothing at all about the first Shayne?"

"Only that it must have been popular, because Fox signed me after it was released."

"Lloyd!"

He knitted his forehead for some moments.

"No. Nothing."

"But, Lloyd, how can you remember all your lines?"

"That's a funny thing. I can remember lines for a week or two when I'm working, but once I forget them, I forget everything."

"Lloyd. Can you remember which picture is your favorite of the many you've made?"

"Oh, that's easy. THE MAN WHO WOULDN'T TALK [20th-Fox, 1940]."

We could not help grinning at each other.

In 1980, when I took a film crew to record Lloyd's remarks for the camera, as preparation the night before I screened one of his Mike Shayne films for him in the projection room he had set up in his basement. Lloyd sat through the film. Afterward, he could not remember anything about the film. He was interrupted by a telephone call. Some one had gotten his number and, although it was late, had called him up to congratulate him on the job he was doing as a spokesman for Poly-Grip denture cream. The caller was obviously drunk and Lloyd had trouble getting him off the line. In addition to being inebriated the caller was also hard-of-hearing and Lloyd had to keep shouting over the line that it was not "Poly-Dent" that he was representing but Poly-Grip. What I ended up recording on film was not Lloyd's reminiscences of his screen work, but his warm, engaging personality, so at odds with the hard guy roles he had usually played.

SLEEPERS WEST (20th-Fox, 1941) was Lloyd's second Mike Shayne film. It was based on a novel by Frederick Nebel who had written for BLACK MASK and which had been previously filmed under its correct title as SLEEPERS EAST (Fox, 1933) with Preston Foster in the lead role. The story was changed to make Mike Shayne the central character who encounters an old flame played by Lynn Bari at a train depot. Shayne is trying to get Mary Beth Hughes, a surprise witness in a murder trial, back to San Francisco to testify. Much of the action takes place aboard the train. Louis Jean Heydt, who is running away from his wife, stumbles into Mary Beth Hughes' compartment. The two of them start drinking and getting to know each other. Lynn Bari is a reporter for a Denver newspaper and is also engaged to a lawyer with Wentworth Industries. Wentworth is a candidate for governor and it is his son who stands to be convicted of murder by Hughes' testimony. Despite all this, Mike still manages to get Hughes through safely. Perhaps the weakest part of the script was the love affair between Hughes and Heydt which results in Hughes' convincing Heydt to return to his wife.

Mary Beth Hughes was back for DRESSED TO KILL (20th-Fox, 1941), also directed by Eugene Forde. It was based on an original screen story by Richard Burke. Hughes is Mike's fiancée. Just as they are leaving the marriage license bureau, they hear a shot and a scream. Mike manages successfully to solve the case but not without arousing Hughes' rancor, and she jilts him.

In BLUE, WHITE, AND PERFECT (20th-Fox, 1941), based on a story by Borden Chase, Shayne gets involved in the war effort. It was directed by Herbert I. Leeds. Mary Beth Hughes, playing yet a different character, is about to marry a phony Russian. Shayne puts a stop to it by calling Cliff Clark cast as a police inspector. Hughes, who is actually in love with Mike, agrees to marry him provided he gives up detective work. No experienced screenwriter, cognizant of screen conventions, would ever have found himself in the predicament Dresser created for himself when he had Shayne and Phyllis Brighton marry in the novels. Shayne goes to work as a riveter in an airplane factory, although, as it turns out, it is actually an undercover detective job. A smuggling ring is stealing industrial diamonds, transferring them to Honolulu in dress buttons, and selling them to Axis agents. Mike has to extort money out of Hughes in order to sail to Honolulu, albeit he is able to capture the head of the ring and bring the story to a successful conclusion.

THE MAN WHO WOULDN'T DIE (20th-Fox, 1942) was the fifth picture in the series. The screen credited the novel THE FOOTPRINTS ON THE CEILING (1939) by Clayton Rawson, but the story actually derives from Rawson's later novel, NO COFFIN FOR THE CORPSE (1942), and it was something of an improvement over earlier entries. Rawson's detective was Merlini, The Great, a character who had previously been brought to the screen in MIRACLES FOR SALE (M-G-M, 1939) based on Rawson's Merlini novel, DEATH FROM A TOP HAT (1938). The earlier film had starred Robert Young in the role of Merlini, only with his name changed to Mike Morgan. Merlini at least makes an appearance as a character in his own right, no matter how briefly, in THE MAN WHO WOULDN'T DIE when Shayne consults him about magicians who are able to practice the art of shallow breathing. This entry opens on the sound stage set from THE HOUND OF THE BASKERVILLES (20th Fox, 1939) with Baskerville Hall serving as the family estate of Marjorie Weaver's father to which she returns to announce her recent marriage. LeRoy Mason pretends to be dead and has been buried that night. When Weaver is shot at by a mysterious figure in the night, she asks help from her old friend Mike Shayne, who impersonates her new husband. Much humor arises from the situation of a man being presumed dead who is not dead, but eventually Mason is really murdered and Mike must get to the bottom of it.

Herbert I. Leeds directed this entry as he did the next one, JUST OFF BROADWAY (20th-Fox, 1942). Phil Silvers was adeptly cast as a free-lance photo-journalist who makes a lot of trouble for Mike empaneled on a jury at Janis Carter's murder trial. Marjorie Weaver is a newspaper reporter. Mike is able to track down the real culprit and in a wholly ludicrous scene is able to cross-examine witnesses and explain the mystery without a single objection being lodged by anyone, although he does draw a sixty-day sentence for his infringement of jury sequestration.

TIME TO KILL (20th-Fox, 1942), also directed by Herbert I. Leeds, was based on Raymond Chandler's THE HIGH WINDOW (1942) and is a better treatment of its plot than the subsequent THE BRASHER DOUBLOON (20th-Fox, 1947) which was a remake in which George Montgomery was cast as a rather colorless Philip Marlowe. If, however, the essential plot of the novel is more effectively presented in TIME TO KILL, the apprehension of Mrs. Murdock is hopelessly inept with her choking on a T-bone steak! The series had started with Mike almost losing his office furniture due to hard times. In this entry, Mike is seen with his feet propped on his desk, large holes in his shoes. After Shayne is hired by Ethel Griffies as Mrs. Murdock to find her rare Brasher Doubloon and to end her son's marriage to stage performer Linda Conquest, Mike is shown again sitting at his desk, but now with new shoes. Sheila Mannors was cast as the wayward wife of nightclub owner Morris Ankrum whose lover is Ralph Byrd who played the screen's Dick Tracy in three chapter plays and four feature films. Richard Lane played a police lieutenant, but his suspicions are not any more reliable here than they are in the Boston Blackie series.

Lloyd Nolan no longer wanted to play Shayne, for obvious reasons. Even before Sol Wurtzel died, Twentieth Century-Fox cut back drastically on ''B'' picture production. The Charlie Chan series, the Laurel and Hardy comedies, and the Mike Shayne series were all victims to the cutback.

In MICHAEL SHAYNE'S LONG CHANCE (1944), Dresser had Mike pack up to leave Miami in order to return to New Orleans where, some years before, he had worked as a private detective. The identical situation prevails there as it does in Miami, with Chief McCracken friendly toward Shayne, Captain Denton his sworn enemy. The police, however, are a little more vicious. '' 'Let Darcy rap him with his stick again,' '' one of them says after Shayne has been felled by a night stick. '' 'The Cap'n said there wouldn't be no comeback if we messed him up a little.' ''[29] The woman Shayne is supposed to watch and protect is bludgeoned to death so brutally that she is scarcely recognizable. In Mike Shayne mystery, as frequently elsewhere, this automatically means the dead person is a substitution and the face has been obliterated to avoid identification. One of the friends of the dead woman is Lucile Hamilton and by the end of the book she has agreed to become Shayne's secretary when he opens his New Orleans office.

In Miami, Shayne had operated out of his apartment. In the next book in the series, MURDER AND THE MARRIED VIRGIN (1944), Shayne has his own office and his relationship to his business and to Lucy indicates that Dresser had gone back to Sam Spade rather than Nick Charles for his prototype. In this opus, as in several others, Mike is retained by an insurance company to find stolen property and he insists on a fee of ten percent of the insured value. Dresser followed this novel with three novelettes which were not collected into book form until MICHAEL SHAYNE'S TRIPLE MYSTERY (1948), but which appeared in paperback in Dell Books in a somewhat different format. DEAD MAN'S DIARY (1945) and DINNER AT DUPRE'S (1946) were included in a single volume while A TASTE FOR COGNAC (1944) was issued separately as part of a series of 10¢ pocket-sized books. A TASTE FOR COGNAC originally appeared in BLACK MASK Magazine. Both DEAD MAN'S DIARY and DINNER AT DUPRE'S involve switches in identity with the information necessary to arrive at a solution concealed from the reader and both are set in New Orleans. A TASTE FOR COGNAC is set in Miami, during the war and during the time, chronologically, when Shayne was married to Phyllis, but she is not a character in the story nor is any mention made of her. Inspired perhaps by Al Capone after he was released from prison, the story concerns a cache of cognac hidden during Prohibition by a bootlegger who has now been released from prison only to find the liquor, because of the war-time economy, is more valuable than ever. It is a story that in terms of style, characterization, incident, and pacing Dashiell Hammett himself might have written and may constitute Dresser's finest achievement in writing a hard-boiled detective story.

MARKED FOR MURDER (1945) has Timothy Rourke working for the MIAMI COURIER, rather than the MIAMI NEWS, and it is stated that he is topping off his twenty-three-year career as a journalist leading a war on crime in Miami. Previously, Dresser had always kept Mike Shayne as the only focus of his books and he was present in every scene. With MARKED FOR MURDER, he introduced a new device, that of setting up the story and mystery prior to Shayne's entrance upon the scene. In this case, Rourke is the point of view until he is found in his apartment nearly dead from gunshot wounds. The case does get Mike back to Miami, and it even concludes with Will Gentry remarking, " 'We could use you around here, Mike. Why don't you come back home?' "[30]

Set, apparently, sometime before MARKED FOR MURDER but not before DEAD MAN'S DIARY, MURDER IS MY BUSINESS (1945) finds Mike Shayne in El Paso. The case involves a mayoral race in which neither candidate is desirable nor honest. Again, there is a switched identity. What is new, and almost unique to this book, is a sense of the past. Shayne had worked in El Paso previously and had come to know some of the characters in this story a that time. One of the candidates for mayor now had then wanted to hire him to frustrate his daughter's intended marriage. Shayne had not co-operated, but the marriage did not take place any way and now, when Shayne encounters the woman, single, unhappy, the reader is told that Carmela Towne's "weeping had an obscene sound. It was as though something had rotted away inside of her, and her tears were a suppurating excrement bubbling up under the pressure of long decay."[31] In imagery and mood, MURDER IS MY BUSINESS could well have been a paradigm for virtually all of Ross Macdonald's Lew Archer novels.

BLOOD ON BISCAYNE BAY (1946) finds Shayne back in Miami on an extended vacation. Shayne has departed his New Orleans office for a period of reflection, "to examine impersonally his feelings toward the dark-haired and brown-eyed girl who was so much like Phyllis."[32] The reference, of course, is to Lucy Hamilton. More is revealed about Phyllis's death when a young woman, Phyllis' best friend, comes to Mike to hire him. " 'I want you to know how happy she was married to you,' " she tells Mike. " 'That fall when she was expecting the baby she made me feel that marriage could be wonderful. Seeing her so happy changed a lot of my ideas. I guess I was pretty cynical about men and marriage. I honestly don't believe I'd be Mrs. Leslie Hudson right now if it hadn't been for Phyllis—and you.' "[33] Mike solves the case and saves Christine Hudson's marriage. At the end, Shayne is on his way to the airport with an imitation pearl necklace he intends to give to Lucy as a peace offering. COUNTERFEIT WIFE (1947) opens with Shayne at the airport. He misses his flight because he becomes involved in another case and Lucy informs him by telephone that she is closing up his New Orleans office and quitting. It is a badly plotted book with two different murderers, one for each of the murders, and with one of them flinging himself out of a window, falling nine stories.

In BLOOD ON THE STARS (1948), Shayne's problems with Lucy have been resolved. She has decided to come to Miami to see how she likes it. Again the plot is developed before Shayne is introduced into the scene. Lucy and Mike enter a swank jewelry store because she does not want the pearls. The plot is improbable with one of the characters having played three different roles in the past eight years, two of them among some of the same people who do not recognize him. A TASTE FOR VIOLENCE (1949) is set in Centerville, Kentucky, a mining town with labor problems. It is Dresser's version of Hammett's RED HARVEST; and, while there are fewer killings in this book, the bleak view of small town corruption is quite as compelling. However, Dresser was fundamentally more of an optimist than was Hammett and the problems are all seen to resolve themselves once Shayne has himself appointed chief of police and imports Timothy Rourke to run the city's newspaper in a campaign to clean up the state.

Production rights to Mike Shayne were acquired in 1946 by Sig Neufeld. Neufeld had been in independent film production since the mid 'Thirties. Most of his extremely poorly mounted films were directed by his brother, who used most often the name Sam Newfield. All of the Mike Shayne films made for release by Producers Releasing Corporation were worse than dreadful. Not only was the dialogue wretched, but the acting and the direction were so soporific as to generate nothing so much as a mounting sense of tedium. Hugh Beaumont, who would later play the role of Ward Cleaver on the LEAVE IT TO BEAVER television series, was cast as Shayne. In the novels, Shayne would sometimes toss a lighted cigarette on the carpet while interviewing a pompous character; and I have already mentioned that cognac, for him, was a marvelous restorative agent which could bring him back to life after enduring the most harrowing physical punishment. In the PRC films, these habits were altered and, instead, Shayne was given the obnoxious habit of eating peanuts all through the pictures, discarding the shells on the floor or street, wherever he happened to be at the moment. In the first entries, Cheryl Walker was cast as Shayne's secretary, Phyllis Hamilton, obviously a combination of Phyllis Brighton and Lucy Hamilton in the stories. She established her self-appointed role in Mike's life early in the series with the line, "But, Mike, I want to be more than a secretary." This "more" was a shrewish, jealous, interfering snoop who resents every pretty female client who comes to consult Shayne. With such a characterization, she could not help but prove a drag on the series.

In the novels, of course, Shayne would customarily tamper with evidence, conceal evidence, destroy evidence, manufacture fraudulent evidence, and in every case he would manage to get away with it. In JUST OFF BROADWAY, Shayne had drawn a light sentence for his illegal activities. Such was not the case at PRC which seconded the novels in giving the impression that a private detective might expect to get away with all manner of felonies if he is shrewd enough. Obviously Dresser wanted this new series to be based on the books he had already published, rather than to go outside for stories as had been done at Twentieth Century-Fox. MURDER IS MY BUSINESS (PRC, 1946) was the first picture in the series, but other than the title, really, it bore no relationship to the novel. The film opens with Shayne taking out his secretary to Lyle Talbot's night club. Shayne eats peanuts and orders milk at the bar! In the next scene, he is hired by a wealthy woman to find out who is sending her threatening letters. The woman turns out to be Talbot's sister. Talbot himself is an ex-con with an inferiority complex about his past. He slugs Shayne on the jaw no less than four times in the course of the picture, twice knocking him out completely. When Talbot's sister is murdered, the identity of the murderer is so painfully evident that the bouts between Talbot and Shayne must have been added as a counter-measure for boredom and to lengthen the development of the plot. Ralph Dunn was cast as Peter Rafferty, the police detective who has it in for Shayne. He goes on the radio and claims outright that Shayne is a front for the underworld.

LARCENY IN HER HEART (PRC, 1946) added Gavin Gordon to the cast in the role of Tim Rourke with Beaumont, Walker, and Dunn. It was based, a bit more faithfully this time, on BODIES ARE WHERE YOU FIND THEM. Phyllis and Mike are going on a vacation to visit Phyllis' aunt. Mike is detained at the last minute by a client who hires him to find his stepdaughter who has vanished. The man gives Shayne a photo of her. When she later stumbles into Shayne's office, she is wearing the identical dress as in the photograph. The girl is murdered while Shayne takes Phyllis to the depot. Her body disappears and reappears, the police being tipped off in each case. The girl, however, proves to be a phony. Shayne locates the real stepdaughter at a sanitarium operated by Douglas Fowley.

Kathryn Adams replaced Cheryl Walker as Shayne's secretary in BLONDE FOR A DAY (PRC, 1946) based on MARKED FOR MURDER. Gavin Gordon as Tim Rourke gets shot while trying to expose a gambling syndicate. Shayne in the film has moved from Los Angeles to San Francisco instead of from Miami to New Orleans and none of the films was ever set in Miami. Fred Myton did the screenplay and the height of the humor which he injected comes when a Negro doorman from whom Shayne wants to buy information tells him, "Yuh came to the rahight mahrket, duh black mahrket." Shayne solves the case in spite of continuous interference from Rafferty, this time played by portly Cy Kendall.

THREE ON A TICKET (PRC, 1947) was based on THE CORPSE CAME CALLING. Cheryl Walker was back as Phyllis, but the peroxide splotches in her hair tended to detract from her appearance. A detective acquaintance of Mike's stumbles into his office and dies. Next a blonde comes to see Shayne, hoping to hire him to rub out her husband, played by Douglas Fowley. Shayne is kidnapped by two thugs and beat unmercifully. There was no need to worry, however, since Shayne suffers only a slight cut to his lip before Phyllis rushes in with the police. Ralph Dunn was back as Rafferty and Gordon portrayed Rourke whose one beat seems to be Shayne's office, reminiscent of the low-budget concept of the newspaper journalist played by Marjorie Reynolds in the Mr. Wong series.

None of the cast regulars appeared in the final entry, TOO MANY WINNERS (PRC, 1947), based on TICKETS FOR DEATH—except, of course, for Beaumont as Shayne. Producers Releasing Corporation was in its death spasm, but not soon enough, since it had inflicted so many bad pictures on the public. William Beaudine directed, replacing Sam Newfield, but in many ways he was worse. Trudy Marshall was cast as Phyllis. Again, Mike and Phyllis are about to embark on a vacation when Shayne is hired to get to the bottom of counterfeit winning tickets at the Santa Rosita racetrack.

In 1949, Mike Shayne came belatedly to radio, played for a single season by Jeff Chandler. Television was already taking over and Shayne had to wait until 1960 before a series of thirty-two episodes was filmed with Richard Denning in the role of Shayne and Patricia Donahue as Lucy Hamilton. The Miami location was used, but the series was not renewed after its first season.

Davis Dresser married three times, always to writers. His first was Helen

McCloy. He co-wrote some fiction with his second wife, Kathleen Rollins, under the pseudonym Hal Debrett. His third wife was Mary Savage. In 1956, Dresser became editor of MIKE SHAYNE'S MYSTERY MAGAZINE and regularly contributed Shayne stories to the pulp publication which enjoyed rather a long run as such publications go. He also founded his own publishing company, Torquil & Company, with Dodd, Mead, his hardbound publishers, doing the distribution.

In the final analysis, I suspect that it was primarily because Mike Shayne was never depicted in films, radio, or television as he appeared in Dresser's stories that he failed to catch on with the public since, after all, the paperback editions of the novels sold in excess of forty million copies. Dresser never changed Mike Shayne, in order to stress the savagery, misogyny, and raw sex which came to characterize Mickey Spillane and the latter generation of hard-boiled detective story writers and, perhaps for this reason, he missed the soaring popularity which met this image of the private detective. In THE CORPSE THAT NEVER WAS, for example, Mike regrets his decision never to marry again and the effect this is having on Lucy Hamilton who is in love with him. At one point he remarks to her, " 'At the very least I could dry the dishes for you so you could come in and relax with a drink. . . . ' "[34] In another snipet of dialogue, Shayne reflects aloud: " 'The woman drank off her cyanide cocktail like a man. . . . ' He paused and frowned. 'Why do I say that? Like a woman, damn it.' "[35] And then, of course, there are moments even as early as BODIES ARE WHERE YOU FIND THEM when Shayne is shown to have an inner dimension. "The thought of his young wife brought an acute sense of loneliness upon him. He needed her bouyant faith tonight, the cool, caressing touch of her hands, the pressure of her smooth cheek against his, the influx of strength from her passionate belief in him. He was, he admitted, becoming increasingly dependent upon Phyllis. He, who had never been dependent upon any person or thing. The hard-boiled dick who had fought his way savagely to the top by a ruthless disregard for everything that stood in his path."[36]

When Davis Dresser died, in 1976, it was perhaps a tribute to his creation of Mike Shayne that other writers continued to write stories about him under the Brett Halliday pseudonym. But here, as is also the case with the many Ellery Queen novels written by other writers, the lack of essential quality only serves to bankrupt the property, not add to its enhancement.

FILM NOIR

> It could well even be a basic condition of existence that complete knowledge brings one to ruin—so that the fortitude of one's spirit might be measured by how much of the "truth" can be endured, and more significantly, to what degree one *might deem it necessary* to dilute it, veil it, sweeten, dampen, even falsify it.
>
> Friedrich Nietzsche[37]

I have already dealt at length with the cultural origins as well as the history and character of this film style in DARK CINEMA. Here I shall only be concerned with it insofar as it exerted an impact on the detective film. The orientation of *film noir* in terms of its narrative structures is indebted to the concept of fate and, hence, is classical in origin. Since fate plays no part in the theology of the Judeo-Christian tradition, and certainly none in what Leibnitz termed theodicy, their tenets are irrelevant to a consideration of *film noir*. This is a distinction often overlooked, especially by American film historians whose background is either Christian or Jewish and who have not had a classical education. The profound difference between Sophocles' OEDIPUS REX and the Book of Job resolves itself not merely into C. G. Jung's observation in ANTWORT AUF HIOB [ANSWER TO JOB] (1952/1961) that "God may be loved and must be feared"[38]; it goes beyond this. There is a wholly different dimension in Sophocles where not only are the ways of the gods unknown to human beings, but they may be forever unknowable and they may at times be blatantly unjust and capricious. Euripides ventured so far as to suggest that perhaps the fundamental principle of the universe is irrational and, therefore, cannot be discerned, much less comprehended, by reason.

It was only when Jung approached the phenomenon of the God of the Old Testament from a psychological point of view informed by his study of Nietzsche and Nietzsche's perspective, derived in turn from the ancient Greek encounter with the irrational, that was born the image of that God's antinomy, the dark God. "From The Apocalypse we learn again," Jung wrote, "that God not only is to be loved, but also is to be feared. *He fills us with good and with evil*, otherwise he would not need to be feared, and because he will become man, the uniting of his antinomy must take place within men. That signifies a new responsibility for mankind. Mankind can no longer now talk about its smallness or its futility, for the dark God has pressed into its hand the atom bomb and chemical weapons and therewith given it the power to pour out vials of apocalyptic wrath upon its fellow human beings. Since man possesses so-to-speak divine power, he can no longer remain blind and unconscious. He must learn about the nature of God and about what has been anticipated by metaphysics so that thereby he may understand himself and recognize the nature of his God."[39]

Film noir is a darkling vision of the world, a view from the underside, born of fundamental disillusionment perhaps, but also invariably the result, no matter how timid, of a confrontation with nihilism. Nietzsche, as Dostoyevsky, knew well the cause of nihilism and, although on the surface in many ways contradictory, their respective works were intended to be an antidote to nihilism. "Othello was not jealous," Alexander Pushkin once wrote; "he was trusting." "This remark in itself attests to that great poet's uncanny insight," Mitya Karamazov says in THE BROTHERS KARAMAZOV (1880), recalling Pushkin. "Othello's heart was broken and his whole understanding of the world was dimmed because *his ideal had been shattered*."[40]

For Nietzsche, "the untenability of one interpretation of the world, upon which a tremendous amount of energy has been lavished, awakens the suspicion that *all* interpretations of the world are false."[41] This comment comes from what has been termed the philosopher's "posthumous legacy," but he had already anticipated it in DIE GÖTZENDÄMMERUNG [THE TWILIGHT OF THE IDOLS] in a passage that I cited in the section on Raffles and which ends with Nietzsche's ironic barb that "for the English morality is still no problem. . . . "[42] But in the Twentieth century, as Nietzsche foresaw, when the keystone of the Christian tradition has been shattered and with it the whole Christian system of moral values, when no tradition, however ingrained, has been able to cope properly with social cataclysms, then, even for the English, and no less for the Americans as revealed in so many *films noirs*: morality is a problem.

It is in this context that the rise of the so-called classical detective story to popularity must be viewed. As John Paterson observed in "A Cosmic View of the Private Eye" (1953), "in the age of the Boom, the Great Depression, flappers and gangsterism, and the Fascist Solution, it recalls the sober gentility and crude optimism of an earlier and more complacent generation; it asserts the triumph of a social order and decorum that have all but passed away."[43] Julian Symons arrived at a similar conclusion when he observed about the supposed "Golden Age" that "in America and also throughout Europe crime literature made its chief appeal to those who had a way of life and a position in society to preserve. So far from being, as some people have suggested, a surrogate satisfaction for murderous desires, typical detective stories of the period were remarkably free from the realities of violence. Victim, murder, investigation— all have a hieratic and ritual quality. What the stories assert is the static nature of society, the inevitableness with which wrongdoing is punished."[44]

What Nietzsche wrote about all interpretations of the world coming to seem false if one is proven false certainly was borne out by the commercial fantasies and wish-fulfillments propounded by Hollywood prior to the advent of *film noir*. The period in American filmmaking between the wars was one in which the happy ending was obligatory and, with the Hays Office in place to guard "public" morality, crime could never be shown to pay. With the rise of National Socialism in Germany, many of the most gifted directors and screenwriters of the Weimar Republic fled Europe and came to Hollywood. They brought with them a tradition utterly alien to the American cinema: the dark, the Gothic, the tragic, in a word: hopelessness. The profound difference between the two film styles is rather aptly symbolized in that little parable Sam Spade tells Brigid O'Shaughnessy in THE MALTESE FALCON about Flitcraft. When the tenuousness of existence penetrated into his consciousness, he became painfully aware of the caprice by which we all live and die, what Quintus Curtius meant when he wrote "*contra Fortunam non satis cauta*" [in fortune's shadow no one stands secure]. Flitcraft fled from the suspicion that perhaps nothing ultimately means anything. But, after acting in accord with the irrational and purposeless nature of life for a couple of years, Flitcraft's mind slowly deadened the shock of awareness and he crept back into his comfortable pattern. It is rather after the fashion of what Nietzsche meant when he observed, "just as one has a certain character, so one also has his typical experience, which perpetually recurs."[45]

If life *is* caprice, if the basis of human existence is irrational and logic a human projection, if order is an illusion, men can still become so busy getting and spending that they can ignore reality, in Nietzche's idiom *what they really know*. Anxiety can be hidden in a quest for wealth, material possessions, security, or power. C. G. Jung, whose psychological theories in many ways might be viewed as a response to a pervasive nihilism, found that even theology itself is an elaborate structure erected to remove safely our fearful and easily unbalanced psyches from the immediacy of religious, which is to say irrational and frightening, experiences. "Extreme positions are not succeeded by moderate ones," Nietzsche declared in his "posthumous legacy," "but by extreme positions, only *reversed*. Thus belief in the absolute immorality of Nature, in the lack of purpose and meaninglessness, is the *affect* psychologically necessary once belief in God and an essentially moral order is no longer supportable."[46]

Hammett initially championed distrust over blind faith, skepticism over belief, cynicism over hope. Yet it is the truly unique individual who can sustain such a mental posture and go on as confidently as the man who relies on all manner of comforting fantasies to get him through. So it was that in the end Hammett could not do it; he turned to Marxism. Ludwig Binswanger whose uncle had cared for Nietzsche at the Jena Clinic after Nietzsche's mental collapse (perhaps better described in German as *eine Umnachtung*: being enveloped in the darkness of night) and who had been a student of both Freud and Jung wrote to me shortly before his own death. He felt that psychoanalysis may have taken a misdirection in its effort to be therapeutically functional. As one of the founders of *Daseinsanalyse* [existential analysis], he summarized his position in a series of questions: What can the analyst do with a life that has been wasted, with a psyche that lives in a body shot up in war, imprisoned in a concentration camp, brainwashed, a psyche that cannot deal competently with deception, exploitation, frustration, and failure? And what of impotence, old age, physical exhaustion, death? What is the therapy for these? If not religion, if not materialism, if not hard work so as to pay taxes, tithes, and interest so others need not work so hard: what then?

Appraising Sam Spade's moral code, William Ruehlmann commented in SAINT WITH A GUN that "Hammett's book is not a novel in praise of that code; it is an examination of its consequences for a man who has nothing else." But for the fact that John Huston made a traditional hero of Sam Spade, *film noir* might have received an early thrust from his version of THE MALTESE FALCON (Warner's, 1941). The Bogart persona, however, to which Huston contributed so much in terms of its projection on the screen in the films he directed with Bogart in the 'Forties and 'Fifties, prevented him from concentrating on the culpability of *all* the characters, the detective included. The American cinema might still have its patriotic films, its family films, its Westerns with super heroes, its musicals with vocalized happy endings, its soap-opera melodramas, and its serials with master criminals dispatched in the final episode, but in certain crime films, those which eschewed being part of a series or part of the convention of a "master" detective or honest agent of a benevolent government fighting organized subversion of many kinds, if there was a detective or agent at all a new spirit was infused into the story, an unsettling, critical, pervasive, pessimistic representation of life, a negation of values that otherwise would have been regarded as commercially unfeasible.

"Dashiell Hammett's dialogues," André Gide remarked in his IMAGINARY INTERVIEWS (1944), "in which every character is trying to deceive all the others and in which the truth slowly becomes visible through a haze of deception, can be compared only with the best in Hemingway."[47] What Gide did not say, but what he could have added, is that the belief in truth is above all a *moral* premise. Faith in the ability to perceive the truth, even if only finally and only after great difficulty, is one moral premise *film noir*, as indeed the detective story, rarely abandons because it does not dare to abandon it. "Sometimes I wake up in the middle of the night," George Raft once described a nocturnal attack of emphysema, "and I am gasping for breath. I turn on the respirator and I breathe, as deeply as I can. I do that for a half hour, maybe an hour. I can breathe a little better then. But I can't get back to sleep." William Barrett in IRRATIONAL MAN (1962) commented that "the American has not yet assimilated the disappearance of his own geographical frontier, his spiritual horizon is still the limitless play of human possibilities, and as yet he has not lived through the crucial experience of human finitude."[48] The classical conception of moderation voiced by Horace—"*est modus in rebus, sunt certi denique fines . . .* " [there is a measure in things, there are certain definite limits]—is a notion almost completely alien to the American worldview. All of these themes come together in *film noir*. It is a gasping for breath, a struggle to hang onto life. It is an essay in personal martyrdom, much in the sense of the highly personal speculations of Friedrich Nietzsche or Søren Kierkegaard, although their names would perhaps not be familiar to most people viewing these films. It is a depiction of the American *mise-en-scène* that tries to arrive at some statement of truth despite the haze of deception. At times, *film noir* almost dares a revaluation of all values, although, by the fade, it usually proves lacking in ultimate courage: the courage, not from conviction, but to attack *all* convictions. Its narrative structure is frequently *de temps perdu*, whether narrated by a character in the story to tell the viewer just how he got into his predicament, or a reconstruction of a man's past through one kind of investigation or another.

Yet, before *film noir* could come to the screen, American fiction itself had to undergo the atmosphere of distrust which informs what has been called the BLACK MASK school: the recognition that the real story is not the story everyone is telling and that the real story, when it comes to light, is not only unpleasant, it is often *worse* than anyone suspected it might be. Through the dark visions of *film noir*, Americans shared Raymond Chandler's consciousness that looming in the streets are forces darker than the night; but—and this came to be the essential difference between Chandler's fiction, and that of the hard-boiled school generally, and true *film noir*—there is no Chandleresque knight to brave the dark evils of the world.

In conversation one day with Howard Hawks, he brought up the story he was fond of telling about THE BIG SLEEP (Warner's, 1946). While he was filming the sequence where Owen's car is pulled out of the water on Warner's tank soundstage, Humphrey Bogart asked him who had killed Owen. After all, if Bogart was playing the detective and the point-of-view character, he really ought to know who had done it. Hawks did not know, but he said he would ask William Faulkner who had worked on the screenplay. Faulkner said he did not know. So Hawks wired Raymond Chandler who had written the novel and Chandler wired back that the butler had done it. It did not matter, of course, because *film noir* was changing the emphasis. One was more concerned with *why* a crime had been committed, why there was a corpse, rather than with who committed the crime. If nothing else made *film noir* unique, this concentration on teleology did.

The term *film noir* was coined in 1946 by Nino Frank, a *cinéaste* who derived it from Marcel Duhamel's SÉRIE NOIRE books. As a film style it commenced in earnest in three films: Boris Ingster's STRANGER ON THE THIRD FLOOR (RKO, 1940), Orson Welles' CITIZEN KANE (RKO, 1941), and H. Bruce Humberstone's I WAKE UP SCREAMING (20th-Fox, 1941). However, while Welles' CITIZEN KANE was one of the founding pictures, it was not until THE LADY FROM SHANGHAI (Columbia, 1948) that Welles produced what might well be taken as a prototype of the style.

Marcel Duhamel in his Preface to PANORAMA DU FILM NOIR AMÉRICAIN (1941–1953) (1955) by Raymond Borde and Etienne Chaumeton admitted the aptness of Frank's term and added, somewhat facetiously, *"lisez donc force romans noirs et voyez des films noirs en abondance. Tant que vous ne vous truciderez qu'en imagination, nous pourrons dormir tranquilles. C'est la grâce que je nous souhaite."*[49] In their Introduction to PANORAMA, Borde and Chaumeton noted that it was first in the spring of 1946 that the Parisian screen began featuring American films *"qui avaient en commun une atmosphère insolite et cruelle, teintée d'un érotisme assez particulier. . . . "*[50] Of course, Nino Frank, in that seminal article *"Un Nouveau Genre 'Policier': L'aventure Criminelle"* [A New Kind of Detective Story: The Criminal Adventure] (1946) had reported that these *films noirs "appartiennent à ce qu'on appelait jadis le genre policier, et que l'on ferait mieux de désigner désormais par le terme d'aventures criminelles, ou mieux encore, de psychologie criminelle."*[51] Borde and Chaumeton accepted this distinction and, if anything, made it even more emphatic, concluding that *"c'est la présence du crime qui donne au film noir sa marque la plus constante.''*[52] They perceived, correctly I believe, that whether *"sordide ou insolite, la mort émerge toujours au terme d'un voyage sinueux. A tous les sens du mot, le film noir est un film de mort.''*[53] They also made a distinction between the police documentary and the true *film noir* which, I think, should be adopted. They recognized that *"le documentaire policier américain est en réalité un documentaire à la gloire de la police et rejoint dans le même sac des productions telles que, en France, IDENTITÉ JUDICAIRE* [(French, 1950) directed by Hervé Bromberger], *ou, en Angleterre, POLICE SANS ARMES* [THE BLUE LAMP (British, 1950) directed by Basil Dearden]. *Rien de tel dans la série noire. S'il y a des policiers, ils sont véreux—comme l'inspecteur de QUAND LA VILLE DORT* [THE ASPHALT JUNGLE (M-G-M, 1950) directed by John Huston], *ou cette belle tête de brute corrompue incarnée par Lloyd Nolan dans LA DAME DU LAC* [THE LADY IN THE LAKE (M-G-M, 1946) directed by Robert Montgomery]—*parfois même meurtriers (CRIME PASSIONNEL)* [FALLEN ANGEL (20th-Fox, 1946)] *et MARK DIXON DÉTECTIVE* [WHERE THE SIDEWALK ENDS (20th-Fox, 1950)] *de Otto Preminger.''*[54]

It was not until the late 1960s that *film noir* began being discussed in English among film critics and historians, followed by a deluge of publications in the 'Seventies and 'Eighties. "The essential question," Nino Frank wrote about *film noir* in Georges Sadoul's DICTIONNAIRE DES CINÉASTES [DICTIONARY OF FILM PROFESSIONALS] (1965), "is not to know who committed the crime, but what the protagonist does. What matters is the enigmatic psychological relationship between the detective and the criminal—at once enemy and friend." A. M. Karimi seemed pretty much to accept this notion in his doctoral dissertation, later published as a book, TOWARD A DEFINITION OF THE AMERICAN FILM NOIR (1941–1949) (1976). Karimi also quoted Graham Greene with obvious approval: "In my books there are crimes, but not criminals."[55] I disagree with both the French critics and with Karimi about the necessity of there being a crime in a *film noir*. There often is a crime, but there need not be one. Rather, what is far more important is that the narrative structure doubly determine the actions of the protagonist. As in Shakespeare's MACBETH, such human actions appear to be both fated *and* consciously willed. In the paradigms of *film noir*, this is invariably the case, along with what might be called the CITIZEN KANE technique: the narrative needs to account for a particular life.

One of the sources of confusion in much that has been written about *film noir* derives from the fact that it is both a style and a type of narrative structure. Because it is a style, it can cut across generic lines and be found in a gangster film such as WHITE HEAT (Warner's, 1949) or a Western such as PURSUED (Warner's, 1947) or a comedy such as UNFAITHFULLY YOURS (20th-Fox, 1948); but what ultimately determines if such films are examples of *film noir*, or not, is the presence of the *film noir* narrative structure. "What keeps the *film noir* alive for us today is something more than a spurious nostalgia,"

Robert G. Porfirio wrote in "No Way Out: Existential Motifs in the *Film Noir*" (1976). "It is the underlying mood of pessimism which undercuts any attempted happy endings and prevents the films from being the typical Hollywood escapist fare many were originally intended to be. More than lighting or photography, it is this sensibility which makes the black film black for us."[56] What *film noir* was, what was so revolutionary about it, was its inherent reaction to decades of forced optimism; *film noir* divorced itself from this ideological obligation with a vengeance. For this reason I tend to agree with Janey Place in her article in WOMEN IN FILM NOIR (1978) that *film noir* is not a genre of film, such as those to which Hollywood filmmakers had become accustomed over the years, but instead a *movement* among individual filmmakers which evoked similar techniques to make anti-generic statements.

Paul Schrader in his "Notes on *Film Noir*" further refined the characteristics of the movement. He felt the narrative structure and its visual component in *films noirs* combined to give an unprecedented, harsh, and uncomplimentary view of American society; that *films noirs*, as German Expressionism and French New Wave, belong to a specific historical period, namely the 'Forties and early 'Fifties; that visually *films noirs* combined the techniques of German Expressionist cinema with cinematic realism; that, just as German Expressionism influenced the visual style of *films noirs*, the hard-boiled writing, especially of the BLACK MASK school, influenced screenwriting and, above all, dialogue. I would agree with him on every one of these points; I would disagree only when he asserted that "*film noir* is more interested in style than theme. . . ."[57] I regard them as inextricable components, one to the other. As Robert G. Porfirio stated in "No Way Out," "to place these films within a specific time period is not enough. . . . Their so-called 'Expressionistic' style was quite literally a combination of impressionistic (i.e., technical effects) and expressionistic (i.e., *mise-en-scène*) techniques, which can be traced back to the period of German Expressionism. The infusion of this style into Hollywood filmmaking was due partly to the talents of the European emigrés and partly to the growth of the classic gangster and horror genres of the 1930s which called for such a style. But the unique development of this style in the *film noir* was most immediately due to CITIZEN KANE. Welles' film not only invigorated a baroque visual style which was later to characterize the period, but also provided a new psychological dimension, a morally ambiguous hero, a convoluted time structure, and the use of flashback and first person narration—all of which became *film noir* conventions."[58]

Socrates, and after him Plato and Aristotle, was convinced that a person confronted with a choice between what was obviously good and what was obviously bad would invariably choose what was good. Euripides saw the matter otherwise and in this century modern psychology has come down on the side of Euripides. "Anybody possessing analytical knowledge," Theodor Reik wrote in THE COMPULSION TO CONFESS (1959), "recognizes the fact that the world is full of actions performed by people exclusively to their detriment and without perceptible advantage, although their eyes were open."[59] This perspective on human nature is evident at once in *films noirs* as is Euripides' conviction that the universe might be *au fond* irrational. Just as Greek drama in terms of narrative structure falls into two basic types, so, too, do *films noirs*: the *film noir* of error and the *film noir* of circumstance. A paradigm of the former, surely, is DOUBLE INDEMNITY (Paramount, 1944) directed by Billy Wilder, while THE BIG HEAT (Columbia, 1953) is a paradigm of the latter. French critics appear to have been more familiar with the classics of the German Expressionist cinema than have their American counterparts and, accordingly, Borde and Chaumeton could remark that "Fritz Lang never forgot the expressionist lessons of his youth," and Georges Sadoul could note in his HISTOIRE GÉNÉRALE DU CINÉMA in Volume IV (1954) that Billy Wilder never forgot Expressionism and the *Kammerspiel* [a private play production for a small audience] in which a guilt complex and all-powerful destiny bring about a catastrophe from which there is no escape.

John Russell Taylor in STRANGERS IN PARADISE (1983) perceived that DOUBLE INDEMNITY, "for all its idiomatic local color, . . . remains in many respects very much in the black German tradition: it does not abandon expressionist lighting, the strongly dramatic use of shadows and such, but instead manages to persuade us to accept them as real, normal even, so convincing is the special world the film creates."[60] Charles Higham and Joel Greenberg in their book, HOLLYWOOD IN THE FORTIES (1968), regarded DOUBLE INDEMNITY as "one of the highest summits of *film noir*, . . . a film without a single trace of pity or love. . . . The film reverberates with the forlorn poetry of late sunny afternoons; the script is as tart as a lemon; and . . . a notable scene is when the car stalls after the husband's murder, the killing conveyed in a single close-up of the wife's face, underlined by the menacing strings of Miklos Rosza's score."[61]

The plot is essentially a variation on the Klytaimnestra story, with this exception: neither in the James M. Cain short novel on which it was based nor in the screen adaptation, written by Billy Wilder in collaboration with Raymond Chandler, are there any extenuating circumstances provided for the wayward wife. The names were somewhat changed in the screenplay. Barbara Stanwyck was cast as Phyllis Dietrichson, Fred MacMurray as the insurance salesman, Walter Neff. Phyllis shows no emotion after the murder of her husband, but, instead, begins to scheme on how to get rid of Neff. Her motivation, in the film as in the short novel, is attributed to a homicidal psychosis. The reason I find the film a superior narrative to the Cain original is that Wilder and Chandler, no doubt instinctively, followed the structure of the five-act tragedy inherited by the Renaissance playwrights from Seneca and perfected by Shakespeare. Employing the flashback technique, the Situation is stated at once by Neff as he enters his insurance company office and begins to dictate his confession to Keyes, the canny head of the claims department played by Edward G. Robinson. The viewer can see that Neff is wounded and, as the camera occasionally cuts back to him throughout his narrative, the blood can be seen to be spreading and the wound soon appears to be fatal. "I killed Dietrichson—me, Walter Neff—insurance salesman—thirty-five years old, no visible scars—till a while ago, that is . . . I killed him for the money—and for a woman. . . . It all began last May." The Conflict soon becomes evident via flashback. Phyllis wants to murder her husband and she wants Neff to help her do it. At first, Neff resists. His psychology is somewhat more complicated than is hers. In terms of the sexual politics of the plot, Phyllis is a woman fully in possession of her own sexuality and capable of using it to achieve her ends. While Neff is attracted to her sexually, the money to be gained through insurance fraud and the sexual possession of Phyllis are compounded for him by the boredom with his job, his rivalry with Keyes who symbolizes the "system," and, most of all, Neff has toyed with the idea of beating the system.

The Crisis section of the plot is concerned with the initial frustrations of killing Dietrichson and then with the mishaps which occur after the deed has been done and Neff must impersonate Dietrichson in order to make it appear that he accidentally fell to his death from the observation deck of a passenger train. The Reversal for Neff comes when he realizes that Phyllis not only has no feeling for him, but that she is both promiscuous (she takes up with her stepdaughter's boyfriend) and intent on removing him as a hindrance to her bid for total independence; at the same time he learns that she has engineered other murders, including that of Dietrichson's first wife, and that he is only the latest in a number of victims to her sexuality and her ambition. The Reversal reaches its peak in the penultimate scene where, quite literally, Phyllis and Neff murder each other. The Recognition scene comes when Keyes enters the office and Neff, still dictating his confession, becomes aware of his presence. Neff tells Keyes: "I know why you couldn't figure this one . . . because the guy you were looking for was too close . . . right across the desk from you." Keyes replies: "Closer than that, Walter." All through the film, Keyes has never had a match with which to light his cigar. At one point, in a jocular tone, Neff had quipped to him, "I love you, too." It is Neff who always lights Keyes' cigar. He lights Keyes' cigar at the most suspenseful moment in the film, when Keyes calls on him at his apartment, when the investigation of Phyllis is at its most intensive, and with Neff in the doorway, Keyes in the hall, Phyllis hiding in the shadows behind the door, the three forming a tableau of crisis in which both Keyes and Phyllis seem to be in pursuit of Neff's soul. Phyllis wins, for a time, at least until the Reversal. In the Recognition, when Keyes bends over and lights Walter's cigarette, as a final, parting gesture, Neff quips again, "I love you, too"; but here the remark is poignant with irony. Trust and love can be found between men; they are impossible with a woman in possession of her sexuality and fired by ambition to break out of the system which, in terms of sexual politics, is the patriarchal society in which Jean Heather, as the stepdaughter, wants nothing more out of life than to live according to the traditional role of loving wife and mother (the right choice in a female companion, which

Neff realizes too late). Neff has made all the wrong choices, and hence his fate. Every *film noir* of error appears to follow this five-part structure of Situation, Conflict, Crisis, Reversal, and Recognition.

THE BIG HEAT is later *film noir* and, therefore, includes many more elements which had become conventions to the style than DOUBLE INDEMNITY had which, much in the manner of an establishing shot, was an "establishing" film. THE BIG HEAT also belongs grouped with a number of films similarly inspired in the early 'Fifties by newspaper exposure of police departments' ignoring the activities of organized crime. Lang himself commented that THE BIG HEAT "is an accusation against crime. But it involves people—unlike other good pictures against crime which only involve gangsters. . . . Glenn Ford is a member of the police department and his wife gets killed. The story becomes a personal affair between him and crime. He becomes the audience."[62]

The narrative structure is that of the *film noir* of circumstance which is modeled on that of the Tragedy of Circumstance as in Euripides' THE TROJAN WOMEN. The film opens with the suicide of a police officer. Ford, cast as homicide sergeant Dave Bannion, is assigned to the case and then told to lay off of it. Bannion is disinclined to listen, especially when he talks with the woman who was the dead man's mistress. She believes that the dead man's wife, played by Jeanette Nolan, is blackmailing gangster Mike Lagana played by Alexander Scourby. Lagana controls the city and it is he who wants all investigation quashed. The mistress' tortured body is discovered—another warning to Bannion to lay off; instead, it only encourages him to pursue his investigation. Bannion goes so far as to confront Lagana in his home, to rough up his bodyguard, and to threaten to tie him to the mistress' murder. Another, even more horrible action must follow this confrontation. A brief domestic scene showing the rapport between Bannion and his wife, played by Jocelyn Brando, concludes with Bannion staying with their child in the child's bedroom telling her a bedtime story while Brando goes out to the car. Sounds alone tell us what she is doing and suspense is created because we half expect to hear the explosion which follows her turning on the ignition. Bannion rushes out to the car which is in flames and desperately tries to pry the door open; it is too late; his wife is dead. When Bannion accuses the police commissioner of deliberately dragging his feet on the investigation, he is removed from the force. Gloria Grahame was cast as hit man Lee Marvin's girlfriend. While playing cards with the police commissioner and other powerful political figures, Marvin throws scalding hot coffee in Grahame's face, permanently disfiguring her. For much of the film, half of her face is covered with bandages, which only serves to intensify the horror. Jocelyn Brando is the good woman of *film noir*, the attractive, loving wife and mother. She is destroyed by the forces of evil. Gloria Grahame is the *femme fatale* of *film noir*, although in this film her ire is turned against Marvin and Marvin's boss and she longs to be the kind of woman Brando was. Realizing that the truth will come out if Jeanette Nolan should die, Grahame goes to her home and shoots her to death. Bannion, in the meantime, suspecting that the life of his daughter will be claimed next, places her with a group of former servicemen for protection. Marvin, entering his dark apartment, pauses to turn on the light, only to be hit in the face with scalding coffee by Grahame who has been hiding in the shadows. Grahame is shot. There is a savage fight between Marvin and Bannion in which Bannion stops himself just short of killing Marvin. Grahame dies. The evidence comes out and the police force has a change of heart: Marvin and Lagana are arrested and Bannion restored to the force.

The violence in each episode is seen to increase as the characters become more and more savage. Borde and Chaumeton recognized in this film one of Lang's favorite themes: "human solitude in a world of steel."[63] They also were cognizant of the ambiguous character of both Bannion and the moll played by Grahame. "Disavowed by his cowardly and corrupt chiefs," they wrote, "Bannion is no more than a machine athirst for vengeance, literally propelled by his instinct for destruction. This fascination provides the narrative its tone. . . . Glenn Ford is sensational as the good cop without mercy and Gloria Grahame, with her face half destroyed, concretizes marvelously the duality of his 'soul.' "[64] It is significant, I think, that the figure of the avenger is regarded as morally ambiguous in this film and in other *films noirs*. Later in the history of the detective film, the avenger would lose this ambiguity; he would instead be cause for admiration by killing those who obviously needed to be killed.

Not all *films noirs* have *femmes fatales*; but many of them do. In those that do, the male protagonist in the film is usually alienated from his environment and one of the principal factors behind this alienation is the fact that the *femme fatale* is in possession of her own sexuality. As a consequence, she is, or behaves as if she is, independent of the patriarchal order. In the course of the film, therefore, or at least by the end of it, the *femme fatale* must be punished for this attempt at independence, usually by her death, thus restoring the balance of the patriarchal system.

I make a distinction between true *film noir* and what might well be termed *film gris* and melodrama. A *film noir*, in terms of its structure, follows either that of the *film noir* of error or that of the *film noir* of circumstance. The destruction is such in a *film noir* that, even if the protagonist survives the end (as, for example, Œdipus survives), he does so in an altered condition. In the *film gris*, the termination is indeterminate: we do not know if the ending will lead ultimately to happiness or not. In the melodrama, by contrast, it is very clear: the ending is invariably happy. Accordingly, an excellent example of a *film gris* done in the *film noir* visual style (not narrative structure) is DEAD RECKONING (Columbia, 1946), about which Borde and Chaumeton wrote that "the direction of John Cromwell, brilliant and expressive, is valuable above all for the rapport between the hero and [Coral] Chandler, a bitch to whom Lizabeth Scott lends her finely edged visage and her singular gaze."[65]

The film opens with Humphrey Bogart backtelling the story to a priest. He tells how he and Johnny Drake, played by William Prince, went through the war together. On a train *en route* to Washington, D.C., where Johnny is to receive the Congressional Medal of Honor and Bogart the Distinguished Service Cross, Bogart accuses Johnny of thinking about "that blonde" again. Johnny admits it: "Remembering how low her voice was, how bad her grammar." "Didn't I tell you," Bogart as Rip Murdock responds, "all females are the same with their faces washed?" And he adds: "Sometimes, chum, you go softheaded. I'd like to see any blonde do that to me." Johnny learns of the honor about to be bestowed upon him and flees. Murdock goes after him, the trail leading to Gulf City. Sitting in a hotel room alone, smoking and drinking, Murdock comments: "What to do on a hot night, wind smelling of night-blooming jasmine and nothing to do but sweat, and wait, and prime the body to sweat some more." Looking through back issues of the newspaper, he learns that Johnny was involved in the murder of an old man who was married to Coral and then, at the morgue, he discovers Johnny's body, burned to a crisp. He sets out to find Coral and goes to the nightclub where she used to sing. "Maybe she was all right," he remarks, "and maybe Christmas comes in July, but I didn't believe it." He invites Coral to dance so he can have her in his arms when he tells her about finding Johnny's body in the morgue: "She tested pure so far, but so did another girl I knew, right up to the dollar point—and it wasn't four million, either." "I don't trust anybody," Murdock tells Coral, "especially women."

The nightclub is owned by a gangster named Martinelli, played by Morris Carnovsky who would eventually be blacklisted by the House UnAmerican Activities Committee for his Communist affiliation. It turns out that Martinelli is married to Coral, that he was married to her when she married Chandler, and that it was Coral, and not Johnny, who killed Chandler. Martinelli has his henchman, Krause, played by Marvin Miller, work over Murdock, but Murdock escapes. He hides in the church, talks to the priest, and the rest of the film is direct action. Murdock has given Coral a pet name. She was Dusty to Johnny; she is Mike to Murdock. Murdock goes to her penthouse. "I'm not the type tears do anything to," he tells her. "I'm the brass knucks in the teeth to dance music type." By the end, the two of them are in the car together. Murdock knows that Coral/Mike killed Martinelli, thinking the gangster was he. "You're going to fry, Dusty," he tells her, significantly reverting to Johnny's pet name for her. Earlier in the dialogue Murdock had told Coral/Mike that women should come pocket-sized and only be allowed to become full-sized when men wanted them that way; all other times they should be kept in a man's pocket. Now Dusty pops the question to Murdock: "Don't you love me?" "That's the tough part of it," Murdock tells her. "But it'll pass in time. Those things always do. Then there is one more thing. I loved him more." At this point, her back against the wall, Dusty, who will not be pushed, pulls a gun. Murdock steps on the gas. She lets him have it. The closing scene is in a hospital. Coral/Dusty/Mike is reclining on a bed, the priest standing over her muttering the last rites in Latin. Rip comes in to say farewell. She does not want to die alone, but all Rip can say to her is the parachutist's jump call: "Geronimo, Mike." "And the final image, completely in documentary fashion," Borde and Chaumeton wrote, "is that of a parachute which opens and then diminishes as it falls. For the first time in the cinema, we have seen death in the first person. The film achieves it by means of a fall into nothingness."[66]

A poetic image, to be sure, but as Janey Place put it, "the *femme fatale* ultimately loses physical movement, and is often actually or symbolically imprisoned by composition as control over her is exerted and expressed visually. . . . The ideological operation of the myth (the absolute necessity of controlling the strong, sexual woman) is thus achieved by first demonstrating her dangerous power and its frightening results, then destroying it."[67] It will be noted that Rip Murdock is a survivor. Yet this motif would seem to be peculiar to the American cinema. Wolfenstein and Leites in MOVIES: A PSYCHOLOGICAL STUDY (1970) observed that "where continued attachment to a loved one would involve serious trouble, feelings become detached. This may happen where the hero has fallen in love with a woman who later turns out to be a criminal (FRAMED [Columbia, 1947], DEAD RECKONING). This pattern contrasts with one which is frequent in French films. The lover may be thrown into self-destructive despair on learning that the previously idealized loved one is criminal (LA PASSIONNELLE [French, 1948]) or be provoked to murder by her infidelity (QUAI DES ORFÈVRES [French, 1947]). But love once committed to this woman cannot be detached."[68] I think the significance of the conclusion of DEAD RECKONING is not a homosexual overtone—"I loved him more"—but the invocation of the buddy system: that men can at least have their buddies even though their relations with women, and above all with independent women, can only end unhappily. The challenge of life is thus how to learn to live without loving a woman.

In the quest for the nurturing woman, Wolfenstein and Leites found a parallel between this situation and what Margaret Mead termed "conditional love." "American children," they wrote, "are often weighed and measured and awarded Mother's love to the extent that they compare favorably with others. The fantasy of the immediate and unconditional award of love by the movie heroine seems related to the suspense and uncertainties of this childhood experience."[69] But just as the nurturing woman is a repudiation of the conditional love of the mother, the male protagonist in a *film noir* might also identify with the mother and withdraw love. "The hero," they wrote, "who withdraws love from the woman who turns out to be bad is exercising the principle of conditional love which he learned from his mother: you have to be good if you want to be loved."[70]

It is very important, I think, to remember that being good, in *film noir* as elsewhere in American films, is to be a nurturing woman. Why, then, is the nurturing woman so little seen in *film noir* and, when she is, why is she so lackluster by comparison with the self-directed woman? What is at the root of this horror and fascination with the *femme fatale* in *film noir*? The obvious answer, to be sure, is the same for the post-war United States as it was for ancient Athens: the fear of women. The fear of women by men would seem to be older than even our cultural representations of it. Yet, when it comes to *film noir*, I would agree with Stephen Farber in his article, "Violence and the Bitch Goddess" (1974), that "during the war years and immediately afterward, strong women flourished in American films, and were often presented as monsters and harpies, hardened by greed and lust, completely without feeling for the suffering they caused. These films undoubtedly reflected the fantasies and fears of a wartime society, in which women had taken control of many of the positions customarily held by men. Fear of the violence that may attend success is a recurring anxiety in American films, but during the war years another psychological dimension was added to this anxiety—fear of the evil, overpowering woman with a shocking ability to humiliate and emasculate men."[71] I think, however, it is vitally necessary to keep in mind what the historical reality was, how really little power and economic independence women were allowed—8.5 percent out of 80 percent of all war-industry jobs—and that the *femme fatale* was a deliberate fantasy reflecting at once a fear and embodying a prescription and a warning. The prescription was that *femmes fatales* do not succeed: they are killed. The warning for men was to avoid them, for women never to be one. American films prior to *film noir*, and the detective film *par excellence*, had usually divided women into victims and vamps when a criminal milieu was part of the background; *film noir* added a new dimension: women who were intent on acquiring money and power.

Virtually all that I have said, however, has been from a contemporary perspective and has been inspired, surely, at least in part, by what female critics themselves have written about the portrayal of women in *film noir*. It is a perspective that the actresses themselves who played *femmes fatales* in these films never for a moment possessed when they were making these films. They tried their best to make these characters, created almost exclusively by male screenwriters, in films directed by men and in which the male voice was almost always dominant, behave as they felt such women would behave in real life.

"I really didn't think you would make it," I said to Lizabeth Scott as she joined me for lunch at the Scandia in Beverly Hills."

"I said I would," she said in a husky, breathless voice. "When I say I will keep an appointment, I always do."

She brushed her long, streaked blonde hair from her face in a nervous gesture. She wasn't wearing a support garment. Her white blouse plunged between her browned breasts, still firm; her whole body was brown beneath her white clothing.

"I love this place. I come here often."

I pulled out her chair for her and she slid into it with a hurried grace. The pupils of her deep blue eyes were dilated, seeming more to take you inside than to look out at you.

"Would you like a drink?" I asked.

"No, I don't drink." Her voice was huskier. "I only had one drink in my whole life." She pulled out a box of long, thin, brown Sherman cigarettes. "But I smoke."

I lit her cigarette.

"You're one of the most difficult people to see in all of Los Angeles."

"I don't know why," she said. "But I wanted to see you. I knew this wouldn't be an interview. I hate interviews. I like to talk to people face to face. Just us, you know? About both of us. You have to try really to talk to each other, to say something."

A waiter hovered near our table.

"We'll order later," I told him.

"It isn't that, sir," he said. "But you'll have to put your jacket on. It's a house rule."

My jacket was draped over the back of my chair.

"But it's warm in here."

"I know, sir. But it *is* a house rule."

I slipped on my jacket. The waiter smiled, then retired. Lizabeth Scott reached over and touched my wrist.

"The food is so good here, it's worth it." Then, looking at my glass, she said, "Have another drink."

I hesitated.

"It's all right. This is on me."

"It isn't that."

She looked at me again, deeply, brushing aside her hair.

"I like to see a man drink," she said, and smiled.

I signaled to the waiter and ordered another Scotch on the rocks.

"I was just at UCLA. They had a Lizabeth Scott day. It was a film course. They showed PITFALL. Afterwards, the students asked me questions. They all wanted to know about *film noir*."

"So would I . . . frankly. What is it?"

Liz smiled again.

"They said almost all my films were examples of *film noir*."

"Yes. But what is it?"

"There's got to be a woman. She can't have a husband. She's smothering inside."

I recalled talking to Jane Wyatt about PITFALL (United Artists, 1948). She had played Dick Powell's wife, the "good" woman. Andre de Toth had directed from a screenplay by Jay Dratler. "I loved Liz Scott," Jane said. "You couldn't help but love her. She was so completely neurotic. She always got on the set early so she could be made up. It always took her so long. And she was always by herself." Raymond Burr was cast as the detective working for Dick Powell's insurance company. He is taken with Liz. Powell is also taken with her when he visits her at her apartment. They sleep together. Liz has been the recipient of stolen property from a man now imprisoned. Powell wants it back. Burr resents Powell's intrusion. Liz hates Burr who is always hanging around. Burr visits Liz' lover in prison and tells him about Powell and Liz. Powell tries to break it off in order to keep his marriage together. Liz will not let him. When Liz' lover is released, Burr picks him up, gets him drunk, and drives him out to Powell's house. Powell shoots the man in self-defense. He tries to cover it up, but it does not work. Burr wants Liz to leave town with him. Terrified, she shoots Burr. Powell confesses to the district attorney, played by John Litel. The district attorney cannot hold Powell but he can, and does, prosecute Liz Scott.

"Whenever I worked on a picture like PITFALL, I would set up the character I was playing in my mind. I wrote down in a notebook how I felt such a character would act in various circumstances. I had to reason out the person I was portraying."

"You played a good girl in THE STRANGE LOVE OF MARTHA IVERS [Paramount, 1946]. Barbara Stanwyck was the murderer. That's an unforgettable scene at the end when Kirk Douglas wants to shoot Stanwyck and cannot, so she puts her thumb over his finger on the trigger and pulls it. Then the camera drops back to see Douglas shoot himself in a double suicide."

"Lewis Milestone directed that film," Liz said, tipping her head, expelling cigarette smoke, and then brushing back her hair. "He was wonderful to work with. But John Cromwell told me he didn't like the picture when I went to work in DEAD RECKONING."

"What was Bogart like to work with?"

"I remember that he never prepared his lines ahead of time. He would always do that in the morning. That way, in the whole picture I only did one take with him before noon. He worked his own way. And he wouldn't work after five. He seemed to find working fun. But one day he said to me, 'I hate coming to work. It's really hard for a male to do this kind of work.' "

"And when you shot him?"

"I had to. The character I was playing had to. He was going to stand in her way. More and more between them would stand in the way. She had to shoot him."

"Personally, I like you best in TOO LATE FOR TEARS [United Artists, 1949] when you cold-bloodedly tell Dan Duryea that if he wants the insurance money, he's going to have to bump your husband, Arthur Kennedy. Up to that point, Duryea thinks he has you scared. But when he hears your plan, he gets scared for himself. And, of course, his face is nothing but surprise and rage when he discovers you've poisoned him, once he does bump Kennedy."

"I had my greatest problem in that picture. In the telephone scene. I had to do all my acting to a telephone. I found that very hard. It took at least six takes before it was right."

Hal B. Wallis had brought Lizabeth Scott to Hollywood in 1946 to work for him in productions he was doing for Paramount release. He invested her money wisely so she could afford to retire to luxury. But she lives alone. I mentioned Mary Astor, with whom Liz had worked in DESERT FURY (Paramount, 1947). "Whatever happened to Mary, I wonder?" she asked vacantly.

"She's living out at the Motion Picture Home."

"No? Really? I have to go out to see her." Liz brushed her hair to one side, then turned her face toward me once more. "You know, a picture is so much like a trip to Europe, on a boat. You get to be so close with everyone while you're working on a picture. You all promise that you will see each other constantly when the picture is over. But once it's over, you never see each other at all. Or, if you do, you're kind of embarrassed, because of all the things you said, and . . . I guess, nobody means what they say, ever . . . do they?"

"They may not mean what they say," I responded, draining my whiskey, "but they definitely mean to get the things they want badly enough for which they say such things."

"I know what you mean. It's like telling someone you love him to get something from him. Or her."

"Have you ever known anyone to say, 'I love you,' who didn't want something?"

Liz smiled demurely. "Let's order lunch," she suggested then. "Try one of their Swedish dishes. They're the best."

John Kobal, in an essay on Rita Hayworth, recorded the fact that Hayworth, and not Lizabeth Scott, was originally intended to play opposite Bogart in DEAD RECKONING and that contractual problems prevented her from doing so. "It is interesting to speculate on what Hayworth might have made of the equally female role opposite Humphrey Bogart . . . ," he wrote.[72] But perhaps we have already come to the point where it has become clear that no matter who appeared in the role—Lizabeth Scott or Rita Hayworth—the result would have been the same: the *film noir* male would find himself humiliated, emasculated, seduced. This was due to the fact that *film noir* required a role reversal between the sexes. As the *femme fatale* took on "masculine" characteristics (as opposed to biological male characteristics), i.e., characteristics assigned to the gender role of masculine by the patriarchy, so it led, covertly if not overtly, to the attribution of "feminine" characteristics to the *film noir* male. The psychosexual dilemma of a *film noir* male is that the surrounding patriarchy has made homosexuality taboo and yet, with the persistent misogynistic attitude toward women, females were also excluded as suitable objects except in those cases where they willingly assumed the narrow roles prescribed for them: hence condemning the *film noir* male to a dull, insipid, and unrewarding life without any deep emotional and sexual commitment.

There is no telling where this ultimate dilemma of *film noir* would have led, to what new forms of human relationship. *Film noir* came to an end, not because of the nature of the dilemma itself, but because the political influence of the House UnAmerican Activities Committee became such that the motion picture industry had to return to its pre-war role of optimism and affirmation. Again, the nuclear American family took the forefront and the habituation to falsehood, so long the staple of American films, once more became predominant in the industry. To question the *status quo* became radical, even revolutionary, and *films noirs* and their makers seemed, increasingly, to imply feelings and attitudes which the new political climate judged unAmerican.

8

Raymond Chandler in Hollywood

> You can live in Hollywood a long time and never see the part they use in pictures.
>
> Philip Marlowe[1]

I

Raymond Chandler was always a solitary man. When, in the second half of his life, he began writing detective stories, he also took to writing, later dictating, lengthy letters to friends, associates, publishers, editors, even strangers. This correspondence has been carefully preserved. In one letter or another, he recorded his reactions to most things going on around him or narrated the events of his life. As secretive as Chandler may have been in person, as socially reticent, as shy with anyone but a very few intimates, in his letters he became expansive, confidential, even at times uninhibited. Some of these letters were collected and published in RAYMOND CHANDLER SPEAKING (1962). Many more were quoted by Frank MacShane in his biography, THE LIFE OF RAYMOND CHANDLER (1976), and some of this vast store upon which MacShane drew were included by him in SELECTED LETTERS OF RAYMOND CHANDLER (1981). The fact of the matter is that Chandler was an uncommonly gifted letter writer and his life and times become vivid in his correspondence with an intensity matched only by the very best in his fiction. The image projected in these letters is that of a man sitting alone in his study at night, the same room where he wrote in the mornings, where he slept, where he revised his work, where he proofread his galleys, where, you might even say, the best and truest part of him lived. Here he could be himself. He talks through these letters in a way he could never have spoken to you if you had known him.

On 11 December 1950, Chandler wrote to Hamish Hamilton, his British publisher, that he had not been happy as a young man. "I had grown up in England and all my relatives were either English or Colonial. And yet I was not English. I had no feelings of identity with the United States, and yet I resented the kind of ignorant and snobbish criticism of Americans that was current at that time. During my year in Paris I had run across a good many Americans, and most of them seemed to have a lot of bounce and liveliness and to be thoroughly enjoying themselves in situations where the average Englishman of the same class would either be stuffy or completely bored. But I wasn't one of them. I didn't even speak their language. I was, in effect, a man without a country."[2] According to Jerry Speir in RAYMOND CHANDLER (1981), "this sense of himself as an outsider plagued Chandler throughout his life. In his personal experience, it contributed to his bouts of bitter loneliness and to his virtually self-imposed social isolation; in his fiction, it is evident in Philip Marlowe's peculiar wit and distant tone."[3]

There was an ingenuous and naive quality about Chandler. For all the posturing which occurs among the characters in his fiction, it would not occur to him that W. Somerset Maugham was only posturing when, at the conclusion of A WRITER'S NOTEBOOK (1949), he observed that "it might seem a poor look-out for the old man, when the young do not want his company and he finds that of his contemporaries tedious. Nothing remains to him then but his own, and I look upon it as singularly fortunate that none has ever been so enduringly satisfactory to me as mine. I have never liked large gatherings of my fellow creatures, and I regard it as not the least of the compensations of old age that I can make it an excuse either to refuse to go to parties or slink away quietly when they have ceased to entertain me. Now that solitude is more and more forced upon me I am more and more content with it. Last year I spent some weeks by myself in a little house on the banks of the Combahee river, seeing no one, and I was neither lonely nor bored. It was indeed with reluctance that I returned to New York when the heat and the anopheles obliged me to abandon my retreat."[4] This was literary posturing of a high order, and Maugham was a master at it; indeed, his finest literary achievement may well have been to create a literary persona far more likeable than he ever was in the flesh. We know now that during those weeks, supposedly by himself, when Maugham was staying in that little house he had with him a youthful male lover who became disillusioned because the master would resort to a Thesaurus when in need of a word and that there was a constant stream of visitors. The image of Maugham at seventy, content with his imposed solitude, was an artifice engendered to gain sympathy, and it certainly worked when it came to Chandler. "I have a feeling that fundamentally he is a pretty sad man, pretty lonely," Chandler wrote to Hamish Hamilton. "His description of his seventieth birthday is pretty grim. I should guess that all in all he has had a lonely life, that his declared attitude of not caring much emotionally about people is a defense mechanism, that he lacks the kind of surface warmth that attracts people, and at the same time is such a wise man that he knows that however superficial and accidental most friendships are, life is a pretty gloomy affair without them. I don't mean that he has not friends, of course; I don't know enough about him to say anything like that. I get my feeling from his writing and that is all. In a conventional sense he probably has many friends. But I don't think they build much of a fire against the darkness for him. He's a lonely old eagle.''⁵ This response to old age and loneliness tells us a great deal more about Chandler than it does about Maugham. Maugham's literary persona as a man alone in the world was, I suspect, a reaction to his compelling attachment to Gerald Haxton, a liberation from bondage albeit only in his imagination. A point that Maugham made over and over in his fiction which might have benefited Chandler more was that invariably a code of honor will destroy those who uphold it. Maugham abandoned his comfortable retreat in the little house, not because of the heat or the mosquitoes, but because Gerald was critically ill and Maugham wanted to be close to him. When at the funeral service Maugham, who was sitting next to Glenway Wescott, broke down and sobbed, Wescott, remembering the incident, wrote to Ted Morgan, who was writing a biography of Maugham, that he had thought of how all these years ''you've been bragging about how tough you are, and you've never displayed emotion, and you've been trying to extend your life into the life hereafter through your work, and here in this church, where the very words 'life hereafter' are being uttered, here you sit blubbering, you can't even keep your composure and you're making a fool of yourself in public. What good was an upper-class Anglo-Saxon manner if it left you weak as a kitten in the common plight, the hour of every man?''⁶

Perhaps it would surprise Chandler to learn that he is generally considered to have been the most important author of detective fiction so far in the history of the genre; and then, again, maybe it would not. When you reflect on how viciously he was denigrated by John Dickson Carr and Anthony Boucher, who reviewed his books as they appeared, it is certainly both a curious and an ironic turn of events. Yet his excellence, as he himself would admit, came about because he tried to overcome the restrictions of the form in which he worked. To the extent that he succeeded, he wrote not detective stories at all, really, but parables of his time, fantasies, nocturnal romances; and he dwelt upon a singular creation, his detective, who as he became more human and probing gained a depth and dimension greater almost than the conventions of his formulary mode might reasonably permit. The two American writers who probably influenced him the most were Dashiell Hammett and Ernest Hemingway. He never equalled the hardness of Hammett at his best, but then he had not wanted to; nor did he attempt to penetrate into the confused darkness of the soul as Hemingway had tried to do. Despair was ineffable in Hammett. Hemingway became a citizen of the world. Chandler never experienced, as Hemingway had, the rubbery sensation of an animal's beating heart and, once having plunged in the knife, the feel of the hot blood spilling over his fingers. Life was never so tenuous for Chandler because he never lived so much of his life on the terrible edge of death and, unlike Hemingway, when he tried to kill himself on more than one occasion he proved ineffectual. All he had was the attendant emptiness. THE LONG GOODBYE (1954) became his epiphany and his masterpiece, his consummate withdrawal from contact with other lives but not from perpetual struggle. All his years as a writer Chandler lived in Southern California. Nearly all of his fiction is set in Southern California. He shared Hammett's insularity. I suspect it was this, far more than the form he chose in which to write, that limited his scope as a novelist. Yet, from what we know of him, travel would not have mattered; it would not have changed anything. He had no home and his detective had only a code of honor which destroyed both of them. Locality bound him as it has so many others, so much so that he seemed unaware that life elsewhere might have a different tempo, existence an alternate throb, the sun a variant light.

Raymond Chandler was born on 23 July 1888 in Chicago. His parents were divorced when he was eight and his mother took him with her to England. He was educated in English public schools; in 1905 he attended Dulwich College. In one of his early stories published in BLACK MASK, narrated in the first person, Chandler's detective remarks: "I had my mouth open and a blank expression on my face, like a farm boy at a Latin lesson."[7] John Houseman, who got to know Chandler when they were both working at Paramount, once told me that in his opinion Chandler's classical education in the English public school system was the most important thing one could know about him. Chandler himself occasionally remarked about it. "I am not only literate but intellectual, much as I dislike the term," he wrote to Hamish Hamilton. "It would seem that a classical education might be rather a poor basis for writing novels in a hard-boiled vernacular. I happen to think otherwise. A classical education saves you from being fooled by pretentiousness, which is what most current fiction is too full of."[8] I have already mentioned how he had once translated Cicero into English and then translated him back into Latin; and how, in a special civil service examination, Chandler was tested in mathematics, English, German, Greek, English history, and French. He placed third among the six hundred candidates and first in the examination in the classics. It had been his family's idea that he should spend a year in Paris learning commercial French and a year in Germany to prepare him for a career in the civil service. To be eligible for the civil service, Chandler had to declare himself a British subject—having been born in the United States, he had an option. He was made an Assistant Store Officer under the Controller of the Navy. Since he had been very young, he had wanted to write. This ambition his family had opposed. He lasted six months in the civil service.

He decided to bite the bullet and became a reporter, but failed at it. He did become a contributor, however, to the WESTMINSTER GAZETTE in which he published some twenty-seven poems between 1908 and 1912. Virtually all of Chandler's early writing, including the poems, was published posthumously in CHANDLER BEFORE MARLOWE (1973) edited by Matthew J. Bruccoli.

The imagery and sentiment of the poems reveal Chandler already then obsessed with a Gothic romanticism and a Victorian prudery. For example, in "The Perfect Knight" (1909), one finds this opening gambit:

> He hath a sword of altar fire,
>   He hath a shield of shimmering air,
> The one to slay his base desire,
>   The one to guard him from despair.[9]

As might well be supposed, Chandler got nowhere with this kind of poetry. When he also began contributing articles and reviews to the ACADEMY, a literary weekly, in 1911 and 1912, his literary fortunes did not much improve. Many years later, reviewing these essays himself, Chandler remarked to Hamish Hamilton that "they are of an intolerable preciousness of style, but already quite nasty in tone."[10] At twenty-three, frustrated in his chosen profession and disappointed in love, Chandler borrowed five hundred pounds from his uncle and decided to emigrate to the United States. Because he was returning within three years of attaining his majority, Chandler found he was able to retain his American citizenship, although this question of dual affiliation would later cause him financial grief with the tax authorities.

On board ship, he met a couple from Los Angeles who invited him to visit them if he made it as far as the West Coast. After passing through New York and staying for a few weeks in St. Louis, Chandler did find himself in Los Angeles and he did seek out the Lloyds. Warren Lloyd helped him secure employment as a bookkeeper. Chandler visited regularly with the Lloyds and it was at their home that he met Julian Pascal and his wife, Cissy. Once Chandler was financially secure, he sent for his mother, who came to live with him. On 14 August 1917, Chandler left California to enlist in the Canadian Armed Forces at Victoria, British Columbia. He had chosen to join in Canada because that way his mother would receive an allowance. He declared himself to be a naturalized British subject. His battalion went first to England and then to France. He did see combat, but he wrote almost nothing about his experiences, and the glimmers one gets from characters in his later books who also have experienced combat, such as Terry Lennox in THE LONG GOODBYE, disclose a similar reticence.

Upon discharge in 1919 Chandler found he was thirty and without a job. At first he went to work for an English bank in San Francisco, but the duties so bored him that he moved back to Los Angeles where, at the top of Angels Flight, he lived again with his mother. Through Warren Lloyd, Chandler became an employee of the Dabney Oil Syndicate in which Lloyd's brother was a partner. He renewed his friendship with Julian and Cissy Pascal and, although Cissy was eighteen years his senior, the two fell in love. He went so far as to it and discuss the whole business with Cissy and Julian just prior to their divorce action which became final in 1920. Yet, even at that, the two did not marry, since Chandler's mother was opposed to the match. Instead, they waited until a few days after Chandler's mother died in 1924. It was a strange relationship, to say the least, although it is usually somewhat charitably glossed over by Chandler's various biographers. In fact, it might even be of negligible psychological significance between some average couple, but not surely where Raymond Chandler was one of the parties. The French have an apt expression for what I suspect it was which held these two together, *psychose à deux*. One parallel which comes to mind is the darkly romantic and passionate marriage of Nathaniel Hawthorne and Sophia Peabody. Their love fed on the same reclusiveness and emotional symbiosis as did that between Ray and Cissy. Frank MacShane in his biography went to great pains to warrant how Chandler's marriage added to his stability and provided him with the inner confidence he needed in order to persevere through the ordeal of becoming a writer. Yet his honesty and objectivity as a biographer could not permit him to overlook the embarrassment Chandler suffered in subsequent years being married to such an old woman, one whose frailty and sickliness caused him untold anguish; how he had to remain reclusive because of Cissy and his sensitivity over their relationship; or how, when Cissy died, Chandler went completely to pieces and could never pull himself together again. "Marlowe was his fantasy image of himself, tough and daring in a world without Cissy," Dilys Powell observed. "In a world with Cissy he showed another kind of gallantry; he shielded her. And he needed her. Without her he had lost not only his accustomed place in the everyday world but the entry to his own world of fable; the decay of his working years after her death is proof of that. Whatever his errancies, she was the stable point in the life of reality."[11] Natasha Spender, who as Dilys Powell knew them both, was of the same opinion and felt that it was "maternal moral support he still both needed and found in her company."[12]

Notwithstanding, there was a part of Chandler which rebelled at his neurotic dependency. As he became more successful as an oil company executive, he courted his secretary and took to week-ending with another girl from the office when his overtures to his secretary were rebuffed. Chandler had not really known his father, but he knew that he was a dissipated alcoholic. He told Natasha Spender that his father had been a swine and his mother an angel, a dichotomy which persisted in all his fiction. "The pressures of the oil business increased with the onset of the Depression," Jerry Speir recorded. "Combined with his domestic difficulties, the pressures became too great. Chandler began to drink heavily (a reaction to adversity which would recur throughout his life), and he made at least one half-serious attempt at suicide. He also began having affairs with secretaries in the office, sometimes not returning from a weekend until Wednesday. Finally, his absences extended into weeks when no one could find him. In 1932, at the age of forty-four, Raymond Chandler was fired."[13] Cissy stayed with him. MacShane, approaching biography with the same frame of mind as one would write a classical detective story, sought a motive for this and gave her the best one of all: she was simply too old to find another man easily. This overlooks a more ambiguous but quite as likely explanation: she was as obsessively dependent on Ray as he was on her.

Chandler made no effort to secure other employment. He had once more decided to write. He was familiar with the pulp detective magazines, BLACK MASK among them, and made an extremely detailed synopsis of a short story by Erle Stanley Gardner. In a variation of what he had once done with Cicero, he rewrote the story from the synopsis, and then rewrote parts of it again. "I found out that the trickiest part of your technique," he later confessed to Gardner, "was the ability to put over situations which verged on the implausible but which in the reading seemed quite real."[14] Yet, if Chandler admired Gardner's gift for adroit plotting, it was Hammett's style and world-view which had the deepest impact on him. "Hammett wrote at first (and almost to the end) for people with a sharp, aggressive attitude toward life," he once summed it up. "They were not afraid of the seamy side of things; they lived there. Violence did not dismay them; it was right down their street. . . . He had style, but his audience didn't know it, because it was a language not supposed to be capable of such refinements. . . . He was spare, frugal, hard-boiled, but he did over and over again what only the best writers can ever do at all. He wrote scenes that seemed never to have been written before."[15] Chandler wanted to write detective stories where the people one meets are more important than the puzzle; and he liked the formula because it permitted him to include people from all stratas of society. He wanted a hero different from those of Hammett who were all hard men lacking, as Hammett did, any kind of sentiment. Chandler's hero—or, in the beginning, heroes—had been the product of another kind of fantasy, an honest man, a lonely man, a protector of women and the helpless, a man with a contempt for the accumulation of money, somewhat adolescent perhaps, but strictly outside his cultural milieu by choice and temperament, liberated (if that is the word) from all binding human relationships. After all, Chandler could face this detective's bleak world because he himself was not alone. He had Cissy. Because he had her and could not shake himself loose of his need for her, in more than one sense we have Cissy to thank for Chandler's having ultimately given us Philip Marlowe.

Chandler submitted his first short story, "Blackmailers Don't Shoot," to Captain Shaw at BLACK MASK. Shaw sent it on to one of the regular BLACK MASK contributors, W. T. Ballard, appending a note to it commenting that its author was either a genius or crazy. Shaw published it in the December, 1933 issue and paid Chandler a penny a word for the eighteen thousand words. The same year Gardner published his first Perry Mason novel, Hammett his last novel, and Raymond Chandler was forty-five years old. The story possesses many ingredients which were to become commonplaces in Chandler's short fiction: a nightclub setting, a handsome, romantic gangster, a vicious gunman, assorted thugs, and a *femme fatale* who is *primum mobile* for much that happens. Mallory is the detective whose activity is described in the third person. The central issue of the story is some phony letters used as part of a publicity stunt by a fading movie star, Rhonda Farr. When Mallory confronts her with the fact that four men got killed because of this stunt, "Rhonda Farr looked at him mildly. 'Two crooks, a double-crossing policeman, make three of them. I should lose my sleep over that trash! Of course, I'm sorry about Landrey.' " Mallory tells her: " 'It's nice of you to be sorry about Landrey.' "[16] Landrey is the handsome, romantic gangster. The story also illustrates Chandler's ambivalent attitude toward the police. Two of the cops are out-and-out crooks; the *soi-disant* "honest" cops are more than willing to cover up things in a most convenient fashion. " 'The coroner don't give a damn about that trash,' " Police Chief Cathcart says to Mallory. " 'If the D. A. wants to get funny, I can tell him about a few cases his office didn't clean up so good.' "[17]

There is too much plot in the story, so much that it almost becomes confusing. Chandler's next story, however, "Smart-Aleck Kill," published in the July, 1934 issue has even more plot. Mallory is back, this time acting as a bodyguard for a film director. The director is being blackmailed. When he is murdered, Mallory goes after the killer. Once the murderer is apprehended and in police custody, he asks to stop off a moment at his home. He is accommodated. Police Chief Cathcart has an office bottle and over a drink with Mallory he explains what happened next. The man's wife, who was jealous because of her husband's adultery, " 'never said a damn word. Brought a little gun around from behind her and fed him three slugs. One two, three. Win, place, show. Just like that. Then she turned the gun around in her hand as nice as you could think and handed it to the boys. . . . ' "[18] Mrs. Sutro was only the first in a long and terrifying line of homicidal females who haunt the pages of all that Chandler wrote. In fact, female murderers outnumber male murderers by a wide margin. Not only is this contrary to reality—since the turn of the century approximately one out of every ten murders committed in the United States has been committed by a female—but even the means of their murders is pure fantasy. Whereas in real crimes, women will most often use poison or a familiar utensil, such as a kitchen knife, in Chandler's fiction they are usually two-gunned hard babies, or they might sap a man down until his skull is flattened, or, in one case, use a hot iron on his feet.

"Finger Man," Chandler's third story published in BLACK MASK in the October, 1934 issue, was reputedly the first story that he wrote with which he felt at ease. It is set in a fictitious city named San Angelo and, as "Killer in the Rain," Chandler's next story published in the January, 1935 issue, it is narrated in the first person by a nameless detective. The model, quite obviously, was Hammett's Continental Op. In "Finger Man," the nameless detective, as the Op, is fast with his gun—" '. . . the big man was already sagging. My bullet had drilled through his neck.' "[19]—and he is as hard-boiled When the girl in the story shows the detective how the gangsters branded her " 'just for a sample of what I'd get' " the detective responds: " 'Okay, sister That's nasty medicine. But we've got some law here now. . . . ' "[20] The gir in "Finger Man" is more or less a victim and compelled to be deceitful. The same cannot be said for Agnes, the blonde in "Killer in the Rain" who works for Steiner in his pornography business and who joins up with Joe Marty after Steiner is killed. When the nameless detective meets her at Marty's apartment, he notices how "nerve tension made her face old and ugly."[21] When Carmen Dravec, the wild daughter of the detective's client, rushes into Marty's apartment with a gun, ready to kill him, the blonde attacks the detective, sinking her teeth into his hand. Then "the blonde took her teeth out of my hand and spat my own blood at me. Then she threw herself at my leg and tried to bite that. I cracked her lightly on the head with the barrel of the gun and tried to stand up. She rolled down my legs and wrapped her arms around my ankles. . . . The blonde was strong with the madness of fear. . . . Then I hit the blonde on the side of the head again, much harder and she rolled off my feet."[22] By the end of the story, the callousness which had once characterized the attitude of the police has become the attitude of the detective. " 'I didn't care a lot about trash like Steiner or Joe Marty and his girlfriend, and still don't,' " he tells the police.[23]

For his next two stories, "Nevada Gas," published in BLACK MASK in June, 1935, and "Spanish Blood," published in November, 1935, Chandler switched back to third person narration and dispensed with a private eye altogether. "Nevada Gas" probably has the strongest opening of any story Chandler ever wrote. Hugo Candless steps into what he believes to be the backseat of his own car, only to find that it is not, that the tonneau is sealed and he cannot get out—and then the cyanide gas is turned on. The protagonist is Johnny De Ruse, a gambler, who admits when he finds his girlfriend with another man that he is " 'not soft, baby—just a bit sentimental. . . . I like games of chance, including women. But when I lose I don't get sore and I don't chisel. I just move on to the next table.' "[24] Candless' wife is in on his murder. When she pulls a gun on De Ruse, "her face was convulsed, her lips drawn back over thin wolfish teeth that shimmered."[25] The protagonist in "Spanish Blood" is a police lieutenant who has long been best friends with the murdered man and his wife. He is pulled off the investigation by party bosses, but promises Belle Marr, the murdered man's widow, that he will stay on the case anyway. There is a blonde in the story—Belle has red-brown hair—but the blonde is a red herring, a junkie who goes gun-happy at the end and shoots down the party bosses. She did not kill Marr. Belle did. Sam Delaguerra, the protagonist, knows that Belle did it; but he agrees to go along with the departmental frame masterminded by the police commissioner because Marr would have wanted it that way. " 'It's my first frame-up,' " he tells Belle. " 'I hope it will be my last.' "[26]

"Guns at Cyrano's" was published in BLACK MASK in January, 1936. In it Chandler introduced Ted Carmady. The story is written in the third person and Carmady is the son of a deceased political boss who lives well off the money he has inherited. He claims to have been once a private dick. At the beginning of the story, he meets Jean Adrian, sapped down in the doorway of her suite in the hotel which Carmady owns. She is the girlfriend of a prize fighter who is supposedly being threatened to throw a fight and who is backed financially by a nightclub owner, Cyrano. When she guns a "red hot"—i.e., a hired killer—brandishing a .45, the fighter gets noble and tries to cover for her. In a rare, sentimental moment at the end of the story, Carmady suggests to Jean that they might run away together. Obviously this did not happen since Ted Carmady was transformed in the next four stories Chandler wrote for BLACK MASK into his first-person private detective narrator.

However, between the appearance of the first of these stories, "The Man Who Liked Dogs," in the March, 1936 issue and the second, "Goldfish," in the June, 1936 issue, Chandler published "Noon Street Nemesis" in the 30 May 1936 issue of DETECTIVE FICTION WEEKLY. "Noon Street Nemesis" introduced Blacks into the metaphor of corruption: there are basically two kinds, those who are docile but secretive and those who are dangerous. In all cases they comprise an alien race. Pete Anglich is the protagonist, an undercover man with the narcotics division. The story is perhaps memorable in that Chandler finally achieved in it that mixture for which he had been striving, dialogue that is in the vernacular and descriptive passages tending toward the grace and elegance of Latin prose, even to the omission of a copula, subsequently a standard practice. "I'm an intellectual snob," Chandler once confessed, "who happens to have a fondness for the American vernacular, largely because I grew up on Latin and Greek. As a result, when I use slang, solecisms, colloquialisms, snide talk or any kind of off-beat language, I do it deliberately. The literary use of slang is a study in itself. I've found that there are only two kinds that are any good: slang that has established itself in the language, and slang that you make up yourself. Everything else is apt to be passé before it gets into print."[27]

Captain Shaw so preferred "The Man Who Liked Dogs" among Chandler's BLACK MASK fiction that it was this story he chose to include in his later anthology. The local chief of police is a crook and some of his picked men are crooks. With the assistance of a crooked doctor who runs a phony clinic, criminals on the lam are provided with protection—for a price. Even the veterinary in the story is a crook. Yet none of them cuts quite the figure of Diana Saint, sister of armed bank robber, Farmer Saint. "Diana Saint came in with a brace of automatics in her hands. A tall, handsome woman, neat and dark, with a rakish hat, and two gloved hands holding guns."[28] For me, however, "Goldfish" is a much better story, although I cannot agree with Frank MacShane's definition of "feminist" when, in THE LIFE OF RAYMOND CHANDLER, he remarked that "Chandler is enough of a feminist to allow some of his women to be crooks, and no one is tougher than Carol Donovan in 'Goldfish.' "[29] It is established already on the first page that Carmady, as a detective, is down on his luck since his blue serge suit shines. Carmady is even identified as the nameless detective from "Finger Man." " 'Right as rain, toots,' " Carol tells Carmady as she enters a room, holding a gun. " 'I'm a lady that wants her own way.' "[30] Even her partner must say of her: " 'I've seen hard women, but she's the bluing on the armor plate.' "[31] At the end, she is shot down by a woman who is a bit faster on the draw. "Then she was a huddled thing on the floor at my feet," Carmady observes, "small, deadly, extinct, with redness coming out from under her, and the tall quiet woman behind her with the smoking Colt held in both hands."[32]

Whiskey is the detective's fuel. In these early stories, every time a corpse is discovered, the detective has to have a drink to get him through it. The atmosphere is always heavy with the tension antecedent to a storm of violence, a violence that once it cuts loose destroys all sense of order. The detective alone is a defense against the darkness and chaos of human malaise. Characters may be dispatched with relentless regularity, but at no point does this methodology reach the bloody extravagance of Hammett's RED HARVEST. Years later, Chandler remarked that it became his objective to exceed Hammett in the kind of detective fiction he was writing: "I thought that perhaps I could go a bit further, be a bit more humane, get a bit more interested in people than in violent death."[33] This new humanity became manifest in the next Ted Carmady story, "The Curtain," published in BLACK MASK in September, 1936. In "The Man Who Liked Dogs" Carmady was capable of rather incredible shooting, as when he knocks a shotgun out of Farmer Saint's hands; in "The Curtain," similarly, he is able to shoot a thug from under his arm. What is different is that Carmady turns down the offer of a thousand dollar fee General Winslow promises him to find Dud O'Mara. " 'He's an old, old man, crippled, half buried already,' " he tells Mrs. O'Mara about her father. " 'One thin thread of interest held him to life. The thread snapped and nobody gives a damn. He tries to act as if he didn't give a damn himself. I don't call that a mood. I call that a pretty swell display of intestinal fortitude.' "[34] Yet, by the end, the humanity has become sentimentality. Mrs. O'Mara's young son is a homicidal lunatic. Instead of exposing him Carmady informs Mrs. O'Mara that she must send him away to be cured because " 'it would kill the general out of hand to know his blood was in that.' "[35] When Chandler reworked this story to create his first novel, THE BIG SLEEP (1939), he changed the sex and familial relationship of the murderer—she is now a sister, the bad sister of the Sternwood family. Marlowe tells Vivian to take her sister, Carmen, away, " 'somewhere far off from here where they can handle her type, where they will keep guns and knives and fancy drinks away from her. Hell, she might even get herself cured, you know. It's been done.' "[36]

The same kind of sentimentality is to be found in "Try the Girl," the last story Chandler submitted to BLACK MASK. It appeared in the January, 1937 issue. Steve Skalla is a giant who does not know his own strength. Carmady encounters him in the Negro section of Los Angeles. He has just gotten out of stir and is looking for his old girlfriend, Beulah. Carmady is able to run her down. Beulah is now singing on the radio and carrying on an affair with a station executive. Skalla finds out where she lives and kills the executive. When the executive's jealous wife shows up, she dives for a gun. "She laughed just before she shot him. She shot him four times, in the lower belly, then the hammer clicked."[37] Carmady tries to help Skalla. "His flat black eyes had something in them that was more than mere pain, something he wanted me to do. Part of the time he was trying to tell me what it was, and part of the time he was holding his belly in one piece and saying again: 'Leave her alone. Maybe she loved the guy.' "[38] When Beulah returns, her heart goes out to Skalla. "She was holding one of his huge, limp fingers . . . ," Carmady remarks at the end of the story, informing the reader that Skalla died of his wounds but doing so with an image perhaps half-intentionally sexual.[39]

Chandler quit writing for BLACK MASK once Captain Shaw left. He switched to DIME DETECTIVE MAGAZINE. His first person narrator detective had the same office Carmady had, only now he was called John Dalmas; and the stories which featured him were the best short fiction Chandler was to write: "Mandarin's Jade," "Red Wind," "Bay City Blues," "The Lady in the Lake," and "Trouble is My Business." Much from the plots of these stories was rewoven into his later novels; and, even when a plot might be left, as with "Trouble is My Business," Chandler would raid it for the similies he so loved. In the short story, Carmady at one point feels as if he were an amputated leg, a simile which Marlowe uses in FAREWELL, MY LOVELY to describe his feelings. Chandler, no less than Hemingway, conceived of a novel as an extended short story. If he was to make a living as a writer, he was convinced he must do it as a novelist. He had served his apprenticeship. He was ready, and so he took the plunge. And he was right. It was as a novelist that he gained international prominence and even several credits as a screenwriter. When Shaw was released from BLACK MASK, he went to work for a literary agent, Sydney Sanders. Chandler reworked "Killer in the Rain," "The Curtain," and fragments of two other stories into THE BIG SLEEP. Sanders became Chandler's agent and placed the novel with Alfred A. Knopf. In retrospect, this may have been a blunder. Knopf was a rather haughty man who preferred to publish what he considered quality fiction which usually, because it was chosen according to his own whim, left the firm in the red. Therefore he had a line of detective thrillers to help pay the bills. Hammett's novels had been published by Knopf, as had those of James M. Cain. It was a relatively easy matter for Sanders to place Chandler with Knopf because the firm was a ready market for hardboiled detective fiction. Yet, given Chandler's personal ambitions, it was a bad place to be. He was only another name on the Knopf thriller list. Knopf did nothing to promote Chandler nor did Knopf see anything in Chandler except a continuation of the formula Hammett had devised. Chandler's correspondence with Knopf appears to have been a constant, pitiful effort to ellicit some sort of understanding from Knopf as to what he was doing. It was wasted. Eventually, Chandler broke with the firm and established a new connection with Houghton Mifflin. This new publisher had no control over Chandler's previous books and, due to Knopf's indifference, Chandler's first four novels had nowhere near the backing they really needed to put them across to the American reading public. He had much better luck in the United Kingdom with Hamish Hamilton and perhaps it was for this reason that, near the end of his life, he went as often as he did to live in London. Just how important a publisher can be is illustrated by William Faulkner who worked on the screenplay for THE BIG SLEEP (Warner's, 1946). By remaining with Random House for most of his years and because of the sympathy his editors had for his fiction despite its lack of real commercial appeal, all the plugging away did finally achieve results and, for a time at any rate, Faulkner did enjoy a certain vogue, especially after his books were taught in schools. All Chandler could say after ten years with Knopf was that "it's a cold show. I have never been able to deal with people at arm's length."[40]

Chandler combined "Try the Girl" with "The Man Who Liked Dogs" and "Mandarin's Jade" to produce his second novel, FAREWELL, MY LOVELY. This became Chandler's plotting technique with all of his subsequent novels, those based on earlier short stories and those which were completely original: he would combine two major plots, weaving them in and out of each other, and try to bring them together at the conclusion. Many of the problems with his plots derive from this technique. Critics chide him for not making everything clear; apologists argue that making things clear was not his aim, but rather to end in a mood of ambiguity. The basic explanation may be less recondite. Chandler was more committed to the scene then he was to the ensemble derived from the totality of scenes. "The scene before the eyes dominates the thought of the audience," he once observed; "the moral individual makes no attempt to reconcile it with the pattern of the story. He is swayed by what is in the actual scene. When you have finished the book, it may, not necessarily will, fall into focus as a whole and be remembered by its merits so considered; but for the time of reading, the chapter is the dominating factor. The vision of the emotional imagination is very short but also very intense."[41] Perhaps, in its way, this tells us why Chandler's stories and novels sparkle in their individual scenes, although in the final analysis the plots in their totalities appear confused and unsatisfying. More than any other BLACK MASK writer he was concerned with the vivid scene and with his characters whom, as Aristophanes and Plautus before him, and Heine, too, he could lampoon, ridicule, flay, satirize, at the same time as over the years he increasingly sentimentalized his detective. He wrote out of a well of loneliness and he wrote well only when he was intensely lonely; then his imagination could best conjure a world in which "the streets were dark with something more than night."[42] In Raymond Chandler all of the strains of Nineteenth century romanticism, its notions of romance and the heroic knight, its Gothic horrors, its obsession with the pathological and with death, decay, and decadence were combined with Baudelaire's revulsion toward women "*s'aimant sans dégoût*," an image reverberant in Keats' vision of "*la belle dame sans merci*"; and he placed them in the mid Twentieth century, set them in the heart of Los Angeles, and from them, with them, out of them, he sought to raise the detective story to the level of art. He objected to Hammett's style which, he felt, "had no overtones, left no echo, evoked no image beyond a distant hill."[43] He tried to write in a style which imparted all of these things, in which the image dominated, even obscured, the linear narrative. In all of this, it would seem, he succeeded to a degree denied all the others in the so-called BLACK MASK school. Much of his fiction is set at night, when he conceived of it if he did not actually write it, and his best scenes are haunted with the vividness of a dream. Indeed, in the words of Russell Davies, "one can feel him at such moments falling in love with his own fantasy; he emerges almost as a decadent figure."[44]

In "Mandarin's Jade," a blonde, Mrs. Prendergast, a woman from the streets who had married a wealthy man, hires a thug, Moose Magoon, to kill her gigolo, Lindley Paul. Paul is beaten to a pulp with a sap. She conspires to have Chandler's detective, John Dalmas, killed. When he exposes her, the reader is told that "her eyes held a warm bitterness like poisoned honey."[45] Her tall husband will protect her. "The blonde laughed crazily and the laugh turned into a screech and then into a yell. The next thing she was rolling on the floor screaming and kicking her legs around. The tall man went over to her quickly and bent down and hit her in the face with his open hand. You could have heard that smack a mile. When he straightened up again his face was a dusky red and the blonde was lying there sobbing."[46] In FAREWELL, MY LOVELY the Beulah character from "Try the Girl" was combined with the murderous blonde from "Mandarin's Jade." In the novel, it is the blonde who saps her former gigolo to death; it is the blonde who guns her former lover, a gigantic ex-con now named Moose Malloy, and who ratted on him in the first place, leading to his imprisonment. The blonde is openly sexual; she loves herself, in Baudelaire's idiom, without disgust. "She fell softly across my lap and I bent down over her face and began to browse on it," Marlowe describes their first encounter. " . . . When I got to her mouth it was half open and burning and her tongue was a darting snake between her teeth."[47] The good girl in the story, Anne Riordan, has to demand of the passive Marlowe: " 'I'd like to be kissed, damn you!' "[48] The blonde in the novel, no less than her prototype in the short story, could have been gotten off because of her wealthy husband's money and influence; but no, she goes into hiding, shoots a cop when he would expose her (rather than offer him a bribe), and kills herself. Marlowe's sentimental explanation for this turn of events is that the blonde did it because she did not want to hurt her husband! A better reason for her suicide is that Chandler did not want her to live.

It cannot really be said that Marlowe in these early novels any more than in the later ones is a fully developed character. In fact, when all is said and done, a reader never learns very much about him at all. Rather, as Jerry Speir suggested, Marlowe is mostly a tone of voice, an attitude toward life. He has what must have been his creator's tendency to over-idealize people only, in turn, to become disillusioned with his ideal projections when they no longer can be seen to conform to the reality. The characters who are most idealized are women and, therefore, it is in connection with them that the disillusionment is most crushing. "Assuming that his intelligence is as high as mine (it could hardly be higher)," Chandler once wrote to John Houseman about Marlowe, "assuming his chances in life to promote his own interest are as numerous as they must be, why does he work for such a pittance? For the answer to that is the whole story, the story that is always being written by indirection and yet never is written completely or even clearly. It is the struggle of all fundamentally honest men to make a decent living in a corrupt society. It is an impossible struggle; he can't win. He can be poor and bitter and take it out in wisecracks and casual amours, or he can be corrupt and amiable and rude like a Hollywood producer. Because the bitter fact is that outside of two or three technical professions which require long years of preparation, there is absolutely no way for a man of this age to acquire a decent affluence in life without to some degree corrupting himself, without accepting the cold, clear fact that success is always and everywhere a racket."[49] This is at the very least Chandler's personal statement of what he was trying to do with his Marlowe character; although it ought also be kept in mind that in making reference to the corruption of Hollywood producers he knew very well that Houseman was functioning in that capacity when he worked for him. It is up to the reader to decide if it is indeed a "cold, clear fact that success is always and everywhere a racket." Certainly, once Chandler became affluent as a result of his work writing for the studios, he was proud of his success. "But even as Marlowe is quick to defend whomever he perceives as helpless," Jerry Speir observed, "so is he—more often than not—disappointed in the results of his own well-intentioned heroics. The world, and other people, simply refuse to conform to his high principles. The typical end of a Marlowe novel finds him disillusioned, drinking or playing chess or both, and unable to assimilate the meaning of his case or of his own role in it."[50]

When it comes to the majority of characters whom Marlowe encounters in his cases, Leigh Brackett was no doubt correct. They are not real people at all, or even based on real people. In Chandler's third Marlowe novel, THE HIGH WINDOW (1942), Marlowe himself confesses as much. " 'What I like about this place is everything runs so true to type,' " he remarks. " 'The cop on the gate, the shine on the door, the cigarette and check girls, the fat greasy sensual Jew with the tall stately bored showgirl, the well-dressed, drunk and horribly rude director cursing the barman, the silent guy with the gun, the night club owner with the soft gray hair and the B-picture mannerisms, and now you— the tall dark torcher with the negligent sneer, the husky voice, the hard-boiled vocabulary.' "[51] These are movie characters; they have no external correspondences; they are products of a collective imagination personalized by Chandler and made vivid in his own fantasy. Without resorting to any of his former stories, Chandler notwithstanding followed the same procedure in this novel and invented two major plots which are interwoven but not seen to be related and actually part of the same case until the conclusion, and Marlowe's explanation requires as much clairvoyance as anything to be found in the Perry Mason books. What makes it distinctly a Chandler plot, beyond the movie characters, is the disillusionment, the fact that the truth is not allowed to come out but must be suppressed, and, of course, the posture toward drinking. " . . . He picked the glass up and tasted it and sighed again and shook his head sideways with a half smile; the way a man does when you give him a drink and he needs it very badly and it is just right and the first swallow is like a peek into a cleaner, sunnier, brighter world."[52] Of all the merits I might attribute to alcohol, this quite definitely would not be one of them. Yet, there is one character in the book, other than Marlowe, who does not owe his presence to the movies or the pulps. Dr. Carl Moss is described as "a big burly Jew with a Hitler moustache, pop eyes and the calmness of a glacier."[53] His similarity to Alfred Knopf is unmistakable.

All of the Marlowe novels are set in Los Angeles. After the first two were published, they brought Raymond Chandler to Hollywood. RKO Radio Pictures purchased FAREWELL, MY LOVELY for $2,000 and used it as the story line for THE FALCON TAKES OVER (RKO, 1942). Knopf's contract with Chandler called for more than the usual apportionment to Knopf for the sale of performing rights. So, even here, at this low asking price, Chandler received less than he would have had he been with another publisher, to say nothing of the picture itself which proved an upsetting experience for Chandler. But then, I do not know what he expected. The Falcon films had their own special formulae for crime detection and the only thing that prevents THE FALCON TAKES OVER from being a wholly successful entry in the series is Chandler's plot. Chandler's nocturnal California characters seem out of place on a studio set of New York being investigated by the debonair George Sanders. The police, represented by James Gleason and Edward Gargan, were intended to be buffoons in contrast to the brutal and secure men who preoccupied Chandler's fantasy. THE HIGH WINDOW was then sold to Twentieth Century-Fox for $3,500 and was used to form the basis for TIME TO KILL (20th-Fox, 1942) in that studio's Mike Shayne series.

Whatever Chandler's personal reaction may have been to both of these films, the sale of the performing rights combined with the fact that Joseph Sistrom, a producer at Paramount who was also a detective story enthusiast and liked Chandler's style, led to his landing a job at Paramount, working first with Billy Wilder in preparing DOUBLE INDEMNITY (Paramount, 1944). Dick Powell, known principally as a singer and dancer, wanted the role of Walter Neff, the co-conspirator in the James M. Cain story. Wilder scoffed at this idea. Fred MacMurray was cast instead. Powell was not to be put off. He heard that RKO had decided to remake FAREWELL, MY LOVELY, this time as a Philip Marlowe story. He was able to persuade the film's director, Edward Dmytryk, that he should be cast in the lead.

"Dick Powell was a hog farmer from Missouri," Dmytryk told me. "He fit the character, as far as I could see. After all, what is Marlowe? He's no Sam Spade. He's an eagle scout among the tough guys. He's a moral, ethical man, with a strong sense of responsibility. I only met Chandler once. He was unusual, not at all what you'd think a detective story writer would be like. He had an off-beat way of looking at things. He hated corruption. Putting Chandler on film, I knew I couldn't improve on his dialogue. I tried my best to be faithful to the spirit of the book.''

Dmytryk paused to light his pipe and reflected for a few moments.

"I had looked at the Falcon picture," he resumed. "I thought it was a great story, but it had been butchered by attempting to make it fit the Falcon formula. As you know, I directed a Falcon picture myself. The whole tone and feel was different. In putting Chandler on the screen, you have to use a lot of shadows. Lenses and lighting were all important. I worked out the camera positions I wanted and I picked the lenses carefully. I employed low-key lighting throughout the picture, getting rid of fills and making more contrasts. The picture was budgeted at $450,000 and we shot it in 44 days.''

Another problem confronting a screenwriter in transposing Chandler's stories to film is the imagistic expressiveness of his first person singular narrative form. Dmytryk solved the difficulty by doing the picture as a series of flashbacks narrated by Marlowe himself. This permitted Powell's Marlowe to tell viewers that he felt awful, that he felt like an amputated leg, that Moose Malloy "looked about as inconspicuous as a tarantula on a slice of angel food." Malloy had been played by Ward Bond in THE FALCON TAKES OVER. Mike Mazurki was given the role in MURDER, MY SWEET (RKO, 1944). RKO had the same reservations about Chandler's original title as Knopf had had, but for a different reason. Whereas Knopf had objected that the title did not suit a murder mystery, RKO did not want anyone to think that the picture was a Dick Powell musical. The sale of the performing rights had been outright, however, so Chandler received no more money, just a credit for the story. The claustrophobic milieu of Chandler's world comes across in MURDER, MY SWEET as in almost no other film based on his fiction. Powell's backtelling of the action makes his Marlowe the constant interpreter of the action, as Marlowe is in the novels, and he has just the right balance of adolescent banter and brash toughness. One of the memorable scenes in THE BIG SLEEP occurs when Bob Steele deliberately poisons Elisha Cook, Jr., with Humphrey Bogart's Marlowe as a silent witness. What MURDER, MY SWEET lacks in this kind of restrained brutality, it compensates for in its penchant for night scenes, its close rooms, narrow hallways, and its shadows. At one point Marlowe is gazing out his office window and every time a neon sign flashes off Mike Mazurki's image is seen reflected in the glass pane.

"That's where my training in science and mathematics at Cal Tech really helped me out," Dmytryk explained. "I had Dick sit at his desk. When light is reflected in glass, the image becomes smaller, not larger. I wanted the effect of it to be larger. So I had a sheet of plate glass placed directly in front of the camera, with Powell sitting way beyond it. As the light goes on and off, Mazurki's image is reflected in the glass, but because it was closer to the camera than Powell is he looks gigantic in comparison. I used glass again in the final scene when I had to have a gun go off near Powell's face. The glass was between Powell and the gun, but on the screen you couldn't tell it.''

"How did you get the spider web effect in the scene where Powell wakes up in the sanitarium?''

"I managed the effect by means of a superimposition. I had stills of cigarette smoke blown up in size and magnified them over the image of Powell returning to consciousness. I used a variant of the falling sequence in MIRAGE [Universal, 1965] where I had a similar scene. I put an actor on a black platform and shot him with a revolving lens, zooming the camera away. A body falling will accelerate as it falls, and there is an amount of air resistance. I then crossed the piece of revolving film with another shot with a camera zooming away faster and faster. To get natural effects effectively, you have to do it unnaturally. When MURDER, MY SWEET came out and Selznick was producing SPELLBOUND [United Artists, 1945], he called me to ask my advice on handling a dream sequence in his picture.''

"How much advice did you give him?''

"Not too much,'' Dmytryk said, and smiled. "It wasn't my picture.''

Claire Trevor was cast by Dmytryk to play Mrs. Grayle. It was a wise choice. In one scene all that indicates her presence in a room is the exhalation of cigarette smoke from where she lies reclining on a sofa. Her appearance only added additional weight to that Chandler fantasy of the 'Forties that blondes are trouble and, if murder is at issue, they are probably at the bottom of it. Yet, what I miss most in Dmytryk's film—and in Dick Richards' third make of the story—is that hilarious scene Chandler wrote in which Marlowe and Mrs. Grayle proceed to get pie-eyed and fall to necking when Marlowe is supposed to be interrogating her. There is a satirical element in Chandler that none of the film versions has ever succeeded adequately in capturing.

When I met with Billy Wilder in the office of his bungalow on the Universal lot in the summer of 1975, it was morning and there was bright sunlight in the room. I glanced at the golden Oscars on one of the library shelves. Billy directed me to a chair alongside his desk which faced windows overlooking a studio street.

"You worked with Raymond Chandler on DOUBLE INDEMNITY,'' I said, "and the only thing you've been quoted as saying about that collaboration is that Chandler was a 'kook.' ''

"Well, he was,'' Wilder said, sitting down in his desk chair. He leaned over in my direction. "Joe Sistrom thought he would be very helpful with the dialogue. A meeting was eventually set up between us. I was to direct the picture.''

Wilder bounced up from his chair and began to pace about, slapping his leg with a short, silver-topped cane.

"Ray was a naive, sweet, warm man," he went on. "He had never worked in this medium before and he didn't know how to collaborate with others. He thought he was supposed to write the whole screenplay. He came back in a few days with an eighty-page screenplay we couldn't use because it consisted mostly of unfilmable descriptions."

He stopped abruptly in his pacing.

"You think that's funny," he accused in his pleasing Viennese accent. "I had to teach him movie techniques. We started really working together."

Chandler was making $750 a week, a sum for him which was incredible. For the first six weeks, he and Wilder simply talked about the story. Wilder would pace. Wilder would talk. Chandler would talk and Wilder would listen. Chandler sat in an easy chair and smoked his pipe. He would smoke and smoke and smoke. The room became filled with tobacco smoke and Chandler would not permit Wilder to open a window because he distrusted Los Angeles air. They were on the fourth floor of the Paramount Writers Building. To get away, Wilder would repair to the toilet and smoke a cigarette in silence, happy just to be away from Chandler. Chandler in the meantime began to become suspicious of Wilder, suspecting that Wilder had a bladder problem. He took advantage of these frequent absences, however. In his briefcase he carried a pint bottle of bourbon. While Wilder was out of the room, he would take a good slug, telling himself that it gave him the strength to endure Wilder's whimsies. "A Paramount press release on Chandler assured readers that he never drank anything stronger than tea," Frank MacShane wrote, "but he was unable to resist the genial alcoholic atmosphere of the Writers Building. Joseph Sistrom was partly to blame for this change in Chandler, for he himself was an expansive drinker, and often at the end of the day he would take Chandler to Lucey's, a famous bar and restaurant on Melrose Avenue across from the Paramount lot. Mrs. Sistrom, who was often present, recalls that Chandler had a very light head. After two or three drinks he would not exactly be drunk but fuzzy and unable to maneuver properly. The Sistroms usually drove him home, and he would have to be guided up the path to his house. The drinking rather inevitably led to women."[54]

John Houseman, who was under contract to Paramount, made Chandler's acquaintance. As a similar product of the English Public School system, the two were drawn together, but Houseman could see that in Chandler's case the system "which he loved had left its sexually devastating mark upon him. The presence of young women—secretaries and extras around the lot—disturbed and excited him. His voice was normally muted; it was in a husky whisper that he uttered those juvenile obscenities at which he would have been the first to take offense, if they had been spoken by others."[55]

Although Chandler's collaboration with Wilder would drag on for six months, already after the first ten weeks the tensions and pressures were almost unendurable.

Billy was still pacing and talking.

"He had a wonderful flair for description. We tried to find some way to use it. That's why we decided to let MacMurray open the picture confessing to the murder plot he was in with Stanwyck. That way he could describe everything. I really thought we were getting on together when one day it was 9:30 and no Chandler. I found out later he had gone to the front office to quit. He had drawn up a long list of complaints against me."

Among Chandler's papers at the UCLA library, in the special collections, there still remains a copy of Chandler's list of complaints. "Item—Mr. Wilder is at no time to swish under Mr. Chandler's nose or to point in his direction the thin, leather-handled malacca cane which Mr. Wilder is in the habit of waving around while they work. Item—Mr. Wilder is not to give Mr. Chandler orders of an arbitrary nature, such as 'Ray, will you open that window?' or 'Ray, will you shut that door, please?' "

Perhaps our conversation helped to refresh Billy Wilder's memory. Whatever was the case, by the time Ivan Moffat interviewed him for an article subsequently titled "On the Fourth Floor of Paramount," Wilder was able to expatiate in much greater detail on this theme than ever he had for me. "But as we all know," he told Moffat, "and he would be the first person to tell you, he was a very peculiar, a sort of rather acid man, like so many former alcoholics are. He was on the wagon, and he was also married to a woman who was considerably older than he was. Suddenly discipline sort of came into his life, because he had to come in the morning and we would write every day, and I would be pacing up and down, and we would have yellow pads. But he didn't really much like me, ever. . . . To begin with there was my German accent. Secondly I knew the craft better than he did. I also drank after four o'clock in the afternoon and I also, being young then, was fucking young girls. All those things just threw him for a loop. But I thought he had an enormous talent and we got along just fine."[56] Then, of course, the blow fell. Chandler not only did not show, wanting to quit, but he sent Wilder the memo with his long list of complaints. "So we got him to come in," he told Moffat, "and said, 'Come on, cut out that shit, come on for Christ's sake, we don't have court manners here.' And I apologized: I will never talk, I will never drink in your presence, and so on. And we finished the script. But in a book of little paragraphs that were put together about Chandler later, he said that he had a miserable time with me because I was a son-of-a-bitch. However, he said that all he ever knew about pictures was what he learned from me. So there was a kind of resentment. Subsequently he stayed on."[57]

The book to which Wilder was referring was RAYMOND CHANDLER SPEAKING, the collection of miscellaneous writings and letters cited earlier. The letter of 10 November 1950 to Hamish Hamilton, excerpted in the book, contains Chandler's comments on the episode from his own viewpoint. " . . . Working with Billy Wilder on DOUBLE INDEMNITY was an agonizing experience and has probably shortened my life, but I learned from it about as much about screenwriting as I am capable of learning, which is not very much. Like every writer, or almost every writer, who goes to Hollywood, I was convinced in the beginning that there must be some discoverable method of working in pictures which would not be completely stultifying to whatever creative talent one might happen to possess. But like others before I discovered that this was a dream. Too many people have too much to say about a writer's work. It ceases to be his own. And after a while he ceases to care about it. He has brief enthusiasms, but they are destroyed before they can flower. People who can't write tell him how to write.''[58] On the face of it, this letter seems cogent, valid, and to the point. Closer to the mark, however, is Maurice Zolotow's assessment of Chandler in BILLY WILDER IN HOLLYWOOD (1977). He believed that Chandler "had become literally insane, and was a well-tempered paranoid. I have read hundreds of his letters to various persons, which are in the Raymond Chandler Collection at the UCLA library of special collections. His letters are brilliant and witty and quite deranged if you know the facts. Chandler would invent incidents and twist facts around to get sympathy from his friends, his editors, his publishers.''[59] Natasha Spender, who knew Chandler as well as anyone and better than most, found it "interesting that in a life so lonely and bare of lasting friendships, some of his most enduring and rewarding ones were with pen-pals, a 'safer' form of communication, for the delay of reply provided a cushioning of impact. His correspondence with Hamish Hamilton, which was a source of great amusement and pleasure to them both, had lasted well over a decade before they ever met.''[60] She also recognized that "both his oil business and his Hollywood careers had ended in débâcles of alcoholism, though he always presented different explanations, denying to himself the true reason for his failures: his inability to cope with colleagues, and the contrast between their invigorating uninhibited social life and the isolation of his marriage, retreat into which provided a therapeutic setting for recovery from these disasters. A healing maternal presence in the home left him free to pursue the interior monologue of fantasy which went into his writing.''[61]

Working every day at Paramount, Chandler became all too painfully aware of the profound difference between the many young women at the studio and his seventy-three-year-old wife living in their home on Drexel Avenue. Chandler became aware of his lost youth and he was often melancholy. He began keeping a bottle in his desk drawer and would begin to drink privately at three or four in the afternoon. He would call in his young secretary and confide to her how unhappy he was with his wife and would explain that the only reason he married her was because she had sufficient money to permit him to write. When his secretary would suggest a divorce, Chandler would dismiss such a notion with the argument that he could not abandon Cissy in her old age. He would become so despairing at night that he would even call up his secretary and ask her to come to his home. Cissy would respond with intense jealousy and their arguments would often last the night through. In physical terms, Chandler's skin was so white that he seemed almost albino and so was not very attractive. At the time of the preview of DOUBLE INDEMNITY, Chandler invited his secretary to go to the screening with him, explaining that Cissy had already seen the picture and did not want to go. His secretary agreed. After the preview, Chandler drove his secretary home to her apartment and then went back to Drexel Avenue. The resulting quarrel lasted until morning. Chandler had forgotten that it was their wedding anniversary. Although his attempt to have an affair with his secretary was unsuccessful, he was able to establish a liaison with another woman on the lot and he went away with her for some weeks. However, as Frank MacShane noted, he always came back, "perhaps because he disliked 'the tawdry imitation of domesticity' in any prolonged relationship of this sort. Cissy and his house remained the center of his life."[62] Ultimately, he kept going back because the strongest need in his life was the need for maternal approval. Natasha Spender recalled that "traces of his need for maternal approval remained in his demeanor in old age, for I remember one afternoon at a swimming pool in Palm Springs when after each dive he made, he would come to where Evelyn Hooker and I were stretched out on chaise-lounges, like two dowagers doing our embroidery, and would stand waiting until we told him what a fine dive it had been."[63] As Thomas Mann once put it, "it comes to this, *who* is sick: an average blockhead, in whom illness is definitely without any spiritual or cultural aspects, or a Nietzsche, a Dostoyevsky."[64] Chandler was no Nietzsche or Dostoyevsky, but he was not an average blockhead, either. At the very least we ought to concede that Natasha Spender might have been correct and he "may have had to pay a very high price for the novels we enjoy."[65]

"Whose idea was it to change the ending and cut out the scene of MacMurray in the gas chamber?" I asked Wilder who was still pacing.

"Mine," he snapped, pausing suddenly. "It was anticlimatic. That's why I deleted the scene. But by that time Ray was already off the picture."

II

While DOUBLE INDEMNITY was still in production, Chandler contributed to the script of AND NOW TOMORROW (Paramount, 1944) and did a polish job on THE UNSEEN (Paramount, 1945). After the release of MURDER, MY SWEET and once the screenplay for DOUBLE INDEMNITY was nominated for an Academy Award, Chandler's stock as a screenwriter rose. The option on his Paramount contract was up in November, 1944. By January, 1945 a new contract was negotiated. Chandler had hoped to return to writing fiction, but he could not turn down the money he was offered. He was to be paid $1,000 a week.

Alan Ladd was going into the service in three months and Paramount wanted another picture for him. In conversation with John Houseman, who had produced THE UNSEEN, Chandler mentioned that he had an unfinished novel of about 120 typescript pages which he felt might work better as a motion picture.

Houseman suggested the property be turned into the Ladd vehicle the studio wanted and Chandler agreed. The result was THE BLUE DAHLIA (Paramount, 1945). Years later the screenplay was published and Houseman wrote a reminiscence of Chandler by way of an introduction. "In Hollywood," Houseman commented, "where the selection of wives was frequently confused with the casting of motion pictures, Cissy was an anomaly and a phenomenon. Ray's life had been hard; he looked ten years older than his age. His wife looked twenty years older than he did and dressed thirty years younger."[66] Chandler set to work at once on the screenplay, after collecting a sizable fee above his salary for selling the property to the studio. He was able to turn in about half the screenplay in three weeks. Shooting commenced under director George Marshall. Then Chandler hit a snag. He could not finish it. The front office, naturally concerned, tried to bribe him with an extra $5,000 bonus if he completed the script on time. This threw Chandler into emotional apoplexy and he thought his honor was at stake. He made a shocking proposal to Houseman. He claimed that he had not been drinking for years, since he became a writer in fact. He was convinced, however, that he could finish the screenplay while drunk. When Chandler drank, he did not eat. He did not suffer from hangovers, he explained, and malnutrition could be avoided through injections. It was coming off a drunk that was such a physical ordeal.

After some consideration, Houseman concurred. Chandler was provided with two limousines with drivers, night and day, to run errands. He had a direct line to the studio switchboard. Six secretaries, in teams of two, were constantly available. Chandler concluded the script and shooting ended with six days to spare. "During those last eight days of shooting," Houseman recalled, "Chandler did not draw one sober breath, nor did one speck of food pass his lips. He was polite and cheerful when I appeared and his doctor came twice a day to give him intravenous injections. The rest of the time, except when he was asleep, . . . Ray was never without a glass in his hand. . . . "[67] Chandler did not overdo it. He drank only enough to keep himself in a perpetual state of euphoria; but it did require a month for his nervous system to absorb the shock when it was all over. THE BLUE DAHLIA, once it was released, grossed almost three million dollars and Chandler received his second nomination for best screenplay.

Chandler stayed on good terms with Houseman for many years but he reacted vehemently to an article Houseman wrote for VOGUE in which he criticized Marlowe as being "a drab, melancholy man of limited intelligence and mediocre aspiration, who is satisfied to work for ten bucks a day and who, between drinks, gets beaten up regularly and laid occasionally."[68] Yet it was Chandler himself, in a letter he wrote to Houseman shortly before his death, who admitted that "I never really thought of what I wrote as anything more than a fire for Cissy to warm her hands at. She didn't even much like what I wrote."[69]

Somehow, despite all of his studio commitments, Chandler did manage to reweave his former short stories, "Bay City Blues" and "Lady in the Lake," into a Philip Marlowe novel during this time, THE LADY IN THE LAKE (1943). It had that remarkable dialogue which sparkled so in Chandler's prose, which was so unique to him, and which has been so greatly imitated since.

" 'I don't like your manner,' " Kingsley said in a voice you could have cracked a Brazil nut on.

" 'That's all right,' " I said. " 'I'm not selling it.' "[70] Metro-Goldwyn-Mayer purchased screen rights to the novel in 1946 for $35,000. Just shortly before this, Warner Bros. paid $10,000 for the screen rights to THE BIG SLEEP.

It was hot in Palm Springs and the heat rose from the city streets in silent eddies as Howard Hawks and I sat together in his living room. He was used to the heat. He walked very slowly. His legs were blistered from cactus poison.

"I've been in the hospital for the last three days," he said as he lowered himself into a leather chair and propped up his legs. He was being very careful. "I was out motorcycling with my son. I made the mistake of riding through a clump of poisonous cactus. I'll be laid up at least another week, maybe ten days."

"You knew William Faulkner," I began.

"Yes, I did," he replied. "I was in New York working on SCARFACE. I read Faulkner. He was employed at the time as a clerk in Macy's bookstore. I later bought his short story 'Turnabout' and made it the basis for the picture TODAY WE LIVE [M-G-M, 1933]. Faulkner was by then living back in Mississippi. I sent him a check and invited him to come to Hollywood to M-G-M, where I was under contract, to assist on the screenplay. He came to my office. 'I'm Howard Hawks,' I told him. 'I know,' he said; 'I saw your name on a check.' He sat there and smoked his pipe while I took a couple of hours to explain what I wanted. He said nothing until I finished. Then he stood up. 'Where are you going?' I asked him. 'I'm going to write your screenplay,' he said. 'It should take me no more than a week.' He didn't know anything about screenwriting. 'Wait a minute,' I said. 'I want to know something about you.' He hesitated. 'Have you got a drink?' he asked. I pulled out a bottle and we began to talk. When we finished that, we went out and visited a few saloons. By three in the morning, when the last cigarette was drowned in a whiskey glass, it was the beginning of a relationship. We were friends from that day until his death."

I remembered a letter Faulkner had sent to Hawks once he returned to Mississippi after his stint at M-G-M. "I'm sitting on the porch with the rain dripping off the eaves, drinking bourbon, and I hear a wonderful sound—the toilet, and it's due to you."[71]

"He worked for you again when you were at Warner's, didn't he?" I asked. "On THE BIG SLEEP?"

"Yes. On that and other pictures. We both liked detective stories and we agreed that Dashiell Hammett and Raymond Chandler were the best. I also hired Leigh Brackett to work on THE BIG SLEEP. I thought she was a man.

She wrote like one. There was no logic in Chandler's story, but the picture proved you didn't need logic. It was a matter of scenes and pacing. It took Jules Furthman, Leigh, and Bill eight days to prepare the screenplay."

I recalled to myself how Leigh Brackett had told me she and Faulkner had split up the novel by chapters, each adapting those which had come his or her way.

"Why did you cast Bogart in the Marlowe role?"

"He was the best of his kind for what we needed," Hawks responded. "His first day on the picture, Bogie had five or six cocktails at lunch. He went off the lot to do it. I threw him up against a wall and told him we were going to Jack Warner's office and either he was going to get a new director or I was getting a new star. Bogie wasn't really tough. I had no more trouble with him after that. He was allowed one beer while shooting."

"And Lauren Bacall?" I inquired.

Hawks looked at me for a moment, but his eyes were distant.

"I will tell you a story I have never told anyone," he said finally. "Her coming to Hollywood was a mistake on my secretary's part. I only wanted to find out about her and my secretary sent her an airplane ticket instead. She showed up in a sweater and gabardine skirt, very excited, with a high nasal voice. I couldn't use her. I told her it was her voice. She asked me what she could do about lowering it. I repeated what I had heard from other people. For two weeks I didn't see her. She went back to the apartment where she was staying and worked on it. When she saw me again, I was amazed. Her voice had become deep, husky. I began to invite her to my home for the Saturday night parties I gave. I always ended up having to drive her home.

" 'Betty,' I told her, 'this isn't going to work. I don't always want to take you home. Can't you interest one of the others in escorting you?'

" 'I've never been very good with men,' she said.

" 'Why not try being insolent?' I suggested.

"The next Saturday night she comes to me and says she has found a ride home.

" 'How'd you do it?' I asked.

"She said, 'I just walked up to him and asked him where he had bought his tie. He asked me why I wanted to know. I told him so I could tell people not to go there. He laughed, and now he's driving me home.'

"It was Clark Gable.

"I got so to like her insolent style that I went to Jules Furthman when I was back on the lot. We were preparing TO HAVE AND HAVE NOT [Warner's, 1944]. Furthman and Bill Faulkner were doing the screenplay. I asked Jules if he could write in a part for an insolent girl. He didn't see why not. I gave Betty a screen test in the purse scene from the picture, opposite Bogart. She was great."

"They fell in love," I said. "Did you try to capture that in the picture, or, later, in THE BIG SLEEP?"

"No. I tried to keep it out. Of course, Bogie's being in love with her helped Betty. He played all his scenes for her."

Howard grew quiet. Outside the sun blazed mutely.

"Did it occur to you that Bogart was falling in love with someone who was to a certain extent your creation?" I asked.

Hawks nodded.

"I even took Betty aside and warned her. 'Bogie is falling in love with you, Betty. He doesn't know it's just a role.' "

He smiled at me.

"But there is a sequel to this story. This last year when I was invited by the Academy to receive a special award, Betty was there. She came up behind me and kissed me. She said, 'I'm still playing the same role.' "

All of which sounds well; in fact, it sounds as well as everything Howard Hawks was inclined to narrate about himself and his life. However, the view one gets from Lauren Bacall's autobiography, BY MYSELF (1978), is dramatically different. Hawks did not want Bacall to fall in love with Bogart at all and did everything he could to prevent it from happening. Bacall told of how Howard and his wife, Slim, "did everything to distract me. Slim called to invite me to dinner one night. 'I've got the most dazzling man you'll ever meet for a fourth—once you meet him, you'll forget all about Bogart.' The man was Clark Gable, in uniform. Imagine meeting Clark Gable—one of these larger-than-life people that you pay your carefully saved money to see. He *was* dazzling to look at, but he stirred me not a bit. I tried to flirt a little, tried to be attractive to him—but it didn't work. He was just a pleasant terrific-looking man without an overabundance of humor who had incredible dimples and was named Clark Gable. There were no sparks flying that night. He even took me home—Clark Gable in uniform standing at the foot of the stairs to my apartment on Reeves Drive—in the moonlight. He kissed me good night, smiled, and walked away. Nothing, but nothing."[72]

In Hollywood, everyone prefers to live by illusions, and, when you come down to it, not just in Hollywood. When Chandler saw THE BIG SLEEP (Warner's, 1946), he was pleased with Bogart in the role of Philip Marlowe. "Bogart can be tough without a gun," he wrote to Hamish Hamilton. "Also, he has a sense of humor that contains that grating undertone of contempt. Alan Ladd is hard, bitter, and occasionally charming, but he is after all a small boy's idea of a tough guy. Bogart is the genuine article. Like Edward G. Robinson, all he has to do to dominate a scene is to enter it."[73] Chandler felt Alan Ladd's touchiness about his short stature was a defect. He referred to Veronica Lake as Moronica when mentioning THE BLUE DAHLIA and the love scenes between Ladd and Lake only served to reaffirm his contempt toward Hollywood films. Notwithstanding, even he could see a difference between Bacall's scenes with Bogart and Lake's scenes with Ladd.

Leigh Brackett hastened to point out to me that Bogart projected an inner power into the Marlowe character which he didn't have in the novels. THE

BIG SLEEP was her second picture with Hawks and she knew beforehand that he intended to cast Bogart in it. She had had him in mind while she worked on her part of the screenplay.

"Bill Faulkner was good at construction," she told me. "But he was too reclusive to ever get to know very well. Then he would just disappear for two or three days at a time."

He was supposedly drinking.

"Yet he was a very hard worker and always courteous. I don't suppose he really liked Hollywood."

Chandler was invited to the Warner Bros. lot while THE BIG SLEEP was in production. He met Leigh Brackett, William Faulkner, Humphrey Bogart, and Howard Hawks. He told them that he was happy with the screenplay and liked the ending Leigh had devised. Hawks would have to shorten that ending, however, due to the fact that Jack Warner wanted the Bogart-Bacall romance stressed. It was becoming one of the most popular off-screen romances in the gossip magazines. The way Brackett wanted the film to conclude was that Carmen Sternwood, played by Martha Vickers, would be machine-gunned by accident. It would certainly be a more decisive and final ending than that in the book. Yet, as it turned out it was Eddie Mars, the gangster played by John Ridgely, who is accidentally shot down in the final scene.

There is a memorable scene in the novel where Marlowe is taken out to a greenhouse to meet General Sternwood who brings him into the case. In "The Curtain" the scene runs approximately 1,100 words which Chandler expanded to 2,500 words for the novel. The physical reality of the humid heat and the decay Chandler made palpable. Yet, it took Hawks' sensitivity to human relationships to get the characters in the film off talking tough and revealing a momentary affection for one another, as in the scenes between Bogart as Marlowe and Charles Waldron as General Sternwood. Throughout the picture, Marlowe is able to relate to people in a way he never can in the novels. The loneliness in which Marlowe perpetually dwells is lifted. THE BIG SLEEP on screen is not haunted by that heavy emotional oppression which the book establishes in the greenhouse and never really relinquishes.

On the other hand, as a detective film THE BIG SLEEP is flawed. I mentioned Hawks' anecdote concerning who killed Owen Taylor in the section on *film noir*. In the novel, Taylor is killed by Brody, played in the film by Louis Jean Heydt. In the film, it never really is clear and the incident, in another sense, only serves to point up how little Hawks or anyone else cared about loose ends—so little that no one even bothered to consult the original novel! The emphasis had changed, but it was not entirely a conscious alteration.

Paramount threw a party for Chandler at which THE BLUE DAHLIA was screened, but following it he became increasingly intractable. After turning down a number of books recommended by the studio, he did work for a time adapting a novel titled THE INNOCENT MRS. DUFF; but his contract expired before he finished and the project was shelved.

George Haight, assigned to produce THE LADY IN THE LAKE at M-G-M, hired Chandler to work on the screenplay. Chandler complained about everything at the Culver City lot, starting off with the fact that writers were not allowed to have couches on which to lie while cogitating. He was eventually permitted to work at home. Haight was displeased with the results. Chandler kept changing the book. He confessed to Haight that he simply could not help it, that it was his story and he was sick of it, so his natural impulse was to create a new story. Haight's rejoinder that the studio had purchased the rights to the novel because it wanted to film the story fell on deaf ears. After thirteen weeks the contract lapsed and Chandler was replaced by Steve Fisher. Fisher did the screenplay the way Haight wanted it done but got in a tussle with Chandler over screen credit, a tussle which led to blows between Chandler and a friend of Fisher's, Frank Gruber.

Chandler's next assignment was for Universal where Joseph Sistrom had gone after leaving Paramount. Chandler was paid $4,000 a week for two years. The original screenplay he did was PLAYBACK. It was never produced. Chandler later used it to form the basis for his last, and perhaps least satisfying, novel which was published by Houghton Mifflin in 1958. Following publication of THE LADY IN THE LAKE, Chandler had had enough of Knopf. The only thing which prevented him from signing with a new publisher was that he had no book to be published and it would be some years before he did have a finished book. His final screen collaboration was for Alfred Hitchcock, adapting Patricia Highsmith's novel for STRANGERS ON A TRAIN (Warner's, 1951). Chandler did not get along with Hitchcock any better than he had with Billy Wilder. He was guaranteed $2,500 a week for five weeks' work. By this time he had moved with Cissy to a large house in La Jolla. Hitchcock drove down for a story conference. Chandler behaved antagonistically from the start. "Look at that fat bastard trying to get out of his car!" he remarked to his secretary so loudly that Hitchcock overheard it.

Hitchcock found his meetings with Chandler difficult, not only because of Chandler's customary rudeness, but also because Chandler could not seem to get the idea of a co-operative enterprise through his head.

"We'd sit together and I would say, 'Why not do it this way?' " Hitchcock told me as we sat in his spacious office on the Universal lot, "and he'd answer, 'Well, if you can puzzle it out, what do you need me for?' " He paused. "A cobbler should stick to his last," he finally summed it up.

Chandler proved Hitchcock right when he complained morosely that the director was "full of little suggestions and ideas, which have a cramping effect on a writer's initiative. . . . This is very hard on a writer, especially on a writer who has any ideas of his own, because the writer not only has to make sense out of a foolish plot, if he can, but he has to do that and at the same time do it in such a way that any kind of camera shot that comes into Hitchcock's mind can be incorporated into it."[74]

Chandler was forced to share screenplay credit with Czenzi Ormonde, a woman writer who worked as one of Ben Hecht's assistants. He did not like that and he did not like the fact that the picture was a success upon its release. "I don't know why it's a success," he wrote to Hamish Hamilton, "perhaps because Hitchcock succeeded in removing almost every trace of my writing from it."[75] Matthew J. Bruccoli put it rather aptly in his Afterword to the published screenplay of THE BLUE DAHLIA when he remarked that "blame also attaches to Chandler, whose contempt for the professionals rendered him incapable of collaborating with them comfortably, even when he was assigned to work with the best in the business. Indeed, this contempt was hardly distinguishable from self-contempt. When he was in the position to write THE BLUE DAHLIA alone, he had to anesthetize himself."[76]

III

When John Ford broke his leg, Robert Montgomery took over direction of THEY WERE EXPENDABLE (M-G-M, 1945). Montgomery wanted to direct films rather than act in them. He then urged the studio to let him make a film based on John Galsworthy's story, "Escape," about the effect an escaped convict has on the people around him. His idea was to do it employing a first person camera technique. No one had yet done a film using this technique throughout, although Orson Welles, when he first came to Hollywood, had wanted to film Joseph Conrad's THE HEART OF DARKNESS in this fashion, only to make CITIZEN KANE (RKO, 1941) instead. The studio offered Montgomery THE LADY IN THE LAKE. He proposed doing this story with the technique. Louis B. Mayer, who was in charge of production, nixed the idea, insisting that it would be impossible to sustain audience interest with such idiocy. Montgomery got Eddie Mannix, Mayer's assistant, to agree to make a test with the technique. The way Montgomery did it was to use a series of fast pans until the camera came to the person or object it was to focus on, very much as natural eye movement. Mannix, once he saw the test, told Montgomery to proceed despite Mayer's hostility toward the proposal.

When I spoke with Montgomery at the Racket Club on Park Avenue, the gentleness which had characterized him all through his career was still evident along with that quiet but firm sense of artistic integrity which had forced him to retire from television production rather than accept network domination.

"Once Mannix gave me the go-ahead," Montgomery recalled, "I started preparing the script at once and casting the picture. Preparing the script was easy."

"Is there any particular reason you can think of that Steve Fisher changed the time setting in the film to Christmas?" I asked.

"None that I can think of. The real challenge was the filming itself. We had to do a lot of rehearsing. Actors are trained *not* to look at the camera. I had to overcome all that training. I had a basket installed under the camera and sat there, so that at least the actors could respond to me even if they couldn't look directly at me. Jayne Meadows, who played the landlady, had a very difficult scene with a half page of dialogue delivered to the camera without being able to look away once. The head of the camera department had to mount the camera on a boom to get me standing up from a sitting position. But the most complicated scene, as I remember, was that where Marlowe crawls into the telephone booth. It took four people just to handle the action. We had to remove all the walls of the phone booth after Marlowe gets inside." He smiled. "But every day we were ahead of schedule. We averaged three minutes of finished film a day. It was an inexpensive film to make. Mannix liked it a lot. So, too, in the end did Mayer. When it turned out that THE LADY IN THE LAKE was M-G-M's third top grossing film that year, Mayer even had an article run in the trades with the heading, 'Mayer Does It Again.' "

To my way of thinking, Montgomery's conception of the role comes closest to the way Marlowe is evoked in the novels. Steve Fisher's screenplay sparkles with wisecracks very much in the Chandler vein, albeit not derived from the text. At one point Audrey Totter, playing the efficient Adrienne Fromsett, is discussing Marlowe's manuscript of a detective story with Leon Ames as Derace Kingsby, head of Kingsby Publications. She relates how full it is of vividness and excitement and then, at a loss for a word, turns to Marlowe and asks sweetly, "What would you say it was full of, Marlowe?" "Short sentences," he responds. Later on, when Marlowe is describing Adrienne's conduct, he makes a few superlative suggestions and then turns to Adrienne. "What would you say you're full of, Miss Fromsett?" When Adrienne tries to prompt Marlowe on how he should express himself in describing her, Marlowe returns bluntly, "I was thinking of a shorter word." From the very outset, Montgomery involves the viewer in the story and with the Marlowe character. On and off throughout the film, in addition to engaging the suspects in conversation or in making observations, Marlowe also builds his own persona, sometimes ruminating to himself, "Quit wondering, Marlowe. Get out of it." In no other Marlowe film does one find quite the same degree of alienation between Marlowe and the world in which he lives. There are also some brilliant effects achieved with the camera technique, such as when Marlowe talks to Jayne Meadows, both of them standing in front of a store window with her face and his seen only in reflection; or when the headlights of the police car driven by the tough cop played by Lloyd Nolan, seen only through the rear-view mirror gain on Marlowe.

"I nearly lost an eye in that picture," Lloyd Nolan told me. "In the final scene, I'm supposed to be shot by a gun fired from outside the window on the fire escape. They had to shoot a pellet gun through the glass to get the splintering effect. The pellet ricocheted at a ninety degree angle." Lloyd motioned with his hands. "One piece flew into my eye, actually curving around the cornea. They rushed me to a hospital where a female doctor carefully removed it."

I studied Leon Ames reservedly before I put the question to him.

"In the novel, Derace Kingsley, Kingsby in the film, is presumably in love with Adrienne Fromsett and carrying on an affair with her. The screenplay changed that."

"Which was all right by me," Ames responded, and grinned. "I thought Audrey's Adrienne okay, but a little too starchy for me."

Marlowe, so alone in the novels, falls in love in MURDER, MY SWEET and in THE BIG SLEEP. In THE LADY IN THE LAKE (M-G-M, 1947), he and Adrienne Fromsett are going to get married by the fade. According to the Hollywood manner of thinking, this kind of romance was necessary in order to appeal to female viewers who were less interested in who had committed the crimes—and, I suppose, it was also a warning to female viewers. After all, the murderers in these films were ambitious women who were assuming masculine behavior patterns. Although it was only intended that Carmen Sternwood would be machine-gunned down at the end of THE BIG SLEEP, the murderous females in the other two films are shot at the end. The moral lesson is obvious: this is what happens to women who would try to be more than domestic helpmates. Surely the weakest aspect of THE LADY IN THE LAKE is the transformation, I might almost better say *reduction*, of the Adrienne Fromsett character, so that she begins to coo with Marlowe about love, "It's scarey, but it's wonderful."

Raymond Chandler's most significant contribution to the cinema of the 'Forties was his dialogue. He was not visual, the way a film director must be visual; but the directors with whom he worked liked best his descriptions of people and tried to retain them in the screenplays. The novelty of Chandler's prose is completely lost in the last Marlowe film to be made during his lifetime, THE BRASHER DOUBLOON (20th-Fox, 1947) with George Montgomery cast as a totally colorless Marlowe. The film was actually no more than a "B" unit effort, the first Marlowe picture *per se* to be that.

Chandler wrote a savage article contra Hollywood screenwriting for THE ATLANTIC. The article combined with his penchant to turn down scripts, his eccentricity, his drinking—above all, his drinking—ruined him in Hollywood. After THE BRASHER DOUBLOON, which was based on THE HIGH WINDOW, Hollywood gave up on Chandler. Even so, there was a long hiatus between books. THE LITTLE SISTER (1949) appeared a full six years after THE LADY IN THE LAKE. THE LONG GOODBYE was published in 1953; PLAYBACK came in 1958.

Insofar as it was Chandler's intention to expand the horizons of the detective story, to remove it as far as it could be removed from the obligations of a formulary mode of fiction, these final books embody his efforts. After completing THE LITTLE SISTER, Chandler wrote to James Sandoe, an historian of the detective story, that he had an unabridged Liddell and Scott "and in my old age I propose to return to Classical Literature—no doubt in Loeb's Library with parallel texts. I hate translations. Those into English from Greek are usually made by classical professors who, I'm sure you'll pardon me, are either pedants or pansies. Greek is a highly intricate language with infinite shades of meaning and in translation about two thirds of it disappears.''[77] Of course, he did add that this was all probably a dream; but the awareness of ambiguity does increase to a surprising degree in both THE LITTLE SISTER and THE LONG GOODBYE, so much so that one can never be certain exactly what did happen and Marlowe's involvement in these cases cannot be said really to have been beneficial. "Consider Steelgrave's murder, for example," Jerry Speir wrote. "Mavis is found with the body and a warm gun and confesses to the murder. But later information suggests Orfamay may have been responsible; Delores supports that theory. But, in the final chapter, Marlowe appears convinced that Delores was herself responsible, though he is never explicit—aside from some circumstantial conjecturing—about why he thinks so. He does suggest, approvingly, that Mavis is the only one of the lot with guts to stand up for principles and that 'last night she proved she was willing to destroy herself' in order to protect her little sister. But Delores undercuts his romantic rhapsodizing with the reminder 'if she was not acting,' and we and Marlowe realize that we are caught in a trap. In a world where illusion has become the coin of the realm, we are not likely ever to uncover the truth about characters' motives.''[78] Speir also observed that if Marlowe "accomplishes anything hopeful in the book, it is to save Mavis Weld's career from being ruined by all the plotting against her. But the nature of the movie business described in THE LITTLE SISTER makes even that accomplishment ring hallow. Marlowe must recognize that there is little he can do about our seemingly inevitable slide toward unreality.''[79] In one vivid scene, there is even an echo of Chandler's association with Billy Wilder. When visiting Mavis Weld's agent, Marlowe tells how he walked "away from me to a tall cylindrical jar in the corner. From this he took one of a number of short thin Malacca canes. He began to walk up and down the carpet, swinging the cane deftly past the right shoe. I sat down again and killed my cigarette and took a deep breath. 'It could only happen in Hollywood,' I grunted. He made a neat about-turn and glanced at me. 'I beg your pardon.' 'That an apparently sane man could walk up and down inside the house with a Piccadilly stroll and a money stick in his hand.' He nodded. 'I caught the disease from a producer at M-G-M. Charming fellow. Or so I've been told.' ''[80]

THE LITTLE SISTER ends with a cover-up; so does THE LONG GOODBYE. It is this, perhaps more than any other single element, which continued to distinguish Chandler's detective fiction. " 'Let the law enforcement people do their own dirty work,' " Marlowe comments in the latter novel. " 'Let the lawyers work it out. They write the law for other lawyers to dissect in front of other lawyers called judges so that other judges can say the first judges were wrong and the Supreme Court can say the second lot were wrong. Sure there's such a thing as law. We're up to our necks in it. About all it does is make business for lawyers. How long do you think the big-shot mobsters would last if the lawyers didn't show them how to operate?' ''[81] Perhaps no other aspect of Chandler's world-view so much needed to be adapted to the screen as his picture of the relentless exclusion of honesty and justice from the American judicial system, but it never happened. In terms of the future of detective fiction, the failure of the court system to administer justice, or even to conceive what justice is, led to a more frustrated and violent solution; but in terms of life and reality, it meant something else more deadly. Justice, where it is not the result of bureaucratic incompetence, has become that opinion bought by the highest bidder. Americans, it would seem, have now come to accept this as a basic fact of life. For a detective to object would be ludicrous, perhaps, but for the movies to portray it thus—with notable exceptions, such as Orson Welles' THE LADY FROM SHANGHAI (Columbia, 1948)—would most often be construed as unAmerican. In THE SIMPLE ART OF MURDER (1950), an anthology of Chandler's short stories which he published in lieu of a novel, Chandler in his Introduction attempted to account for the peculiar power of BLACK MASK fiction and surmised that "possibly it was the smell of fear which these stories managed to generate. Their characters lived in a world gone wrong, a world in which, long before the atom bomb, civilization had created the machinery for its own destruction, and was learning to use it with all the moronic delight of a gangster trying out his first machine gun. The law was something to be manipulated for profit and power."[82] His fiction, to the end, never deserted that perspective.

When Chandler was still at work on THE LITTLE SISTER, he confessed in a letter to James Sandoe that "in the end I was faced with the choice between a clear but boring explanation of who shot who, why and where etc., and more or less letting it hang in the air on the theory that who cared anyway, it wasn't and couldn't pretend to be a proper mystery story. . . . As a constructionist I have a dreadful fault; I let characters run away with the scenes and then refuse to discard the scenes that don't fit. I end up usually with the bed of Procrustes."[83] This tendency became even more marked in THE LONG GOODBYE. As Jerry Speir put it, Marlowe "is unsure, finally, and his uncertainty underscores the book's ambiguity. Either the world is dominated by forces truly beyond individual control or individuals have merely acquiesced to those unprincipled elements of a society whose only measures of value are power and money. Neither alternative is pleasant."[84]

In his perceptive book, HEINRICH HEINE: A MODERN BIOGRAPHY (1979), Jeffrey L. Sammons made the point that in both his poetry and his prose Heine was more concerned with images than with linear narration. Professor Sammons also noted how Heine used his famed *Stimmungsbrechung*, a sardonic breach of mood in which the tone "shifts back and forth from the emotional to the conversational, from the delicate to the blunt, the setting from the realm of the imagination to the banal scenes of modern society. It is all true in Heine's poetry: the feeling and the frustration, the hope and the delusion, the desirability of the beloved and her dimwitted cruelty. But there is no mediation between these contraries in the situation. The resolution is the poetry itself. Thus the poetry and what it is doing for the poet are ultimately the subject of the poetry rather than the beloved or the love story. The poet recovers his shaken dignity through the creative achievement."[85] In Chandler's detective novels—to vary Professor Sammons' phraseology somewhat—there is no mediation between the detective's feelings of compassion and humanity and the frustration he must feel living in a wholly corrupt world. Desirable women, usually blondes, are to be avoided because they are almost invariably corrupt. The "good girls," such as Anne Riordan, are to be avoided because they would cause the detective to forsake his profession and his profession provides him with his first person narratives which, alone, comprise all the meaning he can find in life. The detective retains his dignity by means of his achievement: persisting in his quest until it is resolved.

Even Heine's romantic antinomy between sensuality and asceticism can be found reflected in the world of Chandler's detective. "He is a man in whom the liveliest hopes have died," Russell Davies wrote in "Omnes Me Impune Lacessunt" [Everyone Provokes Me with Impunity] in THE WORLD OF RAYMOND CHANDLER (1977); "but he maintains himself in the face of a world which has let him down. For this he claims our admiration. But it is self-pity that allies him intimately to Chandler. You can see it in the studied dullness of his ordered life: the bottle in the desk, the (admittedly good) coffee in the morning, the trivial round of 'missing persons' business. It's a complete metaphor for the writer's life—but a writer in retreat from the sensuality of the world outside."[86] For Davies, Chandler's Marlowe is no less disillusioned with men than he is with women. But another essay in the same book, "Marlowe, Men and Women" by Michael Mason, contradicts this view and, rightly, I believe. "The general effect," according to Mason, "is that Chandler's world is morally skewed in a way that makes nonsense of the author's claim, which he liked to imply if not actually state, that the Marlowe novels are edifyingly clear-sighted about good and evil. Their moral scheme is in truth pathologically harsh on women and pathologically lenient toward men. For just as the novels are full of homicidal females—gunning men down, beating their brains out, and pushing them out of windows—they are correspondingly devoid of bad males. There is scarcely a dislikeable man to be found, and even the initially dislikeable, especially among the police, often turn out to be less unpleasant than they seemed."[87] On these, as well as other, grounds, Mason concluded that "Marlowe's honor is most clearly a disguise for homosexual feeling."[88] Among Mason's other reasons are "Marlowe's unmasculine assiduity in domestic chores."[89]

What has happened here is that generic cultural roles are being confused with biological sex roles, or inclinations. Cissy was dying while THE LONG GOODBYE was being written and Chandler, despite the anguish generated by the situation, genuinely enjoyed running errands and attending to her. In the novel, it is imperative to recall that Marlowe rejects both the female characters who make overtures to him *and* his friendship with Terry Lennox, the latter because he can no longer admire Lennox' weak character, or what he interprets to be weakness of character. It was only after Cissy was dead that Chandler was confronted with what had been Dashiell Hammett's dilemma. Marlowe put it into words in PLAYBACK. "Alcohol was no cure for this. Nothing was any cure but the hard inner heart that asked for nothing from anyone."[90] Of course, this is the way Marlowe has behaved all along, except that now Chandler himself was in the same condition and he could not bring himself to this resolution any more in his personal life than he could permit Marlowe to live this way. Linda Loring calls Marlowe at the last moment. They had had a sexual encounter near the end of THE LONG GOODBYE. Now she wants to come to Marlowe so that he may, once again, hold her in his arms. In the final Marlowe novel, which Chandler began but did not finish, THE POODLE SPRINGS STORY, Marlowe and Linda are married. Chandler frequently claimed that he was writing "realistic" detective fiction, but, as Philip Durham remarked in DOWN THESE MEAN STREETS A MAN MUST GO: RAYMOND CHANDLER'S KNIGHT (1963), "Chandler was actually writing romantic fiction, [although] by simulating reality through a hard-boiled attitude he could stay within an American literary tradition. The action and violence more or less covered up the fact that everything came out all right in the end."[91] There are those who would have preferred it had Chandler not tried to marry off Marlowe, not taken Hammett's solution in THE THIN MAN; but this can only be because those readers and critics would prefer a Marlowe who was not human and without human needs. It may be, in the final analysis, that this is what constitutes a hero: a person who is not human.

In his own life, it was not quite so simple for Chandler. After Cissy's death, Chandler had a chance to travel and spent as much time as he could in England. Hamish Hamilton provided him with an opportunity to meet both Somerset Maugham and Noel Coward at a party. Yet, once the party was in progress, Chandler rang up to beg off. He used to claim Cissy as his excuse. When he could no longer do that, he still avoided meeting people. He preferred the creations of his own imagination. He would rarely look at a person to whom he was speaking. A skin irritation made him disinclined to shake hands. When an admirer at the Paramount commissary once came over to his table and asked merely to shake his hand, Chandler curtly refused. When the old man turned away, Chandler remarked loudly, "Who's that old bastard? Imagine coming around here and making a nuisance of himself."[92]

While he lived in La Jolla, and when he was writing, it was Chandler's custom to type out his fiction from nine to twelve or one o'clock. He used half-sheets of yellow paper to save on the amount of retyping he might have to do should he decide to add something. Often the night before he would sit for some time and work out in his head what he intended to type the next morning. When a manuscript was completed, Chandler would start the story all over again, many times not even consulting the previous manuscripts. When at last he felt the book was ready, he would have a secretary type it. For a while Carl Brandt, who also represented John P. Marquand, became Chandler's literary agent, but Chandler could not get along with him, so he switched eventually to Helga Greene.

When Cissy died, there were only eight people at the funeral. Chandler had her remains cremated and placed in a vault in the Cyprus View Mausoleum in San Diego. "For thirty years, ten months, and four days," Chandler wrote later, "she was the light of my life, my whole ambition."[93] He insisted that he had never once made an overture to another woman while they had been married. " . . . I sit up half the night playing records when I have the blues and can't get drunk enough to feel sleepy," he described his existence. "My nights are pretty awful. And they don't get any better."[94] He attempted suicide, rather ineffectually; mostly he just drank and drank. He wanted another woman in his life, but he could not find one. For a time, he courted Natasha Spender, pianist wife of Stephen Spender, while, from her point of view, she was trying to make him forget his loss and stop him from drinking. As might be imagined, Spender was not altogether pleased with this situation, but he was surprisingly tolerant all the same. " 'I know what you are all doing for me, and I thank you,' " he once told Natasha, " 'but the turth is I really *want* to die.' "[95]

Chandler's books and subsidiary rights were earning him between $15,000 and $25,000 a year. He spent most of it foolishly on potential candidates for marriage. He made over his will to at least two other women before he finally settled his estate on Helga Greene. She agreed to marry him. She lived in London. Chandler got as far as New York on his way to consummate the marriage when the urgent letters from another woman he had adopted while in La Jolla summoned him back to California. On 23 March 1959 he entered La Jolla Convalescent Hospital with pneumonia. Three days later he died. In "The Pencil," the last Marlowe story of any length, Chandler introduced Anne Riordan again, and this time Marlowe kisses her without being asked. But it cannot go beyond that. " 'I've had too many women to deserve one like you,' " Marlowe tells Anne. The woman in La Jolla was outraged that Chandler had deflected his estate of $60,000 plus copyrights to Helga Greene. Helga Greene was in England, too ill to return to the States. So Chandler's corpse lay alone in the funeral parlour, a testament to the indirections of his life. Although the same minister who had performed Cissy's burial service presided, no one thought to have Chandler's remains cremated, as had been his wish, and he was not even buried in the same cemetery with Cissy.

When Marlowe was revived on the screen, it was in MARLOWE (M-G-M, 1969) and he was played by James Garner. The basis for the film was THE LITTLE SISTER. Yet, given Garner in the role, the prudish detective who in THE BIG SLEEP had torn up the sheets on his bed rather than fornicate with a female suspect and allow his bed to be contaminated by her presence now has a girlfriend and idles away his spare time watching the girls in a modeling school across the way go through their paces. The toughness, the loneliness, the sense of claustrophobic isolation have given way to a superficial wittiness.

When Robert Altman came to direct THE LONG GOODBYE (United Artists, 1973), he felt very strongly about the Marlowe character. He saw Marlowe as a mumbler and a bumbler. He told Leigh Brackett, who worked on the screenplay, that he perceived Marlowe the way Chandler had perceived him, a loser, but a *real* loser, not the fake winner Chandler had made out of him. He was a loser all the way. After the picture was released to such a disappointing box office that it grossed less than a million dollars, I spoke with Leigh Brackett about it.

"The problems for me," she responded, "began with the plot. It broke down. You couldn't really translate it to the screen. It was hackneyed even when Chandler wrote it, riddled with clichés. The big decision we had was whether it should be done as a period piece or if we could update it. I felt we should update it. The Los Angeles Chandler wrote about was long gone; in a sense it never really existed outside of his imagination. Nor do people, even in the movies, talk any more the way they talk in a Chandler novel. Brian Hutton was supposed to be the director, but he got offered another picture. Bob Altman took over. Hutton had wanted Elliott Gould for the part of Marlowe. Elliott Kastner, our producer, went to United Artists and made the deal so Hutton could have Gould. Bob is a good director. But when he got on the picture, he had Elliott Gould and THE LONG GOODBYE."

"I don't think they really go together."

"They're what we had, though," Leigh said. "Bob and I spent a lot of time talking over the plot, who'd done it, who lost what. I wrote one script, and then had to change the construction later. Bob wanted Marlowe to be a loser. I had to agree with him that all Chandler ever wrote had about it the feeling of a loser. I met Chandler only once. I know he wanted Marlowe to be depicted as an honest man and somebody who was his own man. I wanted to get that in my screenplay. But I also had to show Marlowe the way he looked to us in the 'Seventies. The first script I had was too long. I shortened it. But the ending was inconclusive. I had Marlowe shooting Terry Lennox at the end. It was the only way I could think to handle it. The alternative would be for him just to be a louse, to walk away from it. I didn't think that a moral ending. Hutton had wanted to end it this way."

"And Altman?"

"He wasn't so concerned about the ending as how we got there. He conceived of the film as a satire. Bob changed a lot of things. Nina van Pallandt was his idea, as Mrs. Wade. So was Sterling Hayden as Wade. Bob didn't have too much choice. I wrote the part for Dan Blocker, but he died. So when Hayden was cast, the whole plot was thrown off base. The Malibu location was Bob's idea. So was Wade's suicide, walking into the ocean. I had written Blocker in as a large, cowardly type, who would strike his wife. A big man with nothing inside. When Bob came to do the scenes between Marlowe and Wade, he had Gould and Hayden ad lib most of the dialogue."

"Whose idea was the scene where Mark Rydell rams the Coke bottle into his girlfriend's face?"

"Bob Altman's. That's pure Altman. So, really, is the Gould-Marlowe character. Bob built up his character from the bar and cat scenes. Gould isn't tough at all. He looks vulnerable. You have to work with what you have. Marlowe isn't what he was in THE BIG SLEEP, but Elliott Gould isn't Humphrey Bogart.''

"But," I interposed, "when you've changed a character that much, what was the good of basing him on Marlowe at all?"

Leigh sighed. "Because Marlowe, as Chandler saw him, would be unthinkable in the 'Seventies."

Robert Altman was working on a picture titled THREE WOMEN when I visited him on location at Palm Springs. The idea for this picture had come to him in a dream. The scene in the bus terminal was being filmed. Ruth Nelson was cast as an old woman in the film and Altman had talked her husband, John Cromwell, into taking a part as well. During a break, I took the opportunity to speak with Cromwell. He was ninety. He had let the stubble of his beard grow for the part.

"I don't suppose anyone has told you lately that DEAD RECKONING was a good picture," I said.

"What was that?" he asked, stepping closer.

"DEAD RECKONING? It was a good picture."

He screwed up his face into a look of disgust and made a downward motion with his thumb.

"He doesn't like most of the pictures he made," Ruth Nelson explained.

Altman was dressed casually, wearing khaki shorts and a golf cap. His hair and beard were shot with gray. He would track all the shots with the camera himself before he decided on a take.

"Was it your idea to cast Elliott Gould in THE LONG GOODBYE?" I asked, once we had a chance to speak informally.

"No. David Picker who was then president of United Artists had the idea. Jerry Bick, one of the producers, came over to my house one night and asked me what I thought of Gould as Marlowe. United Artists saw in it a way to get Gould through with his contract with them and Bick, if he could get the picture together, had a deal. I thought Elliott was a great idea. I went on for two hours telling Bick why. That was my mistake, I guess. The picture had been offered to Howard Hawks and then Peter Bogdanovich. They had both turned it down. In telling Bick that he should cast Elliott, I just talked myself into doing it."

"Did you really think of Marlowe as Gould?"

Altman smiled. "There's no reality in the Marlowe character. Marlowe can only exist in the minds of the readers or in an audience. He's an anti-character. I tried to play him as if he had been asleep for thirty years. There was a line they cut out which summed him up. Marlowe's friend, Terry Lennox, sees some girls in the next apartment bathing without their tops on. He says to Marlowe, 'I'll bet you have a lot of fun here.' Marlowe replies, 'It's no fun any more, unless I can take off their brassieres.' "

"Did you agree with Leigh Brackett's ending?"

"I wouldn't have done the picture if it'd had a different ending. Marlowe's biggest mistake was depending on friendships. Lennox was his friend. Friendship was all Marlowe had. When his friend betrayed him, he had to kill him."

Altman was called back to the set. Once the scene was completed, the entire company was to return to the motel set. Altman climbed into the car with me.

"Now tell me about this book you're writing," he said.

I told him it was concerned with the detective genre.

"Well," he said, "that's what THE LONG GOODBYE was about. It was about a private detective. It's not a very honorable profession, you know. It's never had anything to do with digging up the truth. A private eye turns over what he finds to whomever hires him and his employer can put it to whatever use he chooses."

As we drove out of the parking lot, Altman glanced back at the bus terminal.

"Whew," he said, "I'm glad that's finished. I feel like such an idiot making a movie in public places. Everyone always stares at you as if you're crazy, or something."

"Leigh told me that you improvised a lot at the Malibu set, especially the dialogue between Gould and Sterling Hayden."

"Just the scenes where they were drinking were improvised. I wanted the Hayden character to represent Chandler. I love Chandler. He didn't think plot was very important, and neither do I. A plot for him was just an excuse to hang onto it a hundred little thumbnail essays. I tried to put myself into Chandler's position, if he was alive in 1973 and doing a movie. I never finished THE LONG GOODBYE. I read the end of the book, and the beginning, but I didn't read it all the way through. I used RAYMOND CHANDLER SPEAKING. I had everyone read it. I wanted to put more of Chandler in the movie than Marlowe. I thought the philosophy of the picture was summed up with the notion of live and let live. That's why I ended it with the theme 'Hooray for Hollywood.' I wanted to say to the audience, 'It's just a movie, folks.' "

"That's one of the things that bothers me. If it was your intention to do THE LONG GOODBYE as a satire, why have the scene where Mark Rydell smashes a Coke bottle in his girlfriend's face?"

Altman gave me a knowing grin. "That was a calculating device," he said. "The audience of today has trouble dealing with drama and humor. They won't allow you to do both together. The Coke bottle sequence brought violence into the film. It was supposed to get the attention of the audience and remind it that, in spite of Marlowe, there is a real world out there, and it is a violent world. It was the same with Hayden's suicide. In the novel, it's faked. It's really murder. But because Hayden was based on Chandler, I put all of Chandler's suicide notions into the character and made the suicide real. It was right out of A STAR IS BORN [United Artists, 1937]."

When we arrived at the motel set, Altman went inside. The rest of the cast and crew was arriving.

"I just don't feel like working today," Altman confessed to an assistant.

"How about a little pool," he suggested, looking at me. He racked the balls and we began to play. He scratched. Then he scratched again. "I'm good at sinking the white ball," he said.

"The critics," I said after I, too, scratched, "have read a great deal of symbolism into the scene at Malibu where Gould is reflected in the glass doors while Hayden is having an argument with Nina van Pallandt."

"That's what symbolism is, isn't it?" Altman asked, preparing his next shot. "Something critics read into a picture that wasn't intended? It works for them. All I wanted to do in that scene was to avoid violating Marlowe's point of view. I didn't want the audience to see anything Marlowe didn't. That's why I superimposed his image over the scene."

"Chandler's fans didn't like the picture."

"I know. It surprised me. It still surprises me. But, you know, people will accept anything as all right in their own lives, but they make strong demands on their heroes. People like to continue to believe in what they once believed. Even if they feel differently than they once did, they don't want to feel differently about their heroes." He laid down his cue stick and faced me. "You might say I have a distorted view of things. But it's my view. And I cherish it."

Having lost any reference at all to Chandler's novel and to his detective, it was probably not too extraordinary that even Chandler's dialogue should also have been excised from THE LONG GOODBYE. Marlowe might rhapsodize in the novels, "I was as dizzy as a dervish, as weak as a worn-out washer, as low as a badger's belly, as timid as a titmouse, and as unlikely to succeed as a ballet dancer with a wooden leg."[96] In Altman's THE LONG GOODBYE, the most inspired Elliott Gould's Marlowe ever gets is to say that the cops have the case "all zippered up like a big bag of shit." Chandler himself had said about the book that "I wrote this because I can do that now. I didn't care whether the mystery was fairly obvious, but I cared about the people, about this strange corrupt world we live in, and how any man who tried to be honest looks in the end either sentimental or plain foolish."[97] In Altman's film, Marlowe is neither; he has surrendered to unmotivated and, therefore, meaningless rage against the world and all that is in it; and, what is more, he has become a killer.

There was no way that, after the disappointing showing of THE LONG GOODBYE, United Artists wanted to distribute the third film adaptation of Chandler's second novel, FAREWELL, MY LOVELY (Avco-Embassy, 1975). In this, the company was mistaken. The picture was a success, in the United States and abroad. It was directed by Dick Richards.

"Bob Altman updated the character," I said as we sat in Richards' office at what used to be the Goldwyn studios on Santa Monica Boulevard. "Why didn't you?"

"I was given an updated script when I was offered the picture," he replied. "I turned it down. I thought it was sacrilegious to screw around with that book."

"What happened then?"

"It was the same producers as on THE LONG GOODBYE, Elliott Kastner and Jerry Bick. They told me to make any changes in the script I wanted to make. David Goodman and I rewrote the whole thing, making it a period piece."

"Well, I have to admit that the way you did it, it worked. When THE LONG GOODBYE was in preproduction, I didn't think it was possible for it to be brought off as a period piece."

"THE LONG GOODBYE is very late Chandler. FAREWELL, MY LOVELY is from Chandler's early period. I think he wrote well in that period. His dialogue is sharper. Everything was better. I tried to stay true to Chandler. The dialogue is what makes Chandler stick. That I wanted to keep. There was a lot about the book that was unbelievable, but not the dialogue."

"You changed the plot. You substituted a cat house for the asylum and a madame for the psychic, Jules Amthor."

"I didn't like Amthor as a villain. That's one of the things I found unbelievable in the novel. It played better, I thought, the way we changed it. And we created a sub-plot. We gave Marlowe a friend. In the novels, he has no one."

"In the novels," I said, "he doesn't trust anyone enough to have a friend."

"Well, that's where Bob Mitchum came in. He played Marlowe as a man of his age. He's tired. Marlowe is tough, smart, but fallible. He can say, almost at the end, 'Now, I get it.' It's nearly too late. But he knows how to get information."

"How did Mitchum take to the role?"

"Oh, he liked the role. But he was worried about how he would be accepted, playing Marlowe. Bob Mitchum is a great sardonic character. That's the way I wanted him to play Marlowe. And, of course, he had always wanted to play Marlowe. We talked over the role quite a bit. But we agreed what kind of guy Marlowe was."

"Did you look at MURDER, MY SWEET?"

"I looked at MURDER, MY SWEET and at the Falcon picture. I wanted Los Angeles to be seedy in my film, the way it had been when Chandler described it. We shot the whole picture right here. I used an old boat for the gambling ship."

"Chandler based Bay City on Santa Monica. Edward Dmytryk told me that they used to lock up Santa Monica at night. Chandler drew his cops as corrupted men. You didn't."

"No. For me, the picture was about Marlowe. Marlowe is a hero. We debated for months how to handle that last scene, where Marlowe gives money to the widow. I wasn't so concerned with corruption. There's plenty of that in the picture. I wanted to stress Marlowe's honesty."

The last Marlowe film also starred Robert Mitchum, THE BIG SLEEP (United Artists, 1978) directed by Michael Winner. The plot was updated and the location was even changed from Los Angeles to London. The meaning and substance of the source were lost. Yet, in Chandler's novels and stories, Marlowe persists, a man to be taken on his own terms, one of the dubious heroes of American popular fiction with his own peculiar but unshakable integrity. Marlowe on the screen should have been so fortunate.

"Well, all this matters nothing," Raymond Chandler wrote to Hamish Hamilton, "except that a writer to be happy should be a good second-rater, not a starved genius like Laforgue. Not a sad lonely man like Heine, not a lunatic like Dostoyevsky. He should definitely not be a mystery writer with a touch of magic and a bad feeling about plots."[98]

9

Crime in the Streets

When men learn to be men maybe they can handle dames.
                                                        Mike Hammer[1]

The development which the private detective underwent after Raymond Chandler was derivative, not original. Rex Stout created a durable combination in the fat, sedentary Nero Wolfe whose cases are described in a humorous, semi-hard-boiled style by his assistant, Archie Goodwin. This team made its first appearance in FER-DE-LANCE (1934) written when Stout was forty-eight and little changed about them over the four decades until their final appearance in the canon, A FAMILY AFFAIR (1975). Only two motion pictures were made based on Stout's creations, both in the mid 'Thirties, and both in his opinion so badly conceived that he never again allowed Nero Wolfe to be brought to the screen during his lifetime. What is perhaps most significant about Stout's Nero Wolfe stories is their combination of elements from the classical and hard-boiled traditions in detective fiction, a balance that no other author seemed able to strike.

The hard-boiled dectective story itself became bifurcated, a circumstance probably best illustrated by the works of Mickey Spillane and Ross Macdonald. Born Frank Morrison Spillane in Brooklyn in 1918, Spillane began his career writing for slick magazines, but he soon changed course and specialized in scripting dialogue for voice balloons in comic books. At the height of this activity, after the Second World War, Spillane was able to make twelve dollars a page and grind out as many as forty or fifty pages a day. During the war, Spillane was in the Air Force, training pilots and himself flying combat missions. When he returned to civilian life, in addition to his work on comic books, he also was a trampoline performer for the Ringling Bros., Barnum, and Baily circus and he had a short stint as a federal agent fighting a narcotics ring. If this last experience provided anything to the milieu of his subsequent books, it was the notion that the major threat to society comes from organizations.

When it seemed that the action comic market was playing out, Spillane decided to write a novel featuring an action character named Mike Danger who became a New York private eye called Mike Hammer in the published draft, I, THE JURY (1947). Hammer has no patience with judges and juries; he knows better. He will knock out teeth, break arms and fingers, gouge eyes, and kill to get what he wants. Already in the first novel, Hammer works over two Blacks and two homosexuals in the first fifty pages and before the end he roughs up two more "pansies" and a college dean, embodying Spillane's right-wing political philosophy and a distrust of minorities and intellectuals. His one friend is Pat Chambers, a police captain. In I, THE JURY Hammer sets out to find the murderer of a pal he knew in the war. Hammer falls in love with Charlotte only to discover that she is the murderer. She strips off her clothes in the final scene, but Hammer will not be enticed. He shoots her low in the belly. When she asks Hammer, "How could you?," he replies before she expires, "It was easy."[2]

This, then, became a prototypical pattern for the Mike Hammer books, all of which became instant bestsellers. "He is on the side of righteousness," Kay Weibel wrote in "Mickey Spillane as a 'Fifties Phenomenon" (1976), "and the city he is attacking, and by inference everyone in it, is evil. The perpetrators of the crime Mike is allegedly solving are always members of a large corrupt group or organization, and Mike merely maims or kills off everybody who is implicated in the group's activities. The last person left standing is presumed most guilty by Mike in the monologue he delivers before the final execution. Significantly, this last person is almost always female."[3]

Whatever misogyny may have been indigenous to Hammett, Chandler, and the BLACK MASK school generally became amplified and intensified in Spillane. Hammer regards all women merely as sex objects. Visiting a model agency in VENGEANCE IS MINE (1950), Hammer remarks of the women he sees that "in the downstairs department they were shipshape from plenty of walking, but upstairs it was hard to tell whether they were coming or going unless they were wearing falsies. They were pretty to look at, but I wouldn't give any of them bed room."[4] In this novel, as in the others, all of the major female characters are attractive and all of them want to go to bed with Hammer about whom the point is made that he is ugly rather than handsome. When Connie offers herself to Hammer and Hammer becomes nasty, she slugs him. At the end of the scene, the blood trickling down his chin, Hammer tells the reader that "I reached up and smacked her across the mouth as hard as I could. Her head rocked, but she still stood there, and now her eyes were more vicious than ever. 'Still want me to make you?' 'Make me,' she said."[5]

This is about as explicit as sexuality ever becomes in the Hammer books; the violence is far more so, as is the narrative rhythm of intercutting scenes of sexual titillation with scenes of brutal violence, a formula which has become standard now in the legion of porno-action books which continue to sell well. Juno is the most beautiful woman in VENGEANCE IS MINE. She tells Hammer why she finds him attractive. " 'I detest people who pamper me. I detest people who insist upon putting me on a pedestal. I think I like to be treated rough and you're the only one who has tried it.' . . . Quite right. I didn't know what the hell was going on in my head, but sometimes when I looked at her I wanted to reach across the table and smack her right in the teeth. Even when I thought of it I could feel the tendons in the back of my hand start twitching. Maybe a goddess was just too damn much for me."[6]

Velda is Mike's secretary and assistant in the novels. She, too, is quite beautiful, with extremely dark hair in contrast to the blondes Mike keeps meeting and taking to bed. What is particularly significant about Velda is that she does not reject violence, nor is she satisfied merely to be excited by Hammer's violence. She is violent herself. In VENGEANCE IS MINE, she kills one villain while the other gets away. " 'You can put a notch on your gun, Velda,' " Mike tells her. "I thought she was going to get sick, but that animal look screwed her face into a snarl. 'I wish I had killed them both.' "[7] All through the book, Hammer is bothered by how much Juno reminds him of Charlotte from I, THE JURY whom he had to kill. At the end, when he exposes Juno as the head of a blackmail ring, he tells her " 'I didn't think it would be this much trouble to kill another woman but it is.' "[8] What saves the situation is when Juno is stripped of her clothing and Hammer discovers that she is actually a male transvestite. "I forgot all my reservations about shooting a woman then."[9].

At the conclusion of KISS ME, DEADLY (1952), Hammer has lost any compunction he might ever have felt about killing a woman. Lily, who has just taken an alcohol bath and with only an alcohol-soaked robe around her, plugs Hammer. Wounded, Hammer tries to light a cigarette as he lies on the floor. Lily comes over for a final, deadly kiss before she finishes him off. This is her great mistake. "The smile never left her mouth and before it was on me I thumbed the lighter and in the moment of time before the scream blossoms into the wild cry of terror she was a mass of flame tumbling on the floor with the blue flames of alcohol turning the white of her hair into black char and her body convulsing under the agony of it. The flames were teeth that ate, ripping and tearing, into scars of other flames and her voice was the shrill sound of death on the loose."[10]

John G. Cawelti in ADVENTURE, MYSTERY, AND ROMANCE observed that "by most traditional literary or artistic standards, the works of Mickey Spillane are simply atrocious."[11] This notwithstanding, in an effort to explain Spillane's tremendous popularity, Cawelti felt that "violence as orgasm is a main theme of Spillane's novels"[12] and that "Mike Hammer is the agonized but final outcry of the evangelistic subculture of rural America about to be swallowed up in the pluralistic, cosmopolitan world of the cities."[13] Cawelti was a poor prophet. Once the vengeance films of Clint Eastwood, Charles

Bronson, and Chuck Norris came upon the scene, Mike Hammer's world-view blazed with an incandescence far surpassing Mickey Spillane's impact. Where Cawelti was correct was in placing Mike Hammer in the American evangelical tradition, although, even here, he was anticipated by William Ruehlmann who remarked two years before Cawelti that the root of Mike Hammer's popularity "is Bible Belt fundamentalism. The powerful rhythms of Spillane's recorded rage show a stylistic debt to the King James text. Hammer is capable of prayer, and he resorts to an Old Testament vision of himself as God's agent in order to justify the carnage."[14] For example, in ONE LONELY NIGHT (1951) Hammer explains to Velda: " 'There's no shame or sin in killing a killer. David did it when he knocked off Goliath. Saul did it when he slew his tens of thousands. There's no shame to killing an evil thing. As long as you have to live with the fact you might as well enjoy it.' "[15]

It should come as no surprise, then, that Spillane became a Jehovah's Witness as early as 1952. In 1965, when a list of the top ten bestselling American fictional works of the Twentieth century included Spillane's first seven novels, he entered into a second marriage to a model whom he had pose in the nude for the cover of THE ERECTION SET (1972). For years before that, Spillane had already been posing himself as his detectives and in the mid 1980s he played himself as a detective in beer commercials on television. Spillane, in fact, has it to his credit that he is the only author of detective fiction who both played himself and then played his detective in films based upon his works.

However, this is to anticipate. United Artists, impressed with Spillane's spectacular sales figures, was quite anxious to bring Mike Hammer to the screen. I, THE JURY (United Artists, 1953) was intended to be the first of a series of films. It was directed by Harry Essex and starred Biff Elliott as Mike Hammer, Preston Foster as Captain Pat Chambers, Margaret Sheridan as Velda, and Peggie Castle as Charlotte Manning, the psychiatrist and murderer. All of the harsh and brutal edges from the book were muted in the screenplay by the film's director, except for its sadistic opening—the repeated shooting of an amputee as he tries to crawl toward his gun—and for the close with the semi-nude Charlotte getting plugged in the stomach while embracing Hammer. The final dialogue exchange between them was also retained. When the film grossed only $1,229,000, United Artists could not discern what was wrong.

Part of the problem may have been the casting. For the second film, KISS ME DEADLY (United Artists, 1955), Ralph Meeker was cast as Mike Hammer. Robert Aldrich was assigned the direction and A. I. Bezzerides did the screenplay. There is a certain irony about this last. Spillane himself was a supporter of McCarthyism and the House UnAmerican Activities Committee and Bezzerides was black-listed because of the findings of HUAC. The screenplay, in fact, is an utter repudiation of the ideology of the novel. In the book, Hammer is up against the Mafia and the object which is being pursued is a cache of narcotics worth two million before the war and which has now doubled in its value. Many of the episodes that shock most in the film originated in the screenplay: Hammer's smiling while a character whimpers when Hammer slams the man's fingers in a drawer or Hammer's breaking another character's valuable Caruso records in a deliberate attempt to get him to talk. In the film, Hammer learns about a box that contains an atomic device that is being sought by various agents. Velda, played by Maxine Cooper, terms it the "great whatsit." She is kidnapped by the enemy agents after the box. In the novel, Hammer kills Dr. Soberin. In the film, Lily kills him in an attempt to get possession of the box. Earlier in the film, Soberin, played by Albert Dekker, makes a reference to Pandora and in dying warns Lily not to open the box. She will not listen to him. She opens the box and a series of explosions ensue, while Hammer and Velda stumble into the nearby ocean surf. Aldrich himself commented in an interview that he intended the film to have political overtones. "It did have a basic significance in our political framework that we thought rather important in those McCarthy times: that the ends did not justify the means."[16] This applies in KISS ME DEADLY not only to the lengths to which the agents, Lily among them, are willing to go to get hold of the box, but as well to Hammer's efforts to thwart them. The world revealed in the film is truly a dark world and the end is definitely no triumph of justice. Upon release, the picture grossed only $726,000 in the United States and a total of $226,000 overseas.

Spillane had every reason to be angered at what was done to his book in Aldrich's film. He was happy for the chance to play himself in RING OF FEAR (Warner's, 1954) directed by James Edward Grant, one of John Wayne's favorite screenwriters. In order to capture a psychopathic killer who is sabotaging his circus, Clyde Beatty asks his old friend Mickey Spillane to take on the case. Spillane solves it. Subsequently, the Mike Hammer series continued with MY GUN IS QUICK (United Artists, 1957) directed by George White and Phil Victor. Robert Bray was cast as Hammer, and the screenplay had him doing more traditional investigating of murders committed by the villain than, as in the novels, where Hammer is almost always not working for a client and simply killing off evil-doers. The gross sank again, this time to $308,000 in the United States and a foreign gross of $602,000.

The fourth and final Mike Hammer film was THE GIRL HUNTERS (United Artists, 1963), which was farmed out to Colorama in England where it was filmed although supposedly it is set in New York. Mickey Spillane was himself cast as Mike Hammer who comes off a seven-year drunk when he learns that Velda, played by Shirley Eaton, may not have met her death at the hands of the Dragon, a Red agent, but may in fact still be alive. Hammer proceeds to take on the Reds single-handedly. Despite an elaborate promotional campaign, the picture grossed less than a million dollars.

"You can write constant action and that is fine if you really enjoy it," Raymond Chandler confided to his literary agent, Bernice Baumgarten, in 1952. "But alas, one grows up, one becomes complicated and unsure, one becomes interested in moral dilemmas, rather than who cracked who on the head. And at that point perhaps one should retire and leave the field to younger and more simple men. I don't necessarily mean writers of comic books like Mickey Spillane."[17] Although he was not overly impressed by Ross Macdonald's first Lew Archer book, THE MOVING TARGET (1949), it was precisely Macdonald who in his Lew Archer saga would carry the private eye detective story far away from the hard-boiled tradition and Mickey Spillane until it did indeed deal with characters and even a detective who were complicated and unsure and he did come to employ plots which were primarily moral dilemmas. Macdonald was convinced that what he wanted to do with the detective story was more valid than what Spillane had done. "In spite of the Spillane phenomenon which has nothing much to do with the mystery but which probably has unsettled paperback publishers' notions of what a mystery is," Macdonald once wrote to Alfred Knopf who was his publisher, "I think the future of the mystery is in the hands of a few good writers like myself."[18] Doubtless Matthew J. Bruccoli put it aptly when, referring to Macdonald under his real name, Kenneth Millar, he wrote in ROSS MACDONALD (1984) that "Millar represented a continuation of the Hammett-Chandler tradition through respectful emulation" whereas "Spillane exaggerated the blatant qualities of the hardboiled movement. Millar subsequently softened his work in reaction against Spillane."[19]

Millar had what strikes me as an exaggeratedly high opinion of Dashiell Hammett whom he considered "the first American writer to use the detective story for the purposes of a major novelist, to present a vision, blazing if disenchanted, of our lives. As a stylist he ranked among the best of his time, directly behind Hemingway and Fitzgerald. As a novelist of realistic intrigue with deep understated poetic and symbolic overtones, he was unsurpassed in his own or any other time."[20] His admiration for Raymond Chandler became more tempered with the passing of time. While early on he admitted "I just can't overestimate the extent he influenced me . . . , turning me in the direction I took . . . as a writer,"[21] he came later to conclude that "I can't accept Chandler's vision of good and evil. It is conventional to the point of occasional old-maidishness, anti-human to the point of frequent sadism (Chandler hates all women and most men, reserving only lovable oldsters, boys and Marlowe for his affection), and the mind behind it, for all its enviable imaginative force, is uncultivated and second-rate."[22] Still later, in an interview, he remarked that Chandler was "too bound up with his hero, who is a self-projection, of course. And he doesn't move freely enough into other lives. He's constantly coming back to the subjective experience of Marlowe. . . . "[23]

"The public eye is always on California," Millar said to me when we met in Santa Barbara. "People are fascinated by it. That's what makes it so interesting. California is the center of world culture. I hope my novels are critical of California. And of Los Angeles. I want them to be." All of the Lew Archer detective stories are centered in California. The farthest Archer ever gets is to Michigan (where Millar studied for an advanced degree) and Canada (where Millar was raised) while investigating a case. He gets to these places in THE

GALTON CASE (1959) which, according to Millar, was the novel which marked a change in his direction, in his detective and in the kind of detective fiction he intended to write. I suppose it was comforting, if one were to focus so exclusively on California as a setting, to think it to be the center of the world.

Millar was a quiet and retiring man. He was capable of attending a party, saying only hello and good-bye and nothing in between. He was born in 1915 near San Francisco. His father abandoned his mother and him when Millar was four. Subsequently, his mother took him to Canada to live where he resided in some fifty different houses while growing up in a state of poverty he could never forget. In 1938 he married Margaret Ellis Sturm who published her first novel, THE INVISIBLE WORM (1941), under her married name three years before Millar had his first novel accepted for publication. He tried teaching and earned advanced degrees, both before and after the war during which he served as a communications officer aboard an escort carrier in the Pacific. After the war, it was his intention to support himself as a professional writer. From 1946 until his death in 1983, he lived with Margaret in Santa Barbara. He told me that he had lived in seven different houses there before the film sale of THE MOVING TARGET permitted him to buy a moderately large home on the Hope Ranch. There was only one daughter, Linda, who was born in 1939. In 1956 she was involved in a vehicular homicide. In 1959 she disappeared, presumably suffering from guilt feelings over the earlier incident, and an extensive search was made to find her. Rather as Laurel Lennox in SLEEPING BEAUTY (1973), when Linda was found, she had only a dim memory of where she had been. She died in 1970 at the age of thirty-one, leaving behind a husband and son. "The moral beatings that people took from their children, I was thinking, were the hardest to endure and the hardest to escape," Millar wrote in THE GOODBYE LOOK (1969).[24] As Matthew J. Bruccoli stated, it is really the figure of Linda Millar who "can be perceived behind the troubled girls in her father's novels."[25] Millar himself felt that "a man's fiction, no matter how remote it may seem to be from the realistic or autobiographical, is very much the record of his particular life. Gradually it may tend to become a substitute for the life, a shadow of the life clinging to the original so closely that . . . it becomes hard to tell which is fiction and which is confession."[26]

THE UNDERGROUND MAN (1971), when it appeared, was acclaimed by critics to be Millar's finest novel. Eudora Welty termed it a stunning achievement in a review for THE NEW YORK TIMES BOOK REVIEW. The plot is typically intricate. Lew Archer, Millar's private detective named after Sam Spade's murdered partner, in the course of his investigations discovers the body of Leo Broadhurst buried for fifteen years in an automobile a short distance from his mountain cabin. Everyone thought he had disappeared but no one suspected foul play. Present the night of Broadhurst's murder was Martha Crandell who was in the midst of sexual congress with him when he was struck in the head by a bullet fired by his wife from outside the cabin. In the loft of the cabin was Martha's daughter, Susan. With Broadhurst's wife was their small son, Stanley. Nearby was Fritz Snow and his criminally inclined friend, Al Sweetner. They buried the body in the automobile through use of a bulldozer but not before Mrs. Snow, Fritz's mother, knifed Broadhurst for good measure since the bullet only grazed him. Also present was Brian Kilpatrick whose wife had run away to Reno to divorce him so as to be free to marry Leo. Kilpatrick sets about blackmailing Mrs. Broadhurst for all her property and money. Eight people inside of two hours knew what had happened and still it was supposedly kept a secret for fifteen years!

In the last decade of his life, when the Ross Macdonald books became bestsellers, reviewers seem to have formed a pact to ignore Millar's convoluted plots. They were more concerned with what they felt to be Millar's perceptive portrait of American life or championed his vision of the degeneration of the American family. These obsessive themes, according to Millar, stemmed from his literary use of the sense of loneliness and deprivation due to his having been raised without a father. "In our society," Millar once remarked, "which is virtually a society of broken marriages (we have almost a fifty percent divorce rate), a man who's really trying to write honestly about the problems of the society will focus on some of these things. In other words, they're not just a personal interest, though they are that, they also reflect, or try to reflect, the truth of what's happening to society. We seem to be moving away from the traditional concept of marriage."[27]

S. S. Van Dine was far more gracious than the BLACK MASK school when it came to the issue of women as murderers. Most of Millar's murderers are women. When asked about this, Millar responded that "I don't base my books on statistics" and added that "in nearly every case the women in my books who commit murders have been victims. People who have been victims tend to victimize."[28] To me, this seems to beg the question, or at least cast doubt on Millar's assertion that he was trying to be a realist about American society. When he learned that in his NEW YORK TIMES obituary he was regarded as both a novelist and an environmentalist, he was pleased; yet, in one of his essays on environmental issues, this man who was so concerned with symbolism in his fiction managed to strike a curious image when he concluded that "everyone, including the Forest Service, knows that a wilderness area, like a woman, loses its character permanently if it is visited by too many lovers."[29]

"Catullus' maxim, *Odi et amo. Excrucior* (I hate and I love. And it hurts), is quoted in WYCHERLY WOMAN [1961] and SLEEPING BEAUTY and acted out in all the other novels," Peter Wolfe wrote in DREAMERS WHO LIVE THEIR DREAMS: THE WORLD OF ROSS MACDONALD'S NOVELS (1976). "Desire is fleeting, a lawless, disruptive emotion. The wheel of love can be a rack that breaks people with its tyranny and caprice. Physically, love demands a total, unguarded self-giving and abandonment. Morally and socially, it rides herd over our civilized arrangements; psychologically, it releases but also creates deep need. In IVORY GRIN [1952], it uncoils as a madness that subverts both reason and responsibility. Dr. Samuel Benning, knowing he can't win the heart of his much younger wife, murders to shock her into loyalty. Similarly, a man tells Archer in WYCHERLY WOMAN, 'You start out with an innocent roll in the hay, and you end up having to kill people.' A wild emotion touching us in our most hidden and vulnerable places, sexual love completes a natural circuit with death. Sexual love and the death-drift have a common source. A character in SLEEPING BEAUTY, describing a lovers' spat, says, 'I wasn't sure if he was talking about killing a woman or making love to her, or possibly both.' In UNDERGROUND MAN a man is shot to death during sex. The title, THE DROWNING POOL [1950], refers to the whirling, down-pulling dangers of sex; a wave thrown back by the pool stuns Archer when a girl picks his pocket while kissing him. The molecular union of sex, crime, blindness, and death, from Sophocles, holds solid. The brutal chemistry of love is to be feared, perhaps even avoided. It is no wonder, during a discussion of sex in DOOMSTERS [1958], the apple Archer is eating suddenly tastes like ashes. Too often has he seen the bright round succulence of sexual promise beckon and then corrupt.''[30]

Millar, following the first problems with Linda, underwent psychotherapy in the years 1956–1957. In conversation he admitted to me that he had long been deeply influenced by Freud and the theories of psychoanalysis. The Œdipus legend is as central to his work as is the California setting. In THE GOODBYE LOOK one character, when he was a boy of eight, actually murdered his father. A crime some fifteen years hence recreates this sense of primal trauma and sends him off the deep end. In THE UNDERGROUND MAN when Susan, present at Leo Broadhurst's murder, witnesses a similar murder fifteen years later when Stanley Broadhurst is killed, the event has an identical effect on her. Stanley, too, was obsessed with finding his father. This theme, in fact, appears as early as THE THREE ROADS (1948). Here a man murders his wife, then suffers from amnesia; upon release from a mental hospital, the man undertakes to find his wife's killer, eventually tracing the crime to himself. I could not see how this plot structure really did have something new or challenging about it as a perspective on American society and I expressed my doubts about it and the despair that seems to be associated with it to Millar.

"An honest critic is always an optimist," he responded, "or he wouldn't write."

"But that's my trouble. I can't really say your novels are particularly optimistic."

"You're misled by my themes," he rejoined, and smiled benignly. "I deal with concealment, self-concealment. That is always depressing."

The past in Millar's books is usually unpleasant. To quote from only a single novel, Archer tends to stress attitudes toward the past when describing the persons he encounters. "His eyes and voice were faintly drowsy with the past."[31] 'She looked as if she were dying under the soft bombardment of the past."[32] 'Her voice had a rueful pride which seemed to belong entirely to the past."[33] ' 'What's hurting, Jean?' 'My whole life.' ''[34] In all of Millar's novels after

THE GALTON CASE (1959), as Matthew J. Bruccoli pointed out, "the past is unreleasable; release from it usually comes in the form of death."[35]

For all of the emphasis on human psychology in his novels, it would not seem that Millar was especially gifted as an interpreter of human behavior. In writing about Dashiell Hammett, he quoted part of the Flitcraft story from THE MALTESE FALCON, including the passage that "his wife and children never saw him again. He had two children, boys, one five and the other three. He owned his house in a Tacoma suburb, a new Packard, and the rest of the appurtenances of successful American living."[36] Instead of drawing the rather obvious conclusion that Hammett was here presenting the ideal vision of the world he had had—only in his case the children were daughters—when he learned that he had tuberculosis and that death made a difference in how one ought to form his values, Millar provided a typically subjective interpretation. " . . . Sam Spade strips away one by one the appearances which stand between him and the truth, and between him and the complete satisfaction of his desires. His story ends in drastic peripeteia with the all but complete frustration of his desires. His lover is guilty of murder; the code without which his life is meaningless forces him to turn her over to the police. The black bird is hollow. The reality behind appearances is a treacherous vacuum. Spade turns for sardonic consolation to the wife of his murdered partner (whose name was Archer). It is his final reluctant act of animal pragmatism."[37]

What Aristotle meant by peripeteia has more application, it would seem, to Millar's novels than to THE MALTESE FALCON. For Aristotle, peripeteia was the sudden change in fortune in classical tragedy, the reversal, and for his paradigm of this process he chose in the POETICS to cite Sophocles' ŒDIPUS TYRANNOUS. One of Millar's genuine contributions to detective fiction was, in Matthew J. Bruccoli's words, the way he "refined the plot twist into the reversal. The twist is arbitrary, whereas the reversal is prepared for—even though it is surprising. The reversal or double reversal would become characteristic of Millar's plotting."[38] Millar himself declared that "all mystery novels by definition have to be constructed in terms of puzzle and solution. What I try to do is to make both the initial statements valid and interesting and the solution even more valid and interesting. In other words, the solution fills out the meaning of what has gone before. The reversal is actually an illumination of what has gone before."[39] Millar really wrote and rewrote his basic plot with a crime in the past being illuminated finally by the solution to a crime or crimes in the present in book after book. Although there are some improbabilities in it, his final novel, THE BLUE HAMMER (1976), comes the closest, I think, to perfecting what it was he was trying (sometimes it seems so desperately) to do in his fiction. This experience of illumination, although engendered by different means, is quite the same as that which S. S. Van Dine achieved in his best books; it is only that in noticing the differences by which the same effect is achieved we realize how far detective fiction has ventured into new territory while remaining somehow so much the same.

"I'm interested in creating moral excitement," Millar once wrote, "which I think will be the successor to physical excitement."[40] This, I believe, was Millar's second outstanding contribution. Peter Wolfe has called attention to Archer's "strenuous attempt to love people without using them" and how "the withholding of moral judgment is, for anybody, an act of love."[41] This was in Millar's fiction. In his personal life it was otherwise. "His convictions," Matthew J. Bruccoli noted, "were unshakable, and he broke off friendships when he found that a friend's principles were contrary to his own. Robert Easton sensed that Millar 'seethed with restrained violence.' "[42] As probably Millar's best friend in Santa Barbara, Easton perhaps knew him better than most.

Millar had one of the most intriguing definitions of tragedy since Aristotle. "Tragedy happens when you lose what is most valuable to you," he wrote. "But that means you have *found out* what is most valuable—and have even *had* it."[43] In stark contrast to Mike Hammer, Archer, rather in the Sherlock Holmes tradition, is not above letting killers go free, if he feels they were somehow justified, as in THE DROWNING POOL, THE BARBAROUS COAST (1956), and THE WYCHERLY WOMAN.

Millar was less successful in what he tried to do with his detective. "I'm deliberately, in my work, trying to get away from the idea, the central idea, that the private detective is a sex hero," he once remarked in an interview.[44] How he chose to accomplish this objective was to make Archer more impersonal, less flamboyant than fictional detectives had been in the past. "He is less a doer than a questioner," he wrote in an essay, "a consciousness in which the meanings of other lives emerge. This gradually developed conception of the detective hero as the mind of the novel is not wholly new, but it is probably my main contribution to this special branch of fiction."[45] The result was a detective who pleads for mercy and not justice, and who does so quietly. It was a subtle conception and it did not lend itself at all well to other media, especially motion pictures.

When Paul Newman was signed to star in the film version of THE MOVING TARGET, he insisted that the detective's name be changed to Harper since previous starring vehicles which had been very successful for him, such as HUD (Paramount, 1963) and THE HUSTLER (20th-Fox, 1961), had included his letter in their titles. HARPER (Warner's, 1966) was directed by Jack Smight with a screenplay by William Goldman. The novel presented a challenge in that Millar already at this point had shifted the emphasis from dialogue to plot whereas Newman's most inspired performances derived from his ability to make a character's psychology memorable and outstanding on its own terms. This required that Harper had to be fleshed out more than Archer is in the novels. Over the years, Archer comments that his wife left him because she objected to detective work. In the film Harper's wife Susan is a major character, played by Janet Leigh. She is a woman frantically determined to divorce the reality of her husband rather than abandon her girlish dream of marital bliss. "Tell him that, lawyer," Susan shouts at one point. "Tell him, he *is not* loved." This situation makes for one of the more humanly touching scenes in the film when Harper, beaten and exhausted, comes home for a night at least, only to leave Susan again the next day because the job, which is finding out the truth, is more important than a false sense of happiness.

When HARPER was released, critics immediately proclaimed that the screen had found a successor to Humphrey Bogart. Such a posture prohibits any appreciation of just how different Newman's portrayal is from any Bogart vehicle. Newman's Harper is neither a tough guy who loses everything including love, the way Sam Spade did; nor is he a Philip Marlowe wise-cracking his way through a case where everyone including the detective is endemically confused. Harper is frightened by life, but he retains his integrity: not by talking tough, not by being tough, but instead by trying to understand what it is all about. There is no wounded cynicism, nor is there sequestered romanticism behind his stance. At the end, when he exposes his best friend, he walks away with a gun pointed at him, ostensibly to turn in his friend which he perhaps can no more do than the friend can shoot him. The picture has to conclude with a freeze-frame of Harper throwing up his hands at the folly of it all.

THE DROWNING POOL (Warner's, 1975) was based on Millar's second Archer novel. It was directed by Stuart Rosenberg. By this time, the Ross Macdonald novels were bestsellers. But ten years had elapsed since the first film. Paul Newman was again in the role and his performance, if anything, was better than it was in the earlier picture. The dialgoue matched the increased depth of character he brought to the role. Yet the intricate plot worked against the characters in the film. The viewer is so busy trying to figure out what happened, who lost what, who was involved, that attention is hopelessly distracted from the characters; and, indeed, this is what happens to a large degree in the novels. The film was neither critically nor commercially successful.

Millar went with Knopf because that firm had published Hammett and Chandler. He did not learn from their experience with him. "Millar was depressed by his publishing situation," Matthew J. Bruccoli noted. "After six hardcover books he felt that he was in effect writing for Pocket Books. Knopf submitted the typescripts to the paperback house before committing itself to publish because the reprint income was a key factor in the decision. Millar was writing on speculation; he received no contract or advance until the book was accepted by Knopf."[46]

In one of the ironies of life, Millar, who had been so long obsessed by the past, once he completed THE BLUE HAMMER began to be haunted by the unmistakable signs of Alzheimer's disease. In an interview in 1982 his wife, Margaret Millar, described what their life had become the year before Millar died. "I said, 'Have you noticed how much friskier the dogs are in the morning?' He listened to me, nodded, then looked up and said, 'Yes, Currier and Ives did some of the best painting as young men.' . . . Mostly we have these long, silent nights now. I never leave him."[47] In mid-life, Millar had quit smoking and lived cautiously, exercised and ate a balanced diet, and died at an earlier age than either Hammett or Chandler. Perhaps everything about him had been just too careful.

The world-view embodied in Mickey Spillane's books had to wait until the 'Seventies and 'Eighties to have its full impact on the way detective films were made and by then it was no longer the private detective who dealt out death to evil-doers, but the professional cop—for the police procedural story had come to replace the rather quaint notion of the private eye, bent on meting out justice. John Wayne, when he had a four-picture contract at Warner Bros., was offered DIRTY HARRY (Warner's, 1971) but turned it down. He claimed the character was not right for him. Clint Eastwood took the role instead and was able to create a popular series hero which persisted for almost two decades. Don Siegel directed the first film. Inspector Harry Callahan is called "Dirty" Harry because he gets all the dirty jobs. As in the subsequent films, there is a major plot and several sub-plots which consist of little else than an opportunity for Harry to kill criminals. The major plot concerns a homicidal maniac who snipes a young girl while she is swimming. The maniac serves notice on the city of San Francisco that there will be another killing unless he is paid $100,000. A black boy is shot before the mayor makes up his mind. Then a fourteen-year-old girl is kidnapped and the ransom goes up to $200,000. Harry is detailed with delivering the money. Harry confronts the maniac after he has already killed his victim and stabs him in the leg, only for the maniac to escape. He is later captured when he enters a hospital for treatment. Harry, who makes the arrest, is summoned to the district attorney's office. The man will be released because his civil liberties were violated by Harry when Harry broke into the killer's room without a warrant. All of the evidence, including the rifle Harry found, including the girl's dead body which was found where the killer confessed to having left it, cannot be used against him. When the maniac then commandeers a school bus and threatens the mayor that he will shoot all the school children unless he is paid $200,000 with a chartered jet waiting for him at the airport, Harry is asked to deliver the money. The mayor promises the maniac immunity. Harry sets the children free and shoots the maniac. At the fade, Inspector Harry Callahan is seen throwing his badge into a pool of water where the killer's body is floating. It is the same kind of ending which concluded HIGH NOON (United Artists, 1952), a film which John Wayne had detested. The message is quite clear. The honest, brave cop is hopelessly hampered in the performance of his duty by the judicial system. Harry solves the problem in the same way that the American cinema has frequently solved social dilemmas: with a bullet.

MAGNUM FORCE (Warner's, 1974), directed by Ted Post, carried on the saga, but with an interesting variation. A distinction is made in the screenplay between Harry, who is still on the force and who only kills criminals in fair fights, and vigilantes. A mobster who had an informer and his family murdered is let off at his trial for insufficient evidence. "Fuck the courts," he boasts to newspaper reporters as he is leaving the San Francisco Hall of Justice. He would appear to be safe. However, his car is stopped by a traffic cop on a motorcycle. When the mobster threatens to have the officer kicked off the force, the officer pulls out a .44 magnum and shoots to death everyone in the car. When another group of gangsters and their women are machine-gunned at a semi-nude bathing party, Hal Holbrook, playing Harry's boss, really becomes concerned. "Someone's trying to put the courts out of business," he remarks. Holbrook assigns Harry to the case, declaring that he suspects that the entire affair may be the result of a new generation of vigilantes who are willing to do what the courts are no longer able to do. In another sequence, a gang leader gets out of his bathrobe and is just about to join a pair of heroin addicts, a beautiful boy and a beautiful girl who want him sexually between them, when a uniformed policeman enters the room and shoots them all. It turns out that Holbrook and four new police recruits are at the bottom of it. The criminals who have been executed by these vigilantes were not armed and dangerous and to kill them when they are helpless is not Harry's way.

In THE ENFORCER (Warner's 1976), directed by James Fargo, Harry is transferred to Personnel after he shoots three armed hoods holding up a liquor store. It is the mayor's idea to bring the police department into the mainstream of Twentieth-century thought. This reduces itself to hiring women and getting rid of Neanderthals such as Harry Callahan. Tyne Daly, a young female policewoman, is made Harry's partner. A gang of terrorists steals a cache of high tech explosives and then kidnap the mayor. Harry, who is on suspension at the time, goes after them with Tyne's help. A woman is no match for this kind of work and Tyne is killed in the process, after saving Harry's life. Harry finishes off the terrorists and releases the mayor just as the police arrive, having acceded to all of the terrorists' demands.

SUDDEN IMPACT (Warner's, 1983) directed by Clint Eastwood has more killings in it than any of the previous Dirty Harry films. The major plot has to do with the character played by Sondra Locke who was gang-raped along with her sister some years before the film opens. She is now out on the vengeance trail. The viewer sees her necking with a man in a car. She pulls a gun and shoots him first in the testicles and then in the brain. Several more men are murdered in this fashion and Harry is assigned to the case. Gender has become even more important in this film than it was in THE ENFORCER. A young murderer is let off by a female judge at the opening of the picture. Women can be as effective as men when it comes to shooting, but when they are in the professions they tend to be soft on crime. One line in the film was used repeatedly in previews on television and was even quoted by President Reagan. After killing three armed hold-up men, Harry holds his gun on the fourth who is hiding behind a female hostage. "Make my day," Harry says, and the viewer is presumed to share Harry's exultation at the power to take human life in a noble cause. This same line is repeated at the end of the film when the last of the rapists has Sondra Locke hostage and would kill her. Harry saves Sondra

Locke's life and then covers up for her, figuring the rapists got just what they deserved.

Eastwood himself once commented on the popularity of the Dirty Harry films. " . . . It's not the blood-letting or whatever that people come to see in the movies. It's vengeance. Getting even is a very important thing with the public. They go to work everyday for some guy who's rude and they can't stand and they have to take it. Then they go see me on the screen and I just kick the shit out of him."[48]

Perhaps Clint Eastwood's best evocation of the milieu of modern crime and a cop who has to do battle in the modern urban jungle is TIGHTROPE (Warner's, 1984) directed by Richard Tuggle. The plot concerns a psychotic killer preying upon prostitutes. Eastwood is cast as Detective Wes Block. Block is a single parent with two daughters, Amanda, played by Eastwood's real daughter, Alison, and Penny played by Jennifer Beck. The basic theme of the film is the male desire for revenge on women as a sex. Wes' wife left him and the children and now he does not want to let any woman get close to him. He seeks sexual companionship with certain prostitutes and it is these women, one after another, who are killed by strangulation. Genevieve Bujold is cast as an independent woman who works at a rape center. In time a relationship develops between her and Wes and it is very significant when he allows her to touch his cheek without pulling away. "There is a dark spot in all of us," a psychologist puts it to Wes. "Some of us try to keep it down. Some act it out. And some of us walk a tightrope between the two." It is Wes' resentment of his ex-wife and his anger and his desire for revenge which constitute his strongest links with the psychopathic killer who, it turns out, wants revenge on Wes. What makes it rather a unique film is the character played by Genevieve Bujold and Eastwood's scenes with his screen daughters, poignant scenes which Tuggle wisely chose to film in silence. Also, compared to the Dirty Harry films, most of the violence takes place off camera.

On the other hand, the simple plot of the Dirty Harry films has given rise to any number of imitations. Some are more violent than others, to be sure, but virtually all films which in the 'Eighties have dealt with the commission of crimes result in the death of evil-doers by a means far more direct than due process. It may be more realistic as in CHINATOWN (Paramount, 1974) for a detective film to conclude with the detective defeated and the criminal triumphant, but such a plot cannot consistently win popular endorsement. Justice defined as sudden death to evil-doers is what the viewing public would seem to prefer and it is a trend likely to remain in detective films for many years to come, just as the transition from the amateur detective to the police procedural seems to be irreversible.

Yet, notwithstanding, I am reminded of Flaubert's admonition concerning the great poet: "*Il ne faut jamais conclure*." No conclusion can really be regarded as final. In having made this transition both detective fiction and detective films appear to have lost some of their peculiar fascination as a creative mental exercise. "Another source of relaxation was reading detective stories, which lay around everywhere and were piled up in stacks on the topmost floor of the house," Aniela Jaffé recalled in her essay, "From Jung's Last Years" (1968). "He liked English thrillers, but Simenon was his favorite. If the picture on the cover was too lurid, I had to shroud the book in a correct wrapper, so that it might appear innocuously on the slate table in the library. For Jung the figure of the detective was a modern version of the alchemical Mercurius, solver of all riddles, and he was entertained by his heroic deeds."[49]

It was no different with the man who had once exerted great influence on C. G. Jung. For Sigmund Freud, according to Paul Roazen in FREUD AND HIS FOLLOWERS (1974), "the beginning of the end came when he stopped seeing patients. For his last two months he could not work any more. He could still read, however. Jones and Schur have discussed in print the significance of the last book Freud read, Balzac's LE PEAU DE CHAGRIN; it fascinated Freud because everything for him was shrinking and diminishing as in the novel, and he knew the end could not be far off. (But Jones was disheartened to hear from Anna Freud of Freud's great love for detective stories, especially following operations; Agatha Christie and Dorothy Sayers were special favorites.)"[50]

While there does seem to have been some reserve on Jung's part and on that of Ernest Jones with regard to Freud's predilection for detective stories, I still think it is significant that two of the great psychologists of this century should have been interested in detective fiction. Perhaps no literary form which is so totally dependent on a plot requiring a solution can aspire to the status of literature; yet it is also true that a few writers have created detective characters that may well be regarded as among the more memorable personalities in modern fiction. There is something very reassuring in the belief that the most perplexing mysteries are capable of solution by a human mind and that, in what may be at bottom an irrational universe, there is nothing in the fictional world of the detective story that cannot be made to yield before human reason. But here, I am addressing detective fiction from its so-called Golden Age, the period between the world wars, and not detective fiction or detective films as they have come to be. Now more than ever the quest to understand has been replaced by the need to be violent and vengeful. The question increasingly is no longer who is a murderer but that killing, depending on who is killed and for what reason, is justifiable, indeed may even be justice itself. This is quite definitely a barbaric devolution and one that cannot but itself be morally suspect.

Notes

INTRODUCTION

1. Macdonald, Ross, SLEEPING BEAUTY (New York: Knopf, 1973), p. 244.
2. Stein, Aaron Marc, "The Mystery Story in Cultural Perspective," contained in Ball, John, editor, THE MYSTERY STORY (New York: Penguin Books, 1976), p. 42.
3. I have dealt at length with the BLACK MASK school of fiction in the chapter, "Hostages of Fate," in DARK CINEMA: AMERICAN FILM NOIR IN CULTURAL PERSPECTIVE (Westport: Greenwood Press, 1984), pp. 46–73.
4. Ruehlmann, William, SAINT WITH A GUN: THE UNLAWFUL AMERICAN PRIVATE EYE (New York: New York University Press, 1974), p. 9.

PROLOGUE: EDGAR ALLAN POE AND THE BIRTH OF THE DETECTIVE STORY

1. Levin, Harry, THE POWER OF BLACKNESS (New York: Vintage Books, 1958), p. 148.
2. Haycraft, Howard, MURDER FOR PLEASURE: THE LIFE AND TIMES OF THE DETECTIVE STORY (1941; New York: Mercury Publications, 1951), p. 11.
3. *Ibid.*, p. 9.
4. Poe, Edgar Allan, "Berenice," in THE COMPLETE POEMS AND STORIES OF EDGAR ALLAN POE WITH SELECTIONS FROM HIS CRITICAL WRITINGS in two volumes (New York: Knopf, 1976), Volume I, p. 149.
5. Zweig, Stefan, DIE WELT VON GESTERN (1944; Frankfurt am Main: Fischer Taschenbuch Verlag, 1982), p. 476.
6. Krutch, Joseph Wood, MORE LIVES THAN ONE (New York: William Sloane Associates, 1962), p. 141.
7. Krutch, Joseph Wood, EDGAR ALLAN POE: A STUDY IN GENIUS (New York: Knopf, 1926), p. 19.
8. Morrison, Claudia C., FREUD AND THE CRITIC: THE EARLY USE OF DEPTH

PSYCHOLOGY IN LITERARY CRITICISM (Chapel Hill: The University of North Carolina Press, 1968), p. 194.

9. Zweig, Stefan, DIE WELT VON GESTERN, *op. cit.*, p. 476.

10. Bonaparte, Maria, "Psychoanalytic Interpretations of Stories of Edgar Allan Poe," contained in Ruitenbeek, Hendrik M., editor, PSYCHOANALYSIS AND LITERATURE (New York: Dutton, 1964), p. 74.

11. Orwell, George, "Benefit of Clergy: Some Notes on Salvador Dali," contained in Volume 3 in Orwell, Sonia, and Ian Angus, THE COLLECTED ESSAYS, JOURNALISM, AND LETTERS OF GEORGE ORWELL in four volumes (New York: Harcourt, Brace, Jovanovich, 1968), pp. 164–165.

12. Poe, Edgar Allan, "The Murders in the Rue Morgue," in THE COMPLETE POEMS AND STORIES OF EDGAR ALLAN POE WITH SELECTIONS FROM HIS CRITICAL WRITINGS, Volume I, *op. cit.*, p. 315.

13. Symons, Julian, MORTAL CONSEQUENCES: A HISTORY FROM THE DETECTIVE STORY TO THE CRIME NOVEL (1972; New York: Schocken Books, 1977), p. 34.

14. *Ibid.*, pp. 34–35.

15. *Ibid.*, p. 35.

16. Poe, Edgar Allan, "Berenice," *op. cit.*, p. 148.

17. Poe, Edgar Allan, "The Mystery of Marie Rogêt," in THE COMPLETE POEMS AND STORIES OF EDGAR ALLAN POE WITH SELECTIONS FROM HIS CRITICAL WRITINGS, Volume I, *op. cit.*, p. 433.

18. Laplace, Pierre Simon de, "Concerning Probability," contained in Newman, James R., editor, THE WORLD OF MATHEMATICS in four volumes (New York: Simon and Schuster, 1956), Volume Two, p. 1333. No translator is named.

19. Quoted in Levin, Harry, THE POWER OF BLACKNESS, *op. cit.*, p. 104.

20. Poe, Edgar Allan, "The Cask of Amontillado," in THE COMPLETE POEMS AND STORIES OF EDGAR ALLAN POE WITH SELECTIONS FROM HIS CRITICAL WRITINGS, Volume II, *op. cit.*, p. 666.

21. *Ibid.*, p. 669.

22. Quoted in Levin, Harry, THE POWER OF BLACKNESS, *op. cit.*, p. 102.

CHAPTER 1: THE ADVENTURES OF SHERLOCK HOLMES

1. Conan Doyle, Sir Arthur, THE ANNOTATED SHERLOCK HOLMES (New York: Clarkson N. Potter, 1967) edited with an Introduction, Notes, and Bibliography by William S. Baring-Gould, Volume I, p. 398.

2. Higham, Charles, THE ADVENTURES OF CONAN DOYLE (New York: W. W. Norton, 1976), p. 58.

3. Conan Doyle, Sir Arthur, "The Captain of the 'Pole-Star,' " in THE WORKS OF A. CONAN DOYLE (Roslyn: Black's Readers Service, n.d.), p. 471.

4. *Ibid.*, p. 493.

5. *Ibid.*, p. 499.

6. Higham, Charles, *op. cit.*, p. 59.

7. Fergusson, Harvey, THE CONQUEST OF DON PEDRO (New York: Morrow, 1954), p. 7.

8. Quoted in Higham, Charles, *loc. cit.*, p. 61.
9. Barzun, Jacques, "Detection and the Literary Art," in THE MYSTERY WRITER'S ART (Bowling Green: Bowling Green University Popular Press, 1970) edited by Francis M. Nevins, Jr., p. 251.
10. Conan Doyle, Sir Arthur, THE ANNOTATED SHERLOCK HOLMES, *op. cit.*, Volume I, p. 196.
11. *Ibid.*, p. 613.
12. Higham, Charles, *op. cit.*, p. 84.
13. Conan Doyle, Sir Arthur, THE ANNOTATED SHERLOCK HOLMES, *op. cit.*, Volume I, p. 655.
14. Quoted in *ibid.*, *loc. cit.*, p. 655.
15. *Ibid.*, p. 656.
16. Quoted in *ibid.*, *loc. cit.*, p. 677.
17. Excerpted in Shreffler, Philip A., editor, THE BAKER STREET READER: CORNERSTONE WRITINGS ABOUT SHERLOCK HOLMES (Westport: Greenwood Press, 1984), p. 13.
18. Conan Doyle, Sir Arthur, THE ANNOTATED SHERLOCK HOLMES, *op. cit.*, Volume I, p. 159.
19. Nordon, Pierre, CONAN DOYLE: A BIOGRAPHY (New York: Holt, Rinehart, and Winston, 1967) translated from the French by Frances Partridge, p. 247.
20. Zweig, Stefan, MEISTERNOVELLEN (Frankfurt am Main: S. Fischer Verlag, 1970), p. 63.
21. Nordon, Pierre, *op. cit.*, p. 257.
22. Conan Doyle, Sir Arthur, THE ANNOTATED SHERLOCK HOLMES, *op. cit.*, Volume I, p. 623.
23. Maugham, W. Somerset, THE VAGRANT MOOD (New York: Doubleday, 1953), p. 114.
24. Conan Doyle, Sir Arthur, THROUGH THE MAGIC DOOR (London: Smith, Elder, 1907), p. 48.
25. Nordon, Pierre, *op. cit.*, p. 271.
26. Higham, Charles, *op. cit.*, p. 94.
27. *Ibid.*, p. 95.
28. Van Dine, S. S., THE BISHOP MURDER CASE (New York: Charles Scribner's Sons, 1929), p. 276.
29. Higham, Charles, *op. cit.*, p. 152.
30. *Ibid.*, pp. 153–154.
31. *Ibid.*, p. 154.
32. Nordon, Pierre, *op. cit.*, p. 178.
33. *Ibid.*, p. 176.
34. Starrett, Vincent, THE PRIVATE LIFE OF SHERLOCK HOLMES (1933; New York: Pinnacle Books, 1975), p. 48.
35. Shreffler, Philip A., *op. cit.*, p. 14.
36. Conan Doyle, Sir Arthur, THE ANNOTATED SHERLOCK HOLMES, *op. cit.*, Volume II, p. 525.
37. *Ibid.*, *loc. cit.*, p. 512.
38. Barzun, Jacques, and Wendell Hertig Taylor, A CATALOGUE OF CRIME (New York: Harper & Row, 1970), p. 488.
39. Haycraft, Howard, *op. cit.*, p. 55.

40. *Ibid.*, p. 54.
41. Wrong, E. M., "Crime and Detection," in Haycraft, Howard, editor, THE ART OF THE MYSTERY STORY (1946; New York: Carroll and Graf, 1983), p. 21. I have added the *"multi"* from Horace's CARMINA, *Liber* IV, ix.
42. *Ibid.*, p. 22.
43. *Ibid.*, p. 29.
44. Nordon, Pierre, *op. cit.*, p. 81.
45. *Ibid.*, p. 82.
46. Higham, Charles, *op. cit.*, p. 266.
47. *Ibid.*, p. 266.
48. *Ibid.*, p. 276.
49. Starrett, Vincent, *op. cit.*, p. 110.
50. Nordon, Pierre, *op. cit.*, pp. 161–162.
51. CARMINA, *Liber* I, xi.
52. Steinbrunner, Chris, and Norman Michaels, THE FILMS OF SHERLOCK HOLMES (Secaucus: Citadel, 1978), p. 10.
53. Shreffler, Philip A., *op. cit.*, p. 12.
54. Steinbrunner, Chris, and Norman Michaels, *op. cit.*, p. 12.
55. *Ibid.*, p. 13.
56. Pointer, Michael, THE PUBLIC LIFE OF SHERLOCK HOLMES (New York: Drake, 1975), pp. 54–55.
57. *Ibid.*, pp. 55–56.
58. Steinbrunner, Chris, and Norman Michaels, *op. cit.*, pp. 20–21.
59. Rathbone, Basil, IN AND OUT OF CHARACTER (New York: Doubleday, 1962), pp. 134–135.
60. Pointer, Michael, *op. cit.*, p. 62.
61. Nordon, Pierre, *op. cit.*, p. 277.
62. Pointer, Michael, *op. cit.*, p. 67.
63. *Ibid.*, p. 67.
64. *Ibid.*, p. 64.
65. Steinbrunner, Chris, and Norman Michaels, *op. cit.*, p. 51.
66. Pointer, Michael, *op. cit.*, p. 73.
67. Rathbone, Basil, *op. cit.*, p. 179.
68. Rubinstein, Artur, MY MANY YEARS (New York: Knopf, 1980), pp. 482–483.
69. Rathbone, Basil, *op. cit.*, p. 181.
70. *Ibid.*, p. 181.
71. Steinbrunner, Chris, and Norman Michaels, *op. cit.*, p. 59.
72. *Ibid.*, p. 60.
73. *Ibid.*, p. 85.
74. *Ibid.*, p. 86.
75. Rathbone, Basil, *op. cit.*, p. 182.
76. Pointer, Michael, *op. cit.*, p. 89.
77. Steinbrunner, Chris, and Norman Michaels, *op. cit.*, p. 194.
78. *Ibid.*, p. 242.
79. Starrett, Vincent, *op. cit.*, p. 58.
80. Shreffler, Philip A., *op. cit.*, p. 6.

CHAPTER 2: THE LIFE AND TIMES OF S. S. VAN DINE

1. Van Dine, S. S., THE "CANARY" MURDER CASE (New York: Charles Scribner's Sons, 1927), p. 343.

2. David R. Smith, who has perhaps the largest collection of memorabilia about Willard Huntington Wright in private hands, contributed an essay to this chapbook titled "S. S. Van Dine at Twentieth Century-Fox." When the chapbook was published, he sent copies of it to Stanton Macdonald-Wright and Beverly Wright which is how I came to know them.

3. The drawing, based on that of James Montgomery Flagg of S. S. Van Dine, was by my former wife, Ruth Tuska.

4. However, Willard's secretary, Y. B. Garden, in her essay "Philo Vance: An Impressionistic Biography," which appeared among the front matter in PHILO VANCE MURDER CASES (New York: Charles Scribner's Sons, 1936), got the correct date for the year of Philo Vance's birth, which is given as 1887. John Loughery who is at work on the first book-length biography of Willard Huntington Wright has confirmed this earlier date in his exhaustive researches into the author's background.

5. Van Dine, S. S., THE "CANARY" MURDER CASE, *op. cit.*, p. 2.

6. *Ibid.*, p. 137.

7. *Ibid.*, p. 138. Translated literally, Willard's Latin in English would read: "All things after death makes a better great age." What he intended to say, surely, was: "Everyone, after death, is made better by virtue of his antiquity."

8. Hammett, Dashiell, review of THE BENSON MURDER CASE in THE SATURDAY REVIEW OF LITERATURE on 15 January 1927, reprinted in Haycraft, Howard, editor, THE ART OF THE MYSTERY STORY, *op. cit.*, p. 382.

9. Van Dine, S. S., THE GREENE MURDER CASE (New York: Charles Scribner's Sons, 1928), pp. 33–34.

10. Van Dine, S. S., Introduction to PHILO VANCE MURDER CASES, *op. cit.*, p. 10.

11. Wheelock, John Hall, editor, EDITOR TO AUTHOR: LETTERS OF MAXWELL E. PERKINS (New York: Charles Scribner's Sons, 1950), letter to Alden Brooks, 2 December 1942, p. 214.

12. *Ibid.*, letter to Alice D. Bond, 17 July 1944, p. 247.

13. Berg, A. Scott, MAX PERKINS: EDITOR OF GENIUS (1978; New York: Pocket Books, 1979), p. 153.

14. Wheelock, John Hall, *loc. cit.*, p. 53.

15. Van Dine, S. S., editor, THE WORLD'S GREAT DETECTIVE STORIES: A CHRONOLOGICAL ANTHOLOGY (1927; New York: Charles Scribner's Sons, 1931), p. 5.

16. Van Dine, S. S., PHILO VANCE MURDER CASES, *op. cit.*, p. 76. Poe in "Berenice" had cited Tertullian's DE CARNE CHRISTI [The Body of Christ] and the famous passage: "*Mortuus est Dei filius; credible est quia ineptum est; et sepultus resurrexit; certum est quia impossible est*" [The Son of God was dead; it was believable because it was absurd; he is resurrected from the grave; it was certain because it was impossible] in THE COMPLETE POEMS AND STORIES OF EDGAR ALLAN POE WITH SELECTIONS FROM HIS CRITICAL WRITINGS, Volume I, *op. cit.*, p. 148. In THE "CANARY" MURDER CASE, Vance cites the same passage (p. 310): " 'And

yet: *Certum est quia impossible est.* I rather like that maxim, don't y'know; for, in the present case, the impossible is true.' " A couple of pages later, Vance assures Markham that " 'when we find the answer it will be reasonable and simple' "; and, if the truth is not altogether reasonable, it is surely material and quite mechanical!

17. *Ibid.*, p. 77.
18. *Ibid.*, p. 20.
19. Manchester, H. F., "How Philo Vance, Clubfoot, and Charlie Chan Were Born," in THE WRITER (Vol. 43, No. 9), September, 1931, p. 251.
20. Van Dine, S. S., THE BISHOP MURDER CASE, *op. cit.*, p. 35.
21. Van Dine, S. S., THE SCARAB MURDER CASE (New York: Charles Scribner's Sons, 1930), p. 7.
22. Van Dine, S. S., THE GREENE MURDER CASE, *op. cit.*, pp. 151. This is the first line of Horace's Ode xiv, Liber II.
23. Van Dine, S. S., PHILO VANCE MURDER CASES, *op. cit.*, pp. 27–28.
24. Van Dine, S. S. THE WORLD'S GREAT DETECTIVE STORIES: A CHRONOLOGICAL ANTHOLOGY, *op. cit.*, pp. 10–11.
25. *Ibid.*, p. 25.
26. Maugham, W. Somerset, editor, TRAVELLER'S LIBRARY (New York: Doubleday, Doran, 1933), pp. 1513–1514.
27. *Ibid.*, p. 1514. However, Maugham had second thoughts. In his essay, "The Decline and Fall of the Detective Story" in THE VAGRANT MOOD, *op. cit.*, he wrote that "readers of detective stories have now grown crafty, and when a gentle, kindly old man who has apparently no motive to commit a murder is presented to them, they have no hesitation in deciding that it was he who committed it. You cannot read many pages of TRENT'S LAST CASE without being sure that Mr. Cupples is the guilty party. But you can still read the book with interest to find out why he should have killed Manderson. Mr. Bentley has deliberately neglected to conform to the canon that the crime should be brought home to the culprit by the detective. The mystery would never have been solved if Mr. Cupples had not obligingly revealed the truth. It must be admitted that it is by a most improbable coincidence that he found himself concealed in a place in circumstances which obliged him to shoot Manderson in self-defence. Nor are these circumstances credible. It is asking us to believe too much that a hard-headed businessman will plot his own suicide to get his secretary hanged and it is futile to adduce the well-known Campden Case in which John Perry accused his mother, brother, and himself of murdering a man, afterwards discovered to be alive, in order to get them hanged even though, as happened, it meant that he would be hanged himself. That something has occurred in real life does not make it a fitting subject of fiction. Life is full of improbabilities which fiction does not admit of." (pp. 108–109). One might hope that Van Dine had taken careful note of this stricture. In THE GREENE MURDER CASE, the fact that the techniques Ada Greene used in implementing her murder scheme had all been used before in Austrian and German criminal cases does not make them *mutatis mutandis* credible, or even viable, in detective fiction.
28. Bentley, E. C., TRENT'S LAST CASE (1913) in 3 STAR OMNIBUS (New York: Knopf, 1934), p. 187.
29. *Ibid.*, p. 188.
30. Based on a personal conversation. For more information, see my career study, "Howard Hawks," in Tuska, Jon, and Vicki Piekarski, editors, CLOSE-UP: THE CONTRACT DIRECTOR (Metuchen: Scarecrow Press, 1976), pp. 391–438.

31. Quoted by Chris Steinbrunner in his Introduction to S. S. Van Dine's THE "CANARY" MURDER CASE (1927; Boston: Gregg Press, 1980), p. xi.
32. Braithwaite, William Stanley, "S. S. Van Dine—Willard Huntington Wright," in PHILO VANCE MURDER CASES, *op. cit.*, p. 31.
33. Larkin, Mark, "The Philosophy of Crime," in PHOTOPLAY (April, 1929), Vol. XXXV, No. 5, p. 137.
34. *Ibid.*, p. 136.
35. Quoted in Burton Rascoe's Introduction to Rascoe, Burton, and Groff Conklin, editors, THE SMART SET ANTHOLOGY (New York: Reynal and Hitchcock, 1934), p. xxii.
36. *Ibid.*, pp. xxvi–xxvii.
37. Letter from Stanton Macdonald-Wright to Jon Tuska dated 24 November 1971. All my correspondence, including that with Stanton Macdonald-Wright, is archived by the Special Collections of the Library of the University of Oregon in Eugene, Oregon.
38. Based on personal conversations. For more information see my career study, "H. Bruce Humberstone," in Tuska, Jon, and Vicki Piekarski, editors, CLOSE-UP: THE CONTRACT DIRECTOR, *op. cit.*, pp. 57–107, and Tuska, Jon, "The Dragon Murder Case" in JOURNAL OF POPULAR CULTURE (Winter, 1971) Vol. V, No. 3, pp. 606–615.
39. Quoted by David R. Smith in his article "The Gracie Allen Murder Case" in VIEWS & REVIEWS Magazine (Winter, 1972) Vol. 4, Issue No. 2, p. 71.
40. Van Dine, S. S., THE GARDEN MURDER CASE (New York: Charles Scribner's Sons, 1935), p. 15.
41. Nietzsche, Friedrich, THE PHILOSOPHY OF NIETZSCHE (New York: Modern Library, 1937) with an Introduction by Willard Huntington Wright, p. 376.
42. Smith, David R., "The Gracie Allen Murder Case," *op. cit.*, p. 69.
43. *Ibid.*, p. 70.
44. Van Dine, S. S., THE GRACIE ALLEN MURDER CASE (New York: Charles Scribner's Sons, 1938), p. 169.
45. *Ibid.*, p. 162 and p. 167. Owen is dying of cardiac disease and, although Willard titled the chapter "A Dying Madman," it is best read as a dialogue between himself as Owen and his creation, Philo Vance.
46. *Ibid.*, p. 14.
47. Smith, David R., "The Gracie Allen Murder Case," *op. cit.*, p. 72. In view of the success of Parker Bros.' PHILO VANCE, the Milton Bradley Co. signed an agreement with Willard for the exclusive right to manufacture and sell a game titled THE GRACIE ALLEN MURDER CASE.
48. *Ibid.*, p. 72–73.
49. Quoted by David R. Smith in his article "S. S. Van Dine at 20th Century-Fox" in Tuska, Jon, PHILO VANCE: THE LIFE AND TIMES OF S. S. VAN DINE (Bowling Green: Bowling Green University Popular Press, 1971), p. 49.
50. *Ibid.*, p. 50.
51. Berg, A. Scott, MAX PERKINS: EDITOR OF GENIUS, *op. cit.*, p. 457.
52. Smith, David R., "S. S. Van Dine at 20th Century-Fox," *op. cit.*, p. 53.
53. *Ibid.*, pp. 53–54.
54. *Ibid.*, p. 54.
55. *Ibid.*, p. 55.
56. *Ibid.*, p. 55.

57. *Ibid.*, p. 56.
58. *Ibid.*, p. 56.
59. *Ibid.*, p. 56.
60. Van Dine, S. S., THE WINTER MURDER CASE (New York: Charles Scribner's Sons, 1939), pp. ix–x. More to the point in THE BISHOP MURDER CASE Van Dine cited a passage from Nietzsche's GÖTZEN-DÄMMERUNG [TWILIGHT OF THE IDOLS] which he had a character quote in German and then appended an English translation. Since there are two typographical errors in the German and no ellipses to indicate passages omitted, let me quote my own translation. The citation occurs in the section titled "Morality for Physicians." "To die proudly once it is no longer possible to live proudly. . . . Death in contemptible circumstances, a death that is not free, a death at the *wrong* time is a coward's death. . . . It is not within our power to prevent when we are born: however we can make good on this error—for it sometimes is an error. When one abolishes himself, one commits the most estimable deed there is: one deserves almost to live for having committed it. . . . " Nietzsche, Friedrich, GÖTZEN-DÄMMERUNG in Volume Two of WERKE IN DREI BÄNDEN (Munich: Carl Hanser Verlag, 1955), pp. 1010–1011. It is a curiosity to me how many of the authors Maxwell Perkins helped bring to prominence were inclined toward alcoholism and suicide, from F. Scott Fitzgerald to Ernest Hemingway to S. S. Van Dine. The Nietzsche passage is cited in THE BISHOP MURDER CASE on pp. 330–331.
61. Millay, Edna St. Vincent, COLLECTED LYRICS (New York: Washington Square Press, 1959), p. 95.
62. Quoted by William Stanley Braithwaite in PHILO VANCE MURDER CASES, *op. cit.*, p. 44.
63. Haycraft, Howard, MURDER FOR PLEASURE: THE LIFE AND TIMES OF THE DETECTIVE STORY, *op. cit.*, p. 168.
64. *Ibid.*, pp. 166–167.

CHAPTER 3: THE MASTER DETECTIVES

1. Queen, Ellery, THE SPANISH CAPE MYSTERY (1935; New York: Pocket Books, 1942), p. 279.
2. Nevins, Francis M., Jr. ROYAL BLOODLINE: ELLERY QUEEN, AUTHOR AND DETECTIVE (Bowling Green: Bowling Green University Popular Press, 1974), p. 17.
3. Queen, Ellery, THE ROMAN HAT MYSTERY (1929; New York: Pocket Books, 1940), p. 79.
4. *Ibid.*, p. 85.
5. Queen, Ellery, THE GREEK COFFIN MYSTERY (1932; New York: Pocket Books, 1942), pp. 309–310.
6. Queen, Ellery, THE EGYPTIAN CROSS MYSTERY (1932; New York: Pocket Books, 1943), p. 172. The line in Pl.Mil. 742 reads in its entirety: "*hospes nullus tam in amici hospitium devorti potest quin, ubi triduom continuom fuerit, iam odiosus siet*" [no guest can be lodged continuously in the house of a friend for a period of three days but he may to some extent now be an annoyance].
7. Queen, Ellery, THE ROMAN HAT MYSTERY, *op. cit.*, p. 151.
8. *Ibid.*, p. 154.
9. *Ibid.*, pp. 154–155.

10. *Ibid.*, p. 155.
11. *Ibid.*, p. 274.
12. *Ibid.*, p. 274.
13. *Ibid.*, p. 235.
14. Queen, Ellery, THE EGYPTIAN CROSS MYSTERY, *op. cit.*, p. 289.
15. Prescott, Peter S., "The Only Legal Way to Make Money from Murder," LOOK, 21 April 1970. According to Francis M. Nevins, Jr., this interview with Dannay and Lee was not printed in all copies of the magazine. The copy I have was supplied to me by Nevins.
16. Nevins, Francis M., Jr., ROYAL BLOODLINE: ELLERY QUEEN, AUTHOR AND DETECTIVE, *op. cit.*, p. 44.
17. Lee, Rand, "Dad and Cousin Fred Entered a Writing Contest . . . ," TV GUIDE, 11 October 1975, p. 22.
18. Nevins, Francis M., Jr., ROYAL BLOODLINE: ELLERY QUEEN, AUTHOR AND DETECTIVE, *op. cit.*, p. 55.
19. I wrote a history of Mascot Pictures and Nat Levine in THE VANISHING LEGION: A HISTORY OF MASCOT PICTURES, 1927–1935 (Jefferson: McFarland, 1981).
20. Queen, Ellery, THE SPANISH CAPE MYSTERY, *op. cit.*, p. 232.
21. *Ibid.*, pp. 209–210.
22. Prescott, Peter S., "The Only Legal Way to Make Money from Murder," *op. cit.*
23. Queen, Ellery, THE SPANISH CAPE MYSTERY, *op. cit.*, p. 53.
24. Queen, Ellery, THE FOUR OF HEARTS (1938; New York: Pocket Books, 1944), p. 9.
25. Nevins, Francis M., Jr., THE SOUND OF DETECTION: ELLERY QUEEN'S ADVENTURES IN RADIO (Madison: Brownstone Books, 1983) with an episode log compiled by Ray Stanich, p. 25.
26. *Ibid.*, p. 26.
27. *Ibid.*, p. 30.
28. Van Dine, S. S., THE GRACIE ALLEN MURDER CASE, *op. cit.*, p. 167.
29. Nevins, Francis M., Jr., THE SOUND OF DETECTION: ELLERY QUEEN'S ADVENTURES IN RADIO, *op. cit.*, pp. 45–46.
30. Nevins, Francis M., Jr., ROYAL BLOODLINE: ELLERY QUEEN, AUTHOR AND DETECTIVE, *op. cit.*, pp. 112–113.
31. *Ibid.*, p. 114.
32. Queen, Ellery, THE ORIGIN OF EVIL (1951; New York: Pocket Books, 1953), p. 209.
33. Symons, Julian, MORTAL CONSEQUENCES: A HISTORY FROM THE DETECTIVE STORY TO THE CRIME NOVEL, *op. cit.*, p. 153.
34. *Ibid.*, p. 152.
35. Pitts, Michael R., FAMOUS MOVIE DETECTIVES (Metuchen: Scarecrow Press, 1979), pp. 119–120.
36. *Ibid.*, p. 120.
37. *Ibid.*, p. 122. However, Frederic Dannay is quoted in Nevins' THE SOUND OF DETECTION (p. 81) as saying: " 'I happened to be home alone, and when I saw [Hutton] on the screen I had the most curious reaction. I had the feeling I was seeing myself, years and years ago."

38. Nevins, Francis M., Jr., ROYAL BLOODLINE: ELLERY QUEEN, AUTHOR AND DETECTIVE, *op. cit.*, p. 211.

39. From unpublished remarks at the convocation supplied to me by Nevins.

40. Nevins, Francis M., Jr., THE SOUND OF DETECTION: ELLERY QUEEN'S ADVENTURES IN RADIO, *op. cit.*, pp. 80–81.

41. Gardner, Erle Stanley, THE CASE OF THE CURIOUS BRIDE (1934; New York: Pocket Books, 1942), p. 196.

42. This incident is narrated by Johnston, Alva, THE CASE OF ERLE STANLEY GARDNER (New York: Morrow, 1947), pp. 60–62.

43. *Ibid.*, pp. 69–70.

44. Quoted in Hughes, Dorothy B., ERLE STANLEY GARDNER: THE CASE OF THE REAL PERRY MASON (New York: Morrow, 1978), pp. 62–63.

45. *Ibid.*, p. 74.

46. *Ibid.*, p. 73.

47. *Ibid.*, p. 77.

48. *Ibid.*, p. 81.

49. *Ibid.*, p. 83.

50. *Ibid.*, p. 83.

51. *Ibid.*, pp. 84–85.

52. *Ibid.*, p. 95.

53. *Ibid.*, p. 26.

54. *Ibid.*, p. 26.

55. *Ibid.*, p. 103.

56. *Ibid.*, p. 102.

57. Haycraft, Howard, editor, THE ART OF THE MYSTERY STORY, *op. cit.*, pp. 205–206.

58. *Ibid.*, pp. 206–207.

59. Hughes, Dorothy B., ERLE STANLEY GARDNER: THE CASE OF THE REAL PERRY MASON, *op. cit.*, p. 100.

60. Gardner, Erle Stanley, THE CASE OF THE VELVET CLAWS (New York: Morrow, 1933) contained in A PERRY MASON OMNIBUS (New York: Morrow, n.d.), p. 14.

61. *Ibid.*, p. 15.

62. Hughes, Dorothy B., ERLE STANLEY GARDNER: THE CASE OF THE REAL PERRY MASON, *op. cit.*, pp. 138–139.

63. *Ibid.*, p. 142.

64. *Ibid.*, pp. 144–145.

65. Gardner, Erle Stanley, THE CASE OF THE VELVET CLAWS, *op. cit.*, p. 160.

66. *Ibid.*, p. 180.

67. *Ibid.*, p. 188.

68. Van Dine, S. S., PHILO VANCE MURDER CASES, *op. cit.*, p. 77.

69. Hughes, Dorothy B., ERLE STANLEY GARDNER: THE CASE OF THE REAL PERRY MASON, *op. cit.*, pp. 24–25.

70. Gardner, Erle Stanley, THE CASE OF THE LUCKY LEGS (1934; New York: Pocket Books, 1941), p. 245.

71. *Ibid.*, p. 144.

72. Conan Doyle, Sir Arthur, THE ANNOTATED SHERLOCK HOLMES, Vol. II., *op. cit.*, p. 277.

Notes 419

73. Van Dine, S. S., PHILO VANCE MURDER CASES, *op. cit.*, p. 80.
74. Gardner, Erle Stanley, THE CASE OF THE HOWLING DOG (1934; New York: Pocket Books, 1941), p. 121.
75. *Ibid.*, p. 239.
76. Hughes, Dorothy B., ERLE STANLEY GARDNER: THE CASE OF THE REAL PERRY MASON, *op. cit.*, p. 123.
77. *Ibid.*, p. 124.
78. *Ibid.*, p. 124.
79. Gardner, Erle Stanley, THE CASE OF THE COUNTERFEIT EYE (1935; New York: Pocket Books, 1942), p. 95.
80. *Ibid.*, p. 228.
81. Hughes, Dorothy B., ERLE STANLEY GARDNER: THE CASE OF THE REAL PERRY MASON, *op. cit.*, p. 163.
82. *Ibid.*, p. 167.
83. Gardner, Erle Stanley, THE CASE OF THE COUNTERFEIT EYE, *op. cit.*, p. 136.
84. Gardner, Erle Stanley, THE CASE OF THE CURIOUS BRIDE, *op. cit.*, p. 244.
85. Gardner, Erle Stanley, THE CASE OF THE CARETAKER'S CAT (1935; New York: Pocket Books, 1942), p. 230.
86. *Ibid.*, p. 177.
87. Gardner, Erle Stanley, THE CASE OF THE CURIOUS BRIDE, *op. cit.*, p. 6.
88. Gardner, Erle Stanley, THE CASE OF THE SLEEPWALKER'S NIECE (1936; New York: Pocket Books, 1944), p. 106.
89. *Ibid.*, p. 113.
90. Gardner, Erle Stanley, THE CASE OF THE LAME CANARY (1937; New York: Pocket Books, 1943), pp. 235–236.
91. Gardner, Erle Stanley, THE CASE OF THE SUBSTITUTE FACE (1938; New York: Pocket Books, 1943), p. 244.
92. Gardner, Erle Stanley, THE CASE OF THE DROWSY MOSQUITO (1943; New York: Pocket Books, 1950), pp. 239–240.
93. Hughes, Dorothy B., ERLE STANLEY GARDNER: THE CASE OF THE REAL PERRY MASON, *op. cit.*, p. 125.
94. *Ibid.*, p. 134.
95. *Ibid.*, p. 134.
96. *Ibid.*, p. 131.
97. *Ibid.*, p. 136.
98. Gardner, Erle Stanley, THE CASE OF THE SUBSTITUTE FACE, *op. cit.*, p. 207.
99. *Ibid.*, p. 192.
100. *Ibid.*, p. 104.
101. Hughes, Dorothy B., ERLE STANLEY GARDNER: THE CASE OF THE REAL PERRY MASON, *op. cit.*, p. 150.
102. *Ibid.*, p. 156.
103. Gardner, Erle Stanley, THE CASE OF THE DROWSY MOSQUITO, *op. cit.*, p. 96.
104. Hughes, Dorothy B., ERLE STANLEY GARDNER: THE CASE OF THE REAL PERRY MASON, *op. cit.*, p. 163.
105. *Ibid.*, pp. 186–187.

106. Gardner, Erle Stanley, THE CASE OF THE FABULOUS FAKE (New York: Morrow, 1969), p. 21.

107. Quoted in MacShane, Frank, THE LIFE OF RAYMOND CHANDLER (New York: Dutton, 1976), p.106.

108. Chandler, Raymond, SELECTED LETTERS OF RAYMOND CHANDLER (New York: Columbia University Press, 1981) edited by Frank MacShane, pp. 8-9.

109. *Ibid.*, p. 69.

110. *Ibid.*, p. 70.

111. Johnston, Alva, THE CASE OF ERLE STANLEY GARDNER, *op. cit.*, p. 15.

112. *Ibid.*, p. 15.

113. Hughes, Dorothy B., ERLE STANLEY GARDNER: THE CASE OF THE REAL PERRY MASON, *op. cit.*, p. 255.

114. *Ibid.*, p. 261.

115. *Ibid.*, p. 267.

116. Christie, Agatha, THE MYSTERIOUS AFFAIR AT STYLES (1920; New York: Avon Books, n.d.), p. 107.

117. Christie, Agatha, SLEEPING MURDER (New York: Dodd, Mead, 1976), p. 169.

118. Morgan, Janet, AGATHA CHRISTIE: A BIOGRAPHY (New York: Knopf, 1985), p. 377.

119. Panek, LeRoy Lad, WATTEAU'S SHEPHERDS: THE DETECTIVE NOVEL IN BRITAIN 1914–1940 (Bowling Green: Bowling Green University Popular Press, 1979), pp. 38–39.

120. Morgan, Janet, AGATHA CHRISTIE: A BIOGRAPHY, *op. cit.*, p. 260.

121. Panek, LeRoy Lad, WATTEAU'S SHEPHERDS: THE DETECTIVE NOVEL IN BRITAIN 1914–1940, *op. cit.*, p. 49.

122. *Ibid.*, p. 51.

123. Morgan, Janet, AGATHA CHRISTIE: A BIOGRAPHY, *op. cit.*, p. 12.

124. Panek, LeRoy Lad, WATTEAU'S SHEPHERDS: THE DETECTIVE NOVEL IN BRITAIN 1914–1940, *op. cit.*, pp. 57–58.

125. Morgan, Janet, AGATHA CHRISTIE: A BIOGRAPHY, *op. cit.*, p. 82.

126. Christie, Agatha, THE MYSTERIOUS AFFAIR AT STYLES, *op. cit.*, p. 20.

127. Van Dine, S. S., PHILO VANCE MURDER CASES, *op. cit.*, p. 77.

128. Panek, LeRoy Lad, WATTEAU'S SHEPHERDS: THE DETECTIVE NOVEL IN BRITAIN 1914–1940, *op. cit.*, p. 50.

129. Quoted in Sanders, Dennis, and Len Lovallo, THE AGATHA CHRISTIE COMPANION (New York: Avenel Books, 1985), p. 18.

130. Christie Agatha, MURDER ON THE LINKS (1923; New York: Dell Books, n.d.), p. 11.

131. *Ibid.*, p. 82.

132. Panek, LeRoy Lad, WATTEAU'S SHEPHERDS: THE DETECTIVE NOVEL IN BRITAIN 1914–1940, *op. cit.*, p. 41.

133. Christie, Agatha, THE MURDER OF ROGER ACKROYD (1926; New York: Pocket Books, 1939), p. 15.

134. *Ibid.*, p. 17.

135. Morgan, Janet, AGATHA CHRISTIE: A BIOGRAPHY, *op. cit.*, p. 158.

136. *Ibid.*, p. 163.

137. Panek, LeRoy Lad, WATTEAU'S SHEPHERDS: THE DETECTIVE NOVEL IN BRITAIN 1914–1940, *op. cit.*, p. 42.

138. Christie, Agatha, THE BIG FOUR (1927; New York: Dell Books, 1965), p. 148.
139. Van Dine, S. S., THE WORLD'S GREAT DETECTIVE STORIES: A CHRONOLOGICAL ANTHOLOGY, *op. cit.*, p. 20.
140. *Ibid.*, p. 36.
141. Chandler, Raymond, THE SIMPLE ART OF MURDER (1950; New York: Ballantine Books, 1972), pp. 10–11.
142. Christie, Agatha, THE MURDER OF ROGER ACKROYD, *op. cit.*, p. 101.
143. Christie, Agatha, THE MYSTERY OF THE BLUE TRAIN (1928; New York: Pocket Books, 1940), p. 49.
144. Quoted in Sanders, Dennis, and Len Lovallo, THE AGATHA CHRISTIE COMPANION, *op. cit.*, p. 88.
145. Christie, Agatha, THE MURDER AT THE VICARAGE (1930; New York: Dodd, Mead, 1976), p. 187.
146. *Ibid.*, p. 375.
147. Christie, Agatha, THE TUESDAY CLUB MURDERS (1932; New York: Dell Books, 1971), p. 7.
148. Christie, Agatha, SLEEPING MURDER, *op. cit.*, p. 18.
149. Sanders, Dennis, and Len Lovallo, THE AGATHA CHRISTIE COMPANION, *op. cit.*, p. 90.
150. Christie, Agatha, AND THEN THERE WERE NONE (1939; New York: Pocket Books, 1944), p. 172.
151. Morgan, Janet, AGATHA CHRISTIE: A BIOGRAPHY, *op. cit.*, p. 328.
152. Porterfield, Waldon R., "Agatha Christie Kept Some Mystery for Herself, Too," THE MILWAUKEE JOURNAL, 1 February 1976, Part 5, Page 2.
153. Morgan, Janet, AGATHA CHRISTIE: A BIOGRAPHY, *op. cit.*, p. 334.
154. Grella, George, "Murder and Manners: The Formal Detective Novel" in DIMENSIONS OF DETECTIVE FICTION (Bowling Green: Bowling Green University Popular Press, 1976) edited by Larry N. Landrum, Pat Browne, and Ray B. Browne, p. 56.
155. Morgan, Janet, AGATHA CHRISTIE: A BIOGRAPHY, *op. cit.*, pp. 250–251.
156. *Ibid.*, p. 324.
157. *Ibid.*

CHAPTER 4: ORIENTAL DETECTIVES

1. Biggers, Earl Derr, KEEPER OF THE KEYS (Indianapolis: Bobbs-Merrill, 1932) contained in CHARLIE CHAN: FIVE COMPLETE NOVELS (New York: Avenel Books, 1981), p. 700.
2. Biggers, Earl Derr, FIFTY CANDLES contained in THE AGONY COLUMN (1916; New York: Avon Books, 1951), p. 161.
3. Steinbrunner, Chris, and Otto Penzler, editors in chief, ENCYCLOPEDIA OF MYSTERY AND DETECTION (New York: McGraw-Hill, 1976), p. 27.
4. Biggers, Earl Derr, BEHIND THAT CURTAIN (Indianapolis: Bobbs-Merrill, 1928) contained in CHARLIE CHAN: FIVE COMPLETE NOVELS, *op. cit.*, p. 303.
5. *Ibid.*, p. 298.
6. *Ibid.*, p. 339.
7. *Ibid.*, p. 431.
8. Biggers, Earl Derr, KEEPER OF THE KEYES, *op. cit.*, p. 634.

9. *Ibid.*, p. 670.
10. *Ibid.*, p. 713.
11. Carter, Howard, THE TOMB OF TUTANKAMEN (1954; London: Sphere Books, 1972), p. 35.
12. Service, Faith, "Charlie Chan at the Interviewer's," MODERN SCREEN (July, 1937), p. 42.
13. *Ibid.*, p. 84.
14. *Ibid.*, p. 84.
15. *Ibid.*, p. 43.
16. Gurko, Leo, "The High Level Formula of J. P. Marquand," AMERICAN SCHOLAR, XXI, No. 4 (October, 1952), pp. 443–444.
17. Gross, John, JOHN P. MARQUAND (New Haven: Twayne Publishers, 1963), p. 26.
18. *Ibid.*, p. 21.
19. Quoted in Baker, Carlos, ERNEST HEMINGWAY: A LIFE STORY (New York: Charles Scribner's Sons, 1969), p. 241.
20. Marquand, John P., NO HERO (Boston: Little, Brown, 1935) reprinted under the title YOUR TURN, MR. MOTO (New York: Popular Library, 1977), p. 8.
21. *Ibid.*, p. 43.
22. *Ibid.*, p. 55.
23. Marquand, John P., THANK YOU, MR. MOTO (Boston: Little, Brown, 1936) contained in MR. MOTO'S THREE ACES: A JOHN P. MARQUAND OMNIBUS (Boston: Little, Brown, 1956), p. 10.
24. *Ibid.*, p. 31.
25. Marquand, John P., THINK FAST, MR. MOTO (Boston: Little, Brown, 1937) contained in MR. MOTO'S THREE ACES: A JOHN P. MARQUAND OMNIBUS, *op. cit.*, p. 212.
26. Marquand, John P., MR. MOTO IS SO SORRY (Boston: Little, Brown, 1938) contained in MR. MOTO'S THREE ACES: A JOHN P. MARQUAND OMNIBUS, *op. cit.*, p. 392.
27. Marquand, John P., STOPOVER: TOKYO (Boston: Little, Brown, 1956) reprinted under the title RIGHT YOU ARE, MR. MOTO (New York: Popular Library, 1977), p. 208.
28. *Ibid.*, p. 208.

CHAPTER 5: THE SONG OF THE THIN MAN

1. Hammett, Dashiell, "Zigzags of Treachery," in THE CONTINENTAL OP (New York: Dell Books, n.d.) edited by Ellery Queen, p. 98.
2. Dooley, Dennis, DASHIELL HAMMETT (New York: Frederick Ungar, 1984), p. xv.
3. Nolan, William F., HAMMETT: A LIFE AT THE EDGE (New York: Congdon & Weed, 1983), pp. 14–15.
4. Hammett, Dashiell, in a letter to BLACK MASK, 10 October 1923, p. 127.
5. An interview quoted in the NEW YORK TIMES, 11 January 1961, p. 47.
6. Alvarez, A., "The Novels of Dashiell Hammett," in BEYOND ALL THIS FIDDLE (New York: Random House, 1969), pp. 211–212.
7. Nolan, William F., HAMMETT: A LIFE AT THE EDGE, *op. cit.*, p. 200.

8. Hammett, Dashiell, "Tulip," in THE BIG KNOCKOVER (New York: Random House, 1966) edited by Lillian Hellman, p. 270.
9. Hammett, Dashiell, "The Gutting of Couffignal," in THE RETURN OF THE CONTINENTAL OP (New York: Dell Books, n.d.), p. 112.
10. *Ibid.*, p. 116.
11. Hammett, Dashiell, "Nightmare Town," in NIGHTMARE TOWN (New York: Dell Books, n.d.), p. 12.
12. *Ibid.*, p. 24.
13. *Ibid.*, p. 26.
14. Hammett, Dashiell, "The Big Knockover," in THE BIG KNOCKOVER, *op. cit.*, p . 302.
15. Hammett, Dashiell, "Nightmare Town," *op. cit.*, p. 42.
16. *Ibid.*, p. 48.
17. *Ibid.*, p. 55.
18. *Ibid.*, p. 58.
19. Hammett, Dashiell, RED HARVEST (1929), in THE NOVELS OF DASHIELL HAMMETT (New York: Knopf, 1965), p. 102.
20. Hammett, Dashiell, "The Scorched Face," in NIGHTMARE TOWN, *op. cit.*, p. 92.
21. *Ibid.*, p. 114.
22. *Ibid.*, p. 117.
23. Shaw, Joseph T., editor, THE HARD-BOILED OMNIBUS: EARLY STORIES FROM BLACK MASK (New York: Simon & Schuster, 1946), p. v.
24. *Ibid.*, p. vii.
25. Layman, Richard, SHADOW MAN: THE LIFE OF DASHIELL HAMMETT (New York: Harcourt Brace, 1981), pp. 78–79.
26. Hammett, Dashiell, THE DAIN CURSE (1929), in THE NOVELS OF DASHIELL HAMMETT, *op. cit.*, 180.
27. *Ibid.*, p. 183.
28. *Ibid.*, p. 185.
29. *Ibid.*, p. 206.
30. Wolfe, Peter, BEAMS FALLING: THE ART OF DASHIELL HAMMETT (Bowling Green: Bowling Green University Popular Press, 1980), p. 99.
31. Hammett, Dashiell, editor, CREEPS BY NIGHT (New York: John Day, 1931), p. 8.
32. Hammett, Dashiell, THE DAIN CURSE, *op. cit.*, p. 285.
33. *Ibid.*, p. 288.
34. Layman, Richard, *op. cit.*, p. 86.
35. Quoted in Lillian Hellman's Introduction to THE BIG KNOCKOVER, *op. cit.*, p. xv.
36. Hammett, Dashiell, "Zigzags of Treachery," *op. cit.*, p. 112.
37. Hammett, Dashiell, Introduction to THE MALTESE FALCON (New York: Modern Library, 1934), p. vii.
38. Layman, Richard, *op. cit.*, p. 108.
39. Dooley, Dennis, *op. cit.*, p. 70.
40. Hammett, Dashiell, THE MALTESE FALCON (1930), in THE NOVELS OF DASHIELL HAMMETT, *op. cit.*, p. 319.
41. *Ibid.*, p. 330.

42. Edenbaum, Robert I., "The Poetics of the Private-Eye: The Novels of Dashiell Hammett," in TOUGH GUY WRITERS OF THE THIRTIES (Carbondale: Southern Illinois University Press, 1968) edited by David Madden, p. 81.
43. *Ibid.*, p. 81–82.
44. Nietzsche, Friedrich, DIE GÖTZENDÄMMERUNG, in WERKE IN DREI BÄNDEN *op. cit.*, volume two, p. 943.
45. Hammett, Dashiell, THE MALTESE FALCON, *op. cit.*, p. 434.
46. Quoted in Layman, Richard, *op. cit.*, p. 106.
47. Nolan, William F., *op. cit.*, pp. 93–94.
48. Cawelti, John G., ADVENTURE, MYSTERY, AND ROMANCE: FORMULA STORIES AS ART AND POPULAR CULTURE (Chicago: University of Chicago Press, 1976), p. 173.
49. Hammett, Dashiell, THE GLASS KEY (1931), in THE NOVELS OF DASHIELL HAMMETT, *op. cit.*, p. 540.
50. *Ibid.*, p. 509.
51. *Ibid.*, p. 583.
52. Wolfe, Peter, *op. cit.*, p. 145.
53. Johnson, Diane, DASHIELL HAMMETT: A LIFE (New York: Random House, 1983), p. 87.
54. Quoted in Nolan, William F., *op. cit.*, p. 21.
55. Quoted in Johnson, Diane, *op. cit.*, pp. 315–316.
56. Quoted in Nolan, William F., DASHIELL HAMMETT: A CASEBOOK (Santa Barbara: McNally & Loftin, 1969), p. 59.
57. Yablonsky, Lewis, GEORGE RAFT (1974; New York: New American Library, 1975), pp. 75–76.
58. Quoted in Johnson, Diane, *op. cit.*, p. 100.
59. *Ibid.*, p. 101.
60. Nolan, William F., HAMMETT: A LIFE AT THE EDGE, *op. cit.*, pp. 108–109.
61. Hellman, Lillian, Introduction to THE BIG KNOCKOVER, *op. cit.*, p. xvi.
62. Hammett, Dashiell, THE THIN MAN (1934), in THE NOVELS OF DASHIELL HAMMETT, *op. cit.*, p. 675.
63. Nolan, William F., HAMMETT: A LIFE AT THE EDGE, *op. cit.*, p. 133.
64. Dooley, Dennis, *op. cit.*, p. 125.
65. Hammett, Dashiell, THE THIN MAN, *op. cit.*, p. 691.
66. Johnson, Diane, *op. cit.*, p . 123.
67. *Ibid.*, p. 117.
68. Cerf, Bennett, AT RANDOM: THE REMINISCENCES OF BENNETT CERF (New York: Random House, 1977), p. 206.
69. Johnson, Diane, *op. cit.*, p. 149.
70. *Ibid.*, p. 145.
71. *Ibid.*, p. 317.
72. *Ibid.*, p. 228.
73. Hellman, Lillian, AN UNFINISHED WOMAN (Boston: Little, Brown, 1969), p. 192.
74. *Ibid.*
75. Nolan, William F., HAMMETT: A LIFE AT THE EDGE, *op. cit.*, p. 177.
76. *Ibid.*, p. 87.

77. Johnson, Diane, *op. cit.*, p. 155.
78. *Ibid.*, p. 217.
79. *Ibid.*, pp. 271–272.
80. *Ibid.*, p. 248.
81. Hellman, Lillian, Introduction to THE BIG KNOCKOVER, *op. cit.*, p. viii.
82. Nolan, William F., DASHIELL HAMMETT: A CASEBOOK, *op. cit.*, p. 127.
83. Johnson, Diane, *op. cit.*, p. 298.
84. Dooley, Dennis, *op. cit.*, p. 28.

CHAPTER 6: ADVENTURERS AND THIEVES

1. McNeile, H. C., BULLDOG DRUMMOND (1920; New York: Doubleday, Doran, 1934), p. 302.
2. *Ibid.*, pp. 27–28.
3. *Ibid.*, p. 33.
4. *Ibid.*, p. 23.
5. *Ibid.*, p. 167.
6. *Ibid.*, pp. 173–174.
7. *Ibid.*, p. 241.
8. *Ibid.*, p. 222.
9. *Ibid.*, p. 206.
10. *Ibid.*, p. 164.
11. Blake, Nicholas, "The Detective Story—Why?" in Haycraft, Howard, editor, THE ART OF THE MYSTERY, *op. cit.*, p. 401.
12. Symons, Julian, *op. cit.*, p. 10.
13. Orwell, George, "Boys' Weeklies," in Volume 1 of THE COLLECTED ESSAYS, JOURNALISM, AND LETTERS OF GEORGE ORWELL, *op. cit.*, p. 482.
14. Orwell, George, "Raffles and Miss Blandish," in Volume 3 of *loc. cit.*, *op. cit.*, p. 218.
15. McNeile, H. C., BULLDOG DRUMMOND RETURNS (1932; New York: Doubleday, Doran, 1934), pp. 311–312.
16. Steinbrunner, Chris, and Otto Penzler, editors in chief, ENCYCLOPEDIA OF MYSTERY AND DETECTION, *op. cit.*, p. 131.
17. Marx, Arthur, GOLDWYN: A BIOGRAPHY OF THE MAN BEHIND THE MYTH (New York: W. W. Norton, 1976), p. 163.
18. Hornung, E. W., THE COLLECTED RAFFLES (London: J. M. Dent & Sons, Ltd., 1985), p. 20.
19. Quoted in the Introduction by Jeremy Lewis in *ibid.*, *loc. cit.*, p. xvi.
20. *Ibid.*, p. xvi.
21. Orwell, George, "Raffles and Miss Blandish," *op. cit.*, p. 216.
22. *Ibid.*, p. 220.
23. *Ibid.*, p. 220.
24. *Ibid.*, p. 222. Italics in the original.
25. *Ibid.*, p. 222–223.
26. Nietzsche, Friedrich, WERKE IN DREI BÄNDEN, *op. cit.*, edited by Karl Schlechta, volume two [GÖTZENDÄMMERUNG, Chapter IX, section 5], p. 993.
27. Orwell, George, "Raffles and Miss Blandish," *op. cit.*, p. 224.
28. *Ibid.*, p. 214.

29. *Ibid.*, p. 224.
30. *Ibid.*, p. 212.
31. Hornung, E. W., *op. cit.*, p. 119.
32. *Ibid.*, p. 76.
33. *Ibid.*, p. 73.
34. *Ibid.*, p. 273.
35. Hamilton, Edith, THE GREEK WAY (1930; New York: Avon Books, 1973), p. 78.
36. Leblanc, Maurice, THE EXTRAORDINARY ADVENTURES OF ARSÈNE LUPIN, GENTLEMAN-BURGLAR (1907; New York: Dover Books, 1977) translated from the French by George Morehead, p. 108.
37. *Ibid.*, p. 139.
38. *Ibid.*, p. 132.
39. *Ibid.*, p. 132.
40. Leblanc, Maurice, "The Red Silk Scarf," in 101 YEARS' ENTERTAINMENT: THE GREAT DETECTIVE STORIES 1841–1941 (1941; New York: Modern Library, n.d.), edited by Ellery Queen, p. 183.
41. Hornung, E. W., *op. cit.*, p. 42.
42. Boyle, Jack, BOSTON BLACKIE (1919: Boston: Gregg Press, 1979), p. 75.
43. Quoted by Edward D. Hoch in his Introduction to the Gregg Press reissue, *loc. cit.*, p. vii.
44. *Ibid.*, p. vii.
45. *Ibid.*, p. vii.
46. *Ibid.*, p. viii.
47. Boyle, Jack, BOSTON BLACKIE, *op. cit.*, p. 282.
48. *Ibid.*, p. 199.
49. *Ibid.*, p. 204.
50. Castle, William, STEP RIGHT UP! (New York: Putnam's, 1976), p. 74.
51. *Ibid.*, p. 75.
52. Vance, Louis Joseph, THE LONE WOLF (1914; New York: Avon Books, n.d.), p. 119.
53. *Ibid.*, p. 206.
54. *Ibid.*, p. 15.
55. *Ibid.*, p. 120.
56. Vance, Louis Joseph, THE FALSE FACES (1918; New York: Avon Books, n.d.), p. 16.
57. *Ibid.*, p. 193.
58. Charteris, Leslie, SAINT'S GETAWAY (1932; New York: Avon Books, 1952), p. 45.
59. Charteris, Leslie, Introduction to THE SAINT MEETS THE TIGER (1928; New York: Charter Books, 1980), no page number.
60. *Ibid.*, p. 201.
61. *Ibid.*, p. 16.
62. Charteris, Leslie, THE LAST HERO (1930; New York: Charter Books, 1982), p. 23.
63. *Ibid.*, p. 47.
64. Charteris, Leslie, Foreword to ENTER THE SAINT (1931; New York: Pocket Books, 1944), no page number.

65. *Ibid.*, p. 23.
66. *Ibid.*, p. 108.
67. Lofts, W. O. G., and Derek Adley, THE SAINT AND LESLIE CHARTERIS (Bowling Green: Bowling Green University Popular Press, 1970), p. 25.
68. Charteris, Leslie, THE MISFORTUNES OF MR. TEAL retitled THE SAINT IN ENGLAND (1934; New York: Avon Books, n.d.), p. 29.
69. *Ibid.*, pp. 61–62.
70. *Ibid.*, p. 148.
71. Lofts, W. O. G., and Derek Adley, THE SAINT AND LESLIE CHARTERIS, *op. cit.*, p. 63.
72. Charteris, Leslie, SAINT'S GETAWAY, *op. cit.*, p. 106.
73. Charteris, Leslie, THE HAPPY HIGHWAYMAN (1939; New York: Pocket Books, 1945), p. 203.
74. Charteris, Leslie, THE SAINT GOES WEST (1942; New York: Avon Books, 1948), p. 46.
75. *Ibid.*, p. 153.
76. Lofts, W. O. G., and Derek Adley, THE SAINT AND LESLIE CHARTERIS, *op. cit.*, p. 57.
77. Symons, Julian, MORTAL CONSEQUENCES: A HISTORY FROM THE DETECTIVE STORY TO THE CRIME NOVEL, *op. cit.*, p. 210.
78. Steinbrunner, Chris, and Otto Penzler, editors, ENCYCLOPEDIA OF MYSTERY AND DETECTION, *op. cit.*, p. 144.

CHAPTER 7: THE DETECTIVE FILM IN TRANSITION

1. Steinbrunner, Chris, and Otto Penzler, editors, ENCYCLOPEDIA OF MYSTERY AND DETECTION, *op. cit.*, p. 110.
2. Van Dine, S. S., "Twenty Rules for Writing Detective Stories," in PHILO VANCE MURDER CASES, *op. cit.*, p. 81.
3. Pitts, Michael R., FAMOUS MOVIE DETECTIVES, *op. cit.*, p. 85.
4. Zinman, David, SATURDAY AFTERNOON AT THE BIJOU, (New Rochelle: Arlington House, 1973), p. 247.
5. *Ibid.*, p. 247.
6. *Ibid.*, p. 249.
7. Quoted by Bodeen, DeWitt, "Richard Dix," FILMS IN REVIEW (October, 1966), Vol. 17, No. 8, p. 495.
8. Castle, William, STEP RIGHT UP!, *op. cit.*, p. 76.
9. *Ibid.*, p. 77.
10. Cameron, Kate, "Rialto Presents New 'Whistler' Episode," NEW YORK DAILY NEWS (11 November 1944).
11. Masters, Dorothy, "New 'Whistler' Not Up to Par for the Series," NEW YORK DAILY NEWS (23 March 1945).
12. Miller, Don, "Private Eyes," FOCUS ON FILM (Autumn, 1975), No. 22, p. 29.
13. Halliday, Brett, MURDER AND THE MARRIED VIRGIN (1944; New York: Dell Books, n.d.), p. 110.
14. Halliday, Brett, MUM'S THE WORD FOR MURDER (1938; New York: Dell Books, 1964), p. 7.
15. *Ibid.*, p. 123.
16. *Ibid.*, pp. 156–157.

17. *Ibid.*, p. 191.
18. Halliday, Brett, DIVIDEND ON DEATH (1939; New York: Dell Books, n.d.), p. 40.
19. Halliday, Brett, THE PRIVATE PRACTICE OF MICHAEL SHAYNE (1940; New York: Dell Books, 1958), p. 26.
20. *Ibid.*, p. 147.
21. Halliday, Brett, TICKETS FOR DEATH (1941; New York: Dell Books, n.d.), p. 44.
22. *Ibid.*, p. 46.
23. Halliday, Brett, WHEN THE CORPSE CAME CALLING (1942; New York: Dell Books, 1964), pp. 62–63.
24. Halliday, Brett, MURDER WEARS A MUMMER'S MASK re-issued under the title IN A DEADLY VEIN (1943; New York: Dell Books, n.d.), p. 72.
25. *Ibid.*, pp. 73–74.
26. Halliday, Brett, BLOOD ON THE BLACK MARKET re-issued under the title HEADS YOU LOSE (1943; New York: Dell Books, 1970), p. 5.
27. Halliday, Brett, BODIES ARE WHERE YOU FIND THEM (1941; New York: Dell Books, n.d.), pp. 186–187.
28. Halliday, Brett, THE CORPSE THAT NEVER WAS (1963; New York: Dell Books, 1964), p. 93.
29. Halliday, Brett, MICHAEL SHAYNE'S LONG CHANCE (1944; New York: Dell Books, 1964), p. 47.
30. Halliday, Brett, MARKED FOR MURDER (1945; New York: Dell Books, n.d.), p. 192.
31. Halliday, Brett, MURDER IS MY BUSINESS (1945; New York: Dell Books, 1963), p. 42.
32. Halliday, Brett, BLOOD ON BISCAYNE BAY (1946; New York: Dell Books, 1960), p. 6.
33. *Ibid.*, p. 10.
34. Halliday, Brett, THE CORPSE THAT NEVER WAS, *op. cit.*, p. 11.
35. *Ibid.*, p. 20.
36. Halliday, Brett, BODIES ARE WHERE YOU FIND THEM, *op. cit.*, p. 66.
37. Nietzsche, Friedrich, JENSEITS VON GUT UND BÖSE [BEYOND GOOD AND EVIL], No. 39, contained in Volume Two of WERKE IN DREI BÄNDEN, *op. cit.*, p. 602.
38. Jung, C. G., ZUR PSYCHOLOGIE WESTLICHER UND ÖSTLICHER RELIGION [ON THE PSYCHOLOGY OF WESTERN AND EASTERN RELIGION] (Zürich: Rascher Verlag, 1963), p. 484.
39. *Ibid.*, pp. 494–495.
40. Dostoyevsky, Fyodor, THE BROTHERS KARAMAZOV (New York: Bantam Books, 1970) translated by Andrew R. MacAndrew, pp. 459–460.
41. Nietzsche, Friedrich, WERKE, *op. cit.*, Volume Three, p. 881.
42. *Ibid.*, Volume Two, p. 993.
43. Paterson, John, "A Cosmic View of the Private Eye," SATURDAY REVIEW (22 August 1953), p. 7.
44. Symons, Julian, MORTAL CONSEQUENCES: A HISTORY FROM THE DETECTIVE STORY TO THE CRIME NOVEL, *op. cit.*, pp. 11–12.
45. Nietzsche, Friedrich, *op. cit.*, Volume Two, p. 626.

46. *Ibid.*, Volume Three, pp. 852–853.

47. Gide, André, IMAGINARY INTERVIEWS (New York: Knopf, 1944) translated by Malcolm Cowley, p. 146.

48. Barrett, William, IRRATIONAL MAN (New York: Doubleday, 1962), p. 9.

49. Duhamel, Marcel, Preface to PANORAMA DU FILM NOIR AMÉRICAIN (1941–1953) (Paris: Éditions D'Aujourd'hui, 1955) by Raymond Borde and Etienne Chaumeton, p. x. In my translation, it reads: "Read, then, *romans noirs* in great quantities and watch *films noirs* in abundance. So long as you do not kill save in your imagination, you will be able to sleep peacefully. It is an indulgence I would wish for you."

50. *Ibid.*, p. 1. In my translation, it reads: "which kept having in common an unusual and cruel atmosphere, tainted by a rather peculiar eroticism. . . ."

51. Frank, Nino, "Un Nouveau Genre 'Policier': L'aventure Criminelle," L'ECRAN FRANCAISE (1946) No. 61, p. 8. In my translation, it reads: "belong to that which one formerly used to call the genre of police detective, and which one might better designate henceforth by the term criminal adventures, or better still, criminal psychology."

52. Borde, Raymond, and Etienne Chaumeton, *op. cit.*, p. 5. In my translation, it reads: "it is the presence of crime that provides *film noir* with its most enduring characteristic."

53. *Ibid.*, p. 6. In my translation, it reads: "sordid or unusual, death always emerges at the conclusion of a picaresque journey. In the full sense of the word, *film noir* is film about death."

54. *Ibid.*, p. 8. In my translation, it reads: "the American police procedural documentary is in reality a documentary glorifying the police and belongs to the same category as such productions as, in France, IDENTITÉ JUDICIARE [LEGAL IDENTITY], or, in England, THE BLUE LAMP. There is nothing of this kind in *noir* films. If there are policemen, they are rotten—as the inspector in THE ASPHALT JUNGLE, or that prime example of a corrupted brute incarnate by Lloyd Nolan in THE LADY IN THE LAKE—sometimes even murderers (FALLEN ANGEL and WHERE THE SIDEWALK ENDS directed by Otto Preminger)."

55. Karimi, A. M., TOWARD A DEFINITION OF THE AMERICAN FILM NOIR 1941–1949) (New York: Arno Press, 1976), p. 26.

56. Porfirio, Robert G., "No Way Out: Existential Motifs in the *Film Noir*," SIGHT AND SOUND (Autumn, 1976), p. 213.

57. Schrader, Paul, "Notes on *Film Noir*," FILM COMMENT (Spring, 1972), p. 13.

58. Porfirio, Robert G., "No Way Out: Existential Motifs in the *Film Noir*," *op. cit.*, p. 213.

59. Reik, Theodor, THE COMPULSION TO CONFESS: ON THE PSYCHOANALYSIS OF CRIME AND PUNISHMENT (New York: Farrar, Straus, and Cudahy, 1959), p. 260–261.

60. Taylor, John Russell, STRANGERS IN PARADISE: THE HOLLYWOOD ÉMIGRÉS, 1933–1950 (New York: Holt, Rinehart, and Winston, 1983), p. 199.

61. Higham, Charles, and Joel Greenberg, HOLLYWOOD IN THE FORTIES Cranbury and London: Barnes/Tantivy, 1968), p. 28.

62. Lang, Fritz, quoted in THE GREAT GANGSTER PICTURES (Metuchen: Scarecrow Press, 1976) by James Robert Parish and Michael R. Pitts, pp. 35–36.

63. Borde, Raymond, and Etienne Chaumeton, PANORAMA DU FILM NOIR AMÉRICAIN, *op. cit.*, p. 127.

64. *Ibid.*, p. 127. Interestingly, the two French critics see Ford and Grahame as aspects of the same soul in contrast to Paul M. Jensen who in THE CINEMA OF FRITZ LANG (Cranbury and London: Barnes/Tantivy, 1969), p. 183, perceived this duality in Bannion and Lagana, "each contains elements of the other, his opposite," and Colin McArthur who in UNDERWORLD U.S.A. (New York: Viking, 1972), p. 79, perceived Bannion as "the avenger, indistinguishable in behavior from the criminals he hunts."

65. *Ibid.*, p. 80.

66. *Ibid.*, p. 80.

67. Place, Janey, "Women in *Film Noir*, in WOMEN IN FILM NOIR (London: British Film Institute, 1978) edited by E. Ann Kaplan, p. 45.

68. Wolfenstein, Martha, and Nathan Leites, MOVIES: A PSYCHOLOGICAL STUDY (New York: Atheneum, 1970), p. 97.

69. *Ibid.*, p. 83.

70. *Ibid.*, p. 98.

71. Farber, Stephen, "Violence and the Bitch Goddess," FILM COMMENT (November-December, 1974), p. 9.

72. Kobal, John, "The Time, The Place, and The Girl: Rita Hayworth," FOCUS ON FILM (Summer, 1972), No. 10, p. 22.

CHAPTER 8: RAYMOND CHANDLER IN HOLLYWOOD

1. Chandler, Raymond, THE LITTLE SISTER, in THE MIDNIGHT RAYMOND CHANDLER (Boston: Houghton Mifflin, 1971), p. 292.

2. MacShane, Frank, editor, SELECTED LETTERS OF RAYMOND CHANDLER, *op. cit.*, p. 250.

3. Speir, Jerry, RAYMOND CHANDLER (New York: Ungar, 1981), p. 4.

4. Maugham, W. Somerset, A WRITER'S NOTEBOOK (London: Heinemann, 1949), pp. 289–290.

5. MacShane, Frank, editor, SELECTED LETTERS OF RAYMOND CHANDLER, *op. cit.*, p. 205.

6. Morgan, Ted, MAUGHAM: A BIOGRAPHY (New York: Simon & Schuster, 1980), pp. 488–489.

7. Chandler, Raymond, "The Man Who Liked Dogs," in KILLER IN THE RAIN (New York: Ballantine Books, 1972), p. 64.

8. MacShane, Frank, editor, SELECTED LETTERS OF RAYMOND CHANDLER, *op. cit.*, p. 238.

9. Chandler, Raymond, "The Perfect Knight," contained in Bruccoli, Matthew J., editor, CHANDLER BEFORE MARLOWE: RAYMOND CHANDLER'S EARLY PROSE AND POETRY, 1908–1912 (Columbia: University of South Carolina Press, 1973), p. 24.

10. MacShane, Frank, editor, SELECTED LETTERS OF RAYMOND CHANDLER, *op. cit.*, p. 171.

11. Powell, Dilys, "Ray and Cissy," contained in Gross, Miriam, editor, THE WORLD OF RAYMOND CHANDLER (London: Weidenfeld and Nicolson, 1977), p. 87.

12. Spender, Natasha, "His Own Long Goodbye," contained in *Ibid.*, p. 133.

13. Speir, Jerry, RAYMOND CHANDLER, *op. cit.*, p. 9.

14. MacShane, Frank, editor, SELECTED LETTERS OF RAYMOND CHANDLER, *op. cit.*, pp. 8–9.
15. Chandler, Raymond, "The Simple Art of Murder," in THE SIMPLE ART OF MURDER, *op. cit.*, pp. 16–17.
16. Chandler, Raymond, "Blackmailers Don't Shoot," in THE MIDNIGHT RAYMOND CHANDLER, *op. cit.*, p. 147.
17. *Ibid.*, p. 161.
18. Chandler, Raymond, "Smart-Aleck Kill," in PICKUP ON NOON STREET (New York: Ballantine Books, 1971), p. 96.
19. Chandler, Raymond, "Finger Man," in TROUBLE IS MY BUSINESS (New York: Ballantine Books, 1972), p. 116.
20. *Ibid.*, p. 130.
21. Chandler, Raymond, "Killer in the Rain," in KILLER IN THE RAIN, *op. cit.*, p. 37.
22. *Ibid.*, pp. 38–39.
23. *Ibid.*, p. 44.
24. Chandler, Raymond, "Nevada Gas," in PICKUP ON NOON STREET, *op. cit.*, p. 170.
25. *Ibid.*, p. 210.
26. Chandler, Raymond, "Spanish Blood," in THE SIMPLE ART OF MURDER, *op. cit.*, p. 73.
27. MacShane, Frank, editor, SELECTED LETTERS OF RAYMOND CHANDLER, *op. cit.*, p. 155.
28. Chandler, Raymond, "The Man Who Liked Dogs," *op. cit.*, p. 70.
29. MacShane, Frank, THE LIFE OF RAYMOND CHANDLER, *op. cit.*, p. 54.
30. Chandler, Raymond, "Goldfish," contained in Ruhm, Herbert, editor, THE HARDBOILED DETECTIVE: STORIES FROM BLACK MASK MAGAZINE 1920–1951 (New York: Vintage Books, 1977), p. 134.
31. *Ibid.*, p. 132.
32. *Ibid.*, p. 159.
33. Quoted in MacShane, Frank, THE LIFE OF RAYMOND CHANDLER, *op. cit.*, p. 51.
34. Chandler, Raymond, "The Curtain," in KILLER IN THE RAIN, *op. cit.*, p. 98.
35. *Ibid.*, p. 126.
36. Chandler, Raymond, THE BIG SLEEP, in THE RAYMOND CHANDLER OMNIBUS (New York: Modern Library, 1975), p. 138.
37. Chandler, Raymond, "Try the Girl," in KILLER IN THE RAIN, *op. cit.*, p. 162.
38. *Ibid.*, p. 163.
39. *Ibid.*, p. 168.
40. MacShane, Frank, editor, SELECTED LETTERS OF RAYMOND CHANDLER, *op. cit.*, p. 120. The many and devious ways in which Knopf exploited Chandler while he was publishing him are provided in detail in MacShane's biography. One example may suffice. Because of the contract Knopf had with Chandler, Knopf made more money on reprint rights than he paid out to Chandler on earnings from the hard bound editions!
41. MacShane, Frank, editor, THE NOTEBOOKS OF RAYMOND CHANDLER (New York: Ecco Press, 1976), p. 40.
42. Chandler, Raymond, Introduction to TROUBLE IS MY BUSINESS, *op. cit.*, viii.

43. Chandler, Raymond, "The Simple Art of Murder," *op. cit.*, p. 17.
44. Davies, Russell, "Omnes Me Impune Lacessunt," contained in Gross, Miriam, editor, THE WORLD OF RAYMOND CHANDLER, *op. cit.*, p. 36.
45. Chandler, Raymond, "Mandarin's Jade," in KILLER IN THE RAIN, *op. cit.*, p. 219.
46. *Ibid.*, p. 220.
47. Chandler, Raymond, FAREWELL, MY LOVELY, in THE RAYMOND CHANDLER OMNIBUS, *op. cit.*, p. 221.
48. *Ibid.*, p. 312.
49. MacShane, Frank, editor, SELECTED LETTERS OF RAYMOND CHANDLER, *op. cit.*, p. 197.
50. Speir, Jerry, RAYMOND CHANDLER, *op. cit.*, p. 109.
51. Chandler, Raymond, THE HIGH WINDOW, in THE RAYMOND CHANDLER OMNIBUS, *op. cit.*, p. 402.
52. *Ibid.*, p. 382.
53. *Ibid.*, p. 434.
54. MacShane, Frank, THE LIFE OF RAYMOND CHANDLER, *op. cit.*, p. 111.
55. Houseman, John, "Lost Fortnight, A Memoir," contained in Bruccoli, Matthew J., editor, THE BLUE DAHLIA: A SCREENPLAY BY RAYMOND CHANDLER (Carbondale: Southern Illinois University Press, 1976), p. x.
56. Moffat, Ivan, "On the Fourth Floor of Paramount," in Gross, Miriam, editor, THE WORLD OF RAYMOND CHANDLER, *op. cit.*, p. 46.
57. *Ibid.*, p. 46.
58. Gardiner, Dorothy, and Kathrine Sorley Walker, RAYMOND CHANDLER SPEAKING (Boston: Houghton Mifflin, 1962), p. 135. Comparison with the text of the letter in the SELECTED LETTERS OF RAYMOND CHANDLER shows the language to have been "edited" a slight bit, but not essentially.
59. Zolotow, Maurice, BILLY WILDER IN HOLLYWOOD (New York: Putnam's, 1977), p. 119.
60. Spender, Natasha, "His Own Long Goodbye," *op. cit.*, p. 132.
61. *Ibid.*, p. 133.
62. MacShane, Frank, THE LIFE OF RAYMOND CHANDLER, *op. cit.*, p. 113.
63. Spender, Natasha, "His Own Long Goodbye," *op. cit.*, pp. 131–132.
64. Mann, Thomas, NEUE STUDIEN (Stockholm: Bermann-Fischer Verlag, 1948), p. 110.
65. Spender, Natasha, "His Own Long Goodbye," *op. cit.*, p. 132.
66. Houseman, John, "Lost Fortnight, A Memoir," *op. cit.*, p. xi.
67. *Ibid.*, p. xix.
68. *Ibid.*, p. xx.
69. *Ibid.*, p. xxi.
70. Chandler, Raymond, THE LADY IN THE LAKE, in THE RAYMOND CHANDLER OMNIBUS, *op. cit.*, p. 473.
71. Blotner, Joseph, "Faulkner in Hollywood," contained in Robinson, W. R., editor, MAN AND THE MOVIES (Baton Rouge: Louisiana State University Press, 1967) p. 272.
72. Bacall, Lauren, BY MYSELF (New York: Knopf, 1978), p. 134.
73. MacShane, Frank, editor, SELECTED LETTERS OF RAYMOND CHANDLER, *op. cit.*, p. 75.

74. MacShane, Frank, THE LIFE OF RAYMOND CHANDLER, *op. cit.*, pp. 174–175.
75. *Ibid.*, p. 177.
76. Bruccoli, Matthew J., editor, THE BLUE DAHLIA: A SCREENPLAY BY RAYMOND CHANDLER, *op. cit.*, p. 136.
77. MacShane, Frank, editor, SELECTED LETTERS OF RAYMOND CHANDLER, *op. cit.*, pp. 192–193.
78. Speir, Jerry, RAYMOND CHANDLER, *op. cit.*, pp. 60–61.
79. *Ibid.*, p. 63.
80. Chandler, Raymond, THE LITTLE SISTER, *op. cit.*, p. 299.
81. Chandler, Raymond, THE LONG GOODBYE, in THE MIDNIGHT RAYMOND CHANDLER, *op. cit.*, pp. 681–682.
82. Chandler, Raymond, Introduction to TROUBLE IS MY BUSINESS, *op. cit.*, p. viii.
83. MacShane, Frank, editor, SELECTED LETTERS OF RAYMOND CHANDLER, *op. cit.*, p. 175.
84. Speir, Jerry, RAYMOND CHANDLER, *op. cit.*, p. 77.
85. Sammons, Jeffrey L., HEINRICH HEINE: A MODERN BIOGRAPHY (Princeton: Princeton University Press, 1979), p. 62.
86. Davies, Russell, "Omnes Me Impune Lacessunt," *op. cit.*, p. 41.
87. Mason, Michael, "Marlowe, Men and Women," in *Ibid.*, *loc. cit.*, p. 95.
88. *Ibid.*, p. 97.
89. *Ibid.*, p. 93.
90. Chandler, Raymond, PLAYBACK (1958; New York: Ballantine Books, 1977), p. 166.
91. Durham, Philip, DOWN THESE MEAN STREETS A MAN MUST GO: RAYMOND CHANDLER'S KNIGHT (Chapel Hill: University of North Carolina Press, 1963), p. 97.
92. MacShane, Frank, THE LIFE OF RAYMOND CHANDLER, *op. cit.*, p. 188.
93. MacShane, Frank, editor, SELECTED LETTERS OF RAYMOND CHANDLER, *op. cit.*, p. 379.
94. *Ibid.*, p. 382.
95. Spender, Natasha, "His Own Long Goodbye," *op. cit.*, p. 141.
96. Chandler, Raymond, THE LITTLE SISTER, *op. cit.*, p. 329.
97. MacShane, Frank, editor, SELECTED LETTERS OF RAYMOND CHANDLER, *op. cit.*, p. 315.
98. *Ibid.*, p. 293.

CHAPTER 9: CRIME IN THE STREETS

1. Spillane, Mickey, KISS ME, DEADLY (1952; New York: Signet Books, 1953), p. 42.
2. Spillane, Mickey, I, THE JURY (1947; New York. Signet Books, 1948), p. 174.
3. Weibel, Kay, "Mickey Spillane as a 'Fifties Phenomenon," in DIMENSIONS OF DETECTIVE FICTION, *op. cit.*, p. 115.
4. Spillane, Mickey, VENGEANCE IS MINE (1950; New York: Signet Books, 1951), p. 29.
5. *Ibid.*, p. 38.

6. *Ibid.*, pp. 66–67.
7. *Ibid.*, p. 150.
8. *Ibid.*, p. 157.
9. *Ibid.*, p. 159.
10. Spillane, Mickey, KISS ME, DEADLY, *op. cit.*, p. 160.
11. Cawelti, John G., ADVENTURE, MYSTERY, AND ROMANCE: FORMULA STORIES AS ART AND POPULAR CULTURE, *op. cit.*, p. 183.
12. *Ibid.*, p. 185.
13. *Ibid.*, pp. 190–191.
14. Ruehlmann, William, SAINT WITH A GUN: THE UNLAWFUL AMERICAN PRIVATE EYE, *op. cit.*, p. 95.
15. Spillane, Mickey, ONE LONELY NIGHT (1950; New York: Signet Books, 1951), p. 99.
16. Greenberg, Joel, "Interview with Robert Aldrich," SIGHT AND SOUND (Winter, 1968–1969), p. 10.
17. MacShane, Frank, editor, SELECTED LETTERS OF RAYMOND CHANDLER, *op. cit.*, pp. 314–315.
18. Quoted in Bruccoli, Matthew J., ROSS MACDONALD (San Diego: Harcourt, Brace, Jovanovich, 1984), p. 49.
19. *Ibid.*, p. 22.
20. Quoted in *ibid.*, p. 19.
21. Quoted in *ibid.*, p. 15.
22. *Ibid.*, p. 48.
23. Grogg, Sam L., Jr., "Interview with Ross Macdonald," in DIMENSIONS IN DETECTIVE FICTION, *op. cit.*, p. 186.
24. Macdonald, Ross, THE GOODBYE LOOK (New York: Knopf, 1969), p. 48.
25. Bruccoli, Matthew J., ROSS MACDONALD, *op. cit.*, p. 72.
26. Macdonald, Ross, SELF-PORTRAIT: CEASELESSLY INTO THE PAST (Santa Barbara: Capra Press, 1981), p. 5.
27. Grogg, Sam L., Jr., "Interview with Ross Macdonald," *op. cit.*, p. 187.
28. Macdonald, Ross, SELF-PORTRAIT: CEASELESSLY INTO THE PAST, *op. cit.*, p. 89.
29. *Ibid.*, p. 67.
30. Wolfe, Peter, DREAMERS WHO LIVE THEIR DREAMS: THE WORLD OF ROSS MACDONALD'S NOVELS (Bowling Green: Bowling Green University Popular Press, 1976), p. 29.
31. Macdonald, Ross, THE GOODBYE LOOK, *op. cit.*, p. 2.
32. *Ibid.*, p. 188.
33. *Ibid.*, p. 110.
34. *Ibid.*, p. 65.
35. Bruccoli, Matthew J., ROSS MACDONALD, *op. cit.*, p. 101.
36. Hammett, Dashiell, THE NOVELS OF DASHIELL HAMMETT, *op. cit.*, p. 334.
37. Macdonald, Ross, SELF-PORTRAIT: CEASELESSLY INTO THE PAST, *op. cit.*, p. 111.
38. Bruccoli, Matthew J., ROSS MACDONALD, *op. cit.*, p. 26.
39. Macdonald, Ross, SELF-PORTRAIT: CEASELESSLY INTO THE PAST, *op. cit.*, p. 44.
40. Quoted in Bruccoli, Matthew J., ROSS MACDONALD, *op. cit.*, p. 50.

41. Wolfe, Peter, DREAMERS WHO LIVE THEIR DREAMS: THE WORLD OF ROSS MACDONALD'S NOVELS, *op. cit.*, p. 52.
42. Bruccoli, Matthew J., ROSS MACDONALD, *op. cit.*, p. 99.
43. Quoted in Wolfe, Peter, DREAMERS WHO LIVE THEIR DREAMS: THE WORLD OF ROSS MACDONALD NOVEL'S, *op. cit.*, p. 242.
44. Grogg, Sam L., Jr., "Interview with Ross Macdonald," *op. cit.*, p. 187.
45. Macdonald, Ross, SELF-PORTRAIT: CEASELESSLY INTO THE PAST, *op. cit.*, p. 121.
46. Bruccoli, Matthew, J., ROSS MACDONALD, *op. cit.*, p. 50.
47. *Ibid.*, p. 115.
48. Quoted in Ruehlmann, SAINT WITH A GUN: THE UNLAWFUL AMERICAN PRIVATE EYE, *op. cit.*, pp. 98–99.
49. Jaffé, Aneila, JUNG'S LAST YEARS AND OTHER ESSAYS (Dallas: Spring Publications, 1984) translated by R. F. C. Hull and Murray Stein, p. 131.
50. Roazen, Paul, FREUD AND HIS FOLLOWERS (1973; New York: New American Library, 1976), p. 541.

Bibliography

BOOKS

Alvarez, A., BEYOND ALL THIS FIDDLE (New York: Random House, 1969).
Bacall, Lauren, BY MYSELF (New York: Knopf, 1978).
Baker, Carlos, ERNEST HEMINGWAY: A LIFE STORY (New York: Charles Scribner's Sons, 1969).
Ball, John, editor, THE MYSTERY STORY (New York: Penguin Books, 1976).
Barrett, William, IRRATIONAL MAN (New York: Doubleday, 1962).
Barzun, Jacques, and Wendell Hertig Taylor, A CATALOGUE OF CRIME (New York: Harper & Row, 1970).
Bentley, E. C., TRENT'S LAST CASE in 3 STAR OMNIBUS (New York: Knopf, 1934).
Berg, A. Scott, MAX PERKINS: EDITOR OF GENIUS (New York: Pocket Books, 1979).
Biggers, Earl Derr, THE AGONY COLUMN (New York: Avon Books, 1951).
———, CHARLIE CHAN: FIVE COMPLETE NOVELS (New York: Avenel Books, 1981).
Borde, Raymond, and Etienne Chaumeton, PANORAMA DU FILM NOIR AMÉRICAIN (1941–1953) (Paris: Éditions D'Aujourd'hui, 1955).
Boyle, Jack, BOSTON BLACKIE (Boston: Gregg Press, 1979).
Bruccoli, Matthew J., editor, CHANDLER BEFORE MARLOWE: RAYMOND CHANDLER'S EARLY PROSE AND POETRY, 1908–1912 (Columbia: University of South Carolina, 1973).
———, ROSS MACDONALD (San Diego: Harcourt, Brace, Jovanovich, 1984).
———, editor, the BLUE DAHLIA: A SCREENPLAY BY RAYMOND CHANDLER (Carbondale: Southern Illinois University Press, 1976).
Carter, Howard, THE TOMB OF TUTANKHAMEN (London: Sphere Books, 1972).
Castle, William, STEP RIGHT UP! (New York: Putnam's, 1976).
Cawelti, John G., ADVENTURE, MYSTERY, AND ROMANCE: FORMULA STORIES AS ART AND POPULAR CULTURE (Chicago: University of Chicago Press, 1976).

Cerf, Bennett, AT RANDOM: THE REMINISCENCES OF BENNETT CERF (New York: Random House, 1977).
Chandler, Raymond, KILLER IN THE RAIN (New York: Ballantine Books, 1972).
———, THE MIDNIGHT RAYMOND CHANDLER (Boston: Houghton Mifflin, 1971).
———, PLAYBACK (New York: Ballantine Books, 1977).
———, PICKUP ON NOON STREET (New York: Ballantine Books, 1971).
———, THE RAYMOND CHANDLER OMNIBUS (New York: Modern Library, 1975).
———, THE SIMPLE ART OF MURDER (New York: Ballantine Books, 1972).
———, TROUBLE IS MY BUSINESS (New York: Ballantine Books, 1972).
Charteris, Leslie, ENTER THE SAINT (New York: Pocket Books, 1944).
———, SAINT'S GETAWAY (New York: Avon Books, 1952).
———, THE HAPPY HIGHWAYMAN (New York: Pocket Books, 1945).
———, THE LAST HERO (New York: Charter Books, 1982).
———, THE SAINT IN ENGLAND (New York: Avon Books, n.d.).
———, THE SAINT GOES WEST (New York: Avon Books, 1948).
———, THE SAINT MEETS THE TIGER (New York: Charter Books, 1980).
Christie, Agatha, AND THEN THERE WERE NONE (New York: Pocket Books, 1944).
———, MURDER ON THE LINKS (New York: Dell Books, n.d.).
———, SLEEPING DEATH (New York: Dodd, Mead, 1976).
———, THE BIG FOUR (New York: Dell Books, 1965).
———, THE MURDER AT THE VICARAGE (New York: Dodd, Mead, 1976).
———, THE MURDER OF ROGER ACKROYD (New York: Pocket Books, 1939).
———, THE MYSTERIOUS AFFAIR AT STYLES (New York: Avon Books, n.d.).
———, THE MYSTERY OF THE BLUE TRAIN (New York: Pocket Books, 1940).
———, THE TUESDAY CLUB MURDERS (New York: Dell Books, 1971).
Conan Doyle, Sir Arthur, THROUGH THE MAGIC DOOR (London: Smith, Elder, 1907).
———, THE ANNOTATED SHERLOCK HOLMES (New York: Clarkson N. Potter, 1967).
———, WORKS (Roslyn: Black's Readers Service, n.d.).
Dooley, Dennis, DASHIELL HAMMETT (New York: Frederick Ungar, 1984).
Dostoyevsky, Fyodor, THE BROTHERS KARAMAZOV (New York: Bantam Books, 1970).
Durham, Philip, DOWN THESE MEAN STREETS A MAN MUST GO: RAYMOND CHANDLER'S KNIGHT (Chapel Hill: University of North Carolina Press, 1963).
Fergusson, Harvey, THE CONQUEST OF DON PEDRO (New York: Morrow, 1954).
Gardiner, Dorothy, and Kathrine Sorley Walker, RAYMOND CHANDLER SPEAKING (Boston: Houghton Mifflin, 1962).
Gardner, Erle Stanley, THE CASE OF THE CARETAKER'S CAT (New York: Pocket Books, 1942).
———, THE CASE OF THE CURIOUS BRIDE (New York: Pocket Books, 1942.
———, THE CASE OF THE COUNTERFEIT EYE (New York: Pocket Books, 1942).
———, THE CASE OF THE DROWSY MOSQUITO (New York: Pocket Books, 1950)
———, THE CASE OF THE FABULOUS FAKE (New York: Morrow, 1969).
———, THE CASE OF THE HOWLING DOG (New York: Pocket Books, 1941).
———, THE CASE OF THE LAME CANARY (New York: Pocket Books, 1943).
———, THE CASE OF THE LUCKY LEGS (New York: Pocket Books, 1941).
———, THE CASE OF THE SLEEPWALKER'S NIECE (New York: Pocket Books 1944).

―――, THE CASE OF THE SUBSTITUTE FACE (New York: Pocket Books, 1943).
―――, THE CASE OF THE VELVET CLAWS (New York: Morrow, 1933).
Gide, Andre, IMAGINARY INTERVIEWS (New York: Knopf, 1944).
Gross, John, JOHN P. MARQUAND (New Haven: Twayne Publishers, 1963).
Gross, Miriam, editor, THE WORLD OF RAYMOND CHANDLER (London: Weidenfeld and Nicolson, 1977).
Halliday, Brett, BLOOD ON BISCAYNE BAY (New York: Dell Books, 1960).
―――, BLOOD ON THE BLACK MARKET (New York: Dell Books, 1970).
―――, BODIES ARE WHERE YOU FIND THEM (New York: Dell Books, n.d.).
―――, DIVIDEND ON DEATH (New York: Dell Books, n.d.).
―――, MARKED FOR MURDER (New York: Dell Books, n.d.).
―――, MICHAEL SHAYNE'S LONG CHANCE (New York: Dell Books, 1964).
―――, MUM'S THE WORD FOR MURDER (New York: Dell Books, 1964).
―――, MURDER AND THE MARRIED VIRGIN (New York: Dell Books, n.d.).
―――, MURDER IS MY BUSINESS (New York: Dell Books, 1963).
―――, MURDER WEARS A MUMMER'S MASK (New York: Dell Books, n.d.).
―――, THE CORPSE THAT NEVER WAS (New York: Dell Books, 1964).
―――, THE PRIVATE PRACTICE OF MICHAEL SHAYNE (New York: Dell Books, 1958).
―――, TICKETS FOR DEATH (New York: Dell Books, n.d.).
―――, WHEN THE CORPSE COMES CALLING (New York: Dell Books, 1964).
Hamilton, Edith, THE GREEK WAY (New York: Avon Books, 1973).
Hammett, Dashiell, editor, CREEPS BY NIGHT (New York: John Day, 1931).
―――, NIGHTMARE TOWN (New York: Dell Books, n.d.).
―――, THE BIG KNOCKOVER (New York: Random House, 1966).
―――, THE CONTINENTAL OP (New York: Dell Books, n.d.).
―――, THE MALTESE FALCON (New York: Modern Library, 1934).
―――, THE NOVELS OF DASHIELL HAMMETT (New York: Knopf, 1965).
―――, THE RETURN OF THE CONTINENTAL OP (New York: Dell Books, n.d.).
Haycraft, Howard, MURDER FOR PLEASURE: THE LIFE AND TIMES OF THE DETECTIVE STORY (New York: Mercury Publications, 1951).
―――, editor, THE ART OF THE MYSTERY STORY (New York: Carroll and Graf, 1983).
Hellman, Lillian, AN UNFINISHED WOMAN (Boston: Little, Brown, 1969).
Higham, Charles, and Joel Greenberg, HOLLYWOOD IN THE FORTIES (Cranbury and London: Barnes/Tantivy, 1968).
Higham, Charles, THE ADVENTURES OF CONAN DOYLE (New York: W. W. Norton, 1976).
Hornung, E. W., THE COLLECTED RAFFLES (London: J. M. Dent & Sons, Ltd., 1985).
Hughes, Dorothy B., ERLE STANLEY GARDNER: THE CASE OF THE REAL PERRY MASON (New York: Morrow, 1978).
Jaffé, Aneila, JUNG'S LAST YEARS AND OTHER ESSAYS (Dallas. Spring Publications, 1984).
Johnston, Alva, THE CASE OF ERLE STANLEY GARDNER (New York: Morrow, 1947).
Johnson, Diane, DASHIELL HAMMETT: A LIFE (New York: Random House, 1983).
Jung, C. G., ZUR PSYCHOLOGIE WESTLICHER UND ÖSTLICHER RELIGION (Zürich: Rascher Verlag, 1963).

Kaplan, E. Ann, editor, WOMEN IN FILM NOIR (London: British Film Institute, 1978).
Karimi, A. M., TOWARD A DEFINITION OF THE AMERICAN FILM NOIR (1941–1949) (New York: Arno Press, 1976).
Krutch, Joseph Wood, EDGAR ALLAN POE: A STUDY IN GENIUS (New York: Knopf, 1926).
———, MORE LIVES THAN ONE (New York: William Sloane Associates, 1962).
Landrum, Larry, Pat Browne, and Ray B. Browne, editors, DIMENSIONS OF DETECTIVE FICTION (Bowling Green: Bowling Green University Popular Press, 1976).
Layman, Richard, SHADOW MAN: THE LIFE OF DASHIELL HAMMETT (New York: Harcourt, Brace, 1981).
Leblanc, Maurice, THE EXTRAORDINARY ADVENTURES OF ARSÈNE LUPIN, GENTLEMAN-BURGLAR (New York: Dover Books, 1977).
Levin, Harry, THE POWER OF BLACKNESS (New York: Vintage Books, 1958).
Lofts, W. O. G., and Derek Adley, THE SAINT AND LESLIE CHARTERIS (Bowling Green: Bowling Green University Popular Press, 1970).
Macdonald, Ross, SLEEPING BEAUTY (New York: Knopf, 1973).
———, SELF-PORTRAIT: CEASELESSLY INTO THE PAST (Santa Barbara: Capra Press, 1981).
———, THE GOODBYE LOOK (New York: Knopf, 1969).
McNeile, H. C., BULLDOG DRUMMOND (New York: Doubleday, Doran, 1934).
———, BULLDOG DRUMMOND RETURNS (New York: Doubleday, Doran, 1934).
MacShane, Frank, editor, SELECTED LETTERS OF RAYMOND CHANDLER (New York: Columbia University Press, 1981).
———, THE LIFE OF RAYMOND CHANDLER (New York: Dutton, 1976).
———, editor, THE NOTEBOOKS OF RAYMOND CHANDLER (New York: Ecco Press, 1976).
Madden, David, editor, TOUGH GUY WRITERS OF THE THIRTIES (Carbondale: Southern Illinois University Press, 1968).
Mann, Thomas, NEUE STUDIEN (Stockholm: Bermann-Fischer Verlag, 1948).
Marquand, John P., MR. MOTO'S THREE ACES: A JOHN P. MARQUAND OMNIBUS (Boston: Little, Brown, 1956).
———, RIGHT YOU ARE, MR. MOTO (New York: Popular Library, 1977).
———, YOUR TURN, MR. MOTO (New York: Popular Library, 1977).
Marx, Arthur, GOLDWYN: A BIOGRAPHY OF THE MAN BEHIND THE MYTH (New York: W. W. Norton, 1976).
Maugham, W. Somerset, A WRITER'S NOTEBOOK (London: Heinemann, 1949).
———, THE VAGRANT MOOD (New York: Doubleday, 1953).
———, editor, TRAVELLER'S LIBRARY (New York: Doubleday, Doran, 1933).
Millay, Edna St. Vincent, COLLECTED LYRICS (New York: Washington Square Press, 1959).
Morgan, Janet, AGATHA CHRISTIE: A BIOGRAPHY (New York: Knopf, 1985).
Morgan, Ted, MAUGHAM: A BIOGRAPHY (New York: Simon & Schuster, 1980).
Morrison, Claudia C., FREUD AND THE CRITIC: THE EARLY USE OF DEPTH PSYCHOLOGY IN LITERARY CRITICISM (Chapel Hill: The University of North Carolina Press, 1968).
Nevins, Francis M., Jr., ROYAL BLOODLINE: ELLERY QUEEN, AUTHOR AND

DETECTIVE (Bowling Green: Bowling Green University Popular Press, 1974).
———, editor, THE MYSTERY WRITER'S ART (Bowling Green: Bowling Green University Popular Press, 1970).
———, THE SOUND OF DETECTION: ELLERY QUEEN'S ADVENTURES IN RADIO (Madison: Brownstone Books, 1983).
Newman, James R., editor, THE WORLD OF MATHEMATICS in four volumes (New York: Simon & Schuster, 1956).
Nietzsche, Friedrich, THE PHILOSOPHY OF NIETZSCHE (New York: Modern Library, 1937).
———, WERKE IN DREI BÄNDEN (Munich: Carl Hanser Verlag, 1955).
Nolan, William F., DASHIELL HAMMETT: A CASEBOOK (Santa Barbara: McNally & Loftin, 1969).
———, HAMMETT: A LIFE AT THE EDGE (New York: Congdon & Weed, 1983).
Nordon, Pierre, CONAN DOYLE: A BIOGRAPHY (New York: Holt, Rinehart, and Winston, 1967).
Orwell, Sonia, and Ian Angus, editors, THE COLLECTED ESSAYS, JOURNALISM, AND LETTERS OF GEORGE ORWELL in four volumes (New York: Harcourt, Brace, Jovanovich, 1968).
Panek, LeRoy Lad, WATTEAU'S SHEPHERDS: THE DETECTIVE NOVEL IN BRITAIN 1914–1940 (Bowling Green: Bowling Green University Popular Press, 1978).
Parrish, James Robert, and Michael R. Pitts, THE GREAT GANGSTER PICTURES (Metuchen: Scarecrow Press, 1976).
Pitts, Michael R., FAMOUS MOVIE DETECTIVES (Metuchen: Scarecrow Press, 1979).
Poe, Edgar Allan, THE COMPLETE POEMS AND STORIES OF EDGAR ALLAN POE WITH SELECTIONS FROM HIS CRITICAL WRITINGS in two volumes (New York: Knopf, 1976).
Pointer, Michael, THE PUBLIC LIFE OF SHERLOCK HOLMES (New York: Drake, 1975).
Queen, Ellery, editor, 101 YEARS' ENTERTAINMENT: THE GREAT DETECTIVE STORIES 1841–1941 (New York: Modern Library, n.d.).
———, THE EGYPTIAN CROSS MYSTERY (New York: Pocket Books, 1943).
———, THE FOUR OF HEARTS (New York: Pocket Books, 1944).
———, THE GREEK COFFIN MYSTERY (New York: Pocket Books, 1942).
———, THE ORIGIN OF EVIL (New York: Pocket Books, 1953).
———, THE ROMAN HAT MYSTERY (New York: Pocket Books, 1940).
———, THE SPANISH CAPE MYSTERY (New York: Pocket Books, 1942).
Rascoe, Burton, and Groff Conklin, editors, THE SMART SET ANTHOLOGY (New York: Reynal and Hitchcock, 1934).
Rathbone, Basil, IN AND OUT OF CHARACTER (New York: Doubleday, 1962).
Reik, Theodor, THE COMPULSION TO CONFESS: ON THE PSYCHOANALYSIS OF CRIME AND PUNISHMENT (New York: Farrar, Straus, and Cudahy, 1959).
Roazen, Paul, FREUD AND HIS FOLLOWERS (New York: New American Library, 1976).
Robinson, W. R., editor, MAN AND THE MOVIES (Baton Rouge: Louisiana State University Press, 1967).
Rubinstein, Artur, MY MANY YEARS (New York: Knopf, 1980).

Ruehlmann, William, SAINT WITH A GUN: THE UNLAWFUL AMERICAN PRIVATE EYE (New York: New York University Press, 1974).
Ruhm, Herbert, editor, THE HARD-BOILED DETECTIVE: STORIES FROM BLACK MASK MAGAZINE 1920–1951 (New York: Vintage Books, 1977).
Ruitenbeek, Hendrick M., editor, PSYCHOANALYSIS AND LITERATURE (New York: Dutton, 1964).
Sammons, Jeffrey L., HEINRICH HEINE: A MODERN BIOGRAPHY (Princeton: Princeton University Press, 1979).
Sanders, Dennis, and Len Lovallo, THE AGATHA CHRISTIE COMPANION (New York: Avenel Books, 1985).
Shaw, Joseph T., editor, THE HARD-BOILED OMNIBUS: EARLY STORIES FROM BLACK MASK (New York: Simon & Schuster, 1946).
Shreffler, Philip A., editor, THE BAKER STREET READER: CORNERSTONE WRITINGS ABOUT SHERLOCK HOLMES (Westport: Greenwood Press, 1984).
Speir, Jerry, RAYMOND CHANDLER (New York: Ungar, 1981).
Spillane, Mickey, I, THE JURY (New York: Signet Books, 1948).
———, KISS ME DEADLY (New York: Signet Books, 1953).
———, ONE LONELY NIGHT (New York: Signet Books, 1951).
———, VENGEANCE IS MINE (New York: Signet Books, 1951).
Starrett, Vincent, THE PRIVATE LIFE OF SHERLOCK HOLMES (New York: Pinnacle Books, 1975).
Steinbrunner, Chris, and Otto Penzler, editors-in-chief, ENCYCLOPEDIA OF MYSTERY AND DETECTION (New York: McGraw-Hill, 1976).
———, and Norman Michaels, THE FILMS OF SHERLOCK HOLMES (Secaucus: Citadel, 1978).
Symons, Julian, MORTAL CONSEQUENCES: A HISTORY FROM DETECTIVE STORY TO THE CRIME NOVEL (New York: Schocken Books, 1977).
Taylor, John Russell, STRANGERS IN PARADISE: THE HOLLYWOOD EMIGRÉS 1933–1950 (New York: Holt, Rinehart, and Winston, 1983).
Tuska, Jon, DARK CINEMA: AMERICAN FILM NOIR IN CULTURAL PERSPECTIVE (Westport: Greenwood Press, 1984).
———, PHILO VANCE: THE LIFE AND TIMES OF S. S. VAN DINE (Bowling Green: Bowling Green University Popular Press, 1971).
———, THE VANISHING LEGION: A HISTORY OF MASCOT PICTURES 1927–1935 (Jefferson: McFarland, 1981).
———, and Vicki Piekarski, editors, CLOSE-UP: THE CONTRACT DIRECTOR (Metuchen: Scarecrow Press, 1976).
Vance, Louis Joseph, THE FALSE FACES (New York: Avon Books, n.d.).
———, THE LONE WOLF (New York: Avon Books, n.d.).
Van Dine, S. S., PHILO VANCE MURDER CASES (New York: Charles Scribner's Sons, 1936).
———, THE BISHOP MURDER CASE (New York: Charles Scribner's Sons, 1929).
———, THE "CANARY" MURDER CASE (New York: Charles Scribner's Sons, 1927).
———, THE GARDEN MURDER CASE (New York: Charles Scribner's Sons, 1935).
———, THE GRACIE ALLEN MURDER CASE (New York: Charles Scribner's Sons, 1938).
———, THE GREENE MURDER CASE (New York: Charles Scribner's Sons, 1928).

———, THE SCARAB MURDER CASE (New York: Charles Scribner's Sons, 1930).
———, THE WINTER MURDER CASE (New York: Charles Scribner's Sons, 1939).
———, editor, THE WORLD'S GREAT DETECTIVE STORIES: A CHRONOLOGICAL ANTHOLOGY (New York: Charles Scribner's Sons, 1931).
Wheelock, John Hall, editor, EDITOR TO AUTHOR: THE LETTERS OF MAXWELL E. PERKINS (New York: Charles Scribner's Sons, 1950).
Wolfe, Peter, BEAMS FALLING: THE ART OF DASHIELL HAMMETT (Bowling Green: Bowling Green University Popular Press, 1980).
———, DREAMERS WHO LIVE THEIR DREAMS: THE WORLD OF ROSS MACDONALD'S NOVELS (Bowling Green: Bowling Green University Popular Press, 1976).
Wolfenstein, Martha, and Nathan Leites, MOVIES: A PSYCHOLOGICAL STUDY (New York: Atheneum, 1970).
Yablonsky, Lewis, GEORGE RAFT (New York: New American Library, 1975).
Zweig, Stefan, DIE WELT VON GESTERN (Frankfurt am Main: Fischer Taschenbuch Verlag, 1982).
———, MEISTERNOVELLEN (Frankfurt am Main: S. Fischer Verlag, 1970).
Zinman, David. SATURDAY AFTERNOON AT THE BIJOU (New Rochelle: Arlington House, 1973).
Zolotow, Maurice, BILLY WILDER IN HOLLYWOOD (New York: Putnam's, 1977).

ARTICLES

Bodeen, DeWitt, "Richard Dix," FILMS IN REVIEW (October, 1966), Vol. 17, No. 8.
Cameron, Kate, "Rialto Presents New 'Whistler' Episode," NEW YORK DAILY NEWS (11 November 1944).
Farber, Stephen, "Violence and the Bitch Goddess," FILM COMMENT (November-December, 1974).
Frank, Nino, "Un Nouveau Genre 'Policier': L'aventure Criminelle," L'ECRAN FRANCAISE (1946) No. 61.
Greenberg, Joel, "Interview with Robert Aldrich," SIGHT AND SOUND (Winter, 1968–1969).
Gurko, Leo, "The High Level Formula of J. P. Marquand," AMERICAN SCHOLAR (October, 1952), XXI, No. 4.
Kobal, John, "The Time, The Place, and The Girl: Rita Hayworth," FOCUS ON FILM (Summer, 1972), No. 10.
Larkin, Mark, "The Philosophy of Crime," PHOTOPLAY (April, 1929) Vol. XXXV, No. 5.
Lee, Rand, "Dad and Cousin Fred Entered a Writing Contest . . . ," TV GUIDE, 11 October 1975.
Manchester, H. F., "How Philo Vance, Clubfoot, and Charlie Chan Were Born," THE WRITER (September, 1931) Vol. 43, No. 9.
Masters, Dorothy, "New 'Whistler' Not Up to Par for The Series," NEW YORK DAILY NEWS (23 March 1945).
Miller, Don, "Private Eyes," FOCUS ON FILM (Autumn, 1975) No. 22.
Paterson, John, "A Cosmic View of the Private Eye," SATURDAY REVIEW (22 August 1953).

Porfirio, Robert G., "No Way Out: Existential Motifs in the *Film Noir*," SIGHT AND SOUND (Autumn, 1976).
Porterfield, Waldon R., "Agatha Christie Kept Some Mystery for Herself, Too," THE MILWAUKEE JOURNAL (1 February 1976).
Prescott, Peter S., "The Only Legal Way to Make Money from Murder," LOOK (21 April 1970).
Schrader, Paul, "Notes on *Film Noir*," FILM COMMENT (Spring, 1972).
Service, Faith, "Charlie Chan at the Interviewer's," MODERN SCREEN (July, 1937).
Smith, David R., "The Gracie Allen Murder Case," VIEWS & REVIEWS MAGAZINE (Winter, 1972) Vol. 4., Issue No. 2.
Tuska, Jon, "The Dragon Murder Case," JOURNAL OF POPULAR CULTURE (Winter, 1971) Vol. V, No. 3.

Index

ABC MURDERS, THE, 152
ABENTEUER, DIE (Fox, 1928), 151
Adley, Derek, 285
ADVENTURES OF ELLERY QUEEN, THE, 94, 97
ADVENTURES OF ELLERY QUEEN, THE (radio program), 99, 100, 105, 106
ADVENTURES OF SAM SADE, THE (radio program), 234, 237
ADVENTURES OF SHERLOCK HOLMES, THE, 18, 89
ADVENTURES OF SHERLOCK HOLMES, THE (Vitagraph, 1903), 30
ADVENTURES OF SHERLOCK HOLMES, THE (20th-Fox, 1939), 43
ADVENTURES OF THE THIN MAN, THE (radio program), 234, 237
Æschylus, xv
AFTER THE FUNERAL, 156
AFTER THE THIN MAN (M-G-M, 1936), 231
AGONY COLUMN, THE, 162
Aldrich, Robert, 396, 397
ALIAS BOSTON BLACKIE (Columbia, 1942), 270, 273
ALIAS THE LONE WOLF, 275
ALIAS THE LONE WOLF (Columbia, 1927), 277
ALIBI (Twickenham, 1931), 152
Allen, Grácie, 80, 81, 84

ALPHABET MURDERS, THE (M-G-M, 1966), 152, 157
Altman, Robert, 386-390
AMATEUR CRACKSMAN, THE, 254, 256-257
AMERICAN WEST IN FICTION, THE, 254
AMERICAN WEST IN FILM, THE, xiii
Ames, Leon, 7, 104, 105, 175, 184-186, 235, 236, 310, 380, 381
AND THEN THERE WERE NONE, 104, 153
AND THEN THERE WERE NONE (20th-Fox, 1945), 153, 157
ANOTHER THIN MAN (M-G-M, 1939), 232-233
APPOINTMENT WITH MURDER (Film Classics, 1948), 304
Aristotle, 339, 402
Arlen, Michael, 295, 297
ARREST BULLDOG DRUMMOND (Paramount, 1939), 251
ARSÈNE LUPIN (Greater Film Company, 1917), 261
ARSÈNE LUPIN (M-G-M, 1932), 261
ARSÈNE LUPIN CONTRE HERLOCK SHOLMES, 260
ARSÈNE LUPIN: GENTLEMAN-CAMBRIOLEUR, 259
ARSÈNE LUPIN RETURNS (M-G-M, 1938), 262

Arthur, Jean, 66
Asquith, Herbert, 27
Astor, Mary, 132, 216, 349
Atwill, Lionel, 42, 44, 186
Austen, Jane, xv
Autry, Gene, xiv, 95, 298, 312

Bacall, Lauren, 375-376, 377
BACKGROUND TO DANGER (Warner's, 1943), 221-222
Balzac, Honoré de, xv, 6, 50, 85, 408
BARBAROUS COAST, THE, 403
Baring-Gould, William S., 36, 44
Barrat, Robert, 75
Barrett, William, 336
Barrymore, John, 32, 33, 34, 35, 80, 249, 250, 251, 257, 261, 281
Barrymore, Lionel, 261, 266
Barzun, Jacques, 14, 26, 259
Baxter, Warner, 309-310, 313
Beaumont, Hugh, 330, 331
Beecham, Sir Thomas, 268
BEHIND THAT CURTAIN, 164-165, 167, 190
BEHIND THAT CURTAIN (Fox, 1929), 165
Bell, Dr. Joseph, 14, 24
Bell, H. W., 36
Bellamy, Ralph, 100, 101, 102, 103, 104, 105, 106, 107
Bennet, Spencer Gordon, 163-164
BENSON MURDER CASE, THE, 51, 56, 63, 65, 76, 80
BENSON MURDER CASE, THE (Paramount, 1930), 68, 69
Bentley, E. C., 61
Berg, A. Scott, 55
BERYL CORONET, THE (Stoll, 1921), 32
BIG BOW MYSTERY, THE, 70, 307-308
BIG FOUR, THE, 149
Biggers, Earl Derr, 94, 161, 162, 163, 164, 165, 166, 167, 177, 178, 180, 189, 190, 191
BIGGER THEY COME, THE, 128
BIG HEAT, THE (Columbia, 1953), 340, 342-343

BIG SLEEP, THE, 361, 363, 374, 377, 386
BIG SLEEP, THE (Warner's, 1946), xvi, 312, 337, 363, 367, 374-376, 377, 381
BIG SLEEP, THE (United Artists, 1978), 391
Birmingham, Stephen, 177, 188
BIRTH OF A NATION, THE (Epoch, 1915), 70, 193
BISHOP MURDER CASE, THE, 49, 58, 63, 68, 76, 108
BISHOP MURDER CASE, THE (M-G-M, 1930), 42, 68, 69
BLACK CAMEL, THE, 165, 190
BLACK CAMEL, THE (Fox, 1931), 166
BLACK COFFEE (Twickenham, 1931), 152
BLACK GANG, THE, 246
BLACK MASK, THE, 256
Blakeney, T. S., 36
BLONDE FOR A DAY (PRC, 1946), 331
BLOOD ON BISCAYNE BAY, 321, 329
BLOOD ON THE BLACK MARKET, 321, 322
BLOOD ON THE STARS, 329
BLUE DAHLIA, THE (Paramount, 1945), 373, 376, 377, 379
BLUE HAMMER, THE, 402
BLUE, WHITE, AND PERFECT (20th-Fox, 1941), 326
BODIES ARE WHERE YOU FIND THEM, 320, 321, 331, 332
BODY IN THE LIBRARY, THE, 127, 151, 157
Boetticher, Oscar, Jr., 272
Bogart, Humphrey, xiv, 216, 335, 337, 344, 348, 349, 367, 375-376, 377, 388, 404
Bonaparte, Maria, 2, 3
BOOMERANG CLUE, THE, 146
Borde, Raymond, 337-338, 343, 345
BOSTON BLACKIE, 262-263, 265
BOSTON BLACKIE (Fox, 1923), 266
BOSTON BLACKIE AND THE LAW (Columbia, 1946), 273
BOSTON BLACKIE BOOKED ON SUSPICION (Columbia, 1945), 272

BOSTON BLACKIE GOES HOLLYWOOD (Columbia, 1942), 271
BOSTON BLACKIE'S CHINESE VENTURE (Columbia, 1949), 273
BOSTON BLACKIE'S LITTLE PAL (Metro, 1918), 264
BOSTON BLACKIE'S REDEMPTION (Metro, 1919), 264
BOSTON BLACKIE'S RENDEZVOUS (Columbia, 1945), 272
Boswell, James, 19
Boyle, Jack, 262, 263, 264, 265, 266, 267, 268, 269
Brackett, Leigh, xvi, 312, 365, 374, 375, 376-377, 387, 388
BRASHER DOUBLOON, THE (20th-Fox, 1947), 327, 381
Bronson, Charles, 396
Brook, Clive, 34, 35, 38, 286, 308
Brooke, Hillary, 44, 45, 105, 281, 311
Brooks, Louise, 64
Brown, Harry Joe, 82, 83
Bruccoli, Matthew J., 354, 379, 398, 402, 404
Bruce, Nigel, 41, 42, 43, 44, 46
BULLDOG DRUMMOND, 241, 242, 243
BULLDOG DRUMMOND (stage play), 42, 244, 246
BULLDOG DRUMMOND (Hodkinson, 1922), 244, 246
BULLDOG DRUMMOND (United Artists, 1929), 246-247
BULLDOG DRUMMOND AT BAY (Columbia, 1947), 251
BULLDOG DRUMMOND COMES BACK (Paramount, 1937), 249
BULLDOG DRUMMOND ESCAPES (Paramount, 1937), 248, 249
BULLDOG DRUMMOND HITS OUT (stage play), 248
BULLDOG DRUMMOND IN AFRICA (Paramount, 1938), 250
BULLDOG DRUMMOND RETURNS, 242, 243, 245
BULLDOG DRUMMOND'S BRIDE (Paramount, 1939), 251
BULLDOG DRUMMOND'S PERIL (Paramount, 1938), 250

BULLDOG DRUMMOND'S REVENGE (Paramount, 1937), 249
BULLDOG DRUMMOND'S SECRET POLICE (Paramount, 1939), 251
BULLDOG DRUMMOND'S THIRD ROUND (Astra-National, 1925), 246
BULLDOG DRUMMOND STRIKES BACK (20th, 1934), 248, 249, 250
BULLDOG DRUMMOND STRIKES BACK (Columbia, 1947), 251
BULLDOG JACK (British-Gaumont, 1935), 248
Burns, George, 80, 81
Burr, Raymond, 139, 143, 222, 305, 348

Caesar, Julius, 96
Cagney, James, 132
Cain, James M., 264, 340, 362, 366
CALAMITY TOWN, 105, 108
CALLING BULLDOG DRUMMOND (M-G-M, 1951), 252
CALLING PHILO VANCE (Warner's, 1940), 85, 301
CAMPUS MYSTERY, THE (Warner's, 1932), 70
"CANARY" MURDER CASE, THE, 49, 50, 56, 57, 58, 63, 76, 96, 150, 307
"CANARY" MURDER CASE, THE (Paramount, 1929), 64, 66, 67, 68
Capone, Al, 218-219
CAPTAIN OF THE "POLE-STAR" AND OTHER STORIES, THE, 12
Carlyle, Thomas, 11
Carr, John Dickson, 28, 307, 353
Carter, Howard, 169
CASEBOOK OF SHERLOCK HOLMES, THE, 26
CASE OF ERLE STANLEY GARDNER, THE, 141
CASE OF THE BLACK CAT, THE (Warner's, 1936), 135
CASE OF THE CARELESS KITTEN, THE, 137
CASE OF THE CARETAKER'S CAT, THE, 129, 135
CASE OF THE COUNTERFEIT EYE, THE, 125, 126-129, 142

CASE OF THE CURIOUS BRIDE, THE, 124-125, 128, 129
CASE OF THE CURIOUS BRIDE, THE (Warner's, 1935), 132-133
CASE OF THE DANGEROUS DOWAGER, THE, 135, 142
CASE OF THE DARING DIVORCEE, THE, 139
CASE OF THE DEMURE DEFENDANT, THE, 139
CASE OF THE DROWSY MOSQUITO, THE, 123, 130
CASE OF THE FABULOUS FAKE, THE, 139
CASE OF THE HOWLING DOG, THE, 124, 125, 136
CASE OF THE HOWLING DOG, THE (Warner's, 1935), 132
CASE OF THE LAME CANARY, THE, 130, 134, 136, 137, 142
CASE OF THE LUCKY LEGS, THE, 124, 125, 133
CASE OF THE LUCKY LEGS, THE (Warner's, 1935), 133
CASE OF THE PERJURED PARROT, THE, 142
CASE OF THE SHOPLIFTER'S SHOE, THE, 142
CASE OF THE SILENT PARTNER, THE, 137
CASE OF THE SLEEPWALKER'S NIECE, THE, 130
CASE OF THE STUTTERING BISHOP, THE (Warner's, 1936), 135
CASE OF THE SUBSTITUTE FACE, THE, 130, 136
CASE OF THE SULKY GIRL, THE, 124, 129
CASE OF THE SUNBATHER'S DIARY, THE, 138
CASE OF THE VELVET CLAWS, THE, 120-121, 123, 124, 136
CASE OF THE VELVET CLAWS, THE (Warner's, 1936), 134
CASINO MURDER CASE, THE, 75, 77
CASINO MURDER CASE, THE (M-G-M, 1935), 76, 95, 175, 228, 229, 231, 280

Castle, William, 237, 271, 312, 313, 314, 315, 316, 318
CAT OF MANY TAILS, 93, 110
Catullus, 400
Cawelti, John G., 211, 395, 396
Cervantes, Miguel de, xv
CHALLENGE, THE (20th-Fox, 1948), 252
CHANCE OF A LIFETIME (Columbia, 1943), 271, 313
CHANDLER BEFORE MARLOWE, 354-355
Chandler, Raymond, xvi, xviii, 51, 66, 140, 150, 279, 297, 316, 319, 327, 337, 340, 351, 352, 353, 354, 355, 356, 357, 358, 359, 360, 361, 362, 363, 364, 365, 366, 367, 368, 369, 370, 371, 372, 373, 374, 375, 376, 377, 378, 379, 380, 381, 382, 383, 384, 385, 386, 387, 388, 389, 390, 391, 392, 393, 397-398, 405
Chaplin, Charlie, 22, 41
CHARLIE CHAN AT MONTE CARLO (20th-Fox, 1938), 175
CHARLIE CHAN AT THE CIRCUS (20th-Fox, 1936), 167, 173
CHARLIE CHAN AT THE OLYMPICS (20th-Fox, 1937), 174
CHARLIE CHAN AT THE OPERA (20th-Fox, 1937), 174, 175
CHARLIE CHAN AT THE RACETRACK (20th-Fox, 1936), 173, 174
CHARLIE CHAN AT THE WAX MUSEUM (20th-Fox, 1940), 190
CHARLIE CHAN CARRIES ON, 165, 189
CHARLIE CHAN CARRIES ON (Fox, 1931), 165, 166
CHARLIE CHAN IN EGYPT (Fox, 1935), 168-171
CHARLIE CHAN IN HONOLULU (20th-Fox, 1938), 188-189
CHARLIE CHAN IN LONDON (Fox, 1934), 167-168, 191
CHARLIE CHAN IN PANAMA (20th-Fox, 1940), 189
CHARLIE CHAN IN PARIS (Fox, 1935), 168

CHARLIE CHAN IN RIO (20th-Fox, 1941), 190
CHARLIE CHAN IN SHANGHAI (20th-Fox, 1935), 170
CHARLIE CHAN IN THE CITY OF DARKNESS (20th-Fox, 1939), 189
CHARLIE CHAN IN THE SECRET SERVICE (Monogram, 1944), 193
CHARLIE CHAN ON BROADWAY (20th-Fox, 1937), 168, 175
CHARLIE CHAN'S CHANCE (Fox, 1932), 167
CHARLIE CHAN'S COURAGE (Fox, 1934), 167
CHARLIE CHAN'S GREATEST CASE (Fox, 1933), 167
CHARLIE CHAN'S MURDER CRUISE (20th-Fox, 1940), 189-190
CHARLIE CHAN'S SECRET (20th-Fox, 1936), 172
Charteris, Leslie, 264, 283, 284, 285, 286, 287, 288, 289, 291, 292, 293, 294, 295, 296
Chaumeton, Etienne, 337-338, 343, 345
CHEATERS AT PLAY (Fox, 1932), 278
Chesterton, G. K., 150
CHINATOWN (Paramount, 1974), xix, 407
CHINESE CAT, THE (Monogram, 1944), 193
CHINESE ORANGE MYSTERY, THE, 93, 97
CHINESE PARROT, THE, 163, 164, 167, 191
CHINESE PARROT, THE (Universal, 1927), 164
CHINESE RING, THE (Monogram, 1947), 195
Christie, Agatha, 104, 105, 127, 128, 144, 145, 146, 147, 148, 149, 150, 151, 152, 153, 155, 156, 157, 158, 159, 252, 408
Churchill, Sir Winston, 27
CITIZEN KANE (RKO, 1941), 99-100, 337, 338, 339, 379
CITY STREETS (Paramount, 1931), 213
CLOSE CALL FOR BOSTON BLACKIE (Columbia, 1946), 272

CLOSE CALL FOR ELLERY QUEEN (Columbia, 1942), 106
CODE OF SILENCE (Orion, 1985), 7
Cohn, Harry, 313, 314
Colman, Ronald, 231, 244, 246, 247, 248, 249, 258, 289, 305
COME-ON GIRL, 131
COMING OF THE FAIRIES, THE, 28
COMING OUT PARTY (Fox, 1934), 42
CONFESSIONS OF BOSTON BLACKIE (Columbia, 1941), 270, 281
Conway, Tom, 43, 252, 291, 297, 298, 299, 300, 301, 302, 303, 304, 305
Cook, Donald, 76, 95
CORPSE CAME CALLING, THE, 320, 331
CORPSE THAT NEVER WAS, THE, 323, 332
Corrigan, Lloyd, 7, 270, 272
Cortez, Ricardo, 135, 215
COUNTER-ESPIONAGE (Columbia, 1942), 281
COUNTERFEIT WIFE, 329
COUNT ON THE SAINT, 293, 294
COURT OF LAST RESORT, THE, 142
Coward, Noel, xvii, 385
CRIME AND DETECTION, 26
CRIME DOCTOR (radio program), 309
CRIME DOCTOR (Columbia, 1943), 310
CRIME DOCTOR'S COURAGE (Columbia, 1945), 311
CRIME DOCTOR'S DIARY (Columbia, 1949), 313
CRIME DOCTOR's GAMBLE (Columbia, 1947), 313
CRIME DOCTOR'S GAMBLE (Columbia, 1947), 313
CRIME DOCTOR'S MANHUNT (Columbia, 1946), 312
CRIME DOCTOR'S STRANGEST CASE, THE (Columbia, 1943), 310
CRIME NOBODY SAW, THE (Paramount, 1937), 97
CRIME ON MY HANDS, 301
Crisp, Donald, 35, 62, 308
CROOKED ALLEY (Universal, 1923), 267

450   Index

Cukor, George, 33
CURTAIN, 146
Curtis, Alan, 85
Curtiz, Michael, 72, 73, 132, 133

DAIN CURSE, THE, 202, 205-207, 239
Dali, Salvador, 4
Dannay, Frederic. See Queen, Ellery
Daniell, Henry, 45
DARK ALIBI (Monogram, 1946), 194
DARK CINEMA: AMERICAN FILM NOIR IN CULTURAL PERSPECTIVE, xiii, 333
Darmour, Larry, 100, 101, 102, 104, 106, 107
DATE WITH THE FALCON, A (RKO, 1942), 196, 304
DEADLIER THAN THE MALE (Universal, 1967), 253
DEAD MAN'S DIARY, 328
DEAD MEN TELL (20th-Fox, 1941), 190
DEAD RECKONING (Columbia, 1946), 343, 344-345, 348, 349, 388
DEATH FROM A TOP HAT, 326
DEATH IN THE AIR, 146
DEATH ON THE NILE, 146
DEATH ON THE NILE (Paramount, 1978), 158
Del Ruth, Roy, 7
Denny, Reginald, 248-249
DESERT FURY (Paramount, 1947), 349
DESPERATE CHANCE FOR ELLERY QUEEN (Columbia, 1942), 107
DETECTIVE IN HOLLYWOOD, THE, xiii, 49
DETECTIVE STORY (stage play), 269
DETECTIVE STORY (Paramount, 1951), 237
DEVIL'S CARGO (Film Classics, 1948), 304
DEVIL TO PAY, THE, 98, 104
Dickens, Charles, xv, 272
DINNER AT DUPRE'S, 328
DIRTY HARRY (Warner's, 1971), 405
D.A. CALLS IT MURDER, THE, 135
DIVIDEND ON DEATH, 319, 320
Dix, Richard, 131, 314, 315, 316, 317

Dmytryk, Edward, 216, 250, 270, 281, 299-300, 301, 306, 366-367, 368, 391
DOCKS OF NEW ORLEANS (Monogram, 1948), 195
Dodd, Claire, 132, 134, 219
Dooley, Dennis, 197, 227, 240
DOOMED TO DIE (Monogram, 1940), 192
DOOMSTERS, THE, 401
DOOR BETWEEN, THE, 95
Dostoyevsky, Fyodor, xv, 6, 333, 372, 392
DOUBLE, DOUBLE, 108, 109
DOUBLE INDEMNITY (Paramount, 1944), 340-342, 366, 368, 370, 372
Douglas, Melvyn, 231, 262, 278
Doyle, Sir Arthur Conan, xix, 9, 10, 11, 12, 13, 14, 15, 16, 17, 18, 19, 20, 21, 22, 23, 24, 25, 26, 27, 28, 29, 30, 35, 36, 37, 38, 39, 40, 41, 42, 43, 45, 47, 48, 50, 56, 57, 66, 70, 89, 125, 148, 254, 260
DRAGON MURDER CASE, THE, 49, 73
DRAGON MURDER CASE, THE (First National, 1934), xvi, 72, 73-75, 81, 132, 173, 280
DRAGON'S TEETH, THE, 98
DRESSED TO KILL (20th-Fox, 1941), 326
DRESSED TO KILL (Universal, 1946), 45
Dresser, Davis. See Halliday, Brett
DROWNING POOL, THE, 401, 403, 404
DROWNING POOL, THE (Warner's, 1975), 404
Duhamel, Marcel, 337
Dupont, E. A., 67
Durham, Philip, 385
DUTCH SHOE MYSTERY, THE, 104
Dvorak, Ann, 132, 135
DYING DETECTIVE, THE (Stoll, 1921), 32

Eastwood, Clint, 395, 405, 406, 407
Edenbaum, Robert I., 209, 212
EGYPTIAN CROSS MYSTERY, THE, 90, 92-93

Index 451

EIGHT STROKES OF THE CLOCK, THE, 260
Eliot, T. S., 6
ELLERY QUEEN AND THE MURDER RING (Columbia, 1941), 104
ELLERY QUEEN AND THE PERFECT CRIME (Columbia, 1941), 104
ELLERY QUEEN, MASTER DETECTIVE (Columbia, 1940), 103
ELLERY QUEEN'S PENTHOUSE MYSTERY (Columbia, 1941), 103
ENCYCLOPEDIA OF MYSTERY AND DETECTION, 50, 111, 294, 307
ENEMY AGENTS MEET ELLERY QUEEN (Columbia, 1942), 107
ENFORCER, THE (Warner's, 1976), 406
ENTER ARSÈNE LUPIN (Universal, 1944), 262
ENTER THE SAINT, 285
ERECTION SET, THE, 396
Euhemerus, 48
Euripides, xv, 333, 339, 340, 342
EVIL UNDER THE SUN (EMI, 1982), 158
EXTRAORDINARY ADVENTURES OF ARSÈNE LUPIN, GENTLEMAN-BURGLAR, THE, 260

FACE IN THE FOG, THE (Paramount, 1922), 266
Fair, A. A. *See* Gardner, Erle Stanley
Fairlie, Gerald, 171, 248, 251, 253
FALCON AND THE CO-EDS, THE (RKO, 1943), 301
FALCON IN DANGER, THE (RKO, 1943), 301
FALCON IN HOLLYWOOD, THE (RKO, 1944), 303
FALCON IN MEXICO, THE (RKO, 1944), 303, 304
FALCON IN SAN FRANCISCO, THE (RKO, 1945), 303, 304
FALCON OUT WEST, THE (RKO, 1945), 301, 302
FALCON'S ADVENTURE, THE (RKO, 1946), 304
FALCON'S ALIBI, THE (RKO, 1946), 304
FALCON'S BROTHER, THE (RKO, 1942), 298, 299
FALCON STRIKES BACK, THE (RKO, 1943), 299, 300-301
FALCON TAKES OVER, THE (RKO, 1942), 297, 366, 367, 391
FALSE FACES, THE, 275, 277
FALSE FACES, THE (Paramount, 1919), 276
FAMILY AFFAIR, A, 393
FAMILY PLOT, THE (Universal, 1976), 181
Farber, Stephen, 346
FAREWELL, MY LOVELY, 297, 362, 363, 364, 366, 391
FAREWELL, MY LOVELY (Avco-Embassy, 1975), 390-391
FATAL HOUR, THE (Monogram, 1940), 192-193
FAT MAN, THE (radio program), 237
FAT MAN, THE (Universal-International, 1951), 237
Faulkner, William, 227, 363, 374, 375, 377
FEATHERED SERPENT, THE (Monogram, 1948), 195
FEMALE OF THE SPECIES, THE, 242
FER-DE-LANCE, 393
Fergusson, Harvey, 12
FIFTY CANDLES, 162
FILMING OF THE WEST, THE, xii, xiv
Film noir, 219, 315, 316, 332-350
FINAL COUNT, THE, 242, 251
FINISHING STROKE, THE, 110-111
Fitzgerald, F. Scott, 55, 398
Flaubert, Gustave, xv, 9, 407
Fleming, Ian, 37, 38, 40, 246
Florey, Robert, 7, 270
Flothow, Rudolph C., 95, 101, 102, 273, 282, 311, 314, 315
FOOTPRINTS ON THE CEILING, THE, 326
Ford, Corey, 59
Ford, Glenn, 342, 343
Forrest, Steve, 7
Foster, Norman, 182-185, 186, 189
FOUR JUST MEN, THE, 246
FOUR OF HEARTS, THE, 98

4:50 FROM PADDINGTON, 155
Frank, Nino, 337, 338
Freeman, R. Austin, 170, 308
Freud, Sigmund, 2, 46, 335, 401, 408

Gable, Clark, 72, 229, 230, 375, 376
Gaboriau, Émile, 13, 15
GALTON CASE, THE, 398-399, 402
GARDEN MURDER CASE, THE, 77, 78
GARDEN MURDER CASE, THE (M-G-M, 1936), 78
Gardner, Erle Stanley, xvii, 24, 79, 102, 105, 112, 113, 114, 115, 116, 117, 118, 119, 120, 121, 122, 123, 124, 125, 126, 127, 128, 129, 130, 131, 132, 133, 134, 135, 136, 137, 138, 139, 140, 141, 142, 143, 144, 308, 357
Gargan, William, 106, 107, 296, 310
Gauguin, Lorraine, 303
GAY FALCON, THE (RKO, 1941), 295, 296, 304
George, Lloyd, 27
Geraghty, Maurice, 294, 295, 297, 298, 299, 300, 301, 303, 304
GETAWAY, 287, 291
Gide, André, 336
Gillette, William, 21, 22, 30, 32, 37, 43
GIRL HUNTERS, THE (United Artists, 1963), 397
GIRL MISSING (Warner's, 1933), 70
GLASS KEY, THE, 131, 211-212, 225, 226, 319
GLASS KEY, THE (Paramount, 1935), 219-220
GLASS KEY, THE (Paramount, 1942), 235, 279
Gleason, James, 73, 296, 297, 299, 366
Goethe, Johann Wolfgang von, xv
GOLDEN EYE, THE (Monogram, 1948), 195
Goldwyn, Samuel, 246, 247, 258
GOODBYE LOOK, THE, 399, 401
Gordon, Mary, 44
GRACIE ALLEN MURDER CASE, THE, 77, 87

GRACIE ALLEN MURDER CASE, THE (Paramount, 1939), 81, 82, 85, 279
Grahame, Gloria, 235, 342, 343
GRANNY GET YOUR GUN (Warner's, 1940), 135
GREEK COFFIN MYSTERY, THE, 90
Greenberg, Joel, 340
Greene, Richard, 42
GREENE MURDER CASE, THE, 49, 55-56, 57-58, 63, 66, 67, 75, 138, 150
GREENE MURDER CASE, THE (Paramount, 1929), 67, 68
Greenstreet, Sidney, 216, 221, 222
Griffith, D. W., 33, 70, 193
Grindé, Nick, 68

Hale, Barbara, 139, 143, 301, 302, 303, 305
Hale, Jonathan, 262, 287, 290
HALFWAY HOUSE, 95
Halliday, Brett, 120, 318-319, 320, 321, 322, 323, 328, 330, 331-332
Hamilton, Edith, 257
Hammett, Dashiell, xviii, 51, 73, 103, 106, 109, 118, 120, 131, 197, 198, 199, 200, 201, 202, 203, 204, 205, 206, 208, 209, 210, 211, 212, 213, 214, 215, 216, 220, 221, 223, 224, 225, 226, 227, 230, 231, 232, 233, 234, 235, 236, 237, 238, 239, 240, 279, 293, 319, 322, 323, 328, 329, 335, 336, 353, 354, 357, 358, 361, 362, 364, 374, 385, 398, 402, 405
HAPPY HIGHWAYMAN, THE, 291-292
HARD-BOILED OMNIBUS: EARLY STORIES FROM BLACK MASK, THE, 205, 360
Harding, Lyn, 37, 39
HARPER (Warner's, 1966), 403-404
Harte, Bret, 15
Hawks, Howard, 62, 63, 100, 215, 217-218, 220, 224, 262, 290, 312, 337, 374-376, 377
Haycraft, Howard, 1, 4, 26, 86, 120
Hayward, Louis, 153, 287, 291, 293

Heine, Heinrich, 363, 383-384, 392
Hellman, Lillian, 103, 208, 212, 213, 224, 225, 226, 227, 230-231, 232, 234, 235, 236, 238, 239
Hemingway, Ernest, xv, 55, 120, 178, 336, 353, 354, 398
Henie, Sonja, 82, 84
Henry, Louise, 76, 175
Hesse, Hermann, xv
Hessler, Gordon, 7
Higham, Charles, 10, 12, 16, 19, 28, 340
Highsmith, Patricia, 319, 378
HIGH WINDOW, THE, 327, 365, 366, 381
Hilliard, Harriet, 70, 270, 300
Hiscott, Leslie S., 38, 39, 152
HIS GIRL FRIDAY (Columbia, 1940), 100
Hitchcock, Alfred, 41, 181-182, 291, 319, 378
Hitler, Adolf, 2, 181, 185
Hoch, Edward D., 262
Hoey, Dennis, 44
Hogan, James, 102, 103, 104, 106, 249, 250, 251
HOLY TERROR, THE, 288
Homer, xv
Horace, xv, 26, 30, 60, 96, 257, 336
Hornung, E. W., 21, 23, 28, 253, 256, 257, 261, 264, 274
HOUND OF THE BASKERVILLES, THE, 24
HOUND OF THE BASKERVILLES, THE (German, 1929), 35, 246
HOUND OF THE BASKERVILLES, THE (Gaumont, 1931), 37
HOUND OF THE BASKERVILLES, THE (20th-Fox, 1939), 41, 42, 45, 191, 326
HOUND OF THE BASKERVILLES, THE (United Artists, 1959), 46
Houseman, John, 294, 365, 369, 372, 373
HOUSE OF FEAR, THE (Universal, 1945), 44
HOUSE WITHOUT A KEY, THE, 162-163, 164, 165, 167

HOUSE WITHOUT A KEY, THE (Pathé, 1926), 163-164
Howard, John, 249, 250
Howard, William K., 39
Hughes, Dorothy B., 128, 131, 142
Humberstone, H. Bruce ("Lucky"), xvi, 73-75, 173, 174, 175, 188, 189, 337
Huston, John, xviii-xix, 215-216, 335, 338

Ingster, Boris, 337
INSPECTOR QUEEN'S OWN CASE, 110
I, THE JURY, 394, 395
I, THE JURY (United Artists, 1953), 396
IVORY GRIN, THE, 400-401

JADE MASK, THE (Monogram, 1945), 194
Jenkins, Allan, 132, 133, 296, 297
JOHN RIDDLE MURDER CASE, THE, 59
Johnson, Diane, 212, 232, 235, 237
Johnson, Julian, 81-82
Johnson, Nunnally, 214
Johnston, Alva, 141
Jung, C. G., 85, 333, 335, 408
JUST BEFORE DAWN (Columbia, 1946), 312, 313
JUST OFF BROADWAY (20th-Fox, 1942), 327, 330

Karloff, Boris, 174, 191, 192, 193, 228
Karimi, A. M., 338
Keaton, Buster, 32
KEEPER OF THE KEYS, THE, 166-167
KENNEL MURDER CASE, THE, 49, 69, 71, 73, 75, 76-77, 138
KENNEL MURDER CASE, THE (Warner's, 1933), 72, 85, 132, 133
KIDNAP MURDER CASE, THE, 77, 78, 79
King, Louis, 171, 249
KISS ME, DEADLY, 395
KISS ME, DEADLY (United Artists, 1955), 396-397
Knopf, Alfred A., 61, 210, 213, 225, 226, 227, 231, 362, 363, 366, 404

Knowles, Patric, 7
Knox, Ronald, 35-36, 125
Krutch, Joseph Wood, 1, 2, 3, 4

Ladd, Alan, 33, 372, 373, 376
LADY FROM SHANGHAI, THE (Columbia, 1948), 337, 383
LADY IN THE LAKE, THE, 374, 378, 381
LADY IN THE LAKE (M-G-M, 1946), xix, 338, 378, 379-381
Lang, Fritz, 340, 342, 343
Laplace, Pierre Simon de, 5, 6
LARCENY IN HER HEART (PRC, 1946), 330
Larsen, Viggo, 30
LAST HERO, THE, 284, 285, 286, 292
LAST LAUGH, MR. MOTO, 180
LAST OF MRS. CHENEY, THE (M-G-M, 1929), 41
LAST OF THE LONE WOLF (Columbia, 1930), 278, 279
Latimer, Jonathan, 279
Laughton, Charles, 152, 154, 158
Layman, Richard, 205, 207
Leblanc, Maurice, 259, 260, 261, 264
Lee, Manfred B. *See* Queen, Ellery
Lee, Rowland V., 38
Leites, Nathan, 345
Leroux, Gaston, 308
Levine, Nat, 95
Lindsay, Margaret, 73, 103, 107, 132, 133, 310
LITTLE SISTER, THE, 381, 382, 383, 386
Livingston, Margaret, 64
Livy, xviii
Lofts, W.O.G., 285
LONE WOLF, THE, 274, 275
LONE WOLF, THE (Selznick, 1917), 276
LONE WOLF, THE (Associated Exhibitors, 1924), 276
LONE WOLF AND HIS LADY, THE (Columbia, 1949), 252, 282
LONE WOLF IN LONDON, THE (Columbia, 1947), 282
LONE WOLF IN MEXICO, THE (Columbia, 1947), 282

LONE WOLF IN PARIS, THE (Columbia, 1938), 279
LONE WOLF KEEPS A DATE, THE (Columbia, 1941), 280
LONE WOLF MEETS A LADY, THE (Columbia, 1940), 280
LONE WOLF RETURNS, THE, 275
LONE WOLF RETURNS, THE (Columbia, 1926), 276
LONE WOLF RETURNS, THE (Columbia, 1936), 279
LONE WOLF'S DAUGHTER, THE (Paramount, 1919), 276
LONE WOLF'S DAUGHTER, THE (Columbia, 1929), 277, 279
LONE WOLF'S LAST PROWL, THE, 276
LONE WOLF'S SON, THE, 276
LONE WOLF SPY HUNT, THE (Columbia, 1939), 280
LONE WOLF TAKES A CHANCE, THE (Columbia, 1941), 280
LONG GOODBYE, THE, 354, 355, 381, 382, 383, 384, 385, 389, 391
LONG GOODBYE, THE (United Artists, 1973), xvi, 386-390
LORD EDGWARE DIES (Real-Art, 1934), 152
Lorre, Peter, xiv, 180-181, 182, 183, 184, 185, 186, 187, 216, 221-222, 323
Lovallo, Len, 151
LOVE FROM A STRANGER (United Artists, 1937), 152
LOVE FROM A STRANGER (Eagle-Lion, 1947), 152-153
Loy, Myrna, 73, 76, 227-228, 229, 230, 231, 232, 233, 234, 235, 236
Lugosi, Bela, 7, 166, 190, 191, 262, 290, 311
Lukas, Paul, 68, 76, 181, 231
Luke, Keye, 168, 172, 173, 174, 175, 176, 184, 188, 193, 194, 195
Lytell, Bert, 99, 264, 265, 276, 277, 278

MacDonald, Philip, 168, 184, 186
Macdonald, Ross, xiii, xvi-xvii, 177, 393, 398, 399, 400, 401, 402, 403, 404-405

Index 455

MacDonald-Wright, Stanton, 50, 51, 52, 53, 71, 78, 84, 85, 168
MacMurray, Fred, 340, 366, 370, 372
MacShane, Frank, 351, 356, 360, 369, 372
McCarthy, Joseph, 238, 396
McNeile, Herman Cyril, 241, 242, 243, 244, 246, 247, 248, 250, 251, 253
MAGNUM FORCE (Warner's, 1974), 405-406
Malden, Karl, 7
MALTESE FALCON, THE, 197, 202, 204, 208, 209, 210, 211, 213, 334-335, 402
MALTESE FALCON, THE (Warner's, 1931), 214, 215
MALTESE FALCON, THE (Warner's, 1941), xix, 215, 221, 335
MANDARIN MYSTERY, THE (Republic, 1936), 97
MAN IN THE BROWN SUIT, THE, 147
Mann, Thomas, xv, 372
MAN WHO KNEW TOO MUCH, THE (Gaumont, 1934), 181
MAN WHO WOULDN'T DIE, THE (20th-Fox, 1942), 326-327
MAN WITH THE TWISTED LIP, THE (Stoll, 1921), 32
Marcin, Max, 309
Marin, Edwin L., 39, 76
MARKED FOR MURDER, 328
Markey, Gene, 41, 234, 236
MARK OF THE WHISTLER, THE (Columbia, 1944), 315
MARLOWE (M-G-M, 1969), 386
Marlowe, Hugh, 99, 105, 110
Marquand, John P., 176, 177, 178, 179, 180, 183, 187, 188-189, 385
Marx, Arthur, 247
MASK OF FU MANCHU, THE (M-G-M, 1932), 228
Massey, Raymond, 37, 39
Maugham, W. Somerset, xv, xvii, 18, 61, 178, 182, 235, 297, 352, 353, 385
Maurier, Sir Gerald du, 42, 244, 257
Mayer, Louis B., 45, 68, 228, 234, 379, 380

MEET BOSTON BLACKIE (Columbia, 1941), 268, 270, 271
MEETING AT MIDNIGHT (Monogram, 1944), 194
MEET THE TIGER, 283, 285
Melville, Herman, xv
MEMOIRS OF A PROFESSIONAL CAD, 290
MEMORIES AND ADVENTURES, 254
Mencken, H. L., 52, 53, 54, 70, 199
Meyer, Nicholas, 46, 48
Michaels, Norman, 31, 33, 42, 43, 44
MICHAEL SHAYNE, PRIVATE DETECTIVE (20th-Fox, 1941), 323, 325
MICHAEL SHAYNE'S LONG CHANCE, 327
MICHAEL SHAYNE'S TRIPLE MYSTERY, 328
MIDNIGHT CLUB (Paramount, 1933), 286
Milhauser, Bertram, 39
Millar, Kenneth. See Macdonald, Ross
Millay, Edna St. Vincent, 85
MILLERSON CASE, THE (Columbia, 1947), 312
Milne, A. A., 308
MIRACLES FOR SALE (M-G-M, 1939), 326
MIRROR CRACK'D, THE (EMI, 1980), 158
MISFORTUNES OF MR. TEAL, THE, 286, 291
MISSING MILLIONS (Paramount, 1922), 265
MISSING REMBRANDT, THE (Twickenham, 1932), 38
MRS. McGINTY'S DEAD, 156
MR. AND MRS. NORTH (M-G-M, 1941), 81
MISTER DYNAMITE (Universal, 1935), 219
MR. JUSTICE RAFFLES, 257
MR. MOTO IN DANGER ISLAND (20th-Fox, 1939), 186
MR. MOTO IS SO SORRY, 179-180
MR. MOTO'S GAMBLE (20th-Fox, 1938), 184, 290
MR. MOTO'S LAST WARNING (20th-Fox, 1939), 186

MR. MOTO TAKES A CHANCE (20th-Fox, 1938), 184
MR. MOTO TAKES A VACATION (20th-Fox, 1939), 186
MR. WONG, DETECTIVE (Monogram, 1939), 191, 195
MR. WONG IN CHINATOWN (Monogram, 1939), 192
Mitchum, Robert, 302, 391
Mohr, Gerald, 251, 281, 282
Monteux, Pierre, 268
Montgomery, Robert, xix, 338, 379, 380
Moore, Roger, 293
Morgan, Janet, 144, 148, 149, 156, 159
Morison, Patricia, 45, 235, 236
Morley, Christopher, 36
Morris, Chester, 102, 268, 269, 270, 271, 273, 323, 324
Morrison, Claudia C., 2
MOUSE TRAP, THE (stage play), 152
MOVING TARGET, THE, 398, 399, 403
Mowbray, Alan, 39, 45, 190
MUM'S THE WORD FOR MURDER, 318, 319
MURDER AHOY (M-G-M, 1964), 156, 157
MURDER AND THE MARRIED VIRGIN, 328
MURDER AT THE GALLOP (M-G-M, 1963), 155-156
MURDER AT THE VICARAGE, 146, 149, 150-151
MURDERER IS A FOX, THE, 106
MURDER GOES TO COLLEGE (Paramount, 1937), 67
MURDER IS MY BUSINESS, 328, 329, 330
MURDER IS MY BUSINESS (PRC, 1946), 330
MURDER MOST FOUL (M-G-M, 1964), 156
MURDER, MY SWEET (RKO, 1944), 316, 367, 368, 372, 381, 391
MURDER OF ROGER ACKROYD, THE, 147-148, 150, 308
MURDER IN THE CALAIS COACH, 146

MURDER ON THE LINKS, 146-147
MURDER ON THE ORIENT EXPRESS (Paramount, 1974), 158
MURDER OVER NEW YORK (20th-Fox, 1940), 190
MURDER SHE SAID (M-G-M, 1962), 154-155, 157
MURDERS IN THE RUE MORGUE (American-International, 1971), 7
MURDER WEARS A MUMMER'S MASK, 320, 321
MY GUN IS QUICK (United Artists, 1957), 397
MYSTERIOUS AFFAIR AT STYLES, THE, 145-146, 147
MYSTERIOUS DR. FU MANCHU, THE (Paramount, 1929), 165
MYSTERIOUS INTRUDER (Columbia, 1946), 316
MYSTERIOUS MR. MOTO (20th-Fox, 1938), 184
MYSTERIOUS MR. QUINN, THE, 151
MYSTERIOUS MR. WONG, THE (Monogram, 1935), 191
MYSTERY OF MARIE ROGET, THE (Universal, 1942), 7
MYSTERY OF MR. WONG, THE (Monogram, 1939), 191
MYSTERY OF THE BLUE TRAIN, THE, 146, 149, 150
MYSTERY OF THE YELLOW ROOM, THE, 308

Nathan, George Jean, 52, 54, 199
Nebel, Frederick, 325
Neill, Roy William, 43, 44, 45, 278
Nevins, Francis M., Jr., 89, 94, 95, 96, 108, 111, 112
NEW ADVENTURES OF ELLERY QUEEN, THE, 98, 109
NEW ARABIAN NIGHTS, 13
Newman, Paul, 403, 404
NICK CARTER—MASTER DETECTIVE (M-G-M, 1939), 252
Nietzsche, Friedrich, 51, 52, 53, 54, 59, 79, 209, 255, 256, 332, 333, 334, 335, 336, 372

NIGHT OF MYSTERY, A (Paramount, 1937), 67, 79
NO COFFIN FOR THE CORPSE, 326
NO HERO, 178-179, 338
Nolan, Lloyd, 185, 323-325, 327, 380
Nolan, William F., 198, 210, 225, 227, 236
Nordon, Pierre, 17, 19, 23, 27, 28
Norris, Chuck, 7, 396
Norwood, Eille, 31, 32
NOTORIOUS LONE WOLF, THE (Columbia, 1946), 282

Oland, Warner, 164, 165, 166, 167, 168, 170, 171, 172-173, 174, 175, 176, 180, 183, 187, 188, 196
ONE DANGEROUS NIGHT (Columbia, 1943), 281
101 YEARS' ENTERTAINMENT, 106, 260
ONE LONELY NIGHT, 396
ONE MYSTERIOUS NIGHT (Columbia, 1944), 272
ORIGIN OF EVIL, THE, 108-109
Orwell, George, 4, 245, 254, 255-256
Owen, Reginald, 39

Paget, Sidney, 19, 20, 22
Pallette, Eugene, 64, 73, 75
Palmer, Stuart, 250, 251, 298, 299, 300
Panek, LeRoy Lad, 144, 147, 149
PARAMOUNT ON PARADE (Paramount, 1930), 69, 165
PASSING OF MR. QUINN, THE (Strand, 1928), 151
PASSPORT TO SUEZ (Columbia, 1943), 282
Patrick, Gail, 139, 140, 278
PEAU DE CHAGRIN, 85, 408
Penzler, Otto, 50, 111
PERFECT CRIME, THE (FBO, 1928), 308
PERIL AT END HOUSE, 149
Perkins, Maxwell E., 55, 69, 79, 82
Perelman, S. J., 99, 223, 225, 230
Perowne, Barry, 258-259
PHANTOM OF CHINATOWN (Monogram, 1940), 193

PHANTOM OF THE RUE MORGUE (Warner's, 1954), 7
PHANTOM THIEF, THE (Columbia, 1946), 272
PHANTOM RAIDERS (M-G-M, 1940), 252
PHILO VANCE RETURNS (PRC, 1947), 85
PHILO VANCE'S SECRET MISSION (Eagle-Lion, 1947), 85
PHILO VANCE'S GAMBLE (PRC, 1947), 85
PICTURE OF DORIAN GRAY, 15
Pigeon, Walter, 137, 252
PITFALL (United Artists, 1948), 347-348
Pitts, Michael R., 110, 309
Place, Janey, 339, 345
Plato, 339
Plautus, 90, 363
PLAYBACK, 378, 381, 385
Poe, Edgar Allan, 1, 2, 3, 4, 5, 6, 7, 10-11, 12, 13, 19, 27, 55, 57
Pointer, Michael, 38, 40, 43
POIROT LOSES A CLIENT, 146
Polanski, Roman, xx
Pollack, George, 153, 155, 156
Porfirio, Robert G., 339
Powell, Dick, 347, 348, 366, 367, 368
Powell, William, 63, 64, 69, 72, 73, 76, 81, 87, 132, 228, 229, 230, 231, 232, 233, 235, 236
POWER OF THE WHISTLER, THE (Columbia, 1945), 315
PRESIDENT'S MYSTERY, THE (Republic, 1937), 79
PRIVATE LIFE OF SHERLOCK HOLMES, THE (United Artists, 1970), 46
PRIVATE PRACTICE OF MIKE SHAYNE, THE, 319, 320, 323
Proust, Marcel, xv
PURSUIT TO ALGIERS (Universal, 1945), 45

Queen, Ellery, 37, 46, 65, 89, 90, 91, 92, 93, 94, 95, 96, 97, 98, 99, 100, 101, 104, 105, 106, 107, 108, 109,

Queen, Ellery (*continued*)
  110, 111, 112, 119, 128, 233, 260,
  307, 311, 323, 332
Quintus Curtius, 334

RAFFLES (United Artists, 1930), 258
RAFFLES (United Artists, 1940), 258
RAFFLES, THE AMATEUR CRACKS-
  MAN (stage play), 257
RAFFLES, THE AMATEUR CRACKS-
  MAN (Hiller-Wilk, 1917), 257
Raft, George, 33, 73, 216-223, 286, 301,
  324, 336
Randell, Ron, 251, 252, 282
Rascoe, Burton, 71
Rathbone, Basil, 33, 34, 39, 40, 41, 42,
  43, 44, 45, 46, 47, 68, 87, 252, 278,
  291
Ratoff, Gregory, 41
Rawson, Clayton, 326
RAYMOND CHANDLER SPEAKING,
  351, 370, 389
Reade, Winwood, 11
RED DRAGON, THE (Monogram,
  1946), 194
RED HARVEST, 202, 203, 204, 205,
  213, 329, 361
RED MASQUERADE, 275, 276
RED HOUSE MYSTERY, THE, 308
Reid, Mayne, 9-10, 14, 15
Reik, Theodor, 339
Renan, Joseph Ernest, 11
RETURN OF BOSTON BLACKIE, THE
  (First Division, 1927), 267
RETURN OF BULLDOG DRUM-
  MOND, THE (British-Wardour, 1934),
  248
RETURN OF DR. FU MANCHU, THE
  (Paramount, 1930), 165
RETURN OF MR. MOTO, THE (20th-
  Fox, 1965), 187
RETURN OF RAFFLES, THE (British,
  1932), 258
RETURN OF SHERLOCK HOLMES,
  THE (Paramount, 1929), 34, 60
RETURN OF THE WHISTLER (Colum-
  bia, 1949), 317
Rice, Craig, 298, 299, 301

Richards, Dick, 368, 390-392
RING OF FEAR (Warner's, 1954), 397
ROADHOUSE NIGHTS (Paramount,
  1930), 213
Roazen, Paul, 408
Robinson, Edward G., 33, 132, 195,
  340, 376
Rohmer, Sax, 94, 242
ROMAN HAT MYSTERY, THE, 90,
  91-92, 93, 96
ROMEO AND JULIET (M-G-M, 1936),
  33
Roosevelt, Franklin D., 36, 79
Rosen, Phil, 7
Ross, Herbert, 46
Rubinstein, Artur, 41
Ruehlmann, William, xviii, 335, 396
Rutherford, Margaret, 154-157

Sadoul, Georges, 338, 340
St. Clair, Malcolm, 64, 65, 67
SAINT GOES WEST, THE, 288, 292
SAINT IN LONDON, THE (RKO,
  1939), 288, 289
SAINT IN NEW YORK, THE, 286, 294
SAINT IN NEW YORK, THE (RKO,
  1938), 288
SAINT IN PALM SPRINGS, THE
  (RKO, 1941), 290
SAINT MEETS THE TIGER, THE (Re-
  public, 1943), 291, 295, 296
SAINT OVERBOARD, THE, 289
SAINT'S DOUBLE TROUBLE, THE
  (RKO, 1940), 289
SAINT'S GIRL FRIDAY, THE (RKO,
  1954), 293
SAINT STRIKES BACK, THE (RKO,
  1939), 288
SAINT'S VACATION, THE (RKO,
  1941), 291
SAINT TAKES OVER, THE (RKO,
  1940), 290
Sammons, Jeffrey L., 383
Sanders, Dennis, 151
Sanders, George, xiv, 186, 252, 288,
  289, 290, 291, 294, 295, 296, 297,
  298, 299, 300, 301, 304, 305-306

SATAN MET A LADY (Warner's, 1936), 215
Sayers, Dorothy L., 94, 148, 159, 307, 408
SCALPHUNTERS, THE, 10
SCARAB MURDER CASE, THE, 59, 67, 69, 76
SCARAB MURDER CASE, THE (Paramount, 1936), 67, 79-80
SCARFACE (United Artists, 1932), 217-218, 219, 220, 374
SCARLET CLAW, THE (Universal, 1944), 44
SCARLET CLUE, THE (Monogram, 1945), 194
Schrader, Paul, 339
Scott, Lizabeth, 343, 346, 349
Scott, Sir Walter, 10, 15
SEARCH FOR DANGER (Film Classics, 1949), 304
SECRET ADVERSARY, THE, 151
SECRET AGENT, THE (Gaumont, 1936), 182
SECRET OF THE WHISTLER, THE (Columbia, 1947), 317
SECRETS OF THE LONE WOLF (Columbia, 1941), 281
Selander, Lesley, 195-196
Selznick, David O., 34
Seneca, 5, 340
SEVEN KEYS TO BALDPATE, 161, 162
SEVEN PERCENT SOLUTION, THE (Universal, 1970), 46, 47, 48
Sen Young, Victor, 188, 189, 190, 194, 195
SHADOW OF THE THIN MAN (M-G-M, 1941), 101, 233
SHADOWS OF THE NIGHT (Columbia, 1944), 311
SHADOWS OVER CHINATOWN (Monogram, 1946), 194
Shakespeare, William, xv, 34, 338, 340
SHANGHAI CHEST, THE (Monogram, 1948), 195
SHANGHAI COBRA, THE (Monogram, 1945), 194

SHANGHAI EXPRESS (Paramount, 1932), 167
Shaw, Joseph T., 205, 357, 360, 362
SHERLOCK HOLMES (stage play), 46
SHERLOCK HOLMES (Essanay, 1916), 30
SHERLOCK HOLMES (Goldwyn, 1922), 32, 60, 64
SHERLOCK HOLMES (Fox, 1932), 38, 39
SHERLOCK HOLMES AND THE SECRET WEAPON (Universal, 1942), 43
SHERLOCK HOLMES AND THE VOICE OF TERROR (Universal, 1942), 43
SHERLOCK HOLMES BAFFLED (Biograph, 1900), xiv, 30
SHERLOCK HOLMES FACES DEATH (Universal, 1943), 44, 273
SHERLOCK, JR. (M-G-M, 1924), 32
SHE WOKE TO DARKNESS, 322
Shockley, Marian, 99, 106
Schreffler, Philip A., 36, 47
SIGN OF FOUR, THE (Associated Radio Pictures, 1932), 38
SIGN OF THE FOUR, THE, 15, 70, 242
SIGN OF THE FOUR, THE, (Stoll, 1923), 32
SILVER BLAZE (Twickenham, 1937), 40
SIMPLE ART OF MURDER, THE, 383
Sinclair, Hugh, 291
SKY DRAGON (Monogram, 1949), 195, 196
SKY MURDER (M-G-M, 1940), 252
SLEEPERS EAST (Fox, 1933), 325
SLEEPERS WEST (20th-Fox, 1941), 325-326
SLEEPING BEAUTY, 399, 400, 401
SLEEPING CARDINAL, THE (Twickenham, 1931), 36, 37, 38
SLEEPING MURDER, 151
Socrates, 339
SOME GIRLS DO (Universal, 1969), 253
SONG OF THE THIN MAN, THE (M-G-M, 1947), 235

Sophocles, xv, 333, 102
SPANISH CAPE MYSTERY, THE, 95-96
SPANISH CAPE MYSTERY, THE (Republic, 1935), 95, 97
SPECIAL INVESTIGATOR (RKO, 1936), 131
SPECKLED BAND, THE (British and Dominion, 1931), 37
Speir, Jerry, 352, 353, 364, 365, 382, 383
Spenser, Edmund, 159
SPIDER WOMAN (Universal, 1944), 44
Spielberg, Steven, 48
Spillane, Mickey, 246, 332, 393, 394, 396, 397, 398, 405
Stanwyck, Barbara, 340, 348, 370
STAR OF MIDNIGHT (RKO, 1935), 76
Starrett, Vincent, 26, 36, 47
Stein, Aaron Marc, xviii
Steinbrunner, Chris, 31, 33, 42, 43, 44, 50, 111
Stendahl, xv
Stevenson, Robert Louis, 13, 14
Stokowski, Leopold, xxi, 41, 268, 311
Stone, John, 167, 168, 184, 186, 188, 189, 272
STOPOVER: TOKYO, 187
STOPOVER: TOKYO (20th-Fox, 1957), 187
Stout, Rex, xiv, xvii, 264, 393
STRANGE LOVE OF MARTHA IVERS, THE (Paramount, 1946), 348
STRANGER ON THE THIRD FLOOR (RKO, 1940), 337
STRANGERS ON A TRAIN (Warner's, 1951), 319, 378
STUDY IN SCARLET, A, 10, 14, 15, 17, 31
STUDY IN SCARLET, A (World-Wide, 1933), 39
STUDY IN TERROR, A (Columbia, 1965), 46, 111
SUDDEN IMPACT (Warner's, 1983), 406-407
Symons, Julian, 4, 109, 294, 334

TASTE FOR COGNAC, A, 328
TASTE FOR VIOLENCE, A, 329
Taylor, Eric, 103, 106, 311, 312, 314, 316
Taylor, John Russell, 340
Taylor, Wendell Hertig, 26, 259
Taylor, William Desmond, 165, 166
TEETH OF THE TIGER, THE (Paramount, 1919), 261
TEMPLE TOWER, 243, 247, 251
TEMPLE TOWER (Fox, 1930), 247
TEN DAYS' WONDER, 108, 109
TEN DAYS' WONDER (Levitt-Pickman, 1972), 110
TEN LITTLE INDIANS (Seven Arts, 1965), 153
TEN LITTLE INDIANS (Avco-Embassy, 1975), 153
Terence, 90
TERROR BY NIGHT (Universal, 1946), 45
Tertullian, 5
THANK YOU, MR. MOTO, 179, 184
THANK YOU, MR. MOTO, 184
THERE WAS AN OLD WOMAN, 106
THIEF IN THE NIGHT, A, 257
THINK FAST, MR. MOTO, 179, 184
THINK FAST, MR. MOTO (20th-Fox, 1937), 183-184
THIN MAN, THE, 207-208, 212, 225, 227, 236, 385
THIN MAN, THE (M-G-M, 1934), 73, 76, 219, 228, 229
THIN MAN GOES HOME, THE (M-G-M, 1944), 234
THIRD ROUND, THE, 246, 250
THIRTEEN AT DINNER, 146, 152
13 LEAD SOLDIERS (20th-Fox, 1948), 252
THIRTEENTH HOUR, THE (Columbia, 1947), 317
THIS IS MURDER, 131
THREE ON A TICKET (PRC, 1947), 331
THREE ROADS, THE, 401
THROUGH THE DARK (Cosmopolitan 1924), 267
TICKETS FOR DEATH, 320, 331
TIGHTROPE (Warner's, 1984), 407
TIME TO KILL (20th-Fox, 1942), 327, 366

Todd, Thelma, 215
Toler, Sidney, 188, 189, 190, 191, 193, 194, 304
Tolstoy, Leo, xv
TOO LATE FOR TEARS (United Artists, 1949), 348
TOO MANY WINNERS (PRC, 1947), 331
TRAGEDY OF X, THE, 93
TRAP, THE (Monogram, 1946), 194
TRAPPED BY BOSTON BLACKIE (Columbia, 1948), 273
Tree, Herbert Beerbohm, 21
TRENT'S LAST CASE, 61, 62
TRENT'S LAST CASE (Fox, 1929), 62, 63
TRENT'S LAST CASE (Eagle-Lion, 1953), 63
TRIUMPH OF SHERLOCK HOLMES, THE (Gaumont-British, 1935), 39
TUESDAY CLUB MURDERS, THE, 151
Tuttle, Frank, 64, 65, 219, 221
Twain, Mark, 254

UNCOMPLAINING CORPSES, THE, 320
UNDERGROUND MAN, THE, 399-400, 401
UNDERWORLD (Paramount, 1927), 213

VALLEY OF FEAR, THE, 39
Vance, Louis Joseph, 264, 273, 274, 276, 277
Van Dine, S. S., xv, 14, 18, 24, 49, 50, 51, 52, 53, 54, 55, 56, 57, 58, 59, 60, 61, 63, 64, 65, 66, 67, 68, 69, 70, 71, 72, 73, 74, 75, 76, 77, 78, 79, 80, 81, 82, 83, 84, 85, 86, 87, 90, 91, 93, 94, 95, 96, 97, 98, 108, 110, 112, 119, 120, 124, 138, 148, 149, 150, 170, 212, 259, 292, 307, 308, 400, 402
Van Dyke, W. S., 72, 228, 232, 233, 234
VANISHING LEGION, THE, xiii
VENGEANCE IS MINE, 394-395
Virgil, xv, 244
VOICE OF THE WHISTLER, THE (Columbia, 1945), 316

Wallace, Edgar, 246
Wallis, Hal B., 73, 74, 76
Ward, Christopher, 59
Warner, Jack L., 69, 72, 73, 74, 75, 215, 377
Weibel, Kay, 394
Welles, Orson, xix, 63, 99, 337, 339, 379, 383
WHISTLER, THE (Columbia, 1944), 314
Wilder, Billy, 46, 153-154, 181, 340, 366, 368-372
William, Warren, 73, 81, 87, 132, 133, 134, 135, 215, 262, 279, 280, 281, 282, 299
WINTER MURDER CASE, THE, 77, 84
Winters, Roland, 194-195, 196
WITNESS FOR THE PROSECUTION (United Artists, 1957), 153-154, 157
Wolfe, Peter, 206, 400
Wolfenstein, Martha, 345
WOMAN IN GREEN, THE (Universal, 1945), 44, 45
WOMAN IN THE DARK (RKO, 1934), 103, 219
Wontner, Arthur, 37, 38, 39, 40, 47
Woods, Donald, 132, 135
Woolrich, Cornell, 315, 317
WORLD'S GREAT DETECTIVE STORIES: A CHRONOLOGICAL ANTHOLOGY, THE, 56, 57, 60, 150, 259
Wright, Williard Huntington. *See* Van Dine, S. S.
Wright, William, 85, 271
Wrong, E. M., 26
Wurtzel, Sol, 62, 167, 168, 173, 174, 176, 182, 183, 184, 185, 187, 188, 190, 191, 323, 327
Wyatt, Jane, 152, 347
WYCHERLY WOMAN, THE, 400, 401, 403
Wyler, William, 102, 237

Young, Roland, 32, 33, 68
YOUNG SHERLOCK HOLMES (Paramount, 1985), 48

Zachary, George, 98, 99, 100, 106, 107
Zangwill, Israel, 70, 307, 308
Zanuck, Darryl F., 41, 45, 168, 174, 176, 248
Zolotow, Maurice, 371
Zucco, George, 105, 188, 231, 251, 262, 311
Zweig, Stefan, 2, 17

About the Author

JOHN TUSKA is a television film writer and producer, and the author of the award-winning book, *The Detective in Hollywood*. He has also written *Billy the Kid, Dark Cinema,* and *The American West in Film* (Greenwood Press, 1983, 1984, 1985).